OMNISCIENCE AND THE RHETORIC OF REASON

Studies in Indian and Tibetan Buddhism

THIS SERIES WAS CONCEIVED to provide a forum for publishing outstanding new contributions to scholarship on Indian and Tibetan Buddhism and also to make accessible seminal research not widely known outside a narrow specialist audience, including translations of appropriate monographs and collections of articles from other languages. The series strives to shed light on the Indic Buddhist traditions by exposing them to historical-critical inquiry, illuminating through contextualization and analysis these traditions' unique heritage and the significance of their contribution to the world's religious and philosophical achievements.

STUDIES IN INDIAN AND TIBETAN BUDDHISM

OMNISCIENCE AND THE RHETORIC OF REASON

Śāntarakṣita and Kamalaśīla on Rationality, Argumentation, and Religious Authority

Sara L. McClintock

WISDOM PUBLICATIONS • BOSTON

Wisdom Publications
199 Elm Street
Somerville MA 02144 USA
www.wisdompubs.org

Library of Congress Cataloging-in-Publication Data
McClintock, Sara L.
Omniscience and the rhetoric of reason : Śāntarakṣita and Kamalaśīla on Rationality, Argumentation, and Religious Authority / Sara L. McClintock.
p. cm. — (Studies in Indian and Tibetan Buddhism)
Includes translations from Sanskrit.
Includes bibliographical references and index.
ISBN 0-86171-661-2 (pbk. : alk. paper)
1. Śāntarakṣita, 705–762. Tattvasaṃgraha. 2. Kamalaśīla, fl. 713–763. Tattvasangrahapañjika. 3. Omniscience (Theory of knowledge) 4. Rhetoric—Religious aspects—Buddhism. 5. Buddhist philosophy. I. Title.
BQ3287.M38 2010
294.3'824—dc22

2010025729

15 14 13 12 11 10
6 5 4 3 2 1
eBook ISBN 9780861719310

Cover and interior design by Gopa & Ted2, Inc. Cover image of Śāntarakṣita. Tibet; 19th century, courtesy of the Rubin Museum of Art.

Wisdom Publications' books are printed on acid-free paper and meet the guidelines for permanence and durability of the Production Guidelines for Book Longevity of the Council on Library Resources.

Printed in the United States of America.

This book was produced with environmental mindfulness. We have elected to print this title on 30 percent PCW recycled paper. As a result, we have saved the following resources: 17 trees, 5 million BTUs of energy, 1,597 pounds of greenhouse gases, 7,691 gallons of water, and 467 pounds of solid waste. For more information, please visit our website, www.wisdompubs.org. This paper is also FSC certified. For more information, please visit www.fscus.org.

for

Winifred May Jolly

and

Alekha Jane Jolly

Publisher's Acknowledgment

THE PUBLISHER gratefully acknowledges the help of the Hershey Family Foundation in sponsoring the publication of this book.

Contents

Preface

यदा किंचिज्ज्ञो ऽहं द्विप इव मदान्धः समभवं
तदा सर्वज्ञो ऽस्मीत्यभवदवलिप्तं मम मनः ।
यदा किंचित्किंचिद् बुधजनसकाशादवगतं
तदा मूर्खो ऽस्मीति ज्वर इव मदो मे व्यपगतः ॥

When I knew just a little bit, I was blind with intoxication
like an elephant in rut;
at that time, I thought, "I am omniscient!" So arrogant was my fancy.
But when, through proximity to wise persons, I gradually understood
just a little bit,
then, I thought, "I am an idiot!" Like a fever, my pride dissolved.

Bhartṛhari, *Nītiśataka* 8

As an enthusiastic graduate student, I became fascinated by the topic of the Buddha's omniscience. I was intrigued by how a tradition with a reputation for a rational and pragmatic approach to the problems of the human condition could postulate what seemed to me such an implausible state for its founder. That the Buddha should have known absolutely everything was absolutely mind-boggling. I was also perplexed by how a tradition that is frequently concerned with a critique of subject-object duality could maintain a coherent theory of omniscience for the awakened Buddha, who supposedly had overcome dualistic knowing. Would not the act of knowing necessarily become something quite different for such a being? Would not the objects of knowledge also disappear in the nondual gnosis of awakening? Such questions drew me in and led me on a quest for the answers that Buddhists have given over the years.

Being young and eager, I naively imagined that I could address these questions for the entire scope of Indian Buddhism. My plan was to write a dissertation that explored both the initial theories of the Buddha's omniscience and the developments of these theories throughout the many literary and philosophical streams of Buddhism in South Asia. Early on in my project, I discovered the *Tattvasaṃgraha* and its commentary, the *Pañjikā*, the monumental works at the heart of this book. The final chapter of these interconnected works is an extended treatment and defense of omniscience. I decided that I would start my research there. Little did I realize the complexity and sophistication of these works at the time. As it turned out, the scope of my research project became progressively smaller, as I took more and more time to try to understand what was happening in these fascinating but quite challenging works.

The history of the idea of omniscience in Indian Buddhism is yet to be written, and it will not be written for many more years. There remain too many works, some surviving only in Chinese or Tibetan, still insufficiently studied. This book is a modest contribution in that regard, as it addresses only one small slice of the larger Indian Buddhist pie. Although I present an overview of omniscience in India in the first chapter of this book, the gaps in that overview are far greater than what it contains. The present book speaks mainly to very specific sets of arguments that were unfolding in and around the eighth century in India. To understand these arguments, one needs to understand a great deal about the metaphysics, epistemology, soteriology, and practical rationality that were in play at the time. Omniscience, as it turns out, is a theme that involves nearly *everything*—which I suppose should not be surprising.

The quotation by Bhartṛhari cited above well describes my experience in writing this book. The more I pursued this outrageous topic, the more I encountered scholars of extraordinary learning. The more I spent time with such erudite persons, the more clearly I comprehended the limits of my knowledge. Slowly, over time, I began to discern a small area where I might make a unique contribution. But it is with utmost humility that I say this. Most of what I have discovered comes directly from others, and none of what I have done here would be possible without them.

Those who have helped me with this project are far too numerous to name, and any attempt at an exhaustive list would be inevitably doomed to failure. The only consolation I can give to those whose names do not appear here is the assurance that I recognize the depths of my dependence on the many of you who have so kindly offered your insights, your material support, and your friendship. Please know that I am profoundly grateful for all the assistance I have received over the years.

A few persons are too central to this project not to be named. At the very beginning, I wish to acknowledge my first teacher of Buddhism, Professor Masatoshi Nagatomi of Harvard University, without whose encouragement this project would never have begun. Similarly, my current colleague and partner for many years, John Dunne, was with me in Sarnath on the day I decided to make omniscience the focus of my doctoral studies. His help over the years has been invaluable. My teachers in Sarnath were likewise all critical to this work. In particular, Ram Shankar Tripathi, whom I always call Guru-ji, was exceedingly generous with his time, wit, and wisdom, tirelessly reading and explicating hundreds of Sanskrit verses and commentary with me over the course of more than one year. I will never forget his teaching to me of the importance of stopping work periodically for a laughter break—a practice that infused great joy into our time together. In Sarnath as well, Geshe Yeshe Thabkhe took considerable time with me to read Indian texts in Tibetan translation. I learned more from him about Madhyamaka than from nearly anyone else. During this time, Venerable Lobsang Norbu Shastri was my faithful companion, accompanying me to Guru-ji's home and offering me meals and tea, thus entirely and selflessly reversing the usual monk-layperson relationship. Another Sarnath connection is Shrikant Bahulkar, one of the most gifted Sanskritists I have had the pleasure to know. His aid in the later stages of this book is greatly appreciated. Most importantly, I want to thank Andy Rotman, whom I met on the steps of the Śāntarakṣita Library in Sarnath and who has since become a trusted advisor and friend. Andy's perpetual counsel and deep-seated *maitri* have seen me through everything, and there are no words to express my thanks for his presence in my life.

Crucial to the direction that my research eventually took is my dissertation advisor, Professor Tom Tillemans of the University of Lausanne. Tom's invitation to John and me to spend two years in Lausanne was a decisive event in my scholarly life. When Professor Nagatomi passed away unexpectedly during that period, Tom's willingness to take on the role of director for my thesis, even though I was still officially a student at Harvard, was an act of great kindness. His careful work with me on the Sanskrit texts as well as his insistence on the highest level of clarity in my writing and thinking were services whose benefits remain with me to this day. It was also Tom who suggested I look into the New Rhetoric of Chaïm Perelman and Lucie Olbrechts-Tyteca, thinkers whose mark can be discerned throughout the whole of this book. For all these reasons, as well as for his relentless philosophical curiosity and unwavering kindness, I thank Tom profoundly from the depths of my heart.

Others who have played a truly central role in the successful completion of this work include Professor Charles Hallisey of Harvard University, a member of my dissertation committee and a source of ongoing intellectual inspiration. Professor Leonard van der Kuijp, also of Harvard, was the third member of my dissertation committee, and his help has likewise been crucial. Sincere thanks are due as well to Professor Ernst Steinkellner of the Austrian Academy of Sciences and to Professor Shōryū Katsura of Ryukoku University, both of whom provided extensive corrections and comments to an earlier draft of this book. For other indispensible help, I wish to acknowledge Dr. Helmut Krasser, Dr. Vincent Eltschinger, and Dr. Toru Funayama. Likewise also Dr. Phyllis Granoff, Dr. Laurie Patton, Mr. Barry Hershey, Ms. Amy Benson Brown, Ms. Constance Kassor, and all the scholars whose works I cite in this book. These names represent just a few of the many to whom I owe a great debt. Needless to say, any errors that remain in the book are entirely my own.

Many institutions have generously allowed my work to proceed by offering scholarships and other material support. These include Harvard University, Columbia University, the American Institute of Indian Studies, the Rocky Foundation, the Whiting Foundation, the Central Institute for Higher Tibetan Studies (now Central University for Higher Tibetan Studies), the University of Lausanne, the Fonds Elisabet de Boer, Emory University, and the Hershey Family Foundation. I extend my gratitude to all of them for their recognition of my efforts.

Thanks are due also to Laura Cunningham and to everyone at Wisdom who helped bring this book to fruition. This is my second book in the *Studies in Indian and Tibetan Buddhism* series at Wisdom Publications (the first is a volume co-edited with Georges Dreyfus). In both instances, the experience has been exceptional. My editor for both projects, David Kittelstrom, is among the most attentive readers I have yet to encounter. The publisher, Tim McNeill, who has great insight into the world of Buddhist publishing, had the courage to create an academic series that has now published some of the best works in our field—it is a great honor to be part of it. My thanks go also to the members of the editorial board of the series for their positive appraisal of my work and for their patience in seeing it come to press.

Finally, I thank my immediate family, especially my daughter, Alekha Jolly, who continues to be among my greatest teachers concerning those inexpressible realities that must remain unwritten, and my mother, Winifred Jolly, who despite her own challenges and personal tragedies, has consistently been there for me whenever I have called. Each of them has contributed more than she can ever know to the successful completion of this book. May they both, and may all beings, find lasting happiness and peace.

Sara L. McClintock
Atlanta, June 2010

1. Introduction

OMNISCIENCE—THE QUALITY or state of infinite, all-encompassing knowledge—has proved a vexing notion for philosophers who proclaim a commitment to reason. Problems with the conception abound, not the least of which is how an ordinary person possessing limited knowledge could ever verify the omniscience of some allegedly omniscient being. However many things a being may appear to know, it nonetheless remains conceivable that there exist still other things of which that being is ignorant. In the face of this recognition, is it not simply folly for a philosopher to attempt to defend omniscience? This thorny issue lies at the heart of the present book, since Śāntarakṣita and Kamalaśīla, the Buddhist authors whose arguments in defense of omniscience we examine here, are not only aware of the conundrum, they fully endorse its basic premise. That is, these philosophers fully accept that the omniscience of one being cannot be verified by another who is not omniscient. Yet they also emphatically maintain that the doctrine that the Buddha is (or was) omniscient can be entirely justified through rational means.

This book aims to discover how this can be, at least with regard to the myriad arguments concerning omniscience in two Indian Buddhist texts of the eighth century: the *Tattvasaṃgraha* written by the Buddhist monk Śāntarakṣita, and its commentary, the *Tattvasaṃgrahapañjikā*, written by Śāntarakṣita's direct disciple, the monk Kamalaśīla.[1] Śāntarakṣita's work is an

1. We are fortunate to be able to date Śāntarakṣita and Kamalaśīla with greater accuracy than is usually possible for Indian philosophers of their era, since Tibetan historical records testify that both figures visited Tibet during the reign of the king Khri srong lde btsan (ca. 740–98). Frauwallner 1961: 141–43 suggests that Śāntarakṣita first went to Tibet for a short visit in 763, and that he returned relatively soon thereafter for a second visit, which lasted until his death in around 788. Kamalaśīla is reported to have been invited to Tibet upon the death of his master. Frauwallner puts Śāntarakṣita's dates as 725–88, and I see no reason to dispute them as a working hypothesis. Further unsubstantiated details of the

encyclopedic verse composition consisting in 3,645 metered stanzas, while Kamalaśīla's prose commentary, to which I will refer simply as the *Pañjikā*, runs to more than 1,000 pages in modern printed editions. Although the extant Sanskrit manuscripts[2] and Tibetan translations[3] preserve the two works separately, the modern editions display them together, with the verses of the so-called "root text" inserted interlinearly in accord with the commentary's explicit and pervasive "indications" (*pratīka*). The presence of these indications attests to the close commentarial nature of Kamalaśīla's work, and I take them, together with the near certainty that Kamalaśīla was indeed Śāntarakṣita's disciple, as a warrant for referring occasionally (mainly in the notes) to the two texts as a single, though admittedly bipartite, work.[4] Taken

two philosophers' lives can be found in various Tibetan sources. See, e.g., Kapstein 2000; Ruegg 1981b; and Tucci 1958.

2. There are two extant sets of manuscripts for the *Tattvasaṃgraha* (TS) and the *Tattvasaṃgrahapañjikā* (TSP) of which I am aware: those preserved in the Pārśvanātha Jaina temple in Jaisalmer (J) and those preserved at the Bāḍi Pārśvanātha Jaina temple in Patna (Pat). My profound thanks go to an anonymous scholar for providing me with a copy of J. Unfortunately, time constraints prevented me from consulting it to the degree that I would have liked, although in a few places I have been able to profit from it (despite the relatively poor quality of the images). There are also two complete modern editions: Krishnamacarya's 1926 edition in Gaekwad's Oriental Series (G), and Shastri's 1981 edition in the Bauddha Bharati Series (B). Krishnamacarya's edition is based on Pat, while Shastri's is based on J, with occasional reference in the footnotes to both Pat and G. Krishnamacarya mistakenly thought that a verse had been elided from his manuscript, so he added this "missing" verse into the root text. As a result, the verse numbering in G (and in Jha's 1937–39 English translation, which is based on G) starting with verse 527 is uniformly one digit greater than the numbering in B. My numbering corresponds to B throughout. My readings are derived from J, G, and B, as well as by means of reference to the Tibetan translations preserved in the Sde dge (D) and Peking (P) editions of the *bstan 'gyur* (see subsequent note). For details on the editions and Jha's translation, see the bibliography. For copious bibliographical references for editions, translations, and articles concerning individual chapters of the two works, see Steinkellner and Much 1995.

3. A Tibetan translation of TS, attributed to Guṇākaraśrībhadra, Dpal lha btsan po, and Zhi ba 'od, is preserved in D, *tshad ma*, vol. *ze*, 1a1–133a7, as well as P 5764, *tshad ma*, vol. *'e*, 1–159a2. A translation of TSP, attributed to Devendrabhadra and Grags 'byor shes rab, is preserved in D, *tshad ma*, vol. *ze*, 133b1–vol. *'e*, 331a7 and P 5765, *tshad ma*, vol. *'e*, 159b2–405a7.

4. In making this move, I do not mean to imply that reading the two works together as a single bipartite text is the only or even the best way to read the works. In fact, in ideal terms, it would probably be best to attempt to disentangle the two works in an effort to see whether and how Kamalaśīla elaborates on or departs from the ideas of Śāntarakṣita. A difficulty with such an approach, however, stems from the fact that Śāntarakṣita writes here in verse, whereas Kamalaśīla explicates the verses in prose. This naturally provides

as a whole, these two massive works comprise a sustained apology for the rationality of Buddhism, including the ultimate Buddhist goal of attaining omniscience.

Śāntarakṣita and Kamalaśīla's arguments in defense of omniscience in these works are in many ways bewildering.[5] First, the arguments are complex, and

occasion for greater ambiguity in Śāntarakṣita's words than it does in Kamalaśīla's, and there is often no obvious way to determine whether the explications in the commentary correspond to Śāntarakṣita's original intent or represent a deviation from it. One way to address this problem would be to turn to Śāntarakṣita's other works, including his prose commentaries on his own and others' verse treatises. But such a method has its own difficulties, in that it presumes that Śāntarakṣita's views did not change over time, so that one may be justified in taking his statements in a prior or a subsequent work as evidence for his intent in the TS. An example of the kinds of problems that can arise when one makes such an assumption may be found in the Tibetan scholar Tsong kha pa's claim that Śāntarakṣita did not write the commentary on his reputed teacher Jñānagarbha's *Satyadvayavibhaṅga* (SDV), since the arguments for the necessity of stating the aim of a treatise (*śāstraprayojana*) contained within that commentary contradict Kamalaśīla's arguments on the same topic in the TSP. As Tsong kha pa holds that Kamalaśīla would not directly contradict his own teacher (especially not at the outset of a commentary on his teacher's work), the inevitable conclusion is that Śāntarakṣita did not write the commentary on the SDV. This conclusion seems problematic, however, in light of the fact that we find Śāntarakṣita taking the same position (in nearly the same words) on the necessity of stating the aim of a treatise in his commentary on Dharmakīrti's *Vādanyāya* (VN) as does the author of the commentary on the SDV. It seems then that we must agree with Funayama (1995: 193) when he says, "... there is no room to doubt that Kamalaśīla's own idea is quite different from that of Śāntarakṣita." But the question remains what conclusion to draw from this fact. Funayama (193) holds that "Kamalaśīla's intention was not the refutation as such of Śāntarakṣita's idea but an endeavor to take a further step toward the correct interpretation, overtaking even his own teacher's view." This seems a reasonable proposition. What we cannot know, however, is whether at the time of the composition of the TS, Śāntarakṣita had already changed his position on this topic, such that Kamalaśīla's arguments in the TSP were in fact in accord with his teacher's current position, even if Śāntarakṣita remains silent on the issue in the TS itself. This is just one illustration of the difficulty involved in seeking to disentangle the viewpoints of the TS and the TSP. In subsequent notes, I will use the abbreviations TS and TSP when referencing the works individually, and the composite abbreviation TS/P when considering the two works as a single entity.

5. Several scholars have examined these arguments to a greater or lesser extent. Most notable is Shinjō Kawasaki (1992b), who dedicates an entire chapter of his impressive book on omniscience in Buddhism to the *Tattvasaṃgraha*, where he provides both a close reading of passages from several related Indian Buddhist authors and an annotated translation of the opponent's views (*pūrvapakṣa*) as presented in the final chapter of the work. See also Kawasaki (1995: 8–11) in which he provides a brief description of the arguments for omniscience in the final chapter of the TS/P, along with a list of previous scholarship on it, but

they are found in several locations, not all of which are included in the lengthy final chapter explicitly devoted to the topic. Second, the arguments are generally expressed in the highly technical idioms of Indian epistemological discourse, thus requiring solid grounding in that elaborate style of reasoning. Third, and most confusing, the authors present what seem to be contradictory visions of omniscience in different parts of the works. Sorting out the nuances of these various positions is pretty tough. On the one hand, it requires a careful examination of a large number of complex arguments scattered throughout the texts. On the other hand, it also requires a more general investigation into the authors' understanding of the nature of rationality, argumentation, and religious authority, since all three of these are profoundly implicated in their arguments concerning omniscience. But this challenging task turns out to have an unexpected reward, for by attending to the broader conceptions of rationality, argumentation, and religious authority that inform the reasoning about omniscience in these works, we come to discern a *rhetoric of reason* in the argumentation overall. It is insight into this rhetoric of reason that is the true fruit of the labor in this book. For it is only once we have understood the deeply rhetorical nature of reason for these Buddhist thinkers that their arguments about omniscience—arguments that are in some respects the pinnacle of all rational inquiry in their philosophical system—begin to make sense.

The Rhetoric of Reason

I first developed the idea of a rhetoric of reason as a result of my encounter with Chaïm Perelman and Lucie Olbrechts-Tyteca's theory of argumentation known as the New Rhetoric. A fundamental tenet of this theory, which the authors articulate in their groundbreaking work, *La nouvelle rhétorique: traité de l'argumentation*, is that central to all forms of argumentation is the enactment of a dialectical process in which some speaker or author

remains silent on the question of Śāntarakṣita and Kamalaśīla's own views. Other contributions include those of Mookerjee 1960; Jaini 1974; Kher 1972; Pathak 1929, 1930–31, 1931; Singh 1974; Shah 1967; Solomon 1962; and Wood 1991. For further references, especially to Japanese scholarship, see Steinkellner and Much 1995. The contributions of all these authors are admirable, and they testify along with others to the importance and interest of the work for the study of Indian Buddhist conceptions of omniscience; nevertheless, none of them is an exhaustive treatment of the question of omniscience in the TS/P, nor do any of them seriously address the rhetoric of reason at play in the work.

seeks to win over an audience.[6] Whether an argument is formal or informal, concerned with facts or with values, coldly calculating or hotly impassioned, it always involves a speaker or author who, through discourse, tries to make an audience accede to a particular point of view. An argument's audience thus holds enormous power over the argument's author, since to persuade or convince an audience, the author must present arguments to which that audience can be made to accede. The centrality of the audience in argumentation thus can never be negated, even in the case of highly rational or rationalized discourse. To reflect this idea of the centrality of the audience, which I felt was essential to Śāntarakṣita and Kamalaśīla's own theories of rationality and argumentation, I coined the term the "rhetoric of reason" and used it in the title of my doctoral thesis.[7]

Later, I discovered the work of James Crosswhite, a philosopher and professor of English, who also draws on the New Rhetoric and who argues persuasively in his book *The Rhetoric of Reason: Writing and the Attractions of Argument* for the rhetorical nature of all forms of human reasoning. I found that Crosswhite's understanding of rhetoric as "the only viable way to explain the possibility of reason itself"[8] resonated strongly with my reading of the premises underlying certain Buddhist approaches to rationality and reasoning, and that it bolstered my reading of Śāntarakṣita and Kamalaśīla as embracing a rhetoric of reason in the *Tattvasaṃgraha* and the *Pañjikā*. In making his claim about rhetoric, Crosswhite begins from the premise that rhetoric "is different from any other field because rhetoric is concerned with the way discursive authority operates wherever it is found."[9] As such, the study of rhetoric has a kind of priority among all fields and disciplines, insofar as rhetoric always plays a critical role in the production of knowledge, no matter the field or the discipline. But rhetoric is not somehow foundational, since rhetoric is neither impervious to critique nor epistemologically prior to the construction of discursive authority. In short, rhetoric, like all forms of discourse, is also rhetorically constructed. Crosswhite compares his understanding of rhetoric to Habermas's view of philosophy as simultaneously interpreting and acting within communicative practices. Likewise, rhetoric involves both the study of discursive authority and the simultaneous

6. The authors describe the aim of all argumentation as the attempt to "gain the adherence of minds." Perelman and Olbrechts-Tyteca, 1969: 14.

7. McClintock 2002.

8. Crosswhite 1996: 15.

9. Crosswhite 1996: 15.

participation in the rules of such authority at particular times and places. It thus can never be absolute.

The notion of a *rhetoric of reason*, then, points primarily to the ways in which philosophy and philosophical argumentation, both of which put a premium on rationality and truth, are nonetheless themselves also circumscribed by particular norms of authority and particular discursive practices which have themselves been rhetorically constructed. A rhetoric of reason does not reject reason as unattainable, but neither does it futilely attempt to cordon reason off from the rest of human discourse. Instead, a rhetoric of reason attempts, as precisely as possible, to attend to the question of discursive authority in relation to questions about such things as what is reasonable, rational, justified, true, or right in a variety of contexts. Crosswhite sums up as follows:

> A rhetoric of reason does not understand itself as describing the necessary a priori features of all reasoning, to which the rhetorician has some kind of priviledged incontestable access. Rather, in its attempt to offer a general account of what happens when people argue, it understands itself as offering an account which is better for particular purposes, and more convincing in the context in which it is offered, than are competing accounts. That's all.

On my reading of these Buddhist thinkers, Śāntarakṣita and Kamalaśīla would definitely assent to this characterization of their philosophical enterprise, though they would also be likely to emphasize their feeling that their own accounts are indeed *better* and *more convincing* for particular purposes than are rival accounts. But by itself, this high degree of confidence in their own analysis does not mitigate their commitment to an account of the authority of reason as a contextual product of particular discursive practices. While their frequent talk of certainty (*niścaya*) lends a veneer of absolutism to their work, there is good reason to hold that for Śāntarakṣita and Kamalaśīla, certainty, like all conceptual constructs, is primarily of pragmatic and not absolute value. For these reasons, which we will explore further below, I maintain that these thinkers engage in a rhetoric of reason, even if they do not explicitly claim to do so.

Specifically, I see two ways in which Śāntarakṣita and Kamalaśīla may be said to employ a rhetoric of reason in the *Tattvasaṃgraha* and the *Pañjikā*. The first way corresponds closely to Crosswhite's understanding outlined above. Here, the idea of a rhetoric of reason depends on a reading of the term *rhetoric* as signifying the contextual aspect of all communicative discourse—including discourses concerning what counts as a rational argument. The term *rhetoric* in this instance draws attention to the fact that there is no neutral playing field upon which arguments may be advanced, but rather that the field of discourse is always being negotiated by the speaker or author and the audience for any given argument. In the works under study in this book, we find Śāntarakṣita and Kamalaśīla continually adjusting their premises, reasoning, and language to accord with the premises, reasoning, and language of a wide variety of audiences. In part, they do so to increase their chances of winning over these diverse addressees. As such, their practice can appear to be a kind of sophistry. But contrary to this, I argue that Śāntarakṣita and Kamalaśīla do not engage in this behavior solely in order to win debates. Rather, they do so because they understand reason and truth to be highly conventional affairs that emerge only in contexts created mutually by author and audience. This philosophical insight not only justifies their method of shifting premises, it actually requires it for reason to function. The indispensability of the author-audience relationship for the very existence of rationality is the first and most important element in Śāntarakṣita and Kamalaśīla's rhetoric of reason.

The second way in which Śāntarakṣita and Kamalaśīla may be said to embrace a rhetoric of reason corresponds to a more common connotion of the term *rhetoric*—one that is perhaps more familiar than is the study and construction of discursive authority. On this reading, the term *rhetoric* points to what Crosswhite calls the "different protocols and styles of reasoning [that] hold sway in different disciplines."[10] That is, we regularly speak of the rhetoric of a given group, discipline, or profession and, when we do so, we mean the ways in which that group, discipline, or profession attempts to shape and define a particular field of discourse through its use of particular forms of language and argument. Śāntarakṣita and Kamalaśīla engage in a rhetoric of reason insofar as they make consistent appeal to reason (*yukti*) as the highest arbiter of belief, and they do so within a context of a style of formal reasoning (*nyāya*) that places extremely high value on reason and rational analysis. Whatever the particular argument being advanced, whomever the particular audience being addressed, the authors' underlying premises always seem to include the idea that reason justifies their arguments and their conclusions. To emphasize this, the authors regularly supplement their general argumentation with formal proof statements, using a highly stylized and prestigious style of reasoning for presenting arguments.[11] This prestigious style of reasoning is

10. Crosswhite 1996: 15.

11. See p. 67–85 below.

based in their understanding of the *pramāṇa*s, the instruments or means by which reliable knowledge may be attained. In this book, I use the translation "means of trustworthy awareness" to refer to the *pramāṇa*s; other common translations include "valid cognition," "means of valid cognition," "instrumental awareness," "instrument for warranted awareness," and so on.

In utilizing the technical idioms of this prestigious form of reasoning rooted in the *pramāṇa*s, the authors appear to enter a kind of denaturalized field of discourse in which arguments and conclusions attain an aura of self-evidence and objectivity.[12] We will have occasion to examine quite a few such arguments in the book, but our general purpose will not be to evaluate the soundness or validity of these formal proof statements *per se*. Rather, we will focus instead on how the authors use such formal proof statements as part of a larger rhetorical strategy aimed at convincing others of the overall rationality of the doctrines they endorse. The authors thus engage in a rhetoric of reason through their insistence on the privileged status of reason, especially when it is encoded in highly stylized proof statements.

These two ways of reading the notion of a rhetoric of reason—one with an emphasis on the conventional nature of rhetoric, the other with an emphasis on the certainty produced by reason—appear in some ways to be in tension. The first reading, that of a *rhetoric* of reason, involves the understanding that reason, like all forms of communicative discourse, is neither self-evident nor absolute, but is rather contigent on a context created mutually by author and audience. The second reading, that of a rhetoric of *reason*, involves the idea that reason is the highest and best arbiter of belief, and also that it is possible to demonstrate which beliefs reason justifies through the presentation of formal, seemingly self-evident, objective proof statements. Are Śāntarakṣita and Kamalaśīla aware of this tension, and if so, do they attempt to resolve it? I do think that Śāntarakṣita and Kamalaśīla are aware of the tension, but I hold that they see the tension as more apparent than real. This is so because they understand the apparent self-evidence of the formal proof statements of their rational discourse as rooted in the mutual conditioning of author and audience. Describing how language functions, Śāntarakṣita says:

12. Perelman and Olbrechts-Tyteca (1969: 193) refer to this kind of move in argumentation as the use of "quasi-logical arguments," which they characterize as arguments that "lay claim to a certain power of conviction, in the degree that they claim to be similar to the formal reasoning of logic or mathematics."

> Indeed, we hold all verbal transactions to be similar to the statement "There are two moons" uttered by a person with eyes distorted by cataracts to another person who is like himself.[13]

In other words, all discourse—including formal rational discourse—is ultimately flawed, as are the concepts it produces.[14] Words and concepts do not refer in any direct or unambiguous manner to anything that can be verified independently of those very words and concepts. Still, words and concepts function (at times quite well) due to the presence of a shared context and conditioning—conditioning that is itself a shared form of ignorance.[15] The situation is thus similar to that of two people with the same eye disease who are able to agree on the presence of two moons. Even categories of philosophical thought such as reason, truth, and validity can function without any form of absolute reason. Reason functions *as if it were absolute*, but only so long as our shared ignorance remains.[16]

13. TS 1210 (*śabdārthaparīkṣā*): *timiropahatākṣo hi yathā prāha śaśidvayam / svasamāya tathā sarvā śābdī vyavahṛtir matā //*.

14. TS 1211cd (*śabdārthaparīkṣā*): *mithyāvabhāsino hy ete pratyayāḥ śabdanirmitāḥ //*. "Indeed, these verbally produced conceptions have false appeareances."

15. Dharmakīrti refers to this shared ignorance as a kind of internal distortion (*antarupaplava*). Dunne (2004: 324–27) discusses the implications of this distortion for the creation of what he calls "karmic worlds," realms inhabited by beings with similar forms of ignorance who, by dint of the similarity of their internal distortions are able to communicate and function quite well in those worlds, at least in some mundane respects. See also Eltschinger 2007c: 464.

16. This assessment corresponds in certains respects to the analysis in a recent article by Richard Nance (2007) on reasoning (*yukti*) in Indian and Tibetan Buddhist scholasticism. Nance points to a section from the "Investigation of the Existence of Other Means of Trustworthy Awareness" chapter of the TS/P (*pramāṇāntarabhāvaparīkṣā*, TSP *ad* TS 1691–97) in which Śāntarakṣita and Kamalaśīla critique the notion, attributed to Caraka, that *yukti* constitutes a separate means of trustworthy awareness (*pramāṇa*). The function of this purported *pramāṇa* is to determine the existence of causal relations, a function that neither perception nor inference can perform. Śāntarakṣita and Kamalaśīla reject this analysis, and state instead that causal relations are made known through conventions (*saṃketa*) and worldly transactions (*vyavahāra*). Nance (2007: 163) nicely sums up his findings on this point: "This leaves the way open to a notion of reasoning that neither Śāntarakṣita nor Kamalaśīla explicitly advocate, but which seems to me a reasonable interpretation of their view: reasoning is a process of acknowledging and attending to discursive convention and the roles it plays in our worldly transactions (*vyavahāra*). Understood in this way, reasoning is not *equivalent* to inference, but may be read as something like its condition of possibility, marking an acceptance of conventions presupposed not only in our inferences and arguments, but in any meaningful speech act...."

This position has a powerful resonance with the New Rhetoric, especially with its understanding of all argumentation as necessarily imprecise due to the vagueness of language. Philosophy *requires* a rhetorical conception of reason since philosophy, like all discourse, is "elaborated not by setting out from an intuition of clear and distinct ideas, but setting out from common language, always confused and susceptible to a large number of interpretations."[17] Although the precise explanations for why language is confused will differ, there is a common recognition that for philosophical argumentation and analysis to take place, people must agree to start with premises that are inevitably tainted by bias and confusion. Clearly, there can be nothing absolute or self-evident in this process. Still, because conditioning is shared, agreement on premises and terms can be attained, such that a speaker or author may be in a position to "gain the adherence of minds" when addressing an audience. And if the speaker or author is not able to win over an audience, he or she always has the option of going back and revisiting the premises and terms in an attempt to find common ground to move the argumentation forward.

There is, however, one possible exception to the general principle that reason is contextual and rhetorically constructed in both the Buddhist texts and the New Rhetoric. The exception is not, as some might initially imagine, an appeal to direct perception or the "given" of sense-datum philosophers. Such appeals exist and possess a strong aura of self-evidence, but they are still not absolute for either the Buddhists or the New Rhetoricians. Appeals to experience remain conditioned, both rhetorically (insofar as they are discursive appeals) and through other forms of conditioning. The one possible exception to the rhetorical conception of reason in both systems comes in the form of what might be described as analytic reason. In the case of the Buddhist thinkers, the one possible form of reason that may not be rhetorical is that which is based on the principle of noncontradiction; for the authors of the New Rhetoric, it is reason that is entirely mathematical and that can be expressed through the symbols of formal logic. Both systems appear to grant such analytic forms of reason an exalted status, although in both cases it remains difficult to say whether these forms of reason can remain insulated from from the critique of contingency that applies to reasoning as carried out in ordinary language. Since all human reasoning requires ordinary language to function, the existence or nonexistence of a type of pure analytic reason that is not contingent on a rhetorically constructed context is more or less moot: even if such reason exists, human philosophers cannot proceed

17. Perelman 1982: 194.

without constructing a field of discourse that includes confusion, bias, and ignorance, and that proceeds through the mutual construction of discursive authority through the interaction of author and audience.

Reason, Rhetoric, and Omniscience

Although Śāntarakṣita and Kamalaśīla understand reason to be rhetorical in this way, this does not lessen their commitment to it. In fact, they see rational analysis as critical to the fundamental Buddhist enterprise they also embrace: the eventual elimination of the primordial ignorance (*avidyā*) that pervades the mindstreams of all ordinary beings. This primordial ignorance is not just an absence of knowledge but involves a fundamental error or misperception of reality.[18] When perfectly accomplished, the eradication of this fundamental error results in perfect knowledge, which the Buddhist tradition calls omniscience (*sarvajña*). The Buddha is necessarily one who has attained this kind of perfect knowledge, and so he is called the Omniscient One (*sarvajña*). This same can also be said for any and all buddhas in the past, present, and future. This much is relatively standard Buddhist doctrine, and in line with their general commitment to reason, Śāntarakṣita and Kamalaśīla hold that the doctrine that the Buddha is (or was) omniscient can and should be justified by reason. The *Tattvasaṃgraha* and the *Pañjikā* contain extended argumentation in defense of this doctrine, nearly all of which is grounded in the notion that it is a rational doctrine that can be defended through rational means.

In comparison with many of the other Buddhist doctrines they defend, however, including such Buddhist ideas as impermanence, selflessness, and even the complicated exclusion theory of linguistic reference (*apoha*), it is extremely difficult to pin down exactly what these authors think omniscience *is* on basis of the evidence in their texts. Śāntarakṣita and Kamalaśīla present more than one model of omniscience in these works, while providing only subtle and indirect clues as to which version of omniscience they ultimately endorse. Not surprisingly, scholars have often been perplexed at the apparently contradictory presentations of the Buddha's omniscience found in the *Tattvasaṃgraha* and the *Pañjikā*.[19] Once we recognize that Śāntarakṣita and

18. Eltschinger (2007c: 469) cites Dharamkīrti's presentation at PV2.213ab, in which ignorance is equated with erroneous perception (*mithyopalabdhi*).

19. Wood (1991) is an example of a modern interpreter whose insufficient grasp of the rhetorical complexity of these works causes puzzlement about the authors' stance on

Kamalaśīla embrace a rhetorical conception of reason, however, their multiple positions on omniscience and the apparent contradictions appear far less troublesome. The key to our understanding is the authors' use of a technique that I call the "sliding scale of analysis."[20] This technique allows that a philosopher may, under certain circumstances, be rationally justified in arguing from diverse and even contradictory metaphysical premises, even within the confines of a single work. The sliding scale of analysis reflects the authors' rhetorical conception of reason, since it is rooted in the notion that rational discourse can and must change in accordance with the premises of the audience addressed.

Although recognizing the widespread use of the sliding scale of analysis in these works helps resolve some issues, it also raises difficult questions about the rhetorical nature of the rationality that these works valorize. Most of these questions cannot be fully answered in this book because they touch on presuppositions so fundamental that they would need another entire work to address them adequately. For example, one could inquire to what degree the sliding scale of analysis operates by playing on the tension mentioned above, whereby the standards of rationality by which arguments may be judged actually depend for their reliable operation on the continued presence of a degree of primordial ignorance in the author's (and audience's) mind. Similarly, one might also ask whether the sliding scale of analysis implies a kind of pragmatic theory of truth, whereby different things can be true for different people at different times. Or, one might consider whether we are dealing here with a form of practical reasoning in which truth *per se* is not the authors' primary concern. These are extremely important questions, and we will continue to touch on them in the pages to come. The primary focus of the investigation, however, will remain the authors' understanding and rational defense of omniscience, and especially the way that rational defense relies upon a rhetoric of reason in both of the senses described above.

Omniscience is a particularly fruitful doctrine to examine in this context for several reasons. First, omniscience has a special connection to the rhetoric of reason through its association with religious authority. That is, as these

---

omniscience. For example, although Wood understands that different statements on omniscience are addressed to different audiences, he does not recognize that this is part of Śāntarakṣita and Kamalaśīla's philosophical *method* and rhetorical *strategy*; he therefore interprets the statements simply as mired in blatant contradiction. See Wood 1991: 142–44.

20. Dunne (2004: 53–79) provides an extended description of this technique in the works of Dharmakīrti. See also Dreyfus 1997: 98–99 and 103–5.

texts state and as is corroborated in other Buddhist and non-Buddhist works, there is a clear supposition on the part of most Indian philosophers that the primary motivation for undertaking a demonstration of the Buddha's omniscience is to provide an unshakable foundation for the truth of the Buddhist scriptures. After all, if one were able to demonstrate that a particular person knew everything, then one could also feel comfortable accepting whatever that person has said to be true. But if this is an accurate description of the authors' motives in undertaking to demonstrate the Buddha's omniscience, would it not then diminish their rhetoric of *reason*? Why would a person who values reason as the highest arbiter of truth care about grounding scriptures? Would not reason alone suffice for deciding all matters? The close connection that omniscience has with religious authority brings such questions into high relief, and presents a conundrum that will occupy us throughout much of this book: if the motive for undertaking a demonstration of the Buddha's omniscience is *not* to establish his religious authority, then why bother to demonstrate it at all? A possible solution—and one for which I argue in this book—is that the authors wish different audiences to come away with different answers to the problem of reconciling reason and religious authority. This connects again to the rhetoric of reason, in that one answer or argument does not fit all audiences. It also opens the door to asking about political, social, or institutional motivations that may lurk behind the arguments for the Buddha's omniscience.[21]

Another important way that omniscience is related to the rhetoric of reason concerns the authors' conception of omniscience as the proper goal of all rational and judicious persons. A result of this conception is that when Śāntarakṣita and Kamalaśīla argue for the possibility of human beings attaining omniscience, they may be seen also as arguing for a special way of life that is specifically designed to lead to this particular goal. Omniscience is thus not just one doctrine among many for these thinkers but rather the highest good and final destination of all those who seriously value and practice rational inquiry. When the authors claim to have demonstrated the Buddha's omniscience through reason, they at the same time claim to have shown the rational justification for the path that has omniscience as its goal. They say, in

21. Relatively little is known about the political, social, and institutional realities within which Śāntarakṣita and Kamalaśīla worked. Research to date, however, indicates that in post-Gupta India (i.e., starting in the sixth century C.E.), Buddhism suffered something of a geographical contraction as well as a loss of patronage from trade guilds and royal patrons. The new realities under which monastic Buddhism operated may well have provided added incentives for undertaking the refutation of non-Buddhist ideas and the rebuttal of attacks on Buddhist doctrines. See Davidson 2002: 75–112.

effect, that the Buddhist path is a rational path, grounded in reason, which any rational person will be bound to follow if only he or she comes to see its rationality for him or herself. This underlying argument corresponds to Perelman and Olbrechts-Tyteca's conception of rhetoric, since those authors hold that an essential aspect of all argumentation involves persuading an audience to adopt a particular action, or at least to open themselves to the possibility of adopting such an action in appropriate circumstances.[22] One way of reading this bipartite Buddhist work, then, is essentially as an apology for Buddhist practice, designed to convince rational persons to take up the Buddhist path with the eventual goal of attaining omniscience themselves.

Buddhist Philosophia

The above assessment of the *Tattvasaṃgraha* and the *Pañjikā* as offering an apology not just for Buddhist doctrines but also for Buddhist practice brings into relief the question of whether these texts should be considered works of religion, philosophy, or something else altogether. Matthew Kapstein has recently addressed a similar question in relation to these and other Buddhist texts from around the same period, asking in particular what it can possibly mean to speak of the works as "Buddhist philosophy."[23] Noting that many of the works in question contain formidable arguments that can be compared with arguments from the Western philosophical tradition, Kapstein nevertheless maintains that the presence of these arguments is not the only or even the most important warrant for speaking of these works as Buddhist philosophy. Instead, he invokes Pierre Hadot's reading of *philosophia* in ancient Greece as "a way of life" whose goal is a kind of personal transformation brought about through a variety of "spiritual exercises" (*exercices spirituels*).[24] In my earlier doctoral thesis, I similarly invoked Hadot, since, like Kapstein, I think that attention to the larger question of how the *practice* of philosophy contributes to the formation of persons is critical to understanding the

22. See Perelman and Olbrechts-Tyteca 1969: 45: "The goal of all argumentation, as we have said before, is to create or increase the adherence of minds to the theses presented for their assent. An efficacious argument is one which succeeds in increasing this intensity of adherence among those who hear it in such a way as to set in motion the intended action (a positive action or an abstention from action) or at least in creating in the hearers a willingness to act which will appear at the right moment."

23. Kapstein 2001: 3–26.

24. Kapstein 2001: 7–9. See also Hadot 1995: 81–109.

nature of *any* form of philosophy.[25] In the case in question, there is good reason to hold that the practices enjoined by the text centrally include the practice of rational inquiry, and that the arguments that make up the bulk of the works are themselves a part of that practice.

In the case of ancient Greek *philosophia*, the parallels to Indian Buddhism are strong. Following Hadot, we can understand *philosophia* to be "a form of life defined by an ideal of wisdom,"[26] where wisdom is "a state of complete liberation from the passions, utter lucidity, knowledge of ourselves and of the world."[27] Wisdom is the goal of this form of life, and approaching or achieving wisdom brings about a transformation of the person that involves liberation from things such as "worries, passions, and desires."[28] To achieve such a transformation, the philosopher undertakes particular exercises of reason "designed to ensure spiritual progress toward the ideal state of wisdom," much as an athlete trains to win a competition or a doctor applies a cure.[29]

Although these exercises of reason may be called *meditations*, Hadot argues instead for calling them "spiritual exercises" on the grounds that they are exercises that "engage the totality of the spirit."[30] According to Hadot, all

25. This is part of what I take Kapstein to be saying when he states (2001: 20), "However, in suggesting that perhaps the richest analogue between traditional Buddhist thought and Western philosophies is to be found not in the comparison of particular arguments so much as in the overriding project of philosophy as a vehicle for the formation of the person through spiritual exercise, as has been emphasized by Hadot, a new perspective may also be disclosed, not only for comparative reflection on arguments and practices elaborated in the past, but in considering also our unactualized prospects. If Buddhism is to emerge as a viable current in Western thought over the long duration, its point of departure will have to be sustained and critical reflection upon its ideals of the good in relation to our contemporary predicaments."

26. Hadot 1995: 59.

27. Hadot 1995: 103.

28. Hadot 1995: 103.

29. Hadot 1995: 59. The reference to philosophy as similar to a medical cure recalls another way in which Buddhist philosophy resembles ancient Greek *philosophia*. As is generally well known, Buddhists frequently refer to their founder, the Buddha, as the "great physician" (*mahābhaiṣajya*), and analogize the nobles' four truths along a medical model of sickness (suffering), diagnosis (the cause of suffering), prognosis (the end of suffering), and cure (the Buddhist path). As Martha Nussbaum has pointed out, a similar understanding of the philosophical enterprise occurs in Hellenistic thought, among both Greeks and Romans. As she so eloquently states (1994: 14): "Philosophy heals human diseases, diseases produced by false beliefs."

30. Hadot 1995: 127. See also the chapter "Spiritual Exercises" in Hadot 1995: 81–125.

ancient Greek philosophical schools practiced such exercises. This is because they all agreed that

> ...man, before his philosophical conversion, is in a state of unhappy disquiet. Consumed by worry, torn by passions, he does not live a genuine life, nor is he truly himself. All schools also agree that man can be delivered from this state. He can accede to genuine life, improve himself, transform himself, and attain a state of perfection. It is precisely for this that spiritual exercises are intended.[31]

Hadot maintains that these exercises are "unlike the Buddhist meditation practices of the Far East," since they are not linked to a specific corporal posture and are instead "purely rational, imaginative, or intuitive."[32] But despite this disclaimer, I see nothing in the above description of philosophy to which Śāntarakṣita and Kamalaśīla would be likely to object.[33] On the contrary, it seems to me they would see his statement as close to encapsulating their own understanding of what they themselves do. For these Buddhists also recommend and engage in specific exercises of reason—including, and especially, the act of rational inquiry itself—as a central element in a way of life in which one seeks to transform oneself through developing and perfecting wisdom in an effort to remove suffering, that unfortunate state of ignorance and "unhappy disquiet."[34]

For Śāntarakṣita and Kamalaśīla, this way of life is the Buddhist path (*mārga*). The goal is intellectual and moral perfection, a state of perfect wisdom and compassion called "awakening" (*bodhi*) or "perfect and complete awakening" (*samyaksaṃbodhi*). This path, like *philosophia*, entails of a way of being in the world whereby a judicious person, the counterpart of the Greek

31. Hadot 1995: 102.

32. Hadot 1995: 59.

33. Conceivably, a Buddhist might question the idea that man, before his conversion, is not "truly himself," on the grounds that there is no Self to which he can be true. But this objection would be trivial, because Hadot's depiction, as I understand it, describes a situation in which a person, before engaging in spiritual exercises and *philosophia*, does not live in accord with the way things truly are (Sanskrit: *yathābhūta*), and is therefore out of step, not only with himself but, in fact, with the universe as a whole. This very general description clearly applies to Buddhist thought.

34. See Hadot 1995: 126, "It is *philosophy itself* that the ancients thought of as a spiritual exercise."

philosopher-sage, seeks to cultivate wisdom by every possible means in order to attain the maximal degree of wisdom attainable by a human being. This also entails that, as part of the cultivation of wisdom, a judicious person on the Buddhist path *must* be unrelenting in subjecting his or her ideas and experiences (his or her "thought") to rational, philosophical analysis. The high degree of confidence that the authors place in the power of rational analysis to remove confusion and ascertain reality leads them to accept that through intensive thought or deliberation (*cintā*), a person may attain certainty (*niścaya*) concerning the way things really are.[35]

It is important to remember that while rational analysis may lead to unshakable certainty concerning the nature of reality, this certainty is still a rhetorically formed linguistic or conceptual construct. As such, this "certainty" is (paradoxically) still connected with ignorance. It is therefore also not the final goal of the path, which involves the complete removal of primordial ignorance and its attendant suffering. Since the removal of ignorance does not take place at the level of language or concepts, the ultimate goal of the path cannot be achieved by rational analysis. Rather, the removal of ignorance requires a transformation of the very structure of the mind itself, which in turn requires one to engage in a process of meditative cultivation (*bhāvanā*). Yet rational analysis still plays a critical role, because it allows one to rule out a whole range of incorrect views and replace them with views that while not able to directly encapsulate reality, can nevertheless be ascertained as in accord with reality. On the basis of such views, one then undertakes the meditative cultivation that gradually eliminates the distortions of primordial ignorance (and hence, also, all "views"), such that one's thought and experience come to be in accord with reality. Eliminating ignorance brings about the elimination of suffering (*duḥkha*)—a term that could arguably be translated as "unhappy disquiet."

*What rational analysis is important.

Thinking of texts like the *Tattvasaṃgraha* and the *Pañjikā* as works of Buddhist *philosophia* and thereby highlighting structural similarities with the practice of philosophy in ancient Greece thus allows us to more clearly see the deeply practical elements of the Buddhist philosophical enterprise. It does not, of course, mean that Buddhist and Greek philosophy are the same nor that the differences between them are unimportant. As Vincent

35. For Śāntarakṣita, Kamalaśīla, and other Buddhists, we can point to the practices of study (*śruti*), thought or deliberation (*cintā*), and meditation or cultivation (*bhāvanā*) as three crucial "spiritual exercises" of the tradition. Analysis (*vicāra*) is also clearly highly valued, as is debate (*vāda*) that is oriented toward the truth. See Scherrer-Schaub 1981: 195–99. See also Eltschinger 2007c for a study of *cintā*.

Eltschinger has recently argued in a lengthy article responding both to Kapstein's use of Hadot and to my own earlier use of Hadot in my doctoral thesis, scholars of Buddhism remain woefully uninformed concerning the details of the social and historical conditions informing the practice of Buddhism, including what we have come to call Buddhist philosophy, in ancient India.[36] Unlike Hadot in his study of *philosophia* in the Hellenistic world, scholars of Buddhism have barely any reliable knowledge concerning the institutional realities and other social conditions under which monks like Śāntarakṣita and Kamalaśīla lived and worked.[37] Nor can we be certain about the actual spiritual exercises in which they engaged. These gaps in our knowledge render problematic any assessment of their work as analogous to the *philosophia* of the ancient world, apparent similarities aside.

Eltschinger further emphasizes that the spiritual exercises of the Hellenistic world differ from those Indian Buddhist practices that we might be tempted to term "spiritual exercises" in Hadot's sense of the term. For example, the spiritual exercise of "training for death," varieties of which Hadot takes as central to several ancient Greek schools, would no doubt look different had it developed in a context, such as that of ancient India, in which philosophers contemplating death envisioned "myriads of births to come."[38] While this is true, Kapstein nevertheless has little difficulty pointing to a number of Buddhist texts—"path texts" like the *Bodhicaryāvatāra* of Śāntideva (eighth century)—in which, to adopt Hadot's idiom, "training for death is related both to scrupulous attention to the moral quality of one's actions and to a general meditation on the nature of all conditioned entities as fleeting and impermanent."[39] These are general characteristics of the Hellenistic practice of training for death, and the doctrine of future births does not negate this, even if it does change how such a practice might affect one's thought about the present life.

The point is not to find the same or similar spiritual exercises in all these disparate philosophical systems and thinkers. It is to see that these particular Buddhist works advocate a form of *praxis* that includes and even glorifies rational analysis, at least to a certain extent. Thus, as Kapstein notes, these Buddhists are perhaps more like Aristotle than they are like Socrates, Plato, or Plotinus. And while it is true that Aristotle, with his emphasis on

36. Eltschinger 2008.

37. Eltschinger 2008: 532.

38. Eltschinger 2008: 537–38.

39. Kapstein 2001: 8.

theoria, is not at the center of Hadot's works, while Plato and the others are, this does not mean that Aristotle should be excluded from the larger scope of "philosophy-as-spiritual-exercise."[40] Indeed, as Kapstein explains:

> ... Hadot does have a position on Aristotle, and it is one that, perhaps to some degree echoing Heidegger, stresses *our* mistaken tendency to read *theoria* as synonymous with what we now mean by "theory," and accordingly to position *theoria* over and against what we call "practice." For Hadot, *theoria* in Aristotle's sense is itself the most highly valued practice; it is, in fact, that practice through which human beings may come to participate in an activity that is characteristically divine. Where Aristotle departs from Plato is not in valuing theoretical knowledge above practice, but in valuing a specific type of practice, *theoria*, and the way of life that it entails, over the life of political practice that had been so dear to his master.[41]

Although Śāntarakṣita and Kamalaśīla clearly differ from Aristotle in numerous respects, there is at least this important point of continuity: that for both traditions rational analysis and inquiry are forms of spiritual exercises in Hadot's sense of the term, the correct practice of which conduces toward the highest good (differently conceived though this may be).

Rightly seeking to explore this claim further, Eltschinger makes reference to two distinct Buddhist schematics that involve rational analysis.[42] The first is the widespread schematic of three successive kinds of wisdom: wisdom arisen from study (*śrutamayīprajñā*); wisdom arisen from deliberation (*cintāmayīprajñā*); and wisdom arisen from meditation (*bhāvanāmayīprajñā*). In this schematic, which we find throughout the *Tattvasaṃgraha* and the *Pañjikā*, it is the middle factor, the wisdom arisen from deliberation, that bears on the theme of rational analysis and inquiry. The second schematic, found mainly in the treatises of the Yogācāra school of Mahāyāna Buddhism but apparently absent in the *Tattvasaṃgraha* and the *Pañjikā*, is that of five "sciences" (*vidyā*). These are the science of logic (*hetuvidyā*); the science of grammar (*śabdavidyā*); the science of medicine (*cikitsāvidyā*); the science of arts (*śilpakarmasthānavidyā*); and the science of the inner spirit

40. Kapstein 2001: 9.

41. Kapstein 2001: 9.

42. In addition to the article on Hadot (2008), see also Eltschinger 2007b: 462–66, where many of the same arguments are presented.

(*adhyātmavidyā*). Eltschinger notes that commentators such as Sthiramati consider the first four sciences to be "worldly" (*laukika*). The science of logic, like that of grammar, is considered to have three main aims: to defeat opponents, to increase faith among those who possess it, and to convert those who do not have faith.[43] From this, Eltschinger concludes that "Buddhist epistemologists denied any soteriological[44] relevance to epistemology as such, which, they contend, has no other *raison d'être* than to discard the heretics' misguiding epistemological doctrines."[45] He then cites a passage from the *Tattvasaṃgrahapañjikā* as evidence for this claim.[46] Although the passage does mention refuting opponents, and thus does attest to a polemical function for the *Tattvasaṃgraha* and the *Pañjikā*, I can see no reason to read it as indicating that logic and reasoning have *no* soteriological relevance. Indeed, it seems to me that even if we focus just on the role of logic to bring about the conversion of non-believers, we must acknowledge its soteriological role.

Eltschinger discusses the passage from the *Tattvasaṃgrahapañjikā* alongside another from Dharmakīrti's *Pramāṇaviniścaya*.[47] In this passage,

43. Eltschinger 2008: 523 and 2007b: 459–63.

44. *Soteriological* is derived from the theological term *soteriology*, meaning "the doctrine of salvation." In the Buddhist context, it relates to the ultimate goals of the Buddhist path, which can be understood as a form of salvation in the sense that one may be "saved" from saṃsāra, albeit generally through one's individual application of the Buddhist teachings and not through the grace or power of a divine being.

45. Eltschinger 2007b: 463.

46. Eltschinger 2007b: 464–65 and 2008: 524. The passage cited from the TSP (B 13,1–12) is part of Kamalaśīla's exegesis of the six opening verses of TS. Translations of most portions of this passage are found later in this book and can be located by referring to "Index of Translated Passages" at the end of the book. The final lines of this passage (TSP *ad* TS 1–6, B 13,10–13) are as follows: *sa cāyaṃ pratītyasamutpādaḥ parair viṣamahetuḥ pramāṇavyāhatapadārthādhikaraṇaś ceṣyate / atas tannirāsane yathāvad eva bhagavatokta iti darśanārthaṃ vakṣyamāṇasakalaśāstrapratipādyārthatattvopakṣepārthaṃ ca bahūnāṃ yathoktapratītyasamutpādaviśeṣāṇām upādānam iti samudāyārthaḥ* //. "And others assert that this dependent arising is a false cause and is a basis for topics refuted by the means of trustworthy awareness. Therefore, when [Śāntarakṣita] refutes them, it is for the sake of demonstrating that what the Blessed One taught is correct; and the enumeration of the many distinctions of dependent arising [in the opening verses] is for the sake of indicating the realities (*tattva*) that are the topics to be explained in the entire treatise that is to be composed. This is the general meaning [of the opening verses, TS 1–6]." For detailed discussion of TS 1–6, see pp. 95–101 below.

47. PVin 1 *ad* PVin 1.58 (Steinkellner ed., 2007: 44): *sāṃvyavahārikasya caitat pramāṇasya rūpam uktam atrāpi pare mūḍhā visaṃvādayanti lokam iti / cintāmayīm eva tu prajñām anuśilayanto vibhramavivekanirmalam anapāyi pāramārthikapramāṇam*

Dharmakīrti contrasts a conventional means of trustworthy awareness (*sāṃvyavahārikapramāṇa*) with an ultimate one (*pāramārthikapramāṇa*), stating those who are confused regarding the conventional means of trustworthy awareness mislead the world (*visaṃvādayanti lokam*). The ultimate means of trustworthy awareness, described as stainless and free from error, is realized by those who have assiduously cultivated the wisdom arisen from deliberation. Eltschinger summarizes his understanding of this passage as follows:

> Since conventional *pramāṇa*s are instrumental in the path to liberation insofar as the whole process of *cintā-mayī-prajñā* resorts to them, Dharmakīrti considers it his duty to refute these misconceptions so that people are not led astray. In other words, epistemology or *hetu-vidyā* as a theoretical concern has no direct bearing on the path to salvation, but misconceived *pramāṇa*s ensure one's failure to achieve liberation, and hence epistemology is a necessary science.[48]

Elsewhere, Eltschinger has shown that Yogācāra treatises understand the wisdom arisen from deliberation to involve four kinds of reasoning (*yukti*), one of which in particular (*upapattisādhanayukti*) may be correlated with the science of logic (*hetuvidyā*) from within the schematic of the five sciences. But if this is the case, then it is difficult to understand his reading of Dharmakīrti. After all, if the science of logic is integral to the cultivation of the wisdom arisen from deliberation, and if that wisdom is in turn critical to the realization of the ultimate means of trustworthy awareness, does it really make sense to say that the science of logic has "no direct bearing" on the path to awakening?

The answer to this question may well lie in our assessment of the authors' own view of their epistemic situation. That is, in linking the *Pramāṇaviniścaya* passage with the passage from the *Tattvasaṃgrahapañjikā* mentioned earlier, Eltschinger states that "Dharmakīrti and Kamalaśīla agree in denying that epistemology itself has any soteriological value whatsoever *provided one is not under the sway of misconceptions*" (emphasis added).[49] But this is precisely the point: on my reading, Indian Buddhists like Śāntarakṣita, Kamalaśīla, and Dharmakīrti maintain that *we all are under the sway of misconceptions* as

abhimukhīkurvanti //. For translations see Eltschinger 2007b: 464; Krasser 2005: 142–44; and Dunne 2004: 315–16.

48. Eltschinger 2007b: 464.

49. Eltschinger 2007b: 465–66.

[handwritten margin notes: double purpose of Reason and logic: 1.) Remove false views re: opponents 2.) to remove false views on the practitioner.]

long as we have not obtained perfect and complete awakening. Thus, while the application of logic and reasoning does serve the purpose of refuting the grossly inaccurate views of opponents, it also has a therapeutic function of helping Buddhist practitioners both to remove gross misconceptions and to begin to correct subtle ones. As Kapstein aptly notes, for Śāntarakṣita and Kamalaśīla, the mistaken views to be counteracted through the application of rational analysis "are not just *others'* views of *themselves,* but that, potentially at least, they are views that any of us may harbor, whether explicitly or not, with respect to *our*selves."[50] Just because the reasoning in question is conventional does not make it ineffective or soteriologically irrelevant.

Returning to the question, then, of whether and how to apply Hadot's analysis of ancient Greek *philosophia* to the works in question, we can see that much depends upon our understanding of the nature of the reasoning at work in these texts. Eltschinger seems to want to separate the highly technical Buddhist treatises of the logico-epistemological tradition, such as the *Tattvasaṃgraha* and the *Pañjikā,* from other forms of Buddhist life and practice. He then advocates that it is these other forms of Buddhist life and practice—what he calls "Buddhism itself"—and not the treatises and ideas that Western scholars have tended to label as Buddhist philosophy, that most resemble the *philosophia* of ancient Greece.[51] The texts of the logico-epistemological school are not concerned with the nondiscursive ethical and soteriological *praxis* that is revealed through the Buddhist scriptures.[52] Instead, they serve a purely polemical function since, apparently, the Buddhist authors have no misconceptions remaining to be put to rest. But this assumes a degree of *hubris* on the part of authors like Śāntarakṣita and Kamalaśīla that belies their own statements concerning both the limitations and the utility of concepts and language, both necessary to the science of logic. The *Tattvasaṃgraha* and the *Pañjikā* may be considered as works of Buddhist *philosophia* insofar as they advocate the use of reasoning as a practice and a way of life that contribute to leading one away from misery and to the attainment of the highest human goal: perfect and complete awakening, buddhahood, omniscience.

50.   Kapstein 2001: 15.

51.   Eltschinger 2008: 529.

52.   Eltschinger 2008: 531–32.

The Contours of Omniscience in India

The defense of omniscience in the *Tattvasaṃgraha* and the *Pañjikā* arises within a complex landscape of competing views and arguments concerning omniscience cutting across the religious traditions of ancient and medieval India. Diverse traditions from ancient times assert and defend some form of omniscience for their founders, sages, or deities. In the Pāli Nikāyas of early Buddhism, we read that the Nigaṇṭha Nātaputta—the founder of the Jain tradition known to his followers as the Jina or Vardhamāna Mahāvīra—as well as the teacher Pūraṇa Kassapa both claimed to possess complete and continuous knowledge.[53] The Jains in particular upheld a very strong version of omniscience for their founder, and Jains were among the earliest systematic defenders of the notion, probably inspiring some later Buddhist arguments.[54] Patañjali in the *Yoga Sūtra* allows that a yogi may become omniscient, although doing so does not seem to be necessary for the attainment of liberation (*mokṣa*).[55] The Sāṃkhyas also give omniscient status to Lord Īśvara (roughly "God," though not necessarily the creator of the world in this system).[56] In the wider Brahmanic literary and religious traditions, great sages and gods from the Veda onward are often said to be all-knowing or all-seeing, although it is not clear whether such epithets are to be understood literally or in some other fashion.[57] Naiyāyikas hold that Īśvara, the creator of the world, is by nature omniscient and that his omniscience is established by virtue of establishing his creatorship.[58] Later Buddhist traditions, both in Pāli and Sanskrit, extol the Buddha's omniscient and inconceivable knowledge. In later Hinduism, major deities like Śiva, Viṣṇu, and Durgā are all described as omniscient, and they are given as examples of omniscience in traditional

53. See, for example, the *Cūḷadukkhakkhanda Sutta* at *Majjhima Nikāya* 14.17 (MN i.92). For a book-length treatment of omniscience in Jainism, see Singh 1974. See also Jaini 1974; Kariyawasam 2001: 135–36

54. See Sin 2000; Singh 1974; and Jaini 1974.

55. Relevant discussions may be found at *Yoga Sūtra* I.24–27; I.48–49; and III.54–55. See Solomon 1962.

56. See Bronkhorst (1983, 1996) for discussions of such a God in the Sāṃkhya and Vaiśeṣika traditions. See also Chemaparathy 1969.

57. Singh (1979) provides a wealth of references to omniscience in the Vedas, Upaniṣads, epics, Purāṇas, and related works.

58. See Chemparathy 1969: 125–30 and 1972: 168–72.

lexicons.[59] In short, omniscient beings abound in India in ways that they do not in the West.

But critics of omniscience can also be found in India. The Buddha himself is seen to reject certain formulations of all-encompassing knowledge in the early strata of the Pāli Nikāyas. Although later Pāli sources uphold certain other forms of omniscience, and Mahāyāna treatises frequently tout the dimensions of the Buddha's omniscience as inconceivable, it is nonetheless clear that Buddhism has a history of ambivalence toward the stronger forms of omniscient knowing. In the era just prior to Śāntarakṣita and Kamalaśīla, the Mīmāṃsaka philosopher Kumārila Bhaṭṭa (sixth or seventh century) launches a formidable attack on the idea, and it is primarily in response to this attack that the bulk of the argumention concerning omniscience in the *Tattvasaṃgraha* and the *Pañjikā* is composed. Around the same time as well, the Lokāyata sceptic Jayarāśi rejects even ordinary knowledge claims, to say nothing of claims concerning the existence of supersensible realities like a buddha's omniscient mind.[60] Dharmakīrti (seventh century), an important predecessor and intellectual influence for Śāntarakṣita and Kamalaśīla, is similarly well known for his remarks dismissing the significance of supersensible knowing—stating that if seeing far is the mark of wisdom, then we might as well worship vultures—though his precise position on omniscience remains something of an open question. There is thus a great diversity of opinion regarding omniscience in India, and many of these opinions are developed in conversation with rival models or attacks.

Terms for omniscience in the Indian texts are also diverse, though in general they are similar to the Latin term *omniscience* in that they are compound words made up of a component denoting some form of totality (e.g., *sarva*; *sabba*) and a component denoting some form of knowing (e.g., *jña*; *ñu*). Note that such terms may denote both omniscience and the omniscient being; abstract endings (e.g., *-tva*) may be added when the discussion is specifically focused on the state of omniscience and not on the omniscient being. The nature of the terms highlights the need to understand the nature of both the totality and the knowledge in question when considering the precise meaning of omniscience for a given text, thinker, or tradition.

This is by no means obvious, however, since extreme differences in the understanding of both components may be found in the diverse religious and philosophical traditions of India. Consider, for example, Jan Gonda's research on the the term *sarva* in early Vedic texts, which indicates that

59. Singh 1979: 1.

60. Franco 1987.

omniscience would originally have meant something like "knowledge that is complete" in the sense of not lacking anything essential, as opposed to a literal "knowledge of all things whatsoever."[61] Similarly, in the *Sabba Sutta*, the Buddha defines "all" or *sabba* as the twelve sense media (*āyatana*): the eye and visual forms; the ear and audible sounds; the nose and smells; the tongue and tastes; the body and tangible objects; the mind and mental objects.[62] While the implications of this claim are not entirely obvious, one possibility is that on this definition of the term *all*, omniscience could turn out to be a kind of exhaustive knowledge of the taxonomy of being, such that by knowing all possible categories of things one is considered omniscient.[63] Another possibility is that the meaning of "all" is unique to each individual, changing from person to person.

Whatever the case, it is clear that specifying the nature of omniscience for a given tradition, thinker, or text requires that we also understand the ontological and epistemological premises upon which that concept of omniscience depends. As philosopher of religion Roy Perrett has argued, these differing premises lead to various kinds of restrictions to the scope of the totality that is known in omniscience, as well as to the ways it may be known.[64] Taking the Western tradition first as an example, Perrett argues that the scope of God's omniscient knowledge will be restricted due to "certain fundamental philosophical and theological beliefs about the nature of God and of the world."[65] He goes on to show that by restricting the scope of the term *all* in the phrase *all-knowing* in various ways, it is possible to come up with a range of degrees of omniscience to combat philosophical or theological problems. As examples, he delineates the concepts of *logical* omniscience, *total* omniscience, and *inevitability* omniscience, each of which corresponds to a different kind of omniscience that might be attributed

61. Gonda (1955) has demonstrated that the earliest (Vedic) meanings for the term *sarva* include such ideas as "undivided," "whole," "complete," while its opposite, *asarva*, means "defective," "incomplete," and "lacking something essential."

62. *Saṃyutta Nikāya* (35.23), discussed in Kariyawasam 2001: 139 and Anālayo 2006: 9. Endo 1997: 61–62 provides information on post-canonical Pāli interpretations of the term *sabba*.

63. Such a view of omniscience was suggested by Luis Gómez in an oral presentation at a conference on the Sāṃkhya tradition held at the University of Lausanne in 1998, in which he delineated a model of "truth as taxonomy" in both the Sāṃkhya and the Abhidharma traditions.

64. Perrett 1989.

65. Perrett 1989: 129.

to God.[66] He then sets out to show that restrictions to the scope of omniscience can also be found in the Indian traditions, although the nature of the restrictions differ from those in the West, due again to differences in the ontological and epistemological premises at play.[67]

Indeed, the contours and philosophical problems associated with omniscience in India are different from those associated with omniscience in the West.[68] In the first place, there is a stark difference in assumptions concerning the *kinds* of beings who may be or become omniscient, with many Indian traditions allowing that humans may become omniscient and Western traditions generally limiting omniscience to a single creator God. Further, unlike in India, omniscience in the West is not generally something beings can *attain* but is rather an essential and inalienable property of the divine. The philosophical problems entailed by accepting omniscience appear distinct as well. Thus, while Indian thinkers have been mostly unperturbed by any-

66. Note that all these terms presume a propositional model of knowledge as justified, true belief. Perrett explains the examples as follows (1989: 130): "The point of these examples is that there is nothing in the use of the term 'all' such that to describe a being as 'all-knowing' or 'all-powerful' in itself entails that there can be no limitations on the powers of such a being. The quantifier might well be being used with an implicit restriction of scope.... Thus a claim that a being is all-knowing is more precisely understood as a claim that a being is all-Φ-knowing, where Φ is a class of propositions. Omniscience is really Φ-omniscience and a being is Φ-omniscient if it knows the truth-value of every proposition in Φ. Specifying the class Φ then enables us to differentiate various sorts of omniscience: *logical* omniscience is where Φ is the class of logical truths; *total* omniscience is where Φ is the class of all propositions; *inevitability* omniscience is where Φ is the class of determined propositions; and so on. We can also ask of the class Φ whether it is closed under deduction. If it is, then Φ-omniscience entails logical omniscience. Hence we have a spectrum with total omniscience at one end, where Φ is the full class of all propositions, and logical omniscience at the other end, where Φ is the class of logical truths. The former is the strongest sort of omniscience, the latter the weakest sort. In between would be inevitability omniscience, where Φ is the class of determined propositions. Thus the thesis that God's omniscience does not include knowledge of future free actions is the thesis that God is inevitability omniscient, but not totally omniscient."

67. As one of his examples from the Indian tradition, Perrett (1989: 135) discusses Śāntarakṣita and Kamalaśīla's restriction of omniscience to the "class of truths necessary for salvation." While I think that Perrett does better justice to Śāntarakṣita and Kamalaśīla's interpretation of omniscience than some others have done, his brief article does not begin to unpack the complexity of their argumentation in the TS/P.

68. For summaries of some of the differences between Western and Indian accounts of omniscience, see Perrett 1989 and Griffiths 1989. For a summary of some of the theoretical problems associated with the notion of omniscience in Christian theology, see Nash 1983: 51–66.

thing like the notorious conflict in Christian theology between divine omniscience and human free will, they were greatly disturbed by the conundrum of how an omniscient being could speak—an issue that does not seem to have struck Western theologians at all.[69] An area for further research is the question of whether and how such differences in the approach to omniscience in India and the West can be related to differences in the approach to knowledge: whereas the Western tradition generally understands knowledge to be propositional and to involve justified true belief, the Indian tradition tends to understand knowledge as a kind of trustworthy or faultless awareness, and this seems to impact the types of problems that theorists discover when considering the possibility of an omniscient mind.

Foundational to all discussions of omniscience in India is a basic understanding concerning knowledge and liberation whereby knowledge or awareness (*jñāna*) of reality (*tattva*) is incompatible with all moral and intellectual faults (*doṣa*). These faults, in turn, are the principal causes of suffering, which for many theorists continues throughout innumerable lifetimes in the seemingly endless cyle of repeated birth, death, and rebirth known as *saṃsāra*. Since the goal of religious practice is ultimate release or liberation (*mokṣa; apavarga*)—in other words, everlasting freedom from suffering—the goal of religious practice requires the elimination of all moral and intellectual faults, including all forms of ignorance and misconception. The main way to eliminate these faults is to gain accurate knowledge of reality.[70] In this way, Indian religious philosophy assigns correct knowledge of reality an exalted position

69. The problem of how an omniscient being can speak results from the idea that the elimination of ignorance requires the elimination of all desire (*rāga*), and speech is generally seen as motivated by the intention or the desire to speak (*vivakṣā*). We treat Śāntarakṣita and Kamalaśīla's approach to this problem in chapter 5. On the question of omniscience and the problem of free will and determinism, both Jayatillike (1963: 469) and Endo (1997: 60–61) see the resistance to the idea that the Buddha knows the future in the early Theravāda texts as compatible with the Buddha's rejection of determinism (*niyativāda*). Later Theravāda and non-Theravāda sources seem unperturbed by this problem, however. On the issue of freedom and determination in Buddhism more generally, see Gómez 1975 and Siderits 1987 and 2008.

70. This idea is clearly shown, for example, by Vātsyāyana in NBh *ad* NS 1.1.2: *yadā tu tattvajñānān mithyājñānam apaiti tadā mithyājñānāpāye doṣā apayanti doṣāpāye pravṛttir apaiti pravṛttyapāye janmāpaiti janmāpāye duḥkham apaiti duḥkhāpāye cātyantiko 'pavargo niḥśreyasam iti //*. "But since false awareness disappears through awareness of reality, then when false awareness is gone, the faults disappear; when the faults are gone, activity disappears; when activity is gone, (re-)birth disappears; when birth is gone, suffering disappears; and when suffering is gone, there is liberation (*apavarga*), the highest good (*niḥśreyasa*)." Translated and discussed in Oberhammer 1984: 3ff.

in the quest for liberation, and controversies among Indian thinkers generally have more to do with disputes about the nature of knowledge and the nature of reality than they do with this widespread and basic structure. The central relevant questions for Indian religious philosophers then become: What is reality? How is it known? When does knowledge of reality reach its perfection so that faults are eliminated and freedom from suffering is obtained? Should such perfection of knowledge be called omniscience, and if so, what does the term imply?

The terms of omniscience naturally fall on the issue of Reality

Omniscience in the Pāli Texts and the Theravāda Tradition

Answers to these questions are extremely diverse in India, and even within the Buddhist tradition we find conflicting models of the Buddha's perfect knowledge of reality. The earliest layers of the Pāli canon do not use the epithet omniscient one (*sabbaññū*) for the Buddha, although the term becomes common in late canonical works and in the commentarial (*aṭṭhakathā*) literature.[71] More typical in the early Pāli works are passages in which the Buddha denies that he or anyone possesses the kind of all-encompassing knowledge in which it is possible to have simultaneous and continuous knowledge of everything in a single moment of cognition. The Buddha's proclamation in the *Kaṇṇakatthala Sutta* is most definitive: "There is no recluse or brahman who knows all, who sees all, simultaneously; that is not possible."[72] A well known passage from the *Tevijjavacchagotta Sutta* furthermore has the Buddha vigorously rebuff the notion that he claims to be omniscient in the sense in which "knowledge and vision are continuously and uninterruptedly present" before him.[73] Instead, he says, his wisdom amounts to a "threefold knowledge" (*tevijja*) consisting of the following: (1) he can recollect any of his former lives (*pubbenivāsa*) in all their details whenever he pleases; (2) he can use his divine eye (*dibbacakkhu*) to see the wanderings of beings in saṃsāra whenever he likes; and (3) he abides in the knowledge that he has realized mental freedom (*cetovimutti*) and the freedom of wisdom (*paññāvimutti*) through the destruction of the defilements (*āsava*).[74] Although such knowl-

71. Endo 1997: 9; 23ff.

72. MN 90.8 (ii.127). Translation by Ñāṇamoli and Bodhi 1995: 735.

73. MN 71 (i.482). Translation by Ñāṇamoli and Bodhi 1995: 587.

74. For discussion, see Jaini 1974: 80–81; Jayatilleke 1963: 467–68; Anālayo 2006: 6–7; and Endo 1997: 17. The three types of knowledge are interestingly described in the *Kandaraka Sutta* (MN 51), where they are not referred to with the term *tevijja* and where the presentation is not linked to a discussion of omniscience as it is in the *Tevijjavacchagotta*

edge is clearly extraordinary, it is not obviously an instance of omniscience. There are plenty of realities (for example, the number of bugs in the world) not covered by this threefold knowledge. And it is also clearly not a simultaneous knowledge of all things (for example, rocks, planets, or stars) in all times and places.

Nothing in this or any other text indicates that the Buddha's threefold knowledge differs in any way from the threefold knowledge attributed to the Buddha's enlightened disciples, the noble ones or arhats (Pāli *arahant*). But other passages do suggest that the Buddha's knowledge greatly surpasses that of his arhat disciples. In the parable of the *siṃsapā* leaves, the Buddha holds up a few leaves and asks his disciples which are more numerous: the leaves he holds or the leaves in the *siṃsapā* grove in which they sit. The disciples answer that the leaves in the grove are more numerous. Just so, the Buddha proclaims, "the things I have directly known but have not taught you are numerous, while the things I have taught you are few."[75] The Buddha goes on to explain that he has not taught those many things because they are irrelevant to the path. What is important, he stresses, is knowledge of the so-called nobles' four truths, and so that is what he has taught and what the disciples must realize. The nobles' four truths, which the Buddha is said to have taught in his first sermon, consist in four salvifically crucial truths: (1) that ordinary life is characterized by suffering; (2) that suffering has a cause, known as thirst or craving; (3) that suffering may cease through the elimination of its cause; and (4) that there is an eightfold path which when followed can bring about the cessation of suffering through the elimination of its cause.

Sutta. Instead, the knowledges are here elaborated in the course of outlining the stages of the path to freedom from saṃsāra. The first two knowledges are described as entailing detailed knowledge of the particulars of one's own and others' myriad previous births, rebirths, and the actions (*kamma*; Sanskrit *karman*) leading to those rebirths. This supersensible knowing precedes and appears to be a prerequistite for the acquisition of the knowledge of the destruction of the defilements. This third knowledge is presented here in conjunction with, and as a variation of, the complete understanding of the nobles' four truths. In the *Kandaraka Sutta*, the Buddhist renunciant, or *bhikkhu*, fully comprehends the reality of these four truths, and then fully comprehends the reality of (1) the defilements, (2) their cause, (3) their destruction, and (4) the path that leads to the destruction of the defilements. The renunciant then understands that "Birth is destroyed, the holy life has been lived, what had to be done has been done, there is no more coming to any state of being." In other words, the *bhikkhu* has become an arhat (Pāli *arahant*), a "noble one" who has attained liberation and everlasting freedom from saṃsāra. See also the *Iddhipādasaṃyutta* at Saṃyutta Nikāya 51.11.

75. SN 56.31. Translation by Bodhi 2000: 1857–58.

Complete knowledge or realization of these four truths is very frequently presented as the heart of the Buddhist path to liberation.

There is thus a kind of pragmatism that seems to permeate the early Buddhist writings, and that makes itself felt in a variety of ways. We see, for example, that the Buddha famously refuses to answer certain speculative questions since they are not conducive to liberation.[76] Although the Buddha's silence on these questions seems to have prompted rivals to question his authority, Buddhists have remained adamant that their teacher's refusal to answer the questions is rooted not in his ignorance but in his knowledge of their uselessness for his followers.[77] Similarly, in the *Cūḷasakuludāyi Sutta*, although the Buddha appears to indicate an ability to know the future, he emphasizes that such knowledge is unimportant, counseling his disciple Udāyin as follows:

> But let be the past, Udāyin, let be the future. I shall teach you the Dhamma: When this exists, that comes to be; with the arising of this, that arises. When this does not exist, that does not come to be; with the cessation of this, that ceases.[78]

Here the Buddha characterizes his core teaching not in terms of the nobles' four truths but rather in terms of dependent arising (*paṭiccasamuppāda*; Sanskrit *pratītyasamutpāda*). The doctrine of dependent arising holds that all conditioned things arise from causes, and that the absence of a cause necessarily involves the absence of an effect. Since the nobles' four truths are the most salvifically relevant of the innumerable causal patterns that make up saṃsāra, the central message remains the same: liberation from saṃsāra requires penetration into the causal nature of reality. Omniscient knowledge is not required.

Despite such passages, however, the early Pāli texts do leave room for a kind of omniscience that, while not necessary for liberation from saṃsāra, may nonetheless be attributed to the Buddha. Obviously, this cannot be the kind of omniscience that entails simultaneous and continuous knowledge of all things, since the Buddha rejects this type of knoweldge in the *Kaṇṇakatthala Sutta* cited above. But the Buddha's claim to far-reaching knowledge in the parable of the *siṃsapā* leaves, together with other passages in which he

76. MN 63 (i.426–32), SN 33, and SN 44.

77. To be more precise, it is not only that the Buddha does not consider the answers to these questions to be conducive to liberation. Rather, he understands that the questions as phrased are in fact unanswerable. See Collins 1982: 132–38.

78. MN 79.8ff. (ii.29). Translation by Ñāṇamoli and Bodhi 1995: 655.

indicates that he knows everything that is seen, heard, sensed, and cognized in the universe,[79] lends support to later canonical texts like the *Paṭisambhidāmagga*, which include omniscient knowledge (*sabbaññutāñāṇa*) as one of the six unique forms of knowledge (*asādhārañāṇa*) that only the Buddha possesses.[80] In this and other similar works,[81] the Buddha's omniscient knowledge is extremely far ranging and includes knowledge of all conditioned and unconditioned things; knowledge of everything past, present, and future; and knowledge of everything that has been seen, heard, sensed, or thought by gods or humans.[82] Toshiichi Endo, whose study of the Buddha in the Theravāda tradition is the most comprehensive to date, sees in such passages a process of "apotheosis or exaltation"[83] of the Buddha. K. N. Jayatilleke has a similar view, holding that "neither did the Buddha claim omniscience nor was omniscience claimed of the Buddha until the very latest stratum of the Pāli Canon...."[84] Several scholars have noted that the increased interest in omniscience in Buddhist texts may well reflect rivalry with the Jain tradition, which holds omniscience to be an indispensible attribute of their founder, Vardhamāna Mahāvīra.[85]

problem of contradiction → Indeed, it is difficult to avoid the impression of a struggle within the Buddhist ranks on the question of how to reconcile scriptural passages in which the Buddha claims to know everything or is extolled as omniscient with other passages in which the Buddha appears to deny knowing everything in a single moment of cognition. Eventually, a model of omniscience emerged that seems to have satisfied many mainstream Buddhist commentators. I call this model *capacity omniscience*. On this model, which we find articulated both in the *Milindapañha* and by Vasubandhu in the *Abhidharmakośabhāṣya*, one may be omniscient in the sense that one may attain an unlimited capacity to know whatever one wishes simply by directing one's attention to the object in question; omniscience is not a matter of knowing all things things simultaneously. According to this model, the Buddha may be called "all-knowing" by virtue of the fact of his unlimited capacity to know any knowable thing to which he directs his attention, just as fire may be called "all-consuming"

79. See the *Kalaka Sutta* of the Anguttara Nikāya 4.24.

80. Endo 1997: 27ff. and Anālayo 2006: 4–5.

81. See especially the *Mahānidessa* and the *Cullanidessa* of the Khuddaka Nikāya.

82. Endo 1997: 27–29; Jayatillike 1963: 380–81; Kariyawasam 2001: 140–43.

83. Endo 1997: 19.

84. Jayatillike 1963: 381.

85. See, for example, Singh (1974: 58), who also cites Sukhlalaji 1957 on this point.

by virtue of its capacity to burn all combustible things and not because it actively burns everything all at once.[86] The sixth-century Theravādin scholar Dhammapāla endorses capacity omniscience in his commentary on the fifth-century scholar Buddhaghosa's *Visuddhimagga*, where he adds an interesting twist by stating that the Buddha may in fact turn his attention to "the entire range of *dhammas*," thus directly knowing all things simultaneously.[87] In other words, the doctrine of the Buddha's capacity omniscience does not preclude that the Buddha also possesses knowledge of all things whatsoever. Following Perrett, we can refer to this later doctrine as *total omniscience*, and we can see Dhammapāla's move to embrace it as part of a larger movement toward the exaltation, or apotheosis, of the Buddha. As we will see, the doctrine of total omniscience becomes increasingly widespread and difficult for Buddhists to reject or temper as time goes on.

Mahāsāṃghika and Sarvāstivāda Perspectives on Omniscience

One of the earliest surviving positive accounts of total omniscience is that found in the *Mahāvastu*, a Buddhist Sanskrit treatise connected with the Mahāsāṃghika school and dating in its earliest strata to perhaps the second century B.C.E. As is well known, the Mahāsāṃghika school maintains that the qualities associated with the Buddha are all supramundane (*lokottara*) and as such are untinged by the defilements of the world.[88] For example, the Buddha's conception is immaculate, and while he appears to engage in ordi-

86. *Milindapañha* 102. We find a direct statement of Vasubandhu's position in the *Pudgala-viniścaya* section of the AKBh (B 1205): *naiva ca vayaṃ sarvatra jñānasammukhībhāvād buddhaṃ sarvajñam ācakṣmahe / kiṃ tarhi / sāmarthyāt / yā hy asau buddhākhyā santatis tasyā idam asti sāmarthyaṃ yad ābhogamātreṇāviparītaṃ jñānam utpadyate yatreṣṭam / āha cātra / santānena samarthatvād yathāgniḥ sarvabhuṅ mataḥ / tathā sarvavid eṣṭavyo 'sakṛt sarvasya vedanāt //*. "And we do not proclaim that the Buddha is omniscient due to having direct awareness in relation to all [things at all times]; rather we do so due to [the Buddha's] capacity [for awareness of all things]. For that mental continuum is called 'awakened' (*buddha*) which has the capacity for a nonerroneous awareness to arise spontaneously in relation to anything that is desired. And here it is said that just as fire is held to be 'all-consuming' because of its continual capacity [to devour combustible things], so, too, is the omniscient one to be asserted [as omniscient] due to knowing everything [but] not simultaneously."

87. For Dhammapāla's view as expressed in his commentary on the *Visuddhimagga*, see the long extract translated in Jaini (1974: 84–85). For further analysis of Dhammapāla's position, see Endo 1997: 65–66.

88. Williams 1989: 18–21. For a discussion of omniscience in the *Mahāvastu* and the *Saṃghabhedavastu*, see Anālayo 2006: 11–12. See also Bareau 1969: 12–13.

nary human activies such as eating, bathing, getting sick, and getting old, he does not do so in reality.[89] In keeping with this exalted vision of buddhahood, his omniscience is total in terms of its scope and also in terms of its immediacy. According to the *Mahāvastu*, the Buddha knows all things whatsoever, and he knows them by means of "wisdom connected with a single moment of cognition" (*ekacittakṣaṇasamāyuktayā prajñayā*).[90] Although this material has not been well studied, Zhihua Yao has made an important start in his book on reflexive awareness (*svasaṃvedana; svasaṃvitti*), where he coins the term *instantaneous omniscience* to refer to the knowledge predicated of the Buddha in the Mahāsāṃghika and related schools.[91] On Yao's reading, the Mahāsāṃghikas are able to uphold this kind of instantaneous omniscience in part because they also maintain that the mind is capable of knowing itself.

In contrast, Yao explores the view of the Sarvāstivāda Abhidharma, a school known best for its doctrine maintaining the existence of past, present, and future. Citing Kātyāyanīputra's *Jñānaprasthāna* (first century B.C.E.) Yao notes that the instantaneous total omniscience upheld by the Mahāsāṃghikas is not possible for the Sarvāstivādins, since without a doctrine of reflexive awareness, at least two moments of mind would be required for knowledge of all dharmas to occur: one moment for knowing all things apart from the mind and its associates, and a second moment for knowing the mind and its associates.[92] At the same time, the Sarvāstivāda Abhidharma seems quite comfortable posting an awareness of all conventional dharmas, though it understands this awareness to require multiple moments. Yao calls this model the *gradual model of omniscience*, and argues that it can only be maintained when past and future are accorded the same reality as the present, such that "the present awareness can take the previous awareness as its object and still consider this previous awareness as *itself*."[93] In addition, this omniscient awareness is considered to be defiled. This is so since it is understood to be conventional. An undefiled awareness of all dharmas consists of the knowledge of the nobles' four truths in all their aspects, a view that Yao attributes to the Vaibhāṣika school as well as the Sarvāstivāda.[94] The view that omniscience requires multiple moments seems also to have been shared by

89. Harrison 1982.

90. Yao 2005: 11.

91. Yao 2005: 10–15.

92. Yao 2005: 44–49.

93. Yao 2005: 47.

94. Yao 2005: 46, 71.

the Pudgalavādins, whose views on the topic are represented and refuted by Vasubandhu in the appendix to his *Abhidharmakośabhāṣya*.[95]

Mahāyāna Developments in Theories of the Buddha's Omniscience

The theories outlined above—many of which deserve much greater study than they have received to date—provide the backdrop for the new theories of omniscience that emerge within the Mahāyāna ("Great Vehicle") schools of Indian Buddhism. As is by now well understood, Mahāyāna Buddhism should not be considered as a singular movement or a unitary phenomenon in India.[96] Just as within the non-Mahāyāna schools, enormous variation exists within the Mahāyāna, and these variations extend to the presentation of the Buddha's omniscience. The formulations of omniscience we find in Mahāyāna texts reflect the new metaphysical and epistemological concerns that are characteristic of the Mahāyāna. We also see an increasing emphasis on the Buddha's omniscience as a mark of his superiority over his enlightened disciples and an increasing use of the epithet Omniscient One (*sarvajña*). Śāntarakṣita and Kamalaśīla are part of the later stream of Indian Mahāyāna Buddhism, and they consciously adopt Mahāyāna rhetoric and dogmas throughout their work. But their approach to omniscience is unique to their particular synthesis of the epistemological, Yogācāra, and Madhyamaka schools of thought, as we will explore in the next section below.

Other Mahāyāna formulations of omniscience were also in play. One of the best-known, though not necessarily well understood, models is found in Maitreya's *Abhisamayālaṃkāra*, a commentary on the *Aṣṭasāhasrikā Prajñāpāramitā*, an important Mahāyāna sūtra. This formulation of omniscience is further codified in the commentaries, including the *Abhisamayālaṃkārāloka* of Haribhadra—a likely contemporary of Śāntarakṣita and Kamalaśīla—and the *Abhisamayālaṃkāravṛtti* of Ārya Vimuktisena. A distinguishing feature of the *Abhisamayālaṃkāra* is its presentation of three kinds of omniscience: knowledge of all aspects (*sarvākārajñatā*), knowledge of the path (*mārgajñatā*), and knowledge of everything (*sarvajñatā*), each of which is held to be obtained by a different kind of Buddhist adept.[97] The root text of the *Abhisamayālaṃkāra* is divided into eight topics, which are described as the three kinds of omniscience, the four methods of realization, and the

95. Duerlinger 2003.

96. Williams 1989: 1–3.

97. For discussions of omniscience in the AA corpus, see Makransky 1997; Naughton 1989; and Obermiller 1933a and 1933b.

final result, the last of which is the *dharmakāya* ("Dharma body") of a buddha. Chapter 7 of the present text takes up the fourth method of realization, the "realization in a single moment," or *ekakṣaṇābhisaṃbodha*, a topic that could be connected with the discussions between the Sarvāstivādins and Mahāsāṃghikas mentioned above. It seems, however, that the main commentators understand this realization in quite different ways.[98] In any case, the scheme with the three forms of omniscience does not appear in the *Tattvasaṃgraha* and the *Pañjikā*, despite the presence of a number of passages in Haribhadra's *Abhisamayālaṃkārāloka* that appear to parallel Kamalaśīla's *Pañjikā*.[99]

Another significant Mahāyāna approach to omniscience is found in several texts associated with the Yogācāra stream of Indian Buddhist thought, including the *Mahāyānasūtrālaṃkāra*, the *Buddhabhūmi Sūtra*, and their commentaries. This approach conceptualizes a buddha's omniscience in terms of four distinct, but interacting, kinds of awareness: mirror-like awareness (*ādarśajñāna*), awareness of equality (*samatājñāna*), discriminating awareness (*pratyavekṣājñāna*), and accomplishing awareness (*kṛtyānuṣṭhānajñāna*).[100] According to the commentaries, mirror-like awareness is connected with a buddha's *dharmakāya* or *svābhāvikakāya* ("essence body"); awareness of equality and discriminating awareness are manifestations of a buddha's *sāmbhogikakāya* ("enjoyment body"); and the accomplishing awareness is identified with a buddha's *nairmāṇikakāya* ("emanation body").[101] Like the theory of the buddha bodies, the theory of the four awarenesses posits that these are not separate realities but rather all aspects of a single reality. Again, despite Śāntarakṣita and Kamalaśīla's association with Yogācāra epistemological traditions, this model of omniscience is not found in the *Tattvasaṃgraha* and the *Pañjikā*.

Models of Omniscience in the *Tattvasaṃgraha* and the *Pañjikā*

All the models of omniscience considered above were likely present to a greater or lesser degree in the intellectual milieu in which Śāntarakṣita and Kamalaśīla composed these treatises. The authors consider several models in

98. Makransky (1997: 188) notes "This requires further study."

99. On the relation between Haribhadra and Kamalaśīla, see Moriyama 1984a and 1984b.

100. For analysis, see Griffiths 1990 and 1994; and Makransky 1997.

101. Makransky 1997: 102–4. Note that the later two terms are alternative forms of the more commonly encountered terms *saṃbhogakāya* and *nirmāṇakāya*.

the works, offering sustained argumentation in support of two models and a more cursory, but ultimately stronger, endorsement of a third model. Their arguments for these distinct models of omniscience are made in different contexts and for different audiences in accord with the authors' sliding scale of analysis and their rhetorical uses of reason.

Although the authors refer to the model we dubbed capacity omniscience above, it is not one of the models they most ardently defend. Instead, their strongest argumentation is devoted to a defense of the models of omniscience to which we will refer in this book as *dharmic omniscience* and *total omniscience*. All of the arguments for these two types of omniscience are found in the final chapter of the *Tattvasaṃgraha* and the *Pañjikā*, which is famous for its treatment of the topic. But ultimately the authors also endorse a third model of omniscience to which we will refer as *spontaneous omniscience*. The arguments for this model of omniscience occur in the twenty-third chapter, which is dedicated not to a treatment of omniscience but rather to the question of the existence of external objects. Their relatively cursory consideration of this model, in conjunction with its less prominent placement in the text as a whole, accounts for the lack of attention that this model has received in scholarly treatments of omniscience in these works to date.

The model of dharmic omniscience emphasizes the Buddha's knowledge of salvifically crucial realities such as the nobles' four truths and dependent arising. This model strongly resonates with the passages in the early Pāli texts that stress not the Buddha's knowledge of a great many irrelevant items but his knowledge of that which would allow his disciples to eliminate ignorance and achieve liberation. Much later, Dharmakīrti takes a similar tack in his *Pramāṇavārttika* as well as in his commentary on that work, the *Svopajñavṛtti*. There, Dharmakīrti appears to be responding to attacks to the Buddha's omniscience that have come to be associated with the Mīmāṃsaka Kumārila Bhaṭṭa. One of Kumārila's main claims is that human beings are incapable of directly knowing the supersensible yet salvifically crucial realities known as Dharma—that which leads to the highest good—and its opposite Adharma. While direct knowledge of these is impossible, indirect knowledge can be obtained through the authorless words of the eternal Veda. Dharmakīrti, in contrast, wants to show that human beings *are* capable of directly knowing all soteriologically significant realities, which for him as a Buddhist means that humans can directly know the nobles' four truths in all their aspects.

Śāntarakṣita and Kamalaśīla closely follow Dharmakīrti in this as in many other matters, and in the final chapter of the *Tattvasaṃgraha* and the *Pañjikā*, the structure of their arguments for omniscience mirrors closely the structure of the arguments for the Buddha's trustworthiness (*prāmāṇya*) or authority in the second chapter of *Pramāṇavārttika*.[102] While Dharmakīrti does not call this knowledge *omniscience*,[103] Śāntarakṣita and Kamalaśīla do. We can refer to this model as *dharmic omniscience*, since the emphasis is on the Buddha's complete knowledge of Dharma in the sense of everything necessary for the removal of ignorance and the attainment of the highest good, freedom from saṃsāra.

The second model of omniscience that Śāntarakṣita and Kamalaśīla defend, total omniscience, refers to an understanding in which the omniscient being can *in some fashion* be said to have simultaneous knowledge of all things whatsoever. Although some version of total omniscience is found in nearly all the major treatises of the Mahāyāna stream of Indian Buddhism, the details can vary considerably. Simultaneous knowledge of all things whatsoever requires a very precise delineation of the referent for "all things," and different Buddhist schools give highly divergent accounts. In the final chapter of the *Tattvasaṃgraha* and the *Pañjikā*, the authors argue mainly from what Kamalaśīla calls a Sautrāntika perspective, in which objects of knowledge are both real and, for the most part, external to the mind. They also occasionally argue from a Yogācāra or Vijñānavāda point of view, wherein external objects do not exist. The consideration of how a buddha can know all things simultaneously necessarily varies depending on the metaphysical premises from which the consideration is undertaken, and in keeping with their rhetorical conception of reason, Śāntarakṣita and Kamalaśīla offer arguments for total omniscience from both these perspectives; they even allow for multiple approaches to the problem within each perspective. At the same time, they continually emphasize the priority of dharmic omniscience, since that is what establishes the authority of the Buddhist tradition.

If the ultimate rejection of real external objects is a hallmark of the Yogācāra stream of Mahāyāna Buddhism, then the rejection of real objects of any kind is a hallmark of the Madhyamaka stream. Śāntarakṣita and Kamalaśīla are closely associated with both schools of thought, and although they do not explicitly argue from the Madhyamaka perspective in these works, we find that the model of omniscience they ultimately defend, spontaneous

102. For studies on Dharmakīrti's approach to the Buddha's authority, see, e.g., Dunne 2004; Franco 1997; Jackson 1991, 1993, and 1999; Hayes 1984; Ruegg 1994a, 1994b, and 1995b; Steinkellner 1982, 1983, and 1994; Tillemans 1993 and 1999a; van Bijlert 1989; van der Kuijp 1999; and Vetter 1964 and 1990.

103. For a study of Dharmakīrti's approach to omniscience, see Jackson 1991. Also see below, pp. 134–38.

omniscience, is one that takes into account this lack of real objects of knowledge. The doctrine of spontaneous omniscience is not unique to these works but appears in a variety of other Mahāyāna sources.[104] In the *Tattvasaṃgraha* and the *Pañjikā*, we find spontaneous omniscience championed in the chapter dedicated to establishing that objects of knowledge external to the mind cannot exist, the "Investigation of External Objects" (*bahirarthaparīkṣā*). In the model of spontaneous omniscience as presented here, the Buddha's omniscience is understood to be a kind of *unknowing* or *nonknowing* that nevertheless appears to unawakened sentient beings to be total omniscience. This paradoxical situation is said to be accomplished through the Buddha's innate power (*ādhipatya*), a natural effect of his previous aspirations (*pūrvapraṇidhāna*) to attain omniscience for the sake of sentient beings. Since this is the solution to the conundrum of the Buddha's omniscient knowledge when the argument is considered at the higher levels of analysis, the spontaneous omniscience model does not get much attention in the final chapter of the *Tattvasaṃgraha* and the *Pañjikā*, which is argued at a lower level of analysis primarily in order to counter the attacks advanced by Kumārila. It is important not to overlook this model, however, as it does represent a position that the authors seem prepared to defend at the highest levels of analysis. Thus, the argumentation in support of dharmic omniscience and total omniscience contained in the final chapter—which is generally advanced on a lower level of analysis—must be understood as in some sense *prior* to the arguments for spontaneous omniscience in the chapter on external objects, even though that chapter comes earlier in the works. Below I will present evidence for this assertion based on my analysis of the structure of the works as divided into two main divisions.[105]

Omniscience and Religious Authority

In advocating multiple versions of omniscience to accord with different metaphysical premises, Śāntarakṣita and Kamalaśīla also advocate a kind of gradual path of rational analysis in accord with their rhetorical conception of reason. Moving up the hierarchy of views, one repeatedly refines one's own previous perspective and one's corresponding understanding of omniscience.

104. Buddhists who promulgate versions of this model include Candrakīrti (seventh century) and Bhāviveka, also known as Bhāvaviveka (sixth century). See Dunne 1996; Eckel 1992 and 2008; and Griffiths 1994. See also chapter 7 below.

105. See pp. 95–105 below.

But while the highest level of analysis—and the corresponding model of spontaneous omniscience—may be the most important for the practitioner, from the point of view of interreligious polemics, it is the lowest level of analysis—and the corresponding model of dharmic omniscience—that holds the most value for these authors. This is because demonstrating the Buddha's dharmic omniscience, understood as the complete knowledge of everything relevant to attaining the highest good of liberation from saṃsāra, is tantamount to demonstrating the religious authority of both the founder and the scriptures of the Buddhist tradition. Indeed, there is a general understanding in India that by claiming omniscience for the founder of one's tradition, one also claims legitimacy for the scriptures attributed to that founder, and legitimacy as well for one's own religious practices. In addition to the early scriptural passages suggesting that the Buddha was omniscient, therefore, later Indian Buddhists were also constrained by the climate of the times to defend and protect the doctrine that their founder was omniscient.

As was noted above, there is some evidence that Jain claims to an omniscient founder were particularly threatening, especially since the Jain scriptures did not contain ambiguous statements, as did the Buddhist, to the effect that it is impossible—or at least pointless—to know all things simultaneously. We see evidence that competition with Jains or similar groups was a factor in provoking Buddhists to delineate and defend a Buddhist notion of omniscience in the sixth-century Buddhist author Bhāviveka's *Tarkajvālā*, his commentary on his own verse composition, the *Madhyamakahṛdaya*. The tenth chapter of that work is entitled the "Demonstration of the Proof of Omniscience" (*sarvajñasiddhinirdeśa*). It presents a series of objections to the Buddha's omniscience under a rubric, found in a variety of early sources, in which episodes from the Buddha's lifestory are offered as evidence against his omniscience. The passage commences with a reference to "naked wanderers" (Tibetan: *gcer bur rgyu ba*), here understood as Jains,[106] who challenge the Buddha's omniscience with a reference to the unanswered questions we

106. The Tibetan here (the text does not survive in Sanskrit) indicates that these wanderers are naked (*gcer bur*), using the standard Tibetan translation for the Sanskrit term *nirgrantha*. Bronkhorst (2000) argues that the Pāli equivalent *nigaṇṭha* (lit., "free from ties") is reserved in the early Buddhist texts not for naked wanderers but for the Jain followers of Pārśva, who wear a single garment. In contrast, the term *acelaka* (lit., "naked ones") applies to the Jain followers of Mahāvīra, who eschew clothing. These Jains appear also to have been included in a larger general class of naked wanderers known to the early Buddhists as the Ājīvikas. By the era of Bhāviveka, however, such distinctions appear to be forgotten, and the term *nirgrantha* comes to refer in Buddhist texts to the whole of the Jain community.

encountered earlier as well as other problematic aspects of the Buddha's life-story.[107] For example, the Buddha is said to have entered a village to beg for alms only to discover that the villagers were attending a festival, and he thus had to return with his begging bowl empty.[108] An omniscient person, it is argued, would have known in advance that begging in that particular village on that particular day was a waste of time, and he would have known the name without asking. Another example includes the Buddha's encounter with a wild elephant; presumably, an omniscient person would have known to take another route and would thus have avoided the dangerous beast. Bhāviveka's resolution of these various challenges to the Buddha's omniscience is based on the resolution found in the *Upāyakauśalya Sūtra*, which Bhāviveka cites, in which it is held that the Buddha only *appears* to undergo unfortunate events as a means of teaching his disciples about the ripening of karma.[109] In no case can such unfortunate episodes be attributed to the Buddha's lack of knowledge or negative karma.[110]

In this way, we see Buddhists like Bhāviveka warding off the attacks of those such as Jains who claim a different omniscient founder. We also see Buddhists like Śāntarakṣita and Kamalaśīla responding to those, like the Naiyāyikas, who claim that omniscience is a quality of God (Īśvara) alone.[111] In these two cases, the debate centers on determining which religious figure should be counted

107. D 320b5–6: *gal te 'dir gcer bur rgyu ba rnams nye bar lhags nas 'di skad du / gang thams cad mkhyen pa nyid des / kho bo cag gi bzhung sun 'byin par nus kyi / 'di ni thams cad mkhyen pa ma yin te / lung tu ma bstan pa'i dngos po bcu bzhi lung ma bstan pa . . . /*. "Here the naked wanderers may approach and say the following: Whoever is omniscient will be able to refute our scriptures; but this one [the Buddha] is not omniscient because he did not explain the fourteen unanswered questions . . ."

108. We find this same example also in the *Sandaka Sutta* of the Majjhima Nikāya, where the supposedly omniscient teacher who gets no alms or has to ask the name of a village is not the Buddha but an unnamed person whom we are led through intertexual references to believe is the Jain leader Nigaṇṭha Nātaputta. In this passage, however, the Buddha explains that following a teacher who claims to be omniscient and is then seen getting no alms or needing to ask the name of a person or village is one of four kinds of "holy life without consolation" (*anassāsikāni brahmacariyāni*). It is interesting to find some of the same list of objections to the Jina's omniscience in the Majjhima Nikāya later leveled against the Buddha in Bhāviveka's work. On the passage from the *Sandaka Sutta*, see Bronkhorst 2000: 518–21 and 2009: 49–51. See also Anālayo 2006: 2–4.

109. See Kawasaki 1977, 1987, 1988, 1992a, 1992b, and 1995.

110. See Harrison 1995 for more on the problem of the Buddha's bad karma.

111. Śāntarakṣita and Kamalaśīla's response to the Naiyāyika assertion that God is omniscient is found in the second chapter of the TS/P, the *īśvaraparīkṣā*. For later Buddhist refutations of Īśvara, see Patil 2008.

as omniscient such that his authored works would then carry the weight of religious authority. In the case of Kumārila, however, the locus of contention is not the founder of a tradition or author of its scriptures: it is rather the scriptures themselves. Because they claim that the Veda is both eternal and authorless, the Mīmāṃsakas are able to advocate a kind of perfection for scripture without having to accept perfection for any being, whether human or divine. A great deal of argumentation in the final three chapters of the *Tattvasaṃgraha* and the *Pañjikā* is therefore devoted to refuting the eternal and authorless nature of the Veda as well as to demonstrating the possibility of the perfectibility of human wisdom. As I argue in chapter 2 of this book, the final three chapters of the *Tattvasaṃgraha* and the *Pañjikā* are primarily focused on the question of religious authority, and the demonstration of dharmic omniscience in particular is in direct response to this question.

The terrain here is tricky, just as it is in Dharmakīrti's demonstration of the Buddha's trustworthiness in the *Pramāṇavārttika*, to which our authors are clearly indebted. At stake is the question of the need for scriptures, and the role of what has come to be called *scripturally based inference* (*āgamāśrayānumāna*) in the Buddhist epistemological tradition. Does a demonstration of the Buddha's dharmic omniscience allow one to then assume that everything he has said about radically inaccessible matters is necessarily true? Does the demonstration of total omniscience allow this? If so, then what is the role of reason for those who have faith in the Buddha? If not, then what is the point of the demonstration of the Buddha's omniscience?

Although the answers to these questions are not easy, we will see that for Śāntarakṣita and Kamalaśīla, much depends upon whether one is to be counted among those judicious persons (*prekṣāvant*) who are inclined toward wisdom or among those who are inclined toward faith. I argue that the *Tattvasaṃgraha* and the *Pañjikā* is ultimately directed toward judicious persons for whom the demonstration of the Buddha's omniscience has nothing to do with grounding scriptures in his transcendent knowledge or authority. Instead, the motivation for demonstrating the Buddha's omniscience is (1) to refute the Mīmāṃsaka claims that humans cannot know Dharma and Adharma and that there can be a reliable scripture that has no author, and (2) to establish that omniscience is possible and therefore a reasonable goal toward which a judicious person may strive. Scripturally based inferences are then understood as a kind of embellishment for rational argument and are to be used rhetorically when arguing with others about radically inaccessible matters. In short, omniscience is demonstrated not so as to justify reliance upon the Buddhist scriptures—which in all significant respects may be entirely verified through ordinary perception and inference—but merely to show omniscience is a viable and worthy goal.

The Path Ahead

Omniscience is thus both a vexing and a critical category of inquiry for the study of Buddhism. As a graduate student, I naively imagined that I could undertake a comprehensive study of the development of the concept of omniscience in Indian Buddhism from the early Pāli texts through the later treatises of the Mahāyāna. Eventually, I realized that even just to unpack the thought of Śāntarakṣita and Kamalaśīla in the *Tattvasaṃgraha* and the *Pañjikā* on this topic would be no small achievement. The remainder of this book contains my findings in this area. As noted earlier, these findings do not concern the doctrine of omniscience alone, but more pertinently they have to do with the problems of rationality, argumentation, and religious authority for these authors. These problems, in turn, entail the exploration of epistemological as well as metaphysical issues, both in order to understand the types of rationality, argumentation, and religious authority at play in these polemical works and to comprehend the various models of omniscience presented there. The study of omniscience in these works thus becomes a window to a much larger vista on the philosophical and religious perspectives of these two eighth-century thinkers.

The remainder of this book proceeds on the premise that understanding the arguments for omniscience in the *Tattvasaṃgraha* and the *Pañjikā* requires that we develop a much better picture of the overall nature of these works than has been available to date. In chapter 2, I seek to enlarge our understanding of these works through an examination of the rhetorical complexity of several elements of the texts. With help from Perelman and Olbrechts-Tyteca, the chapter looks first at the multiple audiences to which the work is addressed, and then at the styles of reasoning employed throughout. Next, we examine a previously unrecognized structural division in the works, one that is crucial for our interpretation of the authors' arguments in defense of omniscience. The chapter closes with a consideration of the various aims of these works, a discussion that can only proceed once the questions of audiences and styles of reasoning have been sufficiently resolved. Throughout this chapter, we remain focused on the high level of prestige that these authors accord to rational inquiry, and to their engagement in a rhetoric of reason in both senses of the term discussed above.

The next chapter continues to provide important background for understanding the argumentation concerning omniscience in the *Tattvasaṃgraha* and the *Pañjikā*, but now the focus narrows specifically to topics relating to omniscience itself. We begin with the notion of Buddhist *philosophia*, taking a cue again from Hadot in understanding the centrality of dogmas to the practice of philosophy in antiquity. Recognizing that Śāntarakṣita and Kamalaśīla write from within a particular stream of Mahāyāna Buddhism, we examine various doctrines, or "dogmas," regarding omniscience which remain more or less unquestioned by the authors, at least in this work. Having explored these dogmas, we then go on to examine the connotations for omniscience in the work, which turn out to be multiple, thus significantly complicating the interpretive task. Finally, the chapter considers some of the same rhetorical aspects that the previous chapter examined in relation to the work as a whole. This time, however, our examination is undertaken specifically in terms of the final chapter of the the *Tattvasaṃgraha* and the *Pañjikā*, the chapter most closely associated with the concept of omniscience, and the final chapter of the first section of the work, the chapter in which the authors present something closer to their own position on omniscience. With the rhetorical structures and dogmatic presuppositions concerning omniscience now more precisely drawn, we next turn to the argumentation concerning omniscience as found in the two works.

Chapters 4 and 5 consider the basic arguments about omniscience that are found in the famous final chapter of the *Tattvasaṃgraha* and the *Pañjikā*. In chapter 4, we explore what I term the *general demonstration* of omniscience, in which the authors argue for the theoretical possibility of omniscience in one of at least two distinct forms. The general demonstration contains three elements or "movements," and the chapter is divided accordingly. As with nearly all of the argumentation in this section of the works, the main person being addressed is Kumārila Bhaṭṭa and his Mīmāṃsaka followers, and our knowledge of this fact helps us to understand these three movements more clearly. The three movements can be further divided according to which model of omniscience they concern. Thus, the first two movements are concerned primarily with establishing the possibility of dharmic omniscience, and this correlates with Kumārila's contention that Dharma and Adharma, which all parties may agree are the keys to salvation, are fundamentally inaccessible to ordinary human knowledge. The third movement in contrast appears aimed to establish the possibility of some vision of total omniscience. Despite this important shift in the third movement, however, all three elements of the general demonstration have in common their concern to establish a general or theoretical possibility of omniscience, and not a particular instance of an omniscient being.

That task is left to another set of arguments, also from the final chapter of the *Tattvasaṃgraha* and the *Pañjikā*. These arguments, which I refer to collectively as the *specific demonstration* of omniscience, comprise the topic of chapter 5 of this book. Unlike the general demonstration, in the specific demonstration the authors wish to show that a particular person, namely, the founder of the Buddhist tradition, the Buddha or Sugata, was himself omniscient. In addition to laying out the mechanism by which this demonstration is conceived to work, chapter 5 also considers a significant tension inherent in the demonstration, namely, that the demonstration of the Buddha as an omniscient being appears to violate the authors' own stated ban on inferring the mental qualities of another person. The tension is not resolved in this chapter, but is soon revisited.

Chapter 6 is an analysis of the motives at play in both the general and the specific demonstrations. In keeping with the theme of the book, I argue that the authors have multiple motives in relation to multiple audiences. For judicious persons, the overall aim appears to be to convince them to convert to Buddhism and then to put the Buddhist teachings into practice and to attain omniscience. For those who are less than judicious, the general goal appears to be to discredit their philosophical thought and religious practice and thus discourage others from adopting their irrational ideas and ways of life. This chapter also takes up the question as to whether and in what way the authors of the *Tattvasaṃgraha* and the *Pañjikā* intend to ground Buddhist scriptures in the omniscience of their founder. Although we will see that Śāntarakṣita and Kamalaśīla are adamant that trustworthy scriptures must have trustworthy authors, they do not accept that a scripture may be determined to be trustworthy on the basis of the omniscience of its author. Rather, the argumentation works in the opposite direction, such that omniscience, at least in the sense of dharmic omniscience, may be determined on the basis of a rationally coherent and salvifically efficacious scripture. Here, again, we see that the commitment to rationality is paramount.

The seventh and concluding chapter includes a discussion of spontaneous omniscience as it is advocated in the *Tattvasaṃgraha* and the *Pañjikā*. Paradoxical as it sounds, I argue that this model of omniscience represents the authors' own favored perspective, at least in the *Tattvasaṃgraha* and the *Pañjikā*, while the arguments in the chapter ostensibly dealing with omniscience operate on lower levels of analysis. Such a conclusion does not diminish the importance and validity of the arguments in the chapter on omniscience, however, since it is these arguments that the authors count on to convince judicious persons—particularly those judicious persons who are not yet committed to the Buddhist path—that omniscience is a worthy and attainable goal. Thus the treatment of omniscience in the *Tattvasaṃgraha* and the *Pañjikā* is in keeping with the authors' rhetoric of reason, insofar as reason is always to be used and valued in relation to particular goals. In the case of the work at hand, the goals appear to include convincing others that omniscience is a viable and important human aim. If the contours of what precisely constitutes omniscience must shift somewhat in the process of the arguments on its behalf, such should not be considered a blemish in the reasoning process. Rather, it is my view that the authors would have us believe such shifts to be the mark of a high level of sophistication in their reasoning process, in that they indicate a dialectical model of reasoning in which the adherence of diverse audiences may be gradually won by means of a large number of interlocking arguments, each of which is individually tailored to counter and remove particular misconceptions of particular persons. Like all good doctors, these authors would certainly agree that the medicine must fit the disease.

2. The Rhetorical Complexity of the Texts

IN A SHORT, insightful excursus on the *Tattvasaṃgraha*, Matthew Kapstein has remarked that "the very dimensions of Śāntarakṣita's work have, I think, caused us to refrain from asking big questions about it."[112] Kapstein is right: the *Tattvasaṃgraha* and its commentary are not simple tracts treating a single topic, but together represent an extensive, complex, and technical exposition treating a wide range of topics and speaking, so it seems, in multiple voices. Diverse sections of the treatise, ranging from as short as a single passage to as long as an entire chapter division, address distinct audiences and argue from a variety of premises and with a seeming variety of rhetorical goals. This practice at times gives rise to what seem to be contradictory statements on various topics, including omniscience. It also contributes to the impression, voiced by several scholars, that the work is no more than a mere collection of unrelated investigations into a variety of topics, strung together like so many flowers on a garland (as one might imagine is implied by the word *saṃgraha* in the title).[113] Yet at the same time, the work exhibits a high degree of cohesion, displaying a clear and coherent structure, a self-declared overall purpose, and numerous instances of self-referentiality. These factors argue for seeing the work as all of a piece, or as Kamalaśīla calls it, a "mega-sentence" (*mahāvākya*),[114] with an overarching

112. Kapstein 2001: 11.

113. K. N. Chatterjee (1988: i), for example, expresses this common misconception when he says, "as a matter of fact, the *Tattvasaṃgraha* is not a single work. It is, on the contrary, a collection of several works severally dealing with all conceivable problems of Buddhism—metaphysical, epistemological, logical and ethical." While Chatterjee's remark accords in some ways with Kamalaśīla's own claims (cf. below, n.250), it does not reflect the carefully wrought structure of the TS/P as seen, for example, in Śāntarakṣita's opening verses, nor Kamalaśīla's own idea that the treatise as a whole has a subject matter (see next note).

114. Kamalaśīla refers to the treatise as a mega-sentence in his answer to an objector's comment that a treatise cannot have a subject matter (*abhidheya*), since subject matter is

subject matter and rhetorical function, the understanding of which is vital to our ability to interpret the work's stance on omniscience or any other topic. For this reason, before we turn to our investigation of omniscience in the *Tattvasaṃgraha* and its commentary, we must first take the time to gain some clarity about the nature of the works, the audience they were intended for, and the purpose for which they were written.

Foregoing such clarity at the outset would be a serious mistake, which could lead us to prematurely dismiss apparently contradictory statements as evidence of the authors' confusion or even dishonesty. This is not to say that the work is *a priori* free of contradictions or that its authors should be held immune to criticism or critique. It *is* to say that we should operate at first on a principle of charity in order to ensure that we do not miss clues in the work that could allow us to resolve seeming contradictions by integrating them into a single religio-philosophical vision that we can justly attribute to the authors. Put another way, what I am trying to do in this chapter is to get at a plausible understanding of what Śāntarakṣita and Kamalaśīla *think* they are doing in this text, so that I can interpret their statements on omniscience in light of that.[115] Four areas of investigation, it seems to me, can yield clues to help us discern the nature of the text: (1) the audiences for the work; (2) the styles of reasoning in the work; (3) the structure of the work as a whole; and

generally understood to be the property of individual sentences. The relevant passage is as follows: TSP *ad* TS 1–6 (B 9,18–24): *nanu ca vākyasyaivābhidheyavattvaṃ nānyasyeti nyāyaḥ na ca sakalaṃ śāstraṃ vākyam api tu vākyasamūhas tat kuto 'syābhidheyasaṃbhavaḥ / naitad asti / yady api vākyasamūhātmakaṃ śāstraṃ tathāpi tāni vākyāni parasparavya pekṣāsaṃbandhāvasthitāni / anyathonmattādivākyasamūhavad asaṅgatārtham eva syāt / tataś ca parasparasaṃbaddhānekaśabdasamūhātmakatvāt tad anyavākyavad vākyam eva śāstraṃ / na hi padair eva vākyam ārabhyate / api tu vākyair api / ato mahāvākyatvād abhidheyavad eva śāstram ity acodyam /*. "[Objection:] Well, isn't it a rule (*nyāya*) that sentences (*vākya*) alone are what contain subject matter? And entire treatises are not sentences but are rather collections of sentences. Therefore, how is it possible for there to be a subject matter of a treatise? [Response:] This is not right. For although a treatise is by its nature a collection of sentences, nevertheless those sentences are arranged in a mutually dependent relationship; otherwise [the treatise] would just have an incoherent meaning, like a collection of sentences [uttered] by a mad person and so on. And therefore, since it consists in a collection of various words that are mutually connected, then like other sentences, that treatise is just a sentence (*vākya*). However, it is not a sentence composed of words but is rather [a sentence composed] of sentences. Thus a treatise contains subject matter because it is a mega-sentence (*mahāvākya*); therefore [this idea is] unobjectionable."

115. This obviously raises the thorny issue of authorial intent; for some brief remarks, see below, p. 50–51.

(4) the function or the purpose of the work. As we will see, each of the first three areas of investigation contributes to our understanding of the fourth, which is in some ways the most crucial point of inquiry.

All four areas of investigation are issues the authors of the *Tattvasaṃgraha* and its *Pañjikā* grapple with as well. Naturally, as modern interpreters, our analysis will differ from the analysis of the ancient authors, but in many ways, our questions do not diverge greatly from those that Śāntarakṣita and Kamalaśīla seem to have expected their contemporary readers to bring to the work. Thus, in the opening pages of the texts, we find that all four areas of investigation are already addressed. As in our analysis, for these authors as well, it is the purpose (*prayojana*) of the treatise that is the most important area of investigation, the one that binds all the others together and gives them meaning. In what follows, then, if we postpone our investigation into the purpose of the work, it is only because we can glean a great deal more about it through a prior exploration of the other three areas of investigation.

Audience

We start with the question of the audience for the work. Of course, in one sense, *we* are the most significant audience in the present context, since the understanding for which we are striving is, necessarily, an understanding *for us*. While we cannot deny this most basic hermeneutical condition, it in no way diminishes the utility of an inquiry into the audience that Śāntarakṣita and Kamalaśīla had in mind when they composed their work. The crucial role of the audience in all forms of argumentation has been extensively pleaded by Perelman and Olbrechts-Tyteca in *The New Rhetoric*.[116] A premise of that work, which I adopt here, is that "all argumentation aims at gaining the adherence of minds, and, by this very fact, assumes the existence of an intellectual contact."[117] Since I take it as too evident to require justification that the *Tattvasaṃgraha* is a work of argumentation (at least rhetorically), my aim in this section is to explore the nature of the intellectual contact that informs and gives shape to the arguments in this work. By learning more about those to whom this work is addressed, I hope to increase our chances

116. Perelman and Olbrechts-Tyteca 1969: 30: "...the nature of the audience to which arguments can be successfully presented will determine to a great extent both the direction the arguments will take and the character, the significance that will be attributed to them."

117. Perelman and Olbrechts-Tyteca 1969: 14.

at attaining some real understanding of the presentation of omniscience in this work.

Now understanding, as I see it, requires some *meaning* as its object, and meaning, on the model I adopt here, always involves an allocutionary, or audience-directed, act of communication (such as a speech-act). Meaning is what the author of the act intends the addressee to understand. Meaning, though not necessarily the *same* meaning, is also what the audience *gets* from its contact with the act; it is that which the audience understands.[118] Seen in this light, all successful acts of communication are perlocutionary, in that they always produce some intended effect—i.e., they always produce some understanding—in their audience. Sometimes the audience for a speech-act will be known, and perhaps chosen, by the author of the act, while in other cases, the audience will be neither known nor chosen, in which case it is obviously not the audience that the author intends to address. Such an audience can still derive meaning from the author's speech, but the chances for an understanding that corresponds to the author's intention increase the closer the audience matches (or can imaginatively approximate) the author's intended audience. Communication is deemed successful when the author acknowledges that the meaning expressed by the addressee as what was understood corresponds to the author's intended meaning. Obviously, this kind of confirmation is possible only when author and addressee are in direct contact. But even in the absence of a living author, the question of audience is important, since every author of a speech-act, if he or she wants that act to be an act of communication, attempts to use language to produce an understanding in some particular audience that conforms as closely as possible with the meaning he or she would like the audience to understand.[119] By considering the

118. This is what I take Ricoeur (1976: 8–12) to be getting at when he speaks of "the dialectic of event and meaning." Ricoeur is pointing to the importance of the audience, not only in shaping what the speaker says, but also in shaping what the audience hears. All speech is directed to an audience—even if, as in a monologue, that audience is oneself—without which there can be no communication and no meaning. As Ricoeur (14) says, "The presence of the pair, speaker and hearer, constitutes language as communication."

119. Here, I adopt a principle of interpretation, sketched out by P. F. Strawson and described by Avramides (1997: 67), that relies on the notion of audience recognition of illocutionary force: namely that "For an audience A to understand an utterance x, A must recognize the speaker S's intention that S's utterance of x produce a certain response in A." Of course, the problem again is confirmation: how do we know that we really *got* S's intention right? While this question may not have an easy answer, I do think the principle that states that S intends to produce an effect in A, and that *understanding* occurs when A recognizes what effect S wishes to produce, is sound.

audience for the work, then, we can gain information that will aid us in interpreting what meaning the authors intended their audience to understand.

This would be complicated enough were there just one audience or one addressee for the work, but, in fact, a variety of audiences of different natures can be discerned. In the present context, what is of primary concern is the *intended* audience, the audience that is both *known* and *chosen* by the authors. We are not here interested in the *unintended* audience, the audience neither known nor chosen by the authors. Although as modern readers we are members of the audience of the work, we more closely resemble an audience eavesdropping on a conversation in which another person or audience is being directly addressed. We inquire about the intended audience because we can be sure that in addressing *that* audience, the authors assume it to possess presuppositions and expectations that we currently lack (though we possess others). To convey their meaning with this audience in mind, the authors must take their view of this audience's presuppositions and expectations into account. Knowing more about this intended audience to whom the authors most directly speak, therefore, will improve our understanding of the authors' meaning.

Alongside the division of the audience into intended and unintended components, there is another way to slice the audience pie, and that is in terms of an *actual* and an *ideal* audience.[120] By an actual audience, I mean the actual readers or hearers of a work, real people who turn their attention to the work and try to understand what the work is saying. These people can be part of the intended or the unintended audience (we, for example, are part of the actual, unintended audience). An ideal audience, in contrast, is comprised of those persons, real or unreal, who in the author's view are the best *kinds* of readers or hearers, the audience the author believes is most likely to understand or *get* the meaning of the work. An ideal audience need not have

120. This way of considering the audience for the work parallels, but is not exactly the same as, Perelman and Olbrechts-Tyteca's division of audiences into particular and universal audiences. A difference is that for Perelman and Olbrechts-Tyteca, both the particular and the universal audience (1969: 19) "as visualized by one undertaking to argue, is always a more or less systematized construction." Although in general I agree with this assessment, and accept that for Śāntarakṣita and Kamalaśīla the actual intended audience is as much a construction as is the universal or ideal audience, my way of dividing the audience allows for a more focused consideration of certain historical realities concerning the production and use of religious and philosophical texts in eighth-century India than would a discussion that adheres more precisely to Perelman and Olbrechts-Tyteca's terms. For an interesting discussion and defense of Perelman's theory of the rhetorical construction of audiences, see Gross 1999.

any actual members; what is needed is only that the author have in mind the type (or types) of person best suited to understand the work. To discern the author's ideal audience is thus to gain some insight into the kinds of dispositions the author hopes that we will bring to her work when we become a member of the actual audience. To whatever degree we share the qualities (presuppositions, expectations, and so on) of the ideal audience, that is the degree that the work will "speak to us," and the degree (so the author hopes) to which we will understand what the author wants us to understand. We return to the ideal audience below, but first, let us consider the difficult question of the actual intended audience of the work.

The Actual Intended Audience

To answer the question of whom Śāntarakṣita and Kamalaśīla *really* intend to address, it seems that we must somehow get inside the heads of these two eighth-century Indian authors. Since this is clearly impossible, we must look for some evidence, textual or otherwise, that will indicate their intentions, and here there are numerous problems as well.

Recently, Paul Griffiths has argued that many, if not all, Indian Buddhist works of various types are probably best interpreted as addressed exclusively to a religious community of Buddhist monks.[121] Griffiths, in a *tour de force* of

121. Griffiths argues for this in his book *Religious Reading* (1999a) and in a separate article (1999b). In the book, he considers four Indian Buddhist treatises of varying sorts and concludes from his study that the works were all intended for what he terms *religious readers*. For such readers (1999a: 42), "the work read is an object of overpowering delight and great beauty. It can never be discarded because it can never be exhausted. It can only be reread, with reverence and ecstasy." In other words, in Griffiths' view, most (if not all) Indian Buddhist treatises were *preaching to the converted*, and lack of appreciation of this fact distorts modern interpretations of them. In the article, where he embarks on a discussion of a text with resemblances to the TS/P, the eleventh-century *Tarkabhāṣā* of Mokṣākaragupta, Griffiths exhibits less surety, though he nonetheless argues for a similar conclusion. In short, Griffiths' argument in the article revolves around the perceived fact that when Buddhists offer antitheistic arguments, they (1999b: 519) "always and necessarily axiomatically assume and deploy the truth of complex claims in metaphysics, epistemology, or logic (or all three)." In other words, Buddhists argue against non-Buddhist ideas but *in Buddhist terms alone*, and this tends (so Griffiths feels) to diminish the persuasive power of their arguments. Griffiths is definitely on to something here, but I think that he may underestimate the ways in which the Indian Buddhist and non-Buddhist philosophers of the classical era participated in a shared intellectual milieu that *did* allow the cross-fertilization of ideas. His statement that Indian Buddhist arguments against God (1999b: 517) "were not persuasively effective" is based on no evidence other than the continued presence of non-Buddhist traditions in India. But conversions to Buddhism on

reason and argumentation, garners a variety of evidence for this conclusion. Much (though not all) of this evidence revolves around an analysis of the supposedly aural medium of the works' transmission and the scholastic—and therefore religious and exegetical—nature of the compositions themselves. The picture Griffiths paints is of a religious community of Buddhist monks whose study consists primarily in reverentially listening to and committing to memory verses and exegetical commentaries. Some of the community's monks become specialists in particular texts and can then be consulted with the expectation that they will exhibit near-total recall of their memorized texts. Although some monks prepare palm-leaf manuscripts, these texts are made not to be read; rather, these texts are to be worshipped as embodiments of the Buddha's speech (*buddhavacana*) in order to aid and inspire learning. Thus, in terms of these written texts, "it matters that they be present but not that they be read."[122]

Griffiths' portrayal of Indian Buddhist monastic education may be accurate—although it does seem clear that numerous manuscripts were transported to foreign lands not as objects of worship but in order to be translated and studied and also that many Mahāyāna sūtras at least were written down right from the beginning—yet I fail to see how the scenario he invokes necessarily entails that the intended audience of the works be limited to Buddhists or Buddhist monks. While there surely are *some* works that are intended exclusively for those who are already committed and practicing Buddhists (prayers, ritual liturgies, and meditation manuals come to mind), there is no reason to think that *all* Buddhist works were so restricted simply because they were (1) aurally received and (2) religious in nature. Griffiths' evidence, it seems to me, is inconclusive.[123]

---

rational grounds may well have occurred (and if Tibetan accounts are correct, they did). In the end, Griffiths is really making a normative more than a historical claim, as he reveals when he wonders (1999b: 520) whether Indian Buddhists "have the modest expectations that I've argued they *ought* to have had for the persuasive power of their antitheistic arguments" (italics added). My position is that the authors of the TS/P, in any case, *did* hold their arguments to have, in Griffiths' words (1999b: 513) "maximal dialectical force," but only for members of their ideal audience, judicious persons, which we discuss below.

122. Griffiths 1999a: 128.

123. The arguments from aurality are found primarily in Griffiths' book (1999a). In his article (1999b), where he treats Mokṣākaragupta's *Tarkabhāṣā*, a work closer in style and tradition to the TS/P than the works treated in the book, he adduces other arguments (see n. 121 above) that have more to do with the embeddedness of Buddhist arguments in forms of reasoning specific to the Buddhist tradition than with their religious or aural nature. Although these contentions are important (and we return to them later), his

One obvious point speaks against Griffiths' argument, at least in relation to the *Tattvasaṃgraha* and its commentary: namely, that many non-Buddhist authors are explicitly quoted and addressed in the works.[124] Bhattacaryya, in his foreword to Krishnamacharya's edition of the *Tattvasaṃgraha* and the *Tattvasaṃgrahapañjikā*, lists more than twenty Naiyāyika, Jain, and Mīmāṃsaka authors who are quoted or otherwise directly cited by Śāntarakṣita or Kamalaśīla in the works.[125] In most of these cases, Kamalaśīla designates the authors by name; in many cases, he addresses them as "you" (*bhavant*). For his part, Śāntarakṣita has quite accurately reproduced (though without naming the authors) a large number of *śloka*s from the works of his

---

arguments based on aurality and the religious nature of Buddhist works highlight what for Griffiths is the most important aspect of these Buddhist works: that they are intended for *insiders* only and do not speak to those outside the tradition.

124. It is still not clear to me to what degree the TS/P elicited any significant *direct* response from later non-Buddhist Indian authors. Pemwieser (1991: 44–47) offers arguments in support of an earlier finding by Steinkellner (1978) to the effect that the TS/P is the probable *indirect* source for a Buddhist *pūrvapakṣa* in the *Nyāyakaṇikā* of Vācaspatimiśra. Kellner (1997: 89–90) cites several later Jain doxographical works that mirror the TSP in their interpretation of Kumārila as upholding a threefold definition of *abhāvapramāṇa*. Since such a threefold definition is absent in all the extant commentaries on ŚV, Kellner surmises that it "can be traced back to TSP . . . but the classification in TSP may of course have been derived from somewhere else" (personal communication). Iwata (1991, vol. 2: 81n82) lists a number of passages in the Jain author Vādidevasūri's *Syādvādaratnākara*, in which "the TSP acts clearly as the *pūrvapakṣa*": "Es ist eindeutig, daß im SyVR (im Rahmen der *sahopalambhaniyama*-Debatte) die TSP als Opponent fungiert." In general, among non-Buddhist traditions, it is the later Jain tradition that seems to have paid the most attention to the TS/P (note also that the two known surviving sets of Sanskrit manuscripts of the TS and TSP were discovered in Jain libraries). In comparison with the TS/P, however, the works of Dharmakīrti (which the TS/P draws upon heavily) appear to have been cited with much greater frequency in later, non-Buddhist texts. Whether this is because later authors understood Śāntarakṣita and Kamalaśīla as expounding essentially the same views as their predecessor, or whether this attests to a relatively scant readership of this work is a question that remains, for the moment at least, unanswered.

125. Bhattacaryya 1926: xxxvii–lxxi. Steinkellner (1963) undertakes an analysis of all the citations attributed to Uddyotakara in the TS/P, demonstrating that Kamalaśīla does not always quote Uddyotakara directly but frequently summarizes or paraphrases his positions, especially when addressing views not particular to Uddyotakara but held by Naiyāyikas in general. Steinkellner further notes that Kamalaśīla is not always correct in his attributions of positions to certain opponents, making it impossible to rely upon his formulations for knowledge about authors whose positions are otherwise unknown. At the same time, Steinkellner maintains that Kamalaśīla, despite such attribution mistakes, does generally give an accurate portrayal of the works he paraphrases and cites.

opponents in the *pūrvapakṣa* (literally, the "antecedent position") sections of most, if not all, of the chapters or "investigations" (*parīkṣā*) in the work.[126]

In the case of two opponents in particular, the Naiyāyika Uddyotakara (sixth to seventh century) and the Mīmāṃsaka Kumārila, the quotations are so extensive that they have led Bhattacaryya to state, "it seems probable that the *Tattvasaṃgraha* was written mainly to refute the arguments and theories of Kumārila and Uddyotakara."[127] Although this assessment rings true, it is probably best judged an exaggeration, since a good number of other opponents, both Buddhist and non-Buddhist, draw repeated and sometimes extended attention from the authors.[128] Still, Bhattacaryya's statement does usefully focus attention on the polemical stance of this work as a whole. The extended citations of opponents' positions and their subsequent refutation in the *uttarapakṣa* (literally, "subsequent position") sections is so pervasive and so relentless that one cannot escape the impression that the work is directed, at least in part, at *those who get it wrong*, whether in terms of ontology, epistemology, or other soteriologically relevant factors.[129] Whether such persons be non-Buddhists or Buddhists, this brazen work aims to set them right.

But what if Griffiths is correct and the texts were studied and learned only aurally? What if Kamalaśīla did not have a manuscript in front of him while quoting Uddyotakara or Kumārila? I do not think that this is particularly important. The fact that he and Śāntarakṣita could quote their non-Buddhist opponents so well shows that they were keenly acquainted with the texts. If their acquaintance came through aural means, so what? We have no reason to assume that these authors did not study non-Buddhist works directly with representatives of non-Buddhist traditions, so that their quotation of these

126. These citations in the *pūrvapakṣa*s are so reliable that Frauwallner (1962: 83), with the aid of auxiliary evidence, is able to convincingly demonstrate that a long string of more than one hundred verses in the final chapter of the TS can be confidently assigned to a now lost work by Kumārila, the *Bṛhaṭṭīkā*.

127. Bhattacaryya 1926: lx.

128. Buddhists whose views are taken as *pūrvapakṣa*s in the TS/P include Dharmatrāta, Vasumitra, Ghoṣaka, Buddhadeva, Yogasena, and Śubhagupta. See Bhattacaryya 1926: xxxvii–lxxi.

129. In glossing the phrase "[that dependent arising] that others do not understand" from the opening stanzas of the TS, Kamalaśīla explains, "This shows that the Buddha alone possesses this unique realization, since all non-Buddhists (*tīrtha*) are addicted to the incorrect vision of a self." See TSP *ad* TS 4 (B 18,13–14): *agataṃ parair iti / sarvatīrthānāṃ vitathātmadṛṣṭyabhiniviṣṭatvād bhagavata evāyaṃ āveṇiko 'bhisaṃbodha iti darśayati /*. For more on the importance of the opening verses, see the section on the structure of the TS/P later in this chapter.

works could be based on an intimate familiarity with those who advocated them. Yet even if their exposure to the texts took place only within Buddhist monastery walls, there is almost no doubt that their study was designed in part for the purpose of devising counter-arguments that could be used in response to non-Buddhist positions in a public debate.[130] To prepare for such debates, the authors and students of the *Tattvasaṃgraha* and the *Pañjikā* and other such texts must have studied their opponents' works, and to do so they would have needed access to *either* a written or an oral text. I think it is less important *how* materials went back and forth across sectarian lines than *that* they did. The fact remains that the *Tattvasaṃgraha* and the *Pañjikā* show a remarkable awareness and understanding of non-Buddhist texts and traditions, as well as a thoroughgoing inclination to try to refute their positions and to come to the defense of Buddhist positions that are attacked therein. It therefore strikes me as absurd to exclude the possibility that at least one component of the intended audience for this work consists of the Buddhist tradition's perceived non-Buddhist detractors.

Although the polemical nature of the work thus appears obvious, one might still wish to argue that its intended audience was exclusively Buddhist. I think that the only plausible scenario on which this hypothesis could hold would require that the texts were intended as pedagogical tools to prepare monks for public debates against non-Buddhist opponents. For it is common sense that to be persuasive in a debate, it is necessary that you get your opponent to agree at the start that you understand the subtleties of his position.[131] Any mistake at the outset could cost one the debate. So the text might conceivably have been used to provide Buddhist monks with the ammuni-

130. Most of the explicit evidence concerning public debates in South Asia is discerned in literary works, starting with the Upaniṣads. One Buddhist literary work, the sixth-century Tamil epic *Manimekhalai*, describes a citywide festival in which debate among representatives of various religious traditions plays a prominent role. Proclaiming the start of the festival, a herald says (Daniélou, 1989: 3), "Let the teachers of civic virtues take their place for their ethics lessons on the fine sand spread under the dais or in the public halls. Let the representatives of the various religions, all of whom claim to hold the truth, gather for debate, seated on the chairs reserved for them in the Hall of Learning." See Solomon 1978: 833–75 for further references to literary works that recount various kinds of debates. See also the reference to Jayanta Bhaṭṭa in the next note.

131. Perelman and Olbrechts-Tyteca emphasize the importance of audience agreement for all stages of argumentation, but especially for the preparatory stages in which the premises of the argument are presented (1969: 65): "When a speaker selects and puts forward the premises that are to serve as foundation for his argument, he relies on his hearers' adherence to the propositions from which he will start." See also Jayanta Bhaṭṭa's ninth-century drama, the *Āgamaḍambara* (Raghavan and Thakur 1964: 17; Dezső 2005: 66–67), where

tion they needed to win intersectarian debates. In this way, even if the non-Buddhist opponents cited in the text never directly encountered (i.e., heard or read) the *Tattvasaṃgraha* and the *Pañjikā*, they could still be expected to encounter their arguments and refutations, perhaps in memorized form, in a public forum. It would thus still be the case that non-Buddhists comprise part of the intended audience, albeit in an indirect fashion.

The textual corpus of this period records a dialectical exchange that crosses the boundaries of individual traditions. In one way or another, Śāntarakṣita and Kamalaśīla were clearly seeking to refute the views of others in their intellectual milieu with whom they disagreed on a wide range of topics. Even if a great many of the actual opponents named in the work were already dead by the eighth century (and we cannot be sure that *none* of the thinkers named were contemporaries), there is no reason to think that Śāntarakṣita and Kamalaśīla were not addressing the followers or would-be followers of those whom they cite, such as Uddyotakara and Kumārila, but also many others, including Vātsyāyana, Aviddhakarṇa, Bhāvivikta, Śabarasvāmin, Umbeka, Bhartṛhari, Praśastamati, and a host of additional named and unnamed thinkers.[132] That

a non-Buddhist challenger must first elicit the Buddhist defender's approval of his prior summary of the Buddhist position before the judges allow him to offer a refutation.

132. In her analysis of the interplay in the TS/P between the voices ("Sprecherrollen") of the proponents (i.e., the authors) and their opponents, Kellner (1997: xxvii–xxviii) points out that the presentation of an apparent back-and-forth dialogue between the two parties in the work has an anachronistic and ahistorical character, since opponents' arguments that are presented as directed at the authors' positions could hardly be so directed *in reality* (a situation which Kellner amusingly describes as requiring that Kamalaśīla relay instantly—in the manner of a modern television reporter—opponents' positions and subsequent rejoinders to Śāntarakṣita's arguments). For Kellner, the dialectical component of the text should be described as an idealized debate constructed through a Buddhist perspective between two idealized and abstracted ideal representatives of a given tradition (Denkrichtung). See Kellner 1997: xxviii: "Dieses Element des Sprecherwechsels im argumentativen Text bedingt einen gewissen 'ahistorischen' Charakter: Wenn Kamalaśīla etwa meint, daß 'der Gegner' ... ein Argument gegen ein zuvor von Śāntarakṣita vorgebrachtes Argument vorbringt, ist das natürlich anachronistisch, weil Kumārila oder ein anderer Mīmāṃsaka wohl kaum *tatsächlich* auf Śāntarakṣita bezug genommen haben kann—es sei denn, Kamalaśīla hätte nach Art eines Fernsehreporters blitzschnell einen in der Nachbarschaft ansässigen Mīmāṃsaka um seine Meinung gefragt. Summa summarum kann man einen Text dieser Gattung also aus einer bestimmten Perspektive (hier der buddhistischen) verfaßte Debatte zwischen zwei zu Idealtypen ihrer Denkrichtung abstrahierten Disputanten bezeichnen." Kellner's portrayal of the debate in the TS/P as an ahistorical and idealized abstraction strikes me as basically accurate; nonetheless, I would reject any attempt to use her portrayal as evidence that the opponents addressed in the work should be necessarily excluded from membership in the intended audience.

the intended audience for the work includes Buddhist monks is not in dispute; that it should be limited to them, however, seems an unnecessary restriction.

The Ideal Audience

In contrast to the actual intended audience, the evidence for specifying the ideal audience of the *Tattvasaṃgraha* and the *Pañjikā* is relatively unambiguous. Throughout the works, starting on the very first page, we encounter a figure who clearly fits the bill of the ideal addressee: the *prekṣāvant* or judicious person.[133] Known also as a *prekṣāpūrvakārin*, or "person who undertakes an investigation prior to acting," the judicious person represents a standard of rationality to which Śāntarakṣita and Kamalaśīla appeal regularly in the defense and promotion of their religious philosophy. The qualities of this person are not laid out in any one place, but they can be gleaned from comments that the authors make throughout the body of the works. In brief, the *prekṣāvant* is eminently rational, and it seems to go almost without saying that such a person respects some version of the laws of contradiction and the excluded middle.[134] But adherence to basic logical

---

While Kumārila, for example, may have been dead at the time of the composition of the TS/P, his tradition (the Bhāṭṭa Mīmāṃsā) appears to have been alive and well.

133. The TSP begins with a protracted defense of the necessity for stating the aim (*prayojana*) of the treatise. Kamalaśīla's argument makes clear that he understands this to be a necessity in relation to an ideal audience of judicious persons. In the first line of the commentary, for example, we read (TSP *ad* TS 1–6, B 2,5): *...śāstre prekṣāvatām abhidheyaprayojanāvasāyapūrvikā pravṛttir* ... /. "Judicious persons act toward a treatise having first determined its subject matter and purpose." Funayama (1995) has shown that Kamalaśīla responds here to the views of his fellow Buddhist, Arcaṭa. Cf. also the first line of commentary in Śāntarakṣita's VNV: *yat prayojanarahitaṃ tat prekṣāpūrvakāribhir nārabhyate* ... /.

134. An example of the application of the law of contradiction occurs at TSP *ad* TS 682 (*guṇapadārthaparīkṣā*, B 281,3–4): *vyāhata iti parasparaviruddhaḥ / bhedābhedayoḥ parasparaparihārasthitalakṣaṇatayā yugapad ekatra viruddhatvāt* /. "Obstructed means mutually contradictory, since it is contradictory for that which is different and that which is non-different to exist simultaneously in a single place because they are [an instance of contradiction that is] characterized as mutually exclusive (*parasparaparihārasthita*)." TSP *ad* TS 3353–54 (*atīndriyārthadarśiparīkṣā*, B 1065,22–24) discusses the two types of contradiction or incompatibility: *tathā hi dvividha eva bhāvānāṃ virodho nirūpyamāṇo 'vatiṣṭhate / parasparaparihārasthitalakṣaṇo vā yathā bhāvābhāvayoḥ kramākramayor vā sahānavasthānalakṣaṇo vā yathāgniśītasparśayoḥ* /. "That is, contradiction between things is described as being just twofold: either it is defined as mutual exclusion, as in the case of existence and nonexistence or gradual and simultaneous, or it is defined as mutual incompatibility, as in the case of fire and an icy touch." Cf. NB 3.73–75. An

intuitions is just one facet of the judicious person. An element of practical reason is also involved, since a judicious person is invariably depicted as a person whose actions are directed toward some purpose or goal.[135] In addition, as the Sanskrit term *prekṣāvant* (literally, "one who possesses investigation") suggests, a judicious person does not act toward some goal in a haphazard or whimsical manner but proceeds only upon completing a suitable investigation into the means for attaining his goal. This shows that a judicious person is intelligent, because it is the mark of intelligence—which, according to Śāntarakṣita, even fishermen possess—to act only after considering the effects of one's actions.[136] Further, since attaining a goal is the driving force behind actions, a judicious person necessarily avoids wasting time in investigating useless things, i.e., things that *a priori* serve no useful function.[137] Nor does such a person resort to mere proclamations to clear

---

example of the application of the law of the excluded middle occurs at TSP *ad* TS 1303–4 (*pratyakṣalakṣaṇaparīkṣā*, B 476,24–477,4): *nāpi tṛtīyaḥ pakṣaḥ / anyo 'nyaparihāreṇa sthiter anyatvatattvayoḥ pakṣayoḥ / yau hi parasparaparihāreṇa sthitalakṣaṇau tayor ya ekaḥ pratiṣedhaḥ so 'paravidhinântarīyakaḥ / parasparaparihāreṇa vānyatvatattve vyavasthite / anyatarasvabhāvavyavacchedenānyatarasya paricchedāt / tasmān nāsti tṛtīyarāśisambandhaḥ /*. "Nor is the third position [i.e., that the universal is both other than and the same as particulars] correct, for the two positions concerning being other and being the same are established as mutually exclusive. And regarding two [positions] that are defined as established through mutual exclusion, when one of the two is negated, that amounts to the affirmation of the other. And being other or being the same are established through mutual exclusion, because one of them is determined by means of the exclusion of the nature of the other. Therefore there is no possibility of a third option (*tṛtīyarāśi*)."

135. See, e.g., TSP *ad* TS 155 (*puruṣaparīkṣā*, B 97,16–17): *prekṣāpūrvakāripravṛtteḥ prayojanavattayā vyāptatvāt /*. "[Śāntarakṣita has asked for what reason the supreme person (*puruṣa*) created the world] because the actions of judicious persons necessarily have a purpose."

136. TS 169 (*puruṣaparīkṣā*): *yathākathaṃcid vṛttiś ced buddhimattāsya kīdṛśī / nāsamīkṣya yataḥ kāryaṃ śanako 'pi pravartate //*. "If the action of [the supreme person (*puruṣa*)] were to be haphazard (*yathākathaṃcit*), then what kind of intelligence would he have? For even a fisherman does not act without considering the effect [of his action]." Kamalaśīla glosses *yathākathaṃcit* by *abuddhipūrvakam*, "without prior intention."

137. Cf. TS 419–25 (*sthirabhāvaparīkṣā*) and TSP *ad cit*. In this passage, Śāntarakṣita claims that only a crazy person (*unmatta*) would undertake an investigation into something that was causally inefficacious (i.e., could serve no purpose), and further, that such causally inefficacious pseudo-entities do not qualify as being real things (*vastu*). Cf. also PV 1.211, cited in TSP *ad* TS 422–24: *arthakriyāsamarthasya vicāraiḥ kiṃ tadarthinām / ṣaṇḍhasya rūpe vairūpye kāminyāḥ kiṃ parīkṣayā /*. "Why would those who seek the [thing in question] bother to analyze something that lacks causal efficacy? Why would

up doubt in some matter; rather, a judicious person relies on *pramāṇa*s, or "means of trustworthy awareness," which in Śāntarakṣita and Kamalaśīla's view are limited to perception (*pratyakṣa*) and inference (*anumāna*).[138] A judicious person, therefore, will only apply the conventions "true" or "untrue" when there exists a *pramāṇa* that respectively establishes or disproves the affair in question.[139] Finally, and perhaps most important of all, a judicious person is antidogmatic, in that he or she will necessarily accept *any* position that is established through reasoning (*nyāya*), even if that position does not accord with the dogmas of the community in which he or she stands.[140]

The combined effect of all of these requirements is to reinforce the idea that the ideal audience for the *Tattvasaṃgraha* and the *Pañjikā* is comprised of persons who proceed on the basis of rational inquiry and not on the basis of the authority of a teacher or scriptures. Although this sentiment is expressed throughout the work, it is epitomized in a famous citation of an unidentified Buddhist sūtra, oft quoted among Tibetans, that is preserved in

---

a lustful woman bother to investigate whether a eunuch is beautiful or ugly?" The same verse appears as MA 8 and at TSP *ad* TS 1610 (*pramāṇāntarabhāvaparīkṣā*).

138. See, e.g., TSP *ad* TS 3009–16 (*svataḥprāmāṇyaparīkṣā*, B 957,11–12): *na hy ākrośamātreṇaiva vinā pramāṇaṃ prekṣāvatām āśaṅkānivṛttir yuktā* /. "In the absence of a means of trustworthy awareness (*pramāṇa*), a mere proclamation alone is incapable of eliminating doubt for judicious persons." For more on the *pramāṇa*s, see the section on *pramāṇa* theory below.

139. For the idea that the convention "true" requires a probative *pramāṇa*, see TSP *ad* TS 652 (*guṇapadārthaparīkṣā*, B 270,21–23): *yasya na kiṃcit sādhakaṃ pramāṇam asti na tat prekṣāvatāṃ sadvyavahāraviṣayo yathā vandhyāsutādi* /. For the idea that the convention "untrue" is likewise also applied on the basis of a *pramāṇa* (i.e., the *pramāṇa* of nonperception of a perceptible entity), see TSP *ad* TS 704 (*karmapadārthaparīkṣā*, B 290,24–291,7): *yad upalabdhilakṣaṇaprāptaṃ san nopalabhyate tat prekṣāvatām asadvyavahāram avatarati* /.

140. TSP *ad* TS 2790–91 (*śrutiparīkṣā*, B 897,21–23): *yady ayam artho yuktyupetaḥ syāt / tadā kim iti bauddho nābhyupagacchet / na hi nyāyopapanne 'rthe prekṣāvato 'nabhyupagamo yuktaḥ* /. "If it is correct that this thing is to be accepted, then why would the Buddhist not accept it? For it is not correct for a judicious person not to accept a thing that has been proved through reasoning." A similar principle can also be seen at work in Dharmakīrti's PV 4, the chapter on inference-for-another (*parārthānumānapariccheda*), where Dharmakīrti holds that proponents in a debate should not be considered responsible for every position accepted by the system or school to which they belong but only for the thesis they advance in the current dispute. See PV 4.42 and PV 4.53ff. Translated in Tillemans 2000.

the *Tattvasaṃgraha* and repeated by Kamalaśīla in the opening pages of the *Pañjikā*:

> Just as wise persons accept gold, having first tested it through heating it, cutting it, and rubbing it on a touchstone, so too, O monks, you should accept my words only after testing them and not out of respect [for me].[141]

The clear implication of this verse is that wise (or judicious) persons accept doctrines only after subjecting them to a process of examination (*pari-√īkṣ*), a process reflected in the titles of the work's twenty-six chapters, each of which is labeled an examination or investigation (*parīkṣā*). The *Tattvasaṃgraha* and the *Pañjikā* can thus be seen as a guide for judicious persons who wish to undertake an examination of the rationality of Buddhist doctrines and not *only* as a polemical work addressed at those who get it wrong.

The emphasis on reasoning (*yukti*; *nyāya*) in the final characteristic of the judicious person hints at another aspect of the ideal audience in this work. That is, at various points the authors of the *Tattvasaṃgraha* and the *Pañjikā* exalt a type of person known as an "espouser of reasoning," or *nyāyavādin*. It is tempting to think of such a person as a "rationalist," but if we do, we must bear in mind that the term *nyāyavādin* here indicates not only a devotion to reason (for this is present in the judicious person as well) but also some training in the formal rules and structures of reasoning used in philosophical treatises and debate.[142] For this reason, a better translation than "rationalist"

141. TS 3587 (*atīndriyārthadarśiparīkṣā*) and TSP *ad* TS 1–6 (B 15,23–24): *tāpāc chedāc ca nikaṣāt suvarṇam iva paṇḍitaiḥ / parīkṣya bhikṣavo grāhyaṃ madvaco na tu gauravāt //*. The same idea appears also at TS 3343 and TSP *ad cit.* (*atīndriyārthadarśiparīkṣā*, B 1063,19–22), where Kamalaśīla explains that "heating it, rubbing it on a touchstone, and cutting it" stands for testing the Buddha's words through perception, inference that functions through the force of real entities, and scripturally based inference: *yathā kaladhautaṃ suvarṇam amalaṃ sarvadoṣarahitaṃ parīkṣyamāṇaṃ tāpādibhir na vikriyāṃ pratipadyate tathā bhagavadvacoratnaṃ pratyakṣeṇa tāpasadṛśena vastubalapravṛttānumānena nikaṣaprakhyeṇāgamāpekṣānumānenāpi chedadṛṣṭāntasūcitena na vikriyate /*. Cf. also Kamalaśīla's comments on the verse in the *Nyāyabindupūrvapakṣasaṅkṣipti* (D *tshad ma*, vol. *ve*, 93a4ff.; translated in Hayes 1984: 664). For the distinction between inference that functions through the force of real entities and scripturally based inference, see the section on *pramāṇa* theory below.

142. TSP *ad* TS 3605 (*atīndriyārthadarśiparīkṣā*), for example, suggests that a *nyāyavādin* is someone who has mastery of the technicalities of how to use a *reductio ad absurdum*, or *prasaṅga*, to defeat an opponent. Cf. also Śāntarakṣita's explanation of the term *nyāyavādin* at VNV *ad* VN 1: *nyāyaḥ trirūpaliṅgalakṣaṇā yuktiḥ ... taṃ vadituṃ śīlaṃ*

might be "espouser of formal reasoning."[143] In contrast to the judicious person, it seems to be part of the definition of an espouser of formal reasoning that he be aligned with a particular tradition or school of thought, whether Buddhist or non-Buddhist.[144] Quite probably, this requirement reflects an actual historical exigency, whereby those who wished to advance oral or written arguments were first obliged to enter into and align themselves with some educational institution in order to learn and master the rules of debate.[145] The fact that Śāntarakṣita and Kamalaśīla appeal to the espouser of formal reasoning emphasizes that their work is not addressed to unschooled persons, no matter how intelligent, but rather to an intellectual elite with whom they share a common dialectical idiom. Their audience consists of persons whom they might face in a public debate, where they would argue about religious and philosophical matters using this common language. If such persons are also judicious, then they will also be members of the work's ideal audience.

---

yasya sa tathoktaḥ /. Note also that the term *vādin*, when used as a suffix, frequently indicates the *systematic* adoption of some set of views.

143. It is important to note that formal reasoning is not the same as formal logic. The difference is that while both are concerned with rules for generating valid inferences, the former does not limit itself to questions of validity but is also concerned with questions of soundness. Formal logic, on the other hand, attempts to divest itself of questions of soundness (i.e., of the truth or falsity of the premises and conclusions) and to limit itself strictly to questions of formal validity. As Matilal summarizes (1998: 16), in formal logic "the conclusion may be validly derived from the premises, if and only if the rules of inference are not violated, while it may still be a false judgment." Matilal contrasts this approach to that found in India, where (1998: 17) "philosophers wanted their 'logically' derived inferences or their conclusions also to be pieces of knowledge." When I use the term *formal reasoning*, I refer therefore to the rules of inference as developed in India, where soundness is understood to occupy an equally important place as validity.

144. Cf. TSP *ad* TS 383–84 (*sthirabhāvaparīkṣā*), which provides evidence that the category *nyāyavādin* may be applied to Buddhists and non-Buddhists alike, since Kamalaśīla refers to "Buddhist espousers of formal reasoning" (*yato nyāyavādināṃ bauddhānām akāraṇam asad eva*), noting that for them that which is uncaused does not exist.

145. As Perelman and Olbrechts-Tyteca point out (1969: 99), some audiences are "distinguishable by their use of a technical language of their own." This language, in turn, represents "an aggregate of acquired knowledge, rules, and conventions" that is only available to those who have training in the appropriate discipline and that "the layman completely fails to understand." If a layman wishes to understand some formalized, technical discourse, it will be necessary to learn from someone who already has mastery of it, and it is for this reason that these authors observe that "entry into a specialized group requires initiation." The audience of espousers of formal reasoning in the TS/P is precisely this kind of specialized audience, whose every member has learned about reasoning (*nyāya*) from a master with institutional affiliations.

Styles of Reasoning and Argumentation

In choosing to discuss the styles of reasoning and argumentation in the *Tattvasaṃgraha* and the *Pañjikā*, I inevitably recall Ian Hacking, who introduces the notion of styles of reasoning in order to rebuff a purely subjective relativism while preserving the insight that "many categories of possibility, of what may be true or false, are contingent upon historical events."[146] The historical events Hacking has in mind are the culturally specific developments of diverse styles of reasoning, which "emerge at definite points and have distinct trajectories of maturation."[147] In this section, I do not assess Hacking's contention (which I think makes good sense) but rather accept it as a starting point for advancing a further claim. That is, my argument here is that not only different cultures but even individual authors may employ diverse styles of reasoning (with diverse standards for what counts as true and false), and that the choice of which style of reasoning to use may depend, in part, on the audience that the author addresses and the conclusions that she wishes to induce that audience to accept. In the *Tattvasaṃgraha* and the *Pañjikā*, I submit, the authors employ several different forms of reasoning and argumentation to a variety of aims, in dependence on the audience they address in a particular passage. In the previous section, we considered two aspects of the audience for the *Tattvasaṃgraha* and the *Pañjikā*, the actual intended audience and the ideal audience; in the present section, we shall explore the styles of reasoning and argument that the authors of the *Tattvasaṃgraha* and the *Pañjikā* employ in relation to these distinct audiences.

Arguments *ad personam* and Arguments *ad hominem*

Our previous discussion of the audience for the work left us with the possibility that there could be some members of the intended audience who were not also members of the ideal audience. In fact, I think we can show that for the authors of the *Tattvasaṃgraha* and the *Pañjikā*, at least *some* members of the intended audience—specifically, the Mīmāṃsakas, and especially Kumārila—are decidedly *injudicious*.[148] Since their lack of judiciousness

146. Hacking 1982: 65.

147. Hacking 1982: 65.

148. There are a number of passages to support this claim. See, for example, TS 2445–46 (*śrutiparīkṣā*) and TS 3581–82 (*atīndriyārthadarśiparīkṣā*), where Śāntarakṣita refers to Mīmāṃsakas as persons who are "made stupid by the study of the Veda" (*vedādhyanajaḍīkṛta*; *vedādhītijaḍa*).

excludes these persons from the ideal audience, we should not be surprised to find that the authors occasionally employ styles of reasoning that differ from what they commonly use in relation to those they hold to be judicious persons. In large part, Śāntarakṣita and Kamalaśīla seem to regard their non-Buddhist intended audience as made up of worthy opponents. While they may disagree strongly, even vehemently, with their opponents' positions, they nonetheless construct their rebuttals of those positions in a manner that makes an implicit appeal to the opponents' own claim to judiciousness. Most of the time, they proceed similarly when addressing Kumārila. That is, they take him seriously as an opponent who himself has a plausible (if ultimately flawed) claim to judiciousness. But on some occasions, the authors slip into another mode of address, one that appears considerably less "judicious" itself and exhibits a degree of disdain generally absent in other parts of the work. At such points, the style of reasoning or argumentation in use is one that could be characterized as *ad personam*, where this is defined as "a personal attack on the opponent . . . which aims essentially at disqualifying him."[149]

Perelman and Olbrechts-Tyteca distinguish this kind of argument from arguments *ad hominem*. Although in common parlance arguments that seek to discredit an opponent are referred to as arguments *ad hominem*, Perelman and Olbrechts-Tyteca reserve the term *ad personam* for that kind of argument. Arguments *ad hominem*, in contrast, are defined more strictly as "arguments which the speaker knows would be without weight for the universal audience, as he conceives it."[150] The universal audience, here, "consists of the whole of mankind, or at least, of all normal, adult persons."[151] It is this audience, according to Perelman and Olbrechts-Tyteca, that philosophers "always claim to be addressing . . . because they think that all who understand the reasons they give will have to accept their conclusions."[152] This amounts to holding that a philosophical argument is necessarily "an attempt to get someone to believe something, whether he wants to believe it or not . . ."[153] where the "someone" in question is a normal, adult human being. In other words, on this view, philosophers necessarily embrace "the claim that an argument (if it is good) ineluctably demonstrates its conclusions, and the claim that all who do not recognize it to be good are thereby irrational."[154]

149. Perelman and Olbrechts-Tyteca 1969: 111.

150. Perelman and Olbrechts-Tyteca 1969: 111.

151. Perelman and Olbrechts-Tyteca 1969: 30.

152. Perelman and Olbrechts-Tyteca 1969: 31.

153. Robert Nozick 1981: 14, as quoted in Griffiths 1999b: 506–7.

154. Griffiths 1999b: 513.

Now, I think it is correct to argue that when Śāntarakṣita and Kamalaśīla address or appeal to judicious persons, they understand the arguments they present to possess this kind of strong persuasive power or cogency. That is, their presupposition seems to be that if the reader or hearer of the arguments contained in the *Tattvasaṃgraha* and the *Pañjikā* is a judicious person, he or she will *necessarily* accept the arguments' conclusions as presented in the work. Failure to accept the conclusions in the work without at the same time convincingly demonstrating *why* they must be rejected can mean only that the addressee is not fully judicious and, thus, not fully rational. In this way, the ideal audience for the *Tattvasaṃgraha* and the *Pañjikā* can be understood as the universal audience on Perelman and Olbrechts-Tyteca's terms, with the understanding that being "normal" for these authors entails nothing less than being "judicious."

Having said that, it is nonetheless true that much of the argumentation in the *Tattvasaṃgraha* and the *Pañjikā* is *ad hominem* in the aforementioned sense. Virtually every chapter is addressed to some particular opponent or philosophical system (*darśana*, *mata*), and the arguments advanced frequently proceed from premises that the opponent alone accepts. But does this mean that Śāntarakṣita and Kamalaśīla should not be seen as "philosophers" in the sense advocated by the authors of *The New Rhetoric*? I think not, primarily because the authors of the *Tattvasaṃgraha* and the *Pañjikā* present *ad hominem* arguments always and only as steps along the way to larger arguments that we can consider as *ad humanitatem*, or addressed to the universal (i.e., ideal) audience. Put another way, we can say that when the authors of the *Tattvasaṃgraha* and the *Pañjikā* advance *ad hominem* arguments, they always do so provisionally, adopting a variant "style of reasoning" that still allows for a subsequent final appeal to their own highest standard of rationality, embodied in the ideal audience of judicious persons.[155] As Perelman and Olbrechts-Tyteca note, "there is nothing improper in this procedure,"[156]

155. In many cases, Kamalaśīla signals the provisional status of an argument by means of the technical term *abhyupagamya*, "having [provisionally] accepted..." For one example, see TSP *ad* TS 587 (*dravyapadārthaparīkṣā*, B 244,20–22): *etac ca sarvaṃ paramāṇūnāṃ siddhiṃ bāhyasya cārthasya pratyakṣatvasiddhim abhyupagamyoktam / yasya tu vijñānavādino na bāhyo 'rtho nīlādirūpatayā pratyakṣasiddhaḥ /*. "And all of this has been stated having provisionally accepted that infinitesimal atoms are established and that external objects are established through perception. But for the Vijñānavāda, external objects are not established through perception as having the form of blue and so on." There are a great many such instances in the TSP.

156. Perelman and Olbrechts-Tyteca 1969: 111. They go on to say (111), "We can even qualify argument of this kind as rational, while admitting that the premises under discussion

even for philosophers, for it can be a method of drawing out agreement from the addressee by revealing contradictions in his positions. Śāntarakṣita and Kamalaśīla's *ad hominem* arguments should be seen, I would argue, in this light. Specific members of the intended audience are addressed directly and arguments relying on the premises *they* accept are advanced with the ultimate aim of showing why these premises are false. Yet throughout the process an appeal is also made to the opponents' claim to judiciousness in the effort to persuade them to abandon their erroneous views. The ideal audience thus acts as a kind of court of appeal before which Śāntarakṣita and Kamalaśīla argue their various cases, and for this reason, the authors are careful to apply their own highest standards when it comes to the ultimate conclusions of their arguments.

Arguments *ad personam* function quite differently. Here, although an appeal is still made to the ideal audience of judicious persons, that appeal is no longer addressed directly to the particular audience but rather only implicitly to those who may witness the debate. The tone of these arguments is one of scorn, exasperation, and calumny; it is not a tone that one would typically use to respectfully submit to one's opponent that his position is wrong for such and such reasons. When the authors of the *Tattvasaṃgraha* and the *Pañjikā* slip into this mode of rhetoric (which they do with relative infrequency), they seem to feel free to employ a looser form of reasoning than that which pervades the rest of the work. The usual marks of their formal reasoning (*nyāya*), such as the formulation of formal proof statements (*prayoga*) and the adducing of suitably qualified evidential signs (*liṅga*), are notably absent from these portions of the work. Far from getting at the truth of the matter, the goal of these passages seems to be to discredit the opponent by casting aspersions on his moral character, on his intelligence, and even on his mother![157] Does this mean that Śāntarakṣita and Kamalaśīla have departed from the realm of philosophy and entered the realm of propaganda when advancing such arguments? The answer should probably be a qualified "yes." This is only a qualified affirmation in that they can no longer maintain the pretense that the arguments stand any chance of convincing the addressee of the error of his ways; nevertheless, the hope is still extended that *some other* members of the audience (i.e., the judicious ones) will understand that the addressee in question is simply *beyond the pale of judiciousness* and thus

are not accepted by everyone. These premises fix the framework within which the argument unfolds...."

157. Kamalaśīla goes so far as to gloss the word *jaḍa* ("stupid") with the name "Kumārila"; see TSP *ad* TS 3564 (*atīndriyārthadarśiparīkṣā*, B 1110,16): *jaḍād iti kumārilāt* /.

his positions are tainted from the start. But there is another reason why the presence of such *ad personam* passages does not discredit Śāntarakṣita and Kamalaśīla as philosophers: that is, although such personal attacks can be found in the work, they are always accompanied by more extensive sober reasoning in which the authors take pains to establish their arguments through appeal to the universal or ideal audience. In other words, the *ad personam* attacks in the *Tattvasaṃgraha* and the *Pañjikā* can be seen as superfluous to the *argument* of the work as a whole, since if they were to be removed from the work, its conclusions would nonetheless remain intact (at least in the eyes of its authors).[158]

Nyāya Reasoning

Apart from the personal attacks we have just been discussing, it is probably fair to say that the rest of the argumentation in the *Tattvasaṃgraha* and the *Pañjikā* is grounded in *nyāya*, or formal reasoning. We have already noted that the authors themselves speak approvingly of espousers of formal reasoning (*nyāyavādin*) and that they include both Buddhists and non-Buddhists in this category. But what precisely *is* this formal reasoning to which they appeal? In short, it consists in the rules for constructing valid arguments and the rules for rebutting invalid ones. These rules no doubt were developed for use in public debates, but they are also seen as applicable to textual arguments. Of course, a problem arises when the debate in question concerns the formulation of the rules themselves. We see in India that various thinkers advanced their own formulations of the rules, and presented arguments as to why their rules were better than those of their opponents. Buddhist treatises on formal reasoning appear to have been known (and to have been influential) in the wider intellectual community, but by no means were they the only option.[159]

158. This is not to say that such passages are rhetorically superfluous. The authors, whether consciously or unconsciously, almost certainly did hope to evoke certain reactions in their audience by means of them. As such, the arguments *ad personam* should not be considered extraneous or insignificant to the work as a whole. My point, however, is that the authors do not seem to expect their readers to attain the same kind of certainty (*niścaya*) through these passages as they do from passages that employ *nyāya*, or formal reasoning and that are addressed *ad humanitatem*.

159. The earliest Buddhist rules for debate are found in the Pāli *Kathāvatthu*. Somewhat later (but still pre-Dignāgean) manuals include works preserved only in Chinese (the **Upāhṛdaya* and the **Tarkaśāstra*), Vasubandhu's *Vādavidhi* (preserved only in Tibetan), and Asaṅga's *Śrāvakabhūmi*. Dignāga's innovative works in this area include the *Nyāyamukha* and the *Hetucakraḍamaru*. Dharmakīrti extends Dignāga's line of thought

Naiyāyikas in particular had their own set of rules, with roots stretching back at least to the *Nyāyasūtra* of Akṣapāda Gautama (second century C.E.).[160] Other early traditions of formal reasoning include that of Caraka (first century C.E.), whose medical treatise, the *Carakasaṃhitā*, analyzes the rules for different kinds of philosophical debates.[161] Jains were also active in this arena.[162] Śāntarakṣita himself is credited with writing a commentary on the Buddhist manual that he and Kamalaśīla adopt as one of their guides in formal reasoning, the *Vādanyāya* of Dharmakīrti.[163] In this work, Dharmakīrti provides an alternative to the Naiyāyika system of rules for rebutting arguments, reducing from three to one the number of valid types of debate, and reducing from twenty-two to two the number of "clinchers" or "downfalls" (*nigrahasthāna*) capable of discrediting a thesis.[164]

It is not my intention to embark on an exposition of the history of formal reasoning in India, or even among the Buddhist epistemological tradition of which Śāntarakṣita and Kamalaśīla are part. Instead, what I wish to show is how the rules of formal reasoning these Buddhist thinkers adopt contain an ideological element that is pertinent to our interpretation of the *Tattvasaṃgraha* and the *Pañjikā*. This ideological element has to do with the kinds of debates that are considered legitimate. The idea, pervasive in India (as in ancient Greece), that there should be different *kinds* of debates reflects an appreciation of the rhetorical elements in debate, since the choice of which kind of debate to use is a function of the kind of opponent one faces

---

with the *Nyāyabindu* and the *Vādanyāya*. For the earlier materials, see Tucci 1929; Wayman 1958; and Matilal 1998: 61–80. For Dignāga and later, consult Steinkellner and Much 1995. For the general history of dialectics in India, see Matilal 1998; Oberhammer 1963; Randle 1930; and Solomon 1976 and 1978.

160. See Oberhammer 1963. Matilal (1998: 58) points out that the *Nyāyasūtra* is more than *just* a manual on debate: properly speaking, only chapters one and five are concerned with debate, while the rest of the treatise is devoted to other issues in epistemology.

161. See Kang 2003; Matilal 1998: 41–43; and Solomon 1976.

162. Subsequent Jain manuals include the *Nyāyaviniścaya* of Akalaṅka (seventh to eighth century). See Matilal 1998: 127–39 and Solomon 1976.

163. Śāntarakṣita's commentary is entitled the *Vādanyāyavipañcitārthā* (VNV). See Much (1991: xxiii–xxx) for the history of the recovery of the Sanskrit text and its publication, as well as details on the available Tibetan translations.

164. The claim that Dharmakīrti reduces the *nigrahasthāna*s to two is misleading only as long as one does not understand that under these two clinchers are subsumed a variety of forms. As Much (1986: 134) points out, various parsings of the introductory verse of Dharmakīrti's VN can yield "two, four, eight or even eleven" different types of *nigrahasthāna*.

and the nature of the audience or witnesses to the debate. At the most basic level, Caraka divides debates into friendly (*sandhāyasaṃbhāṣa*) and hostile (*vigṛhyasaṃbhāṣa*) types in dependence on the mutual dispositions of the two debating parties.[165] The aim of the friendly debate is the ascertainment of truth, while the aim of the hostile debate is victory. Because the second type of debate has victory as its goal, one is permitted to use various forms of sophistry and tricks to defeat one's opponent.[166] In the *Nyāyasūtra*, Akṣapāda Gautama delineates three types of debate: honest debate (*vāda*), devious debate (*jalpa*), and mere refutation (*vitaṇḍā*). Of these, honest debate has truth as its aim; devious debate has victory as its aim; and mere refutation has the demolition of the opponent's thesis without establishing a counter-thesis of one's own as its aim.[167] When engaging in an honest debate, only valid reasons and arguments should be used. But in devious debate and in mere refutation, because one's goal is victory at all costs, one is permitted to use tricks and sophisms, most notably any of numerous varieties of equivocation (*chala*) and illegitimate rejoinders (*jāti*).

In contrast to these widely accepted taxonomies of debate, Buddhist

165. Kang 2003: 55–68; Matilal 1998: 38; Solomon 1976: 74–77; Gokhale 1992: 2–3.

166. Solomon (1976: 76–77) summarizes the permissible procedures: "If the opponent is weak in the scriptures, he should be over-powered by long citations from the scriptures; if he is not very learned, he should be defeated by the use of sentences containing unusual words. An opponent whose memory is not retentive should be defeated by the use of involved, long-strung sentences or periods. An opponent devoid of genius should be defeated through the use of the same word bearing different meanings. An opponent devoid of eloquence should be defeated by a scornful imitation of his half-uttered sentences. An opponent who is nervous, or who has not faced an assembly, should be defeated by putting him to shame on that account. An opponent of irritable temper should be defeated by throwing him into a state of nervous exhaustion by repeatedly angering him. An opponent who is timid should be defeated by frightening him away. An opponent who is inattentive should be defeated by checking him under a certain rule. These devices may be employed in order to defeat an inferior opponent quickly."

167. Matilal (1998: 53–55) ventures a defense of *vitaṇḍā* against the critique of Vātsyāyana, who claims that mere refutation without presentation of a counter-thesis is irrational. Matilal considers skeptics and Mādhyamikas as philosophers who can rationally justify their use of mere refutation. Matilal further points to a precedent for a more positive assessment of *vitaṇḍā* in the Naiyāyika tradition itself. This precedent is preserved by Udayana, who refers to the views of the "old Gauḍa Naiyāyika" who advocated four types of debate: *vāda*, *jalpa*, *vādavitaṇḍā*, and *jalpavitaṇḍā*. The third of these would then be, in Matilal's terms (1998: 55), a "good refutative" debate, which "follows the *vāda* model—where logical reasons are adduced and anything merely masquerading as a good reason (that is, a *hetvābhāsa*) is detected—and nobody is really defeated but truth may be established."

epistemologists (starting at least with Dharmakīrti) maintain that there is only one valid form of debate: the honest one in which the goal is to determine the truth of some matter. Since truth, not victory, is the goal, tricks like equivocation are not allowed.[168] In response to the suggestion that there might be a form of debate that has victory, not truth, as its goal, where equivocation would then be permitted, Dharmakīrti says:

> ...in fact, there is no so-called "debate between those desirous of victory" (*vijigīṣuvāda*) that is endowed with [the rules of] logic (*yoga*). Rather, those good people who are acting in order to help others by pointing out a misunderstanding (*vipratipanna*) should follow formal reasoning (*nyāya*), either through the statement of a correct proof or by pointing out real faults [in the other's reasoning], in the presence of witnesses, in order to bring just that [other person] to knowledge. This very adherence to reasoning (*nyāyānusaraṇa*) is debate for good people.[169]

In rejecting those forms of disputation (such as *jalpa* and *vitaṇḍā*) that value victory over truth, Dharmakīrti stakes a claim to the moral intellectual high ground vis-à-vis his Naiyāyika rivals. It is not that he does away with the idea of victory (*vijaya*) but rather that he advocates a notion of victory as inherently tied to truth. Victory is obtained for the proponent through the revelation of that which is true and for the opponent through the refutation of that which is false.[170] These lofty ideals do not prevent Dharmakīrti from setting down further technical conditions for victory and defeat—such as, for example, the rules by which a proponent may lose a debate through mistakes in his presentation of the proof statement—but they do indicate an ideological (if not an actual) commitment to truth as the only justified goal of debate.

According to Dharmakīrti, the proponent (*vādin*) of a thesis in a debate can

168. VN 21,22: *na hi tattvacintāyāṃ kaścic chalavyavahāraḥ /*. This echoes a sentiment of Vasubandhu, preserved at NV 354.13–14: *traividhyānabhyupagamāt / eka evāyaṃ kathāmārgaḥ / tasya prayojanaṃ tattvāvabodho lābhādayaś ca /*. See Much 1991, vol. 2: xv.

169. VN 22,15–20: *...na yogavihitaḥ kaścid vijigīṣuvādo nāma / parānugrahapravṛttās tu santo vipratipannaṃ pratipādayanto nyāyam anusareyuḥ satsādhanābhidhānena bhūtadoṣodbhāvanena vā sākṣipratyakṣaṃ tasyaivānuprabodhāya / tad eva nyāyānusaraṇaṃ satāṃ vādaḥ....* Much translates this passage as (1991, vol. 2: 51): "Daher gibt es überhaupt kein regelloses (*yogavihita*) sogenanntes 'Streitgespräch von Leuten, die siegen wollen (*vijigīṣuvāda*),'" which seems to misinterpret the term *yogavihita*.

170. VN 23,4–6: *tasmāt parānugrahāya tattvakhyāpanaṃ vādino vijayaḥ / bhūtadoṣadarśanena mithyāpratipattinivarttanaṃ prativādinaḥ /*.

be defeated (i.e., can incur a "downfall") in one of two ways.[171] The first is by failing to offer a justification (*samarthana*) for the necessary members (*aṅga*) of the proof; the second is by presenting that which is not a necessary member (*anaṅga*) for the proof as if it *were* a necessary member for the proof.[172] These two downfalls are classed together under the single description of "the non-statement of the necessary members of the proof" (*asādhanāṅgavacana*). For the opponent (*prativādin*), there are likewise two possible downfalls. The first is the failure to point out faults in the proof statement; the second is to point out faults that were not actually incurred.[173] Both are classified under the rubric of "the non-elucidation of faults" (*adoṣodbhāvana*). The further details of this theory of downfalls cannot detain us here. For our present purposes, it is essential instead that we examine the constraints that adhering to these rules places on the participants in the debate.

For example, if we consider the first type of downfall for the proponent (i.e., "failing to offer a justification for the necessary members of the proof"), it is evident that Dharmakīrti, in Much's words, understands the downfall as "mainly an insufficient usage of the logical forms in terms of his own logical theories."[174] This makes sense when we consider that offering justification for the members of one's proof involves justifying one's logical reason (*liṅga*) in an inference. But to do this successfully, at least in Dharmakīrti's eyes, it is necessary that one accept Dharmakīrti's rules of inference (*anumāna*) as well as his understanding of how logical reasons are justified.[175] This, however, *further* requires that one accept his theory of perception (*pratyakṣa*), since perception is a necessary element of the justification of some forms of inference. Accepting Dharmakīrti's theory of perception, however, is virtually tantamount to becoming a Buddhist oneself, since perception for Dharmakīrti, as for most Indian philosophers, is intimately connected, via its objects, with *the real*. Thus it is hard to understand how the first downfall would make sense if one were not already committed to Buddhist principles about reality.

Does this mean, à la Griffiths, that in adopting the rules of debate

171. VN 1: *asādhanāṅgavacanam adoṣodbhāvanaṃ dvayoḥ / nigrahasthānam anyat tu na yuktam iti neṣyate /.*

172. See Much (1986: 134–35) for a more complete explication.

173. See Much 1986: 135–36 for details.

174. Much 1986: 134.

175. In brief, a reason by an essential property (*svabhāvahetu*) is justified through a *bādhakapramāṇa*; a causal reason (*kāryahetu*) is justified by establishing a causal relation; and a reason by nonperception (*anupalabdhihetu*) is justified by establishing that there is nonperception of that which is capable of being perceived. See Much 1986: 134–35.

contained in the *Vādanyāya*, Śāntarakṣita and Kamalaśīla limit their audience to Buddhists exclusively?[176] Although the answer seems to be yes, two factors caution against this response. First, it must be noted that despite the important differences between the Buddhist and the Naiyāyika rules for debate, there nonetheless exists a sufficient degree of consensus at the time of the *Tattvasaṃgraha* and the *Pañjikā* for Śāntarakṣita and Kamalaśīla to be able to offer refutations of non-Buddhist positions in terms that non-Buddhists could be expected to understand and accept (even if they do not accept the conclusions of the Buddhist arguments).[177] A number of fundamental fallacies of the logical reason (*hetvābhāsa*), for example, were generally accepted (at least since Dignāga) by Buddhists and non-Buddhists alike. When Śāntarakṣita urges, say, the fault of the inconclusiveness (*anaikāntikatva*) of the logical reason, he expects his readers, whether Buddhist or non-Buddhist, to generally understand that he means that the logical reason is in some sense "misleading" or "deviant" (*vyabhicāra*).[178] Second, the disavowal of debates aimed at victory and the insistence on limiting debates to those aimed at truth suggests that although these authors use Buddhist rules, they nonetheless address themselves to a universal audience, understood, as before, as the audience of judicious persons. The underlying assumption in the Buddhist *nyāyavādin* reasoning is that *if* judicious persons investigate the Buddhist *pramāṇa* theory (i.e., its theory of perception and inference), they will inevitably come to accept that *pramāṇa* theory as valid, even if they do not start out as proponents of Buddhism. The use of Dharmakīrti's system of

176. For Griffiths' argument, see above, n. 121.

177. Matilal (1986b: 69), in discussing what he calls the "Nyāya method" supports my thesis: "Although the method was developed initially by the authors of the Nyāya school, one may claim that this was a general philosophic method acceptable also to other schools. Certainly the Buddhist, and sometimes Jaina, authors criticized various aspects of this method, but they offered what may be called 'internal' criticisms and often suggested an improved version of the same. There was thus a tacit agreement among the philosophers of ancient and classical India regarding the efficacy of the Nyāya method." Although there were clearly some differences among the various schools, it seems that enough agreement existed so that rules could be negotiated at the outset of public debates. See Jayanta Bhaṭṭa's drama, the *Āgamaḍambara* 1.25, where the judges (*prāśnikāḥ*) set forth the rules for the debate and elicit agreement to the rules from the proponent and opponent at the outset.

178. A logical reason can be misleading or deviant in various ways. For example, it will be misleading if it occurs in dissimilar (*vipakṣa*) as well as in similar (*sapakṣa*) cases. For the history of the development of the idea of deviance and inconclusiveness, see, e.g., Gokhale 1992.

nyāyavādin reasoning thus does not necessarily exclude non-Buddhists from the audience for the work even though it may appear to do so *prima facie*.

Pramāṇa Theory

In our earlier discussion of the ideal audience, we noted that it is a characteristic of the judicious person that she relies upon *pramāṇas*, the means of trustworthy awareness, to attain certainty and to establish the truth or falsity of any matter. As in the case of *nyāya* reasoning, Śāntarakṣita and Kamalaśīla's appeal to *pramāṇas* is not an idiosyncratic move, but represents a petition to a wider stream of philosophical reasoning beyond the confines of the Buddhist tradition. While it is certainly true that Buddhists developed their own theories for what should count as a *pramāṇa*, it must also be emphasized that they did so within the bounds of a larger context that we can refer to as *pramāṇa* theory or, with some qualification, the Indian epistemological tradition.[179] If *nyāya* reasoning concerns the formal rules of debate, *pramāṇa* theory has to do with the rules of evidence or justification that are at play in *nyāya* reasoning. Both forms of reasoning are aimed at attaining certainty, but whereas *nyāya* reasoning seeks to *convince* an opponent of some position, *pramāṇa* theory aims at demonstrating why that position is *justified*.[180] Clearly, the two forms of reasoning work together, and as noted above, full acceptance of a philosopher's theory of formal reasoning ultimately *requires* full acceptance of his theory of justification as well. At the same time, a sufficient degree of consensus concerning the nature and functions of the *pramāṇas* exists to enable philosophers of different traditions to debate meaningfully about them. In this section, I give a brief overview of the *pramāṇa* theory at work in the *Tattvasaṃgraha* and the *Pañjikā*.[181]

There are a number of problems with casting *pramāṇa* theory as primarily a theory of justification, but these problems arise only when one attempts

179. Dunne (2004: 15–52) gives a good overview of the shared philosophical context in which Dharmakīrti develops his *pramāṇa* theorizing. For the broader context, see Ganeri 2001.

180. The two forms of reasoning mirror, to some extent, the two forms of inference, since inference-for-oneself (*svārthānumāna*) is concerned with demonstrating why a particular cognitive episode is justified, and inference-for-another (*parārthānumāna*) is concerned with convincing others of this same fact.

181. Note that much of this material will appear basic to specialists; my aim here is not so much to advance original research in the area of *pramāṇa* theorizing, but rather to provide the basic background necessary to understand Śāntarakṣita and Kamalaśīla's rhetoric of reason in the TS/P.

too glibly to graft European and American concepts of truth and justification onto *pramāṇa* theory. At the heart of the difficulty is the important question: what are we justifying? European and American epistemological thinkers commonly employ the notion of justification as a component in their theories of knowledge; in the well-known formula, knowledge is defined as "justified true belief."[182] Here, it is a particular kind of belief, namely a true one, that may be justified (or not). In Indian *pramāṇa* theory, however, it is not true beliefs (which are enduring dispositions) but rather momentary cognitive episodes, or awarenesses (*jñāna*), that are justified (or not) by *pramāṇas*.[183] The term *pramāṇa* comes from the verbal root *pra* √*mā*, meaning in this context "to ascertain" or "to know indubitably."[184] A *pramāṇa* in its broadest sense, then, is the instrument or means by which one may be justified in regarding a particular instance of awareness as an instance of certainty or indubitable knowing.[185] All *pramāṇa* theorists are in general agreement about this basic point. As long as we keep in mind the important distinction that the object of justification is a cognitive episode, and not a dispositional

182. Plantinga (1993: 6–11) provides an overview of what he calls "the widely celebrated 'justified true belief' (JTB) account or analysis of knowledge," saying that this account "enjoyed the status of epistemological orthodoxy until 1963, when it was shattered by Edmund Gettier..." Plantinga also points to (1993: 6) "an interesting historical irony," namely that "it isn't easy to find many really explicit statements of a JTB analysis of knowledge prior to Gettier." Despite this alleged difficulty, however, Plantinga goes on to cite a variety of works, both pre- and post-Gettier, that he says exemplify the idea that knowledge is (or is nearly) justified true belief.

183. Potter (1984: 310) makes the case for the difference between *jñāna* and belief: "A *jñāna* is something which happens at a time, an occurrent. If it involves belief, it does so only in the sense of a believing as a fleeting act of awareness. A *jñāna* is not a belief in the dispositional sense. And not all *jñānas* are beliefs even in the occurrent sense—believing is, or may be, only one sort of *jñāna*. Any act of awareness that has intentionality constitutes a *jñāna*. Entertaining a doubt, vaguely sensing the presence of something or other, drawing a reductio ad absurdum inference, and understanding someone's meaning are all *jñāna*. None of them are believings. And since they are not beliefs (in any sense) none of them are true beliefs, and none of them are justified true beliefs. Rather, a *jñāna* is, as indicated, *an* awareness. It is not knowledge or even *a* knowledge *per se*, though it remains open to further scrutiny whether all, some or no acts of awareness constitute instances of knowledge in some sense other than justified true belief."

184. The fundamental meaning of the root *pra* √*mā* is "to measure," from which is derived the further meanings of "to form a correct notion of," "to understand," and "to know." See Monier-Williams, s.v.

185. The word *pramāṇa* is a verbal action noun created through the addition of the *kṛt* suffix *-ana* directly to the root *pra-*√*mā*. See Goldman and Sutherland 1980: 359.

belief, there is nothing wrong with considering *pramāṇa* theory as a theory of justification.

As in so many other areas of their philosophical thought, Śāntarakṣita and Kamalaśīla adhere closely to the views of their predecessors Dignāga and, especially, Dharmakīrti in articulating their *pramāṇa* theory. In contrast to their non-Buddhist contemporaries, these philosophers hold that the *pramāṇa* that serves to justify a cognitive episode as an instance of indubitable knowing does not differ from the episode itself.[186] This presentation deviates significantly from that of most Naiyāyikas, Vaiśeṣikas, Sāṃkhyas, and Bhāṭṭa Mīmāṃsakas, all of whom generally regard the *pramāṇa*, or means of determining that a particular cognitive episode is an instance of indubitable knowledge, as distinct from the resultant instance or action of indubitable knowing (the *pramiti*).[187] This distinction in *pramāṇa* theory has led some modern authors to translate the term *pramāṇa* differently in different contexts.[188] While such a procedure is not without reason, it does tend to gloss over fact that the term *pramāṇa* is used and understood *across* sectarian lines, suggesting that at least some aspects of this term are shared by Buddhist and non-Buddhist authors alike.[189] In this connection, it may also be useful to point out that although for the Buddhists a *pramāṇa* is not different from the cognitive episode that it certifies, it nonetheless does not thereby give up its character of serving as the *means* of arriving at that certification. Thus, even though the means and the end are not distinct, there may still be Buddhist contexts where it is appropriate to speak of a *pramāṇa* as a means of justification, since a cognitive episode is certified as an instance of indubitable knowledge *by virtue of the fact* that it is a *pramāṇa*.

Śāntarakṣita and Kamalaśīla follow Dharmakīrti in defining a *pramāṇa* as a trustworthy awareness that reveals or makes known a previously unknown object.[190] For an awareness to be trustworthy (*avisaṃvāda*) means that it has

186. Dignāga sets out his view on the identity of the *pramāṇa* and its effect (*pramāṇaphala*) in PSV *ad* PS 1.1.8cd–10. See Hattori 1968: 28–29 and 97–107. For Dharmakīrti's presentation, see PV 3.311–19 and PV 3.334–39. For Śāntarakṣita and Kamalaśīla's treatment of this issue, see TS 1343–54 and TSP *ad cit.*

187. See Dunne 2004: 49–50. See also Arnold 2005 and Taber 2005.

188. See, e.g., Dreyfus 1997: 528n23: "I translate *pramāṇa* as 'means of valid cognition' when used in the Nyāya sense of the word and as 'valid cognition' when understood according to Buddhist ideas."

189. Dunne (2004: 22n17) points to NS 1.1.28 with NBh and NV *ad cit.* as the locus for a Naiyāyika discussion of elements common to all philosophical traditions.

190. For the trustworthy component of the definition, see PV 2.1a: *pramāṇam*

some expected (*abhimata*) causal function (*arthakriyā*)[191] as its object. For these thinkers, the capacity for causal function (*arthakriyāsāmarthya*) is the mark of a real thing (*vastu*),[192] such that any awareness of causal function is necessarily an awareness of a real thing. (This assertion is based on a causal theory of perception, whereby awarenesses are the results of causally functioning objects.) Not surprisingly, the causal correspondence between the causal function of the object and the resulting awareness is what accounts for the trustworthiness of that awareness.[193] It is important to note here that when in speaking of *the real* in such contexts, Śāntarakṣita and Kamalaśīla, like most Buddhist philosophers, speak of two sorts of real things: those that are ultimately real (*paramārthasat*) and those that are conventionally real (*saṃvṛtisat*). Of these two kinds of real things, only those that are ultimately real are capable of causal function.[194] It is, therefore, only insofar as a thing

---

avisaṃvādi jñānam / and TSP *ad* TS 2958–61 (*svataḥprāmāṇyaparīkṣā*, B 942,16–17): *pramāṇaṃ hi nāmāvisamvādi jñānam ucyate* /. For the element of "novelty," see PV 2.5c: *ajñātārthaprakāśo vā*. Cf. TS 1549ab (*pramāṇāntarabhāvaparīkṣā*): *vijñātārthaprakāśatvān na pramāṇam iyaṃ* ..., where Śāntarakṣita rejects that memory can be a *pramāṇa* since it lacks this quality of revealing a previously unknown thing. Controversy concerning Dharmakīrti's definition (or lack thereof) of the term *pramāṇa* has erupted in recent years, with the most relevant sources being Dreyfus 1991, 1997; Franco 1991, 1997; Oetke 1999; Dunne 2004; and Ono 2000. This controversy centers on the interpretation of the particle *vā* in PV 2.5c, and especially whether the two elements of trustworthiness and novelty are to be understood as providing the sufficient or merely the necessary conditions for an awareness to be a *pramāṇa*. I will not enter this controversy here, but shall only remark that Śāntarakṣita and Kamalaśīla quite clearly understand both elements to be necessary. See, e.g., TS 1485 (*anumānaparīkṣā*) for a statement that a *pramāṇa* must reveal a previously unknown object.

191. The attempt to interpret and explain the term *arthakriyā* in Buddhist philosophy has generated a sizable body of secondary literature. Important secondary sources on the interpretation of *arthakriyā* in Dharmakīrti's thought include Dreyfus 1997; Dunne 2004; Katsura 1984; Mikogami 1979; Nagatomi 1967–68; and Steinkellner 1971.

192. Dharmakīrti makes this point succinctly at PVSV *ad* PV 1.172: *yad arthakriyākāri tad eva vastv ity uktam* /. Śāntarakṣita and Kamalaśīla reiterate this idea at numerous points in the TS/P. See, e.g., TSP *ad* TS 415–16 (*sthirabhāvaparīkṣā*, B 188,16–17): *idam eva hi vastulakṣaṇaṃ yad arthakriyāsāmarthyam* /. For the corresponding notion that it is the lack of causal functioning that defines unreal things, see TSP *ad* TS 417 (*sthirabhāvaparīkṣā*, B 188,21–22): *tathā hi śaśaviṣāṇādau yad avastutvam iṣṭaṃ tatrārthakriyāsāmarthyaviraha eva nibandhanam* /.

193. See TSP *ad* TS 2958–61 (*svataḥprāmāṇyaparīkṣā*, B 942,16–20), translated on p. 288. Cf. also TS 2965 (*svataḥprāmāṇyaparīkṣā*), translated on p. 291.

194. TSP *ad* TS 2746 (*śrutiparīkṣā*, B 886,7–9): *na ca sāṃvṛtaṃ kasyacit kāryasyārambhakaṃ yuktaṃ tallakṣaṇahāniprasaṅgāt / tathā hi yad arthakriyākāri tad eva param-*

is capable of causal function that it can be held to be a real thing (*vastu*) in an ultimate sense. And such ultimately real things that are capable of causal function are, in Śāntarakṣita and Kamalaśīla's view, limited to momentary, inexpressible, and unique particulars (*svalakṣaṇa*).[195]

On the basis of this analysis, one might conclude that trustworthy awarenesses can have only real particulars as their objects. But such a conclusion does not accord with Dignāga and Dharmakīrti's oft-stated position (adopted by the authors of the *Tattvasaṃgraha* and the *Pañjikā* as well) that the two kinds of *pramāṇa*, perception (*pratyakṣa*) and inference (*anumāna*), each have their own distinctive kind of object: causally functioning real particulars (*svalakṣaṇa*) and causally inefficacious unreal universals (*sāmānyalakṣaṇa*), respectively.[196] If this is the case, the implication seems to be that inference cannot be a trustworthy awareness, since its object is not real. Yet Buddhist *pramāṇa* theorists are adamant that inference *is* a trustworthy awareness, as valid as perception in its power to justify a cognitive episode.[197] The key to their reasoning on this issue is the recognition that although universals are unreal, they nonetheless can be constructed on the basis of real particulars.[198] When a universal is constructed on the basis of a real particular (through

ārthas tadanyat tu saṃvṛtisad iti paramārthasaṃvṛtisator lakṣaṇam /. Note, however, that the equation of causal function and the ultimately real shifts in the authors' Madhyamaka level of analysis to an equation of causal function and the *conventionally* real. See MA 64: *ma brtags gcig pu nyams dga' zhing / skye dang 'jig pa'i chos can pa / don byed pa dag nus rnams kyi / rang bzhin kun rdzob pa yin rtogs //*.

195. For an explicit statement of this equivalence, see TSP *ad* TS 1358–60 (*pratyakṣalakṣaṇaparīkṣā*, B 493,9): *...svalakṣaṇaṃ tad eva vastu....* For a statement by Dharmakīrti, see PV 3.3: *arthakriyāsamarthaṃ yat tad atra paramārthasat / anyat saṃvṛtisat proktaṃ te svasāmānyalakṣaṇe /*.

196. See, e.g., PV 3.1: *mānaṃ dvividhaṃ viṣayadvaividhyāc chaktyaśaktitaḥ / arthakriyāyām ... //*. That inference has a universal (*sāmānya*) as its object is stated, among other places, at TSP *ad* TS 1448–54 (*anumānaparīkṣā*, B 520,11–12): *tasmāt sarvatraiva sāmānyatodṛṣṭam eva kṣaṇakṣayiṣu bhāveṣv anumānaṃ na viśeṣatodṛṣṭaṃ nāma kiṃcid iti /*.

197. See TS 460 and TSP *ad cit.* (*sthirabhāvaparīkṣā*) for an explicit refutation of the idea that perception is "superior" (*jyeṣṭha*) to inference in terms of its status as a trustworthy awareness. See also TS/P 1471–73 (*anumānaparīkṣā*) for a statement on why inference (at least of the *vastubalapravṛttānumāna* variety) cannot be mistaken.

198. Dharmakīrti states that there are three kinds of universals: one that is constructed on the basis of real things, one that is constructed on the basis of unreal things, and one that is constructed on the basis of both real and unreal things. See PV 3.51cd: *sāmānyaṃ trividhaṃ tac ca bhāvābhāvobhayāśrayāt //*.

the process of exclusion, or *apoha*),[199] the universal itself is understood to be unreal, since it can be shown to be *neither the same nor different from* the particular on which it is based.[200] Rather than being a real thing, the universal is then understood to be one way of conceptually *conceiving* the particular through a process of ignoring certain aspects of that particular's differences from all other unique particulars.[201] When one cognizes an unreal universal that is constructed on the basis of a real thing, even though it is not necessary that the real particular on which it is based be right in front of one, it *is* necessary that the particular has been previously known directly through perception.[202] Since inference operates uniquely through universals that are constructed on the basis of real things, inference can be said to depend upon the prior functioning of perception. To emphasize this point, Dharmakīrti asserts that in fact trustworthy awareness has only *one* object, the particular, but is considered to have two objects, depending on whether the particular is known directly in its own form or indirectly through another form.[203]

Thus, although inference does not directly cognize causal function, it does so indirectly, and this is what allows it to function as a trustworthy awareness. The bottom line is that if a cognitive episode is to be counted as trustworthy, it must yield knowledge of causal function. Why do these philosophers put so much emphasis on causal function? For one thing, as we have already seen, they understand causal function to be the mark of the real, and if a cognitive episode is to be justified, it must yield knowledge of the real. But there is another, equally important, reason for the emphasis on causal function, and this is again connected with the ideal of the judicious person. That is, like virtually all *pramāṇa* theorists of their time, Śāntarakṣita and Kamalaśīla hold that a judicious person acts only with some purpose (*prayojana*) in mind.

199. For the theory of *apoha*, see Dreyfus 1997; Dunne 2004; Hattori 1980; Hayes 1988; and Katsura 1991.

200. See, e.g., TS 1029a–c (*śabdārthaparīkṣā*): *yathaivāvidyamānasya na bhedaḥ pāramārthikaḥ / abhedo 'pi tathaiveti ... //*.

201. See, e.g., TS 1056 (*śabdārthaparīkṣā*): *avivakṣitabhedaṃ ca tad eva parikīrtitam / sāmānyalakṣaṇatvena nāniṣṭer aparaṃ punaḥ //*. Kamalaśīla comments at TSP *ad cit.* as follows: *tad eva hi svalakṣaṇam avivakṣitabhedaṃ sāmānyalakṣaṇam ity uktam / sāmānyena bhedāparāmarśena lakṣyate vyavasīyata iti sāmānyalakṣaṇam / nāparaṃ punar iti tīrthikābhimataṃ tasyāniṣṭatvāt /*.

202. PV 3.53b–c: *bhāvagrahaṇapūrvakam / taj jñānam ... //*.

203. PV 3.53d–54: *meyaṃ tv ekaṃ svalakṣaṇam // tasmād arthakriyāsiddheḥ sadasattāvicāraṇāt / tasya svapararūpābhyāṃ gater meyadvayaṃ matam //*. Kamalaśīla cites PV 3.54cd at TSP *ad* TS 1056, just after the commentary given above in n. 201.

Now, the term that we have been translating as causal function, *arthakriyā*, carries with it a significant bivalency, such that in many cases it can convey the meaning of "accomplishment of a goal" in addition to, or sometimes in place of, the more general meaning "causal function."[204] When the term *arthakriyā* has this secondary connotation, it expands the scope of that which is justified through *pramāṇa*s from momentary cognitive episodes to moral and other actions in the world. In this way, as well, *pramāṇa* theory is similar to many European and American theories of justification, which often extend beyond the justification of beliefs to include the justification of actions based on those beliefs.[205] The *pramāṇa* theory of Śāntarakṣita and Kamalaśīla (and likewise that of Dharmakīrti) is thus also a theory of justification in this wider sense.

Goal accomplishment occurs only through causal function, since goals are always attained through the effects of some prior action. The accomplishment of a goal is thus a mark of causal function, which, in turn, is a mark of the real. Thus, the two connotations of *arthakriyā* converge in the actions of judicious persons, since such persons do not act toward (or for the sake of) that which is unreal. Doing so would be pointless, since the unreal, being causally inefficacious, cannot bring about the desired goal. This is why Dharmakīrti states that one should not bother to investigate treatises that discuss "results that are not a human aim" (*apuruṣārthaphalāni*), saying that such texts are "like an investigation into the teeth of crows" (*kākadantaparīkṣāvat*).[206] This pervasive concern with the fulfillment of goals has led some modern scholars to conclude that Dharmakīrti and his followers subscribe to a pragmatic

204. This bivalence is possible due to the well-known multivalence of the term *artha*, which in philosophical writings regularly conveys the meanings "object," "real thing," "referent," "meaning," and "aim" or "goal." For treatments of *arthakriyā* in secondary sources, see the references in n. 191 above.

205. Kirkham (1992), in a contemporary textbook on truth theories, notes that it is in the moral arena that a theory of justification becomes crucially relevant for the majority of people. That is, most of us (1992: 42) "do not want to think that our belief in the wrongness of murder is no more justified than the criminal's belief that murder is morally permissible."

206. See PVSV *ad* PV 1.214: *aśakyopāyaphalāni ca śāstrāṇi phalārthī nādriyeta vicārayitum apuruṣārthaphalāni ca / viṣaśamanāya takṣakaphaṇaratnālaṃkāropadeśavat kākadantaparīkṣāvac ca /*. Drawing on this passage, Kamalaśīla makes the same point at the outset of the TSP *ad* TS 1–6 (B 2,10–12): *tathā saty abhidheye kākadantaparīkṣāśāstravad abhimataprayojanarahitaṃ śāstraṃ prekṣāvantaḥ śrotum api nādriyantaḥ /*. "Thus, even if the subject matter [is stated], if the treatise is devoid of any desired aim, as with a treatise that investigates the teeth of crows, judicious persons will not apply themselves to listening to [i.e., studying] it."

theory of truth.[207] This assessment, however, does not hold up.[208] While it is true that the Buddhist epistemologists understand the *pramāṇa*s in terms of the attainment of desired goals, they also understand the attainment of goals to occur only through causal function, which operates independently of one's hopes, aspirations, and point of view.[209] That which is "true" is here that which is confirmed through trustworthy awarenesses and not simply a belief that is useful, as in many pragmatic theories of truth.[210]

Causal function—in its two senses—is thus the key to the entire system of *pramāṇa* theory for Śāntarakṣita and Kamalaśīla, since the two forms of trust-

207. Although the term "pragmatic theory of truth" has multiple connotations, I use it here in the sense developed by William James, whereby "... an idea is 'true' so long as to believe it is profitable to our lives.... The true is the name of whatever proves itself to be good in the way of belief." Quoted in Tillemans 1999b: 18–19n5. Among modern scholars who assert Buddhism as professing a pragmatic theory of truth is Mohanty (1992: 133), who characterizes the Buddhist epistemologists as having "a sort of pragmatic theory" of truth. See also Potter (1984), who suggests a kind of Buddhist pragmatism when he advocates a definition of *prāmāṇya* as "workability." For the difference between a theory of justification and a theory of truth, see Kirkham (1992: 25): "So theories of justification answer questions like, For any given proposition (or belief or sentence, etc.), when and how are we justified in thinking that the proposition is probably true? It does *not* answer, What are the necessary and sufficient conditions for something's being true? And in no sense could a theory of justification be thought to provide a *definition* of truth." The *pramāṇa* theory espoused by Śāntarakṣita and Kamalaśīla is designed to answer questions closer to the first set than the second, and thus it is closer to a theory of justification than a theory of truth. The explicit connection between trustworthiness and truth, however, suggests that the *pramāṇa* theory may *also* serve as a vehicle for determining the nature of these thinkers' theory of truth. See below, n. 210.

208. Cf. Dreyfus 1995: 671–91 and 1997: 299–315; Jackson 1993: 43–63; and Tillemans 1999b: 6–12.

209. To say that causal function operates independently of mental construction is not to say that one's *determination* of a particular as such-and-such operates independently of such mental construction. On the contrary, mental factors such as desire, expectation, interest, and so on are crucial elements in the process by which a person comes to recognize a given instance of causal function as relevant to her goals. At the same time, however, causal function does not itself depend upon desires, interest, and so on to operate. If it did, then things would only be real if and when they were recognized as such. For an interesting passage in which Śāntarakṣita and Kamalaśīla dispute such a claim, see TS/P 122 (*svābhāvikajagadvādaparīkṣā*), in which it is argued that grass growing in a mountain cave does not become unreal simply because it is not perceived.

210. See TSP *ad* TS 2786–88 (*śrutiparīkṣā*): *satyam iti avisaṃvādi* /. The connection between truth and trustworthiness goes back at least to Nāgārjuna, who links the two at RĀ 2.35a, a verse whose textual variants render an unambiguous interpretation difficult. See Dunne and McClintock 1997: 116n35.

worthy awareness, perception and inference, are both made feasible through causal function. This is especially clear in the case of perception, which operates explicitly on a causal model.[211] That is, following Dharmakīrti, the authors of the *Tattvasaṃgraha* and the *Pañjikā* define perception as an awareness that is nonconceptual (*kalpanāpoḍha*) and nonerroneous (*abhrānta*).[212] Perception occurs when a causally efficacious particular produces an image (*ākāra*) of itself in awareness. This image, insofar as it is the effect of a causally efficacious particular, possesses similarity (*sārūpya*) with its cause, and this is what allows us to classify perception as nonerroneous (*abhrānta*).[213] As nonconceptual (*nirvikalpa, kalpanāpoḍha*), perception possesses a quality of vividness (*spaṣṭatva*) that is absent in conceptual and linguistic cognitive episodes. This vivid quality is known experientially through reflexive awareness (*svasaṃvedana*). Although perception is nonconceptual, it nonetheless gives subsequent rise to definitive ascertainments (*niścaya*) that *are* conceptual and may be expressed in language.[214] Which ascertainments arise

211. Reflexive awareness (*svasaṃvedana*) is an exception to this rule, since it functions non-causally. The other three forms of perception accepted by the Buddhist epistemologists, sense perception (*indriyapratyakṣa*), mental perception (*mānasapratyakṣa*), and yogic perception (*yogipratyakṣa*), all operate causally.

212. For Dharmakīrti's definition, see NB 1.4: *tatra pratyakṣaṃ kalpanāpoḍham abhrāntam /*. Śāntarakṣita and Kamalaśīla accept this characterization throughout the TS/P. See, e.g., TS 1213 (*pratyakṣalakṣaṇaparīkṣā*) and TSP *ad cit.*

213. Kamalaśīla states this principle negatively in a proof statement at TSP *ad* TS 1966–68 (*bahirarthaparīkṣā*, B 672,8–9): *yaḥ pratyakṣābhimate pratyaye na pratibhāsate svenākāreṇa na sa pratyakṣatvena grahītavyaḥ / yathā gaganaṇalinam /*. "Whatever does not appear with its own form in a cognition that is asserted to be a direct perception should not be considered as apprehended by direct perception, like a sky-flower." See also TS 1261cd–1262 (*pratyakṣalakṣaṇaparīkṣā*).

214. This position is stated often in the TS/P. See, e.g., TSP *ad* TS 1272 (*pratyakṣalakṣaṇaparīkṣā*, B 466,17–20): *svabhāvād apare ye niḥśeṣāḥ padārthās tebhyo vyatirekiṇi vyāvṛtte gṛhīte saty asādhāraṇanīlādyākārapratibhāsanāt paścād bhedādhyavasāyī śabdākārānusmṛto bhinnam ity abhilapann utpadyate vikalpaḥ /*. "When one has apprehended [through perception] the excluded [particular] that is distinct from all real things that are different [from that thing] by nature, then after the appearance of the unique (*asādhāraṇa*) image of blue and so on, there arises a conception that determines the difference [of, say, that blue image from non-blue images] expressing [that determination] as '[it is] different,' in accord with the forms of language." A technical term that is sometimes used for the subsequent conceptual determination of the contents of perceptual awareness is *tatpṛṣṭhalabdhaniścaya*. Kamalaśīla also uses the term *pratyakṣapṛṣṭhabhāvī vikalpaḥ*, for example at TSP *ad* TS 1297 (*pratyakṣalakṣaṇaparīkṣā*, B 474,24–475,11): *prayogaḥ / yad gṛhītagrāhi jñānaṃ na tat pramāṇam / yathā smṛtiḥ / gṛhītagrāhī ca pratyakṣapṛṣṭhabhāvī vikalpa iti vyāpakaviruddhopalabdhiḥ /*. "The proof statement is

in the wake of any given perceptual cognitive episode depends not only on the nature of the real thing that has caused the image in perceptual awareness, but also on such factors as one's interests, prior conditioning, intelligence, and so on.[215]

Causal function is also central to the authors' understanding of inference, which, again following Dignāga and Dharmakīrti, they hold is a process by which one ascertains some aspect of a real particular through some evidence or logical sign.[216] Technically, inference is defined as "the vision (or

---

as follows: whatever awareness apprehends what has already been apprehended is not a *pramāṇa*, like remembrance. And the conception that comes about subsequent to perception is an awareness that apprehends what has already been apprehended. Therefore [it is not a *pramāṇa* because] there is the observance of that which contradicts the pervader (*vyāpaka*)." The last phrase refers to the idea that the lack of apprehension of that which is already apprehended is a necessary quality (i.e., "a pervader") of being a *pramāṇa*. Cf. PV 2.3ab.

215. The idea that ascertainment does not automatically arise through perceptual experience is stated, among other places, at TSP *ad* TS 458 (*sthirabhāvaparīkṣā*). In this case, the context is a discussion of the impossibility of a permanent entity. The Buddhist critique (TS 457) holds that the present state of existence of a permanent entity must be either the same as or different from its previous state of existence. If it is different, then the entity's permanence has been disproved. If it is the same, then why is it not apprehended at the time when the previous state of existence is apprehended? In response to this critique, the interlocutor tries to appeal to the Buddhists' own position by suggesting that the previous existence *is* apprehended but is simply *said* not to be apprehended. Kamalaśīla rejects this, noting it is not that some aspects of the real thing (e.g., momentariness) are not apprehended but rather only that they are not conceptually ascertained. See TSP *ad* TS 458 (*sthirabhāvaparīkṣā*, B 201,9–13) *syād etat / yathā kṣaṇikatvaṃ śabdāder avyatiriktam api sat tadgrahaṇe saty apy agṛhītam ucyate / tadvad idam api bhaviṣyatīti / tad ayuktam / na hi śabde dharmiṇi gṛhīte 'pi tadavyatireki kṣaṇikatvam agṛhītam iti vyavasthāpyate / kiṃ tu gṛhītam api tanniścayotpattikāraṇābhāvād aniścitam ity abhidhīyate / na hy anubhavamātrād eva niścayo bhavati / tasyārthitvābhyāsasādguṇyādisāpekṣatvāt /*. "Someone might think the following: Even though momentariness is not different from sound, it is said to be unapprehended, even when there is the apprehension of that [sound]. Likewise, such should be so in this case as well. This is not correct. For we do not postulate that even when the subject (*dharmin*) sound is apprehended, momentariness, which is not different from it, is not apprehended. What then? We say that even though it *is* apprehended, it is not ascertained due to the nonexistence of the causes that would give rise to an ascertainment of it. For it is not the case that just through mere experience (*anubhava*) there is ascertainment, since that [ascertainment] depends upon such things as interest (*arthitva*), habituation (*abhyāsa*), good qualities (*sādguṇya*), and so on."

216. For all of these authors, inference is discussed under the two types mentioned above: inference-for-oneself (*svārthānumāna*) and inference-for-another (*parārthānumāna*). Of these, only the first is a true inference, in the sense of being a trustworthy awareness; the second is not an awareness but a *statement* that can produce a trustworthy awareness

experience) of an inferential object through a triply characterized logical sign (*liṅga*)."[217] The use of inference is restricted to cases where the particular one seeks to ascertain is not perceptible (*pratyakṣa*) but is imperceptible (*parokṣa*) or "remote" in time, place, or nature.[218] In these cases, one has no choice but to resort to inference if one is to ascertain anything about the particular. In inference, one does not directly cognize a particular as one does in perception. Instead, as we saw above, one directly cognizes an abstract *idea*, a conception (*vikalpa*) in the form of a universal (*sāmānya*). Although universals are unreal, in that they are causally inefficacious and lack any actual objective referent, one does *indirectly* know a particular, through the force of the "natural relation" (*svabhāvapratibandha*) that has previously been verified to exist between the evidence and the particular in question. Although inference can thus be defended as trustworthy, its involvement with uni-

in another person. An inference-for-another is thus only metaphorically an inference. In general, when inference is spoken of in this book, it means an inference-for-oneself. The basic underlying structure of an inference in this system can be described as follows: Some subject (S) is some predicate (P) because of some evidence (E). An example is: The mountain is a locus of fire because it is a locus of smoke. Here, smoke is the evidence or logical sign by which one knows that the mountain where the smoke is located is also the locus of fire.

217. TS 1361cd (*anumānaparīkṣā*): *svārthaṃ trirūpato liṅgād anumeyārthadarśanam* /. The specification that the logical sign be "triply characterized" means that in order for the logical sign or evidence to function, it must possess three characteristics (i.e., it must be *trairūpya*). The first characteristic concerns the evidence-subject relation; it is called *pakṣadharmatā*, and means that the evidence must be a property (*dharma*) of the subject (*pakṣa*, *sādhyadharmin*, *dharmin*). In the example from the previous note, this corresponds to the fact that the mountain in question is indeed the locus of smoke. The two remaining characteristics concern two aspects of the evidence-predicate relation, technically called the "pervasion" (*vyāpti*). The two elements of the pervasion are positive concomitance (*anvaya*) and negative concomitance (*vyatireka*). Positive concomitance is understood to mean that wherever the evidence is present, the predicate (*sādhyadharma*) is invariably also present. In the example, this corresponds to the idea that wherever there is smoke, there necessarily is fire. Negative concomitance refers to the restriction whereby the evidence can *only* be present when the predicate is present. In the example, this means that smoke can *only* be present when there is fire. The negative concomitance may also be expressed negatively as follows: wherever the predicate is absent, the evidence is necessarily also absent. In other words, where there is no fire, there necessarily can be no smoke. On this theory, evidence that lacks any of these three characteristics is spurious, and an inference in which such spurious evidence is adduced necessarily fails. See, e.g., TS 1362cd: *ekaikadvidvirūpo 'rtho liṅgābhāsas tato mataḥ* //.

218. See TS/P 1700–1707 (*pramāṇāntarabhāvaparīkṣā*) for an argument that the objects of inference are necessarily remote (*parokṣa*). Cf. also PV 3.63: *na pratyakṣaparokṣābhyāṃ meyasyānyasya sambhavaḥ / tasmāt prameyadvitvena pramāṇadvitvam iṣyate* //.

versals and concepts nevertheless renders it "erroneous" or "incongruent" (*bhrānta*) on Dharmakīrti's view.[219] Śāntarakṣita and Kamalaśīla accept this portrayal of inference as erroneous. Nonetheless, they take pains to point out that *qua* trustworthy awareness, inference should not be characterized as entailing error.[220]

The key to eliminating error from the realm of inference lies in the specification that inference "functions through the force of real entities" (i.e., it is *vastubalapravṛttānumāna*). This is another way of saying that the conceptions by which inference operates must be constructed on the basis of real things (*vastu*). There is one exception to this rule, however, and that is the special case of the so-called "scripturally based inference" (*āgamāśritānumāna*). This somewhat dubious form of inference is reserved only for those objects that are categorized as "extremely remote" or "radically inaccessible" (*atyantaparokṣa*), which means that neither the objects themselves nor any logical sign that can be linked to them are amenable to the perception of ordinary beings. Examples of such entities include Mount Sumeru, the mountain said to be at the center of the universe according to traditional Buddhist cosmology, and the details of the results of one's actions in future lives. Like Dharmakīrti, the authors of the *Tattvasaṃgraha* and the *Pañjikā* appear to allow room for reliance on scripturally based inference "when there is no other way" (*agatyā*).[221] At the same time, they are reluctant to grant scripturally based inference the same status as ordinary inference, since one does not attain ascertainment through it.[222] We return to the notion of scripturally based inference in chapters 5 and 6, where we consider whether the demonstration of omniscience is intended to ground Buddhist scriptures in the authority of the Buddha's extraordinary knowledge.[223] For the moment, however, we can emphasize that when Śāntarakṣita and Kamalaśīla speak of

219. See PVSV *ad* PV 1.70 and PV 1.75; see also PV 1.80–81. The translation "incongruent" for *bhrānta* has been suggested by Tillemans (1999b: 10).

220. See, e.g., TS 3092 (*svataḥprāmāṇyaparīkṣā*): *ātmakāryākhyaliṅgāc ca niścitāvyabhicārataḥ / jāyamāne 'numāne 'pi bhrāntir asti na kācana //*. "And, even when an inference comes about through the logical signs known as identity and effect, because there is no deviance (*vyabhicāra*) in the ascertainment, there is no error at all."

221. PV 1.216: *āptavādāvisaṃvādasāmānyād anumānatā / buddher agatyābhihitā parokṣe 'py asya gocare //*.

222. PVSV *ad* PV 1.318: *nāto niścayaḥ /*. See also Śākyabuddhi (PVT, D 242b5), who states that this form of inference is not real (*bhāvika*). Cf. Karṇakagomin 390.

223. See especially pp. 307–39 below, which takes up the question of the grounding of Buddhist scriptures and the role of scripturally based inference.

inference, they generally mean *vastubalapravṛttānumāna*, which Kamalaśīla states is the form of inference that Buddhists rely upon when seeking the fulfillment of their aims.[224]

The Sliding Scale of Analysis

So far, we have considered the *nyāya* reasoning and the *pramāṇa* theory styles of reasoning in the *Tattvasaṃgraha* and the *Pañjikā*. Already complex, these styles of reasoning are rendered still more complicated by the authors' somewhat unusual method of a sliding scale of analysis.[225] This technique, which is shared by at least a few other Indian epistemologists,[226] permits the authors to move back and forth among distinct ontological and epistemological schemes even within the purview of a single treatise. In the case of Dharmakīrti, Dreyfus has described this method as a "strategy of ascending scales of analysis"[227]

224. TSP *ad* TS 3591 (*atīndriyārthadarśiparīkṣā*, B 1115,23–24): ... *vastubalapravṛttānumānata eva saugatāḥ puruṣārtheṣu ghaṭante na pravādamātreṇa* /.

225. See Dreyfus 1997: 83–105 *et passim* and Dunne 2004: 53–79.

226. Śāntarakṣita and Kamalaśīla's Buddhist predecessors, notably Dharmakīrti and his followers, are the most obvious examples. As for non-Buddhist thinkers, Houben (1995: 16–18) has argued that Bhartṛhari, an innovative fourth- or fifth-century grammarian/philosopher, should be seen as employing a kind of "perspectivism," according to which (1995: 16) "reality is different from different points of view...." Houben also cites Aklujkar in this context, who states (1972: 185) that "a careful reading of the *Trikāṇḍī* [i.e., the *Vākyapadīya*] and its ancient commentaries will reveal that what seem to be different explanations are also statements of different theses and thoughts acceptable to Bhartṛhari on different levels and in different contexts."

227. Dreyfus (1997: 49, 83–105, *et passim*) speaks of four levels of analysis in the works of Dharmakīrti: i) a commonsense level, where objects of awareness are said simply to exist; ii) an alternative interpretation, where objects are reduced to fundamental phenomenological component parts; iii) a standard interpretation, where objects are reduced to infinitesimal component parts; iv) and a Yogācāra level of analysis, where objects external to the mind do not exist at all. Dunne (2004: 53–79) likewise provides an assessment in terms of four levels: i) beliefs of ordinary beings; ii) the Abhidharma typology; iii) External Realism, i.e., *bāhyārthavāda*; and iv) Epistemic Idealism, i.e., *antarjñeyavāda*. Dunne not only gives different names to the four levels, he also emphasizes that the first two levels should not be considered to represent Dharmakīrti's view in any way. Dunne argues that Dharmakīrti's philosophy need not be construed as unified across the levels of analysis, though each level must be seen as exhibiting a systematicity unto itself. Dharmakīrti uses the lower levels of analysis to "lead one up the scale of analysis" (2004: 74), even if his arguments along the way may not be consistent with his final position. This is in contrast with Dreyfus (1997: 99), who states that Dharmakīrti "does not choose between these [four] different levels but uses them in dependence on the context of his inquiry."

and has stated that insufficient attention to this strategy has resulted in an oversimplification of Dharmakīrti's thought by both modern and traditional interpreters.[228] The same can be said for the works of Śāntarakṣita and Kamalaśīla, especially the *Tattvasaṃgraha* and the *Pañjikā*.[229]

We discern in this work two distinct levels of philosophical analysis, each with its own ontological commitments and—to a lesser extent—epistemology. A third level of analysis is also present, though only nascent form, as we will see below. As in the case of Dharmakīrti, the levels of analysis are hierarchical, with each level a refinement and a corrective of the preceding one.[230] The scale is also a sliding one, as the authors liberally move up and down the scale according to the exigencies of various rhetorical situations. Once again, certain basic theorems and principles—those that generally underlie the concerns of judicious persons—apply throughout, as do the *nyāya* reasoning and *pramāṇa* theory styles of reasoning that these concerns entail. Again, the equation of causal function and the real prevails at all levels.[231] To interpret the *Tattvasaṃgraha* and the *Pañjikā*, a reader must pay careful attention to the cues that mark the shifts in the level of analysis. Fortunately, Kamalaśīla's commentary is bountiful in its explicit indications concerning such shifts. In many cases, Kamalaśīla's choice of which level of analysis to use is dictated by the level used in Śāntarakṣita's verses; in other cases, however, Kamalaśīla offers his analysis of a verse or set of verses with arguments made at more than one level. In such cases, he is quite meticulous in informing his readers when he is shifting to another level of analysis.

The two distinct levels of analysis in the *Tattvasaṃgraha* and the *Pañjikā* are the Sautrāntika and the Vijñānavāda. Of these, the Sautrāntika level of analysis operates with an "externalist" (*bahirarthavādin*) ontological

---

Although I cannot investigate this interesting disagreement here, I can note that in the TS/P, Śāntarakṣita and Kamalaśīla seem never to descend below what Kamalaśīla refers to as a Sautrāntika level of analysis, corresponding to Dreyfus's and Dunne's third levels, the "standard interpretation" and "External Realism," respectively.

228. Dreyfus 1997: 83.

229. Somewhat greater, although still insufficient, attention to this method has been paid in relation to Śāntarakṣita and Kamalaśīla's Madhyamaka works, especially the *Madhyamakālaṃkāra* (MA) and its commentaries. See, e.g., Kajiyama 1978.

230. The same is also true for the MA and its commentaries. Kajiyama (1978: 117), for example, has noted in relation to these works "that lower doctrines were not simply rejected but admitted as steps leading to understanding of the highest one."

231. The equation is between causal function and the ultimately real on the lower levels, and between causal function and the conventionally real at the Madhyamaka level of analysis. See above, n. 194.

commitment. In this model, causally functioning real particulars, some of which exist external to the mind, function to produce images (*ākāra*) in awareness. These images are then what awareness knows. The Sautrāntika is the lowest level of analysis, and it is also the one used the most frequently in the *Tattvasaṃgraha* and the *Pañjikā*. The second level of analysis is that of the Vijñānavāda, also known as Vijñaptimātra, Cittamātra, and Yogācāra. This level operates with an "internalist" (*antarjñeyavādin*) ontological commitment. Here, real particulars do not exist outside the mind. That which causes images to arise in awareness is an imprint (*vāsanā*) or "seed" (*bīja*) contained within the beginningless mind itself. The shift from the Sautrāntika to the Vijñānavāda is warranted (in some sense also *required* for judicious persons) since one can demonstrate that it is *impossible* for awareness to know particulars outside the mind. For the authors of the *Tattvasaṃgraha* and the *Pañjikā*, the Sautrāntika level of analysis is therefore *less rational* than the Vijñānavāda position.[232] The Vijñānavāda perspective is explicitly argued for and defended in the twenty-third chapter of the *Tattvasaṃgraha* and the *Pañjikā*, the "Investigation of External Objects" (*bahirarthaparīkṣā*), but it is invoked frequently at other points in the work as well. Two subcategories of this level of analysis, the Sākāravādin ("with images") and Nirākāravādin ("without images") Vijñānavāda, also make an appearance from time to time in the *Tattvasaṃgrahapañjikā*, although Kamalaśīla appears not to endorse either variety.[233]

The third, nascent, level of analysis in the *Tattvasaṃgraha* and the *Pañjikā* is the Madhyamaka. This level operates in an important sense with *no* ontological commitment, in that neither the particular that is known (*jñeya*) nor the awareness (*jñāna*) that knows is ultimately upheld as real. The arguments in support of this view are not presented in the *Tattvasaṃgraha* and the *Pañjikā* but can be found in the authors' Madhyamaka works, including Śāntarakṣita's *Madhyamakālaṃkāra* (MA) and its *Vṛtti* (MAV), and Kamalaśīla's subcommentary on those texts, the *Madhyamakālaṃkārapañjikā* (MAP). Since the Madhyamaka perspective is not explicit in the *Tattvasaṃgraha* and the *Pañjikā*, most interpreters have seen the work as presenting a Vijñānavāda perspective at its highest level of analysis.[234] Certainly, such would seem reasonable given

232. For a statement that it is *more* rational to accept a mentalist (*vijñaptimātra*) perspective than a materialist one, see TS 1887 (*lokāyataparīkṣā*) and TSP *ad cit.*

233. See Funayama 2007 for an analysis of TSP *ad* TS 3626 (*atīndriyārthadarśiparīkṣā*, B 1122,22–1126,19), a highly significant passage treating this distinction.

234. See, e.g., Wood 1991: 219–21 for a strenuous, though not convincing, attack on the idea that the TS/P could be a Madhyamaka work.

the quasi-commentarial nature of the *Tattvasaṃgraha* and the *Pañjikā* vis-à-vis the works of Dignāga and Dharmakīrti,[235] which are generally (though not universally) also understood to propound a Vijñānavāda perspective at the highest level of analysis.[236] When I say that the *Tattvasaṃgraha* and the *Pañjikā* contain a nascent Madhyamaka level of analysis, I base this contention on a number of allusions to Madhyamaka in the works that allow us, in my view, to surmise that the authors do not wish their readers to embrace Vijñānavāda as their final level of analysis.

The first allusion to Madhyamaka comes in the opening verses to the *Tattvasaṃgraha*, which in their structure and language unambiguously recall the opening verses of Nāgārjuna's *Mūlamadhyamakakārikā*, a foundational work for the Madhyamaka tradition. In brief, these two sets of opening stanzas both take the form of a praise of the Buddha, in both cases called "the best of speakers," who is then also said (through the use of a relative phrase) to have taught dependent arising (*pratītyasamutpāda*), which itself is further qualified by a number of (mostly negative) attributes.[237] Of course, there are differences between the two sets of verses as well: the *Mūlamadhyamakakārikā* verses, being only two *śloka*s in length, contain fewer attributes for dependent arising, as well as fewer qualifications of the Buddha. Still, the parallelism between the two sets of verses is too strong to be accidental; by choosing to structure his opening verses in this manner, Śāntarakṣita clearly invokes the Madhyamaka level of analysis, at least for readers who are familiar with Nāgārjuna's treatise.

There also occur two explicit references to Madhyamaka in the body of the work itself. In the first instance, Śāntarakṣita refers to "those who base themselves on the naturelessness that pervades all things," and Kamalaśīla glosses this as a reference to Mādhyamikas.[238] Although the verse neither endorses nor rejects Madhyamaka, readers familiar with the *Madhyamakālaṃkāravṛtti*

235. See n. 252 below.

236. See Steinkellner 1990 for a discussion of some later Indian doxographer's attempts to establish that Dharmakīrti was a Mādhyamika. Steinkellner concludes (1990: 82) that "in relation to our present knowledge of his works these attempts have not produced sufficient evidence to prove their point."

237. MMK 1–2: *anirodham anutpādam anucchedam aśāśvatam / anekārtham anānārtham anāgamam anirgamam // yaḥ pratītyasamutpādaṃ prapañcopaśamaṃ śivam / deśayāmāsa saṃbuddhas taṃ vande vadatāṃ varam //*. "I praise the best of speakers, the Buddha who taught dependent arising, which is peace, the calming of all mental elaboration, [and] which is unceased, unarisen, not limited, not eternal, not single, not multiple, not coming, and not gone." For the Sanskrit of the opening verses of the TS, see n. 259 below.

238. TS 1392 (*anumānaparīkṣā*): *sarvabhāvagataṃ ye 'pi niḥsvabhāvatvam āśritāḥ / te*

will recognize that the verse makes an important statement about what Śāntarakṣita understands Madhyamaka to be: that is, his version of Madhyamaka proceeds through an acceptance of appearances on the conventional level, which is what allows him to integrate his Madhyamaka with Dignāga and Dharmakīrti's *pramāṇa* theory.[239] This passage gives further weight to the idea that the *Tattvasaṃgraha* and the *Pañjikā* is intended to lead judicious persons through the Sautrāntika and Yogācāra levels of analysis as a preparation for the final level of analysis, the Madhyamaka, which receives full expression only in the authors' specifically Madhyamaka works. The second explicit reference to Madhyamaka in the *Tattvasaṃgrahapañjikā* speaks of it with clear approval. The context is a discussion of the continuity of the mind after death. Śāntarakṣita is in the process of refuting the materialist Lokāyata position that the mind ceases at death. The Lokāyatas are shown as objecting that Buddhists themselves understand the mind to end at death, at least in the case of liberated arhats. Śāntarakṣita replies that such is not necessarily the Buddhist view, since "some wise persons" adhere to the doctrine of non-abiding nirvāṇa (*apratiṣṭhitanirvāṇa*).[240] Kamalaśīla glosses the words "wise persons" as meaning Mahāyānists and "some" as indicating Mādhyamikas.[241] Although it is true that the idea of non-abiding nirvāṇa is not a specifically Madhyamaka notion as it is advanced also in Yogācāra works, it seems difficult to avoid the conclusion that Kamalaśīla is here endorsing Madhyamaka.[242]

'pi tattvata ityādi viśeṣaṇam upāśritāḥ //. For Kamalaśīla's commentary see the following note.

239. Cf. TSP *ad* TS 1391–92 (*anumānaparīkṣā*): *ye 'pīti mādhyamikāḥ / te 'pi tattvata iti saviśeṣaṇaṃ sarvabhāvānāṃ niḥsvabhāvatvam āśritā na tu sarvathā yathādarśanam utpādādīnām abhyupagamāc ca / tattvata iti nyāyataḥ* /. This acceptance of appearances is also what prompts later Tibetan commentators to class Śāntarakṣita as a *rang rgyud pa* or Svātantrika. I treat the question of the aptness of this classification in McClintock 2003.

240. On the idea of non-abiding nirvāṇa, see Makransky 1997.

241. TS 1916 (*lokāyataparīkṣā*): *ye ceha sudhiyaḥ kecid apratiṣṭhitanirvṛtīn / jināṃs tadyānaniṣṭhatvaṃ yānayoś ca pracakṣate* //. TSP *ad cit.* (B 657,19–20; G 539,13–15): *sudhiyo mahāyānikāḥ / kecid iti mādhyamikāḥ / te hi buddhānām apratiṣṭhitatvaṃ nirvāṇam āhuḥ / saṃsāranirvāṇayor apratiṣṭhānāt / śrāvakapratyekabuddhayānayoś ca buddhaikayānatiṣṭhatvam āhuḥ* /. Note that B is missing two lines of Sanskrit found in G.

242. The phrase "some wise persons" is clearly not meant to be taken sarcastically. Wood (1991: 219) also points to this passage, but says that it does not mean that the Madhyamaka perspective is "endorsed by either writer as the *siddhānta*." If by this statement, Wood means that the Madhyamaka is not the explicit final level of analysis in the TS/P, then he is correct. However, I do think that Kamalaśīla's equation of Mādhyamikas with wise persons does represent an endorsement, and is an indication that the Yogācāra level of analysis is not truly final for these thinkers even in the TS/P.

The final bits of evidence that the *Tattvasaṃgraha* and the *Pañjikā* contains a nascent Madhyamaka perspective come not from the work itself, but rather from the authors' Madhyamaka treatises, especially the *Madhyamakālaṃkāravṛtti* and *Madhyamakālaṃkārapañjikā*. Although it may seem odd to look outside the *Tattvasaṃgraha* and the *Pañjikā* for evidence concerning its own final level of analysis, there are good reasons for doing so. For one thing, Śāntarakṣita refers to the *Tattvasaṃgraha* in the *Madhyamakālaṃkāravṛtti* in such a way that it is clear that he does not consider his specifically Madhyamaka work as a repudiation of his earlier *Tattvasaṃgraha* but rather as a continuation or refinement of it. Near the end of the *Madhyamakālaṃkāravṛtti*, he tells us that he has already extensively examined dependent arising in the *Tattvasaṃgraha* and another (apparently lost) work, the *Don dam pa gtan la dbab pa* (possibly the *Paramārthaviniścaya*, mentioned in the *Tattvasaṃgraha*), and he advises those who wish to undertake a similarly extensive investigation to turn to those works.[243] Of great interest in this passage is Śāntarakṣita's use of a particular qualification for dependent arising that we find as well in the opening verses of the *Tattvasaṃgraha*: Śāntarakṣita says that dependent arising is "free from the entire mass of conceptual elaborations."[244] This phrase (reminiscent again of Nāgārjuna's opening verses, where dependent arising is said to be the "calming of conceptual elaborations") provides a strong indication that Śāntarakṣita understood the two works, the *Tattvasaṃgraha* and the *Madhyamakālaṃkāravṛtti*, to share the same final view, even if that Madhyamaka perspective is only explicitly argued for in the latter work. Similarly, we can see Śāntarakṣita's citation of a number of verses from Dharmakīrti's *Pramāṇavārttika* 3 in apparent support of the Madhyamaka perspective (or at least of Madhyamaka argumentation) as evidence that he saw the Madhyamaka level of analysis as arising directly out of the final Yogācāra level of analysis as preserved in the epistemological treatises.[245] For all of these rea-

243. MAV *ad* MA 96 (Ichigō, 330): *gzhan yang kho bo bdag cag dang / gzhan gyi gzhung lugs rgya cher dpyad pas rten cing 'brel par 'byung ba spros pa'i tshogs thams cad dang bral ba 'di de kho na bsdus pa dang / don dam pa gtan la dbab pa la sogs par dpyad pa zin gyis / shin tu rgyas par 'dod pa dag gis de dag las khong du chud par gyis shig /*. Cf. TS 2083 (*bahirarthaparīkṣā*): *vijñaptimātratāsiddhir dhīmadbhir vimalīkṛtā / asmābhis taddiśā jātaṃ paramārthaviniścaye //*. The reading: *taddiśā jātam* in place of B and G: *taddiśā yātaṃ* is based on the Tibetan, D 76a3–4: ... *don dam nges par bskyed par byas //*.

244. Tibetan: *spros pa'i tshogs thams cad dang bral ba*; Sanskrit: *sarvaprapañcasandohanirmukta*.

245. MAV *ad* MA 61 (Ichigō, 178). My argument here is not that Śāntarakṣita and Kamalaśīla see Dharmakīrti as aruging for a Madhyamaka perspective in the PV but rather

sons, I take the *Tattvasaṃgraha* and the *Pañjikā* as presenting a nascent Madhyamaka level of analysis. On my reading of the authors' use of the sliding scale of analysis, *all* arguments proceed through a provisional acceptance of real natures in order to gradually lead judicious persons to a Madhyamaka perspective. The *Tattvasaṃgraha* and the *Pañjikā* seems to have been intended to serve, at least in part, as a preparation for a more advanced study of Madhyamaka.

It is difficult to overstate the importance of the sliding scale of analysis for the interpretation of the *Tattvasaṃgraha* and the *Pañjikā*. Without a clear comprehension of this philosophical method, one cannot make sense of what seem to be contradictions in the work. Once the method is taken into account, however, it is possible to see that an appropriate interpretation of any argument in the work requires that we understand the audience to whom the argument is addressed and the level of analysis in play. We return to this point again below, but first we must make one final observation about the styles of reasoning in the *Tattvasaṃgraha* and the *Pañjikā*.

Scholastic Reasoning: Negotiating Tradition and Innovation

A great deal has been made in the secondary literature on Indian philosophical traditions of the tension between tradition and innovation.[246] Halbfass notes that as late as the nineteenth century, Indian intellectuals

that they see Dharmakīrti's neither-one-nor-many arguments in the PV (arguments that also play a prominent role in the TS/P) as ineluctably leading to a Madhyamaka perspective. For Kamalaśīla's remarks, see MAP *ad cit.* (179): *blo gros dkar po rnams kyis zhes bya ba ni slob dpon chos kyis grags pa la sogs pas so // de dang der zhes bya ba ni tshad ma rnam 'grel la sogs par ro // smos te zhes bya ba ni dngos su bshad pa ma yin pa ste / tshad ma rnam par 'grel pa la sogs par ni rnal 'byor spyod pa'i tshul bshad pa'i gnas skabs yin pa'i phyir ro // slob dpon gyis kun tu brtags pa'i ngo bo nyid kyi dbang du byas te de skad du bshad mod kyi / yongs su grub pa nyid ma grub pa'i phyir te / rigs pa thun mong pa'i phyir slob dpon gyi tshig 'di thams cad du rung ba nyid do snyam du bsams pa'o /*. Cf. Steinkellner 1990: 79–81.

246. The extent to which systematic thought in India appears to be "tradition-bound" (cf. our earlier remarks on the necessity of adhering to some tradition in order to participate in *nyāya* reasoning) has led some Europeans and Americans to conclude that India has no indigenous philosophy of its own. By now, this overly stark appraisal of the differences between the tradition of philosophy with its origins in Greece and the tradition of *pramāṇa* theory reasoning is largely discredited (see, e.g., Scharfstein 1997 and Halbfass 1988), so that we may put to rest any qualms in speaking about philosophical traditions in India. Still, the role of the *guruśiṣyaparamparā* in the propagation and spread of philosophical ideas in India must be considered when evaluating traditional Indian philosophical texts.

who strayed from tradition were criticized for their innovation.[247] In classical times as well, Buddhist and non-Buddhist authors seem anxious to dispel the impression that they are innovators, frequently commencing their treatises with the disclaimer that they do not presume to present anything new.[248] Kamalaśīla similarly includes such a disclaimer in his opening verses of the *Tattvasaṃgrahapañjikā*;[249] and he further opines that Śāntarakṣita, in the work upon which he is about to comment, also presents nothing that has not already been established by previous masters (*ācārya*). Instead, in Kamalaśīla's view, Śāntarakṣita merely assembles those previous masters' scattered teachings so that slow-witted persons might more easily understand that they are correct.[250] These statements, if taken at face value, belie the currents of innovation that are present in the *Tattvasaṃgraha* and the *Pañjikā*.

Discerning innovation in the *Tattvasaṃgraha* and the *Pañjikā* is not easy for several reasons. First, and most important, is the work's scholasticism. By scholasticism I mean the presence of a high degree of systematic

247. Halbfass (1988: 211) records that the Hindu reformer, Rammohan Roy, was derided for being a "founder of new doctrines (*nūtanasampradāyakārī*)."

248. Halbfass (1988: 362) points to Jayanta Bhaṭṭa's comments in the *Nyāyamañjarī* to the effect that "he is in no position to expound new ideas or doctrines of his own (*na vayam ātmīyām abhinavāṃ kām api kalpanām utpādayituṃ kṣamāḥ*)." Cf. also the Buddhist author Śāntideva's well-known verse at BCA 1.5: *na hi kiñcid apūrvam atra vācyaṃ na ca saṅgrathanakauśalaṃ mamāsti / ata eva na me parārthacintā svamano vāsayituṃ kṛtaṃ mayedam //*.

249. TSP 2 (B 1,15–18): *vaktuṃ vastu na mādṛśā jaḍadhiyo 'pūrvaṃ kadācit kṣamāḥ kṣuṇṇo vā bahudhā budhair aharahaḥ ko 'sau na panthāḥ kvacit / kiṃ tu svārthaparasya me matir iyaṃ pūṇyodayākāṅkṣiṇas tattvābhyāsam imaṃ śubhodayaphalaṃ kartuṃ samabhyudyatā //*. "People with a dull intellect like myself are never able to state something new. And what path is there anywhere that has not been trod many times, day in and day out, by the wise? Nevertheless, focused on my own aims, I am eager to increase my merit, [and] my mind is ready to compose this meditation on reality (*tattvābhyāsa*) whose fruit is the increase of virtue."

250. TSP *ad* TS 1–6 (B 11,11–13): *tasmāt pūrvācāryaiḥ pratipāditāny api tattvāni yo mandadhīr ativiprakīrṇatayā sukham avadhārayitum aśaktaḥ taṃ prati sukhāvadhāraṇāya tattvasaṃgraha ārabhyamāṇo na viphalatām eṣyatīti manyamānaḥ śāstram idam ārabhate / ata eva kriyate tattvasaṃgraha ityāha / anyathā kriyate tattvaniścaya ity evam uktaṃ syāt /*. "Therefore, [Śāntarakṣita] composes the treatise thinking as follows, 'The *Tattvasaṃgraha* is being composed for the sake of the easy ascertainment on the part of that slow-witted person who is unable to easily ascertain the realities (*tattvāni*) that have been established by the previous masters because they are scattered about [in diverse works]; therefore it will not be purposeless.' And therefore he says, 'I compose this collection of realities (*tattvasaṃgraha*).' Otherwise, he would have said, 'I compose this ascertainment of reality (*tattvaniścaya*).'"

analysis together with a high level of reverence—or, at least, the appearance thereof—for a particular tradition.[251] We have already seen how the *nyāya* reasoning and the *pramāṇa* theory styles of reasoning in the *Tattvasaṃgraha* and the *Pañjikā* are highly systematic and quite complex. Now we may recognize the role of reverence for a tradition in shaping the styles of reasoning in the work. What tradition does the *Tattvasaṃgraha* and the *Pañjikā* revere? Without question, it reveres the tradition of Buddhist *nyāya* reasoning and *pramāṇa* theory styles of reasoning as initially articulated by Dignāga and subsequently refined and supplemented by Dharmakīrti. For the authors of the *Tattvasaṃgraha* and the *Pañjikā*, the works of Dignāga and especially Dharmakīrti appear to have reached a status that John Dunne describes as "inviolable correctness,"[252] whereby it is impossible that anything contained within them be deemed erroneous, or even ill-conceived.[253] Indeed, the reliance upon and deference shown to especially Dharmakīrti's *Pramāṇavārttika* and *Svopajñavṛtti* in the *Tattvasaṃgraha* and the *Pañjikā* are so heavy that the work in many ways takes on the qualities of a scholastic commentary.

Reasoning in the *Tattvasaṃgraha* and the *Pañjikā* thus occurs within the bounds of reverence, and as such the work can justly be described as a kind of scholasticism, but this alone does not imply that the authors of the *Tattvasaṃgraha* and the *Pañjikā* subscribe to what Griffiths has called "scholastic epistemology." Taking his inspiration from the work of William Alston and Alvin Plantinga, Griffiths notes that "scholastics typically will be externalist in epistemology," by which he means that "they claim that what makes a particular instance of believing justified or warranted is something external to believers, some process or method of arriving at the belief in question that is not internal to them, and may not be known, understood, or controlled by

251. Griffiths (1998: 209) defines scholastic intellectual practice first and foremost in terms of a particular kind of *reading*, wherein "the text read is understood as a stable and vastly rich resource, one that yields meaning, suggestions (or imperatives) for action, matter for aesthetic wonder, and much else. It is a treasure-house, an ocean, a mine: the deeper scholastic readers dig, the more ardently they fish, the more single-mindedly they seek gold, the greater will be their reward." While I think that Griffiths overstates the fervor of the scholastic enterprise, his description does support my contention that some degree of reverence is characteristic of scholastic writing.

252. Dunne 2004: 5–6. We should note that Vasubandhu is also occasionally cited as an authority in the TS/P, though his work does not seem to be elevated to the same level of inviolability as that of Dignāga and Dharmakīrti.

253. Dreyfus (1997: 5) claims that the tradition can go even further, to the point where "Not only does it hold that what Dharmakīrti says is right, it also assumes that which is right in logic and epistemology must be said by Dharmakīrti."

them."[254] My reading of Śāntarakṣita and Kamalaśīla leads me to reject such a characterization as applying to them. They seem, in contrast, more like

> internalist epistemologists [who] typically claim that ... "warrant" or "justification" ... is internal to those who have the beliefs under discussion, something to which they have special access: they have had the proper experience, say, or have constructed or understood the proper arguments, and to both of these facts the subject is a better witness than anyone else.[255]

Scholastic reasoning need not be epistemologically externalist in the sense described by Griffiths. That is, it is possible to engage in rational discourse that exhibits reverence for a tradition without thereby relinquishing a claim to the justification of that discourse on grounds that are verifiable for an individual independent of the tradition's received ideas. To put it differently, while the authors of the *Tattvasaṃgraha* and the *Pañjikā* may believe that Dignāga and Dharmakīrti "got it right," they do not expect their audience to accept their position on those grounds but rather to investigate and decide the matter on the same rational grounds that are internal to any rational human being.

Śāntarakṣita and Kamalaśīla depend not only on Dignāga and Dharmakīrti but also on the works of their commentators (most notably, Devendrabuddhi and Śākyabuddhi, but also perhaps others, such as Dharmottara, Arcaṭa, or Haribhadra).[256] In many cases, the authors use the ideas and even explicit words of their predecessors without, however, acknowledging their source. It is thus nearly impossible to isolate any particular idea or doctrine and say with certitude that it represents some new thinking on the authors' part. At the same time, this is perhaps not particularly important. What is more crucial is to note that innovation and change *do occur*, even within the bounds of the scholastic style of reading and composition in which these authors participate.[257] We discern developments and new ideas in the

254. Griffiths 1998: 223.

255. Griffiths 1998: 222.

256. The precise relationship among these thinkers is not fully clear. See Krasser 1992; Funayama 1995; Moriyama 1984a and 1984b; and Ruegg 1981b. Much work needs to be done to determine especially the extent of Kamalaśīla's reliance on Śākyabuddhi. Unfortunately, I have not been able to undertake that research for the purposes of this book, but I am aware that it remains a desideratum.

257. Here it may be pertinent to note that Śāntarakṣita and Kamalaśīla's participation

Tattvasaṃgraha and the *Pañjikā*, and even if many of these ideas do not originate with Śāntarakṣita and Kamalaśīla, it seems likely that at least some of them do. The demonstration of omniscience in the final chapter is one example of an argument that may be of their provenance. But no matter whether we finally judge these authors as innovators or preservers of tradition, there is one area in which their creativity is beyond dispute, and that is in their masterful structuring of the *Tattvasaṃgraha* and the *Pañjikā* as a whole, to which we now turn.

Structure of the Tattvasaṃgraha *and the* Pañjikā

We have already seen that the opening verses for the *Tattvasaṃgraha* take the form of a praise to the Buddha, the teacher of dependent arising, and that they resemble in both language and structure the opening verses of Nāgārjuna's *Mūlamadhyamakakārikā*. But these six verses are remarkable in another way as well, for in them Śāntarakṣita lays out the content and structure of the work as a whole with great elegance and ingenuity. Bhattacaryya enthusiastically describes the stanzas as follows:

> The genius of Śāntarakṣita will be at once apparent if we consider the fact that, with the obvious object of offering his obeisance to Lord Buddha, the first promulgator of the doctrine of Dependent Origination by means of six tiny stanzas, he lays down the whole foundation of his work, which covers very nearly four thousand verses, and anticipates all the twenty-six examinations on various subjects in the stanzas mentioned, where almost each word suggests a new examination.[258]

---

in a tradition does not require that they subscribe to an orthodoxy. Mohanty (1992: 11) describes the difference between tradition and orthodoxy as follows: "Orthodoxy consists in fossilizing tradition into a lifeless, unchanging structure. Tradition, as distinguished from orthodoxy, is a living process of creation and preservation of significations. When a tradition is alive, it continues to grow, to create, and to respond to new situations and challenges. When it is no longer alive, it requires an orthodoxy to preserve its purity against possible distortions and desanctifications. A living tradition is ambiguous in the sense that it allows for growth and development in many different ways. It is false to oppose tradition to freedom from rational criticism, for rational criticism takes place, not within a vacuum but from within a tradition."

258. Bhattacaryya 1926: xiv.

In effect, the opening verses serve as a table of contents for the work, and as such they are invaluable in helping us to understand the work's overall design. Aiding us as well is Kamalaśīla's detailed commentary, in which he correlates the different phrases in the verses with the various chapters or investigations (*parīkṣā*) of the work, showing how each one is an allusion (*upakṣepa*) to one or more of the twenty-six investigations of the work. To get a better idea of how this operates, let us consider the opening verses directly. Śāntarakṣita writes,

> I compose this *Tattvasaṃgraha*, having bowed to that omniscient one, who is the best of speakers, who does not depend on an autonomous scripture, who through his desire to benefit the world inculcated a nature of great compassion throughout many innumerable ages, [and] who proclaimed the dependent arising (*pratītyasamutpāda*) that others do not understand and that is free from the operations (*vyāpāra*) of primordial nature (*prakṛti*), God, both [primordial nature and God], self (*ātman*), and so on; that is in flux (*cala*); that is the basis for the postulation of the relation between actions (*karman*) and their effects and so on; that is devoid of the attributes (*upādhi*) of quality (*guṇa*), substance (*dravya*), action (*kriyā*), universal (*jāti*), inherence (*samavāya*), and so forth; that is the object of words and cognitions with superimposed images; that is ascertained by the two trustworthy awarenesses (*pramā*) whose definitions are clear and whose nature is not mixed with even the tiniest part of anything else; that is not [temporally] concatenated (*asaṃkrānti*); that has neither beginning nor end; that is like a reflection and so forth; [and] that is entirely free from the mass of conceptual elaborations.[259]

Here, in a nutshell, are all of the topics of the *Tattvasaṃgraha* as well as clues about how these topics relate to each other. Despite their complexity, the verses can be easily analyzed into two distinct semantic units: one containing a praise to the Buddha along with important statements about him, and

259. TS 1–6: *prakṛtīśobhayātmādivyāpārarahitaṃ calam / karmatatphalasambandhavyavasthādisamāśrayam // guṇadravyakriyājātisamavāyādyupādhibhiḥ / śūnyam āropitākāraśabdapratyayagocaram // spaṣṭalakṣaṇasaṃyuktapramādvitayaniścitam / aṇīyasāpi nāṃśena miśrībhūtāparātmakam // asaṃkrāntim anādyantaṃ pratibimbādisannibham / sarvaprapañcasandohanirmuktam agataṃ paraiḥ // svatantraśrutinissaṅgo jagaddhitavidhitsayā / analpakalpāsaṃkhyeyasātmībhūtamahādayaḥ // yaḥ pratītyasamutpādaṃ jagāda gadatāṃvaraḥ / taṃ sarvajñaṃ praṇamyāyaṃ kriyate tattvasaṃgrahaḥ //.*

another containing a condensed description of his central teaching, dependent arising (*pratītyasamutpāda*). Significantly, this division corresponds to an important division in the work itself.

To explain, it is possible to see the *Tattvasaṃgraha* as comprised of two distinct segments: one that dispels misconceptions about the nature of reality, understood as dependent arising, and another that dispels misconceptions about the person, i.e., the Buddha, who is credited with having first realized and conveyed this reality. In the verses, the first part of the work (made up of the first twenty-three investigations) is represented by the long string of statements describing the attributes of dependent arising, starting with the statement that it is "free from the operations of primordial nature, God, both, self, and so on" and ending with the statement that it is "entirely free of the mass of conceptual elaborations."[260] The second part of the work (made up of the final three investigations) is represented by the statements concerning the Buddha, namely that he is the "omniscient one" and that he "does not depend upon an autonomous scripture."

Once we have discerned this twofold structure of the work through a study of the opening verses, we can more easily recognize that the two sections of the work serve different purposes. That is, the greater part of the work concerns the nature of reality, and it moves quite clearly from a critique of gross misunderstandings to more subtle ones. This section culminates in the "Investigation of External Objects," in which the authors argue explicitly for the rationality of shifting from an externalist to an internalist ontology (i.e., from a Sautrāntika to a Yogācāra position). It is this chapter that represents most unambiguously the highest explicit level of analysis in the work. The remaining three investigations of the *Tattvasaṃgraha* and the *Pañjikā* do not directly concern the nature of reality but are oriented more toward questions of how that nature can be known and questions of religious authority. These final chapters are directed almost exclusively at the Mīmāṃsakas, and they also involve a conscious stepping back from the Yogācāra perspective and a general re-adoption, for the purposes of persuasion, of the less controversial Sautrāntika system.[261] For this reason, I think it is possible to consider

260. Because the verses together comprise a very tightly structured semantic unit, I have chosen to translate them as a single sentence. To accomplish this with some semblance of elegance, I have rearranged things somewhat, so that the ideas that occur in the final lines of the opening verses in Sanskrit appear at the beginning of the translation. The advantage of this transposition is that it allows us to preserve the emphasis on the Buddha's teaching of dependent arising (*pratītyasamutpāda*) that is evident in the verses.

261. This assessment is based on statements at the outset and at the end of this section of the TS/P.

the final three chapters of the *Tattvasaṃgraha* and the *Pañjikā* as a kind of "appendix" to the body of the work as a whole.[262]

Analysis of Dependent Arising

Let us look in detail at the contents of the first part of the *Tattvasaṃgraha* and the *Pañjikā*. The work starts out by considering mistaken notions of ontology, especially the fundamental ontological errors of imagining that real things can be eternal, be causeless, or have perdurance over time. This section includes investigations of the Sāṃkhya notion that everything is a transformation of a single primordial reality; the Naiyāyika view that everything is a creation of God; the Seśvara Sāṃkhya idea that both are true; the possibility that things arise without a cause; the Grammarian's perspective that everything is the manifestation of primordial sound (*śabdabrahman*); and the Brahmanical view that everything is the creation of a primordial person (*puruṣa*).[263] It then goes on to reject any form of an eternal self (*ātman*), whether according to the systems of Naiyāyikas, Mīmāṃsakas, Sāṃkhyas, Jains, Advaitavādins, or the Buddhist Vātsīputrīyas.[264] In each of these investigations, the conclusion reached is that real things cannot be eternal, since eternality entails changelessness, whereas real things are defined by their causal function, which requires change. To put a cap on this discussion, the work then presents a defense of momentariness.[265]

262. Although I am unaware of their reasons for doing so, it is interesting that the editors of the 1926 Gaekwad's Oriental Series edition of the TS/P decided to publish the final three chapters of the TS/P in a separate volume. Perhaps this decision was dictated by some other exigency, but I wonder whether they, too, might not have noticed the twofold division of the work for which I have argued, and chose to break the work after the "Investigation of External Objects" on that basis.

263. These are the first six investigations of the TS/P: *prakṛtiparīkṣā*, *īśvaraparīkṣā*, *ubhayaparīkṣā*, *svābhāvikajagadvādaparīkṣā*, *śabdabrahmaparīkṣā*, and *puruṣaparīkṣā*. Kamalaśīla explains that the phrase "that is free from the operations (*vyāpāra*) of primordial nature (*prakṛti*), God, both [primordial nature and God], self (*ātman*), and so on" in the opening verses is an allusion to these six chapters, as well as to the seventh investigation, the *ātmaparīkṣā*. See TSP *ad* TS 1 (B 13,14–20): *prakṛtīśobhayātmādivyāpārarahitam iti ... / etena pradhāneśvarobhayāhetukaśabdabrahmātmaparīkṣāṇām upakṣepaḥ /*.

264. These are the six subsections of the seventh investigation of the TS/P, the *ātmaparīkṣā*, which is alluded to in the phrase from the opening verses mentioned in the previous note.

265. This is the eighth investigation of the TS/P, the *sthirabhāvaparīkṣā*. Kamalaśīla explains that this chapter is alluded to by the phrase "that is in flux" in the opening verses. See TSP *ad* TS 1 (B 13,21–14,3): *calam iti ... / ayaṃ ca sthirabhāvaparīkṣopakṣepaḥ /*.

This brings us to an extremely important chapter in the *Tattvasaṃgraha* and the *Pañjikā*, the "Investigation of the Connection between Actions and Results" (*karmaphalasaṃbandhaparīkṣā*).[266] The importance of this chapter lies on two levels. First, the chapter is designed to answer a moral objection, whereby it is charged that on the Buddhist view of momentariness, there would be no incentive to undertake ethically good actions, since there could be no guarantee that the performer of the actions would be the same as the one who experiences the results. Śāntarakṣita and Kamalaśīla's response to this charge is to postulate an ever-changing mental continuum (*santāna*), in which subsequent moments of awareness are the results of causally efficacious previous moments. Those who understand this facet of dependent arising will ascertain that "momentary mental tendencies (*saṃskāra*) capable of giving rise to benefit for oneself and others arise, one after the other in succession from giving and so forth when these are preceded by compassion and so on."[267] With this, the authors clarify their position that the realization of momentariness does not jeopardize morality, since a continuum of momentary awarenesses is adequate to explain the doctrine of karmic retribution. Second, the chapter is important for its insistence that causes and their effects are not connected through any real relation that exists separate from causes and effects themselves.[268] Although causally efficacious things are restricted in terms of the effects to which they may give rise, no further relation need be postulated to make sense of this; that which we designate as a relation between a cause and an effect is a mere conceptual construction and does not correspond to anything real in the world.[269] If a thing is causally efficacious, it is real; thus, to speak of a thing's efficacy or "operation" (*vyāpāra*)

266. For Kamalaśīla, the phrase "that is the basis for the postulation of the relation between actions (*karman*) and their effects and so on" in the opening verses is an allusion to this, the ninth chapter of the TS/P. See TSP *ad* TS 1 (B 14,4–13): *yady evaṃ karmaphalasambandhādivyavasthāyāḥ pratītyasamutpāda āśrayo na prapnoti calatvāt / ity ata āha karmetyādi / . . . ayaṃ ca karmaphalasambandhaparīkṣopakṣepaḥ /*.

267. TSP *ad* TS 540–41 (*karmaphalasaṃbandhaparīkṣā*, B 228,14–15): *karuṇādipūrvakebhyo dānādibhyaḥ svaparahitodayaśālinaḥ saṃskārāḥ kṣaṇikā evāparāpare paramparayā samutpadyante . . . /*. For a translation of this passage in its larger context, see p. 335.

268. In this way, the chapter is a continuation of the discussion in the previous chapter, the *sthirabhāvaparīkṣā*. See Mimaki (1976: 44) for details of how later Buddhists understand the materials in these two chapters to pertain to a single discussion.

269. See TS 518–19 (*karmaphalasaṃbandhaparīkṣā*): *niyamād ātmahetūtthāt prathamakṣaṇabhāvinaḥ / yady ato 'nantaraṃ jātaṃ dvitīyakṣaṇasannidhiḥ // tat taj janayatīty āhur avyāpāre 'pi vastuni / vivakṣāmātrasaṃbhūtasaṃketānuvidhāyinaḥ //*.

is just a convenient way of speaking of the thing itself. Ultimately, however, things do not possess any efficacy or operation at all.[270]

The *Tattvasaṃgraha* and the *Pañjikā* now go on to consider some additional unreal conceptual constructions concerning real things: the six categories (*padārtha*) of the Naiyāyika-Vaiśeṣika tradition. The work consecrates one chapter each to substance (*dravya*), quality (*guṇa*), action (*karman*), universal (*sāmānya*), particularity (*viśeṣa*), and inherence (*samavāya*).[271] With these chapters the authors shift from a critique of eternal entities to a critique of conceptual entities. After refuting them through various attacks on real relations, the work then devotes an important investigation to the problem of linguistic reference.[272] If all real things are momentary, unique, and ultimately devoid of operation, then how does one explain how language operates in the absence of any perduring entity or real universal to which words refer? The solution to this problem involves an elaboration of Dignāga and Dharmakīrti's nominalist theory of exclusion (*apoha*), according to which words refer not to real things but to negations, unreal conceptual constructions that may be based on real things. This chapter marks a shift from ontological to epistemological concerns.

Having entered the realm of epistemology, the authors next contemplate the means of trustworthy awareness (*pramāṇa*) by which a person can correctly ascertain the nature of reality. Three chapters are devoted to this investigation, one on perception, one on inference, and one on other forms of *pramāṇa* propounded by non-Buddhist traditions.[273] Underlying these dis-

270. See, e.g., TS 528 (*karmaphalasaṃbandhaparīkṣā*): *kṣaṇikā hi yathā buddhis tathaivānye 'pi janminaḥ / sādhitās tadvad evāto nirvyāpāram idaṃ jagat //.*

271. These are the tenth through fifteenth chapters of the TS/P: *dravyapadārthaparīkṣā, guṇapadārthaparīkṣā, karmapadārthaparīkṣā, sāmānyapadārthaparīkṣā, viśeṣapadārthaparīkṣā*, and *samavāyapadārthaparīkṣā*. Kamalaśīla states that the phrase "that is devoid of the attributes (*upādhi*) of quality (*guṇa*), substance (*dravya*), action (*kriyā*), universal (*jāti*), inherence (*samavāya*), and so forth" in the opening verses is an allusion to these six chapters. See TSP *ad* TS 2 (B 14,16–23): *guṇetyādi / ... ayaṃ ca ṣaṭpadārthaparīkṣopakṣepaḥ /.*

272. This is the sixteenth chapter of the TS/P, the *śabdārthaparīkṣā*. Kamalaśīla explains that the phrase "that is the object of words and cognitions with superimposed images" in the opening verses is an allusion to this investigation. See TSP *ad* TS 2 (B 14,25–15,15): *āropitākāretyādi / ... ayaṃ ca śabdārthaparīkṣopakṣepaḥ /.*

273. These are the seventeenth through nineteenth chapters of the TS/P: *pratyakṣalakṣaṇaparīkṣā, anumānaparīkṣā*, and *pramāṇāntarabhāvaparīkṣā*. Kamalaśīla explains that the phrase "that is ascertained by the two trustworthy awarenesses (*pramā*) whose definitions are clear" in the opening verses is an allusion to these three investigations. See

cussions is the authors' utter conviction that the nature of reality can be ascertained through correct human reasoning.

The next three chapters take up three further errors concerning reality. The first is the notion that things can possess two contradictory natures; for example, a single thing can simultaneously possess both a specific and a universal nature. The primary target is here the Jain doctrine of indeterminacy (*syādvāda*), although others are addressed as well.[274] The following chapter considers the question of time, with the aim of refuting the Buddhist Sarvāstivādin idea that real things exist in all the three times (i.e., the past, present, and future).[275] The authors conclude that only what is occurring presently can be said to be real. The last of these chapters is a response to those who deny the existence of past and future lives, notably the "materialists," or Lokāyatas.[276] Such persons are described by the authors as "nihilists" (i.e., those who embrace *nāstikatā*), which, as Jha rightly indicates, refers in this context to those who reject future lives (the "other world," or *paraloka*).[277]

With the majority of erroneous conceptions concerning the nature of reality now dispelled, the authors next turn to a more subtle error, the mistaken notion that particulars exist apart from the mind that knows them.[278] The opponents here are Buddhists who accept (more or less) everything that has been presented up until now—especially the doctrine of momentariness and the equation of causal function and the real—but who still maintain a

---

TSP *ad* TS 3 (B 15,18–16,22): *spaṣṭetyādi / ...ayaṃ ca pratyakṣānumānapramāṇāntara-parīkṣāṇām upakṣepaḥ /.*

274. This is the twentieth investigation of the TS/P, the *syādvādaparīkṣā*. Kamalaśīla explains that the phrase "whose nature is not mixed with even the tiniest part of anything else" in the opening verses is an allusion to this investigation. See TSP *ad* TS 3 (B 17,4–12): *aṇīyasāpītyādi / ...ayaṃ ca syādvādaparīkṣopakṣepaḥ /.*

275. This is the twenty-first chapter of the TS/P, the *traikālyaparīkṣā*. Kamalaśīla explains that the phrase "that is not [temporally] concatenated (*asaṃkrānti*)" in the opening verses is an allusion to this investigation. See TSP *ad* TS 4 (B 17,14–20): *asaṃkrāntim iti / ...ayaṃ ca traikālyaparīkṣopakṣepaḥ /.*

276. This is the twenty-second chapter of the TS/P, the *lokāyataparīkṣā*. Kamalaśīla explains that the phrase "that has no beginning or end" in the opening verses is an allusion to this investigation. See TSP *ad* TS 4 (B 17,22–18,2): *anādyantam iti / ...lokāyatap arīkṣopakṣepaḥ /.*

277. Jha 1937: 893.

278. They do this in the twenty-third chapter of the TS/P, the *bahirarthaparīkṣā*. Kamalaśīla explains that the phrase "that is like a reflection and so forth" in the opening verses is an allusion to this investigation. See TSP *ad* TS 4 (B 18,4–9): *pratibimbādisannibham iti / ...ayaṃ ca bahirarthaparīkṣopakṣepaḥ /.*

dualism between the particulars that are known in awareness and the mind that knows them. As noted, in this chapter the authors argue explicitly for the superiority of the Yogācāra or Vijñānavāda level of analysis over that of the Sautrāntika. As the culmination of the part of the *Tattvasaṃgraha* and the *Pañjikā* that is devoted to the nature of reality, this chapter contains the work's final perspective on reality, including its understanding of the nature of a buddha's enlightened awareness or omniscience. This chapter brings to a close the investigation of the nature of reality, understood as dependent arising.

Analysis of Religious Authority

In his commentary on the final three verses of the "Investigation of External Objects," Kamalaśīla explains that the implication of the Vijñānavāda doctrine is that ultimately all cognitions are devoid of an object, since even the aspect of the cognition that appears as an object (i.e., the *grāhyākāra*) does not have any real existence (i.e., any real causal function) separate from the awareness itself.[279] With this remark, we reach the highest explicit level of analysis in the *Tattvasaṃgraha* and the *Pañjikā*, bringing the first part of the work to a close. The next verse, then, marks not only the start of a new investigation but also the opening verse of the second part of the work as a whole. This verse says:

> But here others, with their intellect polluted by ignorance, assert that "this doctrine of mind-only (*cittamātranaya*) is not reasonable, because it is refuted by scriptural revelation."[280]

Kamalaśīla explains that the "others" referred to here are Mīmāṃsakas, or followers of Jaimini (*jaiminīya*), and that the doctrine of mind-only stands metaphorically for a range of Buddhist views, from momentariness and lack of an eternal self to the claims that omniscience and freedom from passion are possible and so on.[281] The rhetorical effect of this verse, coming as it does immediately after the authors have established the Yogācāra perspective,

279. TSP *ad* TS 2081–83 (*bahirarthaparīkṣā*, B 711,17): *paramārthatas tu nirālambanāḥ sarva eva pratyayā iti* /.

280. TS 2084 (*śrutiparīkṣā*): *anye punar ihājñānamalīmasadhiyo jaguḥ / cittamātranayo nāyaṃ yujyate śrutibādhanāt* //.

281. TSP *ad* TS 2084 (*śrutiparīkṣā*, B 714,6–7): *cittamātranaya ity upalakṣaṇam / tathā kṣaṇikatvanairātmyasarvajñavairāgyādipratijñāpi bādhyata eva* . . . /.

is to throw into doubt the judiciousness of the Mīmāṃsakas. The implication is that these persons truly are ignorant, since in spite of all the impeccable Buddhist reasoning concerning the nature of reality in part one of the *Tattvasaṃgraha* and the *Pañjikā*, they remain intractable. According to Śāntarakṣita and Kamalaśīla, the stubbornness of the Mīmāṃsakas is due to their devotion to the idea of an eternal, inherently authoritative, and authorless Veda—an idea whose absurdity has obviously addled their brains.[282]

From this point onward, the aim of the *Tattvasaṃgraha* and the *Pañjikā* is to rebut the Mīmāṃsaka claims concerning the Veda and to draw contrasts between the Mīmāṃsaka and Buddhist understandings of religious authority. The first of the final three chapters—the longest in the entire work—is a consideration of the Mīmāṃsaka claim that the Veda is a means of trustworthy awareness because it is eternal and authorless.[283] Behind this claim lies the idea that the cause of the ultimate or highest good (*niḥśreyasa*) is Dharma, but that we are not capable of knowing Dharma directly because all people are inherently riddled with defects like passion and so on that prevent them from apprehending radically inaccessible entities such as Dharma. Thus the way to happiness can only be found through the eternal, authorless, and inherently trustworthy Veda. Śāntarakṣita and Kamalaśīla attack this position on several fronts in the chapter, most importantly on the grounds that (1) eternal language is impossible, but even it if were to exist it could not be understood; and (2) meaningful language must have its origins in a speaker. In the final paragraph of his commentary on this chapter, Kamalaśīla sums up the basic argument against the Mīmāṃsakas in part 2 of the *Tattvasaṃgraha* and the *Pañjikā*: if the Veda is to be trustworthy, it must have an author, but in that case, there must be an omniscient person (in the sense of one who knows Dharma, which the Mīmāṃsakas explicitly reject). If no such person exists, then the Veda cannot be trustworthy, since its author *ipso facto* could not have known the Dharma of which the Veda speaks.

The second of the final trio of chapters is a consideration of an important epistemological problem, that of intrinsic versus extrinsic trustworthiness.[284]

282. See above, n. 148.

283. This is the twenty-fourth chapter of the TS/P, the *śrutiparīkṣā*. Kamalaśīla explains that the phrase "who does not depend on an autonomous scripture" in the opening verses is an allusion to this investigation, as well as to the following one, the *svataḥprāmāṇyaparīkṣā*. See TSP *ad* TS 5 (B 18,20–25): *svatantraniḥsaṅga iti / ...ayaṃ ca śrutiparīkṣāyāḥ svatantraprāmāṇyaparīkṣāyāś copakṣepaḥ /*. Note that *svatantraprāmāṇyaparīkṣā* is equivalent in meaning to the more common title of the chapter, *svataḥprāmāṇyaparīkṣā*.

284. This is the twenty-fifth chapter of the TS/P, the *svataḥprāmāṇyaparīkṣā*. See previous note.

The placement of this chapter here is due to the fact that Mīmāṃsakas' argument for the trustworthiness of the Veda turns on their understanding of that work as *intrinsically* trustworthy. This, in turn, is related to another Mīmāṃsaka claim, namely, that *all* trustworthy awarenesses must be intrinsically trustworthy. The argument comes down to a question of the justification of *pramāṇa*s, i.e., how can one be sure that a trustworthy awareness is indeed a trustworthy awareness? Śāntarakṣita and Kamalaśīla follow a tradition in which a trustworthy awareness may be justified either intrinsically (i.e., through itself) or extrinsically (i.e., through another awareness), depending on a variety of circumstances. In this chapter, they argue for this understanding of the justification of trustworthy awareness, while they also continue their attack on the Mīmāṃsaka idea that the Veda can be trustworthy in any fashion. Like the previous chapter, this chapter ends with the proclamation that the Mīmāṃsakas must accept either that there is an author for the Veda or that the Veda is not trustworthy; they cannot have it both ways.[285]

This brings us at last to the third and final chapter of this section of the *Tattvasaṃgraha* and the *Pañjikā* and the final chapter of the work as a whole.[286] Like the other two chapters of this section of the work, this investigation continues with the interrelated questions of authorship, trustworthiness, and knowledge of Dharma. Unlike the other two investigations of this section, however, this one is cast not negatively as an attack on the eternal, authorless Veda, but positively in terms of a demonstration of the possibility of knowing Dharma, otherwise understood as a demonstration of omniscience. Since we will be considering this investigation in detail in the subsequent chapters of this book, I will not attempt to summarize it here except to say that the demonstration contains two elements: a general demonstration of the possibility of omniscience and a specific demonstration that concerns the Buddha.

The final three chapters of the *Tattvasaṃgraha* and the *Pañjikā* comprise a unit whose focus is religious authority and whose primary opponent is the Mīmāṃsaka tradition. When this context for the final chapter is thus

285. TS 3122 (*atīndriyārthadarśiparīkṣā*): *atīndriyārthadṛk tasmād vidhūtāntastamaścayaḥ / vedārthapravibhāgajñaḥ karttā cābhyupagamyatām //*.

286. This is the twenty-sixth chapter of the TS/P, the *atīndriyārthadarśiparīkṣā*. Kamalaśīla notes that the phrase "that omniscient one" in the opening verses is an allusion to this investigation. See TSP *ad* TS 6 (B 20,15): *taṃ sarvajñam iti / ayaṃ ca sarvajñasiddhyupakṣepaḥ /*. Although Kamalaśīla elsewhere refers to this chapter as a demonstration of supersensible vision (*atīndriyārthadarśana*), here he simply calls it the "Proof of Omniscience." He repeats this language in his commentary on TS *ad* TSP 1342 (*pratyakṣalakṣaṇaparīkṣā*, B 487,16).

understood, it becomes more readily apparent that we should not allow its impressive length or prominent place at the end of the work to blind us to the other important discussions of omniscience earlier in the *Tattvasaṃgraha* and the *Pañjikā*. We should not, in other words, assume that the final chapter is addressed primarily to the universal audience. For judicious persons, the last truly *crucial* chapter is the final investigation in the first part, the "Investigation of External Objects." This is not to say that there is *nothing* of importance for judicious persons in part 2 of the work overall. It does suggest, however, that (as with the rest of the work) we must evaluate the arguments in this section with reference to the intended audience, and that we must remember that the intended audience may not be coextensive with the ideal audience. As I think is made clear throughout the *Tattvasaṃgraha* and the *Pañjikā*, those who adhere to the Mīmāṃsaka view, and especially Kumārila, should not be seen as judicious at all.

Purposes of the Tattvasaṃgraha *and the* Pañjikā

Our fourth and final area of investigation in this chapter concerns the purposes for which the *Tattvasaṃgraha* and the *Pañjikā* were written. Unlike with the subjects comprising the first three areas of investigation (the audience, styles of reasoning, and structure of the works), Kamalaśīla undertakes an explicit consideration of the aim or purpose (*prayojana*) of his master's treatise over several paragraphs in his long commentary on the opening verses. These paragraphs are a valuable resource for our investigation, and we will examine them before drawing further conclusions based on our findings in the other three areas of investigation. At this point, I should stress that we are dealing now with Kamalaśīla's own views, which may or may not reflect those of Śāntarakṣita, although, as far as I can tell, nothing in the root verses contradicts Kamalaśīla's statements. I thus see no reason to think that Śāntarakṣita would have rejected his student's analysis.

Kamalaśīla's Presentation of the Purpose

In brief, Kamalaśīla proposes a threefold analysis of the purpose of treatises in general: in terms of the work's action (*kriyā*), in terms of the result of that action (*kriyāphala*), and in terms of the subsequent result of the first result of that action (*kriyāphalasya phala*).[287] In speaking of the purpose of the treatise

287. TSP *ad* TS 1–6 (B 10,15): *tac ca prayojanaṃ śāstrasya trividhaṃ kriyārūpaṃ kriyāphalaṃ kriyāphalasya phalam /.*

in terms of an action, Kamalaśīla is pointing to what modern philosophers might call the *illocutionary force* of the work, that is, the treatise as an *act* that is performed through words. For Kamalaśīla, all statements share a common aim in terms of action, which he defines as "the demonstration of their own subject matter."[288] But since this common aim is so obvious as to be trivial, Kamalaśīla dismisses its importance and turns instead to the specific or uncommon aim of the treatise in question.[289] This, he says, is expressed in the opening verses of the *Tattvasaṃgraha* by the word *saṃgraha* in the phrase "I compose this *Tattvasaṃgraha*," by which word, Kamalaśīla maintains, Śāntarakṣita indicates the action that is the aim of the treatise: namely, "the collection, defined as the dwelling in a single intellect, of those realities [or truths, *tattva*] that are scattered here and there [in other treatises]."[290] In other words, the purpose of the *Tattvasaṃgraha* (and by extension, the *Pañjikā*) is to gather into a single mind a comprehensive variety of true realities.

In speaking of the purpose of the treatise in terms of the result of the treatise's action, Kamalaśīla engages in a discussion of what modern thinkers might term the *perlocutionary force* of the work, that is, the treatise as an act that gives rise to a particular effect. Here, the effect in question is the "easy understanding of those realities, which occurs in the mindstream of the one being made to understand."[291] When Kamalaśīla speaks of the aim of the treatise in terms of this result, he confirms a perspective similar to that of Perelman and Olbrechts-Tyteca, who maintain, as we saw, that "all argument aims at gaining the adherence of minds."[292] In the case of the *Tattvasaṃgraha* and the *Pañjikā*, the adherence sought is the understanding (implying also the acceptance on the part of the judicious person) of the various positions, or "realities," presented in the work.

288. TSP *ad* TS 1–6 (B 10,20–21): *tatra sarvavākyānāṃ svābhidheyapratipādanalakṣaṇā kriyā sādhāraṇā /.*

289. TSP *ad* TS 1–6 (B 10,21): *sā cātipratītayā na prayojanatvenopadarśanīyā tasyāṃ śāstrasya vyabhicārābhāvāt /.*

290. TSP *ad* TS 1–6 (B 11,1–4): *tasmād asādhāraṇā yā kriyā sopadarśanīyā / sā tv asya śāstrasya vidyata eva tattvasaṃgrahalakṣaṇā yato 'nena śāstreṇa teṣāṃ tattvānām itastato viprakīrṇānām ekatra buddhau viniveśalakṣaṇaḥ saṃgrahaḥ kriyate / atas tām eva saṃgrahaśabdena darśitavān /.*

291. TSP *ad* TS 1–6 (B 11,5): *asyāś ca tattvasaṃgrahakriyāyāḥ pratipādyasantānagatas tattvasukhāvabodhaḥ phalam /.* The reading *pratipādyasantānagatas* in place of *pratipattṛsantānagatas* is suggested by both B and G, and corresponds to D, vol. *ze*, 139b6: *bstan par bya ba'i rgyud du gtogs pa'i . . .*; the meaning, in any case, is the same.

292. See above, n. 117.

But this is only the first stage of the adherence sought in the work, for as Kamalaśīla tells us, there is a further aim of the treatise, which can be understood as the subsequent result of the understanding that is itself the result of the treatise's action. This subsequent, and final, result of the understanding that the treatise produces in its listener or reader is the attainment of what Kamalaśīla refers to as the "benefit of the world" (*jagaddhita*), which consists in the twin goals of "elevation" (*abhyudaya*) and "the highest good" (*niḥśreyasa*). Elevation generally means rebirth as a god or human, although it can also include health and power in the present life.[293] The highest good is the attainment of liberation from cyclic existence, or *saṃsāra*, specifically, in this text, the liberation of a perfect buddha. Kamalaśīla explains the process by which the treatise brings about these attainments:

> That is, the attainment of elevation and the highest good is said to be the benefit of the world. And the cause of that [attainment] is nonerror (*aviparyāsa*), since the root of all afflictions is error and the removal of the afflictions is the benefit of the world. And therefore, the removal of the cause of that [error] is established to be the cause of that [attainment of elevation and the highest good, which is the benefit of the world]. And nonerror consists respectively (*yathāvat*) in confidence concerning the connection between karmic action and its result (*karmaphalasambandhābhisaṃpratyaya*) and the correct (*aviparīta*) understanding of the selflessness of persons and things. Moreover, that [nonerror] is produced—through the succession of study, deliberation, and meditation—from this treatise that correctly explicates dependent arising. Therefore, we know, "The benefit of the world is accomplished through the action (*kriyā*) of the collection of realities [i.e., through the composition and study of the *Tattvasaṃgraha*]." And when there is the attainment of elevation and the highest good, there is the elimination of longing, since the person has accomplished his intended aim. Therefore, since no other further aim is to be sought, this is the pinnacle of the aim.[294]

293. See TSP *ad* TS 3565 (*atīndriyārthadarśiparīkṣā*): *abhyudayaṃ nityārogyaiśvaryādilakṣaṇam* /. For discussion of this passage, see below: pp. 245–46.

294. TSP *ad* TS 1–6 (B 12,1–8): *tathā hy abhyudayaniḥśreyasāvāptir jagaddhitam ucyate / tasya cāviparyāso hetuḥ sarvasaṃkleśasya viparyāsamūlatvāt saṃkleśaviparītatvāc ca jagaddhitasya / atas taddhetuviparīto 'sya hetur avatiṣṭhate / aviparyāsaś ca yathāvat karmaphalasaṃbandhābhisaṃpratyayaḥ aviparītapudgaladharmanairātmyāvabodhaś ca*

The soteriological tenor of this work and its aim is thus unmistakable. Kamalaśīla clearly states that one who reads the treatise, understands and accepts its arguments, and then cultivates the insights thereby produced will eliminate error and attain the highest possible human aim, liberation from the suffering of saṃsāra (which, as we will see below, occurs in the form of a buddha).

Shortly after the passage just cited, Kamalaśīla clarifies this process even further. Here we learn that the two elements that make up the "benefit of the world," elevation and the highest good, have distinct causes. Elevation is caused by correct confidence in karmic causality, and the highest good comes about through the understanding and cultivation of the vision of selflessness (*nairātmya*), which itself is the antidote to ignorance:

> That is, from the correct teaching of dependent arising, there is the determination of its meaning, from which arises the cause of good rebirth, i.e., reasoned confidence (*abhisaṃpratyaya*) in the connection between karmic action and its result. And the understanding of the selflessness of persons and things, which is the cause of the highest good, is produced through the succession of study, deliberation, and meditation. When that is produced, ignorance, which is the cause of saṃsāra, is destroyed. And when that is destroyed, its root, i.e., the afflictive and epistemic obscurations, is entirely destroyed. Thus, since all obscuration is entirely removed, there is the attainment of liberation (*apavarga*).[295]

Most significant in this passage is Kamalaśīla's reference to the destruction of two kinds of obscurations, the afflictive obscuration (*kleśāvaraṇa*) and the epistemic obscuration (*jñeyāvaraṇa*), for the destruction of these two obscu-

---

/ sa cāsmād aviparītapratītyasamutpādasaṃprakāśakāc chāstrāc chravaṇacintābhāvanākrameṇopajāyata ity ato 'vagamyata eva tattvasaṃgrahakriyāto jagaddhitam api sampadyata iti / abhyudayaniḥśreyasāvāptau ca satyām abhimatārthaparisamāptyā puruṣasyākāṅkṣāvicchedād ato nāparam ūrdhvaṃ prayojanaṃ mṛgyam iti prayojananiṣṭhā /.

295. TSP *ad* TS 1–6 (B 13,4–8): *tathā hi / aviparītapratītyasamutpādadeśanātas tadarthāvadhāraṇāt sugatihetur aviparītakarmaphalasaṃbandhābhisaṃpratyaya upajāyate / pudgaladharmanairātmyāvabodhaś ca niḥśreyasahetuḥ śrutacintābhāvanākrameṇotpadyate / tadutpattau hy avidyā saṃsārahetur nivartate / tannivṛttau ca tanmūlaṃ sakalaṃ kleśajñeyāvaraṇaṃ nivartata iti sakalāvaraṇavigamād apavargasaṃprāptir bhavati /*. The reading *aviparītakarmaphalasaṃbandhābhisaṃpratyaya* in place of *aviparītakarmaphalasaṃbandhādisaṃpratyaya* as found in B and G is based on D, vol. *ze*, 141ab: *las dang 'bras bu phyin ci ma log pa la yid ches pa*.

rations is the necessary and sufficient condition of omniscience for these philosophers. Kamalaśīla states this plainly much later in the treatise, when he says, "omniscience comes about through the elimination of the afflictive and the epistemic obscurations."[296] The import of the above passage is thus clear: the final aim of the *Tattvasaṃgraha* and the *Pañjikā* is the attainment of omniscience on the part of its readers. Of course, what exactly is meant by omniscience is neither immediately obvious nor is it made clear in the opening section of the *Pañjikā*. But what is evident is that, for Kamalaśīla at least, the ultimate aim of the treatise, the final result of the treatise's action, is nothing other than maximal epistemic greatness, or omniscience.

Kamalaśīla's Analysis of the Purpose

In our earlier discussions of the audience, styles of reasoning, and structure of the *Tattvasaṃgraha* and the *Pañjikā*, we have already made a number of observations concerning the various purposes for which the work may have been written. When taken in conjunction with the analysis of the purpose of the work outlined by Kamalaśīla just above, we arrive at something like the following general picture of the purposes of the work as a whole. As expected, the purpose varies in relation to diverse audiences.

In terms of the universal audience of judicious persons, the work clearly intends to convince them of the rationality of the Buddhist teachings and path. If such persons are advocates of a position that conflicts with the Buddhist position (and may be shown, therefore, to be irrational), the work aims to refute that position and to convince such opponents of the errors of their ways. The assumption seems to be that judicious persons who encounter the arguments in the *Tattvasaṃgraha* and the *Pañjikā* will have no choice but to embrace its conclusions as true. Ultimately, this will result in their taking up the Buddhist path, which, if they follow it diligently, will lead them to omniscience. But first, such persons must be convinced of the rationality of the Buddhist teachings and path, and the authors recognize that this is a process of persuasion that occurs in stages. This accounts for the work's various styles of reasoning, the levels of analysis, and the structure of the work as a whole.

Besides convincing others of the rationality of Buddhist positions, the

296. TSP *ad* TS 3337 (*atīndriyārthadarśiparīkṣā*, B 1052,21–22): *kleśajñeyāvaraṇaprahāṇato hi sarvajñatvam* /. Cf. also TS 3338 (*atīndriyārthadarśiparīkṣā*): *sākṣātkṛtiviśeṣāc ca doṣo nāsti savāsanaḥ / sarvajñatvam ataḥ siddhaṃ sarvāvaraṇamuktitaḥ* //. "And due to a special kind of direct realization, neither the fault nor its imprint exits. Therefore omniscience is established since there is freedom from all obscurations."

Tattvasaṃgraha and the *Pañjikā* also clearly seek to defend Buddhist positions against attacks from non-Buddhists. Once again, the audience for such defensive arguments is in general the universal audience of judicious persons, but interestingly, the authors do not always argue for a single Buddhist perspective when defending Buddhist positions that have been attacked. Instead, they argue for a *range* of possible Buddhist responses that can all be defended as rational. For example, the final chapter of the *Tattvasaṃgraha* and the *Pañjikā* argues, as we will see, for several distinct understandings of omniscience, none of which corresponds precisely to the authors' own final position on the topic. To understand how this can be, we must recognize that the arguments for omniscience in the final chapter are a rational defense of omniscience *within the constraints of the opponents' metaphysical commitments*. In other words, on the externalist ontological commitments of the opponents, these are the range of Buddhist arguments for omniscience that can serve to stave off the severe attacks advanced by such opponents as the Mīmāṃsaka Kumārila and others. Although they do not represent the ultimate solution, they are steps along the way to a higher level of analysis, and thus they have a legitimate role.

As for the actual intended audience, we have seen that it is much more difficult to specify than is the universal audience. Our earlier analysis suggests that the intended audience probably includes Buddhists who wish to refine their understanding of Buddhist and non-Buddhist doctrines, perhaps in part as a means of preparing for public debates. Since it seems highly probable that such debates did take place, and that they were an important means of gaining patronage and prestige, it seems a reasonable working hypothesis that at least some of the figures and traditions addressed in the body of the work are part of the intended audience (whether directly through reading or hearing the work itself or indirectly through encountering the work's arguments in debates). In some cases, where members of this intended audience are portrayed as injudicious, we find occasional *ad personam* arguments in the *Tattvasaṃgraha* and the *Pañjikā*. Here, it seems that the purpose is to discredit these opponents in the eyes of others rather than to directly convince them of any Buddhist position. Nonetheless, even here we still see an effort to gain the adherence of minds, for such *ad personam* attacks are uniformly overshadowed by arguments *ad humanitatem* couched in the language of formal reasoning (*nyāya*).

In sum, the *Tattvasaṃgraha* and the *Pañjikā* together form an apologetic tract, by which I mean that they comprise a work of Buddhist *philosophia* that seeks to argue for and defend its religious vision on the basis of canons of rationality that transcend the religious tradition in question. As such, it is not fundamentally a dogmatic work in which received doctrines or tenets are asserted as authoritative without appeal to any canons of rationality outside of the religious tradition in question (this is so despite the presence in the work of a certain number of dogmas, to be discussed shortly). Griffiths has said "Apologetics ... usually uses only methods of argumentation and criteria of knowledge acceptable to the adversary."[297] Throughout the *Tattvasaṃgraha* and the *Pañjikā*, the authors adhere to (or at least offer the pretense of adhering to) this method; and it is their commitment to this kind of argumentation that lies behind the sliding scale of analysis. We have seen above, in our discussions of *nyāya* and *pramāṇa* theory styles of reasoning, that the idea of a common standard of rationality is problematic. Nevertheless, the question here is not whether the authors achieve such a standard but rather whether they make a *bona fide* appeal to such a standard. Did they, in other words, see Buddhist doctrines—including, and perhaps especially, the doctrine of omniscience—as defensible in terms of a belief-neutral form of reasoning? The answer, I think, is undeniably "yes," and the overall aim of the *Tattvasaṃgraha* and the *Pañjikā* is to convince its readers and hearers of this very fact. Having understood this, judicious persons can then be expected to take up the Buddhist path, since it is taken for granted that all rational persons wish to attain elevation and the highest good. For those readers or listeners who, after encountering the arguments in the work, do not come to accept Buddhist doctrines as true, the explanation can only lie in their unfortunate lack of judiciousness.

297. Griffiths 1991: 15.

3. Dogmas, Connotations, and Contexts

TO FURTHER SET the stage for our examination of the arguments for omniscience in the *Tattvasaṃgraha* and the *Pañjikā,* this chapter explores three specific elements crucial to our understanding of omniscience in the work. First, we take an extended look at some of the presuppositions—*dogmas* in Hadot's terms—that inform the religious and philosophical thinking of the authors of the *Tattvasaṃgraha* and the *Pañjikā* as Mahāyāna Buddhist scholastics. These are elements of the discussions of omniscience that are not specifically defended in the work but are in some sense allowed to stand as informing the work from the outset. Second, we examine the semantic range of connotations for the words signaling omniscience in the work, showing that the authors utilize a range of meanings that will impact our analysis of their argumentation. Third, we take a look in some detail at the specific rhetorical contexts in which discussions of omniscience occur in the work, attending again to the central questions of audience and the structure of the arguments.

Dogmas of Omniscience and Buddhahood

One concrete advantage to our earlier consideration of the *Tattvasaṃgraha* and the *Pañjikā* as a form of Buddhist *philosophia* in Hadot's terms reveals itself at this point in relation to another similarity between Buddhist philosophical activity and that of ancient Greece. Hadot maintains that to do philosophy in ancient Greece, it was generally necessary to affiliate oneself with a particular school, whereby one could then undertake spiritual exercises grounded in the dogmas and methodological principles of that school. As Hadot explains:

> The dogmas and methodological principles of each school are not open to discussion. In this period, to philosophize is to choose a school, convert to its way of life, and accept its dogmas.... This does not mean that theoretical reflection and elaboration are absent from the philosophical life. However, this activity never extended to the dogmas themselves or the methodological principles but rather to the ways of demonstrating and systematizing these dogmas and to secondary, doctrinal points issuing from them on which there was no unanimity in the school.[298]

Now, on the face of it, one might imagine that Śāntarakṣita and Kamalaśīla would have a problem with this statement. That is, as the statement stands, the implication is that in order to engage in Buddhist *philosophia*, it is necessary to accept certain doctrines or principles *without question*, so as to have a place to stand in undertaking the philosophizing and other practices that make up the Buddhist path. I think that if we understand Buddhist dogmas to operate in this fashion, then we must reject that the authors of the *Tattvasaṃgraha* and the *Pañjikā* accept them.

On the other hand, there may well be a way in which Hadot's description does apply, and could conceivably even be accepted by Śāntarakṣita and Kamalaśīla. That is, as we have already seen in our discussion of *nyāya* reasoning, to engage in dialectical activity in India in a certain period seems to have required that one join what we might loosely term a school or a particular religio-philosophical tradition. As with the Greek practitioners of *philosophia*, when ancient Indian thinkers join a school, they generally do accept certain basic methodological principles from which moral and other reasoning sets out and that form the background against which the search for wisdom occurs. Examples of such methodological principles include the certain broad values of *nyāya* reasoning and *pramāṇa* theorizing, as well as presuppositions about the purposes of philosophical activity and the goals of rational or judicious persons.[299] If dogmas are understood to refer primarily to such methodological principles, I suspect that Śāntarakṣita and Kamalaśīla would not object to dogmas being ascribed to them.

But there is another kind of dogma present in the *Tattvasaṃgraha* and the

298. Hadot (1995: 60–61).

299. An example of a broadly shared principle in this regard is that the ultimate aim of judicious persons is the complete and irreversible removal of all suffering (*duḥkha*). See Ganeri (2001: 15–17) for some reflections on the connection between rationality and the ends of life in Indian philosophy, especially in Nyāya.

Pañjikā, one that appears to be somewhat more difficult to reconcile with the authors' apparent rationalism and claimed antidogmatism. This type of dogma emerges in certain doctrines characteristic of Mahāyāna Buddhism that are assumed but not explicitly defended at various points in the works. To a reader educated in such matters, the presence of these doctrines stamps the works with the seal of a distinctly Mahāyāna Buddhist perspective, and provides an unambiguous mark as to the stream of Indian Buddhism the authors understand themselves to belong. Since many of these doctrines are used as a basis for further discussion and debate concerning omniscience and its relation to buddhahood, it is necessary that we gain a clear idea about them at the outset of our investigation. This is our aim in the present section.

Bear in mind, however, that the presence of these dogmas in the *Tattvasaṃgraha* and the *Pañjikā* does not imply that the authors accept such doctrines on the basis of either faith or sectarian affiliation. Instead, it is possible and, in my view, quite likely that the authors understand these doctrines to be already established through reasoning in other locations. Since the doctrines in question concern mainly the details of the ultimate goal of Buddhist *philosophia*, the need to discuss and defend them would most naturally arise in intra-Buddhist debate or scholastic settings and not in the more general public arena. In fact, one might even seek to argue that the presence of such doctrines in combination with the authors' various claims to antidogmatism and rationalism is further evidence that this particular work is aimed primarily at non-Buddhists and only secondarily at Buddhists with whom the authors may disagree on various points of specifically Buddhist doctrine. In any case, while I do feel that it is appropriate to consider such doctrines as dogmas in the context of this particular work, I do not believe that we must therefore suppose that Śāntarakṣita and Kamalaśīla hold such doctrines to be beyond the pale of rational grounding.

The first dogma of which we must take account is the obvious one we have already noted: omniscience, whatever else it may mean, is a state of maximal epistemic greatness. It can equally be characterized as the perfection of wisdom (*prajñāpāramitā*).[300] As is also quite clear, omniscience is a form of perfection that is necessarily unique to those who have attained the maximally great state of perfect and complete awakening (*samyaksaṃbodhi*), otherwise known as buddhahood. This being so, omniscience may stand for or represent buddhahood, so that a claim that someone is omniscient amounts to a

300. Cf. TSP *ad* TS 2076–77 (*bahirārthaparīkṣā*, B 708,22–23) for an explicit reference to the Perfection of Wisdom corpus of Mahāyāna Buddhism.

claim that the person has attained all the other forms of maximal greatness that are attributed to buddhas as well.[301]

The Requirement of Great Compassion

In general, the *Tattvasaṃgraha* and the *Pañjikā* as a work is not particularly concerned either to justify or to explain these other forms of maximal greatness apart from omniscience, with one exception: the work makes repeated mention of the Buddha's maximal greatness in the *affective* or *moral* realm—his perfection of great compassion (*mahākaruṇā, mahākṛpā, mahādayā*), understood as the desire and intention to eradicate the suffering of all sentient beings without exception. The position that omniscience or buddhahood is the proper goal of judicious persons is a dogma that the authors do not attempt to justify through reason in the work. Instead, they present it as the obvious choice of a goal for a person motivated by great compassion. Also that one *should* act out of great compassion is not explicitly defended in the work, except indirectly, to the degree that the authors often indicate that great compassion is *required* if one is to reach omniscience. Reviewing this idea will allow us to uncover a number of related dogmas that help form the context of the work as a whole, a context that frames and informs *all* discussions of omniscience in the work.

Great compassion, unlike omniscience, is not the exclusive property of fully awakened buddhas but is possessed as well by bodhisattvas (fledgling buddhas), who are driven by it as their motivation to develop omniscient wisdom and to become full-fledged buddhas. Bodhisattvas are thus distinguished by their motivation from other types of practitioners on the Buddhist path, especially from those "straw men" of the Mahāyāna, the śrāvakas and pratyekabuddhas, who are usually portrayed as seeking the elimination of suffering for themselves alone out of cowardly fear of the suffering of saṃsāra.[302] In the following passage—itself part of a longer argument

301. See Griffiths (1994: 60–82) for a discussion of the many forms of maximal greatness attributed to the figure of the perfect buddha in the Yogācāra and the Abhidharma traditions.

302. The figure of the śrāvaka (literally, "listener"; Pāli: *sāvaka*) has a long history in the Buddhist tradition. Originally, the term seems to have indicated a direct disciple of the Buddha, one who "heard" the teachings or Dharma from the Buddha and then put these teachings into practice with the goal of attaining nirvāṇa (Pāli: *nibbāna*) and becoming an *arhat* (literally, "worthy one"; Pāli: *arahant*). For those later Buddhists who align themselves with the self-styled Mahāyāna (literally, "great vehicle"), the term *śrāvaka* comes to take on a negative connotation, indicating a person who, due to his relative lack of

designed to demonstrate the range of possible motives for engaging in the Buddhist meditation on selflessness (*nairātmya*)—Kamalaśīla highlights the difference in motivation between the two types of practitioners:

> In this regard, first of all, the lack of desire [to engage in this meditation on selflessness] is not established. That is, in the first place, there are those who, their minds tormented by the suffering of birth and so on,[303] strive on their own behalf to pacify that [suffering] because their minds are fearful of saṃsāra; therefore, for such persons who are intent upon the awakening of a śrāvaka and so on, being afraid of saṃsāra is a reason for their desire to meditate upon selflessness. But those who, due to being of a distinctive lineage (*gotra*), are by nature gratified only by causing benefit to others see that the world is tormented by the threefold suffering of being conditioned and so on;[304] they see this, and being under the power of compassion, they are distressed by the suffering of the [world]. Having thrown away any concern for themselves, they accept all the beings in saṃsāra without exception as their own self and resolve [to attain awakening] in order to rescue those [beings]. For these persons, compassion itself is a reason to engage in the meditation [on selflessness], because it is difficult for them to explain the remote goal [i.e., awakening] and its causes [without having first directly realized selflessness].[305]

compassion and fear of saṃsāra, strives for awakening for himself alone. For Mahāyāna thinkers, including Śāntarakṣita and Kamalaśīla, the śrāvaka (and the corresponding figure of the perfected śrāvaka, the arhat) thus becomes an image not of human perfection but of cowardliness and spiritual selfishness. See Jenkins 1999 and Katz 1982.

303. This refers to the suffering of birth, old age, sickness, and death, the four inevitable marks of saṃsāra.

304. The threefold suffering is comprised of the suffering of suffering (*duḥkhaduḥkhatā*), the suffering of change (*vipariṇāmaduḥkhatā*), and the suffering of being conditioned (*saṃskāraduḥkhatā*). See AKBh *ad* AK 6.3.

305. TSP *ad* TS 3337 (*atīndriyārthdarśiparīkṣā*, B 1055,14ff): *tatra na tāvad anarthitvaṃ siddham / tathā hi ye tāvaj jātyādiduḥkhotpīḍitamānasāḥ saṃsārād uttrastamanasas tadupaśamam ātmanaḥ prārthayante / teṣāṃ śrāvakādibodhaniyatānāṃ saṃsārād bhayam eva nairātmyabhāvanārthitvanimittam / ye tu gotraviśeṣāt prakṛtyaiva parahitakaraṇaikābhirāmāḥ saṃskārādiduḥkhatātritayaparipīḍitaṃ jagad avekṣya kṛpāpara tantratayā tadduḥkhaduḥkhinaḥ svātmani vyapekṣām apāsya sakalān eva saṃsāriṇa ātmatvenābhyupagatās tatparitrāṇāya praṇidadhate teṣāṃ karuṇaiva bhāvanāpravṛtti nimittaṃ parokṣopeyataddhetos tadākhyānasya duṣkaratvāt /*. The last clause is virtually

Here, in accord with a pervasive Mahāyāna scheme, Kamalaśīla represents bodhisattvas as belonging to a different lineage, or *gotra*, than śrāvakas and others (e.g., pratyekabuddhas).[306] The members of these different lineages focus on distinct soteriological aims: full-fledged buddhahood for bodhisattvas, and "the awakening of a śrāvaka and so on" (*śrāvakādibodhi*) for śrāvakas and others. The disparity between these final states is great. Not only are buddhas omniscient while śrāvakas and others are not (even after attaining their specific form of "awakening"), but buddhas are also maximally efficacious as teachers in a manner that allows them, through their teaching, to rescue countless sentient beings from the suffering of saṃsāra. And this maximal efficacy as teachers is due to their omniscience, which itself comes about through a practice motivated entirely by great compassion.[307]

The reasoning behind these interlocking claims is as follows. First, great compassion desires the elimination of others' suffering. The only way to remove sentient beings' suffering is through teaching, since in the final analysis, each individual must effect the *actual* elimination of the cause of suffering, understood as ignorance, through his or her own efforts.[308] As is widely agreed, however, it is one thing to comprehend something for oneself, quite another to convey it effectively and skillfully to others. In the Mahāyāna analysis accepted by the authors, the realization necessary to teach others how to eradicate their own suffering requires not only that one has eradicated one's own suffering, but also that one is capable of tailoring one's teaching to the unique circumstances of countless sentient beings in accord with their individual capacities, outlooks, and needs. A Buddhist motivated by great

---

a direct quote from Dharmakīrti's PV 2.132 (on which, see n. 307 below). For a German translation of this passage, see Pemwieser 1991: 79ff.

306. On the theme of *gotra* in Indian and Tibetan Mahāyāna, see the seminal study by Ruegg (1969).

307. Dharmakīrti provides a more detailed picture of how the perfection of others' aims depends upon the perfection of one's own aims. See, e.g., PV 2.131–32ab: *niṣpannakaruṇotkarṣaḥ paraduḥkhākṣamer itaḥ // dayāvān duḥkhahānārtham upāyeṣv abhiyujyate / parokṣopeyataddhetos tadākhyānaṃ hi duṣkaram //*. "Possessing the pinnacle of the excellence of compassion, because he is unable to tolerate the suffering of others, the compassionate one applies himself to [various] methods in order to eliminate [his own] suffering, since it is difficult for one for whom the goal (*upeya*) and its cause (*taddhetu*) are remote (*parokṣa*) to expound that [distant goal and its causes]."

308. Kamalaśīla emphasizes this point in his commentary on the opening verses by evoking a traditional Buddhist maxim at TSP *ad* TS 6 (B 19,21): *yuṣmābhir eva karttavyam ākhyātāras tathāgatāḥ /*. "You yourselves must accomplish [awakening]; the tathāgatas are the instructors."

compassion will then not be satisfied with attaining just enough wisdom to eradicate his or her individual suffering, but will seek the maximum degree of wisdom possible, so as to fulfill the goal of teaching others to help them in turn become free from suffering. Such a Buddhist, in other words, seeks the epistemic maximal greatness that is omniscience (whatever that turns out to mean). And since omniscience, at least of a certain kind, is theoretically possible (as the authors of the *Tattvasaṃgraha* and the *Pañjikā* believe they can demonstrate through reason), a bodhisattva who pursues omniscience with the proper methods and motivation will not fail to attain it.

The Perfection of the Aims of Self and Other

Kamalaśīla's passage above hints also at another way great compassion is thematized in the *Tattvasaṃgraha* and the *Pañjikā*, and that is in terms of the perfection of the aims of both oneself and others (*svaparārthasaṃpat*). This dual perfection is an ancient theme in Buddhist doctrinal thought, found in many of the sources that Śāntarakṣita and Kamalaśīla revere.[309] In the

309. In the Buddhist *pramāṇa* theory tradition, for example, Dignāga invokes the *svaparārtha* theme in his comments on the homage verse (*maṅgalaśloka*) of his *Pramāṇasamuccaya* (i.e., at PSV *ad* PS 1.1). In that famous stanza, Dignāga extols the Buddha through five epithets, one of which—*sugata*, or "well gone"—represents the Buddha's perfection of his own aim, and another—*tāyin*, or "protector"—his perfection of others' aims. Together, these two perfections (i.e., of his own and others' aims) constitute the Buddha's perfection of the result (*phalasaṃpat*), while the perfection of his intention (*āśayasaṃpat*) and of his practice (*prayogasaṃpat*) together constitute his perfection of the cause (*hetusaṃpat*). The coincidence of all these perfections, but especially the perfection of his own aim (i.e., his *sugatatva*), account for the Buddha's superiority over other advanced practitioners, as well as his status as "trustworthy" or an "authority" (*pramāṇabhūta*). See Hattori (1968: 23 and 74) for analysis. On the relationship between this verse, the structure of Dharmakīrti's PV 2, and the TS/P, see below: n. 385. In the MAP *ad* MA (Ichigō ed., 5,11–7,11), Kamalaśīla also analyzes the *svaparārtha* theme in terms of the perfection of cause and of effect, though he does so in a manner that deviates significantly from that of Dignāga in PSV *ad* PS 1.1. On Kamalaśīla's analysis, only the Buddha's perfection of his own aim (*svārtha*) is analyzed in terms of the perfection of the cause and the perfection of the result. Wisdom, understood as omniscience, is then considered to be one aspect of the Buddha's perfection of the result, and his elimination of all mental stains is the second aspect. Regarding the perfection of the cause, it is cast in terms of the perfection of the "near" and the "far," a phrase that may refer to the earlier and the later stages of the ten *bodhisattvabhūmi*s. Others' aims (*parārtha*) are analyzed in terms of their attainment of elevation and the highest good. In his discussion of the *svaparārtha* motif in early Buddhism, Jenkins (1999: 55–59) deflates the Mahāyāna caricature of non-Mahāyāna Buddhists as indifferent to the aims of others.

Tattvasaṃgraha and the *Pañjikā*, we encounter it first when Kamalaśīla comments on Śāntarakṣita's description of the Buddha as one "who through his desire to benefit the world inculcated a nature of great compassion throughout many innumerable ages" by explaining that the Buddha, although he has fulfilled his own aims entirely, does not abandon his activity of accomplishing the aims of others.[310] This activity, we learn, consists in his correct teaching of dependent arising; and since comprehension of this teaching is the means (i.e., the path) by which others may attain maximal greatness in the form of elevation and the highest good, that teaching is called "the accomplishment of [the world's] welfare" (*hitānuṣṭhāna*).[311] Naturally, to teach correctly requires that one have direct knowledge and experience oneself, as Kamalaśīla reminds us with the following statement:

> And the means for this perfection of the correct accomplishment of others' welfare is the direct perception of *dharmas* and great compassion. For if there is compassion but no knowledge of the way things are, one will not be capable of correctly teaching [that which is] the benefit of others. But, if one has knowledge but lacks compassion, then either one will not teach, or if one does teach, one will teach something that is not of benefit. Therefore, the Lord's two perfect means of accomplishing others' welfare are wisdom and compassion.[312]

310. TSP *ad* TS 5 (B 19,6–7): *sā ca mahādayā bhagavataḥ samadhigatāśeṣasvārthasampatter api parārthakaraṇavyāpārāparityāgād avagamyate /*. "And despite having attained the utter perfection of his own aims, one understands that the Blessed One has this great compassion because he has not renounced the activity that accomplishes others' aims." Note that the reading *samādhigatāśeṣa°* at G 15,6 is not supported by D, vol. *ze*, 145b6–7, which has *bcom ldan 'das rang gi don phun sum tshogs pa ma lus pa brnyes na yang*.... For the Sanskrit (and an English translation) of TS 1–6, see p. 96.

311. TSP *ad* TS 5 (B 19,18–19): *yaḥ pratītyasamutpādam evambhūtaṃ jagādetyanena yathāvatparahitānuṣṭhānaṃ bhagavato darśitam / idam eva hitānuṣṭhānaṃ bhagavato yat pareṣām aviparītasvargāpavargamārgopadeśaḥ /*. Śāntarakṣita, too, says that the Buddha's teaching is for the sake of others; see TS 3567 (*atīndriyārthadarśiparīkṣā*): *svārthasaṃsiddhaye teṣām upadeśo na tādṛśaḥ / ārambhaḥ sakala tv eṣa parārthaṃ kartum īdṛśaḥ //*. Kamalaśīla likewise confirms that it is the Buddha's activity as a teacher that constitutes his perfection of others' aims; see TSP *ad* TS 3512–13 (*atīndriyārthadarśiparīkṣā*, B 1099,24–1200,11): *parārthasaṃpadaṃ dīpayann āha sarvalokapiteti / pitā śāstā / sarvasya jagato yānatrayasugatipratiṣṭhāpanāt /*. The reading *yānatraya°* in place of *jñānatraya°* is based on D, vol. *'e*, 316a6: *'gro ba mtha' dag theg pa gsum gyi bde ba la 'god pa'i phyir ro /*.

312. TSP *ad* TS 6 (B 19,22–20,1) *asyāś cāviparītaparahitānuṣṭhānasampada upāyo dharmeṣu sākṣād darśitvaṃ mahākaruṇā ca yataḥ kṛpālur api yathābhūtāparijñānān na*

Here, the direct perception of *dharmas* represents the Buddha's maximal epistemic greatness, which can also be characterized as the perfection of his own aim (*svārthasampat*). Thus, the Buddha's attainment is characterized as the perfection of his own aim in terms of his own realization, while from the perspective of his activity as a teacher, it is characterized as the perfection of others' aims.

In the previous chapter, we saw that Kamalaśīla equates the highest good (*niḥśreyasa*) with liberation (*apavarga*), and that he equates liberation with the removal of two obscurations together with their imprints—which, we know from other passages, is precisely his definition of omniscience, or full-fledged buddhahood. But if liberation, as the highest good, is synonymous with buddhahood, then this must mean that śrāvakas or pratyekabuddhas not only do not accomplish the aims of others, they additionally do not accomplish even their *own* aims, at least not in any authentic sense of attaining awakening and true freedom from saṃsāra.[313] This analysis appears to contradict the idea that while śrāvakas do not fulfill the aims of others in the manner of full-fledged buddhas, they do eliminate ignorance and suffering, attaining freedom from saṃsāra, or "individual liberation" (*pratimokṣa*) and as such they *can* be said to have fulfilled at least their own aims.[314] A resolu-

---

samyakparahitam upadeṣṭuṃ samarthaḥ parijñānavān api kṛpāhīno naivopadiśet upadiśann apy ahitam apy upadiśet / tasmāt prajñākṛpe dve api samyak parahitānuṣṭhānopāyau bhagavataḥ /.

313. Williams (1989: 145–46), in his assessment of the śrāvaka and pratyekabuddha paths according to some Mahāyāna sources, affirms a similar sentiment: "That is, although it is agreed that the Buddha is in certain respects superior to Arhats [i.e., awakened śrāvakas] and Pratyekabuddhas, as regards their having attained liberation, the goal, freedom from rebirth, Arhats, Pratyekabuddhas, and Buddhas are all on the same level [according to certain non-Mahāyāna sources]. They are all enlightened. Now [in certain Mahāyāna sources] the Buddha is portrayed arguing that he taught many provisional ways and goals: his doctrine was taught out of skill adapted to the level of his hearers, with the implied possibility that the goals of Arhatship and Pratyekabuddhahood *are no real goals at all*, they are merely provisional devices, and there is a great gulf separating Arhatship and Pratyekabuddhahood from the true goal of full and complete Buddhahood" (italics added). Mahāyāna sources that explicitly endorse such a perspective include the *Śrīmālādevīsiṃhanāda Sūtra* and the *Laṅkāvatāra Sūtra*. See Ruegg 1969: 177–85.

314. This idea corresponds roughly to what one finds in various Abhidharma sources, where, despite some differences, arhats, pratyekabuddhas, and full-fledged buddhas all have in common the attainment upon their death of a final nirvāṇa "without remainder" (*nirupadhiśeṣanirvāṇa*); Makransky (1997: 28) characterizes this nirvāṇa as "an unconditioned state eternally liberated from the conditioned, mundane world of sentient beings ... lacking any causal connection to the conditioned ... a final salvation from the suffering of the world."

tion to this problem is hinted at in the passage cited earlier, when, through his statement that bodhisattvas throw away selfish concerns and "accept all the beings in saṃsāra without exception as their own self," Kamalaśīla indicates that bodhisattvas engage in an exchange of identity of self and other such that their own aim *becomes*, in some important sense, the fulfillment of the aims of others.[315] Since, in Śāntarakṣita and Kamalaśīla's view, the fulfillment of others' aims is accomplished only through maximally efficacious teaching, and since only an omniscient being or buddha is capable of teaching in this way, accomplishing others' aims entails that the bodhisattva accomplish her own aim, buddhahood, as well.[316] It thus becomes quite difficult to separate

315. The practices of recognizing the equality of self and others (*svaparasamatā*) and of imaginatively exchanging places with others (*parātmaparivartana*) are attested in numerous Mahāyāna sources; see, e.g., BCA 8.90ff. Cf. Dayal (1932: 79) for other sources and discussion. See also Jenkins (1999: 61), who notes that in the bodhisattva's recognition of the equality of self and others, "self and other are not ontologically negated or dissolved here as ethical categories." Rather than seeing an abnegation of his own aims, the bodhisattva's activity is characterized as (80) "enlightened other-interest, according to which the most extreme altruism results in the supreme fruition of the ultimate self-interest."

316. If the aims of self and other cannot be easily distinguished, then what about the śrāvakas and pratyekabuddhas who in Mahāyāna discourse are traditionally said to fulfill their own aims and not those of others? Kamalaśīla would probably answer this question by reference to the *ekayāna* ("one-vehicle") view of the Buddhist path, according to which even śrāvakas and pratyekabuddhas eventually join the bodhisattva lineage and attain full-fledged buddhahood. In this view, śrāvakas and pratyekabuddhas enter a kind of false nirvāṇa, from which they are eventually roused by compassionate buddhas, who incite and encourage them to complete the bodhisattva practices and to attain the true awakening of a full-fledged buddha. In other words, even śrāvakas and pratyekabuddhas are destined for buddhahood. The future buddhahood of these figures does not, however, imply the equality of their lineages with that of the bodhisattva, as the commitment to others' aims that is the bodhisattva's special motivation ensures that the bodhisattva will help many *more* sentient beings to eliminate ignorance, both because the bodhisattva will attain full-fledged buddhahood (and omniscience) *sooner* and because, even before attaining buddhahood, the bodhisattva will be engaged in and focused on helping myriad sentient beings. Of course, even though bodhisattvas attain buddhahood sooner, the śrāvakas and so forth attain their specific "awakening of a śrāvaka and so on" sooner. See TSP *ad* TS 3432 (*atīndriyārthadarśiparīksā*, B 1082,11–17), which indicates that while the mind of a bodhisattva never ceases, the mind of a śrāvaka does come to an end (albeit, it would appear, an end from which they will eventually re-awaken through the urgings of a buddha) when he enters *parinirvāṇa*. For some further reflections on the length of time a śrāvaka will take to attain buddhahood, see Lopez 1992: 169–70. For Kamalaśīla's commitment to the *ekayāna* see, e.g., TSP *ad* TS 1916–17 (*lokāyataparīkṣā*, G 539,14–16; missing in B): *śrāvakapratyekabuddhayānayoś ca buddhaikayānaniṣṭhātvam āhuḥ / ekam evedaṃ yānaṃ yad uta mahāyānam iti vacanāt /*. See also the final section of his MĀ (D

the aims of self and other as distinct goals.[317] The *Tattvasaṃgraha* and the *Pañjikā* proceed without questioning the notion that the desire to fulfill the aims of others is the proper motivation for a judicious person.

The Two Obscurations

The upshot of all of this is that although non-bodhisattva Buddhist practitioners may attain a high level of realization concerning the nature of reality, they do not and cannot attain *maximal* epistemic greatness. This, of course, implies a continued presence of at least some degree of ignorance, some degree of sub-maximal epistemic greatness in such practitioners. This is made clear in the following passage in which Kamalaśīla comments on Śāntarakṣita's homage to the Buddha as "that omniscient one, who is the best of speakers:"[318]

237a4ff.), which offers a sustained explanation and defense of the *ekayāna* theory of the Buddhist path. On the *ekayāna* in general, see Ruegg 1969: 177–235 and Kunst 1977. Lopez (1992) also has a good summary that he derives from Tibetan sources. A typical expression of the idea that śrāvakas attain a kind of false nirvāṇa from which they must be roused is found in Candrakīrti's *Triśaraṇasaptati* 45–47, cited as well by Haribhadra in the AAA (Wogihara ed., 134): *labdhvā bodhidvayaṃ hy ete bhavād uttrastamānasāḥ / bhavanty āyuḥkṣayāt tuṣṭāḥ prāptanirvāṇasaṃjñinaḥ // na teṣām asti nirvāṇaṃ kiṃ tu janma bhavatraye / dhātau na vidyate teśāṃ te 'pi tiṣṭhanty anāsrave // akliṣṭājñānahānāya paścād buddhaiḥ prabodhitāḥ / saṃbhṛtya bodhisaṃbhārāṃs te 'pi syur lokanāyakāḥ //*. Note the reference to *akliṣṭājñāna*, on which see below, n. 327.

317. Williams (1998a: 104) describes Śāntideva's understanding of buddhahood as the fulfillment of a moral imperative as follows: "No one, I think, would deny that to remove one's own pain does not in itself count as a moral act, while to soothe the pains of others would in general count as engaging in actions which are morally virtuous. Our Buddhists however—Śāntideva and his commentators—want to argue that morality requires that I make no distinction at all between removing my own pain and soothing the pains of others, or, put another way, moral consistency requires that in acting to remove my own pain I must also act to remove the pains of others, and no *morally significant* distinction can be drawn between the two imperatives. We find Śāntideva arguing for this as part of his reasoning for the moral (and spiritual) transformation which is called *bodhicittotpāda*, the arising of the mind set on enlightenment, the mind which seeks perfect Buddhahood precisely because only perfect Buddhahood is finally the fulfillment of the moral imperative, the imperative to strive unceasingly to remove the sufferings of all sentient beings *without discrimination*." Although Williams goes on to argue against the possibility of leveling the moral playing field in this way, his analysis does accurately reflect the trend toward the blending of the aims of self and other that we find in many Mahāyāna systematic treatises, including the TS/P.

318. TS 6. For the Sanskrit and an English translation of TS 1–6, see above p. 96.

> [Objection:] Well, the bodhisattvas, śrāvakas, and others have also correctly taught dependent arising, so what is the Blessed One's superiority (*atiśaya*) in that regard? [Answer:] He says, "the best of speakers" and so on. For even if those śrāvakas and others teach dependent arising, nevertheless, it is the Blessed One alone who is the best, i.e., the foremost (*pradhāna*), speaker among them, because [those śrāvakas and others] promulgate the reality of the Dharma that was taught by the Blessed One alone, since they are not capable of teaching the above-described dependent arising independently. Or else, because of his mastery in the accomplishment of the perfection of good qualities and the destruction of faults, the Blessed One alone is the best and not these others, since they are the inverse of that. And this demonstration of the Blessed One's superiority over the śrāvakas and others illustrates the perfection of his own aim (*svārthasaṃpat*), which is defined as the total elimination of the afflictive and the epistemic obscurations together with their imprints. Otherwise, in what sense would the Blessed One be superior to them, if he did not possess the above-mentioned qualities? For this very reason [Śāntarakṣita] says "that omniscient one"; and this is an allusion to [the final chapter of the work,] the "Proof of Omniscience" (*sarvajñasiddhi*).[319]

In addition to serving to connect Śāntarakṣita's praise in the opening verses with the final chapter of the work as a whole, this passage confirms that omniscience, represented by the phrase "the total elimination of the afflictive and the epistemic obscurations together with their imprints,"[320] constitutes the Buddha's perfection of his own aim. It also confirms, in accord with

319. TSP *ad* TS 1–6 (B 20,7–15): *nanu cāviparītaḥ pratītyasamutpādo bodhisattvaśrāvakādibhir api nirdiṣṭas tat ko 'trātiśayo bhagavataḥ / ity āha / gadatāṃvara iti / yady api te śrāvakādayaḥ pratītyasamutpādaṃ gadanti tathāpi bhagavān eva teṣāṃ gadatāṃ varaḥ / pradhānam / bhagavadupadiṣṭasyaiva dharmatattvasya prakāśanān na hi teṣāṃ svato yathoktapratītyasamutpādadeśanāyāṃ śaktir asti / sarvaguṇadoṣaprakarṣāpakarṣaniṣṭhādhiṣṭhānatvād vā bhagavān eva śreṣṭho netare teṣāṃ tadviparītatvāt / etena ca bhagavataḥ śrāvakādibhyo viśeṣatvapratipādanena savāsanāśeṣakleśajñeyāvaraṇaprahāṇalakṣaṇā svārthasampat paridīpitā bhavati / anyathā katham iva tebhyo viśiṣṭo bhaved yadi yathoktaguṇayogitā na syād bhagavataḥ / ata evāha / taṃ sarvajñam iti / ayaṃ ca sarvajñasiddhyupakṣepaḥ /.*

320. As Kamalaśīla has said, "omniscience comes about through the elimination of the afflictive and the epistemic obscurations"; TSP *ad* TS 3337 (*atīndriyārthadarśiparīkṣā*, B 1052,22–22): *kleśajñeyāvaraṇaprahāṇato hi sarvajñatvam /.*

a pervasive Mahāyāna scheme, that while awakened śrāvakas and pratyekabuddhas eliminate the *overt* functioning of ignorance, they do *not* eliminate the *subtle traces* or *imprints* (*vāsanā*) of their previous ignorance (and other afflictions), which remain latent in their mindstreams.[321] Although it is not obvious what precisely constitutes these imprints for Śāntarakṣita and Kamalaśīla, it is clear that they are closely connected with what we have thus far called the *epistemic obscuration*, the *jñeyāvaraṇa*, literally, the "obscuration of the knowable."[322]

Freedom from obscuration or obstruction is common as a way to account for maximal epistemic greatness in Indian religious thought. Jains, for example, generally accept that while the inherent nature of the soul (*jīva*) is knowing, this nature is obstructed in ordinary beings by a covering (*āvaraṇa*) of subtle karmic matter (*dravyakarma*).[323] Once the soul is purified of this karmic veil, the soul attains omniscience, "just as the sun shines in its full splendor when the cloud is removed."[324] Early Buddhist sources also characterize awakening as a process of removing obstruction or obscuration, although they do not appear to understand the obstruction to be necessarily substantial or material in nature.[325] In many Buddhist sources, especially those associated with the systematic treatises of the Mahāyāna, maximal epistemic greatness comes about through the attainment of two freedoms: freedom from the *kleśāvaraṇa*, or afflictive obscuration, and freedom from the *jñeyāvaraṇa*, or

321. See Lamotte (1974), who cites various Mahāyāna and non-Mahāyāna sources that discuss the imprints (*vāsanā*) of afflictions lingering in the mindstreams of arhats (though not buddhas), so that they become like (94) "a prisoner long laden with chains and who, once freed, continues to have a hesitant step" or "a baby's swaddling clothes which have been soiled for a long time and which, even when cleaned, retain the smell of the stains."

322. The term *jñeyāvaraṇa* at first appears structurally similar to the term *kleśāvaraṇa*. But whereas in the case of the *kleśāvaraṇa*, it is easy to understand the compound as a *karmadhārya* compound having the meaning "an obscuration that consists in afflictions," a parallel understanding of *jñeyāvaraṇa* would appear bizarre. For a discussion of some glosses of the compound in various Yogācāra treatises, see Griffiths et al. 1989: 65–66n10.

323. The early Jain author Umāsvāti details the theory of *jñeyāvaraṇa* in his *Tattvārthasūtra*, chap. 8.

324. Singh 1974: 118.

325. See, e.g., *Sutta Nipāta* 6.1.1005a, 193: *anāvaraṇadassāvī yadi buddho bhavissati/*. Cited in Scherrer-Schaub 1991: 104n6. Buddhist accounts of the connection between omniscience and the freedom from obstruction are seen in such Pāli texts as the *Paṭisambhidāmagga* and Dhammapāla's commentary on the *Visuddhimagga*, the *Paramatthamañjūsā*. For discussions and references see Jaini 1974: 83–85 and Kher 1972: 176.

epistemic obscuration.[326] Of these two freedoms, the second is attained only by full-fledged buddhas, and it represents an utter and thorough cleansing of even the traces of ignorance, as a result of which buddhas attain truly *maximal* epistemic greatness, omniscience.[327] This general picture corresponds to what we find in the works of Śāntarakṣita and Kamalaśīla as well.[328]

326. For a typical passage from the Yogācāra corpus, see *Bodhisattvabhūmi* (ed. Dutt: 62): *tatra dvividhaṃ prahāṇam / kleśāvaraṇaprahāṇaṃ jñeyāvaraṇaprahāṇaṃ ca / dvividhaṃ punar jñānaṃ yat kleśāvaraṇaprahāṇāc ca nirmalaṃ sarvakleśaniranubandhajñānam / jñeyāvaraṇaprahāṇāc ca yat sarvasmin jñeye 'pratihatam anāvaraṇaṃ jñānam /*. "Abandonment is twofold in that [i.e., in awakening]: there is the abandonment of the afflictive obscuration and the abandonment of the epistemic obscuration. Knowledge is also twofold: there is the stainless knowledge free from the fetters of all afflictions, which comes about through the abandonment of the afflictive obscuration; and there is the unobscured knowledge unobstructed with regard to all knowable [things], which comes about through the abandonment of the epistemic obscuration." Cf. also MSA (Levi: 44): *kleśajñeyāvaraṇadvayāt sarvadharmatathatāviśuddhilakṣaṇaḥ /*. "Buddha's defining characteristic is the purification of the actuality of all things from the two obstacles: those of affliction and those which obstruct objects of awareness"; translation by Griffiths (1994: 76). Note also that, although this twofold taxonomy of obscuration is most evident in Mahāyāna sources, it is not exclusive to them: it is mentioned, for instance, in the *Mahāvibhāṣā*; see Jaini 1992: 144n14.

327. In some cases, one finds a similar distinction, cast in terms of an afflictive ignorance (*kliṣṭājñāna*) that is eliminated by the arhats and pratyekabuddhas and a non-afflictive ignorance (*akliṣṭājñāna*) that is eliminated only by full-fledged buddhas. See, e.g., AKBh *ad* AK 1.1 and Yaśomitra's SA *ad cit.*, where the *akliṣṭājñāna* is said to remain present (*samudācarati*) in the śrāvakas and pratyekabuddhas, despite having being abandoned (*prahīṇa*) by them. For the Buddha, on the other hand, the *akliṣṭājñāna* is both abandoned and utterly removed or absent from his mindstream. For a useful discussion of this and related passages, see Jaini 1992: 135–41. Authors who specifically connect the elimination of the *jñeyāvaraṇa* with the elimination of *akliṣṭājñāna* include Sthiramati (see Jaini 1992: 144n15), Bhāviveka (see Lopez 1988a: 67–84), Candrakīrti (see above, n. 316), and Jayānanda (MAvT *ad* MAv 6.28: D146a).

328. So far, I have found no direct references to the two obscurations in the works of Dignāga and Dharmakīrti, although the basic structure of a further degree of purification and attainment in the case of buddhas vis-à-vis śrāvakas and pratyekabuddhas is clearly present. The discussion in both authors centers on a certain "remainder" (*śeṣa*) that buddhas alone eliminate, and through which buddhas are distinguished from other advanced Buddhist practitioners. In PSV *ad* PS 1.1, Dignāga delineates three meanings of the term *sugata*, each of which indicates the Buddha's superiority over a different type of being. The third meaning is that of being "complete" (*niḥśeṣārtha*), and Dignāga states that this aspect of *sugatatva* shows the Buddha's superiority over "those who have completed their learning" (*aśaikṣa*). As Hattori (1968: 75n6) points out, the term *aśaikṣa* is used in AKBh to refer to the figure of an arhat, "because he has extinguished the influence of passions (*āsrava-kṣaya*) and no longer needs religious training." Thus, although it is not entirely

Let us consider in greater detail what Kamalaśīla means when he asserts that omniscience "comes about through the elimination of the afflictive and the epistemic obscurations." One of his clearest statements occurs in the following passage:

> Omniscience comes about through the elimination of the afflictive and the epistemic obscurations. Here, the afflictions are passion and so on. They are called the *afflictive obscuration* because they block the vision of what is real. And when a person sees the reality of that which is to be abandoned and that which is to be taken up but does not know it in all of its aspects (*sarvākārāparijñāna*) and is not capable of explaining it to others, that is the *epistemic obscuration*. In that case, because one has directly realized selflessness, there is the elimination of the afflictive obscuration. But the [elimination] of the epistemic obscuration for one who has seen selflessness comes about through the intensive, continuous, and long-term cultivation [of that realization].[329]

Several important elements are presented in this passage. In the first place, and rather obviously, we learn here that removal of the afflictive obscuration entails removal of the afflictions, or *kleśas*. The *kleśas*, which we could also translate as "defilements" or even "troubles," are extremely numerous, but in most Buddhist presentations they can be reduced to three types, sometimes called the *three poisons* (*viṣatraya*): attachment (*rāga*), hatred (*dveṣa*), and

clear what it is about a buddha's attainment that marks it as "complete" for Dignāga, we do know that, as in the case of the elimination of the *jñeyāvaraṇa*, this attainment brings an advancement to a level beyond that of the ordinary arhat. In PV 2, which is often cast as a commentary on PS 1.1, Dharmakīrti also discusses the buddha's superiority in terms of these same three meanings. In PV 2.141bcd–142a, he describes the remainder (*śeṣa*) that buddhas eliminate as consisting in "non-afflictive and non-feverous faults of body, speech, and mind or else the lack of skill in explaining the path," stating that it is "utterly destroyed through practice" (*śeṣam akleśanirjvaram / kāyavāgbuddhivaiguṇyaṃ mārgoktyapaṭutā 'pi vā // aśeṣahānam abhyāsād* ...). Although he does not use the term *jñeyāvaraṇa*, the "remainder" to which Dharmakīrti refers resonates strongly with the epistemic obscuration as understood by Kamalaśīla.

329. TSP *ad* TS 3337 (*atīndriyārthadarśiparīkṣā*, B 1052,21–1053,1): *kleśajñeyāvaraṇaprahāṇato hi sarvajñatvam / tatra kleśā eva rāgādayo bhūtadarśanapratibandhabhāvāt kleśāvaraṇam ucyante / dṛṣṭasyāpi heyopādeyatattvasya yat sarvākārāparijñānaṃ pratipādanāsāmarthyaṃ ca taj jñeyāvaraṇam / tatra kleśāvaraṇasya nairātmyapratyakṣīkaraṇāt prahāṇiḥ / jñeyāvaraṇasya tu tasyaiva nairātmyadarśanasya sādaranirantaradīrghakālābhyāsāt /.*

confusion/ignorance (*moha, avidyā*).[330] Of these three poisons, ignorance is the most basic, for without it the other two are not possible. Given their close dependence on ignorance, it is not surprising to find Kamalaśīla stating that the *kleśa*s "block the vision of what is real."

The vision of what is real is the vision of selflessness (*nairātmyadarśana*), and we know from other passages that the authors hold this vision of selflessness to be the antidote (*pratipakṣa*) to ignorance and therefore to all the afflictions.[331] Now, in the passage above, when Kamalaśīla employs the phrase "that which is to be abandoned and that which is to be taken up" (*heyopādeya*), he means by it all and whatever is necessary to attain liberation, in other words, all soteriologically relevant knowledge.[332] Gaining such knowledge can only occur through the application of the antidote to ignorance, and one effectuates this through the production of a direct realization (*pratyakṣīkaraṇa*) of selflessness (*nairātmya*). This direct realization or vision (*darśana*) of selflessness eliminates the afflictive obscuration, according to the passage above. However, as the passage also indicates, one may destroy the *kleśāvaraṇa* without at the same time destroying the *jñeyāvaraṇa*.[333] Two signs indicate that

330. On the large number of *kleśa*s in some Buddhist treatises, see Cox (1992: 68), who notes, for example, that one early Abhidharma work "begins its discussion of defilements (*kleśa*) by listing over 530 individual defilements or categories of unvirtuous factors (*akuśaladharma*)." See May 1959: n226 for references concerning various classifications of the *kleśa*s.

331. See, e.g., TSP *ad* TS 3342 (*atīndriyārthadarśiparīkṣā*, B 1063,15–16): *tathā hy atra rāgādirūpaṃ tatprabhavaṃ cādharmam uddiśya tatprahāṇāya tannidānātmadarśanavirodhena nairātmyadarśanam eva pratipakṣo deśitaḥ* /. "That is, he first explained the nature of attachment and so on and the nonvirtue that arises from it. Then, in order to eliminate that [attachment and its effect] by means of what contradicts the vision of a self that is that cause of that [attachment], he taught the antidote, which is just the vision of selflessness." The reading *cādharmam* in place of B and G: *vā dharmam* is based on D, vol. *'e*, 302a6–7: *de ltar 'dod chag la sogs pa'i ngo bo dang chos ma yin pa de las byung bar bstan nas*.... See also pp. 319–20 for a translation of this passage in its larger context.

332. The original source for the formulation *heyopādeya* is not certain, although it is clear that the general idea is not restricted to the Buddhist tradition. In NBh *ad* NS 1.1.24, the idea of what is to be avoided and what is to be taken up is connected with one's purpose or aim (*prayojana*), and the action (*pravṛtti*) one takes in relation to that aim is called the means (*upāya*): *yam artham āptavyaṃ hātavyaṃ vādhyavasāya tadāptihānopāyam anutiṣṭhati prayojanaṃ tad veditavyam* /. "One should know the aim to be that goal (*artha*) for which, having determined it as something that should be obtained or avoided, one implements the means (*upāya*) to obtain or avoid it."

333. This reading of Kamalaśīla's position would seem to contradict the claim, found in some Tibetan doxographical sources, that Śāntarakṣita and Kamalaśīla, as members of the so-called Yogācāra-Svātantrika school of Madhyamaka thought, maintain that

one has yet to remove the epistemic obscuration: (a) one does not know what is to be abandoned and what is to be taken up *in all ways*, or *in terms of all aspects* (*ākāra*); and (b) one cannot adequately convey all that is soteriologically relevant to others. These two signs stand in a causal relationship: that is, not being a maximally efficacious teacher is the result of not knowing the soteriologically relevant in all ways or aspects.

What does Kamalaśīla mean when he says that eliminating the *jñeyāvaraṇa* results in one knowing the soteriologically relevant in terms of all aspects or *ākāras*? On my reading, when Kamalaśīla uses the term *sarvākārajña* and related constructions,[334] he does so in order to highlight certain facets of a buddha's omniscience that are of prime importance for the authors. Unlike the simple term *sarvajña*, the term *sarvākārajña* reminds the listener or reader of the thoroughgoing nature of the Buddha's epistemic greatness: that is, it is a greatness that arises through a thorough-going removal of the *jñeyāvaraṇa*, and that entails a thorough-going maximal efficacy for accomplishing others' aims by teaching them the path to awakening. Teaching others "in all ways" (*sarvākāreṇa*) can thus be taken as evidence that one has gained "knowledge

---

the *kleśāvaraṇa* and the *jñeyāvaraṇa* are destroyed simultaneously only at the end of the path (i.e., at the end of the tenth *bodhisattvabhūmi*). This is in contrast with what these same sources hold to be the Prāsaṅgika Madhyamaka position, in which the *kleśāvaraṇa* is destroyed first (at the end of the seventh *bodhisattvabhūmi*) and the *jñeyāvaraṇa* is destroyed subsequently (at the end of the tenth *bodhisattvabhūmi*). See, e.g., Lopez (1988b: 200–206), who draws on both Candrakīrti's presentation of the ten *bhūmis* in the *Madhyamakāvatāra* and that of Kamalaśīla in the first *Bhāvanākrama*. Lopez maintains (200) that "Kamalaśīla's exposition in the first *Bhāvanākrama* does not differ significantly from that of Candrakīrti." In a note, however, he states that (215n91) "They differ on one significant point." He then refers us to another note (216n105) in which he cites the doxographical presentation of the seventeenth-century Dge lugs pa author 'Jam dbyangs bzhad pa along the lines just mentioned as evidence for the distinction; he does not, however, point to anything from Kamalaśīla's original text. My research so far has revealed nothing to support this Tibetan claim, and it is possible that the position has been attributed to Śāntarakṣita and Kamalaśīla due to their perceived connection to their contemporary Haribhadra, who is also classed by the same doxographers as a Yogācāra-Svātantrika Mādhyamika.

334. Kamalaśīla employs the term, among other places, at MAP (Ichigō ed. 9 and 11), where he does not appear to intend by it anything substantially different from what he signals by the more usual words, such as *sarvajña*, for an omniscient being. In this sense, his use of the term *sarvākārajña* does not parallel that of his contemporary Mādhyamika, Haribhadra, who makes a strong distinction between the two forms of omniscience in his commentaries on the AA, on which see Obermiller 1933a. For a discussion of the terms *sarvajña* and *sarvākārajña* in the MSA, see Griffiths 1990.

...ll aspects” (*sarvākārajña*), as Kamalaśīla makes clear in an important passage to which we shall later return:

> And since he expounded the four truths through diverse means, one can infer that his knowledge is complete (*aśeṣa*) because he has eliminated the remainder (*śeṣa*) that is characterized by the inability to expound one’s knowledge in all ways. For one who does not know the good qualities and faults [of things] in all their aspects and one who is not skillful in making them known cannot expound [those topics] in such a manner [i.e., as extensively and thoroughly as the Buddha has done].[335]

Removing the epistemic obscuration is what allows one to become a maximally skillful teacher, and it is this pedagogical and soteriological aspect of omniscience that is highlighted by the use of the term “knowing all aspects” in the *Tattvasaṃgraha* and the *Pañjikā*.

As Kamalaśīla also clarifies in the passage presented earlier above, the removal of the *jñeyāvaraṇa* comes about through an “intensive, continuous, and long-term cultivation” of the vision or realization of selflessness. The picture of the Buddhist path that emerges is one in which the bodhisattva eliminates the *kleśāvaraṇa* through a direct realization of selflessness and subsequently goes on to eliminate the *jñeyāvaraṇa* through an intensive and long period of cultivation of that initial realization. Śāntarakṣita has said:

> And due to a special kind of direct realization, neither the fault nor its imprint exists. Therefore omniscience is established since there is freedom from all obscurations.[336]

335. TSP *ad* TS 3339 (*atīndriyārthadarśiparīkṣā*, B 1062,9–12): *vicitraiś copāyaiś catuḥsatyaprakāśanād aśeṣajñānam asyānumīyate / śeṣasya sarvākārajñānapratipādanāsāmarthyalakṣaṇasya prahāṇāt / na hy aviditasarvākāraguṇadoṣas tatpratipādanākuśalaś ca tathā pratipādayati /*. This passage is part of a longer inference in which the teachings of the Buddha are proposed as evidence of his omniscience. This inference is the subject of chapter 5 below. See also n. 328 above for a similar use of the term remainder (*śeṣa*) in the works of Dignāga and Dharmakīrti.

336. TS 3338 (*atīndriyārthadarśiparīkṣā*): *sākṣātkṛtiviśeṣāc ca doṣo nāsti savāsanaḥ / sarvajñatvam ataḥ siddhaṃ sarvāvaraṇamuktitaḥ //*. Cf. also TSP *ad* TS 3512–14 (*atīndriyārthadarśiparīkṣā*, B 1099,22) where nirvāṇa is characterized as “the attainment of the pacification of all afflictions and their imprints” (*prāptasavāsanāśeṣakleśopaśamalakṣaṇanirvāṇapada*).

Kamalaśīla clarifies in his commentary that a "special kind of direct realization" means a realization that has been continuously and intensely cultivated for a long time. Whether the imprints mentioned are themselves the *jñeyāvaraṇa*, or whether they are merely a part of it, there is no doubt they must be eliminated to attain omniscience. The main point is that it is not sufficient simply to produce the vision of selflessness in one's mindstream to attain the goal of omniscience. Rather, one must cultivate that initial vision of selflessness in such a way that it becomes utterly integral to one's mindstream. Only then will one know the soteriologically relevant in all its aspects, thus enabling one to teach others with a maximal efficacy that corresponds with the maximal greatness of the bodhisattva's intention to fulfill the aims of others, in other words, with her great compassion.

Summary

The preceding section has been an attempt to gather together and briefly examine those inherited ideas concerning omniscience in the *Tattvasaṃgraha* and the *Pañjikā* that, following Hadot with some reservations, I refer to as *dogmas*. These are fundamental ideas that the authors cannot reject without leaving the fold of the tradition within which they work. As I hope has been made clear, these ideas need not be accepted through mere blind allegiance to the revered traditions. At the same time, if these dogmas are perceived to present problems for the interpreters, it is required that those problems be resolved in a way that the ideas are preserved, at least in a nominal fashion.

We have so far exposed the following dogmas concerning buddhahood and omniscience in the *Tattvasaṃgraha* and the *Pañjikā*: (1) omniscience, meaning maximal epistemic greatness, is a necessary quality of buddhahood; (2) great compassion, or maximal moral greatness, is a necessary prerequisite for attaining omniscience; (3) as a symbol or emblem of buddhahood, omniscience involves the twofold perfection of the aims of both oneself and others; (4) the attainment of omniscience occurs through the removal of obscurations in a manner that surpasses their removal by non-bodhisattva practitioners; (5) specifically, omniscience is attained through the removal of the afflictive and the epistemic obscurations together with their imprints, which itself is achieved through the long, continuous, and intense meditation on the antidote to ignorance, the vision of selflessness; (6) the resulting omniscience may be called "knowledge of all aspects" because it is maximally great in terms of what is known as well as in its ability to convey that soteriologically relevant knowledge to a maximal number of suffering beings.

Delineating these dogmas gives us crucial information about the religious context in which the authors write. Since omniscience is the goal of these treatises, as well as of the path that the authors advocate, it is necessary to understand why the authors think omniscience is important and how they believe it may come about. The dogmas concerning compassion and the two obscurations give us some insight into these matters. But the delineation of these dogmas still does not tell us what omniscience actually *is* for these authors. To discover that, it is necessary that we more carefully examine both the central terms and arguments for omniscience in the *Tattvasaṃgraha* and the *Pañjikā*. These tasks form the focus of the remainder of this book.

Once again, the treatises' rhetorical complexity presents an immediate challenge. As we have seen, the *Tattvasaṃgraha* and the *Pañjikā* frequently refrain from directly presenting their final view on any given matter. Instead, they proceed in stages of argument using the sliding scale of analysis, in dependence on the presuppositions of various addressees, in order to convince opponents in a step-by-step fashion through addressing their particular objections and concerns. One consequence of this method is a plasticity of meaning in relation to a variety of terms, including, and quite conspicuously, the terms for omniscience. Opportunities for confusion are rife, and to avoid the more obvious of them, we should now consider the two most significant connotations of the various terms for omniscience at play in these works.

Connotations

The principal term for omniscience in the *Tattvasaṃgraha* and the *Pañjikā* is *sarvajñatva*, although other words with an equivalent lexical meaning (e.g., *sarvajñatā*, *sarvavittva*, and *sarvavijñānatva*) occur as well. The term *sarvajña* refers generally to an omniscient person, in other words, one who possesses omniscience, or *sarvajñatva*, although occasionally, where syntax requires it, I translate even *sarvajña* by the more abstract English expression *omniscience*. Even as a technical term in the *Tattvasaṃgraha* and the *Pañjikā*, *sarvajñatva* does not refer to a single conception of epistemic maximal greatness but rather (and quite confusingly) to a variety of conceptions. As always, care must be taken to determine which meaning is intended in a given context.

We have already glimpsed briefly in the introduction the variation in what *sarvajñatva* can mean in the Indian and Buddhist traditions in general. Many of these diverse significations occur in the *Tattvasaṃgraha* and the *Pañjikā*, but among them two have particular prominence. These two are (1) a connotation in which omniscience refers primarily to the knowledge of all that is soteriologically relevant and (2) a connotation in which omniscience signifies a thoroughgoing knowledge of everything that can possibly be known. The distinction has its roots in Dharmakīrti's previous demonstration of the Buddha's "authority" or "trustworthiness" (*prāmāṇya, pramāṇatā*) in the "Pramāṇasiddhi" chapter of his *Pramāṇavārttika*, a chapter that has clearly inspired much of Śāntarakṣita and Kamalaśīla's thinking on maximal greatness.[337] Later, in the tenth and eleventh centuries, the Buddhist philosophers Jñānaśrīmitra and Ratnakīrti would use the technical terms *upayuktasarvajña* ("knowing all that is useful") and *sarvasarvajña* ("knowing everything whatsoever") for these two connotations of omniscience.[338] In the *Tattvasaṃgraha* and the *Pañjikā*, the two connotations are not indicated by distinct terms but nonetheless may be understood through clues in the contexts where the terms *sarvajñatva* and *sarvajña* occur. In this book, I refer to the two connotations as *dharmic omniscience* and *total omniscience.*

We have already encountered the key elements in the idea of dharmic omniscience above, when we observed Kamalaśīla say that a person who has eliminated the afflictive but not the epistemic obscuration "sees the reality of that which is to be abandoned and that which is to be taken up." Here, the "reality of what is to be abandoned and what is to be taken up" (*heyopādeyatattva*) is a shorthand way of referring to everything that is necessary to attain both elevation (*abhyudaya*) and the highest good (*niḥśreyasa*)—also known as the

337. A growing body of secondary literature treats the problem of what it means for a teacher to be an authority in the Buddhist epistemological tradition. Much of this literature focuses on the question of how to interpret the problematic term *pramāṇabhūta*, which occurs in Dignāga's *maṅgalaśloka* of the PS as well as in Dharmakīrti's PV 2. As the term is not prevalent in the TS/P, I will not enter this debate in this book. I will, however, take up the question of the Buddha's authority and its connection with omniscience in chapter 6 below. Secondary works that discuss the term *pramāṇabhūta* and the related term *pramāṇapuruṣa* (*tshad ma'i skye bu*) include: Dunne 2004; Franco 1997; Hayes 1984; Jackson 1988; Krasser 2001; Ruegg 1994a, 1994b, 1995b; Silk 2002; Steinkellner 1983, 1994; Tillemans 1993; van Bijlert 1989; van der Kuijp 1999; and Vetter 1964.

338. Bühnemann (1980: 92n9) attests that she was able to locate these terms only in the works of Jñānaśrīmitra and Ratnakīrti, although she does note that the term *sarvasarvajñatā* appears in a quotation preserved in the *Tantrālokaviveka*, a commentary on the Kashmiri Śaivite Abhinavagupta's *Tantrāloka*. Despite the rarity of the terms, however, there can be no doubt concerning the long-standing tradition of presenting two distinct connotations for the term *sarvajña* in the Buddhist tradition. As Bühnemann explains (1980: 93n9), the technical terms *upayuktasarvajña* and *sarvasarvajña* probably arose in relation to the practical need of later Buddhists to differentiate these two connotations clearly: "Die Ausdrücke sind deshalb entstanden, weil man ursprünglich nur vom *sarvajña* gesprochen hat und erst durch die Diskussion die Differenzierung notwendig wurde."

pair "heaven and liberation" (*svargāpavarga*)—which are understood here, as in many Indian traditions, to be the natural and appropriate goals of judicious persons. Earlier, we referred to this complex as "soteriologically relevant knowledge."

But mere knowledge of what is to be abandoned and what is to be taken up does not by itself bring about liberation; one also needs knowledge of the means by which one may abandon what is to be abandoned and take up what is to be taken up. To convey this idea, Śāntarakṣita and Kamalaśīla follow Dharmakīrti in qualifying the soteriologically relevant knowledge with the words "together with their means."[339] For a bodhisattva, who is motivated by great compassion, the "means" necessary to achieve the "end" (the highest good) must include the means to achieve the highest good *for all sentient beings* and not only for oneself alone. Naturally, this implies that the means includes the ability to teach sentient beings about what is to be abandoned and what is to be taken up together with the means for doing so. All of this counts as dharmic or soteriologically relevant omniscience.

The second connotation of *sarvajñatva*, that of total omniscience, signifies a state in which one knows all things whatsoever. At first blush, this sounds very much like the kind of omniscience often attributed to God in theistic traditions, although as in those traditions, it is not always obvious what this kind of total omniscience entails for the Buddhists who subscribe to it. As is well known, Dharmakīrti was adamant that only the first type of epistemic maximal greatness—that of dharmic omniscience—is required in order to accept a teacher as an authority. The key verses from the second chapter of the *Pramāṇavārttika* are as follows:

> Some people say that authority (*prāmāṇya*) consists in knowing things that are remote, and since there is no means to attain that [kind of knowledge], there is no accomplishment [of that state].

339. The usual formation in the TS/P, inspired by Dharmakīrti's verse at PV 2.32 (translated just below, p. 135), is *sābhyupāyaheyopādeyatattvajñāna*, literally "knowledge of the reality of what is to be abandoned and what is to be taken up together with their means." See, e.g., TSP *ad* TS 3339 (*atīndriyārthadarśiparīkṣā*, B 1061,22–23): *tasyānayā deśanayā sābhyupāyaheyopādeyatattvasthirāśeṣajñānaṃ sādhyate* /. "This teaching proves his [i.e., the Buddha's] stable and complete knowledge of the reality of that which is to be abandoned and that which is to be taken up together with their means." Cf. also PV 1.217: *heyopādeyatattvasya sopāyasya prasiddhitaḥ / pradhānārthāvisaṃvādād anumānaṃ paratra vā* //. Most commentaries on PV interpret the phrase *sābhyupāyaheyopādeyatattva* as representing the nobles' four truths. See, for example, Devendrabuddhi's comments (PVP, D 15b1ff.).

> [This is not correct.] One seeks some wise person so as to put into practice what that person has taught. Those who suspect that they will be misled if the instruction is the work of an ignorant person should investigate that person's knowledge of that which is to be practiced. Of what use to us is that person's knowledge of the number of bugs [in the world]? One who knows the reality of that which is to be abandoned and that which is to be taken up, together with their means, is asserted to be a means of trustworthy awareness (*pramāṇa*); not, however, one who knows everything. Whether the person sees far or not, let him see the desired reality! If one who sees far is a means of trustworthy awareness, then come, let us show reverence to the vultures![340]

In these rather humorous lines, Dharmakīrti clearly ridicules the notion that religious authority must be grounded in total omniscience. To the contrary, what is important is only that a teacher have the sort of dharmic omniscience that allows him or her to know everything necessary for the attainment of liberation together with the means for doing so. Apparently, in Dharmakīrti's view, this is something that the Buddha can be shown to have; but there is no need or requirement to demonstrate the Buddha's knowledge of such arcane items as the number of bugs in the world.

Assessing Dharmakīrti's Position on Total Omniscience

Some modern commentators have seen in Dharmakīrti's verses an outright rejection of total omniscience.[341] Most, however, have held the verses to

340. PV 2.29–33: *prāmāṇyaṃ ca parokṣārthajñānaṃ tatsādhanasya ca / abhāvān nāsty anuṣṭhānam iti kecit pracakṣate // jñānavān mṛgyate kaścit taduktapratipattaye / ajñopadeśakaraṇe vipralambhanaśaṅkibhiḥ // tasmād anuṣṭheyagataṃ jñānam asya vicāryatām / koṭisaṃkhyāparijñānaṃ tasya naḥ kvopayujyate // heyopādeyatattvasya sābhyupāyasya vedakaḥ / yaḥ pramāṇam asāv iṣṭo na tu sarvasya vedakaḥ // dūraṃ paśyatu vā mā vā tattvam iṣṭan tu paśyatu / pramāṇaṃ dūradarśī ced eta gṛdhrān upāsmahe /.*

341. Singh (1974: 40), for example, states that Dharmakīrti "ridicules the idea of total omniscience," an attitude he contrasts with that of later Buddhists like Śāntarakṣita, whom he suggests were prompted by the challenge posed by the Jain endorsement of total omniscience to "define and prove Buddha's omniscience in terms of knowledge of all objects of all the times." I think Singh has missed the rhetorical force of Dharmakīrti's verses: they do contain scorn; that scorn, however, is not for the idea of the Buddha's omniscience but rather for the idea that one would seek a religious authority on the basis of total, as opposed to dharmic, omniscience. The notion that Dharmakīrti is responding

express a more modest position: that of a *nihil obstat*, or perhaps an indifference, to total omniscience, which can neither be affirmed nor denied by those of ordinary vision.[342] A passage in the *Pramāṇaviniścaya*, however, suggests that Dharmakīrti did accept or at least acknowledge an argument in support of a certain kind of total omniscience. The argument emerges in response to an objection to Dharmakīrti's position that real things (*vastu*) are characterized by their capacity for causal function (*arthakriyāsāmarthya*). The objector states that in this definition, the final moment of an arhat's mindstream would not be a real thing, since it does not produce an effect and thus has no causal function. Dharmakīrti rejects this analysis, on the grounds that the final moment of an arhat's mindstream *does* have an effect: at the very least, it is the cause for the arisal of an awareness in the Buddha's mind that has that final moment of the arhat's mindstream as its object. The objector then suggests that if the Buddha were not paying attention to that particular arhat at that particular time, then the last moment of the arhat's mind would *not* give rise to even the minimal effect of producing an awareness in the Buddha's cognition. Dharmakīrti responds that it is impossible for a buddha not to be paying attention to all things at all times, for otherwise he might miss something necessary—something to be abandoned or something to be taken up—in his quest to help sentient beings.[343]

---

to a Jain position on omniscience is supported by Sin (2000), who argues that the target of several of Dharmakīrti's attacks is Samantabhadra.

342. McDermott 1978: 146; Jackson 1991: 234; Shah 1967: 234. In a later article, Jackson (1999: 489) suggests that Dharmakīrti may well have eschewed such an extraordinary picture of the Buddha's knowledge and capacities, although he acknowledges that this is far from certain: "It seems . . . Dharmakīrti may *not* have regarded the Buddha as fundamentally eternal, omniscient, or non-conceptual, but, rather, simply as the sort of being who has veridical cognitions regarding what is to be avoided or adopted by those intent on freedom—whether this reflects Dharmakīrti's full view or simply his *minimal* description is not, however, clear." That Dharmakīrti holds that omniscience is not amenable to being determined by persons of ordinary vision can be gleaned from his use of the omniscient person as an example in illustrating various logical fallacies in his NB 3.68–71 and 3.93–96.

343. PVin 2 *ad* PVin 2.55 (Steinkellner ed., 2007: 79): *nanv idam apy aniśceyam eva / sarvasāmagrījanmāno naśyantīti / tāsām aniḥśeṣadarśanāt / vicitraśaktayo hi sāmagryo dṛśyante / tatra kācit syād api yā 'naśvarātmānaṃ janayet / na / arthakriyāśaktilakṣaṇatvād vastunaḥ / sarvasāmarthyopākhyāvirahalakṣaṇaṃ hi nirupākhyam // caram asya tarhi kṣaṇasyānupākhyatāprasaṅgaḥ / na / sattvasaṅkhyātakṣaṇāntarānupādānatālakṣaṇatvāc caramatvasya / bhavaty eva hi tasyāpi jñeyavyāpini jñāne 'ntaśaḥ sāmarthyaṃ virūpe 'pi dhātau / dhātvantare tv anekopakāra eva syāt / anābhoge 'sāmarthyam iti ced / na / anābhogāsambhavāt / ekadharmasyāpy ajñāne parārthavṛtteḥ kāryākāryānavabodhāt /*

because it is devoid of the capacity for causal function but rather because not all of the contributing conditions necessary for its effect to come about

---

sarvatra śaṅkotpatteḥ / sarvasya kvacit kathañcid upakārāt / tad ajñāne tad aṅgavikalatvād akṣūṇavidhānāyogāt /. "[Objection:] The statement 'all that is produced from a collection [of causes] is destroyed' is not certain, because their complete passing away is not observed. For collections are observed to have various capacities, and among them there may also be some that would produce [entities] with an imperishable nature. [Answer:] That is not correct, because the definition of a real thing is to be capable of causal function. That which is characterized as devoid of all possibility of capacity is nonexistent (*nirupākhya*). [Objection:] Well then, at the final moment [of an arhat's mindstream, that sentient being] would become nonexistent. [Answer:] No, because the non-appropriation of another moment that is counted as a sentient being is the definition of the final moment. And even in the formless realm, that [final moment] minimally has the capacity to [be an object of] the wisdom that pervades knowable objects. In the other realms, it causally supports many [other effects]. [Objection:] If there is no attention, there will be no capacity. [Answer:] No, because it is not possible for there to be no attention: if even one *dharma* is not known, then when one acts for the sake of others' aims, one will not know what is to be done and what is not to be done. There would be doubt concerning everything, because [that which is not known] is somehow of benefit to something. If [the Buddha] does not know that, then because a necessary component will be lacking, it will not be right that he be one whose means are complete." My reading of this passage is influenced by Dharmottara's commentary on it at D, vol. *dze*, 244a1–244b7. Cf. also Steinkellner (1979, vol. 2: 89–92 and 150–51) and Sakai (2010: 143–53), who edits and translates the Sanskrit of Dharmottara's commentary. Jackson (1999: 505n48) states that he does not see "a completely unambiguous assertion of the Buddha's [total] omniscience" in this passage, although he does not offer an alternative interpretation.

344. The version of total omniscience suggested in the passage appears to be an ingenious twist on what we have referred to as capacity omniscience, i.e., the position found in the AKBh and elsewhere whereby a buddha is omniscient because he is *capable* of knowing anything to which he turns his attention. Dharmakīrti seems to acknowledge that for a buddha to know something, he must turn his attention toward it. Yet he also seems to imply that a buddha may turn his attention to all things simultaneously, a position that probably would not be accepted by the majority of those who advocate a capacity model of omniscience. It is interesting to note that some Indian and Tibetan commentators have understood Dharmakīrti's PV 2 to be advancing more or less the same position found in the PVin passage. See Jackson 1993: 219n106.

are in place.[345] On this alternative explanation, it is possible to maintain that the final moment of an arhat's mindstream is a real thing without having to postulate that it produces an effect (e.g., as an image in the awareness of an omniscient buddha). The earlier argument for total omniscience thus does not necessarily represent Dharmakīrti's final view, although its presence in *Pramāṇaviniścaya* complicates the exegetical task of determining his position regarding omniscience. One point, however, remains abundantly clear: Dharmakīrti does not accept that any argument for total omniscience is *at all* necessary or relevant in the context of deciding whether the Buddha can be considered a religious authority. This is a perspective that Śāntarakṣita and Kamalaśīla advocate as well.

The *Tattvasaṃgraha* and the *Pañjikā* on Dharmic and Total Omniscience

For Śāntarakṣita and Kamalaśīla in the *Tattvasaṃgraha* and the *Pañjikā*, there is no doubt that the most important connotation of omniscience is the pragmatic one of dharmic omniscience. What matters, for those who wish to attain elevation and the highest good, is that the Buddha has taught the means by which one can do so. This, and this alone, is the fundamental warrant for calling the Buddha "that omniscient one," as Śāntarakṣita makes clear in the following verses (reminiscent of Dharmakīrti):

> Due to his clear teaching of just [that which is necessary to attain] heaven and liberation, we understand that "[the Buddha] is omniscient" because he knows the most important things (*pradhānārtha*). What use is knowledge of the innumerable grains of sand in the sea? What use have we for the [omniscient] one's knowledge of things other than this [i.e., what is necessary for attaining liberation]?[346]

345. PVin 2 *ad* PVin 2.55 (Steinkellner ed., 2007: 79) *nāpi caramasyāsāmarthyam eva / kasycit karaṇāt / akāriṇo 'pi pratyayavaikalye syāt / sākalye tu karoty eva //*. "The final [moment] is also not devoid of capacity because it has some activity. If it does not perform [its function], that is because of the absence of contributing conditions. If [those conditions] are not absent, it performs [its activity]."

346. TS3527–28 (*atīndriyārthadarśiparīkṣā*): *svargāpavargamātrasya vispaṣṭam upadeśataḥ / pradhānārthaparijñānāt sarvajña iti gamyate // samudrasikatāsaṅkhyāvijñānaṃ kvopayujyate / tasyāsmākam ato 'nyārthajñānasaṃvedanena kim //*.

such things? Objecting that it is impossible to know all things at all times has no impact at all on the fundamental claim of these Buddhist authors, which is that the Buddha can be shown to have the necessary and sufficient knowledge for attaining the twin goals of elevation and the highest good. No higher degree of knowledge need be claimed nor defended. Clearly, this sentiment resonates strongly with Dharmakīrti's verses from *Pramāṇavārttika* 2 above, although rhetorically the authors of the *Tattvasaṃgraha* and the *Pañjikā* go one step beyond Dharmakīrti in that they allow such soteriologically relevant knowledge to be called "omniscience" and the one who possesses it to be called "omniscient."

The final chapter of the *Tattvasaṃgraha* and the *Pañjikā* also goes beyond Dharmakīrti in another way; it defends not only dharmic omniscience but also (at least one version of) total omniscience. The premise of this defense is that while the most important or fundamental (*mukhya*) demonstration is that of dharmic omniscience, knowledge of all things whatsoever is nonetheless a secondary consequence (*prāsaṅgika*) of that initial and basic demonstration.[348] The idea that total omniscience is a secondary consequence of dharmic omniscience appears structurally similar to the argument we saw above from Dharmakīrti's *Pramāṇaviniścaya*, where knowledge of all things whatsoever was presented as a necessary consequence of the combination of the Buddha's maximal capacity for knowing and his great compassion. Śāntarakṣita and Kamalaśīla, however, do not rely on this type of fundamentally moral argument to construct their demonstration of total omniscience in the *Tattvasaṃgraha* and the *Pañjikā*. Instead, they develop a still more complicated argument based on Dharmakīrti's theory of yogic perception (*yogipratyakṣa*), which does not depend upon the Buddha's compassion. The

347. The *pūrvapakṣa* is found at TS 3194 (*atīndriyārthadarśiparīkṣā*): *na ca sarvanarajñānajñeyasaṃvādasambhavaḥ / kālatrayatrilokasthair narair na ca samāgamaḥ //*.

348. TSP *ad* TS 3308 (*atīndriyārthadarśiparīkṣā*, B 1044,15–17): *mukhyaṃ hi tāvat svargamokṣasaṃprāpakahetujñatvasādhanaṃ bhagavato 'smābhiḥ kriyate / yat punar aśeṣārthaparijñātṛtvasādhanam asya tat prāsaṅgikam //*. Translated in its larger context below on pp. 329–30.

argument from great compassion lurks in the background as an underlying dogma—as we have seen, the motivation for attaining the maximal epistemic greatness of a buddha is held necessarily to be great compassion—but compassion is not put forward as a logical reason for the necessity of the Buddha's total omniscience.

We will deal with these topics more thoroughly in the chapters to come. For now, what is important to recognize is that when Śāntarakṣita and Kamalaśīla use the words *sarvajña* and *sarvajñatva*, the precise connotation of those terms can only be derived from an analysis of the context in which they appear. One may wonder why the authors choose to employ these central terms in such an apparently imprecise manner. Perelman and Olbrechts-Tyteca suggest a possible motive in their discussion of the argumentative usage and plasticity of notions, in which authors may be seen to employ a highly flexible notion that allows them greater opportunity in warding off objections concerning their commitment to that notion.[349] When the opponent attacks omniscience, the authors deflect the objection by insisting that the omniscience they seek to defend is not the omniscience that has been attacked.

Once these authors have defended their minimalist version of dharmic omniscience, however, they go on to argue for a seemingly more grandiose picture of omniscience, a form of total omniscience that they portray as a necessary consequence of the minimalist version. This suggests that the semantic range of the terms for omniscience is part of a strategy that, through a degree of equivocation, seeks to drive back the attacks of Kumārila and others. This would be an impressive, if perhaps somewhat disappointing, conclusion to our investigation of these thinkers, were it to represent their final position. In fact, on the highest level of analysis, even the more grandiose picture of omniscience in which the Buddha knows all particulars without exception in a single cognition is finally rejected, replaced by a totally

349. Perelman and Olbrechts-Tyteca 1969: 138: "The manner of presenting fundamental notions in a discussion often depends on the fact that these notions are connected with the theses defended by the speaker or his opponent. In general, when a notion characterizes his own position, the speaker presents it as being not at all ambiguous but very flexible and rich, that is, with great possibilities of being highly rated, and, above all, as capable of resisting the assaults of new experiences. The notions connected with his opponent's theses will, on the contrary, be fixed and presented as unchangeable. By proceeding in this way, the speaker makes the force of inertia work for him. The flexibility of the notion, postulated at the outset and claimed as inherent to it, makes it possible to minimize, and at the same time underline, the changes that the new experience would impose, that objections would demand: this basic adaptability to new circumstances will enable the speaker to maintain that he is keeping the same notion alive."

... of what the authors understand ... to mean.

The Shifting Nature of the Objects of Knowledge

When the focus remains on dharmic omniscience, the problem of the precise nature of that which is known by an omniscient being remains in the background, for when the primary concern is with soteriologically relevant knowledge, questions concerning the ontological status of objects of knowledge can be, and are, more easily left aside. Likewise, in considering the dogmas of omniscience outlined above, it was possible to avoid the difficult question of precisely what it is that an omniscient being is supposed to know, for even without specifying what constitutes an object of knowledge for an omniscient being, it is possible for the authors to advance such positions as: omniscience comes about through the elimination of the two obscurations, or, omniscience requires great compassion in order to arise. Eventually, however, an interpreter of the meaning of omniscience in the *Tattvasaṃgraha* and the *Pañjikā* is forced to confront the question of the precise nature of what is known in omniscience. Given the complexity of the authors' ontological commitments on the sliding scale of analysis, it is not surprising that the answer turns out to be quite tricky to pin down.

So far, the general picture of omniscience that has emerged is one in which omniscience is a state of maximally great knowing that occurs when all obscurations are cleared away from the mind. As we will see in greater detail below, Śāntarakṣita and Kamalaśīla argue that one clears away obscurations through the application of an antidote, the vision of selflessness (*nairātmyadarśana*). Once this antidote has been fully inculcated, the mind—which may be established as having the nature of perceiving the real—naturally shines forth to illumine objects of knowledge. In Śāntarakṣita's memorable words, the mind automatically functions with regard to "the entire sphere of objects of knowledge" (*jñeyamaṇḍala*).[350] This phrase has an impressive ring, which is strengthened when Śāntarakṣita later states:

350. TS 3419 (*atīndriyārthadarśiparīkṣā*): *tasya cāpacaye jāte jñānam avyāhataṃ mahat*

> An omniscient being is established to be one for whom the entire sphere of objects of knowledge is pervaded by a single moment of cognition.[351]

The addition of the qualification "by a single moment of cognition" simply adds to the mystery of this nearly inconceivable degree of epistemic greatness. Yet it does nothing to clarify what is meant by the "entire sphere of objects of knowledge." One imagines that the phrase must indicate the totality of knowable entities, but this still begs the question of what knowable entities are supposed to be.

We can home in on an interpretation by first considering some other statements concerning omniscience from the final chapter of the work. In his commentary on the verse just cited, for example, Kamalaśīla makes the interesting claim:

> One who apprehends whatever exists as existing and whatever does not exist as not existing is called an omniscient being.[352]

This statement raises the problem of what these authors understand by the verb "to exist." As we saw in the last chapter, Śāntarakṣita and Kamalaśīla follow Dharmakīrti in holding the capacity for causal function to be the mark of a real entity. Since, presumably, the real is that which exists while the unreal is that which does not exist, we can paraphrase Kamalaśīla's statement as meaning that an omniscient being knows the real as real and the unreal as unreal. But what is the real for these philosophers? We know that the meaning of the real shifts on the different levels of analysis in the work, and we know that on each level the authors accept two kinds of reality: ultimate and conventional. For example, on the Sautrāntika level of analysis, that which is ultimately real (and which possesses the capacity for causal function) includes

---

/ *svātantryeṇa pravarteta sarvatra jñeyamaṇḍale* //. "And when the destruction of that [internal obscuration] occurs, the great, unobstructed awareness functions automatically with regard to the entire sphere of objects of knowledge."

351. TS 3626a–c (*atīndriyārthadarśiparīkṣā*): *ekajñānakṣaṇavyāptaniḥśeṣajñeya-maṇḍalaḥ / prasādhito hi sarvajñaḥ ...* //.

352. TSP *ad* TS 3626 (*atīndriyārthadarśiparīkṣā*, B 1124,6–7): *yad asti tad astitvena yan nāsti tan nāstitvena gṛhṇan sarvavid ucyate* /. Cf. also Kamalaśīla's statement at TSP *ad* TS 3319–20 (*atīndriyārthadarśiparīkṣā*, B 1047,23): *yad yathaivāvasthitaṃ vastu sadādirūpeṇa tasya tathaiva jñānāt sarvavid bhavati* /. "A person is omniscient due to knowing a real thing (*vastu*) in just the way that it is established, as [for example] having the nature being existent and so on."

it is indeed a good argument (*śobhate*).[355] The implication is that an argument that runs "omniscience exists, because whatever is real is necessarily perceived" is not ruled out for Śāntarakṣita and Kamalaśīla.[356]

Although it is not obvious that the authors of the *Tattvasaṃgraha* and the *Pañjikā* embrace such an argument, it nevertheless does resonate with their claim, examined below, that the nature of the mind is to perceive reality. For if, in the final analysis, what is meant by the real is just that which is *ultimately* real, then one would have to admit both that the real is necessarily perceived and that omniscience—in the sense of a direct awareness unencumbered by ignorance of that which is ultimately real—is entirely possible. The problem is that the definitions of both conventional and ultimate reality shift on the different levels of analysis, so that the question becomes: on which level of analysis does omniscient knowledge function in relation to the entire sphere of objects of knowledge? This is not a question that we can answer here, but it will be important to bear it in mind when we consider the demonstration of total omniscience in the following chapter. In the meantime, however, we must continue with our investigation of the rhetorical contexts for discussions of omniscience in the work as a whole.

Rhetorical Contexts

Above we have considered the general religious context, in the form of various dogmas, underlying *all* discussions of omniscience in the *Tattvasaṃgraha* and the *Pañjikā*; we turn now to the specific rhetorical contexts in which such discussions occur. One helpful way to classify these contexts is in terms of the audience or addressee in each case. Considered in this light, we discover that there are three distinct rhetorical contexts for discussions about

355. See TSP *ad* TS 93 (*īśvaraparīkṣā*, B 73,14–16): *yadi sāmānyenāsti kaścit sarvajña iti sādhyate tadā nāsmān pratīdaṃ bhavatāṃ sādhanaṃ rājate / siddhasādhyatādoṣāt / kiṃ tu ye sarvajñāpavādino jaiminīyās teṣv eva śobhate //*. "If this [argument] establishes in general that 'there is some omniscient being,' then this demonstration of yours is not directed at us, for it has the fault of establishing that which is already established. But in relation to those Mīmāṃsakas who deny omniscience, it is indeed good."

356. As we will see, there have been a variety of arguments in which knowability (*jñeyatva*)—along with related conceptions like cognizability (*prameyatva*)—has been presented as evidence both for and against the notion of omniscience. In addition to the argument just cited for the omniscience of God, we find cited in the TS/P Jain arguments for the omniscience of Mahāvīra and Mīmāṃsaka arguments refuting omniscience, both using *jñeyatva* and *prameyatva* as evidence. See pp. 179–81 below. See also p. 233.

omniscience in the *Tattvasaṃgraha* and the *Pañjikā*: (1) a strictly rhetorical context, in which omniscience is not the focus of the argument; (2) a context in which the addressees are Mīmāṃsakas; and (3) a context addressing Buddhists and judicious persons more generally.

A Strictly Rhetorical Context

In a strictly rhetorical context, omniscience is not featured as a point of contention but is rather invoked in the course of an argument about some other point not directly related to the question of omniscience.[357] In such contexts, of which there are several in the *Tattvasaṃgraha* and the *Pañjikā*, the authors employ a generalized meaning for omniscience, where one or both elements of the notion (i.e., *sarva* and *jña*) are not clearly defined. The authors take this liberty because the addressee is an adversary who accepts omniscience—even though the one held to be omniscient might be, say, Kapila and not the Buddha.[358] Consider, for example, the authors' response to a certain Naiyāyika argument for the existence of an eternal self (*ātman*). The argument states that a self must exist because cognitions are apprehended by a cognizer who is separate from one's body.[359] Śāntarakṣita and Kamalaśīla reject this reason, saying that it merely "establishes that which has already been established" (*siddhasādhyatā*), because Buddhists already accept that cognitions are apprehended by a cognizer apart from one's body, namely, omniscient persons and so on who are capable of knowing the contents of others' minds.[360] Implicit in this passage is the understanding that since both proponent and opponent nominally accept omniscience (they are both, to

357. In the Buddhist *pramāṇa* theory tradition, Dharmakīrti had already used the idea of omniscience in a strictly rhetorical context to demonstrate various inferential fallacies in NB 3. See above, n. 342.

358. An exception to this general rule occurs at TS 1172 (*śabdārthaparīkṣā*) and TSP *ad cit.*, where the point of the passage is to explain how certain expressions that are meant to apply equally to all existent things (e.g., expressions like *prameya* and *jñeya*) can be explained on the Buddhist theory of reference-as-exclusion (*apoha*). Here, omniscience is used only as part of an example to illustrate that words with universal reference may be meaningfully used when there is some doubt, as when one wonders whether all cognizable things are known by an omniscient person, but there is no suggestion that those addressed necessarily accept (or reject) omniscience.

359. TS 177 (*ātmaparīkṣā*): *jñānāni ca madīyāni tanvādivyatirekiṇā / saṃvedakena vedyāni pratyayatvāt tadanyavat //.*

360. TS 188 (*ātmaparīkṣā*): *tad atra prathame tāvat sādhane siddhasādhyatā / sarvajñādipravedyatvaṃ tvajjñānasyeṣyate yataḥ //.*

…g is a legitimate
…entails are not
…
…such contexts
…tegy. Perelman
…te that ambig-
…when they are
…example, they
…y groups with
…such an agree-
ment is "possible only by the use of ambiguous notions understood and interpreted by each in accordance with his own values."[362] Despite the inherent ambiguity, however, the use of such notions can be useful, as "it encourages a continuation of the dialogue."[363] Śāntarakṣita and Kamalaśīla's use of the notion of omniscience in purely rhetorical contexts is similar to this use of ambiguous notions; by purposefully leaving the notion underdetermined, they hope to solicit agreement on another point, which would then allow the dialogue or debate to go on.

Although this type of strictly rhetorical use of a vague or underdetermined notion of omniscience may be insufficient for clarifying what omniscience means to the authors in the final analysis, it can be revealing with regard to some general features of the authors' view of omniscience. For example, in his commentary on the passage referred to above in which it was claimed that cognitions are cognized by a knower separate from the body, Kamalaśīla states that an omniscient person is one of several kinds of persons, including śrāvakas and pratyekabuddhas, who have knowledge of other people's minds.[364] In another place, we learn that an omniscient person cannot know that which lacks causal function (*arthakriyā*), since only the causally efficacious is real.[365] And we learn that this is no limitation of the omniscient being, since it is not a fault not to know that which is not real (i.e., that which

361. Perelman and Olbrechts-Tyteca 1969: 134.

362. Perelman and Olbrechts-Tyteca 1969: 134.

363. Perelman and Olbrechts-Tyteca 1969: 134.

364. TSP *ad* TS 188 (*ātmaparīkṣā*, B 106,21–23): *tatra siddhasādhyatā bhavadīyapratyayānām asmābhir bhavaccharīrādivyatirekiṇā sarvavidā śrāvakapratyekabuddhais tadanyaiś ca paracittavedibhir vedanābhyupagamāt /.*

365. TS 422 (*sthirabhāvaparīkṣā*): *niḥśeṣaśaktiśūnyaṃ tu yad vandhyāsutasaṃ nibham / sarvajñacetaso 'py eti hetutvaṃ na kadācana //.*

has no causal function or effect).[366] In a passage that we considered ab learn that a certain argument may be advanced to establish omniscienc general, although it cannot succeed as an argument for the omniscience o God.[367] Such, then, are the kinds of general maxims about omniscience that we can extract from the passages concerning omniscience that occur in the first of the three kinds of rhetorical contexts in which omniscience is discussed in the *Tattvasaṃgraha* and the *Pañjikā*.

Two Rhetorical Contexts with Specific Addressees

The second and third rhetorical contexts differ from the first in that they occur when omniscience is directly under debate; they are distinguished from each other in terms of their respective audiences. In the second type of rhetorical context, arguments concerning omniscience are addressed primarily—if not exclusively—at Mīmāṃsakas, especially the formidable Kumārila, whose arguments against omniscience are cited extensively. Since this opponent denies omniscience in all meaningful senses of the term, the authors' goal in relation to him is, in part, to show that his denial of omniscience is wrong. The final chapter of the work, the "Proof of Omniscience" (*sarvajñasiddhi*) or "Investigation of One Who Sees Supersensible Objects" (*atīndriyārthadarśiparīkṣā*) falls almost entirely within this category. Since the addressee in this case is not considered to be fully judicious, we find the occasional use of *ad personam* arguments in this part of the *Tattvasaṃgraha* and the *Pañjikā*, although most of the argumentation cannot be so characterized.

In the third type of rhetorical context, arguments concerning omniscience are addressed primarily to Buddhists or, minimally, to judicious persons who can be expected (after an appropriate investigation) to accept most of the ontological and epistemological theories presented in the *Tattvasaṃgraha* and the *Pañjikā*, as well as (perhaps) the basic dogmas and maxims about omniscience noted above. Here, since the audience already accepts omniscience on at least some definition, the authors' goal is, in part, to rectify misconceptions and solve apparent contradictions in the understanding of omniscience. Most of the discussions of omniscience addressed to this audience are found in the work's twenty-third chapter, the "Investigation of

366. TS 423–24 (*sthirabhāvaparīkṣā*): *kriyate tatra naivedaṃ kāryarūpādyadṛṣṭitaḥ / nirnibandhanam astitvavyavasthānaṃ vicakṣaṇaiḥ // na tasmin sādhitenārthaḥ kṣaṇikatvena kaścana / tatra paryanuyogaś ca kriyamāṇo 'pi niṣphalaḥ //*.

367. TS 93 and TSP *ad cit*. See n. 355 above.

External Objects" (*bahirarthaparīkṣā*), although there are also some passages in the final chapter and in Kamalaśīla's commentary on the opening verses that should be understood as falling under the rubric of this context as well.

In the remainder of this chapter, we will examine especially the second of the three rhetorical contexts outlined above, since it is by far the most complex and potentially misleading. This means, in effect, that we will spend a good deal of time looking at the work's final chapter, inquiring more deeply into its rhetorical function, its place within the work as a whole, and the basic structures that occur there. Once that task is complete, we will take a somewhat more cursory look at the "Investigation of External Objects," a chapter in which discussions of omniscience are overtly addressed directly to Buddhists and other judicious persons.

The Final Chapter of the Tattvasaṃgraha *and the* Pañjikā

Even considered on its own, the final chapter of the *Tattvasaṃgraha* and the *Pañjikā* is a remarkable exposition. Its stated topic and its broad concern is the possibility of a direct perception or "vision" (*darśana*) of that which is beyond the senses or "supersensible" (*atīndriyārtha*). The entire investigation is framed by four introductory verses that together urge an unwanted consequence against the Mīmāṃsakas.[368] The initial premise of the argument is the claim that the Mīmāṃsaka position that the Veda's trustworthiness is due to its unique status as an authorless (*apauruṣeya*) scripture has been thoroughly refuted in the two chapters previous.[369] On this premise,

368. TS 3123–26 (*atīndriyārthadarśiparīkṣā*): *evaṃ sarvapramāṇānāṃ pramāṇatve svato 'sthite / atīndriyārthavitsattvasiddhaye na prayatyate // vedasyāpi pramāṇatvaṃ yasmāt puruṣataḥ sthitam / tasya cātīndriyajñatve tatas tasmin pramāṇatā // anyathājñānasandehaviparyāsānuṣaṅgiṇi / puṃsi kartari naivāsya prāmāṇyaṃ syāt tadanyavat // svargayāgādisaṃbandho jñātvā tad yena bhāṣitaḥ / vispaṣṭātīndriyajñānaḥ so 'bhyupeyaḥ parair api //*. "Thus, it being established that not all trustworthy awarenesses are intrinsically trustworthy, one need not exert oneself to establish the existence of a person who knows supersensible objects. The Veda, too, is established as trustworthy due to some person. And when that [person] has supersensible knowledge, then it [i.e., the Veda] is trustworthy due to that [person]. Otherwise, if the person who was its author were associated with ignorance, doubt, and error, it would have no trustworthiness, just like other [persons and texts]. Having understood the connection between such things as heaven and the sacrificial offerings, that [person] proclaimed it [in the Veda]. [Hence,] his knowledge of things beyond the senses is obvious [and] should be acknowledged by others as well."

369. These are the twenty-fourth and twenty-fifth chapters of the work as a whole, the *śrutiparīkṣā* and the *svataḥprāmāṇyaparīkṣā*.

Śāntarakṣita argues, the Mīmāṃsaka must now accept that the Veda does indeed have an author. And since, on the Mīmāṃsaka view, the Veda is definitely trustworthy with regard to supersensible entities, this means also that the Mīmāṃsaka must acknowledge that the author of the Veda directly knows those entities; otherwise, he must give up the idea that the Veda is trustworthy. In other words, the Mīmāṃsaka must acknowledge "supersensible seeing" on the part of the Veda's author. Of course, supersensible seeing is precisely what the Mīmāṃsaka wants to deny. Kamalaśīla summarizes the argument as follows:

> This is what is being said: if you, sir, definitely accept the trustworthiness of the Veda, then it is right that its trustworthiness is not intrinsic but derives from its author, who is a person. And this has already been proven. And if the author of the Veda is one who sees things beyond the senses, then it is right that it is trustworthy also because of its author and not otherwise. For otherwise, if the author were endowed with erroneous and doubtful cognitions, then the Veda would become untrustworthy, like the speech of a madman! Therefore, the author of the Veda, whose existence has already been established in [the chapter entitled] "The Investigation of Scripture" (*śrutiparīkṣā*), must, by implication, also be accepted by our opponents, the Mīmāṃsakas, as a person who can see supersensible objects. This assertion cannot be denied.[370]

One way of reading this four-verse introduction is as functioning to *diminish* the significance of the chapter's contents to a certain extent. That is, since, on the basis of all that has already been argued, one can establish supersensible seeing "without effort,"[371] the chapter ostensibly does not

370. TSP *ad* TS 3124–26 (*atīndriyārthadarśiparīkṣā*, B 988,8–14): *etad uktaṃ bhavati / yadi bhavadbhir avaśyaṃ vedasya prāmāṇyam abhyupeyate tadāsya puruṣād eva kartuḥ prāmāṇyaṃ yuktam / na svata iti / etac ca pūrvaṃ pratipāditam / sa ca vedasya kartā yady atīndriyadṛg bhavati tadāsya tataḥ kartur api pramāṇatā yuktā nānyathā / anyathā hi viparītasaṃśayajñānādiyukte kartari saty unmattādivākyavad vedo 'pramāṇatām evāśnuvīta / tasmād yo 'sau vedakartā pūrvaṃ śrutiparīkṣāyāṃ prasādhitaḥ parair api mīmāṃsakair atīndriyārthadarśī sāmarthyād aṅgīkartavya iti tat pratikṣepo na kāryaḥ /*. Reading *puruṣād eva* for *puruṣād iva* in accord with G 816,14 and D, vol. *'e*, 258b2: … *byed pa po'i skyes bu nyid las* ….

371. TSP *ad* TS 3123 (*atīndriyārthadarśiparīkṣā*, B 987,22–24): *ato 'yatnenaivātīndriyārthadarśī puruṣaḥ siddha iti na tatsiddhaye pṛthak prayatnāntaram āsthīyate //*. "Therefore the existence of a person who sees things that are beyond the senses is

serve any *necessary* function in relation to Mīmāṃsakas. At the same time, Śāntarakṣita obviously feels he has good arguments to refute the Mīmāṃsaka claims concerning the impossibility of supersensible seeing. Thus, once this basic *prasaṅga*-style argument is in place, he goes on to present various Mīmāṃsaka arguments against supersensible seeing in a long *pūrvapakṣa* of 134 verses, and to respond to those arguments in an even lengthier *uttarapakṣa* of 385 verses.

The final chapter is thus quite extensive, containing a total of 523 verses and filling, when displayed together with Kamalaśīla's commentary, well over one hundred pages in the modern printed editions.[372] This impressive length, along with the tantalizing subject matter ("supersensible seeing") and prominent place at the end of a gargantuan and sophisticated contribution to the Buddhist epistemological tradition, are all-important factors in explaining the chapter's widespread renown among scholars of Buddhism and of Indian religious philosophy more generally.[373] Yet despite the attention the chapter has generated, it nevertheless unfortunately remains the case that the scholarly community has all but ignored its larger structural and rhetorical elements, an oversight that may well account for the current uncer-

established just without effort; hence we make no further, separate effort to establish this fact."

372. In the TS/P, the chapter is the second in length only to the *śrutiparīkṣā*.

373. See n. 5 for a list of scholars who, to varying degrees, have treated this chapter. Interestingly, the chapter is somewhat less acclaimed as a *locus classicus* for the exposition of omniscience among Tibetan scholars, who in this domain generally hold Haribhadra's commentaries on the AA in greater esteem. A possible reason for the apparently lesser value placed on the chapter, and indeed on the TS/P as a whole, may be connected with our argument in this book: that is, the rhetorical force of the chapter is not in what it says about omniscience to a *universal* audience but rather in what it says about omniscience to a *particular* audience of injudicious Mīmāṃsakas. With presumably *no actual* members of this intended audience and perhaps no persons actively interested in the ideas of that intended audience working in Tibet, there is correspondingly lower interest in the chapter and, *inter alia*, the work. A second possible reason is raised by van der Kuijp (1983: 4–5), who maintains that the TS/P was among many texts of the "early transmission" (*snga dar*) of Buddhism to Tibet that were to be "victims of the Glang-dar-ma persecution," which in the early ninth century interrupted the oral teaching lineages related to those works. As evidence that such has occurred in the case of Śāntarakṣita and Kamalaśīla, van der Kuijp (5) cites the eminent fifteenth-century Sa skya pa scholar, Go rams pa Bsod nams seng ge (1429–89), who said, "Although the abbot Śāntarakṣita and the supreme scholar Kamalaśīla appear to have founded an oral tradition (*bshad-srol*), nowadays, apart from the mere book, there does not appear a continuity of its teaching."

tainty regarding Śāntarakṣita and Kamalaśīla's position on omniscience in most scholarly circles.

The purpose of the present section, then, is to take stock of the chapter's pivotal rhetorical elements by asking some of the same questions of the chapter as we previously considered in relation to the work as a whole. Since we have already spoken somewhat about the audience and styles of reasoning, we will only recapitulate briefly our findings here. For the remainder of the section, our focus will be on the chapter's structure. As in the case of the work as a whole, the chapter's purpose is the most difficult element to determine; we will therefore leave aside an in-depth consideration of this question until later in the book, after we have explored in greater detail the specific arguments and counter-arguments contained in the chapter.

Audience and Styles of Reasoning in the Final Chapter

We have seen already that the final chapter of the work is also the final chapter in a group of three chapters addressed to Mīmāṃsakas concerning the question of religious authority. As such, the chapter falls generally into the second rhetorical context outlined above: the context in which injudicious Mīmāṃsakas are the addressees. As is common elsewhere in the *Tattvasaṃgraha* and the *Pañjikā*, however, shifts in the addressee occur throughout the chapter, so that certain sections are not addressed to Mīmāṃsakas but rather to Buddhists and other generally judicious persons. This diversity of audiences for the chapter means that while much of the chapter is addressed *ad hominem*, there are some passages that should be interpreted as addressed *ad humanitatem*. There are also a relatively small number of arguments that appear to be addressed *ad personam*, with Kumārila in particular bearing the brunt of the attacks.

The styles of reasoning at play in the chapter are broadly the same as those in the rest of the work: *nyāya* reasoning argumentation is used within a *pramāṇa* theory framework to urge unwanted consequences on the opponent and to establish the positions favored by the authors. As throughout the text, the works of Dignāga and especially Dharmakīrti are taken as inviolable, and Dharmakīrti's *Pramāṇavārttika* (especially *Pramāṇavārttika* 2 and portions of *Pramāṇavārttikasvopajñavṛtti*) is a particularly significant source for a number of central arguments and for the structure of the argumentation as a whole. On the sliding scale of analysis, the chapter is argued primarily through a Sautrāntika level of analysis, with occasional, temporary shifts to a Vijñānavāda perspective; fortunately, these are quite clearly indicated as such by Kamalaśīla in his commentary. Use of the Sautrāntika level of analysis is what one would expect here, given that the primary addressees—the Mīmāṃsakas—operate with an "externalist" metaphysical commitment in which objects of knowledge are held to exist independent of and external to the mind.

Structure of the Final Chapter (1): *Pūrvapakṣa*

Immediately after the four introductory verses discussed above, Śāntarakṣita presents the *pūrvapakṣa*, which consists of two main parts. The first, and much longer, portion contains the views of the chief opponent in the *pūrvapakṣa*, Kumārila Bhaṭṭa, whose position is laid out in more than one hundred verses, most of which are direct quotations from the extant *Ślokavārttika* and a now lost work, the *Bṛhaṭṭīkā*.[374] The second portion, which occurs just after this presentation of Kumārila's views, sets out a series of objections to omniscience that are attributed to Sāmaṭa and Yajñaṭa.[375] These two figures, who—if they were real historical figures at all—appear also to be Mīmāṃsakas, are depicted as raising a number of astute philosophical problems quite different in nature from the more bookish objections of Kumārila.[376] The responses to these objections near the end of the *Tattvasaṃgraha* and the *Pañjikā* make for some of the most interesting reading in the entire chapter. Nonetheless, the chapter's primary focus remains the views of Kumārila.

Kumārila's objection to the idea of omniscience boils down to a single claim that is fundamental for the Mīmāṃsaka tradition: no one, human or divine, is capable of directly knowing Dharma, which is defined in Śabara's

374. In the TS, Kumārila's *pūrvapakṣa* is found at TS 3127–3245. Frauwallner's seminal article (1962) has been widely accepted as definitively demonstrating that numerous verses attributed to Kumārila in the final chapter of the TS that are not found in the ŚV are from Kumārila's lost work, the *Bṛhaṭṭīkā*.

375. This *pūrvapakṣa* is found at TS 3246–60. See Watanabe 1988 for a Japanese translation.

376. Unfortunately, nearly all of the commentary on the verses in the Sāmaṭa-Yajñaṭa *pūrvapakṣa* is missing in the extant Sanskrit manuscripts. Śāstrī, the editor of B, has provided a reconstruction of this section based on the Tibetan text, but his translation (from Tibetan to Sanskrit) leaves much to be desired. The verses themselves have survived in Sanskrit, however, and with the Tibetan translation of the commentary we are still in a good position to develop a clear picture of the arguments attributed in TS/P to these thinkers. The notion that these figures may represent fictional opponents developed in a Buddhist monastic setting to foster debate was suggested to me by John Dunne. That the figures are meant to be counted rhetorically as Mīmāṃsakas is evident both from a statement in one of the verses (TS 3260) and from Kamalaśīla's commentary.

Bhāṣya as "that by which a person is connected to the highest good."[377] The reason that no one can know Dharma (or, for that matter, its opposite, Adharma) is that Dharma is beyond the range of human perception, which is inherently flawed and limited. To put it in the parlance of the *pramāṇa* theorists, Dharma and Adharma are supersensible (*atīndriya*).[378] This means that the only possible way that one can gain knowledge of Dharma is indirectly, which for the Mīmāṃsaka means through the Veda, whose eternal (*nitya*) and authorless (*apauruṣeya*) nature ensures it to be free from fault in relation even to supersensible realities.[379]

377. ŚBh 1.1.1.2: *tena yaḥ puruṣaṃ niḥśreyasena saṃyunakti sa eva dharmaśabdenocyate /*. Quoted also in TSP *ad* TS 2084. For a useful discussion of the notion of Dharma in early Mīmāṃsaka sources, see D'Sa 1980: 42–54. In the words of Jha (1942: 173), Dharma is used by Kumārila in the sense of "what should be done, i.e., Duty." Perhaps the most famous definition of Dharma in the Mīmāṃsaka corpus is the notoriously difficult-to-translate *sūtra* by Jaimini (JMS 2): *codanālakṣaṇo 'rtho dharmaḥ /*. Jha (1983: 21) suggests "Duty is a purpose having Injunction for its sole authority (means of conceivability)." In any case, the basic sense is clear: Dharma is that aim (D'Sa suggests "Significance" for *artha*) that has its source in the Veda. Of the two formulations of Dharma just above, D'Sa (1980: 51) says that "the former is an eschatological statement about Dharma, the latter is a phenomenological one.... [the latter] tells us where Dharma is traditionally to be found;... [the former] tells us what the inner working of Dharma is;..." See D'Sa (1980: 47) for an argument that Kumārila interprets the technical term *codanā* in the sense of both Vedic injunction and Vedic speech in general.

378. Kumārila makes clear that Dharma is beyond the senses in ŚV2.14 (*codanāsūtra*): *śreyaḥsādhanatā hy eṣāṃ nityaṃ vedāt pratīyate / tādrūpyeṇa ca dharmatvaṃ tasmāt nendriyagocaraḥ //*. "For the fact of those [visible rituals and so on] being a means to attain the good (*śreyas*) is always known from the Veda. And their partaking of Dharma is in terms of that form [i.e., as part of the Veda, not as visible entities]. Therefore [Dharma] is not an object of the senses." Kumārila is ostensibly commenting on ŚBh 1.1.2.2: *codanā hi bhūtaṃ bhavantaṃ bhaviṣyantaṃ sūkṣmaṃ vyavahitaṃ viprakṛṣṭam ity evañjātiyakam arthaṃ śaknoty avagamayitum / nānyat kiñcendriyam /*. "Vedic injunction (or speech, *codanā*) [alone] is capable of making known such things as those that are past, present, future, subtle, hidden, and radically inaccessible; but other things, such as the sense organs, cannot at all [make such things known]." Kamalaśīla cites this statement at the outset of the final chapter of the TS/P (TSP *ad* TS 3124–26, B 988,20–22), where the context indicates that at least some of the items listed in the statement are to be considered as beyond the senses (*atīndriya*).

379. Kumārila ends the ŚV with the claim that the authority of the Veda has been established due to its being eternal and authorless. See ŚV 8.14–15ab (*vedanityatādhikaraṇam*): *nityasya nitya evārthaḥ kṛtakasyāpramāṇatā / unmattavacanatvaṃ tu pūrvam eva nirākṛtam // iti pramāṇatvam idaṃ prasiddhaṃ yuktyeha dharmaṃ prati codanāyāḥ //*. "The meaning (*artha*) of an eternal [scripture] is just eternal; there is no authority for [a scripture] that has been composed. And the fact of being the speech of a madman

However, as we have seen above, Śāntarakṣita and Kamalaśīla, expanding on Dharmakīrti's argument, maintain that the Buddha's dharmic omniscience is constituted *precisely* by the Buddha's knowledge of the means by which one may attain the highest good, including both that which one should avoid as well as that which one should take up. For Kumārila, this claim concerning the Buddha's spiritual knowledge, minimal as it may appear, amounts nevertheless to saying that the Buddha knows Dharma and Adharma, which for Kumārila is impossible. Kumārila's central objection to the Buddhist doctrine of omniscience thus concerns dharmic and not total omniscience: as far as he is concerned, since direct knowledge of Dharma is not possible, total omniscience is ruled out automatically.[380]

As a participant in the *pramāṇa* theorists' style of philosophical reasoning, Kumārila must present some argument or evidence for his claim. He does this in two ways: first, through a demonstration of the impossibility of direct knowledge of Dharma and Adharma; and second, in dependence on a special means of trustworthy awareness—promulgated and accepted only in the tradition founded by Kumārila, i.e., the Bhāṭṭa Mīmāṃsā—called

---

[i.e., any human, since all humans have epistemic and afflictive faults] has already been refuted. Therefore, the fact that the Veda is authoritative with regard to Dharma has been established here through reasoning." Cf. also ŚV 2.242cd–243a: *vihitapratiṣedhatve muktvānyan na ca kāraṇam / dharmādharmāvabodhasya /*. "Apart from being enjoined or prohibited [by the Veda] there is no other means for knowing Dharma and Adharma."

380. See Kumārila's statement (from the *Bṛhaṭṭīkā*, preserved at TS 3143) in which efforts to prove total omniscience are compared to threshing chaff: *ye 'pi vicchinnamūlatvād dharmajñatve hate sati / sarvajñān puruṣān āhus taiḥ kṛtaṃ tuṣakaṇḍanam //*. "And those who, because their root is cut, say that there are omniscient people, even though the knowledge of Dharma has been refuted—such people are threshing chaff." On Śāntarakṣita's response to this verse, see below, p. 169–70. Kumārila has also made some remarks to the effect that he would not object to someone knowing everything else *except* Dharma (see, e.g., ŚV 2.11cd [*codanā*]: *yadi ṣaḍbhiḥ pramāṇaiḥ syāt sarvajñaḥ kena vāryate* and TS 3127 [*atīndriyārthadarśiparīkṣā*]: *dharmajñatvaniṣedhaś cet kevalo 'tropayujyate / sarvam anyad vijānānaḥ puruṣaḥ kena vāryate //*). D'Sa (1980: 193) has opined that such statements indicate that "Kumārila is not against every type of omniscient person." However, Kumārila elsewhere strongly objects to the notion that people can have extraordinary knowledge that transcends the normal limits of human perception (see, e.g., TS 3136 [*atīndriyārthadarśiparīkṣā*]: *ekasyaiva śarīrasya yāvantaḥ paramāṇavaḥ / keśaromāṇi yāvanti kas tāni jñātum arhati //* and TS 3159 [*atīndriyārthadarśiparīkṣā*]: *ye 'pi sātiśayā dṛṣṭāḥ prajñāmedhābalair narāḥ / stokastokāntaratvena na tv atīndriyadarśanāt //*). It therefore seems better to interpret the verses in which Kumārila appears to accept a kind of knowledge-of-everything-except-Dharma as indicating his priorities: the most important point for Kumārila is the impossibility of anyone, even a person with a great deal of ordinary knowledge, having direct knowledge of Dharma; that people cannot know other supersensible (*atīndriya*) objects is a secondary—but no less true—concern.

abhāvapramāṇa, "the means of trustworthy awareness of nonexistence."[381] Kumārila defines *abhāvapramāṇa* as the "nonarisal of [the other *pramāṇas*:] perception and so on,"[382] by which he means the nonarisal of any of the five other *pramāṇas* accepted by the Mīmāṃsakas: perception (*pratyakṣa*), inference (*anumāna*), verbal testimony (*śābda*), analogy (*upamāna*), or presumption (*arthāpatti*). When he claims that an omniscient being is definitively negated by *abhāvapramāṇa*, Kumārila means that such a being cannot be determined to exist by any of these other means of trustworthy awareness.

In the final chapter of the *Tattvasaṃgraha* and the *Pañjikā*, the *pūrvapakṣa* begins with Kumārila's objections to the possibility of human knowledge of Dharma and Adharma and proceeds to his reasons for rejecting that an omniscient being can be ascertained by any of these five *pramāṇas*. Other subsidiary discussions and problems are scattered throughout. As is common in other portions of this work, the *pūrvapakṣa* includes also a number of objections to the Mīmāṃsaka arguments, some of which may represent Śāntarakṣita and Kamalaśīla's positions, while others probably represent the views of other contemporary champions of *sarvajñatva*.[383]

The *pūrvapakṣa* ends, as mentioned, with a short section devoted to the views of Sāmaṭa and Yajñaṭa, who proffer a range of conundrums that omniscience would seem to entail. At the outset of this section, they are portrayed as asking:

> Is the omniscient person asserted to know all things simultaneously, successively, through a single nature, in terms of the most important [things], or due to the capacity [to know all things]?[384]

381. See Kellner 1997 for a study and translation of Śāntarakṣita and Kamalaśīla's refutation of *abhāvapramāṇa* in the *pramāṇāntarabhāvaparīkṣā* of the TS/P, as well as a study of "negative Erkenntnis" in Indian philosophy more generally, especially as it relates to the development of *abhāvapramāṇa* in Kumārila's thought. For a general picture of Kumārila's position vis-à-vis that of Prabhākara and other *pramāṇa* theorists, see Bhatt 1989: 332–57.

382. ŚV *abhāvapariccheda* 11ab: *pratyakṣāder anutpattiḥ pramāṇābhāva ucyate*. Cited at TS 1648ab (*pramāṇāntarabhāvaparīkṣā*) with *iṣyate* for *ucyate*.

383. Pathak (1929) argues that the targets of Kumārila's attack in the verses preserved at TS 3234–36 (*atīndriyārthadarśiparīkṣā*) are the Jain authors Samantabhadra and Akalaṅkadeva. He may well be correct, although the general reasoning under attack in these verses is used by Śāntarakṣita and Kamalaśīla later in the TS/P as well. See pp. 179–80 below.

384. TS 3247 (*atīndriyārthadarśiparīkṣā*): *yugapat paripāṭyā vā sarvaṃ caikasvabhāvataḥ / jānan yathāpradhānaṃ vā śaktyā veṣyeta sarvavit //*.

Here, in a nutshell, are some, if not all, of the major ways of conceiving omniscience in Śāntarakṣita and Kamalaśīla's day; the objectors find problems in all of them. Significantly, when the authors of the *Tattvasaṃgraha* and the *Pañjikā* get around to addressing these charges near the end of the work, they do so without defending just *one* of the paradigms of omniscience mentioned but rather by defending *each* of the paradigms in turn. That they do so is further evidence that the final chapter does not contain the authors' final perspective on omniscience. It is precisely because the chapter represents only a provisional perspective, argued mainly at the Sautrāntika level of analysis, that the authors feel free to offer a variety of solutions to the conundrums raised by Sāmaṭa and Yajñaṭa.

Structure of the Final Chapter (2): *Uttarapakṣa*

Having presented a variety of Mīmāṃsaka objections to omniscience in the *pūrvapakṣa*, Śāntarakṣita and Kamalaśīla next attempt an exhaustive response in the *uttarapakṣa* (*Tattvasaṃgraha* 3261–3645). Despite the impressive length and complexity of the *uttarapakṣa*, we can still discern a structure to the overall argument, in which the authors argue in distinct segments for a series of positions that contribute to a single, larger argument. For now, we will consider these segments somewhat abstractly so as to get a clear sense of the structure of the chapter. Later, we will examine individually many of the arguments that contribute to this larger structure.

Like the *pūrvapakṣa*, the presentation of the *uttarapakṣa* contains within it many voices of protest. These voices represent challenges to the *uttarapakṣa* and may be attributed to some or all members of the opponent school, either theoretically or historically. Since the primary interlocutor in this chapter is Kumārila, it is usually his voice, or in some cases a parody of it, that is portrayed as urging periodic objections in the *uttarapakṣa*. This is similar, though inverse, to the situation in the *pūrvapakṣa*, where Śāntarakṣita allows Kumārila to "speak for himself" (through the direct citation of many of his verses), but where an insistent "judicious" or Buddhist voice returns always to object. As in the *pūrvapakṣa*, arguments are frequently formulated using premises presented as those that the opponent should accept.

In the *uttarapakṣa*, one senses the enthusiasm with which Śāntarakṣita and Kamalaśīla enter into the fray with Kumārila. Śāntarakṣita, for example, frequently parodies Kumārila by reproducing his verses with small, but crucial, alterations that transform the verses into representations of Buddhist positions. He also returns repeatedly to a variety of discussions, and in doing so provides Kamalaśīla with much occasion both to reiterate the authors' positions and to add further force to their previous arguments. All this means that the chapter, while undeniably captivating in its content, meanders a bit, in something like the manner of a protracted argument. As a result, there is a feeling when reading the chapter that one is observing an actual debate between the authors and Kumārila. Of course, it is not an actual debate but only an idealized representation of such a debate presented in the context of a Buddhist apology. Nonetheless, as a representation it is designed to appeal to the judicious person, the *prekṣāvant*, and the careful citation of Kumārila's actual words may in fact be intended in part as a means to increase the final chapter's credibility in the eyes of such impartial judges. In any case, while the great enthusiasm for response and rebuttal that Śāntarakṣita and Kamalaśīla evince here (as elsewhere) does produce a certain prolixity, it is fortunately still possible to isolate several distinct arguments in the chapter. The precise relationship of these arguments to each other is, however, somewhat less easy to determine.

Details of the Structure of the Uttarapakṣa

We can conceive of these arguments as four demonstrations, each of which is a "movement" in a larger argument. Of these four demonstrations, two correspond closely to what Dharmakīrti's successors, including his earliest commentators Devendrabuddhi and Śākyabuddhi, refer to as a "progressive" (*anuloma*) and a "regressive" (*pratiloma*) division in the demonstration of the Buddha's trustworthiness in *Pramāṇavārttika* 2.[385] Although there is

385. The *anuloma-pratiloma* sequence is usually discussed in terms of the five epithets of the Buddha from Dignāga's famous *maṅgalaśloka* at PS 1.1: *pramāṇabhūtāya jagaddhitaiṣine praṇamya śāstre sugatāya tāyine / pramāṇasiddhyai svamatāt samuccayaḥ kariṣyate viprasṛtād ihaikataḥ /*. "Having bowed to the one who has become an authority (*pramāṇabhūta*), who desires to benefit the world, the teacher, the Sugata, the protector, I shall here make a collection of my scattered views in order to establish trustworthy awareness (*pramāṇa*)." Dharmakīrti organizes PV 2 around these five epithets, arguing for them first in a progressive (*anuloma*) sequence and then in a regressive (*pratiloma*) sequence. For alternative translations and explanations of Dharmakīrti's intepretation, see, e.g., Nagatomi 1959; Hattori 1968: 23 and 73–75; Inami and Tillemans 1986: 124–27; Steinkellner 1982: 7–10; Jackson 1988 and 1993: 127–35; Franco 1997: 15–43; van Bijlert 1989: 115–80; and Vetter 1964: 31–34 and 1990: 14–35. In the TS/P, we can see the sequence as a more general style of reasoning about the Buddha's knowledge that appears not to make an explicit connection to the epithets from Dignāga's verse. Although the opening verses of the TS do contain some epithets that could be linked with the five epithets from the PS, I have not been able to discover any overt allusion in the TS/P to the five epithets as they were understood by either Dignāga or Dharmakīrti. A speculative pairing of epithets from PS 1.1 with phrases from TS 1–6 is as follows: *jagaddhitaiṣin* ≈ *jagaddhitavidhitsayā //*

some disagreement about precisely where the break between the progressive and the regressive arguments occurs in *Pramāṇavārttika* 2, surviving Indian commentators appear to be largely unanimous in ascribing this method to Dharmakīrti's proof of the Buddha's authority.[386] According to this schema, Dharmakīrti demonstrates the Buddha's trustworthiness in two steps. First, in the progressive stage, he demonstrates the possibility of the perfection of the good qualities (*guṇa*) of the mind based on certain premises about the nature of the mind. Next, in the regressive stage, he demonstrates that the historical Buddha had in fact attained such perfection of the good qualities of the mind, thus rendering him trustworthy. Devendrabuddhi, the first commentator on Dharmakīrti's *Pramāṇavārttika*, describes the progressive (*anuloma*) argument as establishing that it is "not absolutely impossible" (*shin tu mi srid pa* = *atyantābhāva*) for the Buddha to be trustworthy.[387] The subsequent regressive (*pratiloma*) argument then involves an inference from an effect (the Buddha's teachings) to its cause (his knowledge that produces those teachings).

Although Śāntarakṣita and Kamalaśīla do not use the terms *anuloma* and *pratiloma* in the *Tattvasaṃgraha* and the *Pañjikā*, the similarity of their reasoning with what is found in *Pramāṇavārttika* 2 is clearly not accidental. Not only are two of the central arguments in the final chapter's *uttarapakṣa* analogous to the *anuloma* and *pratiloma* stages of argument in Dharmakīrti, but in addition, many specific arguments, especially those concerning the perfectibility of mental states, are borrowed directly from Dharmakīrti's text.[388] At the same time, the final chapter of the *Tattvasaṃgraha* and the *Pañjikā* is not a commentary on *Pramāṇavārttika* 2, and it contains lines of reasoning not immediately apparent in that chapter, or indeed anywhere in Dharmakīrti's corpus (of which I am aware). Rather than the relatively simple two stages

---

śāstṛ ≈ svatantraśrutiniḥsaṅgo ... analpakalpāsaṃkhyeyasātmībhūtamahādayaḥ // sugata ≈ sarvajñam // tāyin ≈ yaḥ pratītyasamutpāda jagāda gadatāṃ varaḥ //.

386. See, e.g., Vibhūticandra, PVV-n (521,5–13). According to Inami and Tillemans (1986: 126n8), the schematic was not as ubiquitous in Tibet, being mostly absent from pre-fifteenth-century Sa skya pa commentaries. They suggest that "one might provisionally hypothesize that among Tibetan schools this method of approaching PV II was primarily employed by the dGe lugs pas, who took their inspiration on the point from Tsong kha pa's *Tshad ma'i brjed byang chen mo.*"

387. Devendrabuddhi's remarks are from his commentary on PV 2.146 and are found at PVP D 61b6–7. They are translated in Inami and Tillemans (1986: 126).

388. See Pemwieser 1991: 53–101, who in the annotations to her translation of a lengthy and important section of commentary from the final chapter of the TS/P (i.e., TSP *ad* TS 3337) indicates many of the specific instances of dependence on PV 2.

that we find in Dharmakīrti's argument for the trustworthiness of the Buddha, the final chapter of the *Tattvasaṃgraha* and the *Pañjikā* argues for supersensible seeing or omniscience through four demonstrations:

- Rebuttal of Kumārila's refutation of omniscience
- Demonstration of the possibility of omniscience
- Demonstration of the Buddha's omniscience
- Demonstration of total omniscience

These demonstrations are the focus of our study in the following chapters. Here, we may note that although the first demonstration has no corresponding component in *Pramāṇavārttika* 2, it is nonetheless heavily reliant on Dharmakīrti's theory of nonperception (*anupalabdhi*) as presented in *Pramāṇavārttika* 1 and its commentary, *Pramāṇavārttikasvopajñavṛtti*. The general demonstration of the possibility of omniscience and the specific demonstration of the Buddha's omniscience correspond to the progressive and regressive stages of argument in *Pramāṇavārttika* 2. The fourth demonstration appears to be new to the *Tattvasaṃgraha* and the *Pañjikā*.

Relations Among the Four Arguments

The relations among these four demonstrations or "movements" in the larger argument may be analyzed in several ways. For example, one may see them as forming a simple linear progression, where each demonstration takes as its premise the conclusions of the immediately previous demonstration. This is approximately the order in which the demonstrations first appear in the *uttarapakṣa*, and so such an approach is not unwarranted. But it is equally possible to follow Śāntarakṣita and Kamalaśīla and categorize the demonstrations of the argument in terms of a "general" and a "specific" component.[389] If we break things down this way, the four demonstrations could then be represented according to the following table:

389. Śāntarakṣita sums up the procedure he uses to determine the Buddha's omniscience through this twofold division in TS 3335 (*atīndriyārthadarśiparīkṣā*): *tat sambhavy api sarvajñaḥ sāmānyena prasādhitaḥ / tallakṣaṇāvinābhāvāt sugato vyavatiṣṭhate //*. "Therefore, although an omniscient person is established in a general way, the Sugata is established [to actually be omniscient] because of being invariably concomitant with the definition of that [omniscience]." The idea of "invariable concomitance" (*avinābhāvatva*) here indicates that Śāntarakṣita sees the process of proving the Buddha's omniscience as inferential.

General Demonstration	Specific Demonstration
Rebuttal of Kumārila's Refutation	Demonstration of the Buddha's Omniscience
Demonstration of the Possibility of Omniscience	
Demonstration of Total Omniscience	

This is the division of the demonstrations that I will adopt as a guideline for my discussion of the four demonstrations in the following chapters, considering the entire general demonstration in the next chapter and the specific demonstration in the chapter following that.

This is not, however, the only way to conceive the relations among these four demonstrations. Another way, again suggested by the authors, would prioritize the division between the two connotations of omniscience discussed above: dharmic and total omniscience. If we attempt to organize the four demonstrations under these two rubrics, the first three demonstrations should probably be considered as together comprising the fundamental (*mukhya*) demonstration, while the fourth alone would be the consequentialist (*prāsaṅgika*). This could be represented visually as follows:

Fundamental Demonstration of Dharmic Omniscience	Consequential Demonstration of Total Omniscience
Rebuttal of Kumārila's Refutation	Demonstration of Total Omniscience
Demonstration of the Possibility of Omniscience	
Demonstration of the Buddha's Omniscience	

This way of organizing the four demonstrations has the advantage of highlighting the authors' repeated declaration that it is dharmic and not total omniscience that counts as omniscience in this tradition. Yet it also casts into doubt the authors' motives in undertaking the demonstration of total omniscience. What do Śāntarakṣita and Kamalaśīla gain by their efforts to establish total omniscience? They reject that they do so to establish the Buddha as trustworthy or an authority; that task is accomplished by the other three demonstrations alone. We will return to this, and other similar problems, in our closer examination of the four demonstrations.

It is left only to remark that any linear presentation of the four demonstrations is more ideal than reality since, especially in the later sections of the final chapter, the authors move freely back and forth among the four demonstrations, interweaving them as well with detailed considerations of many of Kumārila's specific objections that were presented earlier in the *pūrvapakṣa*.[390] In broad strokes, however, we may say that the *uttarapakṣa* starts off with the rebuttal of Kumārila's refutation of omniscience, before briefly introducing the specific demonstration, which is then almost immediately interrupted by the demonstration of the possibility of omniscience.[391] The authors next return to the specific demonstration, which they follow by various refutations of Kumārila's prior arguments. They then embark on another round of the demonstration of the possibility of omniscience, finally introducing the consequentialist demonstration of total omniscience.[392] After this, the structure of the chapter becomes more difficult to discern; the authors pick up the various demonstrations for longer or shorter passages, often returning to earlier arguments and shoring them up with fresh examples and stronger rhetoric.[393] Finally, near the end of the chapter, the authors advance some *ad personam* attacks that appear to be aimed at discrediting Kumārila rather than at refuting him philosophically.[394] They then take up the objections of Sāmaṭa and Yajñaṭa, setting forth an array of possible solutions to the question of omniscience.[395]

The mix of all these elements: the shifting perspectives, the tolerance of a range of solutions to certain conundrums, the presence of different demonstrations with individual, although related, goals, and the length and complexity of the work as a whole makes for a huge interpretive challenge. Even if

390. In the commentary, Kamalaśīla helpfully indicates the verses to which Śāntarakṣita is responding.

391. The first demonstration is found at TS/P 3261–3305; there is then a section, TS/P 3306–32, in which it is clarified that omniscience includes, paradigmatically, knowledge of Dharma and Adharma; TS/P 3333–36 then begin the specific demonstration, which is interrupted by the demonstration of the possibility of omniscience at TS/P 3337–38 but is picked up again in TS/P 3339–46.

392. The responses to Kumārila's arguments are at TS/P 3347–3405; the authors return to the demonstration of the real possibility in TS/P 3406–48, of which the final portion involves the consequentialist demonstration of total omniscience.

393. So, for example, TS/P 3449–60 returns to the specific demonstration; TS/P 3461–72 picks up the demonstration of the mere possibility of omniscience; the remainder (to TS/P 3645) proceeds similarly.

394. These are at TS/P 3546–90.

395. TS/P 3621–45.

the chapter does not conspicuously argue for the authors' final perspective on omniscience, its importance for our project of understanding omniscience in the *Tattvasaṃgraha* and the *Pañjikā* is undeniable. This is why we spend so much time analyzing the arguments of the "Investigation of One Who Sees Supersensible Objects" in the pages to come. Only after that analysis is complete do we go on to consider the arguments for omniscience as they are advanced on the authors' preferred level of analysis, that of the Vijñānavāda. Most of the discussions of omniscience on this level of analysis occur in the work's twenty-third chapter, the "Investigation of External Objects," to a brief description of which we now turn.

The "Investigation of External Objects"

The *bahirarthaparīkṣā*, or "Investigation of External Objects," is the final chapter of the first section of the work as a whole, the section dealing with the nature of reality. The primary purpose of the chapter is to demonstrate through reasoning that the Vijñānavāda perspective is more rational than the Sautrāntika perspective, and that it should therefore be adopted by judicious persons. As the chapter title suggests, the investigation takes as its focus of refutation the idea that there exist real objects of awareness external to the mind. Here, we encounter arguments against external objects of awareness, along with arguments for the luminous or self-reflexive nature of awareness. The authors argue that awareness is nondual, and, at least on the ultimate level of analysis, devoid of any object of awareness at all. Although not cast in a Madhyamaka frame, much of the argumentation in this chapter is shared with arguments in Śāntarakṣita and Kamalaśīla's Madhyamaka works, especially Śāntarakṣita's *Madhyamakālaṃkāra*, his own commentary thereon, the *Madhyamakālaṃkāravṛtti*, and Kamalaśīla's subcommentary on these, the *Madhyamakālaṃkārapañjikā*.

Unlike many other chapters in the *Tattvasaṃgraha* and the *Pañjikā*, the "Investigation of External Objects" does not neatly divide into two sections, a *pūrvapakṣa* and an *uttarapakṣa*. Instead, the chapter proceeds one objection at a time, presenting the refutation of each objection immediately after first introducing it and then going on to another objection. As usual, Kamalaśīla is forthcoming in his identification of opponents by name. A primary opponent in the chapter is Śubhagupta, a Buddhist thinker who upholds the existence of external objects of awareness and who argues forcefully against the Vijñānavāda perspective in his *Bāhyārthasiddhikārikā*, a verse composition that comes down to us only in Tibetan translation.[396] This work is featured strongly in the "Investigation of External Objects," with Śāntarakṣita and Kamalaśīla directly quoting more than fifteen verses from the work between them.[397] Uddyotakara and Kumārila are also important interlocutors in the chapter, with Śāntarakṣita also quoting a number of verses from the latter's *Ślokavārttika*.

Although the chapter is addressed to both Buddhists and non-Buddhists, the placement in the structure of the work overall and the subject matter combine to create the impression that the audience is composed primarily of Buddhists, or at least of judicious persons, who have followed the reasoning in the *Tattvasaṃgraha* and the *Pañjikā* up to that point and who are now ready to take the step from the Sautrāntika to the Vijñānavāda level of analysis.

Omniscience occurs as a topic in the chapter several times, where it is always raised as part of an objection by Śubhagupta. In short, Śubhagupta argues that without objects of knowledge external to the mind, the Buddha's omniscience would become impossible. Obviously, he is arguing within a Buddhist context that accepts the dogma that omniscience (on some unspecified definition) is an inalienable quality of buddhahood. The answers that the authors of the *Tattvasaṃgraha* and the *Pañjikā* provide to these objections constitute their final perspective on omniscience in the work as a whole. We return to them in the conclusion of this book.

396. On Śubhagupta, see Eltschinger 1999; Frauwallner 1957b; Hattori 1960; Matsumoto 1980; Mikogami 1989; Mimaki 1987–88; and Shastri 1967. Mimaki notes (p. 276) that while the fourteenth-century Tibetan author, Dbus pa blo gsal, considers Śubhagupta to belong to the Vaibhāṣika tradition, Atiśa in the eleventh century classifies him as a Sautrāntika. Frauwallner (1957b) indicates that Śubhagupta was Dharmottara's teacher. See also Steinkellner and Much 1995 for references to Japanese scholarship on Śubhagupta, most notably the contributions of Mikogami, who prepared a critical edition of the BASK.

397. See Hattori 1960 for a list of parallels between the BASK and the *Bahirarthaparīkṣā*. The BASK was also quoted by the eighth-century Jain author Haribhadra Sūri in his *Anekāntajayapatākā*.

4. Omniscience Is Possible: The General Demonstration

We are now ready to focus on those aspects of the demonstration of omniscience found in the final chapter of the work which, taking a cue from Śāntarakṣita, I have called collectively the "general demonstration" of omniscience in the *Tattvasaṃgraha* and the *Pañjikā*. The demonstration is general in that it does not seek to establish the omniscience of any particular person but aims rather to establish the theoretical possibility of omniscience in a general manner (*sāmānyena*). As we outlined above, this general demonstration contains three primary elements: (1) a rebuttal of Kumārila's refutation of omniscience, (2) a demonstration of the possibility of omniscience, and (3) a demonstration of total omniscience. Our procedure will be to describe the three demonstrations as they occur in the final chapter of the *Tattvasaṃgraha* and the *Pañjikā*; later on, in chapter 6, we will analyze the rhetorical force of these arguments through an examination of the audience to which each demonstration is addressed and the strategies of argumentation employed.

Rebutting Kumārila's Refutation of Omniscience

Earlier we saw how, in the *pūrvapakṣa* of the final chapter of the *Tattvasaṃgraha* and the *Pañjikā*, the authors present a series of arguments attributed to Kumārila that are aimed at refuting omniscience through the special negative means of trustworthy awareness called *abhāvapramāṇa*. The first movement in Śāntarakṣita and Kamalaśīla's overall general demonstration of omniscience is the rebuttal to this sustained argument of refutation. This rebuttal contains three primary elements.

The rebuttal starts with a refutation of the position that Dharma is radically inaccessible (*atyantaparokṣa*) or beyond the senses (*atīndriya*). Here the authors reinforce their commitment to the idea that omniscience—whatever else it entails—necessarily and paradigmatically includes knowledge of Dharma and Adharma, the "most important things."

Next comes an attempt to demonstrate that none of the six means of trustworthy awareness accepted by Kumārila is at all capable of refuting omniscience. The argument concedes that an omniscient being is radically inaccessible for those who are not omniscient and that therefore neither the existence nor the nonexistence of such a being can be ascertained through perception or inference.

The last fundamental element in the rebuttal of Kumārila is the conclusion: that the existence or the nonexistence of an omniscient being is objectively a matter of doubt for all ordinary persons of limited vision. We will consider these three elements one by one.

Refuting that Dharma Is Radically Inaccessible

To discredit the Mīmāṃsaka idea that Dharma and Adharma are radically inaccessible, the authors of the *Tattvasaṃgraha* and the *Pañjikā* first invoke an argument in the form of a "presumption" or *arthāpatti*, one of six accepted means of trustworthy awareness in Kumārila's system and a form of inference in the Buddhist system.[398] This argument is the same one with which Śāntarakṣita opens the chapter, and which we examined briefly above. Śāntarakṣita now returns to it at the outset of the *uttarapakṣa*, again emphasizing that he has conclusively established that knowing Dharma and Adharma through an eternal and authorless scripture is not possible:

> Heaven, the sacrifice, and so on, having been understood by that [author] himself, were made known [by him]; therefore, your author of the Veda, too, is that kind of seer of supersensible objects, being either one who knows the most important human aims (*pradhānapuruṣārtha*) or, in fact, one who knows all *dharmas*. Otherwise, if that is not accepted, the Veda would not be trustworthy. But this acceptance of the knowledge of Dharma,

[illegible]ta and Kamalaśīla discuss *arthāpatti* at TS/P 1586–1646 (*pramāṇ*-[illegible]*ikṣā*), where Śāntarakṣita commences by citing Kumārila (TS 1586 = ŚV *arthāpatti*, 1): *pramāṇaṣaṭkavijñāto yatrārtho nānyathā bhavan / adṛṣṭaṃ kalpayaty anyaṃ sārthāpattir udāhṛtā //*. Kamalaśīla further gives a succinct summary of *arthāpatti* at TSP *ad* TS 3267–68 (*atīndriyārthadarśiparīkṣā*, B 1029,5): ... *dṛṣṭaḥ śruto vārtho 'nyathā nopapadyate ity adṛṣṭaparikalpanārthāpattiḥ //*.

> obtained through presumption (*arthāpatti*), contravenes the refutation of that [knowledge of Dharma] that you have so extensively undertaken.[399]

Śāntarakṣita's argument relies on the acceptance of two theses: (1) that the Mīmāṃsaka holds the Veda to be trustworthy in relation to Dharma and Adharma; and (2) that the Buddhist has been successful in demonstrating that the Veda cannot be trustworthy if it is eternal and authorless. The implication of these two statements for the Mīmāṃsaka who will not relinquish the authority of the Veda must be that the Veda *has* an author and that that author sees (i.e., directly knows) Dharma and Adharma. Otherwise, if this is rejected, the Mīmāṃsaka must then give up that the Veda is trustworthy in regard to the most important things, Dharma and Adharma, since verbal testimony derives its trustworthiness or authority from the direct and correct knowledge of its author. The strategy of this argument is to force Kumārila to concede that there is an author of the Veda who sees supersensible objects.

The *degree* of supersensible seeing urged through this presumption is not the most relevant factor in this argument, as the verses just cited make plain. Śāntarakṣita says that in seeing supersensible objects, the author of the Veda is "either one who knows the most important human aims (*pradhānapuruṣārtha*) or, in fact, one who knows all *dharma*s." This is just another way of saying that the author of the Veda must be omniscient—where the meaning of omniscience is left somewhat open, and can indicate either the dharmic or the total variety. But if the degree of supersensible seeing is not very important, the *kind* of supersensible seeing is extremely important; that is, such seeing *must* include seeing Dharma and Adharma, the most important things soteriologically speaking, if that seeing is to be relevant to persons seeking the highest aims. This is the kind of supersensible seeing that the authors of the *Tattvasaṃgraha* and the *Pañjikā* are concerned to defend.

Now, in the *pūrvapakṣa*, Kumārila had been portrayed as allowing for the conventional application of the term *sarvajña* in certain contexts, provided that such applications do not imply knowledge of Dharma and Adharma. In a well-known verse, Kumārila is made to say:

399. TS 3264–66 (*atīndriyārthadarśiparīkṣā*): *svargayāgādayas tasmāt svato jñātvā prakāśitāḥ / vedakāras tavāpy asti tādṛśo 'tīndriyārthadṛk // pradhānapuruṣārthajñaḥ sarvadharmajña eva vā / tasyānupagame na syād vedaprāmāṇyam anyathā // tenārthāpattilabdhena dharmajñopagamena tu / bādhyate tanniṣedho 'yaṃ vistareṇa kṛtas tvayā //*.

> Here the refutation of the knowledge of Dharma alone is appropriate. Who would deny that there are people who know everything else?[400]

There follows immediately after the citation of this verse a number of possible ways in which a person might conceivably be called omniscient, despite lacking knowledge of Dharma and Adharma. For instance, a person could be called omniscient or all-knowing (*sarvajña*) in a purely nominal sense due simply to her knowledge of the word "all" (*sarva*).[401] Alternatively, someone might be considered omniscient by virtue of his knowledge of certain categories thought to epitomize all things, such as the categories "real and unreal" or "being cognizable."[402] Similarly, some might wish to label omniscient that person who has mastered the classification of existent things according to some system or another.[403] On Kumārila's view, these purely nominal applications of the term omniscience are noncontroversial and to argue for them is just to "establish that which is already established."[404]

Kamalaśīla responds in the *uttarapakṣa* that Kumārila's argument here misses the mark, for Buddhists are not interested in defending a form of omniscience that excludes knowledge of Dharma and Adharma, which would be absurd, but only a form of omniscience that minimally includes such knowledge as its most significant and therefore defining element.[405] Kamalaśīla makes this quite clear in a later statement:

> For we do not make an effort to prove omniscience having dispensed with the idea of the knowledge of Dharma. Rather,

400. TS 3127 (*atīndriyārthadarśiparīkṣā*): *dharmajñatvaniṣedhaś cet kevalo 'tropayujyate / sarvam anyad vijānānaḥ puruṣaḥ kena vāryate //*. Quoted with minor variations in Ratnakīrti's SS 1.7–8 and attributed there as well to Kumārila.

401. TS 3129 (*atīndriyārthadarśiparīkṣā*): *arthe cāsaṃbhavāt kāryaṃ kiṃ cic chabde 'pi kalpyate / tatra yaḥ sarvaśabdajñaḥ sa sarvajño 'stu nāmataḥ //*.

402. TS 3131–32 (*atīndriyārthadarśiparīkṣā*): *bhāvābhāvasvarūpaṃ vā jagat sarvaṃ yadocyate / tat saṃkṣepeṇa sarvajñaḥ puruṣaḥ kena neṣyate // evaṃ jñeyaprameyatvasaṃkṣepeṇāpi sarvatām / āśritya yadi sarvajñaḥ kas taṃ vārayituṃ kṣamaḥ //*.

403. TS 3133 (*atīndriyārthadarśiparīkṣā*): *padārthā yaiś ca yāvantaḥ sarvatvenāvadhāritāḥ / tajjñatvenāpi sarvajñāḥ sarve tadgranthavedinaḥ //*.

404. TSP *ad* TS 3128 (*atīndriyārthadarśiparīkṣā*, B 989,17–18): *yadi bhavadbhir api bauddhair dharmādharmajñavyatirekeṇānyasmin puṃsi sarvajñatvaṃ prasajyate tadā siddhasādhyateti ... /*.

405. TSP *ad* TS 3267–68 (*atīndriyārthadarśiparīkṣā*, B 1026,13–14): *na hy asmābhir dharmādivyatiriktavivakṣitāśeṣārthābhijñatayā sarvajño 'bhyupagamyate yena tatra dūṣaṇam āsajyeta /*.

> [we make an effort] to prove that very knowledge of Dharma, which is the most important thing (*pradhānabhūta*). Therefore, earlier, in accord precisely with your opinion, [Śāntarakṣita] stated the means of trustworthy awareness called "presumption" (*arthāpatti*) to prove a person who knows Dharma with the words "this acceptance of the knowledge of Dharma, obtained through presumption."[406] And afterward, he will present the means of trustworthy awareness called inference [to prove knowledge of Dharma or omniscience].[407]

Knowledge of Dharma, defined as that which enables one to attain the highest good, is "the most important thing," and omniscience, insofar as it is maximal epistemic greatness, paradigmatically and minimally must include such knowledge.

Kumārila's primary objection to the doctrine of omniscience rests on his view that knowledge of Dharma is not possible; in their argument against Kumārila, Śāntarakṣita and Kamalaśīla define *sarvajña* as knowledge of Dharma and Adharma first and foremost. A pair of verses from the *Tattvasaṃgraha* illustrates this point. The first verse gives the Mīmāṃsaka position and the second, involving a verbal play on the first, represents the Buddhist response:

> TS 3143: And those who, because their root is cut, say that there are omniscient people, even though the knowledge of Dharma has been refuted—such people are threshing chaff.[408]

> TS 3316: But those who, because their root is *not* cut, say that there are omniscient persons since the knowledge of Dharma is not refuted—they exhibit wisdom.[409]

406. TS 3266 (*atīndriyārthadarśiparīkṣā*): see above, n. 399.

407. TSP *ad* TS 3312–13 (*atīndriyārthadarśiparīkṣā*, B 1045,20–23): *na hy asmābhir dharmajñaviṣayāṃ cintāṃ muktvā sarvajñasādhane prayatnaḥ kriyate / kiṃ tarhi / pradhānabhūtadharmajñasādhana eva / tathā ca pūrvam tenārthāpattilabhyena dharmajñopagamenetyādinā dharmajñasādhane 'rthāpattyākhyaṃ bhavanmatenaiva pramāṇam uktam / paścāc cānumānākhyaṃ pramāṇam abhidhāsyate //*. Reading *asmābhir dharmajñaviṣayāṃ cintāṃ muktvā* in accord with D291a7–291b1 and P355b4: *kho bo cag gis chos shes pa'i yul can gyis bsam pa spangs nas ...*, B and G both give *asmābhiḥ sarvajñaviṣayāṃ*, but J286a5 is exceedingly difficult to read.

408. TS 3143 (*atīndriyārthadarśiparīkṣā*): *ye 'pi vicchinnamūlatvād dharmajñatve hate sati / sarvajñān puruṣān āhus taiḥ kṛtaṃ tuṣakaṇḍanam //*.

409. TS 3316 (*atīndriyārthadarśiparīkṣā*): *ye tv avicchinnamūlatvād dharmajñatve 'hate*

The reference to the "root" which is cut is most likely the "root of virtue" (*kuśalamūla*), an idea found in Buddhist works since early times; in any case, it is clear that in the first verse Kumārila is portrayed as ridiculing the idea of omniscience in the absence of the possibility that Dharma can be known, while in the second verse Śāntarakṣita extols the notion of omniscience precisely for the reason that Dharma *can* be known.

Refuting that Any *Pramāṇa* Can Disprove Omniscience

Once they have laid out the argument by means of *arthāpatti* for the knowledge of Dharma, the authors move to the next phase of the demonstration: the rebuttal of Kumārila's claim that an omniscient being is refuted through *abhāvapramāṇa*, the means of trustworthy awareness of nonexistence. Kamalaśīla presents his version of the formal reasoning behind this Mīmāṃsaka claim early on in the *pūrvapakṣa* of the final chapter:

> That body (*vigraha*) which is an object of the means of trustworthy awareness of nonexistence—the nature of which is to be devoid of the five [other] means of trustworthy awareness [i.e., perception and so on]—is understood by wise people to fall within the convention of nonexistence [i.e., it can be correctly described as nonexistent], like a lotus in the sky. And an omniscient person is a body that is an object of the means of trustworthy awareness of nonexistence; this is evidence by means of essential identity (*svabhāvahetu*).[410]

Kumārila's argument is that an omniscient being does not exist because an omniscient being is not ascertained by any of the five positive means of trustworthy awareness—perception, inference, presumption, analogy, and verbal testimony. Omniscience is therefore, on Kumārila's theory, an object (*viṣaya*) of *abhāvapramāṇa*, which means that omniscience is definitively established

---

sati / sarvajñān puruṣān āhur dhīmattā taiḥ prakāśitā //. Kamalaśīla (TSP *ad cit.*) remarks on the elision (*avagraha*) of the negative particle (*akāra*) in the phrase *dharmajñatve 'hate sati*, and indicates that the word "they" (*taiḥ*) in the verse refers to Buddhists (*buddhaiḥ*).

410. TSP *ad* TS 3124–26 (*atīndriyārthadarśiparīkṣā*, B 988,23–989,9): *yaḥ pramāṇapañcakavirahasvabhāvābhāvapramāṇaviṣayīkṛtavigrahaḥ sa viduṣām abhāvavyavahāragocaratām evāvatarati yathā gaganalinam / abhāvapramāṇaviṣayīkṛtavigrahaś ca sarvadarśī puruṣa iti svabhāvahetuḥ //*. The equivalent for the term *vyavahāra* is missing in Tibetan.

not to exist. In the *pūrvapakṣa*, Śāntarakṣita and Kamalaśīla go on to present detailed arguments from the Mīmāṃsaka perspective showing why omniscience cannot be an object of, and is not therefore established by, any of the other means of trustworthy awareness.[411] We will not enter into these arguments in detail here.

In the *uttarapakṣa*, the authors of the *Tattvasaṃgraha* and the *Pañjikā* seek to rebut these same arguments.[412] The section in which they do so commences with two verses at TS 3267–68, where Śāntarakṣita makes an overt allusion to a verse that he earlier cited and attributed to Kumārila:

> Moreover, the statement "Who is capable of cognizing all head and body hairs..." is utterly without rational ground, like the command of a king, since there might be some person for whom all things are illumined by the lamp of stainless and unflinching knowledge. And to this no contravening [means of trustworthy awareness] has been stated.[413]

Śāntarakṣita's use of the optative mood (*syāt*) in the phrase "there *might be* some person..." reminds us that this demonstration aims to demolish the Mīmāṃsakas' refutation of omniscience. To accomplish this end, the authors of the *Tattvasaṃgraha* and the *Pañjikā* intend to show that the Mīmāṃsakas have no means—whether *abhāvapramāṇa* or any other means of trustworthy awareness—by which to disprove the existence of an omniscient being. Thus, the aim of the argument here is a negative one: to show that no *pramāṇa* is capable of refuting omniscience.

We must remember when considering this section of the *uttarapakṣa* that the authors have already offered what they consider to be convincing arguments to refute Kumārila's general theory of *abhāvapramāṇa*. These arguments rely on a number of objections to Kumārila's formulation of this negative means of trustworthy awareness in the *Ślokavārttika* and are for the

411. See TS/P 3158–3228 (*atīndriyārthadarśiparīkṣā*).

412. See TS/P 3267–3305 (*atīndriyārthadarśiparīkṣā*).

413. TS 3267–68 (*atīndriyārthadarśiparīkṣā*): *kiṃcākāraṇam evedam uktam ājñāprabhor iva / keśaromāṇi yāvanti kas tāni jñātum arhati // yasmān nirmalaniṣkampajñānadīpena kaścana / dyotitākhilavastuḥ syād ity atroktaṃ na bādhakam //*. Amending the fourth *pāda* of G and B to read: *ājñā prabhor iva* instead of *ājñāprabhāvitam* in accord with D 119a6: *rgyal po'i bka' dang 'dra bar smras*. The verse to which Śāntarakṣita alludes here is cited at TS 3136, where it is attributed to Kumārila: *ekasyaiva śarīrasya yāvantaḥ paramāṇavaḥ / keśaromāṇi yāvanti kas tāni jñātum arhati //*.

most part too detailed for us to explicate here.[414] For our purposes, we may focus on a basic conclusion of these arguments, which concerns perception:

> Therefore, the nonperception of something is just the perception of something else; thus, there is no means of trustworthy awareness called nonexistence separate from perception.[415]

For the Buddhist *pramāṇa* theorists like Śāntarakṣita and Kamalaśīla, there is no need for *abhāvapramāṇa* to determine the nonexistence of an entity. That task is instead achieved through nonperception (*anupalabdhi*), which is not a separate means of trustworthy awareness[416] but rather a type of logical sign (*liṅga*, *hetu*) that may serve as evidence in inferences ascertaining the nonexistence of an entity qualified as "amenable to perception" or "perceptible" (*dṛśya*).[417] As one of the three accepted types of logical evidence in this system, nonperception plays its most important role in inference; nonetheless, nonperception itself is understood to be a form of perception (*pratyakṣa*, *upalabdhi*).[418] This seemingly paradoxical assertion is explained by the idea that what we call nonperception of an entity x is in fact just the perception of another entity y (where $y \neq x$). So, for example, nonperception of the moon in the sky does not differ phenomenologically from the positive perception of a sky on a night in which there is no moon.[419]

Therefore, Kumārila's theory of *abhāvapramāṇa*, in the view of the authors of the *Tattvasaṃgraha* and the *Pañjikā*, suffers not only from faults in its formulation but also from the fault of serving no purpose not already accom-

414. See Kellner 1997 for a thorough treatment.

415. TSP *ad* TS 1679–82 (*pramāṇāntarabhāvaparīkṣā*, B 584,19–20): *tasmād ekopalabdhir evānyasyānupalabdhir iti nābhāvo nāma pṛthak pramāṇaṃ pratyakṣāt* //. My translation reverses the order of the words in the first part of the sentence to account for a typical Sanskrit syntactical pattern in which a predicate *precedes* its subject.

416. An exception seems to have occurred in the now lost works of Dharmakīrti's reputed teacher Īśvarasena, who is recorded by Arcaṭa to have upheld nonperception as a separate means of trustworthy awareness. Dharmakīrti rejected this, however, on the grounds that this nonperception, being itself a negation, would need to be verified by a further nonperception, thus leading to an infinite regress. Dharmakīrti's solution is to understand nonperception as a form of "perception of something other," which then, like all perception, is verified through reflexive awareness. See Kellner 1997: 107–8.

417. See PV 1.3cd: *asajjñānaphalā kācid hetubhedavyapekṣayā* //; and PVSV *ad cit.*: *hetur anupalabdhiḥ / bhedo 'syā viśeṣaṇam upalabdhilakṣaṇaprāptasattvam* /.

418. See, e.g., PV 4.274: *tasmād anupalambho 'yaṃ svayaṃ pratyakṣato gataḥ* //.

419. See TS 1687–88 (*pramāṇāntarabhāvaparīkṣā*) and TSP *ad cit.* (B 586,12–587,12).

plished by perception and inference. The upshot is that when Śāntarakṣita and Kamalaśīla address Kumārila's claim that the omniscient being is refuted by *abhāvapramāṇa*, they do not limit themselves to contesting the claim on its own terms, but they include as well a consideration of the opponent's distinct, though related, claim that *anupalabdhi*, or nonperception, *in the Buddhist view* refutes an omniscient being. This explains why the authors spend comparatively more time in this part of the *uttarapakṣa* discussing perception and inference as opposed to the other *pramāṇa*s accepted by Kumārila. After all, the fundamental argument here is that *no pramāṇa* can refute omniscience—whether that be a *pramāṇa* as advanced by the Mīmāṃsakas, the Buddhists, or anyone else—and in the eyes of the authors, as heirs of Dharmakīrti, if any *pramāṇa* were to refute an omniscient being, it would have to be either perception or inference because they do not accept any *pramāṇa*s apart from these.

Perception Cannot Refute Omniscience

The counterattack to Kumārila's refutation of omniscience begins in the commentary on the verses cited above (TS 3267–68), where we find Kamalaśīla going through each of the six means of trustworthy awareness accepted by Kumārila to show that none of them is capable of refuting an omniscient being. Kamalaśīla undertakes this demonstration while simultaneously making clear his conviction that all *pramāṇa*s apart from perception and inference have already been conclusively refuted, saying, for example, that he has no obligation to consider *arthāpatti* as a method of refuting omniscience "since the trustworthiness of [awarenesses] other than perception and inference is not established."[420] Still, he does go on to consider briefly each of these other means of trustworthy awareness, as we will see shortly.

At the same time, Kamalaśīla appears to consider perception to be the most critical means of trustworthy awareness in this investigation. This is not surprising, since in his view, only a particular kind of perception would be capable of establishing the nonexistence of a perceptible entity. Kamalaśīla summarizes his argument near the outset of this section:

> That is to say, there is no refutation by perception, since that [entity in question] is not an object of that [i.e., perception]. For it is only when a real thing that is properly an object of perception is well established as [actually being] perceptible that a contrary quality

420. TSP *ad* TS 3267–68 (*atīndriyārthadarśiparīkṣā*, B 1029,3–4): *pratyakṣānumānavya tirekeṇānyeṣāṃ pramāṇatvāsiddheḥ* /.

> that is being provisionally accepted (*abhyupagamyamāna*) may be refuted through perception. For example, [the quality of] being inaudible [is refuted through perception] in the subject "sound" because [sound] is audible. But [there is] no [refutation] where perception does not occur. And all the mental states occurring in others' mindstreams are not objects of perception for any non-omniscient person, such that the omniscience being proposed (*pratijñāyamāna*) would be refuted through perception, because all of [those non-omniscient persons] are persons of limited vision (*arvāgdarśin*). Or, if [the mental states of others] were objects [of perception], then that [person for whom they were perceptible] would be omniscient. Therefore, [this is] no refutation.[421]

Here, in addition to an assertion that omniscience cannot be refuted by perception since neither it nor its locus (i.e., others' minds) is amenable to perception, we also encounter a concept central to these discussions: the "person of limited vision" (*arvāgdarśin*), i.e., the ordinary person who is capable of cognizing only that which is near (*arvāk*) and who has no access to things radically inaccessible (*atyantaparokṣa*) or supersensible (*atīndriya*). Persons of limited vision are persons who do not know, for example, what is taking place in another person's mind.[422] They are those who cannot see the precise details of karmic causality.[423] And they cannot be sure that a person known

421. TSP *ad* TS 3267–68 (*atīndriyārthadarśiparīkṣā*, B 1027,3–9): *tathā hi na tāvat pratyakṣaṃ bādhakaṃ tasyātadviṣayatvāt / yad eva hi vastu pratyakṣeṇa yathā viṣayīkriyate tatra pratyakṣaprasiddhe viparīto dharmo 'bhyupagamyamānaḥ pratyakṣeṇa bādhyate / yathā śabde dharmiṇi aśrāvaṇatvaṃ śrāvaṇatvena / na tu yatra pratyakṣasyāpravṛttiḥ / na ca parasantānavartīni cetāṃsi sarvāṇi pratyakṣato 'sarvajñena viṣayīkriyante kenacit / yena tatra sarvajñatvaṃ pratijñāyamānaṃ pratyakṣeṇa bādhyeta / sarveṣām evārvāgdarśitvāt / viṣayīkaraṇe vā sa eva sarvajña ity apratikṣepaḥ //*. Cf. PS 3.2 and PSV *ad cit*. For Dharmakīrti's interpretation, see PV 4.131–35, where Dharmakīrti considers the circumstances under which perception may act as a means of refutation, including the example of perception as a refutation for the proposition "sound is inaudible." See Tillemans 2000: 189–94.

422. See, e.g., TSP *ad* TS 1208 (*śabdārthaparīkṣā*, B 447,5–6): *pratyātmasaṃvedanīyam evārvāgdarśanānāṃ jñānam / na hy anyadīyajñānam aparo 'paradarśanaḥ saṃvedayate //*. "The awareness of a person of limited vision is restricted (*eva*) to that which is known by himself [alone], for another's awareness is not known by one who does not see others' [minds]." Although this statement is part of an objection, the following verse and its commentary (TS/P 1209) make clear that Śāntarakṣita and Kamalaśīla accept the principle.

423. See, e.g., TSP *ad* TS 1936–37 (*lokāyataparīkṣā*, B 662,20–21): *...aviprakarṣe 'py arvāgdarśinā so 'yaṃ prāṇī pataṅgādyātmatāṃ gata iti niścetum aśakyatvāt /*. "...because

to them but not in their immediate presence is still alive.[424] In short, these are persons who—intelligent and judicious though they may be—have cognitive limitations typical of most human beings. It is in relation to such persons that we frequently translate the term *atyantaparokṣa* as "radically inaccessible." Kamalaśīla and Kumārila both present their arguments with the understanding that they and their readers are this sort of person.[425]

Śāntarakṣita and Kamalaśīla's argument is that persons of limited vision cannot disprove an omniscient being through perception, because such a being is not an object amenable to perception for them, and because nothing that such persons do perceive can be shown to be incompatible with such a being. When the objector explains that it is not perception *per se* that disproves the omniscient being but rather the fact that perception does not function in relation to such a being, Kamalaśīla retorts that a nonfunctioning perception is not a perception at all.[426] This exchange leads to the following objection and reply:

---

even when [the person in question] is not remote, a person of limited vision is not capable of ascertaining that 'This sentient being has been a bird and so on.'" The context for this remark is an argument that holds that one cannot disprove the theory of rebirth simply because one cannot see either the bodies that went before or that come after the present life.

424. TSP *ad* TS 1640–42 (*pramāṇāntarabhāvaparīkṣā*, B. 572,19–20): *tasya caitrasya jīvane niścāyakapramāṇābhāvād arvāgdarśinaḥ saṃśaya eva* /. "Because the person of limited vision has no means of trustworthy awareness that can ascertain that Caitra is alive, it is just a matter of doubt [for him]."

425. A crucial difference between these thinkers, however, concerns whether ordinary persons may transcend their limited vision. Kamalaśīla would answer "yes," Kumārila "no."

426. TSP *ad* TS 3267–68 (*atīndriyārthadarśiparīkṣā*, B 1027,10–16): *syād etat / na vayaṃ pratyakṣaṃ pravartamānam abhāvaṃ sādhayatīti brūmaḥ / kiṃ tarhi / nivartamānam / tathā hi yatra vastuni pratyakṣasya nivṛttis tasyābhāvo 'vasīyate yathā śaśaviṣāṇasya / yatra pravṛttis tasya bhāvaḥ yathā rūpādeḥ / na ca sarvajñaviṣayaṃ kadācit pratyakṣaṃ pravṛttam ity atas tannivṛttes tadabhāvo 'vasīyata iti / tad etad asambaddham / na hi pratyakṣanivṛtter yo bhavati niścayaḥ sa pratyakṣād bhavati / abhāvābhāvayor ekatra virodhāt / na ca pratyakṣanivṛttir vastvabhāvena vyāptā yenāsau vastvabhāvas tato niścīyate / saty api vastuni vyavahitādau pratyakṣasya nivṛttidarśanāt* //. "[Objection:] Someone might think, 'We do not say that that the nonexistence [of the omniscient being] is established through an occuring perception. Rather, [it is established] through a nonoccurent perception. That is, whenever perception does not occur with regard to a thing, that thing is determined to be nonexistent, like a rabbit's horns. And whenever [perception] does occur, there is the existence of that [object of perception], like form and so on. And a perception that has an omniscient being as its object never occurs. Therefore, the nonexistence of that [omniscient being] is determined due to the nonoccurrence of that

> [Question:] If that is the case, then why have you explained in another location that the nonexistence of a pot and so on is established through a perception called "nonperception"? [Answer:] That is not right. For we do not say in that case that perception establishes nonexistence by taking the nonexistent [thing] as its object [as Kumārila does]. Rather, when there are two things that are both capable of coexisting in a single awareness, then when just one of those is established, the nonexistence of the other is established. This is so because it is not possible that when both of them exist, the cognition would be restricted to a single form, since there is no difference [between the two] in terms of their capacity [to cause an image to arise in awareness, provided that they do exist]. And omniscience has not been determined to coexist in a single awareness with any other [thing] such that we can determine that it does not exist through the mere perception [of just that other thing], because [omniscience] is just always radically inaccessible (*atyantaparokṣa*). In this way, then, it is not possible for perception to be a refuter of omniscience.[427]

Again, we arrive at the bottom line: because omniscience and omniscient beings are not perceived by ordinary persons, they must be counted as

---

[perception].' [Answer:] All of this is incorrect. For it is not the case that the definitive determination that comes about through the nonoccurrence of perception is [also] due to perception, since it is a contradiction for existence and nonexistence to [pertain to] a single thing. Nor is it the case that the nonoccurrence of perception is pervaded by the nonexistence of a thing, such that the nonexistence of that thing would be ascertained from that [nonoccurrence of perception]. For we observe that perception does not occur in relation to things that are hidden (*vyavahita*) and so on, even when [those things] exist." Reading *yathā rūpādeḥ* with B in place of *yathā {a}syādeḥ* in G and in accord with D, vol. *'e*, 280a4: *dper na gzugs la sogs pa bzhin no //*.

427. TSP *ad* TS 3267–68 (*atīndriyārthadarśiparīkṣā*, B 1028,10–17): *yady evaṃ katham anupalambhākhyāt pratyakṣād ghaṭādyabhāvasiddhiḥ pradeśāntare bhavadbhir varṇyate / naitad asti / na hi tatrābhāvaviṣayīkaraṇāt pratyakṣam abhāvaṃ sādhayatīty ucyate / kiṃ tarhi / ekajñānasaṃsargayogyayor arthayor anyatarasyaiva yā siddhiḥ sāparasyābhāvasiddhir iti kṛtvā / yatas tayoḥ sator naikarūpaniyatā pratipattiḥ saṃbhavati / yogyatāyā aviśeṣāt / na caivaṃ sarvajñatvasya kenacit sārdham ekajñānasaṃsargitā niścitā yasya kevalasyopalambhāt tadabhāvaṃ vyavasyāmaḥ / tasya sarvadaivātyantaparokṣatvāt / evaṃ tāvan na pratyakṣaṃ sarvavido bādhakaṃ saṃbhavati //*. In the last line, G (849,9) reads: *evaṃ tāvat pratyakṣaṃ sardhavido (na) bādhakaṃ saṃbhavati /*, which is clearly inferior; the reading in B is confirmed by D, vol. *'e*, 281a2: *de ltar re zhig thams cad mkhyen pa'i gnod par byed pa mngon sum srid pa ma yin no /*.

beyond our perceptual range. But, on the Buddhist understanding of nonperception (*anupalabdhi*), it is only if the omniscient being is "amenable to perception" (*dṛśya*) that nonperception would be able to refute it. And the fact of being amenable to perception can only apply to something that, if it did exist, would be perceived.[428] As Śāntarakṣita seems to enjoy pointing out, an omniscient being is *not* amenable to Kumārila's perception, and it is thus impossible for him to disprove the omniscient being, "for if an omniscient being were refuted through mere nonperception, then the marriage of your mother and so on would also be refuted."[429]

Kamalaśīla continues his commentary on *Tattvasaṃgraha* 3267–68 by considering the remaining means of trustworthy awareness accepted by Kumārila (as we will see in the following section); having done so, he then returns to the problem of nonperception in order to introduce Śāntarakṣita's next verse and the remainder of this part of the *uttarapakṣa*. He starts out by having an opponent claim that it is in terms of the Buddhist's own theory of *anupalabdhi* that the omniscient person is understood to be refuted.[430] In response to this suggestion, Kamalaśīla cites Śāntarakṣita's next verse:

428. In other words, the omniscient being has to be *upalabdhilakṣaṇaprāpta*, "endowed with the characteristic of being perceived (or perceivable)" if nonperception is to function with regard to it. See TSP *ad* TS 3274–75 (*atīndriyārthadarśiparīkṣā*, B 1033,5–8): *na hy apratibaddhasyāhetvavyāpakabhūtasyānyasya vinivṛttāv aparasya niyamena nivṛttir yukteti pūrvam uktam atiprasaṅgāpatter iti / na cāpy aniścitasvahetuvyāpaka vyatirekasyārthasya kāraṇavyāpakayor vyatirekād vyatirekaḥ siddhyatīti atas tatrāpy upalabdhilakṣaṇaprāptasyeti viśeṣaṇam āśrayaṇīyam / evaṃ sarvajñe 'pi syāt //*. "As has been stated earlier, the definitive nonfunctioning of one thing is not reasonable in the absence of another thing that is unconnected [to that thing], being neither its cause nor its pervader; for that is an overextension [of the pervasion]. Nor does the absence of a cause or pervader establish the absence of some thing, the absence of whose own cause and pervader is not certain (*aniścita*). Therefore, one should supply the qualification 'endowed with the characteristic of being perceived (or perceivable)' in regard also to that [entity whose absence one is currently trying to establish]. And this would be the case for omniscience also."

429. TS 3281 (*atīndriyārthadarśiparīkṣā*): *yadi tv adṛṣṭimātreṇa sarvavit pratiṣidhyate / tadā mātṛvivāhādiniṣedho 'pi bhavet tava //*. See TS 3578–79 (*atīndriyārthadarśiparīkṣā*) and TSP *ad cit.* for more disparaging remarks about the opponent's mother, discussed in n. 634 below.

430. TSP *ad* TS 3269 (*atīndriyārthadarśiparīkṣā*, B 1030,18–19): *syād etat anupalambho yo yuṣmābhir upavarṇito 'numānatvena sa eva sarvajñasya bādhako bhaviṣyati / kim atrāsmākam anyena pramāṇeneti //*. "Someone might think, 'just that nonperception that you describe as a form of inference will refute the omniscient being; what need have we of another means of trustworthy awareness?'"

> Mere nonperception cannot ascertain the unreality of that [imperceptible entity], since perception does not have the quality of being either the cause or the pervader of real things.[431]

This is a technical way of saying that perception, on its own with no qualifications, does not possess a "natural relation" (*svabhāvapratibandha*) with all real things, such that the absence of perception in relation to some things can serve as evidence for the unreality of those things.[432] To argue against an omni-

431. TS 3269 (*atīndriyārthadarśiparīkṣā*): *na cāpy adṛṣṭimātreṇa tadasattāviniścayaḥ / hetuvyāpakatāyogād upalambhasya vastuṣu //*.

432. The natural relation may be that of a causal connection (*tadutpatti*) or of identity (*tādātmya*), and according to Śāntarakṣita and Kamalaśīla, neither one pertains between perception and all real things. If one's own perception were the cause of all real things, then all real things would be just that which one perceived—a position Śāntarakṣita and Kamalaśīla clearly reject elsewhere (see, e.g., TS/P 122, discussed above in n. 209). If one's own perception were a pervader of all real things, it would again mean that all real things are necessarily perceived by oneself—this is manifestly not the case, at least for persons of limited vision, such as ourselves. In his commentary on TS 3270–71 (*atīndriyārthadarśiparīkṣā*), Kamalaśīla cites Dharmakīrti on this aspect of Buddhist *pramāṇa* theory. PV 1.23–24: *tasmāt tanmātrasaṃbandhaḥ svabhāvo bhāvam eva vā / nirvarttayet kāraṇaṃ vā kāryam avyabhicārataḥ // anyathaikanivṛttyānyavinivṛttiḥ kathaṃ bhavet / nāśvavān iti martyena na bhāvyaṃ gomatāpi kim //*. "Therefore, an essential quality is only excluded by the exclusion of another essential quality that is invariably related to the mere presence of that first essential quality; likewise, only the exclusion of a cause excludes the effect. [Such is the case] because [the relationship between essential qualities and causes and effects] is not misleading. Otherwise, how could the exclusion of one thing entail the exclusion of another? Should we conclude that a man must not have cows just because he has no horses?" Translation supplied by John Dunne. Cf. also TS 2411 (*śrutiparīkṣā*): *pramāṇānāṃ nivṛttyāpi na prameyaṃ nivartate / yasmād vyāpakahetutvaṃ teṣāṃ tatra na vidyate //*. "The cognizable object is not negated through the mere nonoccurrence of a means of trustworthy awareness, since it is not found to be the case that those [means of trustworthy awareness] are either the pervader (*vyāpaka*) or the cause (*hetu*) of that [object]." Kamalaśīla elaborates at TSP *ad* TS 2411 (*śrutiparīkṣā*, B 802,8–13): *tathā hi deśakālasvabhāvāt viprakṛṣṭasya vastuno vināpi pramāṇena saṃbhavān na tena vyāptiḥ / nāpi kāraṇaṃ pramāṇam ata eva pramāṇasyaiva ca prameyakāryatvāt / na ca kāryaṃ nivartamānaṃ kāraṇamātraṃ nivartayati vyabhicāradarśanāt / na cāhetvavyāpakayor nivartakatvaṃ yuktam atiprasaṅgāt / tasmāt pramāṇamātrābhāvo vyabhicārī prameyamātrābhāve sādhya iti sthitam //*. "That is, even without a means of trustworthy awareness [to confirm it], there is the possibility of a real thing that is distant in place, time, or nature, because there is no pervasion [of that object] by that [means of trustworthy awareness]. Nor is the means of trustworthy awareness the cause [of that object], since in fact the means of trustworthy awareness is just the effect of its object. And the mere removal of an effect does not cause the removal of a cause, because it is observed that that would be misleading. Nor does it make sense that that which is neither a cause

scient person on the basis of a mere absence of perception, Kumārila would have also to assert not only that perception *does* possess a natural relation to all real things but also that he himself is capable of verifying this fact. But this would require that he himself be omniscient, as Śāntarakṣita explains:

> When through your own knowledge you somehow determine that your own perception is either a cause or a pervader of all things, then you yourself are effortlessly established to be omniscient. So why are you angry with yourself? For according to you, you yourself are omniscient![433]

The point is that since an omniscient person is not amenable to the perception of the person of limited vision, then no relationship—no causal relation, relation of pervader and pervaded, or relation of contradiction—may be ascertained to pertain to it, such that there could be some evidence for or against its existence.[434] If one wishes to assert one's own nonperception as evidence for the nonexistence of omniscience, then one would absurdly have to be omniscient oneself, since only then would one be able to verify that one's own perception possesses an invariable relation with real things, as either their cause or their pervader.

Inference Cannot Refute Omniscience

Returning now to the commentary on *Tattvasaṃgraha* 3267–68, we find Kamalaśīla responding to the Mīmāṃsaka who wants to argue that the refutation of an omniscient being comes about through inference or some other means of trustworthy awareness. Kamalaśīla's first response is that, according to Kumārila's own view, these other means of trustworthy awareness are

---

nor a pervader [of something else] removes [that other thing], for that would be an overextension [of the definitions of cause and pervader]. Therefore, it remains the case that the absence of a means of trustworthy awareness alone is misleading when the thing to be proved is the absence of a mere object of knowledge (*prameya*)."

433. TS 3272–73 (*atīndriyārthadarśiparīkṣā*): *svopalambhasya cārtheṣu nikhileṣu viniścaye / kutaścid bhavato jñānād dhetutvavyāpakatvayoḥ // bhavān eva tadā siddhaḥ sarvārthajño 'prayatnataḥ / tataś ca svātmani dveṣaḥ kas te sarvavidi svataḥ //*. Kamalaśīla explains in the commentary that the genitive case ending in *hetutvavyāpakatvayoḥ* is to be understood in semantic dependence on the term *viniścaye*.

434. See TS 3279–80 (*atīndriyārthadarśiparīkṣā*): *kāryakāraṇatāvyāpyavyāpakatvavirodhitāḥ / dṛśyatve sati siddhyanti yaś cātmā saviśeṣaṇaḥ // sarvajño na ca dṛśyas te tena naitā adṛṣṭayaḥ / tannirākaraṇe śaktā niṣedhāṅgaṃ na cāparam //*.

not understood to ascertain an absence or a lack.[435] If the opponent suggests that inference *can* ascertain a negative fact—such as, for example, that non-omniscience is a quality of all persons—Kamalaśīla responds that there is no evidence for the non-omniscience of all persons whereby one could attain certainty of this negative fact; and he promises to demonstrate this later in the work in relation to two logical reasons suggested by Mīmāṃsakas to refute omniscience, namely, the reasons "because of being cognizable" (*prameyatvāt*) and "because of being a speaker" (*vaktṛtvāt*).[436]

The logical reason "because of being cognizable" has a complex history in the demonstrations for and against omniscience in Indian religious philosophy.[437] Its use is complex as well in the *Tattvasaṃgraha* and the *Pañjikā*,

435. TSP *ad* TS 3267–68 (*atīndriyārthadarśiparīkṣā*, B 1028,18–19): *nāpy anumānaṃ sarvajñābhāvaṃ sādhayati / tasya vidhiviṣayatvābhyupagamāt / yato 'bhāvam eva pramāṇam abhāvaviṣayam upavarṇyate bhavadbhiḥ nānyat //*. "Nor does inference establish the nonexistence of an omniscient being, since it is accepted [by you] that the object [of inference] is an affirmation (*vidhi*), because you maintain that only the means of trustworthy awareness known as 'nonexistence' [i.e., *abhāvapramāṇa*] has nonexistence as its object, and no other [means of trustworthy awareness] does."

436. TSP *ad* TS 3267–68 (*atīndriyārthadarśiparīkṣā*, B 1028,21–1029,2): *athāpi syāt / nāsmābhiḥ prasajyarūpeṇa sarvajñābhāvaḥ prasādhyate / kiṃ tarhi / sarvanarān pakṣīkṛtya paryudāsavṛttyā teṣv asarvajñatvaṃ sādhyate tenānumānādīnāṃ vyāpāro bhavaty eveti / bhavatv evam / tathāpy anumānaṃ tāvan na saṃbhavati / sarvanareṣv asarvajñatvāvya bhicāriliṅgāprasiddheḥ / yad api ca prameyatvavaktṛtvādikam uktaṃ tad api vyabhicārīti paścāt pratipādayiṣyate //*. "Now someone might also think, 'We do not establish the nonexistence of omniscience by means of a "sentence negation" (*prasajya*), but rather, having taken all persons as the locus [of the inference], we establish the non-omniscience of them through the application of a "term negation" (*paryudāsa*), whereby there is the operation of inference and so on.' That may be so. Nevertheless, inference is in any case not possible, because no non-misleading evidential sign (*liṅga*) for the non-omniscience of all persons is recognized. And moreover, we will demonstrate later that those [signs] such as 'being cognizable' and 'being a speaker' that have been mentioned are misleading." A *term negation* (*paryudāsa*) indicates a type of negation where the negation applies to a term, not to a verb or entire sentence, as is the case in a *sentence negation* (*prasajyapratiṣedha*).

437. Such an argument for omniscience is (to my knowledge) first encountered in the Jain author Samantabhadra's *Āptamīmāṃsā* (also known as the *Devāgamastotra*). The fifth verse of that text reads: *sūkṣmāntaritadūrārthāḥ pratyakṣāḥ kasyacid yathā / anumeyatvato 'gnyādir iti sarvajñasaṃsthitiḥ //*. "Things that are subtle, concealed, or far away are perceived by someone because they are inferable (*anumeya*), like fire and so forth. Thus the omniscient being is established." This verse represents a proof statement where the evidence is "because they are inferable" (*anumeyatvataḥ*). Akalaṅkadeva, in his commentary on the *Āptamīmāṃsā*, the *Aṣṭaśatī*, introduces another reason with an equivalent force, *prameyatvāt*, "because of being cognizable." The logical reason *prameyatva* is also used in the *Vyomavatī* on the *Padārthadharmasaṃgraha* to prove the existence of *yogis*. See VV

where it is discussed, along with related reasons—"because of being a real thing" (*vastutvād*), "because of being real" (*sattvād*), and so on—in a variety of contexts relevant to omniscience. The first such context occurs in the *pūrvapakṣa*, when Kumārila is seen to parrot an opponent's position, probably that of the Jain authors Samantabhadra and Akalaṅka.[438] The argument is presented as follows:

> Everything in this world is indeed perceived by someone, because [everything] is cognizable (*prameya*), knowable (*jñeya*), and is a real thing (*vastu*), like the form and taste of yogurt and so on.[439]

Kumārila is then seen to dismiss this argument as inadequate to the proposition that there is someone who is omniscient, and especially to the idea that it is a particular person, namely, the Buddha who is shown to be omniscient by such an argument.[440] We return to this objection in the next chapter, when considering the specific demonstration of the Buddha's omniscience.

The second context in which the reasons "because of being cognizable" and so on are presented in connection with omniscience is a negative one, in which Kumārila is portrayed as offering these reasons as evidence *against* omniscience. The key verse is as follows:

> For who would imagine [as existent] that [omniscient being] for whom there exist reasons—characterized as being knowable

---

560.9ff. *ad* PDS 240–41: *asti ca yogināṃ sadbhāve 'numānam / tathāhi asmadādīnāṃ pratyakṣeṇānupalambhyamānāḥ paramāṇvādayaḥ kasyacit pratyakṣāḥ prameyatvāt ghaṭādivad iti //*. A reference is made also to the use of the reason *jñeyatva* to establish Cittamātra in BASK 29: *blo tsam nyid du bsgrub pa la / shes phyir la sogs bsgrub pa gang / mi mthun rigs dang mi 'gal phyir / thams cad lhag dang bcas shes bya.*

438. See Pathak 1931.

439. TS 3234 (*atīndriyārthadarśiparīkṣā*): *yat sarvaṃ nāma loke 'smin pratyakṣaṃ tad dhi kasyacit / prameyajñeyavastutvair dadhirūparasādivat //*. For precedents in the Jain literature, see the previous two notes. Later in the TS/P, Śāntarakṣita and Kamalaśīla defend a proof of total omniscience that relies upon a similar reason (e.g., TSP *ad* TS 3440–42: *vastutvajñeyatvādi* and TS 3446: *vastusattvādi*), although it is not clear to me in what ways their argumentation is the same as or differs from that of the Jain authors.

440. TS 3235–36 (*atīndriyārthadarśiparīkṣā*): *jñānamātre 'pi nirdiṣṭe pakṣanyūnatvam āpatet / sarvajña iti yo 'bhīṣṭo netthaṃ sa pratipāditaḥ // yadi buddhātirikto 'nyaḥ kaścit sarvajñatāṃ gataḥ / buddhavākyapramāṇatve tajjñānaṃ kvopayujyate //*.

> (*jñeya*), being cognizable (*prameya*), being a real thing (*vastu*), being real (*sat*), and so on—capable of refuting [that being]?[441]

In explicating this verse, Kamalaśīla gives another, similar list of reasons, starting with "being cognizable" and ending with "being a speaker," "being a person," and so forth, accompanied by the example "like the man in the street."[442] The rationale for the latter two reasons is easier to grasp: speakers and persons in general have desire, which on many Indian views prevents them from seeing things clearly. The earlier reasons, starting with "being cognizable" and so on, seem intended to apply not to the person but rather to the objects of the person's knowledge.[443] According to the *Pañjikā*, Kumārila's idea is that objects of knowledge (*prameya*, *jñeya*, and so on) are restricted both in terms of being known by particular faculties (e.g., visual consciousness for visible objects) and in terms of being known at particular times and places. It is therefore not conceivable that a single person could know all knowable objects.[444]

441. TS 3156 (*atīndriyārthadarśiparīkṣā*): *yasya jñeyaprameyatvavastusattvādilakṣaṇāḥ / nihantuṃ hetavaḥ śaktāḥ ko nu taṃ kalpayiṣyati //*. Cited in Ratnakīrti's SS 23.16–17, where it is attributed to Kumārila's lost *Bṛhaṭṭīkā*.

442. TSP *ad* TS 3156 (*atīndriyārthadarśiparīkṣā*, B 997,17–18): *sugato 'sarvajño jñeyatvap rameyatvavastutvasattvavaktṛtvapuruṣatvādibhyo rathyāpuruṣavad iti //*. These same reasons are considered together at NB 3.93–96.

443. Cf. also ŚV, *codanāsūtra*, 132: *pratyakṣādyavisaṃvādi prameyatvādi yasya ca / sadbhāvavāraṇe śaktaṃ ko nu taṃ kalpayiṣyati //*.

444. TSP *ad* TS 3156–57 (*atīndriyārthadarśiparīkṣā*, B 997,19–998,11): *tathā hi sarvapadārthajñānāt sarvajña iṣyate / tac ca sakalavastuparijñānaṃ kadācid indriyajñānena vā bhaven manojñānena vā / na tāvad indriyajñānena tasya pratiniyatārthaviṣayatvād ayuktam aśeṣārthaviṣayatvam / tathā hi cakṣurādijñānāni pratiniyata viṣayagrahaṇasvabhāvāny eva svakāraṇair indriyair niyāmakair janitāni / tataś cānatikrāntasvaviṣayamaryādāni loke 'tipratītānīti na yuktam etair aśeṣārthagrahaṇam / anyathā hy anekendriyavaiyarthyaprasaṅgaḥ syāt / tataś caikenaiva jñānena sarvadharmān bhinnendriyagrāhyān api rasarūpādīn jānātīty evaṃ yena bauddhena kalpyate ekena sarvaṃ jānāti sarvam ekena paśyatīti vacanān nūnaṃ sa vādī bauddhaś cakṣuṣā karaṇabhūtena taddvārapravṛttena jñānena sarvadharmān rasādīn avagacchatīti prāptam / na caitac chakyate vaktum / mā bhūd ekena jñānena yugapad aśeṣārthasya grahaṇam anekena bhaviṣyatīti / yato yugapad anekavijñānāsaṃbhavāt / saṃbhave 'pi na sarvapadārthagrahaṇam asti paracittasyendriyajñānāviṣayatvāt agocaraprāptasya ca dūrasūkṣmavyavahitāder arthasya tena grahītum aśakyatvāt //*. "That is, a person is asserted to be omniscient due to knowing all real things. And that knowledge of all things should come about either through some [single] sense awareness or through mental awareness. Now, first of all, it cannot be through [a single] sense awareness, since that is restricted in terms of its objects; therefore, it does not make sense that it can have everything as its

Śāntarakṣita and Kamalaśīla respond to the charge that "being cognizable" and "being an object of knowledge" can serve as evidence against omniscience by challenging the Mīmāṃsaka to explain the nature of the contradiction that he sees between "being cognizable" and the omniscient being.[445] In this context, the authors seem to leave purposefully vague exactly *what* is meant to be qualified as "being cognizable." Instead, they focus on the technical problem of how the Mīmāṃsaka is going to demonstrate that there is a contradiction between the qualities mentioned and the omniscient being. The discussion relies on a distinction between two kinds of contradiction: that of mutual exclusion (*parasparaparihārasthita*), like the contradiction between being and nonbeing, and that of mutual incompatibility (*sahānavasthāna*), like the contradiction between fire and a cool sensation. The authors then argue that neither kind of contradiction can be established to exist between the qualities of being cognizable and being omniscient. The first kind of contradiction does not apply, since it is not the case the qualities "being cognizable" and so on are based on an exclusion of an omniscient being and vice versa. And the second kind of contradiction does not apply, for it requires that both elements be verified to exist independently (although never in each other's presence). Since this would require the Mīmāṃsaka to admit that an omniscient being exists, it is clearly faulty as an argument against omniscience.

---

object. That is to say, the awarenesses of the eye and so on, whose natures are to grasp those objects to which they are restricted, are produced through the particular sense organs that are their own causes. And since it is extremely well known in the world that they do not pass beyond the limits of their own objects, it does not make sense that they should apprehend every object. Otherwise, there would be the undesirable conclusion that the plurality of sense organs would have no purpose! And thus, whatever Buddhist imagines that [some person] knows in a single cognition all things, tastes, forms, and so on, even though they should be apprehended by different sense organs—saying 'Through one [cognition] he knows everything, through one [cognition] he sees everything'—that Buddhist philosopher, since he speaks thus, ends up saying that one understands all things, tastes, and so on through a cognition whose cause is the eye and by means of the operation of that [eye]. And it is not possible to say that. Or let it not be the case that there is the simultaneous apprehension of all things through a single cognition, but let it be through various [cognitions], since the simultaneity of various cognitions is not possible. But even if that were possible, there would be no cognition of all real things, since the cognitions of the sense organs do not have as their objects the minds of others and since it is not possible to cognize through that [sense awareness] things that are far away, subtle, or hidden, and so on, which are not included in the scope [of the sense organs]." The text goes on to dispute that all things can be the object of mental awareness, citing again the reasons that mental awareness cannot apprehend things that are far away, subtle, hidden, and so on.

445. See TS 3353–58 (*atīndriyārthadarśiparīkṣā*) and TSP *ad cit.*

Finally, there is also another context in which the authors consider the reasons "being cognizable" and so on, this time offering arguments to show that these reasons may, in fact, be used as evidence *in favor* of omniscience. We will consider these arguments later in this chapter, in the section on the demonstration of total omniscience. Arguments that take up the reason "because of being a person" are considered in the next section, in the context of the demonstration of the possibility of omniscience. And arguments concerning the reason "because of being a speaker" will be considered in the final chapter of this book.[446]

The Other Pramāṇas *Cannot Refute Omniscience*

Moving on from inference, Kamalaśīla takes up the remaining means of trustworthy awareness accepted by Kumārila. Presumption (*arthāpatti*) cannot disprove omniscience, because there is nothing that is presently observed that could not be explained unless omniscience did not exist.[447] Analogy (*upamāna*) also cannot disprove omniscience. On Kumārila's view, analogy is a means of trustworthy awareness whose object is either (a) something that is remembered as similar to something that is presently perceived; or (b) the similarity itself.[448] Neither of these is possible in relation to non-omniscience, which has never been ascertained and so cannot be remembered nor made the locus of any similarity with anything else.

Last, verbal testimony (*śābda*) cannot disprove omniscience, for several reasons. First, as the Mīmāṃsaka himself maintains, human speech is not reliable in regard to supersensible entities. Second, the Veda, which the Mīmāṃsaka does accept as trustworthy, does not assert the non-omniscience of all persons. Third, the mere lack of being mentioned in the Veda does not imply the nonexistence of something. Finally, because the Veda has numerous recensions (*śākhā*), it is always possible that one of them speaks of the omniscient person; Kamalaśīla actually asserts that one recension *does* speak clearly of the omniscient person, a fact that he again says will be demonstrated later on.[449]

446. See pp. 355–57 below.

447. TSP *ad* TS 3267–68 (*atīndriyārthadarśiparīkṣā*, B 1029,5–6): *na cāsarvajñatvam antareṇa sarvanareṣu kaścid artho dṛṣṭādir nopapadyate, yatas tadarthāpattyā kalpyeta //*.

448. ŚV, *upamāna*, 37: *tasmād yat smaryate tat syāt sādṛśyena viśeṣitam / prameyam upamānasya sādṛśyaṃ vā tadanvitam //*. Cited at TSP *ad* TS 3267–68 (*atīndriyārthadarśiparīkṣā*, B 1029,10–11) and at TS 1534 (*pramāṇāntarabhāvaparīkṣā*), where the final *pāda* reads: *vā tadāśritam*.

449. TSP *ad* TS 3267–68 (*atīndriyārthadarśiparīkṣā*, B 1030,1–4): *na caikadeśe kvacit*

The Nonperception of an Omniscient Being Is Not Certain

There is one more argument contributing to this part of Śāntarakṣita and Kamalaśīla's rebuttal of the claim that the omniscient being is an object of *abhāvapramāṇa*. This is an argument that stresses the uncertainty of the proposition that an omniscient being is not ascertained by any means of trustworthy awareness for anyone at all. This proposition is addressed in two ways: as indicating that an omniscient being is radically inaccessible *tout court*, and as indicating that an omniscient being is radically inaccessible *for Kumārila*.[450] We first encounter this bifurcation in the commentary when, in response to the opponent's suggestion that the omniscient being might be refuted through the Buddhist theory of nonperception, Kamalaśīla questions:

> Is the nonperception intended by you for the establishing of the nonexistence of an omniscient being the nonfunctioning of your own perception? Or, alternatively, is it the nonfunctioning of the perception of all persons?[451]

The authors of the *Tattvasaṃgraha* and the *Pañjikā* then offer arguments to show that neither of these two alternatives is capable of refuting an omniscient being. If the nonperception is in terms only of Kumārila's own perception, then the evidence is inconclusive (*anaikāntika*), for if an omniscient being does exist, that being would certainly know of his or her own omniscience, even if Kumārila himself is ignorant of it.[452] If the nonperception is proposed

---

pāṭhādarśanāt sarvatrāpāṭhaniścayo yuktaḥ / anekaśākhāśatāntarhitaśravaṇād anyatrāpi pāṭhasya saṃbhāvyamānatvāt / nimittanāmni ca śākhāntare sphuṭataram eva sarvajñaḥ paṭhyata iti paścāt pratipādayiṣyāmaḥ //. "It is not reasonable to ascertain that because a [particular] reading is not observed in one place that it therefore does not occur anywhere. It is surely possible for the reading to occur elsewhere since the Veda (*śravaṇa*) is contained in hundreds of different recensions. In fact, in another recension called Nimitta the reading 'an omniscient one' is very clear. We will demonstrate this later." For our discussion of the passage treating the Vedic recension that speaks of the Buddha, his birth, and his omniscience, see pp. 277–79 below.

450. TS 3280a (*atīndriyārthadarśiparīkṣā*): *sarvajño na ca dṛśyas te ... /*. "An omniscient being is not amenable to perception *for you* ...."

451. TSP *ad* TS 3269 (*atīndriyārthadarśiparīkṣā*, B 1030,19–20): *kiṃ svopalambhanivṛttis tvayā sarvajñābhāvasiddhaye 'nupalambho 'bhipretaḥ / āhosvit sarvapuruṣopalambhanivṛttir vā /*.

452. TS 3288–89 (*atīndriyārthadarśiparīkṣā*): *anyathā saṃśayo yukto 'nupalambhe 'pi sattvavat / kecit sarvavidaḥ santo vidantīti hi śaṅkyate // svayam evātmanātmānam ātmajyotiḥ sa paśyati / ity apy āśaṅkyate 'taś ca sarvādṛṣṭir aniścitā //*. "Otherwise, it is

in terms of the perceptions of all beings, then the evidence is unestablished (*asiddha*), for without being omniscient himself, the Mīmāṃsaka cannot verify that the omniscient being has never been an object of trustworthy awareness for any person.[453] So the assertion that no one has ever ascertained an omniscient being at any time must remain open to doubt.

Conclusion: It Is Best to Let There Be Doubt

Everything we have examined thus far has aimed to show that the existence of an omniscient being is, at the very least, a matter that must remain open to doubt. The positive value these authors attribute to doubt in this case can be discerned in Śāntarakṣita's summation of his response to Kumārila's arguments:

> For when one's eyes and so on are defective, there is no means of trustworthy awareness with regard even to an existent thing; likewise when one's eyes and so on are not defective, [there is no means of trustworthy awareness] because of the nonexistence of a thing, as in the case of a pot and so on. Hence, the mere fact of nonapprehension is observed in both cases [i.e., in relation to both existent and nonexistent things]. Therefore, it is best to let there be doubt concerning the omniscient person due to the absence of a means of trustworthy awareness.[454]

reasonable that there be doubt [concerning the omniscient being's existence or nonexistence] even though [such a being] is not perceived, like the existence [of some things]. Some good people [claim to] know that an omniscient person exists; hence there is doubt in this matter. Or it might be the case that the [omniscient person] himself, being self-luminous (*ātmajyotis*), sees his own self by himself. Hence there is this doubt also, and thus it is not certain that [the omniscient person] is not seen by anyone."

453. TS 3286–87 (*atīndriyārthadarśiparīkṣā*): *mā vā bhūd upadeśo 'sya prāmāṇyaṃ vā tathāpi vaḥ / kuto 'yaṃ niścayaḥ sarvaiḥ sarvavin nopalabhyate // evaṃ hi niścayo hi syāt sarvasattvātmadarśane / taddṛṣṭau sarvavidbhūto bhavān iti ca varṇitam //*. "Or let there be no [such] teaching [that an omniscient person exists]; or let it not be trustworthy. Nevertheless, whence comes this certainty of yours that an omniscient person is never perceived at all? For if such certainty exists, it occurs when one sees the inner natures of all sentient beings; if you see that, then you yourself will become omniscient! And this has [already] been explained." Reading *kuto 'yam niścayaḥ* in place of the reading in B and G: *kṛto 'yam niścayaḥ* in accord with D 120a1: *gang las skyes //*. My reading of TS 3287ab follows that found in G rather than that given in B: *ity evaṃ niścayas tasmāt sarvasattvāt pradarśane /*.

454. TS 3300–3301 (*atīndriyārthadarśiparīkṣā*): *netrādīnāṃ hi vaikalye vastusattve 'pi na*

As Kamalaśīla explains, it is "best" to have doubt because doubt "is the cause for developing the root of virtue."[455] The idea is that the openness that accompanies doubt toward omniscience is an initial step necessary for the generation of a special kind of faith—a faith that, for these authors, allows one to rationally engage in the Buddhist path.

Doubt, however, is only the first step. The next step is to determine that omniscience is actually possible for humans and therefore a goal toward which a judicious person may be justified in striving. After concluding the rebuttal of Kumārila's refutation of omniscience, therefore, Śāntarakṣita and Kamalaśīla turn to the next demonstration: that of the possibility of omniscience.

Demonstrating that Omniscience Is Possible

As we turn to the next "movement" in the demonstration of omniscience in the *Tattvasaṃgraha* and the *Pañjikā*, that of the possibility of omniscience, we do well to remind ourselves that our exploration in this chapter concerns only the *general* demonstration of omniscience in the work, not the specific demonstration, in which omniscience is established as a quality of a particular person, the Buddha. Any attempt to show that a particular person has attained omniscience presupposes that omniscience is a state that potentially exists, as the authors of the *Tattvasaṃgraha* and the *Pañjikā* recognize, and it is in order to demonstrate this potential existence that the authors advance the arguments we will examine here. As we have already noted, this stage of the argumentation in the *Tattvasaṃgraha* and the *Pañjikā* corresponds closely to the "progressive" or *anuloma* stage of argumentation in Dharmakīrti's *Pramāṇasiddhi* chapter (*Pramāṇavārttika* 2), where the intention is to show that it is "not absolutely impossible" for the Buddha to be trustworthy (or, in the case of the *Tattvasaṃgraha* and the *Pañjikā*, for the

pramā / teṣām avikalatve 'pi vastvabhāvād ghaṭādivat // tataś cānupa[redacted]
dvidhekṣaṇāt / tat pramābhāvato 'py astu sarvajñe saṃśayo varam //.

455. TSP *ad* TS 3300–3301 (*atīndriyārthadarśiparīkṣā*, B 1042,14–16): *tathā hi mithyādṛṣṭyā samucchinnakuśalamūlānāṃ kuśalamūlapratisandhānaṃ saṃśayāstidṛṣṭibhyāṃ varṇyate //.* "For indeed, for those who are completely disassociated from the root of virtue due to wrong views, the connection to the root of virtue is said to be through the two views of doubt and existence." The reading *saṃśayāstidṛṣṭibhyāṃ* is instead of B and G's *kāṅkṣā 'sti dṛṣṭibhyāṃ* on the strength of the Tibetan, D, vol. *'e*, 290a: *'di ltar log pa'i lta bas dge ba'i rtsa ba rgyun bcad pa rnams la the tshom dang yod par lta ba dag gis dge ba'i mtshams sbyor ba brjod par 'gyur ro /.*

Buddha to be omniscient). At its base, this demonstration involves showing that the nature of the mind and the nature of omniscience are such that it is possible for omniscience to be a quality that, under certain circumstances, may be predicated of the mind.

Here, again, the primary connotation for omniscience is dharmic, not total, omniscience. Dharmic omniscience, as we have said, means knowledge of all that is soteriologically relevant. For Dharmakīrti, demonstrating knowledge of all that is soteriologically relevant is equivalent to demonstrating trustworthiness or authority (*prāmāṇya*). In the *Tattvasaṃgraha* and the *Pañjikā*, the authors make a shift from demonstrating trustworthiness to demonstrating omniscience. Although the focus on knowledge of the soteriologically relevant remains, the emphasis is now on the manner in which such soteriologically relevant knowledge necessarily applies *to all things*. That is, the central aspects of soteriologically relevant knowledge are "that which is to be abandoned" (*heya*) and "that which is to be taken up" (*upādeya*). As it turns out, that which is to be abandoned and that which is to be taken up are particular *ways of apprehending the world*. One way of apprehending the world is wrong, and leads to suffering; another way is correct, and leads to liberation. And when the correct way of apprehending the world is applied *to all things*, it then qualifies as omniscience. Śāntarakṣita says, "One is omniscient due to correctly knowing the reality of all things."[456] This shift in emphasis becomes vitally important in the demonstration of total omniscience. However, it is also significant in the present context, as it is the element that transforms a demonstration of trustworthiness into a demonstration of omniscience.

Inference of Capacity: *Kāryānumāna* and *Saṃbhavatpramāṇa*

Although Śāntarakṣita and Kamalaśīla do not say so directly, their argumentation in this movement attests that it is only omniscience as a reality made actual by a particular omniscient being that is radically inaccessible to ordinary, judicious persons of limited vision. Omniscience as a potential entity—or, put differently, the possibility of omniscience—is not radically inaccessible (*atyantaparokṣa*) but merely remote (*parokṣa*) and, thus, inferable. In the Buddhist *pramāṇa* theory tradition, Dharmakīrti accounts for inference of a capacity or potential in his *Pramāṇavārttika* 1 and *Svopajñavṛtti*, where he explains that one may infer the "capacity to produce an effect" (*kāryotpādanayogyatā*) from the presence of a cause (or, more

456. TS 3329ab (*atīndriyārthadarśiparīkṣā*): *samyak sarvapadārthānāṃ tattvajñānāc ca sarvavit /*.

precisely, from the presence of a complete collection of all requisite causes).[457] In Dharmakīrti's terminology, this is called an "inference of the capacity [of a causal complex] to produce an effect" (*kāryotpādanayogyatānumāna*), or more simply, an "inference of capacity" (*yogyatānumāna*) or an "inference of an effect" (*kāryānumāna*).[458] The idea is that although it is not possible to indubitably infer an effect from a cause, one can indubitably infer the property of "being capable to produce an effect" on the basis of a complete or sufficient causal complex (*samāgrī*). As Steinkellner and others have noted, this means that the inference in question is, properly speaking, one based on the identity (*tādātmya*) relation, and the evidence is that of an essential property (*svabhāvahetu*).[459]

Several modern commentators have speculated that Dharmakīrti's motive in promoting this *kāryānumāna* as a means of trustworthy awareness is rooted in his desire to provide a rational ground for the Buddhist path.[460] The connection has also been made to the *anuloma* portion of *Pramāṇavārttika* 2, where Dharmakīrti advances arguments for the capacity of positive mental qualities, such as wisdom and compassion, to be perfected by the Buddhist practitioner. Steinkellner summarizes these arguments as follows:

> The progress toward Buddhahood laid out in PV II is based upon the idea that the good qualities (*guṇa*) of the mind, e.g. compassion (*kṛpā*), can be developed by continuous practice

457. PV 1.7–8 and PVSV *ad cit.*

458. PVSV *ad* PV 1.8. For a brief explanation of *kāryānumāna*, see Steinkellner (1999: 349–50), who explores the Buddhist epistemological tradition's use of the notion to establish the soteriological possibility of yogic perception and of tantric practice.

459. Steinkellner (1999: 350) notes that technically the causal complex is only complete in the last moment before the production of the effect, and that strictly speaking, therefore, "an inferential process is no longer possible, because the presence of the effect will outrun every inferential process." Despite this problem, however, Dharmakīrti and his followers allow for a qualified inference of capacity as long as it is accompanied by a conditional statement barring the arisal of unforeseen hindrances.

460. Steinkellner (1999: 350) has suggested that "the real motive for Dharmakīrti to deal with the possibilities of an inference 'from cause to effect' ... [is not] ... a logical motive primarily, but a soteriological one." A similar point is also made by Gillon and Hayes (1991: 67), who state by way of an explanation for the presentation of *kāryānumāna* in the PVSV that "Dharmakīrti evidently felt obliged, in discussing the limits within which the process of inference is capable of yielding certain knowledge, to keep open the possibility of preserving the basic teachings of Buddhism intact ... [namely,] that certain kinds of unwholesome (*akuśala*) mental properties are causes of discontent (*duḥkha*), and when these unwholesome causes are eradicated, their unwanted effect does not arise."

> towards perfection thereby becoming the "highest inner nature" (*atyantasātmatā*) of a mental continuum (PV II 129). The result of this development is a transformation of the basis (*āśrayaḥ parivartate*) (PV II 205b), i.e. of the mental continuum (*cittasantāna*), which can no longer be reversed due to a complete elimination of the bad qualities (*doṣa*) (PV II 205–10). An elimination of bad mental qualities, on the other hand, is possible because they do not correspond to true reality, because they can be analyzed as to their causes and conditions, and because they can be overcome by applying the appropriate means for the destruction of their causes (PV II 144).[461]

As this passage indicates, Dharmakīrti is concerned to defend two different potentials: first, the potential for good mental qualities to attain perfection, and second, the potential for negative mental qualities to be utterly eliminated. These same concerns and lines of argument are found extensively in the final chapter of the *Tattvasaṃgraha* and the *Pañjikā*, as we will see.[462]

Steinkellner points out that the role of the logical tool of *kāryānumāna* "in explaining the progression towards Buddhahood is not reserved a

461. Steinkellner 1999: 351.

462. The basic argument in the TS/P is the same as that in Dharmakīrti's PV 2, although most of the preliminary arguments in Dharmakīrti's demonstration are found not in the final chapter of the TS/P but rather earlier in the work. For example, Dharmakīrti spends considerable time (see PV 2.8–28) demonstrating that a creator God, or Īśvara, cannot be an authority, in large part because such an entity, being permanent, cannot exist. Prior to the final chapter, the authors of the TS/P have already undertaken extensive refutations of various permanent entities, including Īśvara, and they do not repeat those efforts in their demonstration of omniscience (see, especially, the *īśvaraparīkṣā*). Dharmakīrti also undertakes arguments in PV 2 to establish past and future lives and to refute materialism—arguments he deems necessary for showing that wisdom and compassion may be developed to a very great degree (see PV 2.34–119). Many of these arguments occur earlier in the TS/P in the *lokāyataparīkṣā*. Some of Dharmakīrti's arguments in support of the nobles' four truths (see PV 2.176–205) are repeated in the *karmaphalasaṃbandhaparīkṣā* of the TS/P, while counterparts to the various refutations of opponents' views of the path to liberation (see PV 2.205–80) may be found scattered in the various chapters devoted to the refutation of other religious systems in the TS/P. In this way, the bulk of the argumentation in PV 2 has already been presented in TS/P by the time the reader arrives at the work's final chapter. We should also note that some of the argumentation in the final chapter of the TS/P relies on passages found in Dharmakīrti's PV 1 and PVSV.

conspicuous place"[463] in *Pramāṇavārttika* 2 or in the final chapter of the *Tattvasaṃgraha* and the *Pañjikā*. Nonetheless, despite finding no direct reference to the logical forms *yogyatānumāna* or *kāryānumāna*, we do find unambiguous reference to the notion of the proof of the possibility (*saṃbhavasādhana*) of omniscience, an idea that appears to be closely related to the inference of capacity. In particular, Kamalaśīla makes repeated use of the terms *saṃbhavat* ("possible") and *saṃbhavatpramāṇa* ("means of trustworthy awareness regarding the possible") in his formal proof statements (*prayogas*) concerning the perfectibility of the mind.[464] Thus, rather than seeking to establish that that mental qualities are perfect, the authors seek instead to show that they are perfectible. With this in mind, we can confidently assert that in the general portion of their proof, Śāntarakṣita and Kamalaśīla are arguing not so much for any particular instantiation of omniscience as for the possibility of the perfection of wisdom in general.[465]

Ignorance as the Vision of a Self

In the previous chapter, we saw that Kamalaśīla defines omniscience as the removal of two obscurations: the afflictive obscuration (*kleśāvaraṇa*) and the epistemic obscuration (*jñeyāvaraṇa*). Underlying this definition is the idea that the afflictions (*kleśas*) are what keep one ensconced in the suffering of

463. Steinkellner 1999: 352.

464. See, e.g., TSP *ad* TS 3409–12, TSP *ad* TS 3415–17, TSP *ad* TS 3418–19, TSP *ad* TS 3420–23, TSP *ad* TS 3440–42, and TSP *ad* TS 3443–44 (all from the *atīndriyārthadarśiparīkṣā*). This usage of the term *saṃbhavat* calls to mind a comment made by Śākyabuddhi in his PVT. The context is Dharmakīrti's discussion (*ad* PV 1.201ab) of why nonperception does not indicate nonexistence in the case of supersensible entities. Much like Śāntarakṣita and Kamalaśīla, Dharmakīrti insists that in such cases doubt is appropriate, adding that there might ultimately be a means to establish the entity in question "since eventually some things become manifest" (*paryāyeṇa keṣāmcid abhivyakteḥ*). In commenting on this passage, Śākyabuddhi indicates that the entities Dharmakīrti has in mind here are radically inaccessible things such as a mind free from desire (*viraktacitta*) and omniscience (*sarvajñatva*), and he states that Dharmakīrti will provide a *saṃbhavatpramāṇa* for these entities in PV 2 (*ata eva bādhakasā ... [iti virakta]cittasarvajñatve bhaved vā pramāṇam iti apratikṣepaḥ / tac ca saṃbhavatpramāṇaṃ dvitīye paricchede 'bhidhāyiṣyate*). Cf. also Vibhūticandra's comments at PV 2.124: *anulomataḥ pūrvapūrvāj jagaddhitaiṣitvāder uttarottarasya saṃbhāvanānumānenātyantābhāvanirāsaḥ / nāvaśyaṃ kāraṇaṃ kāryavad iti niyamahetuḥ //*.

465. TSP *ad* TS 3508 (*atīndriyārthadarśiparīkṣā*, B 1098,19–22) is a clear statement of the fact that the primary focus of the proof is the perfection of wisdom and not the omniscient person *per se*. See pp. 271–72.

saṃsāra. Earlier in the *Pañjikā*, Kamalaśīla cites a Buddhist source to this effect:

> For saṃsāra is just the mind, impregnated (*vāsita*) with the afflictions of passion and so forth; that same [mind], purified of those [afflictions], is called "the end of existence" (*bhavānta*).[466]

Here, "the end of existence" means the end of saṃsāra (i.e., nirvāṇa), and reaching that is a matter of purifying one's mind of the afflictions. Now, in the eyes of the authors of the *Tattvasaṃgraha* and the *Pañjikā*, the root cause of all afflictions is a kind of primordial ignorance called the "vision of a self" (*ātmadarśana*) or the "view that the aggregates constitute an essential self" (*satkāyadṛṣṭi*).[467] To remove the afflictions, one must remove this cause, and this one does by applying the antidote to that cause—the "vision of selflessness" (*nairātmyadarśana*).

Kamalaśīla lays out the basic arguments used to establish this claim in a lengthy excursus in his comments on a key verse in the final chapter of the *Tattvasaṃgraha*:[468]

> There is no room for fault when one has directly realized selflessness (*pratyakṣīkṛtanairātmye*) since it is contradictory to that, like darkness when a lamp is blazing.[469]

We have already had a look at the first few lines of Kamalaśīla's commentary on this verse, in which he defines omniscience as the removal of the two obscurations. Kamalaśīla then reiterates his claim that the afflictions have their root in the vision of a self (*ātmadarśana*):

466. TSP *ad* TS 543 (*karmaphalasaṃbandhaparīkṣā*, B 230,8–9): *cittam eva hi saṃsāro rāgādikleśavāsitam / tad eva tair vinirmuktaṃ bhavānta iti kathyate //*.

467. See, e.g., TSP *ad* TS 3342 (*atīndriyārthadarśiparīkṣā*); cited above (n. 331). See also. PV 1.222: *sarvāsāṃ doṣajātīnāṃ jātiḥ satkāyadarśanāt / sāvidyā tatra tatsnehas tasmād dveṣādisaṃbhavaḥ /*. "All types of faults arise from the view that the aggregates constitute an essential self. That is ignorance (*avidyā*). When that [is present, one experiences] clinging (*sneha*) to that [alleged self], and from that [clinging] comes anger and so on." Cf. PV 2.212. For Dharmakīrti's emphasis on *satkāyadṛṣṭi*, see Vetter (1990: 42, n. 1, 112 n.2, and 113 n. 3).

468. For a critical edition of the Sanskrit and a German translation of this passage, see Pemwieser (1991: 53–108).

469. TS 3337 (*atīndriyārthadarśiparīkṣā*): *pratyakṣīkṛtanairātmye na doṣo labhate sthitim / tadviruddhatayā dīpre pradīpe timiraṃ yathā //*. Cf. PV 2.135: *ātmātmīyagrahakṛtaḥ snehaḥ saṃskāragocaraḥ / hetur virodhi nairātymadarśanaṃ tasya bādhakam //*.

> That is, these afflictions such as attachment and so on are ascertained to have their root in the false vision of a self, since there is positive concomitance (*anvaya*) and negative concomitance (*vyatireka*) [between the presence of the false vision of a self and the presence of the afflictions]. They do not come about through the force of external objects, since even when an external object exists, [the afflictions] do not arise without the existence of a negative mental outlook (*ayoniśomanaskāra*). And even without [external] objects, when the fabrications of a negative mental outlook are present, they do arise. And it is not logical that that which does not depend upon the existence or nonexistence [of something else] can have that [other thing] as its cause, since that would entail an overextension [of the relation between cause and effect].[470]

Kamalaśīla here makes a rather bold claim, namely, that it has been definitively determined or ascertained (*niścita*) that the vision of a self is the root cause of the afflictions. Apparently, Kamalaśīla believes that one can be certain that there pertains a "natural relation" (*svabhāvapratibandha*) of the causal type (*tadutpatti*) between the vision of a self and the afflictions, such that whenever afflictions are present, one knows that the visio[illegible] present. The implication here is that even an ordinary person [illegible] required positive and negative concomitance (*anvaya* and *vy*[illegible] ascertain the natural relation.

Following Dharmakīrti's argument and wording closely, Kamalaśīla then clarifies the process by which the natural relation may be ascertained. The basic idea is that it is possible to determine that the afflictions of attachment (*rāga*) and hatred (*dveṣa*) depend upon the notion of "mine" (*ātmīya*) to function, and the notion of "mine," in turn, operates only in the presence of the notion of a self (*ātman*). The topic in the passage is the afflictions (*kleśa*s):

> Nor are they produced through the power of external things. Rather, they arise due to the false vision of a self (*abhūtātmadarśana*). That is, self-cherishing does not arise for one who does not see an "I." Nor will attachment [to things] as one's own arise for the person who does not perceive "mine," insofar as one does not

470. TSP *ad* TS 3337 (*atīndriyārthadarśiparīkṣā*, B 1053,1–5): *tathā hy amī rāgādayaḥ kleśā vitathātmadarśanamūlakā anvayavyatirekābhyāṃ niścitāḥ na bāhyārthabalabhāvinaḥ / yataḥ saty api bāhyārthe nāyoniśomanasikāram antareṇotpadyante / vināpi cārthenāyoniśovikalpasaṃmukhībhāve saty utpadyante / na ca yat sadasattānuvidhāyi na bhavati tat tatkāraṇaṃ yuktam atiprasaṅgāt /*.

> perceive things as being conducive to one's own happiness. Also, aversion will not manifest at all for one who has no attachment, insofar as things are not perceived as inimical to one's self or possessions, because that [aversion] is not possible for one who is not impeded by [that notion of] "I" and "mine" and for one who has eliminated that impediment. The same should be said for arrogance and so on. Therefore, since beginningless time, the vision of a self that has arisen through the cultivation of each preceding similar [view] produces the perception of "mine." And those two [produce] the love of "I" and "mine." And that [love of "I" and "mine" produces] aversion and so on. Thus, through positive concomitance (*anvaya*) and negative concomitance (*vyatireka*), it is very clear that those [faults such as attachment and so on] have their root in the perception of "I" and "mine," which arises through the perception of a self; everyone up to and including the wife of a cowherd determines it thus.[471]

As this passage makes clear, the vision of a self is a primordial mistake; it is an erroneous perspective (*darśana*) produced in the mind through a process of continuous cultivation (*abhyāsa*) of that perspective since beginningless time. It is thus not primarily a philosophical view but something much deeper; in *Pramāṇavārttika* 1, Dharmakīrti equates it with ignorance.[472] These authors refer to this perspective variously as the vision of a self (*ātmadarśana*), the false vision of a self (*vitathātmadarśana*), the view that the aggregates constitute an essential self (*satkāyadṛṣṭi*), the view that sentient beings are real (*sattvadṛṣṭi*), the view of non-Buddhists (*tīrthadṛṣṭi*), and so on. Its basic characteristic is to see an unchanging "self" or nature (*ātman*) where none exists.

471. TSP *ad* TS 3337 (*atīndriyārthadarśiparīkṣā*, B 1053,10–17): *nāpi bāhyārthabalabhāvinaḥ / kiṃ tv abhūtātmadarśanabalasamudbhāvinaḥ / tathā hy aham ity apaśyato nātmasneho jāyate nāpi mamety agṛhṇata ātmasukhotpādānukūlatvenāgṛhīte vastuny ātmīyatvenābhiṣvaṅgaḥ samudbhavati / dveṣo 'pi na hi kvacid asaktasyātmātmīyapratikūlatvenāgṛhīte vastuni prādurbhāvam āsādayati / ātmātmīyānuparodhini taduparodhapratighātini ca tasyāsaṃbhavāt / evaṃ mānādayo 'pi vācyāḥ / tasmād anādikālikaṃ pūrvapūrvasajātīyābhyāsajanitam ātmadarśanam ātmīyagrahaṃ prasūte tau cātmātmīyasnehaṃ so 'pi dveṣādikam ity anvayavyatirekābhyām ātmagrahād ātmātmīyagrahamūlatvam eṣāṃ sphuṭataram āgopālāṅganam avasitam eva //*. Reading *ātmātmīyānuparodhini* instead of *ātymīyānuparodhini* on the basis of D, vol. *'e*, 295b: *bdag dang bdag gi la mi gnod pa dang de la gnod pa'i gnyen po can la de mi srid pa'i phyir ro.* Cf. PVSV 115–20.

472. PVSV 111,19–20: *satkāyadarśanajāḥ sarvadoṣāḥ / tad eva cājñānam ity ucyate //.*

The Antidote to Ignorance: The Vision of Selflessness

Eliminating this ignorance is primarily a matter of applying the antidote, the vision of selflessness. This process can perhaps best be thought of as the replacement of a faulty perspective with one that is correct. Since the faulty perspective is the cause of the afflictions, eliminating it also serves to eliminate the afflictions (or, put in Kamalaśīla's more technical vocabulary, the afflictive obscuration). Kamalaśīla explains how this is envisioned to work in the next segment of commentary:

> And the vision of selflessness contradicts the vision of a self, because its [epistemic] objective basis (*ālambana*) is an image (*ākāra*) that is the opposite of that [vision of a self]. For [both] the simultaneous coexistence and the identity of both [these images] in a single mental stream is a contradiction, just as [it is a contradiction for] the cognition of a snake and of that [rope] to exist [either simultaneously or as identical] in relation to an [actual] rope. Therefore, since the vision of a self is contradicted by the vision of selflessness, then passion and so on, which have that [vision of a self] as their root, are also contradicted [by the vision of selflessness], just as the quality of goosebumps caused by the cold [is contradicted] by the quality of burning heat. Thus, when one has perceived directly (*pratyakṣīkṛte*) the vision of selflessness, which contradicts all faults, then the crowds of passion and so on that are contradicted by that find no place to stand, like darkness in a place that is pervaded by light. Hence, the elimination of the afflictive obscuration comes about through the vision of selflessness. The proof statement (*prayoga*) is as follows: wherever there occurs something that contradicts something [else], then in that place that other thing will not find room to dwell, like darkness when the earth's surface meets with a flood of splendor from a blazing lamp. And this is the case when there occurs the vision of selflessness that contradicts the crowds of faults when a person sees selflessness through direct perception; this is [evidence in the form of] a perception of that which contradicts [the cause of something else].[473]

473. TSP *ad* TS 3337 (*atīndriyārthadarśiparīkṣā*, B 1053,18–1054,4): *ātmadarśana-viruddhaṃ ca nairātmyadarśanam tadviparītākārālambanatvāt / anayor hi yugapad ekasmin santāne rajjau sarpatajjñānayor iva sahāvasthānam aikyaṃ ca viruddham / ato*

The vision of selflessness dispels the vision of a self as a lamp dispels darkness. The two visions are utterly incompatible and cannot exist simultaneously within the same mindstream. Since the vision of a self is the cause of the afflictions, replacing it with the vision of selflessness rids one of the afflictions. After presenting this basic argument, Kamalaśīla then consolidates it into a formal argument (*prayoga*) that relies on evidence in the form of a perception of that which contradicts the cause of something.[474] In other words, upon observing the vision of selflessness in some mindstream, one understands that the afflictions cannot arise there, since the vision of selflessness is incompatible with the cause of the afflictions, the vision of a self.[475]

At this point, however, some objections are raised. That is, if the vision of a self and the vision of selflessness are mutually contradictory, and if the presence of one dispels the other, then assuming the vision of a self is present primordially in our minds, how can the vision of selflessness ever arise in the first place? Further, even if the vision of selflessness were somehow to arise, how can we be sure that it will eliminate the vision of a self completely and not just suppress it temporarily? Kamalaśīla gives voice to these doubts:

> [Objection:] Someone might think: "Just as there is no opportunity for the vision of a self to arise in a mind beset by the vision of selflessness, since [the two visions] are contradictory, so, too, the vision of selflessness [cannot arise] in a mind beset by the vision of a self, since the contradiction [between the two] is equal. And therefore, since any instance of a vision of selflessness is impossible,

---

nairātmyadarśanasyātmadarśanavirodhāt tanmūlair api rāgādibhiḥ saha virodho bhavati dahanaviśeṣeṇeva śītakṛtaromaharṣādiviśeṣasya / tena sarvadoṣavirodhinairātmyadarśane pratyakṣīkṛte sati na tadviruddho rāgādidoṣagaṇo 'vasthānaṃ labhate timiravad ālokaparigate deśa iti / ato nairātmyadarśanāt kleśāvaraṇaprahāṇaṃ bhavati / prayogaḥ yatra yadviruddhavastusamavadhānaṃ na tatra tadaparam avasthitim āsādayati yathā dīprapradīpaprabhāvaprasarasaṃsargiṇi dharaṇitale timiram / asti ca doṣagaṇaviruddhanairātmyadarśanasamavadhānaṃ pratyakṣīkṛtanairātmyadarśane puṃsīti viruddhopalabdhiḥ //. With Pemwieser 1991: 55, the reading *dahanaviśeṣeṇeva* is instead of *dahanaviśeṣe*, and *kleśāvaraṇaprahāṇaṃ* is instead of *kleśāvaraṇagrahāṇaṃ*.

474. The evidence in the form of a perception of that which contradicts the cause of something else (*viruddhopalabdhi*) is explained at NB 2.40: *kāraṇaviruddhopalabdhir yathā nāsya romaharṣādiviśeṣāḥ saṃnihitadahanaviśeṣatvād* /. Cf. also PVSV 6,13–15.

475. Technically, a person of limited vision would not be able to observe the vision of selflessness in another person's mindstream but only in his or her own mindstream. In that case, however, the person would also be able to observe that the afflictions are not operative there, and so reliance upon an inference would not be necessary. Kamalaśīla's proof statement, therefore, seems limited to a theoretical and not a practical value.

the evidence is unestablished. Even if the vision of selflessness were possible, nonetheless, although the two [visions] are contradictory, the relation of refuted and refuter is not established to exist in the highest degree, just as, for example, [the contradiction] between attachment and aversion or pleasure and pain [is not established as contradictory in the highest degree, such that the existence of one utterly eliminates for all time the existence of the other]. But here [you] wish to establish that [one of the pair of contrary visions] is utterly eliminated, not merely that it does not operate during the time [that the other one is present]. Therefore, your evidence is inconclusive. And it is observed every day that attachment and so on arise with unmitigated strength even for those persons for whom the reality of selflessness that pervades all things has been ascertained through the force of inference. For this reason also the evidence is inconclusive."[476]

The objector here attacks Kamalaśīla's evidence, claiming that it is either unestablished (*asiddha*) or inconclusive (*anaikāntika*). The evidence, recall, is the perception of the vision of selflessness, which contradicts the cause of the afflictions. But if the vision of selflessness cannot arise due to the primordial presence of the vision of a self, then the evidence will be unreal, hence unestablished. On the other hand, even if the vision of selflessness can arise, the evidence will still be faulty because it is inconclusive, as there is no guarantee that the vision of selflessness will actually eradicate the vision of a self and not merely suppress it temporarily. Finally, the objector points out another reason the evidence should be regarded as inconclusive: namely, it is regularly observed that even those who have ascertained the vision of selflessness through inferential reasoning are not free from the afflictions.

The last point is critical, and Kamalaśīla's response is quite interesting, for in it, he reveals that there is a significant difference between *recognizing* that the vision of selflessness is a correct or accurate perspective and internally

476. TSP *ad* TS 3337 (*atīndriyārthadarśiparīkṣā*, B 1054,5–12): *syād etat / yathā nairātmyadarśanasamākrānte cetasi viruddhatayātmadarśanasyotpattum anavakāśas tathā nairātmyadarśanasyāpy ātmadarśanasamākrānte manasi virodhasya tulyatvāt / tataś ca kasyacin nairātmyadarśanasyāsambhavād asiddho hetuḥ / saṃbhavatu vā nairātmyadarśanam tathāpy anayor virodhe saty api nātyantaṃ bādhyabādhakabhāvaḥ siddhyati yathā rāgadveṣayoḥ sukhaduḥkhayor vā / yato 'tyantaprahāṇam iha sādhayitum iṣṭam / na tu tāvatkālāsamudācāramātram ity ato 'naikāntikatā hetoḥ / dṛśyante pratidinam anumānabalāvadhāritasamastavastugatanairātmyatattvānām api satām akhaṇḍitamahimāno rāgādayaḥ samudayam āsādayanta ity ato 'pi hetor naikāntikateti //.*

realizing that perspective in the thoroughgoing manner that eliminates primordial ignorance. He begins by responding to the objection that the vision of selflessness cannot arise for one who is presently ensconced in the vision of a self, and then quickly moves on to the second point:

> [Answer:] This is not right. If it were not possible for the concept (*vikalpa*) of selflessness to arise in the mindstream of a person for whom the afflictions have not been eliminated, then there would be no opportunity for the vision of selflessness to arise. But insofar as it is established through experience, the concept of selflessness *can* be directly encountered by everyone. And then because that [concept] is capable of reaching a pinnacle when it is cultivated, just like the concept of the beloved [in the mind of the lovesick man], then at the end [of the period of cultivation] it becomes extremely clear, and it is perceived as an object that is cognized by a means of trustworthy awareness. And through these [two criteria,] it ends up being [the means of trustworthy awareness called] perception (*pratyakṣa*). Hence, how is the arisal of the vision of selflessness impossible?[477]

This passage introduces a nuance to the claim that the vision of selflessness is the antidote to ignorance: that is, we learn here both that the vision of selflessness is necessarily nonconceptual and that the process by which that vision arises starts out from an initial *conceptual* understanding, which is transformed into a nonconceptual vision through a process of cultivation or meditation (*bhāvanā*). The vision of selflessness, in other words, is an instance of yogic perception (*yogipratyakṣa*)—as the reference to the vision of the beloved on the part of the lovesick man makes clear—a special form of perception for these authors, to a brief account of which we now turn.[478]

477. TSP *ad* TS 3337 (*atīndriyārthadarśiparīkṣā*, B 1054,13–17): *naitad asti / yadi nairātmyavikalpasyotpādo 'prahīṇakleśasya santāne na saṃbhavet tadā na saṃbhaven nairātmyadarśanodayāvakāśo yāvatānubhavasiddhas tāvan nairātmyavikalpasaṃmukhībhāvaḥ sarveṣām eva / sa eva ca bhāvanayā kāminīvikalpavat prakarṣagamanasaṃbhavād ante sphuṭapratibhāsatayā pramāṇapratītārthagrāhitayā ca pratyakṣatām āpadyata iti kathaṃ nairātmyadarśanodayāsaṃbhavaḥ /.*

478. The *locus classicus* for Dharmakīrti's theory of *yogipratyakṣa* is PV 3.281–87. Dignāga discusses the topic at PS 1.6 and PSV *ad cit*. For secondary sources, see Bühnemann 1980; Dunne 2007; Pemwieser 1991; Prévèreau 1994; and Steinkellner 1978.

The Vision of Selflessness as Yogic Perception

Yogic perception is one of four types of perception accepted in the Buddhist *pramāṇa* theory tradition.[479] For Śāntarakṣita and Kamalaśīla, this means that yogic perception corresponds to Dharmakīrti's basic definition of perception as nonconceptual (*kalpanāpoḍha*) and nonerroneous (*abhrānta*). Two things are distinctive about yogic perception as compared to other forms of perception. First, it always serves a soteriological function, contributing to the elimination of the afflictions in some manner. Second, its object starts out as a conceptual mental image and is transformed into a nonconceptual mental image through intense meditation. What is significant about this process for Dharmakīrti and his followers is that *any* mental image upon which one meditates long enough and with enough intensity eventually comes to have the vividness (*sphuṭatva*) and nonconceptuality associated with perception. As Dharmakīrti has said,

> Therefore, whatever one meditates upon, whether real or unreal, results in a cognition that is vivid and nonconceptual when the meditation is perfected.[480]

From the phenomenological perspective, the initial image may be real (i.e., trustworthy) or unreal (untrustworthy). The classic example of a meditation on an unreal object is the one that we saw in Kamalaśīla's passage above, that of a lovesick man who focuses so intensely on an image of his beloved that he eventually comes to "see" her with all of the vividness of an actual perception. In short, Dharmakīrti refers to a process by which an obsession leads eventually to a hallucination.

Now, the same process is held to occur with mental images such as the concept of selflessness, whereby prolonged meditation on the concept eventually gives rise to a clear and nonconceptual awareness (i.e., the "vision") of selflessness. The difference between the vision of selflessness on the part of the yogi and the vision of the beloved on the part of the lovesick man is that the vision of selflessness is trustworthy while the vision of the beloved is not. That is, in Śāntarakṣita and Kamalaśīla's understanding, selflessness has already been determined, by means of inference, to be necessarily true of

479. The other forms of perception are sense perception (*indriyapratyakṣa*), mental perception (*mānasapratyakṣa*), and reflexive awareness (*svasaṃvedana*).

480. PV 3.285: *tasmād bhūtam abhūtaṃ vā yad yad evābhibhāvyate / bhāvanāpariniṣpattau tat spuṭākalpadhīphalam //*.

all *dharma*s. And this is why, once the mental image has been transformed into a nonconceptual awareness, the awareness of selflessness is classified as perception while the hallucination of the beloved is not. Both experiences have the vividness and nonconceptuality of perception, but only the former is nonerroneous.

Śāntarakṣita and Kamalaśīla do not offer any sustained rational defense of the process by which conceptual images become nonconceptual through habituation. Instead, they indicate that this is a process that can be observed,[481] and they take that observation as their warrant for asserting the process as a matter of fact. In itself, this is not out of the ordinary for these thinkers. A great deal of their theorizing rests on observations concerning everyday experiences, and about which they clearly expect agreement from their audience. The process by which a concept attains clarity—illustrated by the stock examples of a lover's hallucination of his beloved, a grieving father's hallucination of his dead son, and a fearful person's hallucination of a thief—is just another appeal to experience of this kind. Although it may not satisfy many modern readers, I think we can assume that the authors believe that their audience (or at least the ideal audience of judicious persons) would assent to the proposition without many qualms.

Response to Objections Concerning the Antidote

We have now seen Kamalaśīla's basic position, according to which liberation and omniscience both come about through the utter elimination of ignorance, which may be achieved by thoroughly inculcating in one's mindstream, by means of meditation (*bhāvanā*), the antidote to ignorance, i.e., the vision of selflessness. The end result of this process is a direct yogic perception, a clear awareness of the selflessness of all *dharma*s, which, by its nature, is incompatible with all afflictions. This means that the end result of the proper meditation on selflessness is liberation, the highest good (*niḥśreyasa*), knowledge of how to attain which we have seen to be a requirement of dharmic as well as total omniscience. The state of omniscience itself is an extension of liberation that occurs for those who have great compassion, and who

481. See, e.g., TSP *ad* TS 1360 (*pratyakṣalakṣaṇaparīkṣā*, B 493,23–25): *abhūtam api bhāvayatāṃ kāmaśokabhayādyupaplutacetasām anapekṣitasādharmyādismṛter abhyāsasya sphuṭapratibhāsasya jñānotpādanasāmarthyam upalabhyata eva /*. "The capacity of cultivation (*abhyāsa*)—which is memory that does not depend on similarity and so on—to produce an awareness of a vivid image is indeed observed in those who, their minds deranged by desire, grief, fear, and so on, are meditating on even an unreal [object]."

extend their meditation sufficiently to remove even the subtle traces of ignorance that remain in the mindstream.

Returning now to the lengthy excursus on *Tattvasaṃgraha* 3337, we find Kamalaśīla presenting a list of eleven objections to the Buddhist theory, each of which is an ostensible reason for the impossibility of the meditation on selflessness as described by Kamalaśīla.[482] The objections ensue progressively one from the other as follows:

1. If no one were to wish [to engage in the meditation], then that would be a reason for the non-engagement with the meditation, since the activity of wise persons is pervaded by the desire [to undertake the action].
2. Or, even if there were some desire [to engage in the meditation], due to not knowing the nature of that which is to be abandoned, a wise person would not engage in it, because it is not possible to eliminate a fault whose nature is not known.
3. Or, even if one did know the nature of that, understanding that the faults are permanent, one would not undertake any effort to eliminate them, since it is not possible to eliminate a permanent thing.
4. Or, even if [the faults] are not permanent, nonetheless, understanding that they were without a cause, one would not engage [in the meditation], since it is not possible to destroy something that is independently existent.
5. Or, even if [those faults] possess a cause, because one has not definitively determined the nature of the cause of those [faults], one does not apply oneself to the meditation, since it is not possible to eliminate something of which the cause is not known, as for example an illness.
6. Or, even if we grant that the cause of those [faults] is known, nevertheless, understanding that that cause is permanent, a wise person will not exert him or herself to eliminate it, since it is not possible to block a cause that is fully present.
7. Or, even if the cause of those [faults] it is not permanent, knowing that the faults are the very nature (*dharmatā*) of living beings, one will not make an effort [to engage in the meditation to eliminate those faults], since it is not possible to destroy a nature (*svabhāva*) [of something without destroying the thing itself].
8. Or, even if the faults are not the nature [of living beings], nevertheless,

482. Pemwieser (1991, 73–74n19) points to NK 1,8–16 and SS 2,1–6 as analogous passages and suggests that PV 2.143 might serve as a source for this catalogue of questions. See her subsequent notes for specific instances of parallel arguments in NK and SS.

since there is no method for their elimination, one will not engage [in the meditation], because without a method one does not obtain the goal.

9. Or, even if there is a method, because one does not know that [method], its application will be impossible, because it is not possible to apply something whose nature is not known.
10. Or, even if [the method] is known, because its highest point is fixed, as in jumping and so on, or because a future life is impossible, the complete perfection of the meditation will not be possible, hence one will not engage [in that meditation].
11. Or, even if we grant that it is possible to reach the complete perfection [of the meditation] and from that the faults are eliminated through the arisal of the antidote, nevertheless, since it is possible that the faults will arise again, like the solidity of copper and so on [will arise again even after the copper has been melted in a fire], therefore one will not begin to engage [in the meditation].[483]

We have already seen the greater part of Kamalaśīla's answer to the first of these eleven objections when we considered the bodhisattva's great compassion. Great compassion provides the motivation for undertaking the meditation on selflessness, since it is only by means of a thorough realization of the vision of selflessness that a person becomes enabled to help others eliminate their own suffering.

483. TSP *ad* TS 3337 (*atīndriyārthadarśiparīkṣā*, B 1054,21–1055,13): *tathā hi bhāvanāyām aprayoge sarveṣām evānarthitvaṃ vā kāraṇaṃ bhavet / prekṣāvataḥ pravṛtter arthitayā vyāptatvāt / saty apy arthitve praheyasvarūpāparijñānād vā na pravartate prekṣāvān / anirjñātasvarūpasya doṣasya hātum aśakyatvāt / saty api tatsvarūpajñāne nityatvaṃ vā doṣāṇāṃ paśyaṃs tatprahāṇāya na yatnam ārabhate / nityasya prahāṇāsaṃbhavāt / asaty api vānityatve nirhetukatvam eṣām avagamya nirvartate / svatantrasyāsaṃbhavaducchedatvāt / saty api vā kāraṇavattve tatkāraṇasvarūpāniścayād api nādriyate bhāvanāyām / avijñātanidānasya vyādhir iva prahātum aśakyatvāt / bhavatu vā tatkāraṇaparijñānaṃ kiṃ tatkāraṇaṃ nityam avagamya notsahate tatprahāṇāya prekṣāpūrvakārī / avikalakāraṇasya pratibaddhum aśakteḥ / anityatve 'pi vā tatkāraṇasya doṣāṇāṃ prāṇidharmatām avetya na prayatate / svabhāvasya hātum aśakyatvāt / asvabhāvatve vā doṣāṇāṃ kṣayopāyāsaṃbhavān nivartate / na hy upāyavikalasyopeyasaṃprāptir asti / sattve 'pi copāyasya tadaparijñānād asaṃbhavattadanuṣṭhāno bhavet / aparijñātasvarūpasyānuṣṭhānāsaṃbhavāt / parijñāne 'pi vā laṅghanād iva vyavasthitotkarṣatayā janmāntarāsaṃbhavena vā bhāvanāyā atyantaprakarṣam asambhāvayan nābhiyogavān bhavati / bhavatu vātyantaprakarṣagamanasaṃbhavāt pratipakṣodayena doṣāṇāṃ kṣayas tathāpi tāmrādikāṭhinyavat punar api doṣodayaṃ sambhāvayan nābhiyogam ārabhata iti //.*

The remaining ten objections fall into three main categories: those dealing with the afflictions (here called the "faults"), those dealing with the cause of the afflictions, and those dealing with the method for eliminating the cause of the afflictions. Three objections (2, 3, and 7) deal with the afflictions themselves. The first of these (2) states that the afflictions are not known. Kamalaśīla rejects this on empirical grounds, stating that anger, lust, arrogance, pride, and so on are recognized by those who experience them.[484] The next objection concerning the afflictions (3) states that the afflictions are permanent. Kamalaśīla likewise appeals to experience to dispel this objection, in that our experience of the afflictions is only intermittent.[485] The third objection that deals with the afflictions (7) states that the afflictions are the very nature (*dharmatā*) of living beings. Kamalaśīla's answer to this objection is somewhat more complex, and we will treat it in a subsequent section.[486]

The next set of objections deals with the cause of the afflictions. As we have seen, the Buddhist theory of the meditation on selflessness argues that the vision of selflessness is the antidote to the cause of the afflictions, the vision of a self. Here, an opponent raises possibilities concerning the cause of the afflictions that would nullify the Buddhist theory. The first objection is that the afflictions have *no* cause (4), making the removal of their cause impossible. Kamalaśīla rebuts this by referring to his and Śāntarakṣita's theory of causality, whereby whatever is observed to be restricted in time and place is understood to necessarily have a cause.[487] Kamalaśīla next skips to the objection that the cause of the afflictions is permanent (6) and thus impossible to eliminate, stating that this cannot be the case, for it would mean that the afflictions would always arise simultaneously instead of one by one, as

484. TSP *ad* TS 3337 (*atīndriyārthadarśiparīkṣā*, B 1056,8–10): *nāpi doṣasvarūpāparijñānaṃ yato 'bhiṣvaṅgaparighātātmātmīyonnatyādyākāreṇa rāgadveṣamohamānamaderṣyāmātsaryādayaḥ kleśopakleśagaṇā viditasvarūpā evodayante vyayante ca //*. "Nor is the nature of the faults not known, since the host of afflictions and subsidiary afflictions such as lust, aversion, delusion, pride, arrogance, jealousy, and envy, which are forms of such things as attachment, hatred, and the conceit of 'I' and 'mine,' arise and subside with their natures known [by those in whom they are arising and subsiding]."

485. TSP *ad* TS 3337 (*atīndriyārthadarśiparīkṣā*, B 1056,11–13): *nāpi ca te nityāḥ kādācitkatayā saṃvedyamānatvāt //*. "And neither are those [afflictions] permanent, since they are only experienced occasionally."

486. See below, pp. 212–19.

487. TSP *ad* TS 3337 (*atīndriyārthadarśiparīkṣā*, B 1056,13–14): *ata eva nāhetukatvam eṣām ahetor anapekṣitatvena deśakālasvabhāvaniyamāyogāt //*. "Hence, neither are they causeless, since by virtue of its independence, it does not make sense for a causeless thing to be restricted in its nature to any [particular] time or place."

they are seen to do.[488] Having addressed the problem of a permanent cause, Kamalaśīla then turns to the last objection concerning the cause of the afflictions, that its nature is not known (5). He responds that its nature *is* known, in that it is determined to be impermanent and to consist in the incorrect notions of "I" and "mine."[489] Once again, the basic appeal is to experience.

Finally, there are four objections dealing with the method for the elimination of the cause of the afflictions. The first objection (8) claims that there is *no* such method. Kamalaśīla responds that there is such a method, which is to cultivate that which contradicts the cause of the afflictions. That which contradicts the cause of something is the antidote (*pratipakṣa*), and cultivating the antidote is the method.[490] The second objection (9) is that the method is not known.[491] The third objection (10) states that the method is inade-

488. TSP *ad* TS 3337 (*atīndriyārthadarśiparīkṣā*, B 1053,13–16) *ato 'pi nityahetutvam eṣāṃ pratikṣiptaṃ tatkāraṇasyātmādeḥ sadā saṃnihitatvād anādheyātiśayasya paraiḥ sahakārinirapekṣatvāt / tanmātrabhāvināṃ sarvadā yugapac cotpattiprasaṅgāt / ataḥ sāmarthyād anityahetava evaite //*. "And from this, moreover, the idea that their cause is permanent is refuted, since their cause, the self and so on, would always be [fully] present, since something whose perfection is not provided by others is not dependent upon contributing conditions. And there would be the undesired consequence that the things that are produced by just that [cause] would always arise simultaneously. Hence, by implication, those [faults] are [known to have] just impermanent causes."

489. TSP *ad* TS 3337 (*atīndriyārthadarśiparīkṣā*, B 1056,17–18): *anityo 'pi hetur eṣāṃ viditasvarūpa eva ātmātmīyaviparyāsahetukatvād rāgāder doṣagaṇasya tadanvaya-vyatirekānuvidhānād iti pūrvaṃ pratipāditatvāt //*. "Also, we know that the nature of the cause of these [faults] is just to be impermanent, because the cause of the host of faults such as lust and so on is the incorrect [apprehension of] 'I' and 'mine,' and because [those faults] are regulated by the positive concomitance and the negative concomitance to that [apprehension of a self and possessions]. These statements have already been proven."

490. TSP *ad* TS 3337 (*atīndriyārthadarśiparīkṣā*, B 1057,19–22): *nāpi kṣayopāyāsaṃbhavaḥ / svahetuviruddhasvabhāvapadārthābhyāsasya kṣayopāyatvena saṃbhavāt / tathā hi ye saṃbhavatsvahetuviruddhasvabhāvābhyāsās te saṃbhavadatyantasantānavicchedās tad yathā vrīhyādayaḥ / tathā cāmī rāgādaya iti saṃbhavaty evaiṣāṃ kṣayopāyaḥ //*. "Nor is it the case that there is no method for the elimination [of those faults], because it is possible for the cultivation of things whose nature is contradictory to the cause [of those faults] to be a method for their elimination. That is, things for which the cultivation of [other] things whose nature is contradictory [to those things] is possible may become such that their continuum is utterly interrupted, as in the case of rice and so on. And this is so for those [faults] such as attachment [i.e., they are things for which the cultivation of other things whose nature is contradictory to them is possible]. Therefore, there is a method for eliminating them."

491. TSP *ad* TS 3337 (*atīndriyārthadarśiparīkṣā*, B 1057,23–1058,2): *nāpi tadaparijñānaṃ yato hetusvarūpajñānād eva yat tadviparītālambanākāraṃ vastu sa tasya pratipakṣa iti*

quate, in that it cannot achieve the full eradication of the cause of the afflictions either because there is an inherent limitation in the human capacity to eliminate faults or because humans are limited to one lifetime only, which is insufficient for eliminating all faults. Kamalaśīla dismisses the second point by stating simply that past and future lives have already been demonstrated.[492] His response to the first part is to say that wisdom, which is the goal of the meditation on selflessness, is not like physical endeavors, such as jumping, in which the degree of excellence that one may obtain is inherently fixed and limited. Kamalaśīla indicates that this will be explained subsequently, and we, too, will treat this topic in a separate section below.[493] Finally, the last objection (11) holds that while the afflictions may be dispelled temporarily, they may also re-arise, thus rendering the antidote ineffective.[494] Kamalaśīla denies this in his response, saying, in essence, that a person who has eliminated the faulty vision of a self will never go back, since the negative consequences of doing so will be obvious.[495]

Having presented his responses to each of these eleven objections, Kamalaśīla says, "Therefore, the evidence is not unestablished."[496] Here, we should recall the initial proof statement, which is as follows:

> Wherever there occurs something that contradicts something [else], then in that place that other thing will not find room to dwell, like darkness when the earth's surface meets with a flood

---

sphuṭam avasīyata eva / nairātmyadarśanaṃ ca tatra viparītālambanākāratvāt pratipakṣa iti pradarśitam etat //. "Nor is it the case that [that method] is not known, since the nature of the cause is known; [and] it is clearly determined that whatever has an objective basis and image that is contrary to some [cause] is the antidote for that [cause]. And it has been shown that the vision of selflessness has an objective basis and image that is contrary to that [vision of a self that is the cause of the faults]."

492. TSP *ad* TS 3337 (*atīndriyārthadarśiparīkṣā*, B 1058,6): *nāpi janmāntarāsaṃbhavaḥ pūrvajanmaprasarasya prasādhitatvāt //*. "Nor is it the case that future lives are not possible, since the stream of previous lives has been established." Kamalaśīla refers to the *lokāyataparīkṣā* of the TS/P.

493. The explanation for why cultivation of the vision of selflessness is not inherently limited occurs at TS 3401–48 and TSP *ad cit.*, with the discussion of jumping and so on occurring at TS 3420–26 and TSP *ad cit.* See pp. 208–12 below.

494. The objection corresponds to an objection raised by Dharmakīrti at PVSV (Gn 110,23–25): *kathaṃ nirdoṣo nāma / yāvatā doṣavipakṣasātmatve 'pi doṣasātmano vipakṣotpattivad yathāpratyayaṃ doṣotpattir api //*. Translated in Yaita 1988: 434.

495. Cf. PVSV *ad* PV 1.221.

496. TSP *ad* TS 3337 (*atīndriyārthadarśiparīkṣā*, B 1059,5): *tasmān nāsiddho hetuḥ /*.

> of splendor from a blazing lamp. And this is the case when there occurs the vision of selflessness that contradicts the crowds of faults when a person sees selflessness through direct perception; this is [evidence in the form of] a perception of that which contradicts [the cause of something else].[497]

The evidence in this proof statement is "the vision of selflessness," insofar as it contradicts the cause of the afflictions, the vision of a self. Kamalaśīla has now set out the primary arguments he feels are necessary for a basic defense of this evidence, showing that the evidence is not unestablished (*asiddha*).

In the remainder of the excursus on *Tattvasaṃgraha* 3337, Kamalaśīla presents two arguments as to why the evidence is not inconclusive (*anaikāntika*). First, he argues that the vision of selflessness is indeed able to dispel the afflictions, since the vision of selflessness is strong (*balavat*) due to its object being real (*bhūta*), while the vision of a self is the opposite of that, i.e., it is weak due to its object being unreal (*abhūta*).[498] If someone objects that just as passion (*rāga*) and hatred (*dveṣa*), or pleasure (*sukha*) and suffering (*duḥkha*), are opposite to each other and yet nonetheless one does not definitively dispel the other, Kamalaśīla argues that there is no such deviance (*vyabhicāra*) in the evidence, since passion and hatred or pleasure and suffering are not in fact contradictory in the sense of one being the antidote to the other.[499] From the point of view of their cause, passion and hatred are equal in that both are caused by the vision of a self; and from the point of view of their object, pleasure and suffering are equal in that their objects are the same (that is, the same thing gives rise at times to pleasure and at times to suffering). So, unlike the vision of selflessness and the vision of a self, there is no difference in strength between these other opposing pairs of mental states.

Second, Kamalaśīla argues that the fact that those who have ascertained the truth of selflessness through inferential reasoning still experience afflictions like passion and hatred does not render the evidence inconclusive.

497. See above, n. 473.

498. TSP *ad* TS 3337 (*atīndriyārthadarśiparīkṣā*, B 1059,5–7): *nāpy anaikāntiko yato nairātmyadarśanasya bhūtārthaviṣayatvena balavattvam ātmadarśanasya tu viparyayād viparyaya iti bhavati vipakṣapratipakṣabhāvaḥ* //. "Nor is it inconclusive, since the vision of selflessness is strong due to having a real object. But the vision of a self is the inverse because it is the opposite [i.e., it is not strong since its object is not real]. Therefore, the relationship of the opposite and its antidote exists [between these two]." Cf. PVSV *ad* PV 1.221.

499. Cf. PV 2.211.

For the mere inferential ascertainment of selflessness is not the same as the vision of selflessness that the yogi inculcates through meditation. Kamalaśīla records the following exchange:

> [Objection:] But the following might be urged: passion and so on arise even for those for whom selflessness has been ascertained by the strength of inference. [Answer:] This is not right. For we describe the antidote that completely uproots the vision of a self to be that vision of selflessness that is produced through meditation (*bhāvanāmaya*), which, because it appears clearly, is a nonconceptual awareness that directly apprehends the real thing, "selflessness" (*nirātmaka*), and which, because its object has been established by a trustworthy means of awareness, is nonerroneous (*abhrānta*). We do not [so describe the vision of selflessness] that is produced through study and deliberation.[500]

As is quite evident here, the vision of selflessness is a *perception* (*pratyakṣa*) that arises through meditation. It is thus a form of yogic perception, as we have already learned. Mere intellectual knowledge of the fact that all things are selfless is not the antidote to the afflictions. Only the direct perception of selflessness, obtained through meditation, can uproot the erroneous vision of a self that has been inculcated since beginningless time. To seal the argument, Kamalaśīla presents one last proof statement, topped off by a rhetorical question:

> Whatever things are diminished through the presence of some other thing become eliminated without a trace when there is the development [or increase] of that [other thing] to the highest degree, like flames of fire when there is an increase in water. And the faults are things that are diminished by the presence of the awareness of selflessness. Therefore, when there is the development of that [awareness of selflessness] to the highest degree, how could [the faults] obtain any place [in the mind]?[501]

500. TSP *ad* TS 3337 (*atīndriyārthadarśiparīkṣā*, B 1060,3–6): *yat punar utkam anu mānabalāvadhāritanairātmyānām api samutpadyante rāgādaya iti tad ayuktam / yasmād bhāvanāmayaṃ sphuṭapratibhāsatayā nirātmakavastusākṣātkārijñānam avikalpakaṃ pramāṇaprasiddhārthaviṣayatayā cābhrāntaṃ tan nairātmyadarśanam ātmadarśanasyātyantonmūlanena pratipakṣo varṇito na śrutacintāmayam //.*

501. TSP *ad* TS 3337 (*atīndriyārthadarśiparīkṣā*, B 1060,13–15): *ye hi yadupadhānād*

With this, Kamalaśīla completes his defense of the evidence in the abbreviated proof statement that Śāntarakṣita first gave in *Tattvasaṃgraha* 3337 except for his response to the tenth objection (10), which states that the method for eliminating the afflictions is inadequate because the highest point of the cultivation of the vision of selflessness is inherently limited or fixed, a point he has promised to explain subsequently. We turn to this objection and response now, before undertaking a fuller explication of Kamalaśīla's response to objection 7, which states that the cause of the faults is the very nature of living beings and so impossible to eliminate.

The Perfectibility of the Vision of Selflessness

The tenth objection in the above list of eleven objections states that there is a limit to the degree to which the meditation on selflessness can be perfected. This is an objection advanced (apparently) by Kumārila in a verse preserved in the *Tattvasaṃgraha* and in Ratnakīrti's *Sarvajñasiddhi*. Kumārila is credited with saying:

> One who, having jumped, goes up to ten cubits (*hasta*) in the air is not able to go a league (*yojana*), even after practicing hundreds of times.[502]

Dharmakīrti also raises the objection in *Pramāṇavārttika* 2:

> Even if cultivation (*abhyāsa*) may bring about excellence (*viśeṣa*), the transcendence of [a thing's] nature does not occur, as [is observed in the cases of] jumping and heating of water.[503]

---

apakarṣadharmāṇas te tadatyantavṛddhau niranvayasamucchittidharmāṇo bhavanti yathā salilāvṛddhāv agnijvālā / nairātmyajñānopadhānāc cāpakarṣadharmāṇo doṣā iti tadatyantavṛddhau katham avasthāṃ labheran //.

502. TS 3167 (*atīndriyārthadarśiparīkṣā*): *daśahastāntaraṃ vyomno yo nāmotplutya gacchati / na yojanam asau gantuṃ śakto 'bhyāsaśatair api //*. Cited in SS 9,16–17, where it is attributed to the *Bṛhaṭṭīkā*. A *hasta* (literally, a "hand") is a measurement "from the elbow to the tip of the middle finger," i.e., a cubit, while a *yojana* is a measurement of variable but always considerable length, ranging from two-and-a-half to eighteen miles. See Monier-Williams s.v.

503. PV 2.120a–c: *abhyāsena viśeṣe 'pi laṅghanodakatāpavat / svabhāvātikramo mā bhūd iti ced āhitaḥ ... //*.

Like Kumārila, Dharmakīrti here uses the example of jumping, according to which it is granted that repeated practice may lead one to jump higher, but no amount of practice will allow one to jump miles into the sky. Dharmakīrti also includes a second example, that of the heating of water. According to this example, water can be heated only to a certain point. No matter how much fuel one adds to the fire, water will never be induced to burst into flames. These two examples are designed to show that there are limits on the development of things as a way of illustrating that an extreme or total perfection of the meditation on selflessness is also not possible.

Śāntarakṣita and Kamalaśīla follow Dharmakīrti in their response to this problem.[504] In brief, they claim that mental qualities such as wisdom, compassion, and so on, meet certain criteria that allow them to develop to an extraordinarily high degree, whereas jumping, heating water, and so on do not meet these same criteria. The criteria in question are (1) that the quality to be developed must naturally continue at the level already obtained, without depending on repeated further efforts; and (2) that the basis for the quality to be developed be stable. The case of jumping violates the first condition. That is, one may jump to a certain height, but the height obtained does not remain, such that the next jump can start off where the previous jump left off. Instead, one returns to the earth and must make a renewed effort to jump again. Thus, as every height obtained depends upon a renewed effort, it is not possible to develop jumping to an extraordinarily high degree. The case of heating water violates the second condition. That is, although one may heat water until it is quite hot, because water evaporates when heated, the basis in which the quality of heat is developed is inherently unstable. Thus, one is again prevented from developing heat in water to the highest degree.[505]

This argument comes at a point in the *Tattvasaṃgraha* and the *Pañjikā* where the authors are defending the general principle that knowledge of

504. Dharmakīrti's response is found in PV 2.120d–2.131.

505. As usual, Kamalaśīla expresses the argument in a formal proof statement. See TSP *ad* TS 3420–23 (*atīndriyārthadarśiparīkṣā*, B 1079,19–22): *ye sthirāśrayavartinaḥ sakṛc ca yathākathaṃcid āhitaviśeṣāḥ santo 'sati virodhipratyaye tadbhāvāyāpunaryatnāpekṣiṇas te saṃskārotkarṣabhedena sambhavatprakarṣaparyantavṛttayas tad yathā kanakaviśuddhyādayaḥ / yathoktadharmāṇaś ca prajñākṛpādaya iti svabhāvahetuḥ //*. "Whatever qualities subsist in a stable basis and, once they have somehow been acquired, do not depend upon a further effort for their production, may develop, provided there is no contradictory condition, to the highest degree of excellence (*prakarṣaparyanta*) through a distinction in the superiority of their cultivation (*saṃskāra*), like the purification of gold and so on. Wisdom, compassion, and so on are qualities of this kind; this is evidence by means of an essential property."

supersensible entities (*atīndriyārtha*) may come about through the cultivation (*abhyāsa*) of wisdom. Other arguments are offered as well. For instance, following Dharmakīrti, Śāntarakṣita states:

> Or, whatever things arise from a prior seed of a similar type are qualities [capable] of extreme development due to a distinction in the superiority of their refinement.[506]

Kamalaśīla invokes this argument when explaining why the example of jumping does not invalidate the premise that mental qualities may be developed to the highest degree. That is, following Dharmakīrti again, Śāntarakṣita has stated that jumping does not arise from jumping but rather from strength and effort.[507] Commenting on this statement, Kamalaśīla explains that it indicates that "arisal from a prior seed of a similar type" (*samānajātīyabījavṛtti*) is a further necessary criterion (*viśeṣa*) for the kinds of things that may increase to an extraordinarily high degree.[508]

If at this point an opponent objects that excellence in jumping *does* arise from jumping, for otherwise practice would not improve one's ability in this domain, Kamalaśīla responds by saying that what happens when one practices jumping is that one conditions one's body, thereby eliminating certain infirmities (such as too much phlegm) that before the conditioning prevented one from jumping as high as one can after practice.[509] This, however, does not mean that each new jump arises from the previous jump, for if it did, there would be no limit to the degree to which a person could jump.

Up to this point, the argumentation in the *Tattvasaṃgraha* and the *Pañjikā*

506. TS 3413 (*atīndriyārthadarśiparīkṣā*): *ye vā samānajātīyapūrvabījapravṛttayaḥ / te 'tyantavṛddhidharmāṇaḥ saṃskārotkarṣabhedataḥ //*. Cf. PV 2.126: *yasmāc ca tulyajātīya pūrvabījapravṛddhayaḥ / kṛpādibuddhayas tāsāṃ saty abhyāse kutaḥ sthitiḥ //*.

507. TS 3423cd (*atīndriyārthadarśiparīkṣā*): *na hi tallaṅghanād eva laṅghanaṃ balayatnayoḥ //*. Cf. PV 2.127ab: *na caivaṃ laṅghanād eva laṅghanaṃ balayatnayoḥ /*.

508. See TSP *ad* TS 3420–23 (*atīndriyārthadarśiparīkṣā*, B 1079,24–1080,7): *yadi vātrāpi samānajātīyabījavṛttitve satīti viśeṣaṇāpekṣaṇād avyabhicāro laṅghaneneti manyamāna āha na hi tallaṅghanād eveti /*.

509. TSP *ad* TS 3420–23 (*atīndriyārthadarśiparīkṣā*, B 1080,11–15): *syād etad yadi balayatnābhyām eva laṅghanaṃ bhavati na laṅghanād evaṃ saty abhyāse yādṛśaṃ laṅghanaṃ puruṣasya bhavati tādṛg abhyāsāt prāg api prāpnotīti / naiṣa doṣaḥ / prāktanasya śleṣmādinā dehasya viguṇatvāt paścādvan na laṅghanam upajāyate / paścāt tu śanaiḥ prayatnena dehavaiguṇye 'panīte sati yathābalam evāvatiṣṭhate laṅghanam / avaśyaṃ caitad evaṃ vijñeyam /*. Cf. PV 2.128: *tasyādau dehavaiguṇyāt paścādvad avilaṅghanaṃ / śanair yatnena vaiguṇye niraste svabale sthitiḥ //*.

on this issue has followed that of Dharmakīrti quite closely. Now, however, Śāntarakṣita and Kamalaśīla make a move that, while quite characteristic of them, seems less so of their master. That is, they appeal again to the idea that mere nonperception cannot disprove that which is beyond the senses, raising the possibility that an extraordinary person perhaps *could* jump several miles into the air. The key verses are as follows:

> Or, if jumping, too, were to have the quality of developing to the limit of perfection due to a particular kind of movement and so on [arising] through the force of meditative concentration (*samādhi*) that comes about through its own cause [then the example of jumping could not invalidate the reason]. And such is the supreme superhuman attainment called "swift as thought" (*manojavā*) that is heard of [in scriptures] according to which the Lord goes even long [distances] just through a thought. And one also cannot demonstrate the nonexistence of that [superhuman attainment] merely through not seeing it. And regarding it, others also are not able to state any refutation.[510]

As in the earlier rebuttal of Kumārila's refutation of omniscience, the authors here emphasize the impossibility of disproving even extraordinary things merely because one has not seen them. When it comes to the superhuman attainments (*ṛddhi*) that one hears of in scriptures, the best stance for an ordinary person to adopt is one of an open-minded agnosticism, in which one neither affirms nor denies that for which one has no evidence one way or the other.

So far, we have examined the arguments for why the vision of selflessness should be regarded as a quality capable of being developed to an extraordinarily high degree focusing on the first criterion mentioned above: that the quality in question, once attained, must continue without any further, repeated effort. In other words, the quality must be produced from a prior cause of a similar type.

Now we will consider the argument that focuses on the second criterion: that the quality in question must have a stable basis. The counterexample is of heating water. Śāntarakṣita says:

510. TS3424–26(*atīndriyārthadarśiparīkṣā*):*yadivālaṅghanasyāpikāṣṭhāparyantavṛttitā / samādhibalagatyādiviśeṣāt syāt svahetutaḥ // ṛddhir manojavāsaṃjñā tathā ca śrūyate parā / yayā cintitamātreṇa yāti dūram api prabhuḥ // na cāpy adṛṣṭimātreṇa tadabhāvaḥ prasiddhyati / na cātra bādhakaṃ kiṃcid vaktum atra paraḥ kṣamaḥ //.*

> And water that is being heated is destroyed. Therefore, since the basis is not stable, where and of what would there be perfection?[511]

In contrast to water, mental qualities, of which wisdom or the vision of selflessness is one, reside in a stable or lasting basis, the mindstream or mental continuum that is connected to a receptacle.[512] Kamalaśīla clarifies that when Śāntarakṣita speaks of a "receptacle" in this context, he means a particular kind of person, namely a bodhisattva, whose mindstream is particularly stable due to the bodhisattva's vow to remain until the end of saṃsāra to help sentient beings.[513] Here again, we are reminded that the perfection of wisdom cannot come about for one who lacks great compassion, which is a *sine qua non* for maximal epistemic greatness, or omniscience, although in this case the reason is not that one without great compassion lacks the motivation to fully develop the perfection of wisdom but rather that such a person will not have sufficient time. The mindstream of a bodhisattva, then, is a stable basis in which, once it has been established there, the mental quality defined as the vision of selflessness will naturally persist.

The Nature of the Mind: Luminous and Seeing Reality

Having demonstrated to their own satisfaction the possibility of developing the vision of selflessness to an extraordinarily high degree, the authors now emphasize that such realization is also made possible by the very nature of the mind itself. Echoing Dharmakīrti again, Śāntarakṣita says:

511. TS 3431 (*atīndriyārthadarśiparīkṣā*): *uṣṇatāṃ nīyamānasya kṣayo bhavati cāmbhasaḥ / asthairyād āśrayasyātaḥ kasya kasmin prakṛṣṭatā //*.

512. See TS 3432 (*atīndriyārthadarśiparīkṣā*): *mānasānāṃ guṇānāṃ tu cittasantatir āśrayaḥ / sādhārayogato vṛtter na kathaṃcin nivartate //*. "But the basis for mental qualities is the mental continuum. And because that functions through its connection with its receptacle, it never ceases."

513. TSP *ad* TS 3432 (*atīndriyārthadarśiparīkṣā*, B 1082,13–17): *tathā hi paralokasya prasādhitatvād bodhisattvānāṃ ca sātmībhūtamahākṛpāṇām āsaṃsāram aśeṣasattvoddharaṇāyāvasthānāt tadāśrayavartinī cittasantatir atitarāṃ sthirāśrayā / yā tu śrāvakādīnāṃ santānavartinī sā na sthirāśrayā teṣāṃ śīghrataraṃ parinirvāṇān mandatvāt kṛpāyās teṣām avasthāne yatnābhāvād iti bhāvaḥ //*. "That is, since future lives (*paraloka*) have been established, and because the bodhisattvas who are infused with great compassion remain until the end of saṃsāra in order to rescue all sentient beings, the mental continuum that functions as the basis of that [vision of selflessness] is an extremely stable basis. But that which functions as the mental continuum of the śrāvaka and so on is not a stable basis, since they enter into final nirvāṇa quite quickly since, due to their smaller compassion, they make no effort to remain [in saṃsāra]. That is the idea."

> This mind is luminous, [and] its nature of seeing reality is established just naturally, since stains are held to be adventitious.[514]

In his commentary on this verse, Kamalaśīla states that this has already been explained. His explanation of this point occurs in response to the seventh objection (7) in the eleven objections listed above. The objection states that the meditation on selflessness cannot be successful since faults (*doṣa*)—which stands for afflictions (*kleśa*) and are here called "stains" (*mala*)—are the very nature of living beings, and thus it would not be possible for beings to become free of them. Kamalaśīla's first response has a Madhyamaka-like flavor (although it is perfectly in concert with Yogācāra thought as well). He states that the faults cannot be the nature of living beings since one can find no living beings who could be said to possess the faults as their nature! Instead, all that one can find is the mere fact of things being conditioned (*idampratyayatāmātra*), since all talk of entities and their qualities is conventional and arises through a superimposition of imaginary concepts.[515] Not surprisingly, this answer does not satisfy the hypothetical opponent, who then alters the objection to state that faults are the nature of the mind, or that they arise from the mind.[516]

Kamalaśīla tackles the reformulated objection by first determining some basic ideas about the nature of the mind. He starts by stating a condition: if one accepts a real relation between object and subject (*viṣayaviṣayibhāva*), then one must accept that the mind has the nature of apprehending or grasping objects, for that is the only way that such a relationship could obtain between awareness and an object.[517] Starting from this premise,

514. TS 3434 (*atīndriyārthadarśiparīkṣā*): *prabhāsvaram idaṃ cittaṃ tattvadarśanasātmakam / prakṛtyaiva sthitaṃ yasmān malās tv āgantavo matāḥ //*. Cf. PV 2.208: *prabhāsvaram idaṃ cittaṃ prakṛtyāgantavo malāḥ / tatprāg apy asamarthānāṃ paścāc chaktiḥ kva tanmaye //* and PV 1.221 = PV 2.210: *nirupadravabhūtārthasvabhāvasya viparyayaiḥ / na bādhā yatnavattve 'pi buddhes tatpakṣapātataḥ //*.

515. TSP *ad* TS 3337 (*atīndriyārthadarśiparīkṣā*, B 1056,18–20): *nāpi prāṇidharmatvam eṣāṃ tasyaiva dharmiṇo 'siddeḥ / na hi prāṇī nāma dharmī vidyate kaścit yasyāmī rāgādayo dharmā bhaveyuḥ / kevalam idaṃpratyayatāmātram idaṃ vikalpasamāropitatvād dharmadharmivyavahārasya /*.

516. TSP *ad* TS 3337 (*atīndriyārthadarśiparīkṣā*, B 1056,20–21): *atha cittasvabhāvatvena tatrotpattyā vā prāṇidharmatvam eṣāṃ tathāpy asiddhir anaikāntikaś ca /*.

517. TSP *ad* TS 3337 (*atīndriyārthadarśiparīkṣā*, B 1056,21–22): *tathāpi viṣayaviṣayibhāvam icchatā cittaṃ viṣayagrahaṇasvabhāvam abhyupeyam anyathā viṣayajñānayor na viṣayaviṣayibhāvaḥ /*. "That is, for one who asserts a real relation between object and subject, it must be accepted that the mind has the nature of apprehending an object.

Kamalaśīla then launches into a fairly dense argument to show that the nature of the mind is to apprehend things as they truly are. Let us consider his formulation:

> When one accepts that [the mind] has the nature of apprehending things, then one must say that the thing is apprehended by that [mind] as having the very nature that [in fact] is the nature of that [thing]. Otherwise, how would that [thing] be apprehended? If [the thing] were to be apprehended as an unreal image, then there would be no real relation of object and subject. For the way the awareness takes the thing as an object is not the way that thing [exists]; [and] the way that thing [exists] is not the way [the awareness] takes that [thing] as an object. Therefore, awarenesses would be just objectless. And from that there would be the undesired consequence that all entities would be unestablished. Therefore, it is established that the innate nature of that [mind] is to apprehend a true (*bhūta*) image of the object. And it has been proven that the true nature of the object is the nature of being momentary, selfless, and so on. Therefore, the mind just has the nature of apprehending selflessness; it does not have the nature of apprehending a self.[518]

Although Kamalaśīla phrases things in a rather complex fashion here, the point he is making is relatively simple. In short, he is saying that as long as one holds that the mind apprehends objects, one must also hold that apprehension to be *accurate*, for otherwise it is absurd to say that the mind apprehends the object. This is a position that Dharmakīrti advocates in *Pramāṇavārttika*

Otherwise, the relation of object and subject would not apply to the object and the awareness."

518. TSP *ad* TS 3337 (*atīndriyārthadarśiparīkṣā*, B 1056,23–1057,5): *arthagrahaṇasvabhāvatvenāṅgīkriyamāṇe yas tasya svabhāvas tenaivātmanā so 'rthas tena gṛhyata iti vaktavyam / anyathā katham asau gṛhītaḥ syāt / yady asatākāreṇa gṛhyeta tataś ca viṣayaviṣayibhāvo na syāt / tathā hi yathā jñānaṃ viṣayīkaroty arthaṃ na tathā so 'rthaḥ yathā so 'rtho na tathā taṃ viṣayīkarotīti nirviṣayāny eva jñānāni syuḥ / tataś ca sarvapadārthāsiddhiprasaṅgaḥ / tasmād bhūtaviṣayākāragrāhitāsya svabhāvo nija iti sthitam / bhūtaś ca svabhāvo viṣayasya kṣaṇikānātmādirūpa iti pratipāditam etat / tena nairātmyagrahaṇasvabhāvam eva cittam nātmagrahaṇasvabhāvam //*. I follow Pemwieser (1991: 60) in her emendation of the text, in accord with the Tibetan, to read: *tenaivātmanā so 'rthas tena gṛhyata iti vaktavyam /* instead of *tenaivātmanoṃ 'śo 'rthas tena gṛhyata iti vaktavyam /*.

2 as well.[519] If such were not the case, and one were to accept that the apprehension of objects was, at bottom, erroneous, then no entity could ever be established because nothing would ever be accurately apprehended. To the degree that one asserts the nature of mind to be one of apprehending or knowing objects, to that same degree must one also assert that the nature of the mind is to know objects as they truly are. In Kamalaśīla's view, it has been established through inferential reasoning that things are necessarily momentary and selfless, and so, *ipso facto*, the mind must naturally apprehend them as such.

Of course, this claim leads immediately to the thorny problem of how it is, in the Buddhist view, that people are so frequently mistaken about the true nature of things, if the nature of the mind is to apprehend things as they truly are. Kamalaśīla's answer to this problem again corresponds to that of Dharmakīrti, whereby error is accounted for by the presence of adventitious afflictions:[520]

> But the nature of that [thing] which appears otherwise [than it really is] to the confused (*mūḍha*) exists by dint of the force of adventitious conditions. It does not [appear] according to its [true] nature, like the perception of a snake when there is [just] a rope. Therefore, even though the host of afflictions is extremely intense, it is not able to uproot the [mind's] capacity for the vision of selflessness, since it is unstable due to having been formed through adventitious conditions. But the awareness of selflessness is the nature [of the mind], and trustworthy awareness is its friend, therefore it is strong. Hence, even though the contradiction [between the vision of selflessness and the vision of a self] is equal, [the vision of selflessness] is resolved to be the antidote to the vision of a self. And the vision of a self is not [resolved to be

519. See PV 2.206: *viṣayagrahaṇaṃ dharmo vijñānasya yathāsti saḥ / gṛhyate so 'sya janako vidyamānātmaneti ca //*. "Apprehending an object is a quality of awareness. That [object] is apprehended in the manner in which is exists. And that [object] is productive of that [awareness] through its actual nature."

520. Cf. PV 2.207: *eṣā prakṛtir asyās tu nimittāntarataḥ skhalat / vyāvṛttau pratyayāpekṣam adṛḍhaṃ sarpabuddhivat /*. "This is the nature [of the mind]. But an erroneous [awareness] comes about through causes that are other than that [nature]. [Such an erroneous awareness] depends on conditions (*pratyaya*) for [its] elimination [and] is [therefore] not stable, like the cognition of a snake [that is superimposed upon a rope]."

> the antidote] of that [vision of selflessness], because it is the opposite of it.[521]

Although bare perception is inherently accurate, the perception of ordinary persons is distorted by the presence of the afflictions, the most significant of which is ignorance. It is ignorance that prevents one from seeing things as they truly are. Through analysis, one can definitively determine that things are really momentary and selfless; and on the basis of *that* knowledge, one can be sure that the nature of perception is to perceive things as momentary and selfless, and not as endowed with an unchanging essential nature or self. Hence, when one purifies one's mind of adventitious defilements, one will naturally perceive all as momentary and selfless. This vision will be stronger than one's prior, distorted view of things, in which one saw them as permanent and endowed with a self, because this new vision will correspond with the way things really are and also with the true nature of the mind. The vision of selflessness thus overcomes the vision of a self in the way in which a lamp brought into a room overcomes darkness; but the vision of a self cannot overcome the vision of selflessness, just as one cannot bring darkness into a lighted room to dispel the light.[522]

Kamalaśīla's commentary in response to the seventh objection goes on to consider the same problem from the perspective of a Yogācāra level of analysis, and it concludes that even when external objects are not accepted, it can still be shown that the nature of the mind is to apprehend selflessness and not to apprehend a self (that does not exist). In the discussion, Kamalaśīla emphasizes his commitment (and that of his teacher) to the notion of reflexive awareness (*svasaṃvedana, svasaṃvitti*), which really is another way of speaking about the luminous quality of the mind.

Although Kamalaśīla's argument in this passage is coherent, it is quite

521. TS *ad* TSP 3337 (*atīndriyārthadarśiparīkṣā*, B 1057,6–11): *yat punar anyathāsvabhāvo 'sya khyātir mūḍhānāṃ sāmarthyād āgantukapratyayabalād evety avatiṣṭhate na svabhāvatvena yathā rajjvāṃ sarpapratyayasya / ata eva kleśagaṇo 'tyantasamuddhato 'pi nairātmyadarśanasāmarthyam asyonmūlayitum asamarthaḥ / āgantukapratyaya kṛtatvenādṛḍhatvāt / nairātmyajñānaṃ tu svabhāvatvāt pramāṇasahāyatvāc ca balavad iti tulye 'pi virodhitva ātmadarśane pratipakṣo vyavasthāpyate / na cātmadarśanaṃ tasya tadviparītatvāt //*. Reading *mūḍhānāṃ sāmarthyād* ... instead of B: *tadā tām sa sāmarthyād* ... or G: *khyātimūḍhānāśa(mūḍhānāmasa ?) sāmarthyād* in accord with the Tibetan: *rmongs pa rnams la 'di'i rang bzhin du snang ba ni shugs kyis* ... /. See also Pemwieser 1991: 60.

522. This example was suggested to me by my teacher Rām Śānkar Tripāṭhi of the Central Institute of Higher Tibetan Studies, Sarnath, India.

brief, and I prefer to focus therefore on his comments occurring somewhat later in the chapter.[523] We can examine first Śāntarakṣita's verses, which occur just after the verse we cited at the beginning of this section:

> For if the mind were restricted to having a nature that is cognized by another [awareness], then since perception would be unestablished, there would be no knowledge of anything. Therefore, the nature of the mind is reflexive awareness, since [its nature is] illumination. And it is established that this reflexive awareness is the unimputed (*anāropita*) nature [of the mind].[524]

This argument requires some unpacking. Śāntarakṣita is saying that awareness must be reflexively aware, that is, it must be self-aware, for otherwise nothing could ever be known. If the mind were such that, as the Mīmāṃsaka holds, awareness illumined its object but did not illumine itself, then this would mean that awareness would require a *further* awareness in order for one to gain actual knowledge of the original object. This, however, would lead to an infinite regress, where every awareness would require yet another awareness to gain knowledge of the contents of the previous awareness. Unless

523. Here are Kamalaśīla's comments on this topic from the response to objection 7. TSP *ad* TS 3337 (*atīndriyārthadarśiparīkṣā*, B 1057,12–16): *yasyāpi na bāhyo 'rtho 'stīti pakṣas tasyāpi mate nairātmyagrahaṇasvabhāvam eva jñānaṃ nātmadarśanātmakaṃ tasyātmano 'sattvāt / tathā hi yadi nāma tena viṣayasyābhāvāt tadgrahaṇātmakaṃ jñānaṃ neṣṭaṃ svasaṃvedanātmakaṃ tu tad avaśyam aṅgīkartavyam / anyathā jñānasyāpi vyavasthā na syāt / sa cātmā vidyamānenaivānātmādvayādirūpeṇa saṃvedyo nānyathā pūrvavad doṣaprasaṅgāt / tasmāt prāṇidharmatvam eṣām asiddham //*. "In addition, according to the opinion that holds that there are no external objects, it is also the case that knowledge has the nature of the apprehension of selflessness; it does not have [the nature of] the apprehension of the self, since the self does not exist. That is, if one does not assert that awareness has the nature of grasping the [object] because that object does not exist, one must nevertheless accept that it has the nature of reflexive awareness. Otherwise, one could not even determine that awareness exists! And that nature should be known to have the existent nature of being selfless, nondual, and so on and not otherwise. Because [if it were understood to exist in some other fashion] there would be an undesired consequence like that explained earlier. Hence, the fact that those [faults and so on] are the nature of living beings is unestablished."

524. TS 3435–36 (*atīndriyārthadarśiparīkṣā*): *parabodhātmaniyataṃ ceto yadi hi saṃbhavet / tadāsiddhopalambhatvād arthavittir na saṃbhavet // tasmāt svasaṃvedanātmatvaṃ cetaso 'sti prakāśanāt / anāropitarūpā ca svasaṃvittir iyaṃ sthitā //*. Cf. TS 1351ab (*pratyakṣalakṣaṇaparīkṣā*): *sarvāvittiprasaṅgena sā niṣeddhum na śakyate /*. "That [i.e., reflexive awareness] cannot be refuted, because [there would be] the undesired consequence that there would be no knowledge at all."

some awareness eventually were self-aware, knowledge of the original object would never be possible.[525] Thus, for Śāntarakṣita and Kamalaśīla (following Dignāga and Dharmakīrti), awareness is necessarily reflexively aware.[526]

Kamalaśīla's comments on the above verses clarify the significance in their present context. That is, after explaining that mind is necessarily reflexively aware, for the reasons we have just outlined,[527] he states, "Therefore, the primary nature of the mind is just the illumination of itself."[528] Why is this relevant to the discussion of the nature of the mind as seeing or perceiving reality? Kamalaśīla explains:

> And that "self" of that [mind] has a nature that is impermanent and so on. Therefore, by implication, the mind is established to have just the nature of seeing reality. This is the idea.[529]

At the Yogācāra level of analysis, awareness is nothing other than reflexive awareness. The duality of object and subject that appears to ordinary persons is illusory and is the result of ignorance and the other afflictions. Only reflexive awareness is real. Since what is known in reflexive awareness is nothing

525. See TS 2022–27 (*bahirarthaparīkṣā*).

526. The way in which awareness is aware of itself differs from the way in which awareness is aware of other objects, for it is not causal. That is, unlike all other forms of perception, the object of reflexive awareness is not something other than itself that has then causally produced an image to arise in perceptual awareness. See TS 2000 (*bahirarthaparīkṣā*) = MA 17: *kriyākārakabhāvena na svasaṃvittir asya tu / ekasyānaṃśarūpasya trairūpyānupapattitaḥ //*. "The self-reflexivity of that [awareness] is not in terms of the relationship of an action and its causes (*kriyākārakabhāva*), since it does not make sense for a single, partless entity to have a threefold nature." The threefold nature mentioned in the second line indicates the *kartṛ* (agent), *karman* (patient), and *kriyā* (action in general). The point is the reflexive awareness does not operate like other kinds of action where the agent, the patient, and the activity may be seen as separate entities.

527. TSP *ad* TS 3435–36 (*atīndriyārthadarśiparīkṣā*, B 1083,12–14): *mukhyaṃ hi tāvac cittasya svasaṃvedanam eva rūpam ity avaśyaṃ sarvavādibhir abhyupeyam anyathā yadi pareṇa jñānāntareṇa budhyata iti syāt tadāprasiddhopalambhatvenārthavittir na siddhyet* /. "For in the first place, the primary nature of the mind is reflexive awareness. Certainly all disputants must accept that. For otherwise, if [they held that] it was known by another, separate cognition, then knowledge of things (*artha*) would not be established because perception would be unestablished."

528. TSP *ad* TS 3435–36 (*atīndriyārthadarśiparīkṣā*, B 1083,14–15): *tasmān mukhyaṃ cetasa ātmaprakāśanam eva rūpam* /.

529. TSP *ad* TS 3435–36 (*atīndriyārthadarśiparīkṣā*, B 1083,15–16): *sa cātmā tasyānityādirūpa iti sāmarthyāt tattvadarśanātmakam eva cittaṃ siddham iti bhāvaḥ* //.

other than awareness itself, and since awareness itself has already been shown to be momentary, selfless, and so on, and since it is only the momentary, the selfless, and so on that are real, it is thus established that awareness has the nature of seeing reality.

Conclusion: The Perfection of Wisdom *Is* Possible

We have now covered all of the major elements of the demonstration of the possibility of omniscience, the second of the three "movements" in the overall general demonstration of omniscience in the *Tattvasaṃgraha* and the *Pañjikā*. Unlike the first movement, which aimed to show merely that omniscience could not be ruled out, the concern here has been to establish the real capacity for the attainment of omniscience on the part of human beings. Once again, the connotation of omniscience in play in this movement of the demonstration has been that of dharmic omniscience. The authors will judge themselves successful if they can establish that the mind is capable of directly knowing all that is soteriologically relevant, i.e., everything that must be abandoned and taken up in order to attain elevation and the highest good. In other words, the primary concern in this demonstration is to show that the human mind is capable of having a direct intuition of Dharma and Adharma, where these are understood as meaning that which leads to and prevents liberation, respectively.

Śāntarakṣita and Kamalaśīla argue that the nature of the mind is such that it is capable of directly realizing Dharma, and they hold this realization, when it is developed to its most extreme degree, to constitute omniscience. To demonstrate that such a realization may be cultivated to such an extreme degree, the authors rely on the theory of yogic perception, which states that any conceptual notion may be transformed into a vivid and nonconceptual experience through intense and uninterrupted meditation on it. They then argue that the notion of selflessness, when it is cultivated to an extreme degree, will act as an antidote to all the afflictions, since these latter can be shown to be rooted in the erroneous notion of a self.[530] When

530. For a succinct expression of these ideas, see TS 3487–91 (*atīndriyārthadarśiparīkṣā*): *samastadharmanairātmyadarśanāt tatprakāśitāt / satkāyadarśanodbhūtakleśaughasya nivartanam // ātmātmīyadṛgākārasattvadṛṣṭiḥ pravartate / ahaṃ mameti māne ca kleśo 'śeṣaḥ pravartate // sattvadṛkpratyanīkaṃ ca tannairātmyanidarśanam / abhyāsāt sātmyam āyāte tasmin sā vinivartate // tanmūlakleśarāśiś ca hetvabhāvāt prahīyate / tasminn asati taddhetur na punar jāyate bhavaḥ // tadatyantavinirmuktir apavargaś ca kīrtyate / advitīyaśivadvāram ato nairātmyadarśanam //*. "The elimination of the flood of afflictions that comes from the belief that the aggregates constitute an essential self is

the notion of selflessness is transformed through meditation into the vision of selflessness, one attains liberation, which for these authors may also be equated with omniscience.

Unlike the rebuttal of Kumārila's refutation of omniscience, the arguments for the possibility of omniscience have as their premise the idea that the selflessness of all things has already been established through inference. Since the authors extensively undertake to refute the notion of an eternal and unchanging self in the early chapters of the work, they now proceed on the premise that such a self has indeed been refuted. The arguments in this movement of the demonstration therefore are not designed to hold sway with those who are not persuaded by the arguments there and who continue to insist on the existence of an unchanging self. For this reason, one might say that the arguments here are no more than "preaching to the converted." While there is certainly a sense in which this is true, it does not diminish the fact that the authors have made a *bona fide* effort to refute the notion of a self and to establish momentariness by appeal to canons of rationality that are not unique to the Buddhist tradition. Thus, if the authors preach to the converted here, it is with the understanding that their audience is only converted in the sense of being *convinced* by prior arguments that operate through the force of *reason*.

We return to the question of what the authors of the *Tattvasaṃgraha* and the *Pañjikā* are trying to achieve by the various movements in the general and the specific demonstrations of omniscience in our concluding chapter. Now, however, we must continue our examination of the arguments that make up the general demonstration by turning the final movement of that demonstration, the consequentialist demonstration of total omniscience.

---

brought about through the vision (*darśana*) that has been demonstrated by the [Buddha], i.e., that all entities are selfless. The belief in [the existence of] sentient beings occurs in the form of a belief in 'I' and 'mine,' and when one believes in 'I' and 'mine,' all the afflictions arise. And the vision of selflessness is the antidote to the belief in beings. When through habituation inculcation is reached, that [belief in beings] ceases in that [vision of selflessness]. And the mass of afflictions, which have that [belief] as their root, are eliminated because [their] cause no longer exists. And when the [mass of afflictions] do not exist, then saṃsāric existence (*bhava*), which is caused by those [afflictions], does not arise again. And it is well known that liberation (*apavarga*) is the complete freedom from that [saṃsāric existence]. Hence, the vision of selflessness is the peerless door to peace." Reading °*vinimuktir* in place of °*vinimukter* in accord with the commentary.

Demonstrating Total Omniscience

Earlier, when discussing the semantic range of the term *omniscience* in the *Tattvasaṃgraha* and the *Pañjikā*, we saw that Śāntarakṣita and Kamalaśīla hold the demonstration of dharmic omniscience to be primary (*mukhya*), while the demonstration of total omniscience is understood to be a secondary consequence (*prāsaṅgika*) of that. Like Dharmakīrti (and like the Buddhist tradition more generally), the authors of the *Tattvasaṃgraha* and the *Pañjikā* clearly place a much higher value on soteriologically relevant knowledge than they do on knowledge of such arcane niceties as the number of grains of sand in the world, the number of bugs in the world, whether crows have teeth, and so on. But just as we found it was not entirely clear whether Dharmakīrti accepts some variety of total omniscience as either possible or necessary in the case of buddhas, it is not easy to pin down Śāntarakṣita and Kamalaśīla's position on this question either. We do know that the authors of the *Tattvasaṃgraha* and the *Pañjikā* hold that dharmic omniscience somehow entails knowledge of all things, and that this knowledge is a necessary correlate of dharmic omniscience. What is less clear, however, is what the authors understand by this knowledge of all things—i.e., whether it includes knowledge of each and every detail of the universe, or whether there is some other way of understanding what it means to know all things. In this section, we examine arguments from the final chapter of the *Tattvasaṃgraha* and the *Pañjikā* that touch on this issue to try to get a better sense of what the authors understand by total omniscience and how they think it can be demonstrated.

The Logic of Perfectibility

We have already seen that Śāntarakṣita and Kamalaśīla argue extensively that mental qualities such as wisdom and compassion may be cultivated to an extraordinarily high degree, or as the authors put it, "to the limit of their perfection" (*prakarṣaparyanta*). When the goal was to demonstrate the possibility of dharmic omniscience, this potential perfection was offered as part of a larger body of evidence as to why ignorance (defined as the vision of a self) can be definitively and permanently overcome. When the emphasis shifts from the demonstration of dharmic omniscience to the demonstration of total omniscience, however, there is a corresponding shift in that which the authors are trying to establish. In this new context, the authors take advantage of ambiguities in the definition of both *wisdom* and *perfection* to argue that the potential perfection of wisdom may serve as evidence for the potential for total omniscience as well.

Consider the following verses, in which Śāntarakṣita responds to Kumārila's objection that mastery of one domain of knowledge or one treatise does not entail mastery of other domains or other treatises:

> Nor is it the case that we say that one is omniscient due to knowledge of just one domain (*ekadeśa*) such that [for example] heaven and so on would become perceptible through one's knowledge of the Veda and so on. But rather, having observed that there is the growth of wisdom, compassion, and so on through cultivation, one recognizes [that there is] another excellence as well due to that growth [of those mental qualities]. Being mental qualities, it is possible for them to reach the limit of their perfection; therefore, through great cultivation, the knowledge of all things reaches its pinnacle, as in the case of cruelty. For the definition of wisdom is established as having the nature of knowing things (*dharmas*); [and] that wisdom is incomplete when there is lack of knowledge of even a single thing (*dharma*).[531]

Śāntarakṣita's argument here turns on what I call the "logic of perfectibility." That is, Śāntarakṣita has already demonstrated, at least to his own satisfaction, that mental qualities such as wisdom, compassion, cruelty, and so on, may be perfected, in the sense of being developed to an extraordinarily high degree. In the earlier demonstration, perfection of a particular mental quality was understood to imply a deep inculcation (*sātmya*) of a "vision" that transforms the attitudes and actions of the one who cultivates it. In the case of wisdom, the transformation is particularly strong, since wisdom, understood as the vision of selflessness, is in accord with reality.

Now, however, Śāntarakṣita introduces another aspect of wisdom. Wisdom is no longer characterized in terms of the vision of selflessness but rather in terms of the knowledge of things (*dharmāvabodha*). But if wisdom is characterized as the knowledge of things, then its "perfection" cannot be

531. TS 3409–12 (*atīndriyārthadarśiparīkṣā*): *na caikadeśavijñānāt sarvajñānāstitocyate / yena vedādivijñānāt svargādyadhyakṣatā bhavet // kiṃ tu prajñākṛpādīnām abhyāsād vṛddhidarśanāt / anyo 'py atiśayas tasmād vardhamānāt pratīyate // manoguṇatayāpy eṣāṃ kāṣṭhāparyantasaṃbhavaḥ / nairghṛṇyavan mahābhyāsān niṣṭhāśeṣārthabodhanāt // dharmāvabodharūpā hi prajñā lakṣaṇataḥ sthitā / ekasyāpy aparijñāne sāsamāptaiva vartate //.*

complete without the knowledge of *all* things. Kamalaśīla, in glossing the argument, slightly refines the newly introduced definition of wisdom in his proof statement:

> The proof statement is: Whatever mental qualities exist are capable of reaching their ultimate perfection when there is cultivation [of them], like the cruelty of the *brāhmaṇa*s and *jodiṅga*s. And wisdom is a mental quality. This is evidence by means of an essential property. And this evidence is not inconclusive, because it is not possible for wisdom, which is defined as the knowledge of the natures of things, to attain its ultimate perfection without the knowledge of all things! Nor is this evidence unestablished due to the [specified] qualification not being recognized, since we earlier extensively established the possibility of a special kind of cultivation [that could bring about the perfection of a mental state].[532]

In this passage, wisdom is now defined as the "knowledge of the natures of things" (*padārthasvabhāva*). This refinement is important, for it corresponds to one of the fundamental moves in the argument for total omniscience, which we will examine in detail below. The basic idea, however, remains the same as that found in the verses: that is, lack of knowledge of any entity whatsoever constitutes a lack in wisdom that is incompatible with the perfection of wisdom. And wisdom has been demonstrated to be perfectible. By this logic of perfectibility, the authors argue it is not reasonable for any entity to be left unknown for one who has attained perfect wisdom.

Omniscience as Knowing the Selflessness that Pervades All Things

Kamalaśīla's refinement of Śāntarakṣita's definition of wisdom is reflective of a pervasive ambiguity in the final chapter of the *Tattvasaṃgraha* and the *Pañjikā* concerning the nature of what is known in omniscience, with the

532. TSP *ad* TS 3409–12 (*atīndriyārthadarśiparīkṣā*, B 1077,20–25): *prayogaḥ / ye ye manoguṇās te 'bhyāsātiśaye sati saṃbhavatprakarṣaparyantavṛttayo yathā śrotriyajodiṅganairghṛṇyam / manoguṇaś ca prajñeti svabhāvahetuḥ / na cānaikāntikatā hetoḥ prajñāyāḥ padārthasvabhāvabodhalakṣaṇāyāḥ prakarṣaparyantagamanaṃ nāśeṣārthaparijñānam antareṇa saṃbhavati / nāpy aprasiddhaviśeṣaṇatayā hetor asiddhatā pūrvam abhyāsaviśeṣasaṃbhavasya vistareṇa prasādhitatvāt //*. The term *jodiṅga* is somewhat mysterious. The Tibetan translation (D, vol. *'e*, 308a6) of *ro bsreg mkhan* implies some connection with cremation practices. The term appears again in a similar locution at TSP *ad* TS 3437–39 (*atīndriyārthadarśiparīkṣā*, B 1083,22).

authors asserting in some cases that the omniscient being knows the *reality* or *nature* of all things, and elsewhere that such a being knows all things whatsoever. At one point, for example, Śāntarakṣita says, "One is omniscient due to the correct knowledge of the reality of all things,"[533] while Kamalaśīla glosses this statement as meaning that "omniscience is asserted to be the perfectly correct knowledge of all things whatsoever."[534] Clearly, we cannot account for this difference by means of a distinction in the two authors' views, for, as we have just seen, the situation is reversed elsewhere, when Śāntarakṣita defines wisdom as "knowing things," while Kamalaśīla defines it as "knowing the nature of things." Although this ambiguity is at first disconcerting, it is possible to see it as holding a key to understanding the authors' claim that total omniscience is a necessary consequence of dharmic omniscience. The key is in recognizing that there is a relationship between the two kinds of knowing, such that knowing the reality or nature of all things somehow *entails* knowledge of all things. Of course, it remains to be shown how and in what sense such a relationship obtains, as well as to specify the precise nature of the objects of knowledge that are supposed to be known in total omniscience.

The first crucial element in the argument by which Śāntarakṣita and Kamalaśīla attempt to demonstrate that total omniscience is a consequence of dharmic omniscience is the notion that the reality directly realized in dharmic omniscience—namely, selflessness—may be inferentially established to pertain to all real things. Putting this in the language of the *pramāṇa* theory tradition, one can say that selflessness is a quality that "pervades" (*vyāpnoti*) all real things. For the authors of the *Tattvasaṃgraha* and the *Pañjikā*, this fact may be determined through a series of inferences starting from the initial premise that the capacity for causal function (*arthakriyāsamartha*) is the mark of the real. Causal function is then shown to be incompatible with an eternal or unchanging self (i.e., nature), leading to the position that whatever is real is necessarily selfless. Selflessness is thus shown to be a quality of all real things. Furthermore, selflessness is not just a quality like other universal qualities. As we have seen, selflessness for these authors is a quality that, when directly recognized, is deeply transformative, leading both to freedom from saṃsāra and to dharmic omniscience. This is because selflessness is the quality at which one arrives when one pushes the analysis of the real to its

533. TS 3329ab (*atīndriyārthadarśiparīkṣā*): *samyak sarvapadārthānāṃ tattvajñānāc ca sarvavit /*. Cf. also TSP *ad* TS 3322–23 (*atīndriyārthadarśiparīkṣā*, B 1049,16–17): *ya evaṃ yathoditatattvavedī sa eva sarvavid iṣyate nānyaḥ /*.

534. TSP *ad* TS 3329 (*atīndriyārthadarśiparīkṣā*, B 1050,13–14): ... *samyagaśeṣapadārtha parijñātṛtvena sarvajñatvam iṣyate /*.

ultimate limit. It is therefore that which is *ultimately* real, and it cannot be gainsaid in relation to anything.

If such is the case, then one may also say that selflessness is the ultimate *nature* of all things—even though, as a concept, selflessness is designed to point to the very *lack* of nature in all things. Let us put the unsettling aspects of this conclusion aside for the moment and simply accept that for Śāntarakṣita and Kamalaśīla selflessness is the ultimate nature, or reality (*tattva*), of all things. For the authors of the *Tattvasaṃgraha* and the *Pañjikā*, it appears that knowing this ultimate nature or reality of all things somehow leads to knowing all things themselves, as we intuit from the following verse:

> The sugatas are all-seeing, because they directly know the reality that pervades all things and that is established as their nature.[535]

Śāntarakṣita here presents a clear example of an approach to omniscience that, in an earlier article, I dubbed the *knowing all through knowing one* approach to omniscience.[536] Even though it is still not clear how we should construe the "all" that is known when one knows the "one" nature or reality that pervades everything, it is still possible to recognize this verse as an example of this basic approach to omniscience.

In fact, we find this approach throughout the final chapter of the *Tattvasaṃgraha* and the *Pañjikā*. It first surfaces in an obvious way in an objection attributed to Sāmaṭa and Yajñaṭa to the effect that knowledge of a single nature cannot bring about knowledge of the individual natures (*svalakṣaṇa*) of all things:

> One who understands everything in terms of a nondifferent nature does not know the individual natures (*svalakṣaṇa*) of all things.[537]

When Śāntarakṣita and Kamalaśīla get around to addressing this objection nearly two hundred verses later, they make it quite clear that the Buddha's

535. TS 3333 (*atīndriyārthadarśiparīkṣā*): *pratipāditarūpasya sarvavastugatasya ca / sākṣāt tattvasya vijñānāt sugatāḥ sarvadarśinaḥ //*.

536. McClintock 2000. Much of the remainder of this section is based on the latter half of this article.

537. TS 3250 (*atīndriyārthadarśiparīkṣā*): *svabhāvenāvibhaktena yaḥ sarvam avabudhyate / svalakṣaṇāni bhāvānāṃ sarveṣām na sa budhyate //*.

knowledge of a nondifferent, i.e., a single and universal, nature *does* imply knowledge of all individual natures. In a deliberate mirroring of the objectors' statement, Śāntarakṣita quips:

> One who understands everything in terms of a nondifferent nature understands precisely the individual natures (*svarūpa*) of all things.[538]

Now, the most pressing question that this approach to omniscience raises is: how does knowing a single nature, i.e., selflessness, lead to the knowledge of everything? Before we can attempt to answer this question, it is necessary that we first understand something of the Buddhist *pramāṇa* theory tradition's theory of exclusion, or *apoha*, and how it functions in yogic perception. We will therefore undertake a quick examination of this topic.

The *Apoha* Theory and Yogic Perception

The theory of exclusion was introduced by Dignāga and Dharmakīrti in order to account for linguistic reference in the absence of real natures or universals. As we have already seen, for these thinkers, only particulars (*svalakṣaṇa*) are causally efficacious and therefore real, while universals (*sāmānyalakṣaṇa*) are causally inefficacious, and therefore unreal, mental constructs. These mental constructs are fabricated by the mind through a process of exclusion (*apoha*), which these philosophers feel allows them to account for the validity of the conventional usage of universals while simultaneously denying their ultimate reality. The mechanism for this process depends upon the fact that one can class certain particulars together, even though in reality each one is utterly unique, because one can validly ascertain that they are all equally "excluded from everything that does not perform the expected function of *x*."[539] In this way, one is able to use a kind of shorthand for the sake of communication and say that certain groups of particulars possess a certain universal property, or *x*-ness. In this way, the Buddhist theorist feels free to use the positive language of universals and properties, while understanding that the universal *x* actually just indicates that the particular in question shares with certain other particulars a common negation—namely, the exclusion from all other

538. TS 3631 (*atīndriyārthadarśiparīkṣā*): *svabhāvenāvibhaktena yaḥ sarvam avabudhyate / svarūpāṇy eva bhāvānāṃ sarveṣāṃ so 'vabudhyate //*.

539. See Dunne (2004: 117–18; 124–25) on the role of expectations in the formation of universals in Dharmakīrti.

particulars that do not behave in the manner necessary for the construction of that universal *x*. Universals are then simply a way of construing particulars, apart from which they have no independent or real existence.

In the context of the proof of omniscience, this last fact is critical. That is, Śāntarakṣita and Kamalaśīla want to point out that knowledge of selflessness, a mentally constructed unreal universal, cannot take place without knowledge of a particular that can conventionally be said to be "qualified" by the exclusion that is selflessness. In the parlance that they take over from Dharmakīrti, the exclusion (the universal) is not separate from the excluded thing (the particular). Hence, in the verse that we just read by Śāntarakṣita, the idea is that a person who knows a "nondifferent" or universal quality of things must also have knowledge of the particular things themselves. But Śāntarakṣita's retort still does not explain how knowledge of selflessness leads to knowledge of all individual particulars. To explain how such can occur, Śāntarakṣita and Kamalaśīla resort to an element we have already encountered, namely the theory of yogic perception or *yogipratyakṣa*.

Recall that the Buddhist theory of yogic perception is designed to show how anything that one meditates upon long enough and single-pointedly enough eventually achieves the clarity (*sphuṭatva*) and nonconceptuality (*nirvikalpatva*) that Dharmakīrti and his followers associate with direct perception. Whether the object of such a meditation is real or unreal (*bhūta* or *abhūta*) is irrelevant to the meditative process: focusing long enough and hard enough on anything leads one to experience it as if it were right in front of one. Dharmakīrti cites a lover overcome by desire or a father grieving for a lost son as examples of meditations on unreal objects that can lead to visions that are the equivalent of perceptions in terms of their clarity, though not in terms of their trustworthiness. Selflessness, however, has already been demonstrated to be true of all *dharma*s. Hence, at the end of one's meditation on the mentally constructed exclusion that is selflessness, one comes to have a direct and trustworthy perception of just that selflessness, which, as we know through inferential knowledge, is a true attribute of those things.[540] And, as

540. See TS 3440–42 (*atīndriyārthadarśiparīkṣā*): *kiṃ ca ye ye vibhāvyante te te bhānti parisphuṭam / bhāvanāpariniṣpattau kāmādiviṣayā iva // sarvadharmāś ca bhāvyante dīrghakālam anekadhā / śūnyānātmādirūpeṇa tāttvikena mahātmabhiḥ // śūnyānātmādirūpasya bhāvikatvaṃ ca sādhitam / bhūtārthabhāvanodbhūteḥ pramāṇaṃ tena tanmatam //*. "Whatever is meditated on appears clearly when the meditation reaches its perfection, like [the meditation] whose object is a lover and so on. And the great ones meditate on all *dharma*s for a long time and in various ways as ultimately having the nature of being empty, being selfless, and so on. And it is established that being empty and having no self is the true (*bhāvika*) nature [of all things]. Therefore, that

we have seen, this direct perception of selflessness is understood to be a powerful antidote to beginningless ignorance, which functions through imposing individual natures (*svabhāva*) where none exist.

We can now see how Śāntarakṣita and Kamalaśīla attempt to put it all together. The key move is to extend the argument based on yogic perception such that the object of meditation is no longer simply the selflessness of a *single dharma* but is instead the selflessness of *all dharmas*. In following the demonstration, it is important to remember the specification described above: that is, since selflessness is an exclusion, it cannot occur in isolation from a particular. Kamalaśīla expresses the argument, accompanied by a proof statement (*prayoga*), as follows:

> That [awareness of emptiness, selflessness, and so on] is [an instance of] the trustworthy awareness [called] perception, like visual awareness and so on, because it is free from conceptuality due to its having a vivid appearance, [and] because it is not misleading (*avisaṃvāditā*) since its object is established through a means of trustworthy awareness. And therefore, when it is established that that which is merely cultivated mentally possesses a clear appearance, then the simultaneous, clear appearance of all *dharmas* in a single cognition is established. Thus the pervasion is established. And thus, one should understand that the simultaneous clear appearance of all *dharmas* in a single awareness is possible. The proof statement is as follows: Whatever things are meditated upon, it is possible that they will have a clear appearance all at once in a single cognition, like a woman [who is meditated upon by a lovesick man]. Now, all dharmas are meditated upon. This is evidence by means of an essential property.[541]

[perceptual awareness] is held to be trustworthy because it arises from a meditation on a real thing (*bhūtārtha*)." The reading *bhānti parisphuṭam* as found in G is preferable to *bhrāntiparisphuṭam* as found in B; it is also supported by D 125b2: *gsal snang 'gyur …/*. The reading *mahātmabhiḥ* as found in G is preferable to *mahānmatiḥ* as found in B; it is also supported by D 125b3: *bdag nyid chen pos …/*.

541. TSP *ad* TS 3443–45 (*atīndriyārthadarśiparīkṣā*, B 1048,21–1049,15): *sphuṭapratibhāsitvenāvikalpatayā pramāṇaprasiddhārthaviṣayatvenāvisaṃvāditayā cakṣurādijñānavat pratyakṣapramāṇam etat / tataś ca bhāvanāmātrabhāvini sphuṭapratibhāsitve siddhe siddham eva sarvadharmāṇām ekajñāne yugapat sphuṭapratibhāsanam iti siddhā vyāptiḥ / evaṃ pratīyatām iti saṃbhavaty ekavijñāne sarvadharmāṇāṃ sakṛt spaṣṭāvabhāsanam iti / prayogaḥ / ye ye vibhāvyante te saṃbhavatsakṛdekavijñānasphuṭapratibhāsanāḥ / yathāṅganādayaḥ / sarvadharmāś ca bhāvyanta iti svabhāvahetuḥ //.*

Kamalaśīla here argues that because it has already been established through inference (*anumāna*) that the exclusion "selflessness" does indeed validly apply to all *dharmas*, one may therefore be equally assured that when meditating on the selflessness of all *dharmas*, one will also be meditating on the real particulars that are not different from the exclusion, selflessness. To become omniscient, then, it seems that the key is to meditate long enough and with enough concentration not just on the selflessness of one thing but on the selflessness of everything! In so doing, one will, *ipso facto*, be meditating on *all dharmas*, since even though selflessness is a negation and unreal, it nonetheless possesses a connection to all particulars such that by fully knowing selflessness, one comes to fully know particulars as well.[542]

An Equivocation in the Term *All Dharmas*?

The above argument looks like a logical trick that relies upon an equivocation in the denotation of the term *all dharmas*. That is, at the start of the yogi's meditation, the term *all dharmas* denotes a mental image; but at the end of the meditation, the term *all dharmas* seems to denote all entities (*vastu* or *bhāva*) without exception. Do Śāntarakṣita and Kamalaśīla endorse this double signification? I think that ultimately they do not, although it is possible that they may not be averse to allowing an apparent sleight-of-hand to stand in order to bedazzle some of their readers. My reason for saying this is that at the end of the *Tattvasaṃgraha* and the *Pañjikā*, when summarizing the argument for omniscience based on *yogipratyakṣa*, the authors do nothing either to refute such an equivocation or to more fully explicate the nature of the particular that is known when one knows the selflessness of all *dharmas*. On the contrary, Śāntarakṣita and Kamalaśīla almost seem to encourage a reading in which the meaning of *all dharmas* undergoes a mysterious change. This they accomplish not only through their insistence on the fundamental point

542. Although the above reading is clearly implied by the passage, Śāntarakṣita and Kamalaśīla are not explicit on this point, a fact that may reinforce my reading of them as ultimately resisting such an interpretation. A Buddhist *pūrvapakṣa* contained in the *Nyāyakaṇikā*, Vācaspatimiśra's commentary on Maṇḍanamiśra's *Vidhiviveka*, however, does present the argument succinctly and clearly: *samastavastuviṣayaṃ ca tannairātmyasākṣātkārarūpatvāt / na ca nairātmyaṃ nāma bhāvebhyo bhinnaṃ kaścid asti yad apratyakṣagocareṣv api teṣu pratyakṣagocaraḥ syāt /*. "And [the meditation that leads to omniscience] has all things as its object, since its nature is the direct apprehension (*sākṣātkāra*) of the selflessness of that [i.e., of everything]. For selflessness cannot exist apart from real things, such that it could become the object of perception even when those [real things] were not the objects of perception." See Pemwieser 1991: 115 and 141.

that meditation on the exclusion *selflessness* entails meditation on the particular from which the exclusion does not differ,[543] but also through an immediately subsequent explicit reference to the notion that omniscience entails knowledge of such normally hidden entities as karmic causes and effects.[544]

These moves at first seem to support a reading in which the term *all dharmas* does change in meaning. Nonetheless, despite these statements in the closing passages of the *Tattvasaṃgraha* and the *Pañjikā*, I think that in the authors' minds no real equivocation in the meaning of *all dharmas* has occurred. For, earlier in the chapter, Kamalaśīla has already explained that what appears clearly in this kind of yogic perception is actually nothing other than the mind (*manas*) or mental consciousness (*manovijñāna*) that takes as its object (*ālambana*) the "selflessness of all *dharmas*" and so on. Omniscience is then equated with this clear appearance and not with the knowledge of individual entities. Kamalaśīla first lays out the proof statement and then elaborates on why it is justified:

> The proof statement is as follows: That meditation with the qualities of being intense, uninterrupted, and of long duration results in an awareness in which the object appears as [if it were] held

543. In TS 3632–33 (*atīndriyārthadarśiparīkṣā*), Śāntarakṣita clarifies that although the object of the yogi's meditation is referred to as the universal "emptiness," the actual object is not the unreal universal *per se* but rather a particular that can be construed as a universal, that is, the particular *as* conceptually excluded (*vyāvṛtta*) from such properties as "possessing a self" and "being non-momentary." Although the authors are not explicit on this point, it seems clear that the particular in this instance is not, for example, the external cause of a perceptual image but rather that image itself. We can safely make this claim because it is that image that is the direct cause of the cognition of sameness (*samotprekṣa* or *abhinnākārapratyaya*) to which the authors refer in this passage. Thus, as Kamalaśīla explains, although that mental image is a particular, it can be called a universal insofar as it serves as a cause for that cognition of sameness. See TSP *ad cit.* (B 1127,18–19): *tad eva hi svalakṣaṇaṃ vijātīyavyāvṛttam abhinnākārapratyayahetutayā śāstre sāmānyalakṣaṇam ity ucyate* /. The cognition of sameness corresponds to what Dharmakīrti calls *ekapratyavamarśajñāna* ("judgment of sameness"). See Dunne 2004: 119–26; 158–59.

544. Immediately after arguing that the object of yogic perception cannot be a universal, Śāntarakṣita goes on to equate omniscience with knowledge of karmic causes and effects. See TS 3637 (*atīndriyārthadarśiparīkṣā*): *sahetu saphalaṃ karma jñānenālaukikena yaḥ* / *samādhijena jānāti sa sarvajño 'padiśyate* //. This would seem to imply that a literal and total omniscience arises through the practices associated with yogic perception; but see chapter 7 below for an alternative vision of omniscience that would account for the Buddha's display of knowledge of the details of karma without requiring that he actually *know* them in any ordinary sense of that term.

> in the palm of the hand, like the lovesick man's meditation on his beloved. And a compassionate person's meditation on the all-pervasive selflessness in all its aspects is endowed with the above-stated three qualifications. This is evidence by means of an essential property. And this evidence is not unestablished, since it has been established that it is possible to engage in this kind [of meditation] due to the fact that a compassionate person is desirous [of engaging in it]. Nor is it inconclusive, for the following reason: the fact of possessing a clear appearance is that which is to be proved (*sādhya*); [this predicate applies to] the subject (*dharmin*), which is a mental consciousness (*manovijñāna*) that takes as its object the selflessness of all *dharmas*; [this is to be proved] by means of the evidence, namely that [the subject, the mental consciousness,] is mingled (*saṃspṛṣṭa*) with a meditation endowed with the three-fold qualification mentioned above; and the pervasion (*vyāpti*) of the above-stated establishing property (*sādhanadharma*) by that probandum (*sādhyadharma*) is established, since possessing a clear appearance does not depend on any other cause.[545]

This rather technical presentation is Kamalaśīla's attempt to show that what one is really establishing in the demonstration of omniscience is the fact that at the end of the yogi's long meditation on selflessness, the yogi's mind comes to possess a clear appearance that has taken as its object "the selflessness of all *dharmas*." Now, it is clear that when the yogi takes the exclusion "the selflessness of all *dharmas*" as the object of meditation, that exclusion is a mental image; the yogi does not (because he or she *cannot*) meditate on an image that *literally* contains all *dharmas*. When, at the end of the meditation, the conceptual construction of "the emptiness of all *dharmas*" is transformed into a clear appearance, the thing that is directly perceived or known at that

545. TSP *ad* TS 3338 (*atīndriyārthadarśiparīkṣā*, B 1060,22–1061,8): *prayogaḥ / yā sādaranairantaryadīrghakālaviśeṣaṇā bhāvanā sā karatalāyamānagrāhyāvabhāsamāna-jñānaphalā / tad yathā kāmāturasya kāminībhāvanā / yathoktaviśeṣaṇatrayayuktā ca sarvākārasarvagatanairātmyabhāvanā kāruṇikasyeti svabhāvahetuḥ / na cāsiddho hetuḥ / kāruṇikasyārthitvena tathā pravṛttisaṃbhavasya pratipāditatvāt / nāpy anaikāntikatvam / yataḥ sarvadharmagatanairātmyālambanasya manovijñānasya dharmiṇo yathoktaviśe-ṣaṇatrayayuktabhāvanāsaṃspṛṣṭatvena hetunā sphuṭapratibhāsitvaṃ sādhyam / etena ca sādhyadharmeṇa yathoktasādhanadharmasya vyāptiḥ siddhā / kāraṇāntarānapekṣitvāt sphuṭapratibhāsitvasya //*. Reading *sarvākārasarvagatanairātmyabhāvanā* with B 1061 instead of *sarvākārasarvamatanairātymabhāvanā* as in G 876 on the strength of D300b and P366b: *rnam pa thams cad kyi chos thams cad la yod pa'i bdag med pa bsgom pa /*.

time is just the yogi's mind itself in a particular configuration, namely, as meditating upon the selflessness of all *dharmas*. The particular that is known (and that is not different from the exclusion) is the yogi's mind, or rather only the momentary mental consciousness that takes the selflessness of all *dharmas* as its meditational object, and there is therefore no mysterious transformation of the meaning of the term *all dharmas*.[546]

To be sure, the authors believe the perfection of this form of yogic perception to be worthy of the name *omniscience*, both because the selflessness that is directly known therein is nondifferent from the selflessness of all things, and because the arisal of that clear appearance eliminates all traces of ignorance. Kamalaśīla goes on to explain:

> And therefore, the pervasion [of that mental consciousness] by omniscience is also indirectly established, since that clear appearance possessed by the subject, i.e., the mind that takes as its object the selflessness and so on that are possessed by (*gata*) all things, is nothing other than the omniscience of that [person]. That is, since it has been generally established that meditation is pervaded by a clear appearance of the thing that is being meditated upon, therefore, by implication, it is indeed established [that the mind that is meditating on the selflessness of all *dharmas*] is pervaded also by omniscience, since it is not possible for that clear appearance [of the selflessness of all *dharmas*] to exist in anything other than the above-stated subject [i.e., the mind meditating on that very selflessness of all *dharmas*].[547]

In other words, the mind is the locus of the clear appearance of the selflessness of all *dharmas*. The direct perception of the selflessness of all *dharmas* is one way of defining omniscience, as Śāntarakṣita makes clear elsewhere when he says, "That person who knows the entire world as it truly is, that is,

546. This reading of Śāntarakṣita and Kamalaśīla's position thus corresponds with Steinkellner's findings concerning Jñānaśrīmitra's understanding of the particular that is known in yogic perception. See Steinkellner 1978: 132–33.

547. TSP *ad* TS 3338 (*atīndriyārthadarśiparīkṣā*, B 1061,8–12): *tataś ca sāmarthyāt sarvajñatvenāpi vyāptiḥ siddhā / yasmāt sarvavastugatanairātmyādyālambanasya manaso dharmiṇo yat sphuṭapratibhāsitvaṃ tad evāsya sarvajñatvaṃ nānyat / tathā hi bhāvyamānavastusphuṭapratibhāsitvena bhāvanāyāḥ sāmānyena vyāptau siddhāyāṃ sāmarthyāt sarvajñatvenāpi siddhaiva / yathoktadharmiṇy anyasya sphuṭapratibhāsitvasyāsaṃbhavāt //*.

as selfless and so on, is omniscient."[548] Therefore, the mind in which the clear appearance of the selflessness of all *dharmas* occurs may be called omniscient. On this reading, no equivocation in the term *all dharmas* occurs, whereby the yogi starts off meditating on a mentally constructed image and ends up by knowing literally everything.

If this analysis is correct, it means that for Śāntarakṣita and Kamalaśīla, even total omniscience does not entail knowledge of all individual entities, including such apparently useless items as the number of grains of sand or the number of bugs in the world. How does this fit with the idea that the mind of the omniscient being spontaneously engages with the entire sphere of objects of knowledge? Is total omniscience really so banal that it can be achieved merely through meditating on a quality that pertains to all things? It seems so. Consider, for example, that a clear appearance of "all *dharmas*" may come about through a meditation not only on the qualities of selflessness or emptiness, but even on more mundane universal qualities, such as being a real thing (*vastutva*), being existent (*sattva*), or being produced (*utpāda*), as we discover in these verses by Śāntarakṣita:

> Due to the reasons "being a real thing" or "being existent," [it is established that] all *dharmas* appear clearly in a single cognition that is the pinnacle of the perfection of cultivation, like a beloved [woman appears in the cognition of a lovesick man]. And thus, who would not demonstrate that [omniscience] for which there exists logical reasons—characterized as "being a real thing," "being existent," or "being produced"—which are capable of ascertaining [that omniscience]? The omniscient being, the crown jewel of humans and divinities, for whom a single moment of awareness pervades the entire sphere of objects of knowledge things, is here established.[549]

The advantage of meditation on selflessness, of course, is that selflessness is the antidote to primordial ignorance. Meditating on the selflessness of all *dharmas* allows for a particularly thoroughgoing inculcation of wisdom,

548. TS 3336cd (*atīndriyārthadarśiparīkṣā*): *yo yathāvaj jagat sarvaṃ vetty anātmādirūpataḥ //*. For Kamalaśīla's commentary on this statement, see n. 573 below.

549. TS 3446–48 (*atīndriyārthadarśiparīkṣā*): *bhāvanotkarṣaniṣṭhaikabuddhispaṣṭaprakāśanāḥ / vastusattvādihetubhyaḥ sarvadharmāḥ priyādivat // evaṃ ca yasya vastutvasattvotpādādilakṣaṇāḥ / niścaye hetavaḥ śaktāḥ ko na taṃ sādhayiṣyati // ekajñānakṣaṇavyāptaniḥśeṣajñeyamaṇḍalaḥ / surāsuraśiroratnabhūtaḥ siddho 'tra sarvavit //*.

which can be characterized as omniscience. But here Śāntarakṣita tells us that even meditating on the "fact of being a real thing" as that applies to "all *dharmas*" will bring about the clear appearance of "all *dharmas*" that characterizes total omniscience. Of course, these authors undoubtedly would not wish to characterize such an appearance as omniscience, because unless one eliminates ignorance by meditating on selflessness, one clearly would not merit the title of an omniscient one. But in terms of the demonstration of total omniscience, it is difficult to discern any significant difference between a meditation on the selflessness of all *dharmas* and a meditation on the existence (*sattva*) of all *dharmas*.

Conclusion: Omniscience as Reflexive Awareness

The passage just cited concludes with the now-familiar notion that the omniscient person's awareness pervades the "entire sphere of objects of knowledge." Śāntarakṣita and Kamalaśīla never really come clean regarding the precise nature of this sphere of objects of knowledge. But a clue may be gleaned from a passage late in the final chapter of the *Tattvasaṃgraha* and the *Pañjikā* in which the authors respond to an argument from the *pūrvapakṣa* that was promulgated to explain why, in some Brahmanical sources, various deities are called "omniscient" if, as Kumārila argues, omniscience does not exist. The Mīmāṃsaka argument is to suggest that, in such contexts, omniscience must indicate the deity's unobstructed knowledge in relation to certain unique objects such as, in one interpretation, his own self.[550] Responding to this idea, the authors of the *Tattvasaṃgraha* and the *Pañjikā* claim that this is "nothing undesirable" for them, as such a description applies in the case of the buddhas as well. When the opponent objects that the Buddhist interpretation differs from the Brahmanical interpretation insofar as the Buddhists assert reflexive awareness and not knowledge of an eternal "person" (*puruṣa*) functioning within, Śāntarakṣita dismisses the quibble by emphasizing that any knowledge of the purified self is (and can be) nothing more than reflexive awareness. He says:

> For that seeing of the purified self is just that awareness of that

550. See TS 3204 (*atīndriyārthadarśiparīkṣā*): *yad vātmany eva taj jñānaṃ dhyānābhyāsapravartitam / tasyaivāpratighātena jñānāpratighatocyate //*. "Or else, that knowledge—which is with regard to the self [and] is brought about through meditation and study—is [the knowledge] called *unobstructed knowledge* since there is no obstruction of that very [knowledge of the self]."

> [mind itself] that comes through knowing the mere mind (*cittamātratvavedana*) from which the adventitious stains have been removed. Previously, cognition (*buddhi*) was established to be without [either] the aspect of what is known or the aspect of the knower, and [it was established to be] devoid of the distortion of duality (*dvayopaplava*). That [is the type of cognition that] the buddhas promulgated. Therefore, the great wise ones are established to be ones whose awareness is inimical to saṃsāra.[551]

A "self" that is purified is a mind that is not deluded by the false duality of subject and object. It is a mind that is free from the primordial ignorance that imposes natures where none exist. It is also, *qua* awareness, necessarily reflexively aware. This is the kind of awareness that the buddhas have, and it is this awareness that frees one from saṃsāra.

This argument is clearly advanced at the highest explicit level of analysis in the *Tattvasaṃgraha* and the *Pañjikā*, that of the Yogācāra. We have seen that, on this level of analysis, there can be no other "object of knowledge" than the mind itself. Any other object of knowledge is by definition false, appearing to be an object of knowledge only through the force of the "distortion of duality." Those who have purified their minds through meditation on selflessness are not affected by the distortion of duality. Hence, it is quite reasonable to maintain that their insight extends to the entire sphere of objects of knowledge, since this sphere extends no further than awareness itself. One who meditates on the selflessness of all objects of knowledge thus meditates on the selflessness of awareness itself. Likewise, one who realizes the selflessness of awareness itself realizes also the entire sphere of objects of knowledge—the particulars from which this selflessness is not different—since they turn out to be nothing other than awareness itself. When approached in this fashion, that which we have been calling *total omniscience* appears vastly diminished in scope when compared with dharmic omniscience, which at least seems to have knowledge of certain definite things: what to abandon, what to adopt, and the methods for doing so.

551. TS 3534–36ab (*atīndriyārthadarśiparīkṣā*): *etad eva hi taj jñānaṃ yad viśuddhātmadarśanam / āgantukamalāpetacittamātratvavedanāt // avedyavedakākārā buddhiḥ pūrvaṃ prasādhitā / dvayopaplavaśūnyā ca sā saṃbuddhaiḥ prakāśitā // saṃsārānucitajñānās tena siddhā mahādhiyaḥ /*. The reading *āgantukamalāpeta°* instead of *āgantukamalopeta°* is based on D 129a1: *blo bur dri ma spangs pa can /*.

5. Omniscience Is Actual: The Specific Demonstration

Having concluded our discussion of the three elements in the general demonstration, we are now ready to consider the fourth and last component in the overall demonstration of omniscience in the final chapter of the *Tattvasaṃgraha* and the *Pañjikā*, a demonstration I have dubbed the specific demonstration. This demonstration, which, as we noted earlier, corresponds to the "regressive" or *pratiloma* stage of Dharmakīrti's arguments for the Buddha's trustworthiness in *Pramāṇavārttika* 2, takes as a premise that omniscience has been conclusively established to be theoretically possible. Now the task that the authors set for themselves is to show that the Buddha, or Sugata, himself had attained omniscience. As usual, they attempt to do so for the most part by recourse to the idioms of Buddhist *pramāṇa* theory and *nyāya* reasoning, although as we shall see, they seem also ready to use a number of less strict arguments to sway their audience.

The problems inherent in Dharmakīrti's attempt to establish the trustworthiness of the Buddha are well known, and similar problems arise for the authors of the *Tattvasaṃgraha* and the *Pañjikā* as well. My approach in this chapter will be to first lay out the elements of the specific demonstration and then to consider the tensions these elements provoke. I will begin with what the authors clearly understand to be the most important and "rigorous" of their arguments: those that are grounded in and explicitly expressed through the language of *pramāṇa* theory. But since these arguments are supplemented by other arguments that are not so clearly grounded in the certainty (*niścaya*) of the *pramāṇa* theorists' methods, I also devote a section at the end of the chapter to a consideration of these supplementary arguments, whose persuasive power the authors may believe derive less from their strict cogency than from other rhetorical considerations. Although the authors would no doubt urge us to pay greater attention to the more rigorous forms of reasoning, the considerable time and attention they have devoted to these supplementary arguments is sufficient reason for us to conclude that to ignore them would be to disregard a significant element of the authors' creativity and genius in arguing for the Buddha's omniscience.

First, however, we should look more closely at the rhetorical context in which these arguments are made. We have already indicated that the final chapter is, on the whole, addressed to Mīmāṃsakas, especially to Kumārila and his followers. How might this affect our understanding of the specific demonstration? More precisely, what do the two principal parties to the debate understand to be the primary subject under contention? And what exactly is at stake? To answer this we commence this chapter with a brief consideration of the figure of the "person who sees things that are beyond the senses" (*atīndriyārthadṛś*).

The Subject of the Debate: Supersensible Seeing

The opening gambit of the final chapter of the *Tattvasaṃgraha* and the *Pañjikā* is, as we have seen, a rhetorical move designed to force the Mīmāṃsaka into accepting the existence of a person who sees things that are beyond the senses (*atīndriyārthadṛś*), where the supersensible is understood paradigmatically to include the categories of Dharma and Adharma. We see this gambit in play from the very first verse of the chapter:

> Thus, it being established that not all trustworthy awarenesses are intrinsically trustworthy, one need not exert oneself to establish the existence of a person who knows supersensible objects.[552]

This rather mysterious-sounding statement presumes that the reader is familiar with the arguments in the previous two chapters, the "Investigation of Scripture" (*śrutiparīkṣā*) and the "Investigation of Intrinsic Trustworthiness" (*svataḥprāmāṇyaparīkṣā*), in which it was shown that any trustworthiness a scripture may have cannot be intrinsic (*svataḥ*) but must be extrinsic (*parataḥ*); in other words, any trustworthiness a scripture may have must be derived from a source outside of itself, namely, the trustworthiness of its

552. TS 3123 (*atīndriyārthadarśiparīkṣā*): *evaṃ sarvapramāṇānāṃ pramāṇatve svato 'sthite / atīndriyārthavitsattvasiddhaye na prayatyate //*. Jha's translation (1939: 1391) is quite misleading: "Thus, it having been proved that the validity of all cognitions is not inherent in themselves, no attempt is made to prove the existence of the person cognisant of things beyond the reach of the senses." The implication of this translation is that all means of trustworthy awareness are extrinsically trustworthy (*parataḥprāmāṇya*), which is very clearly *not* the position advocated by the authors of the TS/P.

author. Kumārila, in contrast, famously holds that *all* means of trustworthy awareness are *inherently* trustworthy; scripture—by which he intends, of course, only the authorless Veda—is no exception. The above verse indicates that Śāntarakṣita takes as a premise in the final chapter of the *Tattvasaṃgraha* that, *pace* Kumārila, it has been conclusively established that in fact it is *not* the case that all means of trustworthy awareness are intrinsically trustworthy, and in particular that scriptures, if they are to be trustworthy at all, *cannot* be intrinsically so. Hence, if one admits that some scriptures are trustworthy with regard to the supersensible, one has effectively, i.e., *de facto*, established that those scriptures have as their source some person who knows the supersensible.

Kamalaśīla helpfully summarizes the argument in the verses immediately subsequent to the verse above, setting forth the Mīmāṃsaka position as he understands it, and quoting from *Śābarabhāṣya* of Śabarasvāmin and perhaps also from an unidentified source. He says:

> Therefore, [the Mīmāṃsakas think:] a person who desires to understand Dharma and Adharma—having understood that there is no one who can see things that are beyond the senses due to the fact that every person's mind's eye is obscured by the cataracts of the faults of lust and so on, and hence having no grounds for hope in the trustworthiness of the scriptures composed by this kind of person—is like a bird who cannot see the shore; thus he should take the Veda alone as authoritative. Thinking thus, or else because their conviction is impaired by the poverty of their qualities, the followers of Jaimini [i.e., the Mīmāṃsakas] reject the notion of a person who sees supersensible objects [as follows]: All people are defiled by lust and so on and by ignorance. Since they lack a method to remove those [faults], therefore, no one at all can see things that are beyond the senses. Consequently, "the Dharma that is useful is brought about by the Vedic injunctions and not brought about by the sense organs and so on. For the Vedic injunctions alone are capable of making known such things as those that are past, present, future, subtle, hidden, and remote; but other things—such as the sense organs—cannot [make such things known] at all."[553]

553. TSP *ad* TS 3124–26 (*atīndriyārthadarśiparīkṣā*, B 988,15–22): *tathā hi sarveṣām eva puṃsāṃ rāgādidoṣatimiropahatabuddhilocanatayā nātīndriyārthadarśitvam astīty avagamya tatpratīteṣv āgameṣv apratiṣṭhitaprāmāṇyapratyāśo dharmādharmāvagamārthī*

The most important thing about this passage is that it makes abundantly clear that in the Mīmāṃsaka view, *only* the Veda gives reliable information about things that are beyond the senses and that, of these supersensible entities, Dharma and Adharma are the most important. The basic argument is: if you want to get insight into Dharma and Adharma, your only choice is to turn to the Veda.

These are all ideas we have encountered before. We emphasize them again here, however, because they provide an interesting initial challenge for our interpretation of the final chapter of the *Tattvasaṃgraha* and the *Pañjikā*. That is, the final chapter of the *Tattvasaṃgraha* and the *Pañjikā* ostensibly refutes the claim that there is no one who sees things that are beyond the senses—Dharma and Adharma in particular. But we also know that for Śāntarakṣita and Kamalaśīla, Dharma (and therefore also Adharma) is in fact held to be *not* beyond the senses. Kamalaśīla makes this clear, among other places, in the last line of his commentary on the "Investigation of Scripture":

> And the statement [made by the Mīmāṃsaka] "Nor is Dharma and so on to be known through yogic perception [because yogic perception is perception]" is also insufficient (*śeṣavat*) [as a logical reason], since the yogi [who knows Dharma] will be demonstrated later on through inference.[554]

In contrast to the Mīmāṃsaka view, for these Buddhist thinkers, Dharma is *not* supersensible, at least not for all persons. So it would seem that these Buddhists are not in fact establishing that there is someone who sees supersensible entities and so on, as they appear to claim.

---

naras tīrādarśīva śakunir vedam eva kila pramāṇayiṣyatīti manyamānair yad vā guṇadraviṇadāridryopahatādhimokṣatayā jaiminīyair atīndriyārthadṛk pratikṣipyate / sarva eva hi puruṣā rāgādibhir avidyayā ca tadupaśamopāyavaikalyād viplutās tasmān nāsty atīndriyārthadarśī kaścid iti codanālakṣaṇa evārtho dharmo nendriyādilakṣaṇaḥ / codanā hi bhūtaṃ bhavantaṃ bhaviṣyantaṃ sūkṣmaṃ vyavahitaṃ viprakṛṣṭam ityevaṃjātīyakam arthaṃ śaknoty avagamayituṃ nānyat kiṃcanendriyam iti //. Reading *guṇadraviṇadāridryopahatādhimokṣatayā* with B instead of *guṇadraviṇadāridryopahatā vimokṣatayā* with G. The final statement in the passage is from ŚBh 1.1.2.2.

554. TSP *ad* TS 2809 (*śrutiparīkṣā*, B 902,20–22): *yac coktaṃ yogipratyakṣasamādhigamyo 'pi dharmādir na bhavatīti tad api śeṣavad anumānena yoginaḥ paścāt sādhayiṣyamāṇatvād iti bhāvaḥ //*. D, vol. *'e*, 216a6–7 seems to confirm the alternative reading *anumānayoginaḥ*: *rnal 'byor pa rjes su dpag pa ni phyis bsgrub par 'gyur pa'i phyir ro ... /*. Cf. TSP *ad* TS 2084 (*śrutiparīkṣā*, B 713,10–11) for a statement encapsulating the Mīmāṃsaka rejection of *yogipratyakṣa* as a means for knowing Dharma.

One explanation for this apparent anomaly is that, when the authors of the *Tattvasaṃgraha* and the *Pañjikā* claim that they are establishing the existence of a person who sees things that are beyond the senses, they do so *on their opponent's terms*. The authors actually state this explicitly. Kamalaśīla emphasizes that when Śāntarakṣita urges the undesired consequence on the Mīmāṃsaka to the effect that he must accept that the author of the Veda is one who sees supersensible objects, the argument is carried out "through the provisional acceptance of the opponent's point of view."[555] From a strictly Buddhist perspective, however, the omniscient person is

> ...asserted to be one for whom all knowable objects, including Dharma and so on, appear [in the mind] due to the mind being entirely freed from the stains of the afflictive and the epistemic obscurations....[556]

This implies that the argument in the final chapter is understood to be in relation to an omniscient being who knows all manner of what are supersensible entities for ordinary beings, with Dharma and Adharma foremost among them. Of course, this position accords well with what we have already seen is the authors' preference for dharmic omniscience over the total variety. It further suggests that the aim of the chapter is really to show that the Buddha knows Dharma and Adharma, entities that in any case are only to be understood as supersensible from the opponent's perspective.

The Buddha as a Knower of the Hidden Capacities of *Mantras*

The situation, however, is somewhat more complicated than just this much might lead one to believe. That is, the final chapter of the *Tattvasaṃgraha* and the *Pañjikā* also contains passages that make quite clear that Śāntarakṣita and Kamalaśīla believe that certain persons, including the Buddha, *can* be determined to have knowledge of *truly* supersensible entities, not merely entities

555. TSP *ad* TS 3264–66 (*atīndriyārthadarśiparīkṣā*, B 1025,24–26): *tatra dharmajñābhāvapratijñāyā arthāpattipramāṇabādhitatvaṃ hetoś cāsiddhatvaṃ parābhyupagamenaiva pratipādayann āha* ... //. "Showing by means of a provisional acceptance of the opponent's [views] that [1] the thesis 'the knower of Dharma does not exist' is refuted by the means of trustworthy awareness of presumption (*arthāpatti*) and [2] that the evidence is unestablished, [Śāntarakṣita] says...."

556. TSP *ad* TS 3264–66 (*atīndriyārthadarśiparīkṣā*, B 1026,14–16): *yasya sakalakleśajñeyāvaraṇamalavyapagatena cetasā sakalam eva dharmādikaṃ jñeyam avabhāsate sa sarvajño 'bhīṣṭaḥ* //.

such as Dharma and Adharma erroneously considered supersensible by the Mīmāṃsaka opponents. In particular, the supersensible entities in question are the hidden capacities (*sāmarthya*) of certain utterances (*mantra*), gestures (*mudrā*), or esoteric designs (*maṇḍala*) that may be perceived by extraordinary persons (*puruṣaviśeṣa*), who may then teach these utterances, gestures, and designs to others for purposes such as counteracting the effects of poison and so on. Vincent Eltschinger has shown that in Dharmakīrti's *Pramāṇavārttika* and *Pramāṇavārttikasvopajñavṛtti*, and among Dharmakīrti's commentators, the terms *puruṣaviśeṣa* and *puruṣātiśaya*, both of which convey a literal meaning of an "extraordinary person," are understood to indicate a person who sees things that are beyond the senses, where such supersensible entities paradigmatically include these normally hidden capacities.[557] The extraordinary person, by knowing such supersensible capacities, is then in a position to become an author or propounder of *mantras* (*mantrakartṛ*, *mantrapraṇetṛ*), and to then teach the *mantras* to others.[558]

In the *Tattvasaṃgraha* and the *Pañjikā*, both Śāntarakṣita and Kamalaśīla appeal to what they see as the obvious efficacy of the *mantras* and so on promulgated by the Buddha as evidence of his supersensible knowledge. At the same time, they appear ready to concede, along with Dharmakīrti, that such knowledge does not in and of itself imply or require knowledge of "the most important things," i.e., the soteriologically relevant knowledge that constitutes dharmic omniscience.[559] Instead, it appears that knowing normally hidden capacities is something that even non-Buddhists may achieve. As Śāntarakṣita says,

> The capacities of the *mudrās*, *maṇḍalas*, and *mantras* that are for [such purposes as obtaining] freedom from ghosts (*piśāca*) and witches (*ḍākinī*) and for eradicating poison are beyond the senses (*atīndriya*). If the sages, Garuḍa, and so on did not have stainless

557. Eltschinger 2001: 18. It should be noted, however, that the terms do not always or necessarily carry precisely this connotation. For example, at PVSV *ad* PV 1.217, Dharmakīrti glosses the term *puruṣātiśaya* with the term *āpta*, meaning a credible or trustworthy person. Approximately the same connotation seems to occur in the opening section of the TSP, where Kamalaśīla emphasizes that a judicious person does not act on the basis of scriptures authored by an extraordinary person (*puruṣātiśaya*), since it is not possible to determine that a given person is in fact extraordinary. We return to this important issue on p. 326 below.

558. See Eltschinger 2001: 18 and 43.

559. Dharmakīrti and his commentators allow that there may be authors of *mantras* among Brāhmaṇas, Jains, Śaivas, Buddhists, and so on. See Eltschinger 2001: 45–46.

> knowledge [of those capacities] by means of direct perception independent of scripture or inference, then how did they speak about those [*mudrā*s, *maṇḍala*s, and *mantra*s]?[560]

Garuḍa is the legendary bird and traditional mount (*vāhana*) of the god Viṣṇu, who may be especially associated with *mantra*s used to protect one from poisonous snakes.[561] The important thing for our purposes here is that Śāntarakṣita is making a direct appeal to the notion that the Buddha knows entities that are truly supersensible, and that this fact can be ascertained because of the efficacy of the *mantra*s and so on that he propounded.

Why do the authors of the *Tattvasaṃgraha* and the *Pañjikā* bring up the Buddha's purported knowledge of the hidden capacities that underlie *mantra*s in the final chapter?[562] Strangely, the authors seem to imply that they do so in order to establish the Buddha's knowledge of Dharma, despite their apparent acceptance of the above-mentioned principle that knowledge of *mantra*s and so on does *not* imply knowledge of Dharma. Consider the following verses, which Kamalaśīla maintains are for "establishing the Blessed One's knowledge of Dharma":[563]

560. TS 3451–52 (*atīndriyārthadarśiparīkṣā*): *mudrāmaṇḍalamantrāder yat sāmarthyam atīndriyam / piśācaḍākinīmokṣaviṣāpanayanādiṣu // śrutānumānabhinnena sākṣājjñānena nirmalam / munitārkṣyādivijñānaṃ na cet tad gaditaṃ katham //*.

561. See Eltschinger 2001:45. Cf. also TS 2786–88 (*śrutiparīkṣā*), which concerns *mantra*s in the Veda and makes reference to Vainateya as a propounder of *mantra*s. Eltschinger suggests that this Vainateya may be identical to Garuḍa, as Vinatā is the name of Garuḍa's father.

562. Eltschinger argues that Dharmakīrti's demonstration of supersensible seeing in the PVSV is designed at least in part to undermine the Mīmāṃsaka claim that the Veda cannot have a human author. To accomplish this aim, Dharmakīrti attacks the purportedly Mīmāṃsaka notion that *mantra*s possess an inherent or natural capacity (called *bhāvaśakti* by Dharmakīrti) that accounts for their efficacy, and that cannot be known by human beings. Śāntarakṣita and Kamalaśīla present similar arguments in the TS/P in the "Investigation of Scripture" concluding, as does Dharmakīrti in PVSV, that the Veda *must* have a human author. Since this conclusion has already been reached in the TS/P, it seems unlikely that the authors are hoping to establish that point again in the present context.

563. TSP *ad* TS 3458–61 (*atīndriyārthadarśiparīkṣā*, B 1087,23–24): *syād etat yadi nāma sāmānyena siddham tathāpi sugate dharmajñatvaṃ sādhayitum iṣṭaṃ tat te kathaṃ siddhyati / ity āśaṅkya bhagavati dharmajñatvaṃ sādhayann āha .../*. "Someone might think, 'Well, even if you establish [omniscience] generally, nevertheless it was the Sugata's knowledge of Dharma that you intended to prove. How will you prove that?' Establishing the Blessed One's knowledge of Dharma, he responds to this doubt as follows...."

> A person who proclaims a true thing that was [previously] unheard and uninferred, being dedicated to that [thing], should be known as the kind of person who has direct knowledge of that reality (*rūpa*). He points it out just as another who has directly perceived water and so on points that out. And also (*vā*) the great sage, being dedicated to that, stated a true thing that was unheard of and uninferred, that is characterized by *mudrā*s, *maṇḍala*s, ritual rules (*kalpa*), and so on because he had ascertained the capacity that is beyond the senses and that others do not know. Therefore, those who possess extraordinary knowledge, who proceed through the power of skillful means, are capable of knowing *all* else that remains, even that which is beyond the senses.[564]

The reasoning in this passage seems to go something like this: it is possible to verify that the Buddha has knowledge of some supersensible entities, namely the capacities that allow him to promulgate efficacious *mantra*s and so on. Therefore, since it is established that he knows *some* supersensible entities, it is equally established that he is capable of knowing *all* supersensible entities, including those which you, our opponents, hold to be the most important of all supersensible entities, Dharma and Adharma. (And this is so even though we Buddhists do not accept the status of Dharma as a supersensible entity.) Despite Kamalaśīla's introductory remarks, it seems then that the passage is intended only to establish the Buddha's capacity to know Dharma, though the reader is not in fact here being urged to accept the Buddha's knowledge of the supersensible capacities of *mantra*s as strict *evidence* for his knowledge of Dharma.

The argument in the above passage is nonetheless very striking for its structural similarity to the argument at the core of the specific demonstration. In particular, the notion that something that has been previously unheard of and uninferred can only be taught by one who has direct knowledge of it is a key element in the specific demonstration, as we will soon see. But if the specific demonstration is meant to establish the Buddha's omniscience with certainty though the mechanisms of *pramāṇa* theory, this argument

564. TS 3458–61 (*atīndriyārthadarśiparīkṣā*): *yo 'śrutānumitaṃ satyaṃ tatparo 'rthaṃ prakāśate / pratyakṣajñātatadrūpaḥ sa tādṛkpratipādakaḥ // pratyakṣadṛṣṭanīrādir yathānyaḥ pratipādakaḥ / aśrutānumitaṃ satyaṃ tatparas vārtham uktavān // atīndriyaṃ parājñātasāmarthyaṃ pariniścayāt / mudrāmaṇḍalakalpādilakṣaṇaṃ munisattamaḥ // tasmād atiśayajñānair upāyabalavarttibhiḥ / sarva evādhiko jñātuṃ śakyate yo 'py atīndriyaḥ //*. Both D and P give extremely problematical readings, which do not help with the relatively difficult Sanskrit.

hovers somewhere between the strict argumentation of *pramāṇa* theory and a less rigorous form of argument occurring sporadically throughout the final chapter of the *Tattvasaṃgraha* and the *Pañjikā*. For this is an argument from personal experience, which argues, in essence, that because the Buddha's teachings, when properly followed, *work* in relation to the hidden capacities of *mantras*, they therefore indicate that the Buddha may well have knowledge of Dharma and Adharma.

Śāntarakṣita and Kamalaśīla, like the Mīmāṃsakas, accept that Dharma may be defined as that which leads to elevation and the highest good.[565] And in another place, Śāntarakṣita even goes as far as to argue that putting the Buddha's teachings into practice leads to these positive results in a manner *that can be verified in this very lifetime*. The relevant statement is laced with sarcasm:

> And therefore that one [i.e., the Buddha] has undertaken a supreme delusion of those [i.e., his disciples] who have attained, even in this very life, elevation and the highest pacification of mental faults.[566]

Kamalaśīla explains that the term *elevation* (*abhyudaya*), which more typically carries a connotation of higher rebirth as a human or god, in the present context indicates such visible benefits as perpetual health, power, and so on in this very life.[567] This is a striking argument, for it seems to say that those who put the Buddhist teachings into practice gain empirically observable benefits, both temporal and spiritual, and this testifies to the fact that what the Buddha taught is Dharma. At the same time, the relative rarity of this argument and others like it in the final chapter of the *Tattvasaṃgraha* and the *Pañjikā*

565. Cf. also TS 3485 (*atīndriyārthadarśiparīkṣā*): *yato 'bhyudayaniṣpattir yato niḥśreyasasya ca / sa dharma ucyate tādṛk sarvair eva vicakṣaṇaiḥ //*. "That from which there is the perfection of elevation and of the highest good is called *Dharma*; all wise persons say the same."

566. TS 3565 (*atīndriyārthadarśiparīkṣā*): *dṛṣṭe 'py abhyudayaṃ cittadoṣaśāntiṃ parāṃ tathā / tataś cāpnuvatāṃ tena paraṃ vyāmohanaṃ kṛtam //*. Kamalaśīla unpacks the sarcasm: TSP *ad cit.* (B 1110,22–23): *yadīdṛśaṃ vyāmohaṃ bhavān manyeta tadā bhavān eva vyāmūḍhaḥ syād avyāmoham evaṃ vyāmoham iti gṛhṇan /*. "If you were to consider this sort of thing to be a delusion, then it would really be *you* who are deluded, as you understand that which is just nondelusion as delusion."

567. TSP *ad* TS 3565 (*atīndriyārthadarśiparīkṣā*, B 1110,19–21): *dṛṣṭa iti / asminn eva janmani / abhyudayaṃ nityārogyaiśvaryādilakṣaṇam / avāpnuvatām iti saṃbandhaḥ / doṣaśāntiṃ ceti / rāgādidoṣopaśamam //*.

may indicate that the authors see it as somewhat weak. In concert with their desire to gain the adherence of minds through arguments grounded more obviously in a stricter style of reasoning, they spend more time developing arguments they feel can be backed by *pramāṇa* theory discourse, such as the inferential arguments that make up the specific demonstration.

The *Sādhya* Is Supersensible Seeing on Mīmāṃsaka Terms

In conclusion, it seems fair to say that the final chapter of the *Tattvasaṃgraha* and the *Pañjikā* is primarily designed to demonstrate that there is a person who sees supersensible entities, where the supersensible entities in question are Dharma and Adharma. Again, although properly speaking these are *not* supersensible from the Buddhist perspective, they are supersensible from the Mīmāṃsaka perspective. Put another way, we could say that the chapter is designed to establish the Buddha's dharmic omniscience, which is equivalent to his knowledge of Dharma and Adharma. Although the chapter does contain arguments to support the idea that the Buddha has knowledge of entities that are *truly* supersensible (that is, supersensible from a Buddhist perspective), these arguments are not the focus of the chapter, and they play only a supplemental role in the larger and more significant quest to demonstrate that the Buddha has the crucial, soteriologically necessary, knowledge. The final chapter of the *Tattvasaṃgraha* and the *Pañjikā* is fundamentally concerned with questions of religious authority, and these questions are understood in relation to the attainment of the twin goals of elevation (*abhyudaya*) and the highest good (*niḥśreyasa*). Supersensible seeing of entities that is *not* relevant to these goals is admitted as possible but is not defended with the same vigor or attention as is the seeing of the most important things. It is thus to those more vigorous and more rigorous arguments that we now turn in our examination of the specific demonstration.

Overview of the Specific Demonstration

In this section, we present an overview of the specific demonstration of the Buddha's omniscience in the final chapter of the *Tattvasaṃgraha* and the *Pañjikā*. As already noted, this demonstration corresponds to the regressive, or *pratiloma*, phase of Dharmakīrti's demonstration of the Buddha's authority in *Pramāṇavārttika* 2. In this portion of the defense of omniscience, Śāntarakṣita and Kamalaśīla shift from the progressive (*anuloma*) style of causal reasoning that they used to establish the possibility of dharmic omniscience, and now argue on the basis of an inference from effect to cause in order to demonstrate that the Buddha must be considered to have attained omniscience, understood again as the dharmic variety. The evidence in this inference is the Buddha's teachings, which are considered to be evidence in the form of an effect (i.e., they are a *kāryahetu*) of the Buddha's omniscience.[568] More specifically, according to Śāntarakṣita and Kamalaśīla, these teachings serve as a valid indicator for the fact that the Buddha possessed a type of awareness that entails his omniscience.

Śāntarakṣita introduces this regressive style of argument at *Tattvasaṃgraha* 3335:

> Therefore, although an omniscient person is established in a general way, the Sugata is established [to actually be omniscient] because of being invariably concomitant with the definition of that [omniscience].[569]

The term "invariably concomitant" (*avinābhāva*) is a technical term used by Buddhist *pramāṇa* theorists to describe the natural relation (*svabhāvapratibandha*) between the evidence and the thing to be established in a valid inference.[570] Its presence in this verse is an indication that the authors desire their argument to be evaluated by the standards of inference as articulated in *pramāṇa* theory discourse.

Kamalaśīla has little to say about this verse and quickly introduces the next verse, indicating that it is meant to answer the objection: "Well, without demonstrating a particular [person to be omniscient], how can that one be known [as such]?"[571] The reply, presented in *Tattvasaṃgraha* 3336, is that "whoever knows the entire world as it truly is, that is, as selfless and so on," is omniscient.[572] Kamalaśīla's commentary on this verse gives us the first broad presentation of the specific demonstration in the chapter:

568. The authors do not seem concerned to differentiate among the Buddha's various teachings. Nor do they seem to consider the possibility that some (but not other) teachings attributed to the Buddha may not have in fact been authored by him. In this way, they appear rather naive from the perspective of modern, historical sensibilities.

569. TS 3335 (*atīndriyārthadarśiparīkṣā*): *tat saṃbhavy api sarvajñaḥ sāmānyena prasādhitaḥ / tallakṣaṇāvinābhāvāt sugato vyavatiṣṭhate //*.

570. See PV 1.1.

571. TSP *ad* TS 3336 (*atīndriyārthadarśiparīkṣā*, B 1052,12–13): *nanu viśeṣanirdeśam antareṇa katham asau labhyata iti . . . //*.

572. TS 3336cd (*atīndriyārthadarśiparīkṣā*): *yo yathāvaj jagat sarvaṃ vetty anātmādirūpataḥ //*.

> That person who knows the entire world as it truly is, that is, as selfless and so on, is omniscient. Since the definition of omniscience has been construed thus in a general way, then in whomever that [definition] is observed, that one is consequently understood to be a particular [instance of omniscience]. Therefore, it is unnecessary to mention a particular [person]. And that definition of omniscience is observed in just the Blessed One, not in the others. The idea is that [it is observed in him] since he promulgated through diverse means the reality of that which is to be abandoned and that which is to be taken up together with the methods [for doing so], which is the definition of the perfect (*avikala*) four truths. For one who does not know reality is not able to correctly and fully demonstrate that [reality] in accord with how it truly is. As it is said [at PV 2.132], "When the goal and its cause remain hidden, one cannot then explain them."[573]

In this passage we encounter again the familiar idea that omniscience consists in knowing that which is soteriologically necessary, or "the reality of that which is to be abandoned and that which is to be taken up together with the methods [for doing so]" (*heyopadeyatattvasābhyupāya*); this reality is then further held to be the definition or characteristic (*lakṣaṇa*) of the nobles' four truths. The idea here is that the Buddha could not have taught the Buddhist path, epitomized by the nobles' four truths, without having known those truths directly and not merely through inference. In addition, the fact that he taught so extensively is further evidence of the thoroughgoing nature of his realization.

Immediately following this statement come two verses (TS 3337–38) concerning the nature of omniscience; we have seen in the previous chapter on the general demonstration that Kamalaśīla's extensive commentary on these verses contains the chapter's basic demonstration of the possibility of omniscience. It is as if the specific demonstration that begins with TS 3335 has been interrupted in order to clarify that omniscience, as it is understood by these authors, is indeed possible. This task once accomplished, Śāntarakṣita

573. TSP *ad* TS 3336 (*atīndriyārthadarśiparīkṣā*, B 1052,13–19): *yo hi sarvaṃ jagad anātmādirūpeṇa yathāvad avagacchati sa sarvajña ity evaṃ sāmānyena kṛte 'pi sarvajñalakṣaṇe yatra tad upalabhyate sa sāmarthyād viśeṣo 'vagamyata eveti viśeṣopādānam anarthakam / etac ca sarvajñalakṣaṇaṃ bhagavaty evopalabhyate nānyatra vicitrair upāyair avikalacatuḥsatyalakṣaṇasābhyupāyaheyopādeyatattvaprakāśanād iti bhāvaḥ / na hy aviditaṃ vastu tathābhāvais tathāvat tadaviparītam avikalam upadeṣṭuṃ śakyate / yathoktam parokṣopeyataddhetos tadākhyānaṃ hi duṣkaram iti /.*

returns to the specific demonstration in *Tattvasaṃgraha* 3339, where he refers to the Buddha by the epithets Sugata and Tathāgata:

> And this [omniscience] is asserted for the Sugata, since he proclaimed selflessness first. Therefore, the Tathāgata is superior to all non-Buddhist philosophers.[574]

Kamalaśīla's commentary on the verse commences as follows:

> "This" means the above-described omniscience. It is asserted, or established, only for the Sugata, not for Kapila and the others. Why? Because he proclaimed selflessness first. This is what is being said: the one who first, i.e., at the beginning, proclaimed selflessness in all its aspects (*sarvākāram*), through the teaching that all things have the nature of five aggregates and so on, is established to be the exceptional person (*puruṣaviśeṣa*),[575] whom we call the Sugata, by means of the effect-evidence (*kāryaliṅga*), which consists in the fact that he proclaimed the selflessness of all things in various ways (*vicitraprabheda*) at the beginning. This teaching proves his stable and complete knowledge of the reality of that which is to be abandoned and that which is to be taken up together with their methods (*sābhyupāyaheyopādeyatattva*). For those who wish to put into practice that which was said by that one [i.e., the Buddha], it is reasonable to prove that he is omniscient and an authority (*pramāṇabhūta*)[576] on the basis of his being endowed with

574. TS 3339 (*atīndriyārthadarśiparīkṣā*): *etac ca sugatasyeṣṭam ādau nairātmyakīrtanāt / sarvatīrthakṛtāṃ tasmāt sthitāṃ mūrdhni tathāgataḥ //.*

575. On this term, see above, n. 557.

576. Kamalaśīla's use of the term *pramāṇabhūta* in this passage is noteworthy. The term, as we have seen above (see n. 385), plays a conspicuous role in the *maṅgalaśloka* of Dignāga's PS, upon which is based Dharmakīrti's defense of the Buddha's authority in PV 2. In some later Buddhist sources, the term comes to be equated with the concept of dharmic omniscience or even total omniscience (see Jackson 1988: 349–50). Given this, the relative rarity of the term *pramāṇabhūta* in TS/P is striking. To my knowledge, Śāntarakṣita never uses the term; it appears in the commentary mostly in reference to the Veda, with Kamalaśīla at one point (TSP *ad* TS 2399–2400, *śrutiparīkṣā*, B 797,20) using the locution *pramāṇabhūtapuruṣa* to describe the kind of author that would be necessary if the Veda were to be authoritative or trustworthy (*prāmāṇya*). Kamalaśīla's use of the term in this context, just when the argument for omniscience is shifting from a progressive to a regressive strategy, is strongly evocative of Dharmakīrti's PV 2, where the explicit focus of

> knowledge. But it is not [reasonable to prove his omniscience and authority] on the basis of [his] knowledge of the number of bugs and so on. The possibility of his knowledge of such things as the number of bugs is, however, established, but [his] stable and complete knowledge of reality is overwhelmingly [established].[577]

This passage presents us with a number of central themes we have encountered before. Most significantly for the present context, we learn here that it is not only the content of the Buddha's teachings that allows it to serve as a valid indicator for his omniscience, but it is also the fact that he "proclaimed selflessness first" and did so "in various ways." These two added specifications are significant because they are taken to show that the Buddha has removed both the afflictive and the epistemic obscurations. As explained earlier, removal of the two obscurations is a process that, for these authors, necessarily results in omniscience.[578]

According to the implicit reasoning here, we can be sure that the Buddha has removed the afflictive obscuration (*kleśāvaraṇa*) and directly understood selflessness because he teaches about it in a clear and correct manner despite he himself not having heard about it from any other teacher. This indicates the Buddha's direct realization of selflessness, since as Dharmakīrti has stated and Kamalaśīla has quoted, "it is difficult for one for whom the goal (*upeya*) and its cause (*taddhetu*) are remote (*parokṣa*) to expound that [distant goal and its causes]."[579] For ordinary persons, the fundamental teachings of the Buddhist path, the nobles' four truths, which consist in teachings about liberation and its causes, are epistemically remote (*parokṣa*) and hence only knowable through inference. For one who has attained nirvāṇa, the goal of the path, however, that final goal and its causes are amenable

the demonstration is not the Buddha's omniscience but his "authority" (*pramāṇatā*). For references to studies that take up the term *pramāṇabhūta*, see n. 337 above.

577. TSP *ad* TS 3339 (*atīndriyārthadarśiparīkṣā*, B 1061,19–1062,6): *etad yathoktaṃ sarvajñatvaṃ sugatasyaiveṣṭaṃ siddham / na kapilādeḥ / kasmāt / ādau nairātmyakīrtanāt / etad uktaṃ bhavati / yenedaṃ sarvapadārthānāṃ skandhapañcakatvādideśanayā sarvākāram ādau prathamato nairātmyaṃ kīrtitaṃ sa evādau sarvadharmāṇāṃ vicitrap rabhedanairātmyakīrtanāt kāryaliṅgāt siddhaḥ puruṣaviśeṣo 'smābhiḥ sugata ity ucyate / tasyānayā deśanayā sābhyupāyaheyopādeyatattvasthirāśeṣajñānaṃ sādhyate / jñānayogād evāsau sarvajñaḥ pramāṇabhūtaś ceti taduktapratipattikāmaiḥ sādhayituṃ yuktaḥ / na tu kīṭasaṅkhyādijñānāt / kiṃ tu kīṭasaṅkhyādāv api tasya jñānasaṃbhavaḥ sādhyate / tattvasthirāśeṣajñānaṃ tv āhatya //.*

578. See pp. 123–31 above.

579. PV 2.132. Cf. TSP *ad* TS 3337, cited in n. 305 above.

to direct perception (*pratyakṣa*); hence, since a liberated person such as a buddha directly experiences the final goal and its cause, he or she is able to explain those realities even without the benefit of having heard about them from a teacher.

We also know that the Buddha has removed the epistemic obscuration (*jñeyāvaraṇa*) because it is only through the removal of that obscuration that one is able to teach about selflessness "in all aspects" (*sarvākāra*) and "in various ways" (*vicitraprabheda*). The fact that the Buddha has given so many different teachings on selflessness in so many different ways is taken as evidence that his realization is especially deep, and includes even the removal of the imprints (*vāsanā*) of ignorance that still remain in other realized beings such as śrāvakas and pratyekabuddhas. The Buddha's direct realization (*sākṣātkaraṇa*) is of a special kind (*viśeṣa*); it is beyond that attained even by other liberated Buddhist practitioners. Kamalaśīla explains the nature of this special kind of direct realization in his commentary on *Tattvasaṃgraha* 3338:

> Of what [does the omniscient one] directly realize, i.e., [of what does the omniscient one have a] direct realization? One should understand from the context that it is "of selflessness." "A special kind" of that [i.e., direct realization] means that it is manifold, with many kinds of methods, over much time, in all ways. Regarding that and its opposite, the good qualities and the faults are exceedingly clear. Therefore, even though the śrāvakas and others perceive selflessness, they are not omniscient; [this is so] because they have not eliminated the epistemic obscuration since they do not possess this special kind of inner cultivation.[580]

This statement paves the way for Kamalaśīla's subsequent presentation of a proof statement in which yogic perception is declared as the method by which omniscience may be developed, and which we have examined already in some detail above.[581] The fundamental idea is that by meditating long enough and with sufficient concentration on the selflessness that pervades

580. TSP *ad* TS 3338 (*atīndriyārthadarśiparīkṣā*, B 1060,18–22): *sākṣātkṛtiḥ sākṣātkaraṇaṃ kasya / nairātmyasyeti prakṛtatvād gamyate / tasyā viśeṣo bahuśo bahudhopāyaṃ kālena bahunā sarvākāreṇa tatra tadvipakṣe ca guṇadoṣāṇām atyantaprakāśībhāvaḥ / ata eva śrāvakāder nairātmyadarśane 'pi na sarvajñatvam / tathāvidhāntarābhyāsaviśeṣābhāven a jñeyāvaraṇasyāprahāṇāt /*. For a translation of TS 3338, see above, n. 296.

581. See pp. 226–29 above.

all real things, one comes to have a direct perception of it, a direct perception that eliminates ignorance and all its traces, resulting in omniscience. The reader is reminded that the object to be established in the demonstration (i.e., the *sādhya*) is a particular mental state.

Putting these various elements together, we arrive at the following picture of the specific demonstration. It is, first of all, an attempt to demonstrate that a particular type of mental state, a special kind of direct realization, was attained by the Buddha. The evidence for this claim is the Buddha's teachings. In order for these teachings to serve as evidence, they must be shown to possess a number of interrelated characteristics. In the first place, the teachings must be shown to be rationally correct according to the dictates of *pramāṇa* theorizing and *nyāya* reasoning. This the authors understand to have been accomplished in the earlier chapters of the *Tattvasaṃgraha* and the *Pañjikā*. Next, the teachings must have been given independently of the direct aid of any prior teacher, in other words, they must be given "first." This is not something the authors doubt;[582] in fact, it is the primary reason given in Śāntarakṣita's formulation of the demonstration in *Tattvasaṃgraha* 3339: "...because he proclaimed selflessness first" (*ādau nairātmyakīrtanāt*).[583] Along with this specification comes the understanding that the Buddha must have had a direct realization of the contents of his teachings, since it is not possible for such extensive and correct teachings *not* to stem from a profound direct realization or direct perception (*pratyakṣa*). Finally, although the authors do not dwell on this, one may also deduce that the Buddha must be compassionate, since it is only through compassion that he could have been motivated to undertake the arduous meditative practices that lead to omniscience.[584]

582. Although see pp. 268–70 below for some consideration of the possibility that the Buddha was not first.

583. The specification that the Buddha taught selflessness first corresponds to one aspect of Dharmakīrti's definition of a means of trustworthy awareness, or *pramāṇa*, namely that it must have the quality of revealing something that was previously unknown. Although Śāntarakṣita and Kamalaśīla do not make an explicit connection between the idea that the Buddha taught selflessness first and his trustworthiness (*pramāṇabhūtatva*), this does seem to enter into Dharmakīrti's reasoning in PV 2.

584. While such an idea is a relatively standard Mahāyāna Buddhist doctrine, the authors of the TS/P do not make this argument directly, nor do they seem highly motivated to establish that the Buddha was compassionate. The argument that the Buddha must be compassionate is more clearly present in PV 2.

The Status of Verbal Testimony

With this sketch of the specific demonstration in place, we can now examine more carefully the mechanism by which Śāntarakṣita and Kamalaśīla conceive of this demonstration as an inference relying on the effect-evidence of the Buddha's speech. As is well known, and as we have already seen, the Indian Buddhist *pramāṇa* theorists, unlike most other religious philosophers of their time, reject verbal testimony (*śābda*) as a separate means of trustworthy awareness. Instead, they classify verbal testimony strictly as a form of inference. Starting with Dignāga and Dharmakīrti, Buddhist *pramāṇa* theorists argue that under no circumstances can speech be held to be trustworthy in relation to the external entities and ideas to which it appears to refer.[585] This is so, they claim, even in the case of the speech of ordinary beings, not to mention the case of speech embodied in religious scriptures. Simply put, speech in itself can *never* serve as reliable evidence for external states of affairs, and even the so-called "scripturally based inference" (*āgamāśritānumāna*) is not a real inference but is rather expedient and provisional. A mere statement, such as "there is fire here," neither entails nor prevents the state of affairs to which it seems to refer—in this case, the fact of there actually being a fire in the place where the speaker is located. It is perfectly possible for a speaker to make a statement like "there is fire here" even in the absence of fire, whether due to an error in perceptual judgment, an intention to deceive the listener, or the desire to employ a metaphor or some other poetic trope. The point is that verbal expressions are not inherently trustworthy with regard to that which they purport to state.[586]

Nonetheless, these Buddhist philosophers agree that there is one area in

585. For Dharmakīrti's basic position, see PV 2.1cd–2: *śābde 'py abhiprāyanivedanāt // vaktṛvyāpāraviṣayo yo 'rtho buddhau prakāśate / prāmāṇyaṃ tatra śabdasya nārtha-tattvanibandhanam //*. "This [i.e., the fact of being a *pramāṇa*] is also the case with linguistic awareness because it makes one aware of the intention [in the speakers' mind]. An expression is a *pramāṇa* [in that it indicates] the *artha* that appears in awareness as the object of the speaker's linguistic intention. [But] it is not connected to a real *artha*, [so it is not a *pramāṇa* for the alleged referent of the speaker's intention]."

586. In more technical terms, speech cannot serve as evidence for external states of affairs because there is no necessary relation (*svabhāvapratibandha*) between the two. Speech is not necessarily related to external states of affairs by either of the two accepted kinds of relations, the relation of identity (*tādātyma*) or the causal relation (*tadutpatti*). As Śāntarakṣita says, the relation of identity cannot obtain, since speech and the external states of affairs to which it supposedly refers are apprehended by different sense organs (i.e., speech is heard whereas fire is seen or felt) and in different times and places and so on. Nor can the causal relation be right, since speech concerning certain things can occur

which speech universally *can* yield reliable knowledge, albeit of a rather limited scope. That is, for all cases of verbal testimony, it is possible to infer the speaker's intention to speak. This supposed state of affairs is what allows these thinkers, including Śāntarakṣita and Kamalaśīla, to classify *śābda* as a type of inference.[587] It is legitimate to classify it as such, they claim, because it is possible to definitively ascertain that speech is invariably the effect of an intention to speak. Śāntarakṣita says:

> But this intention to speak (*vivakṣā*) is inferred from every instance of speech, since that [intention to speak] is ascertained to be the cause of that [speech] through perception and nonperception.[588]

The phrase "through perception and nonperception" is a reference to the method for ascertaining that the necessary relation (*svabhāvapratibandha*) of produced-and-producer (*kāryakāraṇabhāva*) that pertains between speech and the intention to speak. The details of this method, although very interesting, need not delay us now;[589] what is important here is that Śāntarakṣita and Kamalaśīla accept that it is possible to empirically ascertain that (a) wherever there is speech, there is the intention to speak and (b) wherever there is no intention to speak, there is no speech.[590] In this way, these philosophers accept that speech may serve as evidence of the type known as effect-evidence (*kāryahetu*) by which one can reliably infer the existence of the speaker's intention to speak.

Now, Śāntarakṣita and Kamalaśīla's understanding of this process is that one infers not only the speaker's intention to speak in general but also the

---

even in the absence of those things. For a statement and explication of these claims, see TS 1412–13 (*pramāṇāntarabhāvaparīkṣā*) and TSP *ad cit.* (B 538,10–539,17).

587. Cf. PV 1.213 and PV 2.1–2. See also PV 4.16.

588. TS 1514 (*pramāṇāntarabhāvaparīkṣā*): *vacobhyo nikhilebhyo 'pi vivakṣaiṣānumīyate / pratyakṣānupalambhābhyāṃ taddhetuḥ sā hi niścitā /*.

589. On this controversial subject see, e.g., Gillon 1991; Kajiyama 1963; and Lasic 1999.

590. In other words, they accept the positive concomitance (*anvayavyāpti*) and the negative concomitance (*vyatirekavyāpti*) that allows for a natural relation between speech and the intention to speak. Note also that this formulation precludes the possibility of an authorless (*apauruṣeya*) scripture, as one of the defining characteristics of speech is that it has been uttered by a speaker. See, e.g., TSP *ad* TS 1514 (*pramāṇāntarabhāvaparīkṣā*, B 539,25): *nikhilebhya ity apauruṣeyatvenāpy abhimatebhyaḥ /*. "All [words] means even those regarded as being authorless." Reading *apauruṣeya°* in place of *pauruṣeya°* on the strength of D, vol. *'e*, 45b3: *skyes bus ma byas la....* Cf. also TSP *ad* TS 2619 (*śrutiparīkṣā*, B 854,8–11).

specific concept that the speaker has in mind when he or she utters a sentence or word.[591] For example, Śāntarakṣita states that when a speaker utters the word "tree," one is justified in inferring that the speaker is one who has (or in any case had) the intention of speaking about a tree.[592] Śāntarakṣita and Kamalaśīla concede that there may be cases where a person, out of confusion, may say something that does not accord with what she intended to say. Nonetheless, they defend the basic principle by which speech is a legitimate indicator of the intention to speak by noting that intelligent people are capable of discerning when speakers are confused, by relying on such things as the context, facial expressions, and so on.[593] The point simply is that for speech to be a reliable indicator of a *particular* intention, it must be measured, sane, and free from confusion.[594] But in all cases, speech indicates the general

591. See, e.g., PV 2.2. Translated in n. 585 above.

592. TS 1520–21 (*pramāṇāntaraparīkṣā*): *vivakṣāyāṃ ca gamyāyāṃ vispaṣṭaiva trirūpatā / puṃsi dharmiṇi sā sādhyā kāryeṇa vacasā yataḥ // pādapārthavivakṣāvān puruṣo 'yaṃ pratīyate / vṛkṣaśabdaprayoktṛtvāt pūrvāvasthāsv ahaṃ yathā //*. "And it is very clear that the triple characteristic (*trirūpa*) [of a valid inference] applies to the intention to speak, which is [the thing] to be inferred: that [intention] is the thing to be proved (*sādhya*) in relation to the subject (*dharmin*)—the person—by means of the effect—[his or her] speech. For example, one understands 'this person has the intention to speak about a tree because [the person] is employing the word "tree," just as I [have done] on a previous occasion.'"

593. TS 1515–16 (*pramāṇāntaraparīkṣā*): *bhrāntasyānyavivakṣāyāṃ vākyaṃ ced anyad īkṣyate / yathāvivakṣam apy etat tasmān naiva pravartate // bhrāntābhrāntaprayuktānāṃ vailakṣaṇyaṃ parisphuṭam / vidagdhāḥ prakṛtādibhyo niścinvanti girām alam //*. "[Objection:] It is observed that although a confused person makes a statement, it is different from what he intends to say; thus that [statement] is also not what was intended. Therefore, that [statement] does not at all operate in the way that was intended [by the speaker]. [Answer:] Intelligent people are capable of determining by means of the context and so forth the clear disparity that pertains between speech that is employed by persons who are confused and by those that are not confused." See also TSP *ad cit.* (B 540,17–20): *avaśyaṃ hi bhrāntābhrāntaprayuktānāṃ vailakṣaṇyam aṅgīkartavyam / anyathā na kāraṇabhedo bhedakaḥ syāt / tac ca vailakṣaṇyaṃ kuśalāḥ puruṣā niścinvanty eva prakṛtādibhyaḥ / prakṛtam prakaraṇam / ādiśabdenāvyākulatā mukhaprasannatādi gṛhyate //*. "For certainly we must accept that there is a disparity between [words] that are employed by persons who are confused and those who are not confused. Otherwise, a difference in the cause would not produce a difference [in effect]. And skillful persons indeed determine that disparity through the context and so on ... The words 'and so on' mean such things as the fact of not being disturbed [and] having a tranquil countenance."

594. TS 1517–18 (*pramāṇāntaraparīkṣā*): *vailakṣaṇyena hetūnāṃ viśeṣaṃ tāsu ye na tu / avagacchanti doṣo 'yaṃ teṣāṃ liṅgasya nāsti tu // saṃdihyamānavapuṣo dhūmasyāpy ekadā 'nyathā / bhāvān niścayakāle 'pi na syāt tejasi liṅgatā //*. "But the fault lies with those who

intention to speak.[595] These, then, are the strict limitations that Śāntarakṣita and Kamalaśīla place on speech as a source of knowledge.[596] Under these conditions, the authors of the *Tattvasaṃgraha* and the *Pañjikā* hold that the Buddha's teachings constitute evidence of the Buddha's intention to speak about those things; and since the Buddha did not hear about those things from anyone else, he must have had direct knowledge of them.

A Tension in the Specific Demonstration

The present section aims to take account of a fundamental tension in the specific demonstration, a tension stemming from the status of the entity that is being established, that is, the person who sees supersensible entities or the omniscient being. As we have earlier seen, Śāntarakṣita and Kamalaśīla argue vigorously in their initial rebuttal of Kumārila's refutation of omniscience that the mere nonperception of an omniscient being cannot serve as

---

do not recognize in those [instances of speech] the distinction of the causes by means of their disparity; [the fault] does not lie with the evidence. Otherwise, from a single instance of a form that was being confounded with smoke, [it would ensue that] at the time of ascertaining [smoke] definitively, [the smoke] would not count as evidence for fire." Kamalaśīla explains that if we do allow for the mistakes of confused persons to be disregarded as evidence for their intentions, then we would similarly be forced to abandon all inferential reasoning in which mistakes regarding the nature of the evidence ever occur. For example, the fact that steam is sometimes confused with smoke would mean that even when we have a true definitive determination of smoke, our perception could not be considered as evidence for the presence of fire. As Kamalaśīla says (TSP *ad cit.*, B 541,7), "We do not assert that the evidence is an indicator (*gamaka*) just by being present; rather, [it is an indicator when it has been] definitively determined" (*na hi liṅgaṃ sattāmātreṇa gamakam iṣyate / kiṃ tarhi / niścitam*). In short, confused speech or babble is not actual speech, since actual speech is always preceded by the intention to say a particular thing. As an example, consider the words uttered by a dreaming person; certainly, no one would hold a person to statements made in such a circumstance, nor would one be likely to credit the person with the intention, at least in the usual sense of that term, to speak of the things uttered out loud while asleep.

595. TS 1519 (*pramāṇāntaraparīkṣā*): *teṣām api vivakṣāyāḥ kevalāyā virudhyate / nānumaikāntasadbhāvāt prāṇitādiprasiddhaye //*. "Also for those [instances of speech employed by confused persons,] there is no contradiction in an inference of the mere intention to speak [in general] in order to establish [that the speaker is] alive and so forth, since there is conclusivity (*ekāntasadbhāva*) [between being alive and having the intention to speak]."

596. Of course, like all inferential knowledge, the result of the inference is considered true only conventionally.

evidence for the nonexistence of such a being, since such a being is always radically inaccessible (*atyantaparokṣa*) for ordinary beings. Subsequent to this, in the second movement of the general demonstration of omniscience, Śāntarakṣita and Kamalaśīla attempt to establish the possibility of omniscience, and we theorized that in doing so, they must distinguish between omniscience as instantiated in a particular being, which is radically inaccessible, and omniscience as a theoretical possibility, which is merely remote (*parokṣa*). In this way, they may infer that omniscience is possible without violating the Buddhist *pramāṇa* theory principle that an *atyantaparokṣa* entity cannot be inferred. However workable this interpretation appears in terms of the general demonstration, it finds no purchase when it comes to the specific demonstration. That is, if the very aim of the specific demonstration is to inferentially establish that a particular person, the Buddha, had attained omniscience, then it is difficult to get around the fact that this presents a blatant contradiction with the reasoning used previously to rebut the Mīmāṃsaka claims, since earlier the omniscient being was said to be radically inaccessible and now it is precisely such an omniscient being that the authors claim to be able to establish through inference.

How are we to make sense of this tension in the final chapter of the *Tattvasaṃgraha* and the *Pañjikā?* It is unsatisfactory to state that in this case the authors have simply slipped up. The tension in the proof is too obvious and the authors themselves are too sophisticated for us to reasonably argue that they simply did not notice the problem. Instead, we must search for an interpretation that takes into account the idea that the authors formulated the specific demonstration in full awareness of the apparent conflict it presents, but that they did so in a manner that, in their own eyes at least, actually does not entail a contradiction with their earlier statements concerning the radically inaccessible nature of omniscient beings.

Two potential avenues of interpretation present themselves. The first involves the possibility that we have misinterpreted the authors' intent in the specific demonstration, and that they do not in fact undertake to establish the existence of a particular omniscient being, but rather that they are actually attempting to establish something other than the Buddha's omniscience in this demonstration. If this turns out to be the case, then the authors could preserve their initial statement that the omniscient being is "always just radically inaccessible" intact, because a particular omniscient being is not in fact what they are trying to demonstrate. Although this possibility seems at first unlikely, there do exist a number of reasons for considering it seriously, as we shall see below.

The second avenue of interpretation involves the possibility that we have not correctly understood the parameters of some of the technical terms in play in the two demonstrations. That is, it is conceivable that the status of the omniscient being as radically inaccessible is not fixed for all persons but rather depends on the audience addressed—being radically inaccessible (*atyantaparokṣa*) for one group but merely remote (*parokṣa*), and therefore inferable, for another. This possibility requires us to relativize our understanding of these basic epistemological categories, so that they become not absolute distinctions or necessary properties of things but rather classifications that operate and apply only in relation to particular cognizers.

We investigate the viability of both these interpretations in the following. But before doing so directly, we first investigate a related tension, one parallel to the fundamental tension in the specific demonstration in the *Tattvasaṃgraha* and the *Pañjikā*. This is the tension between the position that the mental qualities of others are *atyantaparokṣa* for ordinary beings and the claim that one can nonetheless infer that the Buddha is compassionate and an authority, a tension at the heart of Dharmakīrti's demonstration of the Buddha's authority in *Pramāṇavārttika* 2.

Dharmakīrti on Inferring Mental Qualities

Dharmakīrti considers the problem of the inferability of others' mental qualities in the first chapter of the *Pramāṇavārttika*, among other places.[597] He makes his statements concerning this problem when discussing the criteria according to which one may be justified in relying upon a scripturally based inference (*āgamāśritānumāna*). Specifically, the question is raised as to whether the credibility (*āptatva*) of a scripture's author is a legitimate reason to accept the scripture's statements on radically inaccessible entities as true.

Now, *credibility* is a quality of authors that is frequently cited in Indian philosophical sources as a warrant for the trustworthiness of scriptural statements, and the term carries a number of connotations. The Naiyāyika tradition, for example, proposes three criteria for a credible person: knowledge of reality, compassion, and a desire to communicate things as they truly are.[598] In the Buddhist tradition of *pramāṇa* theory, credibility is first discussed by Dignāga, who allows for the classification of the speech of a cred-

597. See also PVin 2.

598. The seminal statement is at NBh *ad* NS 2.1.68: *sākṣātkṛtadharmatā bhūtadayā yathābhūtārthacikhyāpayiṣā ceti* /. Translated by Eltschinger (2001: 101) as follows: "[Leur authorité consiste en] cela qu'[elles] réalisent directement le *dharma* (*sākṣātkṛtadharmatā*), qu'[elles] éprouvent de la compassion pour les êtres (*bhūtadayā*)

ible person as a form of inference.[599] Dharmakīrti quotes Dignāga's statement in *Svopajñavṛtti*, where he seems to allow the speech of a credible person to qualify as a scripturally based inference in regard to radically inaccessible entities.[600] Although Dharmakīrti says that such an inference is "not without problems" (*anapāya*), he nonetheless admits that it may be used "when there is no other way" (*agatyā*).[601]

We return to many of these issues in the next chapter. Of immediate interest here is the fact that Dharmakīrti ends his discussion of scripturally based inference by rejecting the criterion of the credibility of the scripture's author on the grounds that such credibility is impossible to ascertain. The relevant passage begins as follows:

> Others [such as the Naiyāyikas] think that a statement dependent for its origin on a superior person (*puruṣātiśaya*) is in accord with reality (*yathārtha*). This point is admitted if one is able to know that that person has that superior quality.[602]

In his commentary, Dharmakīrti makes clear that a "superior person" here means a credible person (*āpta*).[603] Dharmakīrti does not dispute that the words of a credible person are authoritative or trustworthy. What he disputes is that one can ever definitively determine that any particular person is in fact credible, since, as he says, "it is impossible to know that that [person] is like that."[604]

---

et qu'[elles] sont animées de l'intention de communiquer les choses telles qu'elles sont (*yathābhūtārthacikhyāpayiṣā*)."

599. PS 2.5a: *āptavādāvisaṃvādasāmānyād anumānatā* /. "Because the speech of a credible person (*āptavāda*) is generally trustworthy, it is [classified as] inference." For the interpretation of *sāmānya* as "generally," see Dunne 2004: 239n25. For Tillemans' understanding of *sāmānya* as "similar to," see, e.g., his article "Dharmakīrti, Āryadeva, and Dharmapāla on Scriptural Authority," in Tillemans 1999b: 33n2.

600. PVSV *ad* PV 1.214. Translated in Dunne 2004: 361–62 and Yaita 1987.

601. PVSV *ad* PV 1.217. Translated in Dunne 2004: 365–66 and Yaita 1987.

602. PV 1.218: *puruṣātiśayāpekṣaṃ yathārtham apare viduḥ / iṣṭo 'yam arthaḥ śakyeta jñātuṃ so 'tiśayo yadi* //. Translation by Dunne 2004: 243. Cf. also the translation in Yaita 1988.

603. Elsewhere, as we saw on pp. 241–43 above, the term seems to connote a person who can see things that are beyond the senses.

604. PVSV *ad* PV 1.218: *puruṣaparīkṣayā tu pravṛttāv apravṛttir eva / tasya tathābhūtasya jñātum aśakyatvāt / nāniṣṭeḥ / tādṛśām avitathābhidhānāt* /. "But were one to act only due to an examination of the [special qualities of] the person, one would not act at all,

The next verse clarifies the problem with grounding scriptures in the credibility of their author:

> Others [namely, we Buddhists] know that it is extremely difficult to know (*durbodha*) whether others have faults or are faultless, as when one responds to the question, "Is this person like this or not?" It is extremely difficult to know because the *pramāṇas* [for determining such issues] are almost unobtainable (*durlabha*).[605]

In this translation, Dunne renders the term *durlabha* as "almost unobtainable," although elsewhere Tillemans has interpreted the term more strictly as "unavailable" in his translation of the same verse.[606] Tillemans's translation, though less literal, is certainly defensible in light of Dharmakīrti's claim cited just above that "it is impossible to know that that [person] is like that." Such would also seem to be the case if the mental qualities that define credibility are indeed supersensible, as Dharmakīrti states that they are.

Nonetheless, one wonders what Dharmakīrti may be up to here, since he appears to leave room for some kind of exception to the prohibition in his immediately following statement. That is, just after claiming that others' mental states are inaccessible for ordinary beings, Dharmakīrti explains that if one were to be able to determine the mental qualities of another, the only way to do so would be through an inference based on the person's speech and behavior (in other words, such mental states are definitely not perceptible, *pratyakṣa*). And, as he notes, virtually all speech and behavior can be deliberately manipulated. The available evidence—the speech and behavior of the person in question—thus lacks the invariable or natural connection that would be necessary for an inference of that person's good and bad mental qualities to take place.[607] Yet in adding the qualification "virtually all" or

---

since it is impossible to know that that [person] is like that. It is not [that one would not act] because of not accepting [that there *could* be such a person], since the statements of such [persons] are [indeed] not false." Translated also in Dunne 2004: 367 and Yaita 1988.

605. PV 1.219: *ayam evaṃ na vety anyadoṣānirdoṣatāpi vā / durlabhatvāt pramāṇānāṃ durbodhā ity apare //*. Translation by Dunne 2004: 244. Cf. translation in Yaita 1988.

606. Tillemans 1993: 19. In a note (2004: 244n32), Dunne also discusses the challenge posed by the translation of the *duḥ-* prefix: "The prefix *duḥ-* is often translated simply as 'difficult,' but this English word is too weak for the sense that the prefix conveys. In nearly every case, *duḥ-* expresses something more than English 'difficult' but not necessarily quite as strident as 'impossible.'"

607. See PVSV *ad* PV 1.219: *caitasyebhyo hi guṇadoṣebhyaḥ puruṣāḥ samyaṅmithyāpra-*

"most" (*prāyaśaḥ*) in the statement "virtually all speech and behavior can be manipulated," it seems plausible that Dharmakīrti may have been trying to allow for a highly particular situation in which some *special* kind of speech could *only* come about as the result of *particular* mental qualities, and thus could not be the result of a deliberate manipulation. This seems, at any rate, to be the implication of the demonstration of the Buddha's authority in *Pramāṇavārttika* 2, where the Buddha's teachings are understood to require both compassion and the direct realization of selflessness in order to arise.

What, then, should we make of the prohibition on the inference of mental states in *Pramāṇavārttika* 1? At this point it seems at least plausible that the prohibition was intended to apply in all cases, apart from those exceptional cases in which the speech that serves as the evidence for the mental qualities can be shown to have a fixed and unmanipulable connection to those mental qualities. And according to the reasoning in *Pramāṇavārttika* 2, the case of the inference of a buddha's mental qualities on the basis of his teachings is just such an exceptional case. If we reject this interpretation as too strained, then we are in the difficult (though familiar) circumstance of trying to account for what Dharmakīrti thought he was up to in *Pramāṇavārttika* 2.[608] Again, the situation exhibits parallels to that found in the final chapter of the *Tattvasaṃgraha* and the *Pañjikā*. With the Dharmakīrtian background in mind, let us consider how Śāntarakṣita and Kamalaśīla deal with this problem.

---

vṛttaḥ te cātīndriyāḥ svaprabhavakāyavāgvyavahārānumeyāḥ syuḥ / vyavahārāś ca prāyaśo buddhipūrvam anyathāpi kartuṃ śakyante puruṣecchāvṛttitvāt teṣāṃ ca citrābhisandhitvāt / tad ayaṃ liṅgasaṃkarāt katham aniścinvan pratipadyeta /. Dunne (2004: 244) translates: "The truthful (*samyag*) and deceitful actions of persons are due to their good mental qualities and their mental flaws. Those mental attributes are supersensible, and they would have to be inferred from the physical and vocal behavior that arises from them. And most behavior can also be performed deliberately (*buddhipūrvam*) in a way other than the mental state they seem to reflect because those behaviors occur as one desires and because those behaviors may be intended for various aims. Thus, there is an overlap of the alleged evidence for faults and faultlessness. Therefore, not having made a definitive determination, how is one to establish that the author of the scripture is flawless?" See also PVSV *ad* PV 1.318: *na kvacid askhalita iti sarvaṃ tathā / vyabhicāradarśanāt / tatpravṛtter avisaṃvādena vyāptyasiddheś ca //*. Translated in Tillemans 1999b: 43: "It is not so that because [someone] is unmistaken about some things he will be so for all, for deviance is observed (*vyabhicāradarśanāt*) and it is not established that there is any pervasion (*vyāpti*) between his [verbal] activity and being non-belying."

608. Various scholars have attempted to resolve the apparent tension at the heart of PV 2. See the list given above in n. 385.

Śāntarakṣita and Kamalaśīla on Inferring Mental Qualities

We start again with the question of the credible person. In the *Tattvasaṃgraha* and the *Pañjikā*, Śāntarakṣita and Kamalaśīla appear to accept a modified version of the three Naiyāyika criteria for credibility. That is, although they accept that the three criteria—i.e., knowledge of reality, compassion, and truthfulness—are all required if a credible person is to be credible, they see the third criterion, truthfulness, as ultimately rooted in the other two, which they call, using terminology typical of the Buddhist tradition, wisdom (*prajñā*) and compassion (*kṛpā*), respectively. As Kamalaśīla explains,

> Just as it is observed that one endowed with passion and so on speaks falsely and therefore faults are ascertained to be the causes of false speech through positive and negative concomitance, so too it is observed that one endowed with good qualities such as compassion speaks the truth, and therefore good qualities such as compassion and so on are [ascertained to be] the causes of truth.[609]

We know that wisdom is included with "compassion and so on" as a cause for truthfulness because Śāntarakṣita and Kamalaśīla specifically say so just a few lines later.[610] The idea here is that it is possible to ascertain a natural relation between compassion and wisdom on the one hand and speaking the truth on the other. Presumably, the authors hold that this ascertainment comes through introspective observation of one's own mind, since, like Dharmakīrti, they reject direct knowledge of others' mental states, at least for ordinary persons. In any case, based on this and other such passages, we know that Śāntarakṣita and Kamalaśīla accept the principle that a person endowed with extraordinary wisdom and compassion will necessarily speak the truth and will thus be a credible person (*āpta*).

Despite accepting that the speech of an *āpta* will be authoritative or true, these thinkers are similar to Dharmakīrti in their apparently staunch

609. TSP *ad* TS 2352 (*śrutiparīkṣā*, B 786,20–22): *yathā rāgādiyukto mṛṣāvādī dṛṣṭa ity anvayavyatirekābhyāṃ girāṃ mithyātvahetavo doṣā niścitās tathā kṛpādiguṇayuktaḥ satyavāk dṛṣṭa iti kṛpādayo guṇāḥ satyatvahetava iti* /. The reference to the determination through positive and negative concomitance most likely indicates that one has made this determination on the basis of an observation of one's own mental states and subsequent vocal behavior.

610. TS 2354 (*śrutiparīkṣā*) and TSP *ad cit.* (B 787,9–11).

resistance to the idea that one can determine that any *particular* person is credible. The authors of the *Tattvasaṃgraha* and the *Pañjikā* discuss the question of the determination of an *āpta* in the "Investigation of the Existence of Other Means of Trustworthy Awareness" (*pramāṇāntarabhāvaparīkṣā*), in a section in which the primary concern is to refute that scripture or any other verbal testimony (*śādba*) is a separate means of trustworthy awareness. The *pūrvapakṣa* presented represents a Mīmāṃsaka position, in which speech is defended as an independent means of trustworthy awareness in two cases: (1) when the speech in question has no author and (2) when the speech in question is authored by a credible person.[611] In the commentary on the second point, the *Pañjikā* cites the Mīmāṃsaka Śabarasvāmin and explains that his position allows for the possibility that a trustworthy person (*pratyayitapuruṣa*)—treated as equivalent to a credible person, or *āpta*, by Śāntarakṣita and Kamalaśīla—could be a means of trustworthy awareness in terms of worldly, perceptible matters, though not, of course, in terms of things that are beyond the senses (*atīndriya*).[612]

In responding to this position, Śāntarakṣita first objects that the Mīmāṃsakas contradict themselves by referring to a trustworthy or credible person, since they themselves do not accept that it is possible for people to eliminate their afflictive and epistemic faults.[613] He then goes on to say that in any case the speech of a credible person cannot be accepted as yielding knowledge of external entities "because there is no definitive determination that 'this [person] is that [i.e., credible].'"[614] Kamalaśīla elaborates:

611. TS 1488 (*pramāṇāntarabhāvaparīkṣā*): *śabdajñānāt parokṣārthajñānaṃ śābdaṃ pare jaguḥ / tac cākartṛkato vākyāt tathā pratyayinoditāt //*. Reading *pratyayinoditāt* with G in favor of *pratyayitoditāt* in B.

612. A version of Śabara's statement is given at TSP *ad* TS 1498 (*pramāṇāntarabhāvaparīkṣā*, B 533,17–20): *yat tu laukikaṃ vacanaṃ tac cet pratyayitāt puruṣād indriyaviṣayaṃ vā tad avitatham eva / athāpratyayitād atīndriyaviṣayaṃ vā tatpuruṣabuddhiprabhavam apramāṇam aśakyaṃ hi puruṣamātreṇa jñātum iti /*. "But with regard to worldly speech, if it comes from a trustworthy person and has a perceptible object, then it is not wrong. But if it comes from one who is not trustworthy or has a supersensible object, then it is not a means of trustworthy awareness since it has its origin in the mind of that person. For it is not possible to know [supersensible entities] just through a person." Cf. ŚBh 1.1.2.

613. TS 1509a–c (*pramāṇāntarabhāvaparīkṣā*): *āptānaṅgīkṛter eva dvitīyam api na kṣamam / śābdalakṣaṇam iṣṭo vā /*. "Also, it is not possible [for you] to assert [your] second definition of verbal testimony (*śābda*) [as a means of trustworthy awareness], since you do not accept a credible person."

614. TS 1509d (*pramāṇāntarabhāvaparīkṣā*): *so 'yam ity aviniścitaḥ /*.

> But even if a credible person is accepted [in general], still when there is a search (*iṣṭi*) for the credible person, a credible person is not definitively determined directly (*śṛṅgagrāhikayā*) as in "this [person] is that [i.e., credible]." Hence it is just as if that [credible person] did not exist. For there is no means of trustworthy awareness for the ascertainment of the good and bad [mental] qualities of another person, since those are beyond the senses. Moreover, the conventions of body and speech are [sometimes] deliberately done otherwise [from what corresponds to the real mental qualities of the person]. So how could there be any trustworthiness in that speech, since those who lack transcendental vision cannot determine those [mental qualities] clearly?[615]

In this passage, in which we find strong echoes of Dharmakīrti, we find what seems to be an insistent statement that others' mental qualities, as radically inaccessible entities, are not amenable to ordinary persons' perception or inference. If this is so, then even though it is true that the speech of credible persons can be trusted, a judicious person will still be unable to rely on this fact to ground scripturally based inference, for it will not be possible to determine which authors are in fact credible and which are not.

But what of Kamalaśīla's use of the term *śṛṅgagrāhikayā*, which literally means "in the manner of grasping a horn," as a qualifier on his prohibition against determining a particular person to be credible? Does this odd-sounding adverb afford any openings for a resolution to the tension under discussion? Let us consider some other instances of the term *śṛṅgagrāhikayā* in the *Pañjikā*.

The Term *Śṛṅgagrāhikayā* in the *Pañjikā*

We find the term *śṛṅgagrāhikayā* first of all in the Mīmāṃsaka *pūrvapakṣa* at the outset of the "Investigation of Scripture" (*śrutiparīkṣā*). In this section, we learn that in order to demonstrate that the Veda is without an author, the Mīmāṃsakas employ a reasoning—similar to that levied again the omniscient being as presented in the final chapter of the *Tattvasaṃgraha* and the

615. TSP *ad* TS 1509 (*pramāṇāntarabhāvaparīkṣā*, B 567,17–21): *athāpy āpta iṣyate tadā tasyāptasyeṣṭau satyāṃ śṛṅgagrāhikayāyam asāv ity āpto na niścita ity asatprakhya eva / na hy anyaguṇadoṣaniścaye pramāṇam asti teṣām atīndriyatvāt / kāyavāgvyavahārāś cānyathā 'pi buddhipūrvaṃ kriyanta iti kutas tadvacanasya prāmāṇyam asāṅkaryeṇārvāgdarśibhis teṣām anavadhāraṇāt //*. Cf. PVSV *ad* PV 1.219, cited above in n. 607.

Pañjikā—in which *abhāvapramāṇa*, the means of trustworthy awareness of nonexistence, is said to establish that the Veda is authorless. Showing first that perception cannot establish such an author, the passage asserts that "it is not possible to demonstrate directly (*śṛṅgagrāhikayā*) that "this [person] is that [i.e., the author of the Veda]."[616] This statement clearly recalls the one made above in the context of the impossibility of determining that a particular person is credible, although in this case the term *śṛṅgagrāhikayā* is associated explicitly only with direct perception and in the earlier passage there is no such association.

The term returns in the final chapter of the *Pañjikā*. We find it first in the *pūrvapakṣa*, in a statement that is meant to represent a Buddhist position on the demonstration of omniscience. Kamalaśīla writes in the voice of Kumārila expressing a Buddhist position:

> Now some people [i.e., some Buddhists] think, "We do not establish an omniscient person directly (*śṛṅgagrāhikayā*). Rather, we establish the mere possibility in general terms: there is some omniscient person, or omniscience exists somewhere, because the perfection (*prakarṣa*) of wisdom and so on are observed." To such people, [Kumārila] responds by [the verse that begins] "*naraḥ* and so on" [i.e., *Tattvasaṃgraha* 3229].[617]

Here, we see a condensed sketch of an anonymous Buddhist (or possibly Jain) attempt to resolve the tension at the heart of the specific demonstration by giving priority to the general demonstration, the proof of "the mere possibility in general terms." Kumārila's response to these Buddhists or Jains (in the verse that begins "*naraḥ* and so on") is to accuse them of constructing a faulty proof, one that attains "the fault of the thesis (*pakṣadoṣa*) known as the inadequacy of the proposition (*pratijñānyūna*)," which comes about "when one proposes (*pratijñāyate*) one thing while desiring to prove something

616. TSP *ad* TS 2087 (*śrutiparīkṣā*, B 715,13–14): *na tāvat pratyakṣataḥ kartā vedasya siddhaḥ / tathā hi / ayam asāv iti na śakyate śṛṅgagrāhikayā pratipādayitum idānīm anupalabhyamānatvāt //*. "First, an author of the Veda is not established through perception. That is, it is not possible to demonstrate in the manner of singling something out (*śṛṅgagrāhikayā*) that 'this [person] is that [i.e., the author of the Veda],' because [such an author] is not presently perceived."

617. TSP *ad* TS 3229 (*atīndriyārthadarśiparīkṣā*, B 1016,19–21): *ye 'pi manyante / nāsmābhiḥ śṛṅgagrāhikayā sarvajñaḥ prasādhyate / kiṃ tarhi / sāmānyena sambhavamātraṃ prasādhyate / asti ko 'pi sarvajñaḥ kvacid vā sarvajñatvam asti prajñādīnāṃ prakarṣadarśanād iti / tān pratīdam āha nara ityādi /*.

else."[618] Kumārila's point here is that a mere general demonstration of omniscience is inadequate when one's actual purpose is to ground the scriptures authored by one's teacher through the proof that one's teacher is omniscient. Śāntarakṣita answers this charge much later in the chapter, when he rejects Kumārila's underlying assumption about the motive of the demonstration of omniscience.[619] We will return to this but for now we have one last instance of the qualifier *śṛṅgagrāhikayā* to consider.

This instance comes directly after a section in the final chapter of the *Tattvasaṃgraha* and the *Pañjikā* where Śāntarakṣita and Kamalaśīla reject that non-Buddhist teachers, such as Kapila and Vardhamāna, are omniscient. They make this rejection on the grounds that those non-Buddhist teachers have taught things that can, through *nyāya* and *pramāṇa* theory styles of reasoning, be shown to be false, such as the doctrine of a self (*ātmavāda*) and the doctrine of possibility (*syādvāda*). Kamalaśīla then has an objector suggest that these teachings do not necessarily indicate ignorance on the part of the promulgators, since those teachers may have purposely given false teachings for particular purposes.[620]

618. TS 3229 (*atīndriyārthadarśiparīkṣā*): *naraḥ ko 'py asti sarvajñas tat sarvajñatvam ity api / sādhanaṃ yat prayujyeta pratijñānyūnam eva tat //*. "But that proof which would be put forward as 'There is some omniscient person, or that omniscience [exists],' is just [faulty by virtue of incurring the point of defeat known as] the inadequacy of the proposition." On this point of defeat (*nigrahasthāna*), see NS 5.2.12ff., where the meaning seems simply to be that the proponent has neglected to mention a thesis, one of the necessary components of a valid proof statement. In the Buddhist tradition, Dharmakīrti has followed Dignāga in arguing that not mentioning the thesis is not necessarily a downfall. See Tillemans (2000: 37), who offers the following explanation in connection with Dharmakīrti's verses at PV 4.23, "Dharmakīrti opens his refutation of the Naiyāyikas by invoking their notion of 'incompleteness,' a point of defeat (*nigrahasthāna*) that, following the *Nyāyasūtra* (NS), occurs when one or more of the five members of a proof are missing. Dharmakīrti, in k.23, is in effect virtually reproducing a line from Dignāga's PSV [*ad* PV 3.1] where the latter invokes the fault of incompleteness, but redefines it as meaning not stating any one of the three characteristics of the logical reason." In VN (Much ed., 49,11–12), however, Dharmakīrti does allow for a kind of downfall in which a proponent offers a pointless statement as the thesis. Cf. TSP *ad* TS 3229 (*atīndriyārthadarśiparīkṣā*, B 1016,21–23): *hetos tāvat pūrvam anaikāntikatvaṃ pratipāditam ity ata pakṣadoṣam eva tāvat pratipādayati / anyasmin sādhayitum iṣṭe yad anyat pratijñāyate tat pratijñānyūnaṃ pakṣadoṣaḥ /*. See p. 328 for a translation of this passage in its larger context.

619. See TS 3590–91 (*atīndriyārthadarśiparīkṣā*), translated in n. 728 below.

620. TSP *ad* TS 3330 (*atīndriyārthadarśiparīkṣā*, B 1050,16–18): *syād etat yadi nāma viparītārthaprakāśanam eṣām / tathāpi mithyājñānānuṣaṅgitvam ato 'vasātuṃ na śakyate yato 'nyathāpi vyavahārāḥ śakyante kartuṃ vicitrābhisandhitvāt puruṣāṇām / tena hetoḥ saṃdigdhāsiddhatā //*. "Someone might think, 'Well, even if they promulgated incorrect

Śāntarakṣita responds to this suggestion by asking a question:

> If their doctrine of possibility and so on are of interpretable meaning (*ābhiprāyika*), then what do they hold to be the real (*tāttvika*) form of all things?[621]

Kamalaśīla has the opponent answer that the true meaning of the teachings of these other teachers is exactly the same as that of the Buddha's teaching of the doctrine of selflessness![622] In that case, Śāntarakṣita says, "Let them also be [omniscient],"[623] and Kamalaśīla comments, using the term *śṛṅgagrāhikayā* once again:

---

things, it is still not possible to definitively determine thereby that they possess false knowledge—conventional designations can be [construed] in more than one way, since people have diverse intentions. Therefore, the evidence is unestablished due to uncertainty.'"

621. TS 3330 (*atīndriyārthadarśiparīkṣā*): *ābhiprāyikam eteṣāṃ syādvādādivaco yadi / tāttvikaṃ sarvavastūnāṃ kim ebhī rūpam iṣyate //*. Śāntarakṣita and Kamalaśīla here employ the well-known Buddhist hermeneutical division between teachings that are interpretable (*ābhiprāyika*) and teachings that are definitive (*tāttvika*), ideas that are also frequently expressed in the respective Sanskrit terms *neyārtha* and *nītārtha*.

622. TSP *ad* TS 3330 (*atīndriyārthadarśiparīkṣā*, B 1050,19–1051,11): *yadi hy anyābhiprāyeṇa tair etat syādvādādi pramāṇaviruddham apy uktam ity abhidhīyate / abhidhīyatām / na hy asmābhiḥ svātantryeṇa vardhamānādīnām asarvajñatvaṃ sādhayitum iṣṭam / kiṃ tu bhavatā parasparaviruddhamatāvasthitena kapilādiṣu yadi sugataḥ sarvajñas tadā kapilo neti kā pramety uktam / atrāsmābhiḥ pramāṇaṃ bhavanmatyā teṣāṃ matabhedam aṅgīkṛtyābhidhīyate tena nāsiddhatā hetoḥ / tathā hi yady eṣām ābhiprāyikaṃ vaco varṇyate tadā kim eṣāṃ pāramārthikaṃ vasturūpam iṣṭam iti vaktavyam //*. "If you explain moreover that it is due to some other intention that they proclaimed the doctrine of indeterminacy (*syādvāda*) and so on—which [doctrines] are contradicted by the means of trustworthy awareness—then let it be explained like that! For we do not seek to establish the non-omniscience of Vardhamāna and others capriciously. Rather, you have stated that Kapila and others possess mutually contradictory opinions; therefore, regarding them you said [at TS 3148], 'If the Sugata is omniscient, then what is the means of trustworthy awareness by which one knows that Kapila is not omniscient?' Hence, we explain the means of trustworthy awareness [by which Kapila and others are shown to not be omniscient] having accepted the difference in their opinions in accord with *your* thinking. Therefore, our evidence is not unestablished. That is, if their doctrines are explained as being of interpretable meaning, then you must explain what they assert as the ultimate and true nature of things." My translation of *svātantryeṇa* as "capriciously" is bolstered by the Tibetan rendition at D, vol. *'e*, 293b7: *rang dgar . . . /*.

623. TS 3332 (*atīndriyārthadarśiparīkṣā*): *santu te 'pi samastānām aikamatyena saṃsthiteḥ / parasparaviruddhārthaṃ nītārthaṃ na hi te jaguḥ //*. "Let them also be [omniscient]! But because they all adhere to a single point of view, they would not proclaim mutually contradictory things to be of definitive meaning."

> We do not claim to prove just the statement "This one is omniscient" in the manner of singling something out. Rather, we do so generally.[624]

My translation "in the manner of singling something out" instead of "directly" for *śṛṅgagrāhikayā* is meant to highlight a slight difference in meaning here. Rather than saying something about the reasoning in the proof, this statement appears more concerned with warding off an acusation of partisanism. It is meant to emphasize once again that as far as these authors are concerned, the really important demonstration is of omniscience in general, while the specific case of the Buddha is simply a collorary of that. If others can be shown to be invariably concomitant with the qualities that define omniscience, then they will be omniscient also.

What are we to make of this? The various instances of the term *śṛṅgagrāhikayā* may not all mean precisely the same thing or be used in precisely the same way, but they all have the connotation of directly showing a particular person to be omniscient or credible (*ayam asau sarvajñaḥ* or *ayam asāv āptaḥ*) and not just of showing omniscience in general. Consistently, Śāntarakṣita and Kamalaśīla deny that they are engaged in this kind of specific demonstration, all the while eagerly pointing out that they *are* engaged in a general demonstration. But if we are to take them at their word here, then what do we make of the specific demonstration of omniscience in which the Buddha's teachings are taken as effect evidence for his omniscience? Can we really accept that the specific demonstration is *not* an instance of proving omniscience directly, that it is not a matter of singling something or someone out, that it does not say "this person [the Buddha], is that, [omniscient]"? There is only one clue that I have found to indicate that such may indeed represent the authors' own understanding of the demonstration of omniscience, and it is in a passage in which the authors acknowledge the Buddha may not have been the first to give the Buddhist teachings after all.

Acknowledging that the Buddha May Not Have Been First

Earlier we saw that, using the model of speech-as-inferential-sign, Śāntarakṣita and Kamalaśīla conclude that the Buddha intended to speak of all of the things that he spoke of in his various teachings. In addition, these thinkers also claim that since what the Buddha taught is correct (as they feel they

624. TSP *ad* TS 3331–32 (*atīndriyārthadarśiparīkṣā*, B 1051,14–15): *na hy asmābhiḥ śṛṅgagrāhikayāyam asau sarvajña ity evaṃ sādhayitum iṣṭaḥ / kiṃ tu sāmānyena //*.

have demonstrated by verifying his teachings through perception and inference), and since he did not learn about those things from anyone else (at least as far as we know), it is therefore also justified to conclude that the Buddha did possess direct (i.e., noninferential) knowledge of those things. The two qualifications—that what he taught was true and that he did not hear the teachings from someone else—together provide the warrant for the inference at the heart of the specific demonstration, or so it seems. It is interesting, therefore, that although much of the argumentation about the Buddha's omniscience and his attainment of supersensible knowledge is based on the idea that what he taught to his disciples was not something that he had learned from someone else, the authors of the *Tattvasaṃgraha* and the *Pañjikā* seem to recognize that this position is inherently weak. That is, Śāntarakṣita and Kamalaśīla recognize that it is not possible to verify that the Buddha did not have a teacher, and they clearly confront this fact.

Their approach to the problem is somewhat surprising. In effect, they say that it does not matter that we cannot know that the Buddha gave the Buddhist teachings first. In answering the objection that the Buddha might have given teachings on supersensible entities having first heard them from someone else, Kamalaśīla responds as follows:

> No [that is not a fault], because the objection would be the same in relation to that [other person] as well. That is, the following investigation would necessarily ensue: Well, how did the other person know [those supersensible objects]? For it would not be possible that he taught [them] in that manner not having known [them previously]. If you say he also knew them from another [person], then that would simply be an infinite regress. And thus, it would be a case of a lineage of [spiritually] blind persons, none of them would have extraordinary knowledge and therefore the teaching would not be correct (*samyak*).[625]

This passage comes in the context of a discussion of the Buddha's knowledge of normally supersensible entities such as the hidden capacities of *mantras* and so on. The idea is that if the *mantras* and so on are efficacious, then at some point in time the supersensible capacities that allow them to be

625. TSP *ad* TS 3454 (*atīndriyārthadarśiparīkṣā*, B 1086,22–25): *na tasyāpi tulyaparyanuyogāt / tathā hi tathāpy ayaṃ vicāro 'vatarati / tenāpi pareṇa kathaṃ jñātaṃ na hy ajñātvā tathopadeśaḥ saṃbhavet tenāpy anyato jñātam iti cet / evaṃ tarhy anavasthā syāt tataś cāndhaparamparāyāṃ satyāṃ sarveṣām anabhijñatvān na samyag upadeśaḥ syāt //.*

efficacious were directly known by someone, and this person must then be accepted as the author or promulgator of the *mantras*. The same principle can be equally applied to the Buddha's teachings of the nobles' four truths and so on. That is, we can be confident that when true teachings are conveyed by speech, especially those that are extensive and extremely profound, this cannot be merely random or accidental but must be the effect of some actual profound and direct knowledge of those teachings on the part of some teacher.[626]

For Śāntarakṣita and Kamalaśīla it is less important to show that it was a particular person, i.e., the Buddha himself, who had some particular knowledge than it is to show that all knowledge, extraordinary or otherwise, is by definition something that has been instantiated in a (human) knower. In other words, the important point to take away from the specific demonstration is not that some particular person (i.e., the Buddha) is credible but rather that all scriptures, including the trustworthy Buddhist scriptures, have their origin in an author (who, in the case of the Buddhist scriptures, must be counted as a credible person).

Because the most important things (*pradhānārtha*), that is, the matters crucial for liberation, may all be verified through perception and inference even by ordinary beings, the Buddha's teachings, once they have been established to be true, provide the warrant for an assertion that he, or in any case *someone* before him, was omniscient in the sense of possessing dharmic omniscience. In this way, the specific demonstration is only specific in the sense that it insists that some original promulgator of the Buddhist teachings was omniscient. On this reading, the authors would avoid the problem that they were somehow singling a specific person out as omniscient while still maintaining that the author of the Buddhist scriptures (whomever he or she may be) was omniscient.

626. See TSP *ad* TS 3450 (*atīndriyārthadarśiparīkṣā*, B 1086,15–16): *na hy ajñātvā yadṛcchayā pramāṇāviruddhaṃ niyamena bahu śakyaṃ bhāṣitum* /. "For it is not possible to explain greatly and in an orderly fashion that which does not contradict the means of trustworthy awareness just by mere accident, without having known it [beforehand]." See also TS 3457 (*atīndriyārthadarśiparīkṣā*): *vikṣiptacetasām etan mūḍhānāṃ na ca bhāṣitam / niyatānukramaṃ hīdaṃ prakṛṣṭaṃ phalasādhakam* //. "Nor is this [true teaching] the speech of idiots whose minds are deranged, since it possesses an orderly structure (*niyatānukrama*) [and] is eminent at establishing results."

The Specific Demonstration as a Corollary of the General

The above interpretation suggests that the specific demonstration is not quite as specific as it first appears. Further evidence that this may be the case can also be found in the final chapter of the *Tattvasaṃgraha* and the *Pañjikā* in a passage that responds to the Mīmāṃsaka position that omniscience cannot be established through inference since no evidence can be adduced that will allow one to infer its existence (*sattā*).[627] Responding to this objection, Śāntarakṣita and Kamalaśīla appear to make an astonishing concession—they agree that such evidence cannot be adduced, but they also claim that this is not a problem, since the existence of omniscience is not the target of their proof.[628] Kamalaśīla comments:

> By the statement that begins "Or, whatever things arise from a prior seed of a similar type..." [*Tattvasaṃgraha* 3413] he adduces the evidence having set forth wisdom and so on as the subject. Thus, it is not established that there is no evidence. Nor is it the case that we establish the existence [of an omniscient person]. Rather, [we establish] the property (*dharma*) that is called the *extreme perfection* (*atyantotkarṣa*) of wisdom and so on. And that itself *is* omniscience. Thus, whatever faults [apply] when one establishes the existence [of an omniscient person] do not apply here at all.[629]

627. See TS 3185 (*atīndriyārthadarśiparīkṣā*): *sarvajño dṛśyate tāvan nedānīm asmadādibhiḥ / dṛṣṭo na caikadeśo 'sti liṅgaṃ vā yo 'numāpayet //*. "After all, an omniscient person is not presently observed by us or others; nor is any logical evidence that is a part [of omniscience] observed that could lead us to an inference [of omniscience]." The first two *pāda*s of this verse are equivalent to ŚV 2.117ab. The second two *pāda*s are found (attributed, perhaps mistakenly, to ŚV) quoted in Ratnakīrti's SS (29,26).

628. TS 3508 (*atīndriyārthadarśiparīkṣā*): *prajñādīnāṃ ca dharmitvaṃ kṛtvā liṅgam udīritam / tan nāma dṛśyate liṅgaṃ na ca sattā prasādhyate //*. "The evidence is stated having construed wisdom and so on as the logical subject (*dharmin*). And the evidence that is observed does not establish the existence [of an omniscient person]." There are some philological difficulties in the last two *pāda*s. B reads *na nāma dṛśyate liṅgaṃ na ca sattā prasādhyate //*. G reads *nanā* (*tannāma* ?) *dṛśyate liṅgaṃ na ca sattā prasi* (*sā* ?) *dhyate //*. The Tibetan (D 128a2 and P 152b7–8) exhibits significant variation as well, so I include the whole verse here for comparison: *shes rab la sogs chos can du / byas nas rtags ni bshad pa yin / rtags ni mi snang ma grub yin / des na kun mkhyen med mi 'grub //*.

629. TSP *ad* TS 3508 (*atīndriyārthadarśiparīkṣā*, B 1098,19–22): *ye cāsamānajātīyetyādinā prajñādīnāṃ dharmitvaṃ vidhāya liṅgam udīritam ato liṅgaṃ nāstīty etad asiddham*

Kamalaśīla first makes reference to a verse that we saw above, one where Śāntarakṣita argues that since mental qualities are produced from prior similar moments, they (unlike some other qualities, such as skill in jumping) are "[capable] of extreme development due to a distinction in the superiority of their refinement."[630] By referring to this verse, Kamalaśīla makes quite clear his conviction that Śāntarakṣita is intent on establishing omniscience as a theoretical entity *as opposed to* omniscience as a truly existent or instantiated thing. In other words, the blunt message of this statement is that the authors are *not* attempting to establish or demonstrate that omniscience *exists* but rather only that the potential for the perfection of wisdom exists.

What is the implication of this passage for our interpretation of the specific demonstration? It seems to me that we should take this as a further piece of evidence to the effect that the authors do not wish to consider the specific demonstration to be the real or truly important demonstration, but rather that they see it as a mere corollary of the general demonstration. In this way, *the authors again attempt to avoid the charge that they are establishing a specific person as omniscient, for that is not the aim nor the force of their demonstration.* If, once they have established that omniscience as a mental state is a real possibility, it is then shown that there was someone, namely the author of the Buddhist scriptures, who had attained that state, then so be it. But this should not constitute, so the authors appear to argue, a fault in their reasoning, since they have not directly established that a particular person has a particular mental state. Rhetorically, it is a hard sell, but I do think this is what the authors are trying to argue.

This constitutes our exploration of the first avenue of interpretation concerning the fundamental tension in the specific demonstration of omniscience in the final chapter of the *Tattvasaṃgraha* and the *Pañjikā*, namely, the avenue of interpretation according to which the omniscient being in the figure of the Buddha is not in fact what the authors are aiming to establish in the specific demonstration. We now turn to the other avenue of interpretation mentioned above.

Who Can Infer the Buddha's Omniscience?

The second avenue of interpretation for dealing with the tension at the heart of the specific demonstration involves the possibility that the epistemological

/ nāpi sattā sādhyate / kiṃ tarhi / prajñādīnām atyantotkarṣākhyo dharmas tad eva ca sarvajñatvam ataḥ sattāsādhane 'pi ye doṣās te 'py atra nāvataranty eva //.

630. TS 3413. See p. 210.

category of radically inaccessible (*atyantaparokṣa*) must be understood in relation to particular audiences. In the previous chapter, when examining Śāntarakṣita and Kamalaśīla's rebuttal of Kumārila's refutation of omniscience, we saw that the argument was often framed in terms of the "person of limited vision" (*arvāgdarśin*). In that context, I noted that the authors write as if they include both themselves and their readers in this epistemic category. The question now presents itself, however, as to whether there may not be *degrees* of limitation, and whether Śāntarakṣita and Kamalaśīla might not consider themselves to be just a bit *less limited* than their Mīmāṃsaka counterparts. One begins to suspect such a perspective when Śāntarakṣita mentions that some intelligent persons, even though they are of limited vision, might ascertain the existence of an omniscient being through inference:

> Moreover, even some persons of ordinary vision might cognize [the omniscient person] through inference, for sometimes there are some people whose intellects are sharp. That is, although the previously stated proofs for the momentary nature of the Veda, the earth, and so on are extremely clear, dullards do not recognize them. Therefore, even the absence of a cognition [of the existence of an omniscient person], by which [absence] the twice-born [i.e., followers of the Veda] might confidently establish the nonexistence [of the omniscient person], is not certain, because there is doubt [about its nonexistence for all persons].[631]

Kamalaśīla tells us that Śāntarakṣita is demonstrating here that the Mīmāṃsaka position that an omniscient being is an object of the means of trustworthy awareness of nonexistence (*abhāvapramāṇa*) is doubtful (*saṃdigdha*). In other words, Śāntarakṣita is raising the possibility that some ordinary person, somewhere, *might* infer the existence of an omniscient being—although he does not here tell us how this would be done. This seems a strange argument for him to make, for it appears to cast into doubt the statements already encountered that stress the radically inaccessible (*atyantaparokṣa*) nature of

631. TS 3292–94 (*atīndriyārthadarśiparīkṣā*): *kecid arvāgdṛśo vāpi prapaśyante 'numānataḥ / kāścid eva hi keṣāṃcin nipuṇā matayaḥ kvacit // tathā hi vedabhūmyādeḥ kṣaṇikatvādisādhanam / puraḥ proktaṃ suvispaṣṭam api no lakṣitaṃ jaḍaiḥ // tad evaṃ śaṅkayā nāsya jñānābhāvo 'pi niścitaḥ / yato 'sattvaṃ prapaśyante nirviśaṅkā dvijātayaḥ //*. Reading *dvijātayaḥ* for *hi jātayaḥ* in accord with D 120a5: *gnyis skyes /*. Reading *prapaśyante* with G in place of *prapatsyante* in B.

the omniscient being. As such, it perfectly highlights the tension we have isolated as being at the heart of the specific demonstration.

Now, it is true that in the immediate context of the passage in which Śāntarakṣita and Kamalaśīla raise the possibility that persons of ordinary vision might verify the existence of an omniscient being through inference, the authors seem neither to accord it much likelihood nor to defend this idea. That is, immediately after the verses just cited, they return to the more familiar notion that the omniscient being is *not* an object of inference for ordinary persons, reiterating their position that this in no way disproves the existence of such a being. But later in the chapter, in a section summarizing the results of the rebuttal of Kumārila's refutation of omniscience, Śāntarakṣita makes another intriguing linguistic shift when he says:

> Since a person who knows all objects is never perceptible *for those whose mental vision is dull*, the proof of his existence will not come about through inference [for them].[632] [Emphasis added.]

Here, in place of the usual formulation that rules out inference of an omniscient being for persons of limited vision (*arvāgdarśin*), we find instead that such an inference is ruled out for persons whose mental vision is dull (*jaḍadhīdṛś*). The word translated as "dull" in this compound is *jaḍa*, a derogatory term implying stupidity and torpor. It is not a term that one normally applies to oneself, at least not if one's aim is to convince others of the superiority of one's reasoning. Kamalaśīla does not gloss the term,[633] and so an ambiguity remains: does Śāntarakṣita include himself in the category of those whose mental vision is dull and for whom the inference of an omniscient being is impossible? Or does he rather see himself as one whose vision, while perhaps still limited, is nevertheless not quite so dull as that of Kumārila, and who is in some way capable of using inference to ascertain an omniscient being?

The strong implication of the passages in the final chapter of the *Tattvasaṃgraha* and the *Pañjikā* that lay out the inference that grounds the specific demonstration is that Śāntarakṣita and Kamalaśīla do understand themselves as being in a different epistemic situation from that of their

632. TS 3304 (*atīndriyārthadarśiparīkṣā*): *sarvārthajño yato 'dṛśyaḥ sadaiva jaḍadhīdṛśām / nāto 'numānatas tasya sattā siddhiṃ prayāsyati //*. See also 3344–46 translated on p. 275.

633. In another location, however, Kamalaśīla glosses the term *jaḍa* as referring specifically to Kumārila. See n. 157 above.

Mīmāṃsaka counterparts. That is, as we noted earlier, although the authors of the *Tattvasaṃgraha* and the *Pañjikā* generally exhibit respect for their philosophical opponents, they seem less inclined toward courtesy in the case of Kumārila and his like. We find numerous references to the idea that *brāhmaṇa*s have been made stupid by their study of the Veda, and the final chapter of the *Tattvasaṃgraha* and the *Pañjikā* also contains a lengthy digression on the question of caste, in which *ad personam* arguments are mounted against the Mīmāṃsaka.[634] In sum, it seems that Śāntarakṣita and Kamalaśīla may finally conclude that their Mīmāṃsaka opponents are beyond the pale of understanding, being too burdened by erroneous and even harmful ideas.

Śāntarakṣita sums up his feelings in the following verses:

> Those who possess many impurities cannot obtain the jewel of the Tathāgata's speech, which when produced is conducive to the destruction of the darkness of all wrong opinions. Therefore, those who are conversant with [philosophical] opinions call just the Sugata omniscient. And they call just him the best physician, who knows the principal aims of human beings. Thus, there *is* a means of trustworthy awareness by which one can say that the Sugata is omniscient whereas Kapila is not; although it has been clearly expounded directly above, stupid people do not comprehend it.[635]

634. TS 3573–89 (*atīndriyārthadarśiparīkṣā*) and TSP *ad cit.* (B 1111,26–1115,18). The outset of this discussion of caste specifically links the philosophical notion of *jāti*, or "universal," with the social sense of this same word as "caste" (see TS 3574ab). The charged nature of this topic becomes evident in Śāntarakṣita's sardonic reply to the notion of the superiority of the *brāhmaṇa* caste. Not only does Śāntarakṣita reject this notion, he even throws into doubt the moral character of his opponent's mother! The jibe concerning Kumārila's mother is rather witty, and not entirely gratuitous. Śāntarakṣita knows that in traditional Brahmanism, *jāti* is passed to children through their fathers. But without the kind of supersensible knowledge that the Mīmāṃsaka rejects, it is impossible to know for certain that the husband of one's mother is in fact one's father (this is all the more so since women are "extremely restless" [*aticāpalam*] and hence by nature not likely to remain faithful for long!). Hence, Śāntarakṣita concludes, even if the *brāhmaṇa* caste could be shown to be superior, one could never know for certain that one was in fact of that caste (unless, of course, one admits supersensible knowledge). See TS 3578–79. See also TS 3281 (*atīndriyārthadarśiparīkṣā*) and TSP *ad cit.* (B 1037,10–14), verse translated above on p. 177. For a study of caste in the Buddhist epistemological tradition, see Eltschinger 2000.

635. TS 3344–46 (*atīndriyārthadarśiparīkṣā*): *samastakumatadhvāntavidhvaṃsānuguṇodayam / tathāgatavacoratnam alabdhaṃ bahukalmaṣaiḥ // tataḥ sugatam evāhuḥ sarvajñaṃ matiśālinaḥ / pradhānapuruṣārthajñaṃ taṃ caivāhur bhiṣagvaram // sugatas*

These verses occur not long after the major presentation of the specific demonstration. Clearly, they lend support to the idea that the omniscient being is *not* beyond the reach of inference (and therefore is *not* a radically inaccessible entity) for those whose mental vision is not quite so dull as that of the Mīmāṃsakas. Thus, we have significant evidence in support of the second avenue of interpretation, which speculates that the category of radically inaccessible must be judged in relation to specific audiences.

Reconciling the Two Interpretations

The two possible solutions that we have explored for resolving the tension at the heart of the specific demonstration are quite different, and the question remains whether there is good reason to favor one over the other. Both solutions seem to rely on a degree of equivocation. In the first case, the authors hope both to establish the Buddha as omniscient and to deny that they are establishing the Buddha as omniscient. The argument relies on a shift in the understanding of what it means to establish something to be the case. The Buddha's omniscience is not the primary focus of the overall proof, which is rather omniscience itself as a theoretical entity. The fact that the Buddha, or in any case someone (i.e., the author of the Buddhist scriptures), can be determined to be invariably concomitant with the definition of omniscience is merely incidental, an unintended, although welcome, corollary to the actual proof. It is in this sense that the authors can maintain that they are not really establishing that the Buddha is omniscient. In the second case, the argument relies on a shift in the meaning of the technical term *atyantaparokṣa*. Here, the authors appear to claim greater epistemic access to reality than their non-Buddhist counterparts, who have been rendered stupid by the idiotic doctrines that they continually study. This interpretation requires that the specific demonstration really hold up as an inference. Since, as we have seen, the authors acknowledge that it is possible that the Buddha was *not* first (and therefore by implication that he was not omniscient, although someone else surely was), it seems as though they recognize a weakness in the inference that forms the basis for the specific demonstration. In this case, it is understandable that they should attempt to pull away from a full commitment to

---

tena sarvajñaḥ kapilo neti tu pramā / anantaroditā vyaktāpy eṣā mūḍhair na lakṣitā //. Reading *sarvajñaṃ matiśālinaḥ* instead of *sarvajñam atiśālinaḥ* in accord with D 122a: *blo gros rgyas pas … /*. The final verse mirrors that presented at TS 3148 (*atīndriyārthadarśiparīkṣā*), which is also reproduced in the commentary on TS 3330 (*atīndriyārthadarśiparīkṣā*), and is translated above in n. 622.

that demonstration by relegating it to the status of a mere corollary of the actual demonstration.

In fact, I see no obvious way to allow both avenues of interpretation to stand, but perhaps this is not necessary. After all, it is not our job to reconcile all possible tensions in the *Tattvasaṃgraha* and the *Pañjikā*. Rather, our job is to show how the authors deal with the tensions that do arise. In this case, I think it is fair to say that they employ a variety of arguments, not all of which are entirely compatible, in an attempt to cover their bases.

In the following chapter of this book, we will consider the possible motivations behind the elements of the various demonstrations of omniscience in the *Tattvasaṃgraha* and the *Pañjikā*. For the moment, we will leave the question of the fundamental tension in the specific demonstration behind and turn to a couple of supplementary arguments for the Buddha's omniscience also found in the final chapter of the *Tattvasaṃgraha* and the *Pañjikā*.

Supplemental Arguments in the Demonstration

In addition to arguments for the Buddha's omniscience that make up the basic specific demonstration, the *Tattvasaṃgraha* and the *Pañjikā* also contain some supplemental arguments that are not directly tied to the specific demonstration but that do aim to demonstrate the Buddha's maximal greatness in some fashion. Unlike the arguments that make up the general and the specific demonstrations, these arguments are less clearly grounded in *pramāṇa* theory. They also appear to be offered somewhat tongue-in-cheek, thus making them less convincing, perhaps, for judicious persons, but also adding to the overall persuasiveness of the argument by shoring up the Buddhist position through humor and *ad personam* arguments.

The Buddha's Omniscience Is Attested in the Veda

The first of these supplemental arguments maintains that Buddhists do not seek to establish the Buddha's omniscience by recourse to scripture, since it is pointless to do so when an inference that functions through the force of real entities (*vastubalapravṛttānumāna*) is available to accomplish the task;[636] nonetheless, the Buddha's omniscience is attested in the Mīmāṃsaka's sacred

636. TSP *ad* TS 3509 (*atīndriyārthadarśiparīkṣā*): *na hi vastubalapravṛttānumānasambhave sati kaścid icchāmātrānuvidhāyino vacanād vastusiddhim anvicchet / ato na vayam āgamāt sarvajñaṃ sādhayāmaḥ / kiṃ tarhi / anumānāt //.*

scripture, the Veda, and so should be accepted by Kumārila. Śāntarakṣita states the claim boldly:

> However, if you assert that the Veda is trustworthy, then can you idiots not comprehend that the Blessed One is omniscient? For in another Vedic recension (*śākhā*) called "Nimitta," wise *brāhmaṇas* clearly read that the greatest sage, the Blessed One, is omniscient.[637]

Kamalaśīla clarifies in his commentary that the Blessed One or "Lord" in question here is the Buddha Śākyamuni.[638] But Śāntarakṣita does not stop at a mere assertion but goes so far as to quote the text as evidence:

> That one who, having appeared in a dream as a six-tusked white elephant, was born as the bodhisattva, that ocean of good qualities, whose name is widely proclaimed, who is omniscient and compassionate, will become one who attains the stage of immortality, pure, the father of all the world.[639]

The image of the Buddha as a six-tusked white elephant appearing in a dream is an obvious reference to traditional Buddhist hagiographical literature in which it is frequently said that the Buddha's mother dreamed of such an elephant on the night that she conceived her son.

At this point, the authors of the *Tattvasaṃgraha* and the *Pañjikā* confront an obvious problem: the Vedic recension known as "Nimitta" is not accepted by the *brāhmaṇa* community. Śāntarakṣita dismisses this problem as being due to nothing other than hostility (*dveṣa*). As for the Vedic accents (*svara*), which are used for the recitation of Vedic texts, these may be freely applied in the present case as well.[640] In short, Śāntarakṣita insists that the opponents

637. TS 3510–11 (*atīndriyārthadarśiparīkṣā*): *kiṃ tu vedapramāṇatvaṃ yadi yuṣmābhir iṣyate / tat kiṃ bhagavato mūḍhaiḥ sarvajñatvaṃ na gamyate // nimittanāmni sarvajño bhagavān munisattamaḥ / śākhāntare hi vispaṣṭaṃ paṭhyate brāhmaṇair budhaiḥ //.*

638. TSP *ad* TS 3510–11 (*atīndriyārthadarśiparīkṣā*, B 1099,18–20): *tathā hi nimittaṃ nāma śākhāntaram asti tatra sphuṭataram ayam eva bhagavān śākyamuniḥ sarvajñaḥ paṭhyate tat kim iti mūḍhair vedaṃ pramāṇayadbhir api bhavadbhir asau pratikṣipyate /.*

639. TS 3512–13 (*atīndriyārthadarśiparīkṣā*): *yo 'sau ṣaḍdantam ātmānam avadāta-dvipātmakam / svapne pradarśya saṃjāto bodhisattvo guṇodadhiḥ // vighuṣṭaśabdaḥ sarvajñaḥ kṛpātmā sa bhaviṣyati / prāptāmṛtapadaḥ śuddhaḥ sarvalokapitāpi ca //.*

640. TS 3514–16 (*atīndriyārthadarśiparīkṣā*): *atha śākhāntaraṃ nedaṃ vedāntargatam*

must be prepared to make clear through solid reasoning on what basis the text is rejected as being part of the Veda; if the opponent cannot do so, then his claim that the Buddha's omniscience is not attested in the Veda remains doubtful at best.[641]

Finally, at the end of this section, Śāntarakṣita gives another reason why it is doubtful that the Veda does not assert that the Buddha is omniscient. For this argument, he returns to an idea that he had developed extensively in the "Investigation of Scripture," namely, that an eternal Veda would be incapable of communicating meaning.[642] In that case, if the opponent still insists that the Veda is eternal, then his assertion that the Veda does not speak of the Buddha's omniscience must be rejected, for there will be no way to be certain that the well-known Vedic injunction *agnihotraṃ juhuyāt svargakāmaḥ* means what it appears to mean in standard Sanskrit, namely, "one who desires heaven should offer the fire sacrifice" and that it does not mean instead "the Victor is omniscient."[643]

The authors of the *Tattvasaṃgraha* and the *Pañjikā* therefore offer two basic arguments for why their Mīmāṃsaka opponents should accept that the Veda teaches that the Buddha is omniscient. The first asserts that there is a Vedic recension in which such is explicitly stated. Since the authors of the *Tattvasaṃgraha* and the *Pañjikā* claim not to accept scripture as a means of trustworthy awareness, this argument is clearly one that is meant to be offered on the opponents' terms. Nonetheless, as I think was no doubt quite obvious to any educated reader of the time, the authors of the *Tattvasaṃgraha* and the *Pañjikā* were quite aware that the Vedic recension called "Nimitta"

---

iṣyate / tad atra na nimittaṃ vo dveṣaṃ muktvāvadhāryate // svarādayaś ca te dharmāḥ prasiddhāḥ śrutibhāvinaḥ / kartum atrāpi śakyās te narecchāmātrasambhavāt //.

641. TS 3520 (*atīndriyārthadarśiparīkṣā*): *jñāpanīyam avedatvaṃ yad vā yuktyā dhruvaṃ tvayā / anyathā śrutyanuktatvaṃ saṃdigdhaṃ tasya te bhavet //.*

642. That is, Śāntarakṣita and Kamalaśīla hold that meaning is a function of human convention (*vyavahāra*), whereas the Mīmāṃsakas hold meaning to arise through an eternal potency (*śakti*) inherent in words. The authors of the TS/P, however, find the notion of an eternal potency to be a contradiction in terms, since potency implies causal function, and causal function requires change, which is inimical to eternality. They further argue that even if such an eternal potency were to exist, its meaning could still only be determined through convention, which is not fixed but depends upon human interests. See, e.g., TS 2651–66 (*śrutiparīkṣā*) and TSP *ad cit.* (B 861,22–866,7).

643. TS 3525–26 (*atīndriyārthadarśiparīkṣā*): *tadā ca vedavākyānāṃ svātantryeṇārthaniścayaḥ / vedāt svataḥ parasmāc ca mohādivivaśātmanaḥ // tenāgnihotraṃ juhuyāt svargakāma iti śruteḥ / jinaḥ sarvajña ity evaṃ nārtha ity atra kā pramā //.* Cf. also TSP *ad* TS 2331–33 (*śrutiparīkṣā*, B 780,18–781,18).

to which they refer would not have been recognized by their opponents as having the status of Veda (if such a work existed at all). The argument, then, must be seen as including a subtle dig at the Mīmāṃsakas for their lack of rational criteria by which to judge which texts may be considered authentic scripture (*śruti*). The second argument holds somewhat closer to *pramāṇa* theory style of reasoning, although it, too, comes across as mocking rather than as serious debate. The linchpin of the argument is again the irrationality of holding that the Veda is both eternal and that it may provide guidance for humans. For Śāntarakṣita and Kamalaśīla, the consequence of such a notion is that the Vedic sentences may mean anything (hence nothing) at all![644] Together these arguments form a supplement to the specific demonstration in that they argue for the omniscience of the Buddha, although not in terms that judicious persons would be likely to accept.

The Buddha's Compassion as a Mark of His Superiority

The other supplementary argument involves a demonstration of the Buddha's compassion. Śāntarakṣita and Kamalaśīla discuss the Buddha's compassion in response to a verse quoted earlier in the *pūrvapakṣa* and attributed to Kumārila. The context of the remark is the hypothetical situation in which the Buddha's teachings might be thought to derive from the Veda and thus gain their authority from them. Kumārila is reported to have said:

> If that teaching had its basis in the Veda, then [the buddhas] would bestow it on just those who expound the Veda, just as Manu and so on [did]. But since, however, it is known they [i.e., the buddhas] gave that teaching to stupid *śūdra*s, it is evident that it is false (*sāṃvṛta*), like a counterfeit coin.[645]

644. See TS 2808 (*śrutiparīkṣā*), which indicates that the eternal Veda cannot make known Dharma because its meaning cannot be determined at all: *dharmaṃ prati na siddhātaś codanānāṃ pramāṇatā / svato 'nyebhyaś ca mandebhyas tadarthānavadhāraṇāt //.*

645. TS 3225–26 (*atīndriyārthadarśiparīkṣā*): *yady asau vedamūlaḥ syād vedavādibhya eva tu / upadeśaṃ prayaccheyur yathā manvādayas tathā / yatas tu mūrkhaśūdrebhyaḥ kṛtaṃ tair upadeśanam / jñāyate tena dṛṣṭaṃ tat sāṃvṛtaṃ kūṭakarmavat //.* TSP *ad cit.*: *yadi hi buddhādīnāṃ dharmādyupadeśo vedamūlaḥ syāt tadā brāhmaṇebhya eva vidvadbhyo manvādivad upadiśeyuḥ / na ca tair brāhmaṇebhya evopadiṣṭam / kiṃ tu vaṭharaśūdrebhya eva / ato 'vagamyate sāmvṛtam alīkam tat upadeśanam yathā kūṭadīnārādikam iti //.* Reading *vaṭharaśūdrebhya* with G in place of *jaraṭhaśūdrebhya* as found in B. Śāntarakṣita and Kamalaśīla's response to this statement comes at TS/P 3574–89 (*atīndriyārthadarśiparīkṣā*). See n. 634 above.

Śāntarakṣita's response to this assault is to insist that the fact that the Buddha taught impartially to all, including *śūdras*, is an indication of not of his delusion but of his compassion.[646] In contrast,

> That teaching of those who are devoid of compassion, [and] who are under the sway of greed, fear, anger, and jealousy, would be partisan.[647]

Compared with the intricate reasoning in the general demonstration discussed above, where compassion is established to be a necessary cause for omniscience, this argument is considerably looser. No proof statement is given, although a distinct line of reasoning can be discerned. This seems to be an argument that the authors advance not specifically on rational grounds but rather as an indignant response to what they perceive as the exclusivism and arrogance of their Brahmanical opponents.

As a matter of fact, it is shortly after the verse just cited that Śāntarakṣita and Kamalaśīla launch into their cutting critique of the arrogance of caste superiority. There they employ a variety of arguments—again, not presented through the *pramāṇa* theory idiom—in order to discredit the notion that the *brāhmaṇa* caste is somehow superior. Kamalaśīla refers, for example, to "artificial, imagined *brāhmaṇas*,"[648] stating that they, too, follow the rites (*saṃskāra*) and so on that are supposed to be marks of the superiority of the *brāhmaṇa* caste. Likewise, the authors cast aspersions on Manu and others, implying that they lacked the courage and intelligence to share their teachings with a wider community:

> I suspect that somehow Manu and the others ascertained the irrationality of the Veda's meaning, which is by its nature impossible to make known, and thinking that the *brāhmaṇas*, stupefied by

646. TS 3567–68 (*atīndriyārthadarśiparīkṣā*): *svārthasaṃsiddhaye teṣām upadeśo na tādṛśaḥ / ārambhaḥ sakalas tv eṣa parārthaṃ kartum īdṛśaḥ // tasmāj jagaddhitādhānadīkṣitāḥ karuṇātmakāḥ / anibandhanabandhutvād āhuḥ sarveṣu tat padam //.*

647. TS 3569 (*atīndriyārthadarśiparīkṣā*): *ye hi lobhabhayadveṣamātsaryādivaśīkṛtāḥ / prādeśikī bhavet teṣāṃ deśanā niḥkṛpātmanām //.*

648. TSP *ad* TS 3577 (*atīndriyārthadarśiparīkṣā*, B 1113,9): *kṛtrimābhimatabrāhmaṇeśv iva /.* The reference here is likely to persons who follow brahmanic rites and claim to be *brāhmaṇas*, but whose status as *brāhmaṇas* is rejected by other *brāhmaṇas*.

> their recitation of the Veda, were incapable of investigating [it], they taught the Veda and so on to *brāhmaṇa*s alone.[649]

And Śāntarakṣita goes on:

> The Purāṇas, the Mānavadharma [law books], the Veda and its limbs, and the medical treatises: these four are established as commands (*ājñā*) and are not to be challenged by reasoning. I think that they [i.e., Manu and the rest] bequeathed this scare tactic on stupid persons precisely for the reasons [given just above], for otherwise how could [those works be] established as a command just through speech?[650]

As Kamalaśīla clarifies, the reason for the "scare tactics" of Manu and others can be traced to the irrationality of the Veda and the stupidity of the *brāhmaṇa*s.[651]

In contrast to the cowardice of Manu and his like, the Buddha stands as the paragon of confidence, readily encouraging rational investigation of his teachings since he knows that they will always withstand such analysis. Śāntarakṣita expresses his admiration poetically when he says,

> But the great ones clearly ascertained the rationality of their own words, and being able themselves to explain that [teaching], being therefore unshaken by fear, they proclaimed the lion's roar that removes the debility of the elephant's rut [i.e., pride] of the opinions of bad teachers as follows: Just as wise persons accept gold, having first tested it through heating it, cutting it, and rubbing it on a touchstone, so too, O monks, you should accept my words only after testing them, and not out of respect [for me].[652]

649. TS 3581–82 (*atīndriyārthadarśiparīkṣā*): *niryuktikatvaṃ vedārthe jñāpanāśaktatātmani / vedādhītijaḍā viprā na parīkṣākṣamā iti // kutaścin niścitaṃ śaṅke nūnaṃ manvādibhis tataḥ / viprebhya eva vedādeḥ kṛtaṃ tair upadeśanam //.*

650. TS 3583–84 (*atīndriyārthadarśiparīkṣā*): *purāṇaṃ mānavo dharmaḥ sāṅgo vedaś cikitsitam / ājñāsiddhāni catvāri na hantavyāni hetubhiḥ // manye tenaiva datteyaṃ jaḍebhyas tair vibhīṣikā / ājñāsiddhatvam anyatra vāṅmātrāt kiṃ nu vā bhavet //.*

651. TSP *ad* TS 3583–84 (*atīndriyārthadarśiparīkṣā*, B 1114,18–19): *tenaiveti / kāraṇena / niryuktikatvam eṣāṃ purāṇādīnāṃ bhavatāṃ ca jāḍyam avadhāryeti yāvat //.*

652. TS 3585–87 (*atīndriyārthadarśiparīkṣā*): *yaiḥ punaḥ svoktiṣu spaṣṭaṃ yuktārthatvaṃ viniścitam / tat pratyāyanasāmarthyam ātmanaś ca mahātmabhiḥ // kutīrthyamattamā-*

The "lion's roar" is the Buddha's call to examine his teachings through reason. As we saw above, Kamalaśīla cites this call at the outset of the *Pañjikā*.[653] All of these arguments are designed to lend credibility to the Buddhist case for the superiority of their tradition through an appeal to the integrity, including the compassion, of the Buddha (and a corresponding denigration of the integrity of the non-Buddhist players). Again, while it seems that the authors of the *Tattvasaṃgraha* and the *Pañjikā* do not expect their audience to be *convinced* by these arguments, which typically are not accompanied by proof statements in the *pramāṇa* theoretical vein, their inclusion in the work is evidence for the shrewdness with which both Śāntarakṣita and Kamalaśīla approach their rhetorical task.

taṅgamadaglānividhāyinam / evam astākhilatrāsāḥ siṃhanādaṃ nadanti te // tāpāc chedāc ca nikaṣāt suvarṇam iva paṇḍitaiḥ / parīkṣya bhikṣavo grāhyaṃ madvaco na tu gauravāt //. See also p. 61 above.

653. See n. 141 above.

6. Motives for the Two Demonstrations

MUCH EARLIER in this book, we saw that omniscience itself can be construed as the ultimate aim of Śāntarakṣita and Kamalaśīla's treatise. The reasoning was as follows: Kamalaśīla explicitly states that the ultimate aim of the *Tattvasaṃgraha* and the *Pañjikā* includes the attainment of a kind of *summum bonum*, the so-called highest good (*niḥśreyasa*), understood as liberation (*apavarga*) from the suffering of saṃsāra. He further equates this highest good with the eradication of the two obscurations, the afflictive obscuration (*kleśāvaraṇa*) and the epistemic obscuration (*jñeyāvaraṇa*). The removal of these two obscurations, as we have seen, constitutes the necessary and sufficient conditions for the attainment of omniscience (*sarvajña*) for these authors. We concluded that the ultimate aim of the work may be construed as the attainment of omniscience on the part of those judicious persons who engage with the text.[654]

The present chapter is an attempt to gain deeper insight into how the authors understand the way the two basic demonstrations comprising the overall demonstration of omniscience in the final chapter of the *Tattvasaṃgraha* and the *Pañjikā* contribute to this ultimate goal. In other words, just as we earlier asked about the purpose of the work as a whole, we ask here about the purpose or motives behind the general and the specific demonstrations of omniscience. According to our division of the overall demonstration of omniscience into a general and a specific demonstration, we have understood the general demonstration to contain three distinct elements: the rebuttal of Kumārila's refutation of omniscience, the demonstration of the possibility of dharmic omniscience, and the demonstration of total omniscience. We examined these three elements or "movements" in the general demonstration in chapter 4 above. In the present chapter, we will consider the motives behind the general and the specific demonstrations without at

654. See pp. 105–9 above.

first taking the demonstration of total omniscience into account. For, as we have seen, the authors understand the demonstration of total omniscience to be a consequence of the demonstration of dharmic omniscience and do not consider it central to the overall demonstration. We therefore reserve a separate section of the chapter for our analysis of its aims. The bulk of our analysis will assume that the omniscience in question is of the dharmic variety.

Motives for the General Demonstration

We start by considering the motives behind the first two elements in the general demonstration: the rebuttal of Kumārila's refutation of omniscience and the demonstration of the possibility of dharmic omniscience. On my reading, these two aspects of the general demonstration work together as part of a strategy aimed at convincing judicious persons that it is indeed rational to put into practice the teachings that comprise the Buddhist path and to take as their goal the attainment of omniscience. In other words, even though we have said that the first element of the demonstration, namely, the rebuttal of Kumārila's refutation, is directed at Mīmāṃsakas, it can also be seen as the first step in an argument addressed to the universal audience of judicious persons. As such, the engendering of doubt that occurs through the rebuttal should be construed not as an end in itself but as part of a process by which the judicious person becomes convinced first to study and then to put into practice the Buddhist teachings aimed at the eventual attainment of omniscience.

Trustworthy Awareness as a Justification of Action

Let us return for a moment to our initial characterization of the judicious person, or *prekṣāvant*, in order to determine what the authors understand to be the conditions under which such a person will be prompted to act. First, let us remember that judicious persons are held always to act with some goal in mind and never to act whimsically or haphazardly. Instead, such persons act only after fully investigating the means to the goal and having determined its plausibility and usefulness. The indispensable tools for this investigation are the means of trustworthy awareness—perception and inference—whose very trustworthiness ensures that the results of the investigation will be reliable. It is because judicious persons proceed in this manner, relying always on the means of trustworthy awareness, that their actions may be considered justified or rational.

As we have noted, Śāntarakṣita and Kamalaśīla follow Dharmakīrti in characterizing a means of trustworthy awareness as an awareness that has some expected (*abhimata*) causal function (*arthakriyā*) as its object. We have also noted that the term *arthakriyā*, in addition to indicating causal function, also connotes the meaning of the accomplishment of a goal. This makes a certain amount of sense, since the capacity for causal function (*arthakriyāsamartha*) is, for these thinkers, the mark of a real thing (*vastu*), and to be plausible and useful, a goal (*artha*) must also be a real thing (*artha*). The judicious person's reliance upon the means of trustworthy awareness to attain his or her goals is rooted, therefore, in the idea that it is only by such means of trustworthy awareness that one will be assured of attaining something real. The importance of the *pramāṇa*s in relation to the attainment of goals is emphasized by Śāntarakṣita and Kamalaśīla, who, following Dharmakīrti, state that the means of trustworthy awareness is the most powerful factor governing a judicious person's actions with regard to goals.[655]

But how precisely do the means of trustworthy awareness function so as to allow the judicious person to accomplish his or her goals? Śāntarakṣita holds that an awareness is trustworthy if it contains an appearance of causal function:

655. Dharmakīrti's statement is found at PV 2.3b–d: *dhīpramāṇatā / pravṛttes tatpradhānatvād dheyopādeyavastuni /*. Kamalaśīla's relevant comments are found at TSP *ad* TS 3122 (*atīndriyārthadarśiparīkṣā*, B 983,22–984,5): *yata iṣyata evāsmābhiḥ pramāṇam avisaṃvādivijñānam iti vacanād arthāvisaṃvāditvaṃ jñānasya prāmāṇyam / kiṃ tu jñānam iti viśeṣeṇopādānād brūyād dhūmāder ajñānasvabhāvasya mukhyataḥ prāmāṇyaṃ neṣṭam ity arthāvisaṃvāditvamātraṃ prāmāṇyam asiddham / jñānasyaiva heyopādeyavastuni pravṛttau prādhānyāt / tathā hi saty apy avinābhāvini dhūmādau na tāvat puruṣasyārthe pravṛttir bhavati yāvad vijñānotpādo na bhavati tasmāt pravṛttau jñānasyāvyavahitaṃ kārakatvam iti tadeva pramāṇam / yad āha dhīpramāṇatā / pravṛttes tatpradhānatvād dheyopādeyavastuni iti //*. "For we indeed assert that a means of trustworthy awareness is a trustworthy awareness, and by this statement [is meant that] the trustworthiness (*prāmāṇya*) of an awareness is its trustworthiness in relation to a real thing (*arthāvisaṃvāditva*). But one should speak about [trustworthiness] by mentioning the qualification 'awareness,' [since] trustworthiness is not primarily asserted of smoke and so on whose nature is nonconscious. Therefore, it is not established that trustworthiness is merely in terms of the trustworthiness in relation to an object, because awareness is primary when it comes to engaging with a real thing that is to be relinquished or that is to be taken up. That is, even if it is the case that smoke and so forth are invariably concomitant [with fire and so on], as long as there does not arise a consciousness [of that object], for that long there is no activity with regard to a human aim. Therefore, since awareness is the immediate (*avyavahita*) cause (*kāraka*) when it comes to engagement, that [awareness] alone is a *pramāṇa*. As it has been said (PV 2.3) 'awareness (*dhī*) is trustworthy, since it is the chief factor in action toward a real thing that is to be relinquished or taken up.'"

> It is said that [an awareness] that is correspondent with real things is called trustworthy (*prāmāṇya*), and there is no definition of that apart from being an awareness in which causal function appears.[656]

Kamalaśīla offers the following commentary:

> For a trustworthy awareness alone is called a *pramāṇa*, since it was said [by Dharmakīrti] that a *pramāṇa* is a trustworthy awareness. And this trustworthiness is defined simply as causal function (*arthakriyā*), since the consideration of [whether a particular awareness is or is not] a *pramāṇa* is done for the sake of that [causal function]. For this reason, the judicious person who seeks a [particular] causal function investigates whether [an awareness] is a *pramāṇa* or is not a *pramāṇa*; [such a person] does not do so wantonly. That causal function is characterized by the arisal of an awareness in which appears [such causal functions as] burning, cooking, and so on. And it is just through the arisal of that [awareness] that there is the cessation of the quest (*ākāṅkṣa*) on the part of the person who desires that [particular] causal function [and] who acts [toward that thing].[657]

656. TS 2958 (*svataḥprāmāṇyaparīkṣā*): *ucyate vastusaṃvādaḥ prāmāṇyam abhidhīyate / tasya cārthakriyābhāsajñānād anyan na lakṣaṇam //*. [For the reading *arthakriyābhāsajñānād* in place of *arthakriyābhyāsajñānād*, see Krasser 1992: 156n22.] See also n. 193.

657. TSP *ad* TS 2958–61 (*svataḥprāmāṇyaparīkṣā*, B 942,16–20): *ayam atra saṃkṣepārthaḥ / pramāṇaṃ hi nāmāvisaṃvādi jñānam ucyate / pramāṇam avisaṃvādi jñānam iti vacanāt / sa cāvisaṃvādo 'rthakriyālakṣaṇa eva tadarthatvāt pramāṇacintāyāḥ / yato 'rthakriyārthī pramāṇam apramāṇaṃ vānveṣate prekṣāvān na vyasanitayā / sā cārthakriyā dāhapākādinirbhāsajñānodayalakṣaṇā tadutpādād evārthakriyārthinaḥ pravṛttasyākāṅkṣānivṛtteḥ /*. Reading *sa cāvisaṃvādo* in place of *na cāvisaṃvādo* on the strength of the Tibetan (D, vol. *'e*, 235b4–5): *mi slu ba de yang don byed pa'i mtshan nyid can kho na yin te /*. Although Kamalaśīla here presents trustworthiness rather loosely as causal function, he soon makes clear in the continuation of the commentary on TS 2958–61 that his understanding comes close to that of Dharmakīrti's more technical definition of trustworthiness as the *cognition* of causal function (PV 2.1bff.: *arthakriyāsthitiḥ / avisaṃvādam....* See PVP for the gloss of *sthitiḥ* as *rtogs pa* ≈ *pratipatti*). Kamalaśīla continues the commentary as follows (TSP *ad* TS 2958–61, *svataḥprāmāṇyaparīkṣā*, B 942,20–23): *tac cārthakriyājñānam ātmasaṃvedanapratyakṣatayā svayam evāvirbhavati / spaṣṭānubhavatvāc cānantaraṃ yathānubhavaṃ parāmarśajñānotpattyā niścitam iti svata eva siddham /*. "And that awareness of causal function appears just intrinsically (*svayam*)

This passage appears in a context in which the main topic of discussion is the question of when a given means of trustworthy awareness is to be considered intrinsically trustworthy (*svataḥprāmāṇya*) and when it is to be considered extrinsically trustworthy (*parataḥprāmāṇya*), but this is not what is of principal concern to us here. Instead, our attention should be drawn to the idea that when the desired causal function (in other words, one's goal) "appears" in awareness, that is tantamount to one's having attained one's goal. For example, if one's goal is warmth, then when a real, i.e., causally functioning, source of heat, such as a fire, appears in one's awareness, and when one determines that this is so,[658] one will at that time also rightly determine that one has attained one's goal. On the other hand, if some unreal or non-causally functioning source of heat—such as a holographic image of fire—appears in one's awareness, then because this image of fire does not have the expected or desired causal function, one will not determine that one has attained one's goal, and one's quest will go on.

The situation is not quite as simple the above explanation suggests, however, since it is frequently the case that even though the desired causal function appears in awareness, and even though one determines that this is so, one still has *not* attained one's desired goal. For example, if the warmth-giving fire that one seeks is located far away across a field, then the mere arisal of an image of the fire in awareness and the determination of that image as an image of a causally functioning, i.e., real, fire, do not immediately bring about the goal of getting warm, for one still must traverse the distance between oneself and the fire in order to feel its warmth. Kamalaśīla addresses this problem in the following passage, dealing specifically with the question of the trustworthiness of perception:

> That is, inasmuch as it causes the person who desires a [particular] causal function to obtain the desired thing, [perception] is called a means of trustworthy awareness. But it does not make one attain [the desired causal function] by transporting the person to the place where the thing exists, nor by leading the thing to

---

due to being perceived through reflexive awareness (*ātmasaṃvedana*). And because it is a vivid experience, certainty follows immediately thereafter, through the arisal of a judgment (*parāmarśajñāna*) that accords with that experience. Therefore, it is established that [that awareness] is just intrinsic."

658. The "appearance" of the causal function is an instance of perception (*pratyakṣa*) and therefore it is nonconceptual. The determination that the appearance is fire is an instance of a subsequent conceptual definitive determination. See n. 214 above.

> the place where the person exists. Instead, it causes the person to act. Nor does it cause the person to act by taking him by the hand. Rather, [it causes him to act] by revealing to him the object of his action (*pravṛttiviṣaya*). And that revelation comes about through the determination (*avasāya*) of the thing that is appearing [in the perceptual awareness] and not otherwise.[659]

The point of all this is that a means of trustworthy awareness has a twofold function: on the one hand, it is that which causes one to obtain (*prāpaka*) the desired causal function or goal; on the other hand, it is that which causes one to act (*pravartaka*) in such a way that one will be able to attain the desired causal function or goal. But it is only in some cases that the means of trustworthy awareness will itself constitute the attainment of the desired causal function and the immediate justification to engage with that thing; in other cases it will constitute only the justification for taking certain actions that are designed to lead to the *eventual* attainment of the desired causal function.

It is because the means of trustworthy awareness does not always result in an immediate attainment of the desired causal function that the authors introduce the idea of capacity (*śakti*) into their definitions of the means of trustworthy awareness. For example, at one point, Kamalaśīla states that the trustworthiness of a means of trustworthy awareness consists in the fact that it is "correspondent" (*saṃvāda*) with real things, meaning that it has the "capacity to attain a real thing."[660] In another place, he says:

> And being correspondent (*avisaṃvāditva*) consists in having the capacity to attain the thing that is capable of the desired causal function; but it does not consist in necessarily attaining [that thing], because there may be [unforeseen] hindrances.[661]

659. TSP *ad* TS 2972 (*svataḥprāmāṇyaparīkṣā*, 946,15–18): *tathā hy arthakriyārthino 'bhimatam arthaṃ prāpayat pramāṇam ucyate / na cārthadeśaṃ puruṣam upasarpayad arthaṃ vā puruṣadeśam ānayat tatprāpakaṃ bhavati api tu puruṣaṃ pravartayat / taṃ ca puruṣaṃ na hastena gṛhītvā pravartayati / kiṃ tarhi / pravṛttiviṣayam upadarśayat / tac copadarśanaṃ pratibhāsamānārthāvasāyān nānyat /*.

660. TSP *ad* TS 1628 (*pramāṇāntarabhāvaparīkṣā*, B 569,13–14): *arthaprāpaṇaśaktiḥ saṃvādaḥ prāmāṇyam /*.

661. TSP *ad* TS 1311 (*pratyakṣalakṣaṇaparīkṣā*, B 479,23–24): *avisaṃvāditvaṃ cābhimat ārthakriyāsamarthārthaprāpaṇaśaktir na tu prāpaṇam eva pratibandhādisaṃbhavāt /*. Cf. also TSP *ad* TS 2958–61, translated on p. 288 above. See Krasser 1992: 156n22.

To continue with our example: if the arisal of an image of a real, causally functioning fire in awareness is a sufficient justification for the judicious person to begin walking across the field in order to achieve the goal of getting warm, it nevertheless does not guarantee that the person will in fact attain that goal. Some unforeseen event could occur before the person ever reaches the fire, thus preventing him or her from reaching that goal. For example, the person could be struck by lightning and killed. On Śāntarakṣita and Kamalaśīla's view, this unfortunate event would nevertheless not annul the trustworthiness of the initial perception, even though the person never reached the goal. Nor would the event render the person injudicious, since on the basis of the initial perception and subsequent determination of the fire, the person was indeed justified in walking toward the fire to fulfill the goal of getting warm.

Doubt as a Justification for Action

The above example of the person who sees fire from across the field presumed that the person was able to have a genuine subsequent conceptual determination that what he or she was seeing was indeed fire. In other words, the above example presumed there arose for the person a definitive determination (*niścaya*) as to whether the contents of the perception are capable of accomplishing the desired goal. But there are other cases where a definitive determination of the capacity for goal accomplishment does not immediately appear—whether due to lack of experience, confusion, a damaged sense organ, or some other reason—and as long as that determination has not occurred, there will be doubt about whether one's awareness is trustworthy. Acknowledging this state of affairs, Śāntarakṣita says:

> Therefore, for as long as there does not arise an awareness in which the causal functioning [of the desired goal] appears, a doubt concerning the trustworthiness of the initial [awareness] will arise, due to [the possible existence of] causes for error.[662]

The context for this statement is a discussion of an initial perceptual awareness that does not immediately give rise to a definitive determination of its capacity for goal accomplishment. As an example, think of a person who wishes to get warm and who sees what vaguely appears to be a fire (but

662. TS 2965 (*svataḥprāmāṇyaparīkṣā*): *tasmād arthakriyābhāsaṃ jñānaṃ yāvan na jāyate / tāvad ādye 'pramāśaṅkā jāyate bhrāntihetutaḥ //*.

which could, in fact, be a clump of red flowers) from a distance. At this point, the person cannot be certain that what he or she is seeing is a real fire capable of fulfilling his or her goal of getting warm (and not something else that is not so capable, such as a holographic image or a clump of red flowers). In this case, the person will have a doubt, thinking something like, "It looks like there might be a fire over there. If I go near it, I will be able to determine if it is indeed a fire, and if it is, I will be able to fulfill my goal of getting warm. Therefore, I should go over there to determine whether it is a fire." The point here is that not all perceptual awarenesses are capable of immediately giving rise to a determination of the causal capacities of the object of the awareness, and in such cases, it is necessary to take extra steps to come to such a determination.

Given all this, the astute observer might object that Śāntarakṣita and Kamalaśīla appear to have embraced a contradiction. That is, on the one hand they have insisted that a judicious person acts toward a goal as a result of the certainty concerning causal function that is attained by a trustworthy awareness. On the other hand, in the example just cited, it is only through making some initial action toward the thing in question—e.g., in this case, moving toward the fire-like object—that one can come to determine whether the contents of one's awareness are trustworthy. And since one would be acting on the basis of awarenesses whose status as trustworthy was in doubt, one could no longer consider oneself a judicious person. Kamalaśīla, aware of this problem, sums it up as follows:

> That is, there should be action on the part of judicious persons when there has been a definitive determination (*niścaya*) of the trustworthiness [of an awareness]; and the definitive determination of the trustworthiness [of the awareness] comes about [only] when there is activity! Therefore, because there would be a mutual dependence [of these two processes], how could there be any activity on the part of a judicious person when there is no [immediate] definitive determination of the [capacity for the accomplishment of the] desired goal?[663]

This objection is no mere quibble, since it has ramifications for the fundamental claim that the authors are committed to a rationalist expression of their religious philosophy.

663. TSP *ad* TS 2973 (*svataḥprāmāṇyaparīkṣā*, B 947,15–18): *tathā hi prekṣāpūrvakāriṇaḥ prāmāṇyaniścaye sati pravṛttyā bhavitavyam / pravṛttau ca satyāṃ prāmāṇyaniścaya itītaretarāśrayāt kathaṃ prekṣāvata īpsitārthāviniścaye sati pravṛttiḥ syāt /.*

Recall Śāntarakṣita's statement in the opening verses of the *Tattvasaṃgraha* that the Buddha's teaching of dependent arising "is ascertained by the two means of trustworthy awareness, which possess clear definitions."[664] The strong implication of this statement is that it is possible to verify the truth of the Buddha's teaching through rational inquiry. But at the same time, the opening verses also enumerate a whole host of predicates that are said to be true characteristics (*tattva*) of dependent arising, including such things as "being free from the operations of primordial nature, God, both [primordial nature and God], self, and so on" and "having no beginning and no end."[665] Clearly, the verification of all these predicates through rational inquiry will take a significant period of time (witness the considerable length of the *Tattvasaṃgraha* and the *Pañjikā*, which profess to examine all these predicates). And during this long period of inquiry, until such time as the inquirer—whose goal it is to determine the truth of the Buddha's teachings—has obtained a definitive determination that his or her perceptual and inferential awarenesses are indeed capable of accomplishing that goal, the inquirer cannot be sure whether the awarenesses upon which he or she is relying are trustworthy or not! If the person relies upon the awarenesses without knowing whether they are trustworthy, he or she can no longer be considered a judicious, or rational, person, since one of the marks of a judicious person is that he or she relies upon the means of trustworthy awareness to motivate action.

Śāntarakṣita and Kamalaśīla's answer to this objection turns out to be a pivotal point in sorting out the nature of their defense of the Buddha's omniscience as well as in the evaluation of their religious philosophy as a whole. Briefly put, their response is that despite what was earlier said about judicious persons acting on the basis of the certainty or definitive determinations (*niścaya*) generated by the means of trustworthy awareness, it is also accepted that judicious persons sometimes act out of doubt, but only in situations where there is no other way. As Kamalaśīla explains, judicious persons undertake actions of two distinct sorts. The first type of action is oriented toward the accomplishment of some causal function or goal (*arthakriyā*), whereas the second type of action is oriented toward the ascertainment of the trustworthiness (*prāmāṇyaviniścaya*) of some previous awareness. In the case of the first type of action, doubt occurs when the goal one seeks is sufficiently removed in time or space from the initial awareness, so that even though one may have a definitive determination of the capacity of the contents of one's

664. TS 3ab: *spaṣṭalakṣaṇasaṃyuktapramādvitayaniścitam* /.

665. TS 1ab: *prakṛtīśobhayātmādivyāpārarahitam* //; TS 4a: *anādyantam* //.

awareness to fulfill one's goals, some unforeseen obstacle could still arise and thwart the attainment of one's goal. This is like the case of the fire which one sees across the field that we examined earlier.

The example that Kamalaśīla cites is of farmers, and even though the details of the process are not spelled out, they are nonetheless fairly clear. That is, farmers know that certain seeds, when planted and tended, have the capacity to produce desired crops. When they examine their seeds at the beginning of the planting season, there arises for them a definitive determination that the seeds that appear in their present awareness are capable of fulfilling their goal of raising crops. However, because the goal is distant in time, the farmers cannot be sure that some obstacle to the development of the crops will not arise between the time of their planting and the time of their harvest. In this sense, the farmers can be said to have doubt, despite the presence of the definitive determination of the capacity for the accomplishment of their goals. Nonetheless, for Śāntarakṣita and Kamalaśīla, the farmers are not irrational to plant their crops. Indeed, as Śāntarakṣita explains, in such cases "the intelligent person acts precisely due to doubt, and no diminishment of that [person's] intelligence is entailed thereby."[666] The idea seems to be that the doubt "it is possible that these seeds will yield a crop" is a legitimate motivator for planting and tending the seeds for the farmer who wishes to harvest a crop.

In the case of the second type of action, doubt *always* plays a role. An example is the case when one is not sure whether what one is seeing is fire or a clump of red flowers. In such cases, when one's goal is to determine whether a particular awareness is trustworthy or not, one is *necessarily* motivated by doubt. If one has no doubt about whether an awareness is trustworthy, one will not bother to investigate it. Śāntarakṣita and Kamalaśīla do not spend much time defending this view, presumably because it corresponds with a widely held principle of Indian philosophical inquiry that holds doubt to be a prerequisite for any investigation.[667]

Summing up the role of doubt as a motivator for action, then, Śāntarakṣita makes the following statement:

> If, acting out of doubt, I were to obtain my goal, in that case the trustworthiness of the awareness [that initially prompted my action] would be ascertained, [and it would] not [be ascertained]

666. TS 2974 (*svataḥprāmāṇyaparīkṣā*): *ucyate saṃśayenaiva vartate 'sau vicakṣaṇaḥ / vaicakṣaṇyakṣatis tasya na caivam anuṣajyate //*.

667. See NS 1.1.1 and NBh *ad cit.*

otherwise. And therefore, also, it is not right to inquire in this [regard] "Why [should a person] engage in a means [that is not certain]?" because there is no other way. For without a means, no one can accomplish an end; therefore, even though one acts out of doubt, one does not lose one's judiciousness.[668]

Why does one not lose one's judiciousness? The answer seems to be that one is justified in acting in relation to some means even when there is doubt about its outcome *because there is no alternative*. To reject such action would lead to paralysis, for it would mean that whenever one's goal was remote or whenever one wished to verify the trustworthiness of any awareness, one could not act toward that goal.

But there is a second, equally important reason why judiciousness can be preserved when one acts out of doubt. That is, when a rational person acts out of doubt, he or she nevertheless does not do so randomly; instead, the person generally acts in reliance upon precisely the kind of inference that we saw that the authors use in their demonstration of the possibility of omniscience, namely, an "inference of capacity" (*yogyatānumāna*), or "inference of the capacity to produce an effect" (*kāryotpādanayogyatānumāna*).[669]

668. TS 2976–78 (*svataḥprāmāṇyaparīkṣā*): *saṃdehena pravṛttau me phalaprāptir bhaved yadi / prāmāṇyaniścayas tatra jñāta eva bhaviṣyati // nānyatheti na cāpy evam anuyogo 'tra yuktimān / upāye vartate kasmād iti na hy anyathāgatiḥ // na hy upāyād vinā kaścid upeyaṃ pratipadyate / iti saṃdehavṛtto 'pi prekṣāvattāṃ jahāti na //*.

669. Steinkellner (1978) finds explicit evidence that some post-Dharmakīrtian Buddhists conceived of the proof of yogic cognition in terms of the *kāryānumāna* model in a *pūrvapakṣa* preserved in Vācaspatimiśra's *Nyāyakaṇikā* (see also Pemwieser 1991: 138n94). After presenting a proof statement (*prayoga*) for yogic perception that is nearly identical with one preserved in the TSP (*ad* TS 3338, *atīndriyārthadarśiparīkṣā*, B 1060,22–1061,3), the passage goes on to state that the type of reasoning used in the proof is an "inference of the capacity to produce an effect" (*kāryotpādasāmarthyānumāna*), a clear reference to Dharmakīrti's theory in PVSV *ad* PV 1.7–8. Despite the parallels with the TSP, however, Steinkellner (1999: 355) notes, "This application of Dharmakīrti's logical form has no parallel in Kamalaśīla's commentary." I believe that this statement should be qualified. That is, while it appears to be true that neither Śāntarakṣita nor Kamalaśīla refer to the specific logical form of *kāryānumāna* in the context of their proof of yogic perception and omniscience in the final chapter of the TS/P, we have seen above that Kamalaśīla does explicitly discuss it at the outset of the TSP, in his discussion of statement of the aim of a treatise. As I have tried to show, Kamalaśīla's treatment of the question of the aim of a treatise is related to the question of the motives behind the proof of omniscience in the TS/P, since both concern goals whose eventual fulfillment is presently in doubt and since—as Kamalaśīla makes clear—the ultimate aim of the treatise is in any case precisely the arisal of the reader's omniscience. It is therefore significant that Kamalaśīla speaks of the logical

Kamalaśīla refers to this type of inference when speaking of doubt in another context, that of the doubt concerning the aim (*prayojana*) of a treatise. Here, too, he mentions the example of farmers, and he notes that although one cannot know that "it is definite that this [means] will establish just that kind of future result," one *can* reasonably posit that "as long as there is no hindrance or insufficiency in the causal complex, it is definite that this [means] will be sufficient for the production of the desired result."[670] When judicious per-

form of *kāryānumāna*, or as he calls it, "inference of capacity" (*yogyatānumāna*), when discussing the aim of the treatise. Likewise, it is important also to note that Kamalaśīla is emphatic that the inference of capacity does not lead to certainty about a future result, since "those who lack transcendental vision cannot ascertain the nonexistence of hindrances and so on" (TSP *ad* TS 1–6, B 4,16: *pratibandhādyasattvasyaivāparadarśanair niścetum aśakyatvāt*). This is entirely in accord with a Dharmakīrtian reading of the *kāryānumāna* theory. See especially PVSV *ad* PV 1.8. Translated in Gillon and Hayes 1991: 11–12.

670. The context is a discussion of the necessity to state the aim (*prayojana*) of a treatise and the role that stating the aim plays in motivating people to engage with (i.e., read and study) the text. The statements quoted are contained in TSP *ad* TS 1–6, B 4,4–16, wherein is also found a quotation of PV 1.8: *api ca sādhananiścayo 'pi teṣāṃ bhāviphalāpekṣayā bhavann avaśyam etad anāgatam evaṃvidhaṃ phalaṃ sādhayiṣyatītyevaṃrūpo bhavet yad vā pratibandhakasahakārivaikalyayor asaṃbhave saty avaśyam abhimataphalasaṃpādanāyālam etad ityevaṃrūpaḥ / na tatra tāvad ādyo yuktarūpaḥ saṃbhavatsahakārivaikalyapratibandhakopanipātasya kasyacid upalabdhatathāvidhaphalasyāpi śālyāder anāgataphalaṃ praty asādhanatvadarśanena sarvatrāśaṅkāyā avyāvṛtteḥ / yad āha / sāmagrīphalaśaktīnāṃ pariṇāmānubandhini / anaikāntikatā kārye pratibandhādisaṃbhavāt // iti / atha dvitīyas tadā yuktataram etat / evaṃrūpatvād eva sarvasyāḥ pramāṇapūrvikāyāḥ pravṛtteḥ / ata eva cācāryās tatra yogyatānumānena viśeṣaṇaṃ vidadhati / asati pratibandhe yogyam etad iti / kiṃ tu phalam apy anena rūpeṇa niścitam eveti na sādhanasyaiva niścayaḥ / na cāpy evaṃpravṛttau paramārthataḥ phalaniścayapūrvikā pravṛttiḥ siddhyati / pratibandhādyasattvasyaivāparadarśanair niścetum aśakyatvāt //* "Furthermore, their certainty about the means also being construed in terms of a future result, it would take the form of the idea 'it is definite that this [means] will establish just that kind of future result.' Or else, [it would take] the form of the idea 'as long as there is no hindrance or insufficiency in the causal complex, it is definite that this [means] will be sufficient for the production of the desired result.' Concerning these, first of all, the first one is incorrect, since it is observed that some rice and so on, even though it has been perceived to have a particular kind of effect, has been unexpectedly afflicted by some potential hindrance or else by a insufficiency in the supporting conditions [and therefore] is not a means for [producing] the future effect. Hence that [means] does not eliminate doubt in all cases. As [Dharmakīrti] has said [at PV 1.8], '[A complete causal complex] is inconclusive evidence for an effect which is invariably connected with the development of the potentials which are themselves the effect of that complex. [It is inconclusive] because a hindrance might occur.' And as for the second [idea concerning the certainty of the means], it is quite correct, because all action that is preceded by a trustworthy awareness is just of that kind. And thus the *ācārya*

sons act on the basis of doubt, therefore, they do not do so indiscriminately; instead, they act only in cases where their doubt in informed by a definitive determination of the causal capacities of that which is presently appearing to their perceptual awareness. That is, there may be a doubt as to whether one will in fact reach one's goal, but there is no doubt that the means one is taking up are *theoretically capable* of allowing one to reach that goal.

In the context of this discussion of the reasons for stating the aim of a treatise, Kamalaśīla explains that one engages in the act of studying a treatise due to a doubt (in the sense of a suspicion) that the treatise might lead one to the accomplishment of one's aim, a goal that is clearly remote. Since one would initially have the same doubt in relation to all treatises, the statement of the subject matter and the aim of the treatise allow one to orient one's doubt toward the means in question, namely the study of that particular treatise. Kamalaśīla seems to recognize that this process does not ensure either that one's aim will be fulfilled or that the text will in fact discuss what one hopes it will (a treatise could claim to be about liberation and turn out to be about medicine, or worse, crows' teeth). But, as he notes, since "it is not possible to obtain an undesired result from a treatise," desisting from reading the text on the basis of a doubt that misfortune might befall one is not very reasonable.[671] The idea seems to be that one is taking a calculated and reasonable risk in reading a text whose stated aim corresponds to one's own. Certainly there is a chance that one's aim will remain unfulfilled, but the chances that it will be fulfilled are also increased by the fact that the aim of the text is stated to be one that corresponds with one's own.

Not all doubt is equal in its capacity to induce action in judicious persons. On Kamalaśīla's analysis, the key criteria for determining when acting on the basis of doubt is justified is that the doubt be the cause for the adoption of specific or distinct means (*pratiniyatasādhanopādānahetu*).[672] In a case where

---

[Dharmakīrti] establishes a qualification in this regard [which consists of being] an inference of the capacity [to produce a future effect, and which takes the form of] the idea 'if there is no hindrance, there is this capacity.' But not [in the form] 'in this way the result is also certain.' There is certainty only of the means. And neither is it the case that at the time of action, the action is ultimately established to be preceded by certainty with regard to the effect, because those who lack transcendental vision cannot be certain that no hindrance and so on exists." Translation of PV 1 quotation by John Dunne.

671. TSP *ad* TS 1–6 (B 5,15): *nāpy anārthāvāptiśaṅkā śāstrād aniṣṭaphalāvāptyasaṃbhavāt* /.

672. See, e.g., TSP *ad* TS 1–6 (B 5,19–22): *na ca prayojanamātrasaṃdehāt pravṛttir yuktā sarvatraiva pravṛttiprasaṅgāt / prayojanamātrasya cānarthitatvāt / kiṃ tu pratiniyatasādhanopādānahetoḥ prayojanaviśeṣaviṣayāt saṃśayāt pravṛttir dṛśyate* /. "And

one is equally doubtful about all possible means, one's doubt cannot act as a cause for taking up some particular means as opposed to all others. Lacking knowledge of the means for attaining one's goal, one has no basis to choose between, say, practicing generosity and eating rocks![673] In such a situation, a judicious person would never act at all, since it is not possible to act on all possible means. It seems that the only solution, if one is to act in such a situation, is to rely upon a statement—whether of a scripture or an ordinary treatise—to orient one's doubt toward particular means. We saw an example of this type of situation just above when we considered Kamalaśīla's theory

---

it is not reasonable that one act through a doubt concerning a mere goal [in general], because there would be the undesired consequence that one would act toward everything, and because there is not the desire [on the part of the actor] for a mere goal. Rather, it is observed that [people] act through a doubt that is oriented toward a particular goal, which [doubt] is the cause for taking up specific means." That doubt must be oriented toward a particular goal may be a pan-Indian assumption. For some speculation on the general lack of interest in "bare possibilities" in Indian philosophy, see Mohanty (1992: 20), who suggests that we adopt Husserl's notion of a "motivated possibility" as a model for interpreting possibility in Indian thought.

673. The reference to eating rocks comes in a passage in which Kamalaśīla compares the practice of promulgating scriptures (*āgama*) concerning radically inaccessible entities with the practice of stating the purpose at the beginning of a treatise; we discuss this analogy of the statement of the purpose to the promulgation of scripture just below. For the passage on eating rocks, see TSP *ad* TS 1–6 (B 7,1–7): *avaśyaṃ caitad evaṃ vijñeyaṃ / anyathātyantaparokṣārthaviṣayāgamapraṇayanam api vyarthaṃ syāt / prāg apy āgamapraṇayanād dānādiṣu phalaviśeṣārthināṃ sādhakabādhakapramāṇābhāvena tatsaṃśayasya vidyamānatvāt / kiṃ tv asāv avyutpannasvargādiphalānāṃ naivotpadyate / tatkāraṇabhūtāyāḥ phalaviśeṣārthitāyā asaṃmukhībhāvāt / yeṣāṃ copajāyate teṣām api sarvatropalādibhakṣaṇe 'pi pravṛttihetutayā sādhāraṇatvād upalādibhakṣaṇaparihāreṇa na pratiniyatadānādiparigrahahetur bhavatīti matvā tadartham āgamapraṇetṛbhir āgamaḥ praṇīyate tadvat prayojanavākyam api śāstrakārair ity acodyam etat /*. "And it should definitely be understood in this manner. Otherwise, the promulgation of a scripture whose object is a radically inaccessible entity would be pointless, because even before the promulgation of the scripture there exists doubt concerning that [radically inaccessible] entity on the part of a person who desires a particular result, due to the lack of any probative or contravening trustworthy awareness in relation to [the ascertainment of] giving and so on [as a means for accomplishing the goal]. But this doubt does not even arise for those who have not learned about results such as heaven and so on, because the desire for the particular result that is the cause of that [doubt] is not apparent [to them]. But even for those in whom [the doubt] does arise, because it would be a cause for action with regard to all things, including even eating rocks and so on, it is a [cause for action] in general; therefore, [it] is not a cause for taking up specific [means] such as giving, while avoiding the eating of rocks and so forth. Thinking this, the scripture is quoted by the one quoting it for the sake of those [persons]. Likewise, the author of the treatise makes the statement of the aim. This is undeniable."

that the reason for stating the aim of a treatise is to induce a person whose aim corresponds to that treatise to adopt the specific means of reading the treatise.

The situation with regard to omniscience is different, however. For one thing, unlike engaging with reading a text, putting into effect the practices aimed at attaining omniscience *could* prove harmful (at least in the sense of proving to be an extraordinary waste of an enormous amount of time) if it turns out that they do not in fact lead to the desired goal. Fortunately, however, judicious persons are in a better circumstance with regard to omniscience, at least if they have taken the time to study the *Tattvasaṃgraha* and the *Pañjikā*. For, as we have seen, the work's general demonstration of omniscience contains both a demonstration of the possibility of dharmic omniscience and a demonstration of the specific means that are supposed to bring it about. Thus, although a judicious person may wonder whether he or she will ever in fact arrive at omniscience, he or she may be certain that the means to attain omniscience do exist and that those means may be determined through rational inquiry. As such, the judicious person may be justified in taking up these means with the intention of attaining omniscience, the ultimate goal of the treatise as a whole.

Faith and Judicious Persons

At the very outset of the *Pañjikā*, when Kamalaśīla first mentions the purpose of the treatise, he clarifies his opinion that Śāntarakṣita wrote the opening verses of the *Tattvasaṃgraha* in order to induce judicious persons to read and study his treatise, since he recognized that such persons will engage with a text only after they have determined its subject matter (*abhidheya*) and purpose (*prayojana*). But, as we have seen above, in addition to setting forth the contents and purpose of the text that is to follow, Śāntarakṣita's opening verses also contain an homage to the Buddha, praising him as "that omniscient one." In Kamalaśīla's view, Śāntarakṣita includes this homage because he knows that "the primary cause of obtaining the highest good is faith (*prasāda*) in the great beings."[674] The implication is

674. TSP *ad* TS 1–6 (B 2,5–8): *iha hi śāstre prekṣāvatām abhidheyaprayojanāvasāyapūrvikā pravṛttir mahatsu ca prasādaḥ sarvaśreyo 'dhigateḥ kāraṇaṃ prathamam ity ālocya bhagavati prasādotpādanārthaṃ śāstre cāsminn ādareṇa śrotuḥ pravṛttyarthaṃ svaśāstṛpūjāvidhipūrvakam asya śāstrasya prakṛtītyādibhiḥ ślokais tattvasaṃgraha ityetatparyantair abhidheyaprayojane prāha* /. "Having perceived that judicious people act toward a text having first determined its subject matter (*abhidheya*) and aim (*prayojana*) and that the primary cause of obtaining the highest good (*sarvaśreya*) is faith in great beings,

that faith in the Buddha and other such great beings is a necessary condition for obtaining the highest goal of this tradition; in short, faith is a prerequisite for attaining omniscience.

Later, however, when elaborating on this idea that Śāntarakṣita's homage is for the purpose of inducing faith in the Blessed One (i.e., the Buddha), Kamalaśīla divides the potential audience for the *Tattvasaṃgraha* and the *Pañjikā* into two distinct groups: those inclined toward faith (*śraddhānusārin*) and those inclined toward wisdom (*prajñānusārin*). Kamalaśīla explains that for audience members of the first type, a mere statement in which the greatness of the Buddha is proclaimed is sufficient to give rise to unshakable faith in the Blessed One:

> The act of worshiping the teacher, however, is for the sake of engendering faith in the Blessed One, which [faith] is the cause of the attainment of everything good. That is to say, by that undertaking of the statement of the host of good qualities, the supreme greatness of the Blessed One is proclaimed. And having heard that, there will first of all quickly arise for those who are inclined toward faith a faithful mindset (*cittaprasāda*) free from doubt [and] directed toward the Blessed One.[675]

But for audience members of the second type, i.e., those who are inclined toward wisdom, producing faith is considerably more complex, because for such persons it is necessary to first ascertain through rational means that the extraordinary qualities attributed to the Buddha are indeed possible. As Kamalaśīla says:

> But those who are inclined toward wisdom, not seeing any refutation (*bādhaka*) of these kinds of [qualities], and understanding that good qualities such as wisdom and so on [can reach] perfection (*prakarṣa*) through habituation (*abhyāsa*), [will

[Śāntarakṣita] states the subject matter and the aim of the treatise, preceded by the act of honoring his own teacher, by means of the first six verses [literally: the verses that begin with *prakṛti* and end with the word *Tattvasaṃgraha*] in order to generate faith in the Blessed One and to cause the listener to respectfully engage with this."

675. TSP *ad* TS 1–6 (B 9,1–3): *śāstṛpūjāvidhānaṃ tu bhagavati sarvaśreyo 'dhigatihetoḥ prasādasyotpādanārthaṃ / tathā hi guṇagaṇākhyānavidhināmunā bhagavato 'tiśāyo māhātmyam udbhāvyate / tad upaśrutya ca śraddhānusārimanasāṃ tāvad asaṃśayaṃ bhagavati jhagiti cittaprasādaḥ samudeti /*.

> determine]—through the means of trustworthy awareness that will be stated [and] which establishes the seer of supersensible objects—that "certainly these kinds of sages are possible in the world." [And] having determined this, they indeed produce faith in the Blessed One.[676]

The reference to the trustworthy awareness that establishes the seer of supersensible objects is a clear allusion to the final chapter of the *Tattvasaṃgraha* and the *Pañjikā*, the "Investigation of One Who Sees Supersensible Objects." The implication of this statement in the opening pages of the *Pañjikā* is that the final chapter of the work was written for those who are inclined toward wisdom, in order that they might ascertain the possibility of supersensible seeing, in other words, omniscience. It is this ascertainment of the real possibility of their goal that is termed "faith" for those who are inclined toward wisdom. In other words, for those who are inclined toward wisdom, faith is really a particular kind of certainty.[677]

It might seem odd that those who are inclined toward wisdom have need of faith at all. Yet Kamalaśīla tells us twice that faith (*prasāda*) in great beings is the primary or chief cause of the attainment of everything good, up to and including the highest good. How this is so becomes clear in the following passage:

> And due to [their] faith in that [Blessed One], those who desire the good qualities of that [Blessed One] apply themselves to the words of that [sage] and to the treatises and so forth that are based on those [words], having first investigated them, in order to memorize them and so on. Thus, through the sequence of producing the wisdom that arises through study and so on, they attain [all goodness] up to the highest good. Hence, the chief cause for the attainment of the highest good is faith in the great beings.[678]

676. TSP *ad* TS 1–6 (B 9,4–6): *ye 'pi prajñānusāriṇas te 'pi tathāvidheṣu bādham apaśyantaḥ prajñādīnāṃ ca guṇānām abhyāsāt prakarṣam avagacchanto vakṣyamāṇād apy atīndriyārthadṛksādhakāt pramāṇān nūnaṃ jagati saṃbhāvyanta eva tathāvidhāḥ sūraya ity avadhārya bhagavati prasādam upajanayanty eva* /.

677. It is worth noting that Śāntarakṣita and Kamalaśīla appear to use the terms *prasāda* and *śraddhā* interchangeably, though this merits further investigation. See Rotman 2009 for a study of faith in Indian Buddhist *avadāna* literature, including the ways in which these two terms may be seen to diverge significantly.

678. The first sentence is translated from the Tibetan, as the Sanskrit is unintelligible. TSP *ad* TS 1–6 (D, vol. *ze*, 138b2–3): *de la dang bas kyang de'i yon tan mngon par 'dod*

The principal role of faith—and the reason that it is considered so important—is that faith allows one to apply oneself to the practices that have been set forth by the Buddha and his followers and thus to begin to generate three kinds of wisdom: wisdom arisen from study (*śrutamayīprajñā*), wisdom arisen from deliberation (*cintāmayīprajñā*), and wisdom arisen from meditation (*bhāvanāmayīprajñā*). Faith, in other words, allows one to move beyond a mere intellectual curiosity about Buddhist texts to an engagement with those texts that involves a more deeply committed application of the teachings and the eventual realization of its ultimate goals.

The role of faith, then, is to act as a catalyst in getting judicious people to undertake the practices that will lead to worldly and spiritual advancement; and this is the reason that Kamalaśīla says that faith is "the chief cause for the attainment of the highest good." But this is the only sense in which faith is primary. For as Kamalaśīla also says, the actual cause of both worldly and spiritual attainments is freedom from error (*aviparyāsa*), which consists in the correct reasoned confidence (*abhisaṃpratyaya*) in the laws of actions and their effects and in the correct understanding (*avabodha*) of the selflessness of persons and things.[679] And it is precisely this freedom from error that one achieves through the study of, deliberation upon, and meditation on the teachings found in texts, such as the *Tattvasaṃgraha* and the *Pañjikā*, that accurately make known the Buddhist teaching of dependent arising. One needs faith in order to begin to study, contemplate, and meditate on the teachings, but it is the reasoned confidence and understanding that arise from that study, deliberation, and meditation that eliminate error or ignorance.

It seems then that those who are inclined toward faith are not to be counted among judicious persons at all, since they are swayed by hearing a mere proclamation of the Buddha's great qualities. Judicious persons, as we know, do not generally act on the strength of mere proclamations but rely on the means of trustworthy awareness instead. Those who are inclined toward wisdom, however, are clearly judicious. For such persons, faith is really a kind of certainty concerning the possibility of their own future omniscience and

---

pa rnams de'i gsung rab dang de la brten pa'i bstan bcos la sogs pa la brtag pa sngon du 'gro bas 'dzin pa la sogs pa'i don du gus par byed do. The second sentence is from the Sanskrit at TSP *ad* TS 1–6 (B 9,8–9): *tataḥ śrutamayyādiprajñodayakrameṇa yāvat paraṃ śreyo 'dhigacchantīti mahatsu prasādaḥ sarvaśreyo 'dhigateḥ pradhānaṃ kāraṇaṃ /*. For the other location where Kamalaśīla states that faith is the primary cause of obtaining the highest good, see n. 674 above.

679. See p. 107 above.

the means by which they believe they shall get there. It is this kind of faith that Kamalaśīla has in mind when he says that faith is the principal cause of all that is good.

Summation: Motives for the General Demonstration

In sum, it seems fairly clear that the motive behind the general demonstration is to provide a rational justification for judicious persons to begin to practice the Buddhist teachings with the aim of attaining the highest possible state, that of a perfect, omniscient buddha. Because judicious persons will not act toward that which is impossible or unreal, it was necessary that the authors establish the theoretical possibility of omniscience, a feat they accomplish in two stages. On the first stage, they show that at the very least omniscience is a matter of doubt, in that it is not possible to establish that omniscience cannot exist. Next, on the second stage, they demonstrate the causes by which omniscience may be reached, thereby establishing its theoretical possibility. For the judicious person who follows and accepts this reasoning, it is now possible to take up the practices designed to lead to omniscience (e.g., the meditation on selflessness) without thereby losing his or her judiciousness. For even without certainty concerning the ultimate result, it is not irrational to act toward a future goal if one has certainty about the capacity of certain causes to lead to that goal. Although some unexpected obstacle may still arise, one can be certain that omniscience is possible, and one is therefore justified in setting out to obtain it as one's goal.

Motives for the Specific Demonstration

In turning to the question of the motives behind the formulation of the specific demonstration of omniscience, we should recall our earlier discussion of the fundamental tension inherent in it. This tension revolves around the question of the status of the omniscient person's mental qualities as radically inaccessible for ordinary beings. As we saw above, there is no obvious solution to this tension, although a couple of possibilities do present themselves. That is, the tension may be resolved by reference to the claim that the *real* object of the demonstration is not, in fact, the mental qualities of the omniscient person but only the theoretical possibility of omniscience in general, such that the specific demonstration becomes a mere corollary of the real—that is, the general—demonstration. Or, the tension may be resolved by reference to the intelligence of the person to whom the argument is directed, whereby the omniscient person's mental qualities are radically inaccessible only for those who are dull-witted but are actually inferable for those of greater acuity.

Whether we accept one, both, or neither of these solutions, there is a further version of the tension that appears even more troubling. That is, the prohibition against the inferring of mental qualities occurs in the *Pramāṇavārttika* as well as the *Tattvasaṃgraha* and the *Pañjikā* in the context of the respective discussions of scripturally based inference (*āgamāśritānumāna*), i.e., discussions about whether it is possible to rely on the statements found in scriptures authored by a credible person (*āpta*) to gain knowledge of radically inaccessible matters. According to some readings, both the demonstration of the Buddha's authority and the demonstration of the Buddha's omniscience are intended to guarantee that the Buddha can be trusted on radically inaccessible matters. But if such is the case, then the tension in the specific demonstration becomes more acute, since the purpose of the proof would be to ground the teachings that concern radically inaccessible things and yet the object of the proof would itself *be* a radically inaccessible thing.

As in the general demonstration, we face the problem that the authors do not clearly and unambiguously state their motives for presenting the specific demonstration of the Buddha's omniscience. But whereas in the case of the general demonstration we are able to rely upon various statements concerning the nature of doubt and faith, as well as on an interpretation of the authors' theories of the justification of action, and thereby to arrive at a theory concerning the motive of the proof, a clear picture of the rationale for the specific demonstration is significantly more elusive. In this section we will consider three hypotheses concerning the authors' purpose or purposes in presenting the specific demonstration. Each hypothesis has advantages and problems, and I have found it impossible to settle on any one of them as representing the single most plausible motivation of the authors. Possibly, all three theories are valid—although if they are, it is probably best to see them as being so in relation to distinct audiences.

Briefly, here are the three hypotheses for the motivation behind the specific demonstration. The first follows closely on our findings concerning the motivation for the general demonstration. According to this hypothesis, the specific demonstration is intended to allow those judicious persons who wish to practice the Buddhist path to go for refuge in the Buddha. Although the evidence for this theory is relatively scant, it is nonetheless compelling in that it suggests a motivation for the proof that is not at all in tension with other aspects of these authors' thinking. The second hypothesis is the thorny one mentioned just above, according to which the purpose of the specific demonstration is to ground the Buddhist teachings in the omniscience of the Buddha. This hypothesis accords closely with a number of modern interpretations of the motivation of the regressive or *pratiloma* portion of Dharmakīrti's proof for the Buddha's authority in *Pramāṇavārttika* 2. It is also the most difficult of the three hypotheses to evaluate, since, as we will see, the evidence is not only scant but also problematic. The third hypothesis is that the specific demonstration is not intended for Buddhist practitioners but is designed to address those non-Buddhists who insist that the authority or credibility of scriptures may only be known by reference to the credibility of their author. Indirect evidence for this theory can be garnered from several passages, though there is nothing that would speak in favor of this theory alone. We will consider each hypothesis in turn.

First Hypothesis: Causing Judicious Persons to Go for Refuge

In the previous chapter, we said that the audience for the *Tattvasaṃgraha* and the *Pañjikā* as a whole consists of judicious persons whose aim corresponds with that of the treatise, namely, the attainment of elevation and the highest good. Of these two goals, the later one—the highest good—is the ultimate goal and is equivalent to liberation and omniscience. We next saw that the general portion of the defense of omniscience is directed at those judicious persons inclined toward wisdom whose aim is liberation but who have not yet ascertained that omniscience and its causes are possible. Assuming that Śāntarakṣita and Kamalaśīla hold their proofs to have persuasive power, it is not absurd to imagine that they consider the next portion of the defense, the specific demonstration, to be for the benefit of those judicious persons who *have* ascertained that omniscience and its causes are possible.

Evidence to this effect is available in the long passage describing the specific demonstration that we cited earlier, where Kamalaśīla says:

> For those who wish to put into practice that which was said by that one [i.e., the Buddha], it is reasonable to prove that he is omniscient and an authority (*pramāṇabhūta*) on the basis of his being endowed with knowledge.[680]

From this statement, we can readily recognize one component of the audience that Śāntarakṣita and Kamalaśīla have in mind for this portion of the defense of omniscience: namely, judicious persons who desire omniscience,

680. TSP *ad* TS 3339 (*atīndriyārthadarśiparīkṣā*, B 1061, 23–24). See n. 577 above.

who have faith in—in other words, who have ascertained through the means of trustworthy awareness—the possibility of omniscience and its causes as they are explained in Buddhist texts, and who now wish to engage in the practices (i.e., study, deliberation, and meditation) that will allow them to accomplish their goal. Once again, we can note that the context is one of the justification of action—the emphasis is on the "wish to put into practice" what the Buddha taught—and not only the justification of belief.

Postulating this characterization of the audience for the specific demonstration does not, however, provide an answer to the question of why Śāntarakṣita and Kamalaśīla might think that the specific demonstration would be necessary for those who "wish to put into practice" what the Buddha taught. Another passage we can cite, again from the introductory section of the *Pañjikā*, may give a clue. The statement comes in a section where Kamalaśīla is explaining why Śāntarakṣita chose to praise the Buddha in terms of his teaching of dependent arising. Kamalaśīla says:

> That is, because of possessing the perfection of these kinds of good qualities, [i.e., an "immeasurable host" of good qualities], he causes [others] to attain elevation and the highest good; therefore the Blessed One is the teacher of the world. And that itself should be stated to be the reason that those who desire elevation and the highest good go for refuge and so on in the Blessed One, as well as [the fact that] the Blessed One causes [others] to attain elevation and so on through teaching dependent arising.[681]

In this passage, we see an indication of a possible motive for stating the specific demonstration of the Buddha's omniscience, namely, to allow those who desire the aims of the treatise and of the Buddhist path to "go for refuge" (*śaraṇagamana*) in the Buddha. The act of "going for refuge" in the three jewels—the Buddha, his teaching (the Dharma), and the Buddhist community (the Saṅgha)—is frequently seen as a necessary first step in becoming fully engaged with the Buddhist path.[682] For some, it is the act of going

681. See TSP *ad* TS 1–6 (B 13,1–4): *tathā hi yathābhūtaguṇasaṃpadyogād abhyudayaniḥśreyasaprāpaṇatojagataḥśāstābhavatibhagavān / saevābhyudayaniḥśreyasārthināṃ bhagavaccharaṇādigamanahetur abhidhānīyaḥ / pratītyasamutpādadeśanayā cābhyudayādisaṃprāpako bhagavān /*. Kamalaśīla goes on after this to describe a process that proceeds from taking refuge all the way up to the attainment of buddhahood. See n. 295 above.

682. See, e.g., AKBh *ad* AK 4.32.

for refuge that marks one as a Buddhist.[683] In this passage, Kamalaśīla states explicitly that the Buddha's perfection of various good qualities, and his ability to impart the teachings necessary to attain those same qualities, provide the warrant for "going for refuge" to the Buddha.[684] The demonstration of the Buddha's omniscience in the specific portion of the proof, according to this hypothesis, may best be understood as being for the purpose of allowing judicious persons to go for refuge in the Buddha, thus initiating their full engagement with the Buddhist path. And this make sense, for in order that one go for refuge in someone or something (in the sense of deciding to rely upon that thing in some sense), it is necessary that one know what the qualities of that thing are and that one deem those qualities useful to one's goals.

Second Hypothesis: Grounding Buddhist Scriptures

The second hypothesis concerning the motives for the specific demonstration is that Śāntarakṣita and Kamalaśīla mean for it to ground Buddhist scriptures in the Buddha's authority. According to this theory, the motivation behind the demonstration for omniscience is structurally the same as the motivation behind the demonstration of the credibility (*āptatva*) of a tradition's founder that is commonplace in Indian sources and that we have already briefly encountered above.[685] In both cases, the argument goes, the author of the demonstration uses rational argumentation to ground scriptures in the credibility of their author. A scripture whose author can be shown to be a credible person (*āpta*), with all of the extraordinary qualities that this credibility entails, is then considered to be a reliable source of knowledge. Such, in any case, is the generally accepted analysis of the motivation behind the theories of *āptatva* among Indian philosophical schools like the Jain, the Naiyāyika,

683. E.g., Lcang skya rol pa'i rdo rje, *Grub mtha' thub bstan lhun po'i mdzes rgyan* (*Krung go bod kyi shes rig dpe skrung khang* ed., p.58).

684. Vasubandhu expounds a view according to which going for refuge in the Buddha is understood as going for refuge in the perfect (*aśaikṣa*) qualities that make one a buddha; it is interesting that in this context Vasubandhu specifically mentions omniscience, albeit in the form of the capacity omniscience that he prefers. See AKBh *ad* AK 4.34: *yo buddhaṃ śaraṇam gacchati / aśaikṣān asau buddhakarakān dharmāñ charaṇaṃ gacchati / yeṣāṃ prādhānyena sa ātmabhāvo buddha ity ucyate / yeṣāṃ vā lābhena sarvāvabodhasāmarthyād buddho bhavati //*. "One who goes for refuge in the Buddha goes for refuge in the perfect qualities that make one a buddha; [one goes to refuge in those qualities] due chiefly to which that person is called *buddha* and due to the attainment of which [that one] is capable of knowing everything and therefore is a buddha."

685. See pp. 258–61 above.

and the Vaiśeṣika.[686] The question is whether a similar analysis applies in the case of the *Tattvasaṃgraha* and the *Pañjikā* or not.

On the face of it, one might easily assume that the motivation behind the specific demonstration of the Buddha's omniscience in the *Tattvasaṃgraha* and the *Pañjikā* is, at least in part, to show that the Buddha was a credible person and that whatever he said must be true. Certainly, this seems to have been recognized as Kumārila's basic assumption, as he is reported to have said, "Omniscience is claimed in order to establish the truthfulness of the scriptures of a particular person."[687] More recently, Richard Hayes, in his article on doctrinalism in the Buddhist *pramāṇa* theory tradition, cites some

686. See, e.g., NS 2.1.69: *mantrāyurvedaprāmāṇyavac ca tatprāmāṇyam āptaprāmāṇyāt* /. Translated in van Bijlert 1989: 31 as follows: "And the fact that the [Vedas] are a means of valid cognition [i.e., have authority] like the fact that incantations and medical science are a means of valid cognition [i.e., have effective authority, is derived] from the fact that experts are a means of valid cognition." For the Jain position, see Singh 1974: 47–48, who states, "Jainism denies both God and the Vedas, but it is nonetheless a religion. Hence, it needed the *Tīrthaṅkaras*, who would function as the source of its scripture. The *Tīrthaṅkaras* in order to be reliable (*āpta*) must be omniscient, the knower of the universal principles ... Unless a *Tīrthaṅkara* is all-knowing, how can he create a reliable *āgama*?" Singh cites several Jain sources on the question of *āptatva*, including the *Tattvārthasūtra* of Umāsvatī with Pūjyapāda's commentary, the *Āptamīmāṃsā* of Samantabhadra, and the *Āptaparīkṣā* of Vidyānanda. The Jain contribution to the role of the *āpta* and to the question of omniscience has unfortunately been generally understudied in the modern academy. In the case of the Mīmāṃsakas, as we have seen, there can be no proof of the authority of a founder, since they assert that their scripture, the Veda, is eternal and does not have an author, either human or divine. This theory of the authorlessness (*apauruṣeyatva*) of the Veda, however, does not prevent the Mīmāṃsakas from claiming authoritative status for their scriptures. Indeed, it is this very fact that the Veda has no author that ensures its credibility for the Mīmāṃsakas, since unlike the eternal speech of the Veda, human authors are held to be always and necessarily fallible. Thus, although the authority on which the scriptures are grounded is not a personality, the basic structure of seeking to rationally ground scripture in an infallible source remains the same. For more on the theory of *āptopadeśa* in various Indian traditions, see Oberhammer 1974. For the Nyāya-Vaiśeṣika tradition, see Biardeau 1964: 120–27; Chemparathy 1983; and Franco 1997. For the Jain tradition, see Soni 1996.

687. TS 3231ab (*atīndriyārthadarśiparīkṣā*): *yadīyāgamasatyatvasiddhyai sarvajñatocyate* /. This statement, which is presumably from the *Bṛhaṭṭīkā*, is also preserved in the Jain author Anantakīrti's *Bṛhatsarvajñasiddi* (see Frauwallner 1962: 82–83). Cf. also Kumārila's verse preserved at TS 3139 (*atīndriyārthadarśiparīkṣā*): *svadharmādharmamātrajñasādhanapratiṣedhayoḥ / tatpraṇītāgamagrāhyaheyatve hi prasiddhyataḥ* //. "For the establishment and the refutation of [whether] one's own [teacher] knows just Dharma and Adharma establishes whether the scriptures composed by that person are to be taken up or to be abandoned." Reading °*heyatve* with G instead of °*hetutve* with B.

verses close to the end of the *Tattvasaṃgraha* to reinforce his contention that the aim of the demonstration of the Buddha's omniscience is to anchor the authority of the Buddhist teachings in the Buddha's extraordinary knowledge (although Hayes does acknowledge that for these thinkers "each doctrine must stand up under empirical and rational investigation").[688] The verses that Hayes cites are as follows (in my translation):

> The following statement is supported by the means of trustworthy awareness: distinguished among all persons through having obtained a unique method (*asādhāraṇopāya*), that one [i.e., the Buddha] is the peerless omniscient Lord, whose stainless teaching is this well-cultivated (*svabhyasta*) selflessness of *dharma*s, which is proved by the whole treatise [i.e., the *Tattvasaṃgraha*] and which is not refuted by any means of trustworthy awareness ... And in this way, since it is reasonable that there is someone who

688. Hayes 1984: 665. Hayes' general interpretation, which applies to his reading of Dharmakīrti's proof of the Buddha's authority as well, is that these thinkers were trapped in the confines of dogma in a rationalist guise. As he explains (1984: 666), "in Śāntarakṣita we seem to have come full circle to a situation in which the overriding concern is with doctrine—specifically, the Buddhist doctrine that everything necessary for salvation is within the reach of human beings without a need for divine help or divinely inspired knowledge—rather than with a genuinely disinterested philosophical investigation into the limits of knowledge." The notion that these thinkers were dogmatic about their rationality is an interesting one. In effect, Hayes is saying that they upheld the dogma that their religious philosophy was free from dogma. While Hayes may be right about this, it seems highly unlikely that Śāntarakṣita and Kamalaśīla would accept this description of their approach to religious and philosophical truth. Of course, Hayes could still be correct in the sense that Śāntarakṣita and Kamalaśīla could be deluded about the degree to which their religious philosophy is nondogmatic. My concern here is not to decide whether Śāntarakṣita and Kamalaśīla were dogmatic. Rather, I am interested in showing that Hayes's statement (1984: 663) that "Śāntarakṣita's central thesis is that the authority of Buddhist scriptures derives from the omniscience of the Buddha" is incorrect. I grant, however, that I may be placing too much emphasis on this single statement in Hayes's article. Perhaps Hayes did not mean to imply that Śāntarakṣita and Kamalaśīla wish to *ground* the truth of their religious philosophy in the words of the Buddha but rather merely wished to point out that for the authors of the TS/P, the truth of the Buddhist scriptures necessarily requires the Buddha's own, individual realization of that truth (which is a different point that in fact *does* correspond to what we find in the TS/P). When he states, however, that the *authority* of the scriptures derives from the Buddha's omniscience, it is difficult to avoid the impression that Hayes did indeed want to argue for such a grounding of the Buddhist scriptures in the Buddha's omniscience. In any case, I don't think that such a claim is warranted.

> is omniscient, therefore human speech *is* a cause for the understanding of Dharma and so on.[689]

These verses, along with other passages,[690] seem to lend support to the hypothesis that the purpose of the specific demonstration is to ground what is stated in the Buddhist scriptures in the Buddha's omniscient authority and thus credibility. After all, Śāntarakṣita *seems* to be saying that *because* the Buddha is omniscient, *therefore* we can trust that what he says about Dharma must be true.

There remains, however, another possibility for how to interpret passages such as these, one that would not take Śāntarakṣita's statement that the Buddha's speech is the cause for the understanding of Dharma and so on as implying that a Buddhist practitioner's belief in Dharma and so on is *justified* because she has heard it from the Buddha. Instead, on this interpretation, the statement would indicate only that the Buddha, with his direct knowledge of things that are only inferentially available to ordinary beings, teaches the Dharma, which the disciples then examine to see if it is correct. It is the result of the individual disciple's own rational inquiry that ultimately justifies his or her acceptance of what is stated in the scriptures. Since Śāntarakṣita and Kamalaśīla hold all of the important matters (*pradhānārtha*) taught in the Buddhist scriptures to be definitively determinable through ordinary

689. TS 3640 and 3643–44 (*atīndriyārthadarśiparīkṣā*): *svabhyastadharmanairātmyā yasyeyaṃ deśanāmalā / sādhitā sarvaśāstreṣu sarvamānair abādhitā // … // labdhāsādhāraṇopāyo 'śeṣapuṃsāṃ vilakṣaṇaḥ / sa ekaḥ sarvavin nātha ity etat sapramāṇakam // itthaṃ yadā ca sarvajñaḥ kaścid evopapadyate / dharmādyadhigame hetuḥ pauruṣeyaṃ tadā vacaḥ //*. Reading °*śāstreṣu* in TS 3640 with G in place of °*śāstreṇa* as found in B; and reading *vilakṣaṇaḥ* in TS 3643 with G in place of *vilakṣaṇāt* as found in B; both readings are supported by the Tibetan at D 133b. Hayes (1984: 665) translates these lines as follows: "This is a statement for which there is good evidence, namely, that the omniscient lord who has acquired unique talents that distinguish him from the rest of mankind is none other than him whose faultless teaching, in which selflessness is the constantly repeated thesis, is established throughout the present work and is not overturned by any means of knowledge. That being the case, it turns out to be plausible that someone is omniscient, from which it follows that *human* teachings can result in an understanding of truth." The verb "is" in the final sentence of my translation is emphasized to indicate that this verse is a mirroring of the final verse from the Mīmāṃsaka *pūrvapakṣa* in the final chapter of the TS (i.e., TS 3260), in which it is stated that because there is no omniscient person, "therefore human speech is *not* a cause for the understanding of *Dharma* and so on"; *itthaṃ yadā na sarvajñaḥ kaścid apy upapadyate / na dharmādhigame hetuḥ pauruṣeyaṃ tadā vacaḥ //*.

690. Cf., e.g., TSP *ad* TS 3126 (*atīndriyārthadarśiparīkṣā*), where we see Kamalaśīla agreeing, even insisting, that the authority of a scripture is rooted in the authority of its author. See n. 370 above.

perception and inference, the Buddhist practitioner is well positioned to ascertain whether what the Buddha said on these matters is correct or not. While the disciple would admittedly not be able to verify whether what the Buddha said concerning radically inaccessible entities is true or not, this would not be particularly problematic, since all the important things (in other words, all that leads to the highest good, or Dharma) can be tested. This analysis seems to be very much more in keeping with the overall emphasis on the rationality of the judicious person that one finds in the *Tattvasaṃgraha* and the *Pañjikā*.

The Buddha, on this reading, may then be fairly said to be *a* cause (in the sense of a contributing factor) for the understanding of the Dharma, in that he provides the initial impetus for the disciple's rational inquiry, but he is not the only, or even the principal, cause. The principal cause of the disciple's understanding and acceptance of Dharma is the certainty that arises in relation to the Dharma through the process of rational analysis to which the disciple subjects it. Proving the Buddha's credibility or authority, then, could *at most* serve the limited purpose of grounding scriptures on radically inaccessible matters and would not at all be necessary for grounding the Buddhist scriptures or teachings more generally.

This interpretation is an example of what we may call the *linear approach*, as opposed to the *circular approach*, to the grounding scriptures hypothesis. Although an analysis of these two approaches to the question of the grounding of Buddhist scriptures in the omniscience of the Buddha has not, to my knowledge, appeared in the secondary literature in relation to the *Tattvasaṃgraha* and the *Pañjikā*, examples of both these approaches can be found in the secondary literature on Dharmakīrti's demonstration of the Buddha's authority or trustworthiness in *Pramāṇavārttika* 2. Since the structure of the demonstration of omniscience in the *Tattvasaṃgraha* and the *Pañjikā* is so similar to, and appears to be based upon, the structure of Dharmakīrti's demonstration of the Buddha's authority in *Pramāṇavārttika* 2, it may help to review some of the secondary literature that interprets Dharmakīrti's chapter in terms of these two interpretive schemes.

The Circular Approach

By now, a considerable body of secondary literature has appeared debating the question of the degree to which Dharmakīrti is or is not invested in the project of grounding Buddhist scriptures in the authority of the Buddha.[691]

691. See especially Dunne 2004; Eltschinger 2001; Franco 1997; Hayes 1984; Jackson 1988, 1993, 1999; Nagatomi 1959; Ruegg 1994a, 1994b, 1995b; Steinkellner 1982, 1983; Tillemans 1990, 1993; van Bijlert 1989; and Vetter 1964, 1990.

At the heart of the debate is the question of the significance of Dharmakīrti's demonstration of the Buddha's authority or trustworthiness (*prāmāṇya, pramāṇabhūtatva, pramāṇatā*) in *Pramāṇavārttika* 2, which, as we have seen, provides an important model for the arguments in the final chapter of the *Tattvasaṃgraha* and the *Pañjikā*.[692] The first and most obvious problem is simply the tradition's insistence that the means of trustworthy awareness are necessarily restricted to perception (*pratyakṣa*) and inference (*anumāna*). Verbal testimony or scripture (*śābda*) is not considered to be an independent means of trustworthy awareness but rather only a rather limited type of inference that yields knowledge of a speaker's intention to speak of something, as we saw above.[693] Given this, Dharmakīrti's attempt to prove the Buddha's authority or trustworthiness at first appears superfluous. This impression diminishes to some extent when one takes into account Dharmakīrti's theory of scripturally based inference, in which, on some readings, certain statements—namely, those uttered by a credible person—can be accepted as yielding knowledge of external entities. If this is the case, then Dharmakīrti's proof of the Buddha'a authority might after all have the rational grounding of Buddhist scripture as its goal.

This seems to be the conclusion that a number of modern interpreters have settled on—a few of whom have chosen to cast this scenario in terms of the circularity that it implies. Nagatomi speaks of the "reciprocal relation" that obtains between the *pramāṇa* theory system and the faith that Buddhist *pramāṇa* theory philosophers have in the Buddha's words.[694] Stein-

692. Dharmakīrti states that he has proven the Buddha's authority (*pramāṇatā*) at PV 2.282: *dayayā śreya ācaṣṭe jñānād bhūtaṃ sasādhanam / tac cābhiyogavān vaktuṃ yatas tasmāt pramāṇatā //*. "He proclaims the highest good due to compassion, the truth together with its methods due to [his] knowledge; and he exerts himself for the sake of stating that [truth that conforms to the highest good together with the methods for achieving the highest good]; therefore he is an authority." Unfortunately, Dharmakīrti does not seem to ever tell us *why* he undertook this proof nor precisely what is implied by it.

693. See pp. 253–56 above.

694. Nagatomi 1979: 246: "The testing of the validity of the Buddha's words requires a tool which was for Dignāga and Dharmakīrti the *pramāṇa*, the valid means of cognition. Such a tool, at least in principle, may be expected to be one which is universally acceptable to all and free from dogmatic premises and presuppositions. Both Dignāga and Dharmakīrti struggled to achieve that end by polemically refuting the number and definitions of *pramāṇa*s of the non-Buddhist schools which were contradictory to their own. We must note, however, that the final authority by which they claimed the validity of their *pramāṇa* system was none other than the Buddha's words which they accepted as authentic by faith. Thus the Buddhist *pramāṇa* system and the authenticity of the

kellner and Vetter envision a "historical-factual circle" (*historisch-sachlicher Zirkel*) in which "[the Buddha's] authority legitimizes the trustworthiness of perception and inference," although they appear to understand this circularity at least partially in the historical sense that it was the Buddha who first introduced the idea of a religious system in which the means of trustworthy awareness were limited to perception and inference.[695] Hayes is less forgiving, stating that in offering a proof for the authority of the Buddha, Dharmakīrti has not been able to avoid a "vicious circularity" that sets the stage for "the post-Dharmakīrtian tendency to deal with questions of logic and epistemology merely as components within a much larger systematic apology of Buddhist dogma...."[696] Although they differ in their judgment of the appropriateness of Dharmakīrti's demonstration, these scholars all share the idea that its purpose is in some sense to ground the entire range of

Buddha's words stood, in reality, in a reciprocal relation: the structuring of the former was done within the limits of the latter, and the latter was meant to be supported by the former."

695. See Vetter (1964: 27) and Steinkellner (1982: 11) for the reference to the "historical-factual circle." See also Vetter (1964: 33–34) for the idea that the circularity is primarily a question of historical precedence: "Es mag etwas künstlich erscheinen, die Wahrheit über die Erkenntnismittel aus der Lehre des Buddha abzuleiten. Aber Dharmakīrti is historisch im Recht. Nur durch das Auftreten des Buddha gibt es in Indien ein religiöses System, das nur Wahrnehmung und Schlussfolgerung anerkennt und jede Überlieferung, die als solche schon massgeblich sein will, ablehnt." Assessing Vetter and Steinkellner's position is rather more difficult than it at first appears. The introduction of the historical component could indicate a shift toward something closer to what I call the "linear approach" to the problem of the Buddha's authority. Still, a significant number of quotations remain in which the entire range of Buddhist teachings (including those that are not radically inaccessible to ordinary beings) are said to gain their legitimacy from the Buddha's authority. See, e.g., Vetter 1964: 27: "Er gilt as Erkenntnismittel, weil seine Autorität die Massgeblichkeit von Wahrnehmung und Schlussfolgerung legitimiert." Cf. also Steinkellner 1982: 11: "The structural scheme of these ideas of Dharmakīrti turns out to be a true circle: The decisive defining characteristic of a means of valid cognition (*pramāṇa*) is the demand that it must stand the test of meaningful practice (*avisaṃvādana*), and connects it with the Buddha as the one on whose authority one knows what meaningful practice is. The reciprocity then is brought about by the need to prove this authority of the Buddha. For the words of the Buddha (*āgama*), as such, have neither guarantee for their truth nor for success on following their advice. Their validity has to be accounted for, and it is accounted for by the Buddha himself: 'The statement that the Buddha is a means of valid cognition is proven through reference to the means by which he has become one.'" The final statement in this sentence is from Vetter 1964: 32.

696. Hayes 1984: 661 and 663.

teachings found in Buddhist scriptures by means of an appeal to the authority or credibility of their author.

The Linear Approach

Not everyone is satisfied with this circular approach to Dharmakīrti's demonstration of the Buddha's authority. Tillemans, for example, taking his cue in part from the Mongolian Dge lugs pa author Ngag dbang stan dar, rejects the circular interpretation in favor of a linear depiction in which "it is the teaching which must invariably be judged first to assess a religious teacher's worth."[697] Tillemans argues that understanding the proof for authority as unidirectional accords better with Dharmakīrti's own insistence on the priority of "belief-neutral" reasoning (especially the so-called "inference that functions through the force of real entities" or *vastubalapravṛttānumāna*) in assessing the truth of any matter, including that of scriptural sources.[698] On this view, which Tillemans shares with his Tibetan and Mongolian sources, one first establishes (in the *anuloma* phase) that the Buddhist teachings are "faultless" (*skyon med*) using the ordinary means of trustworthy awareness of perception and inference, and subsequently (in the *pratiloma* phase) one uses the teachings as effect-evidence (*kāryahetu*) to infer that the teacher was also faultless.[699] The point here is that although one can and does use Buddhist scriptures as evidence to infer the Buddha's authority, one does so using only the tools of perception and inference, which themselves are rationally justified through human reasoning that functions independently of any scriptural or personal authority.[700] In this way, the question of the "vicious circle"

697. Tillemans 1993: 19. Ngag dbang bstan dar, or A lag sha Ngag dbang bstan dar, lived from 1759–1804 and was a Mongolian author who wrote in Tibetan. Tillemans' annotated translation of this author's work on the "person of authority" (*tshad ma'i skyes bu* = *pramāṇapuruṣa*), the *Ston pa tshad ma'i skyes bur sgrub pa'i gtam*, was reviewed in van der Kuijp 1999.

698. Tillemans (1993: 22) cites PV 4:48–59 as the location of one passage where Dharmakīrti argues for the need for *vastubalapravṛttānumāna* to "function without any dependence upon the words of writers of treatises (*śāstrākāra*)."

699. Cf. Ngag dbang bstan dar's *Ston pa tshad ma'i skyed pur sgrub pa'i gtam* in Tillemans 1993: 39–43.

700. Tillemans (1993: 22) sums up understanding on this point as follows: "If we take Dharmakīrti's own views, there seems to me to be little evidence that he held that inference and perception were in any way *dependent* on the authority of the Buddha. On the contrary, *Pramāṇavārttika* seems to go to great lengths to establish that *vastubala*-inference has to function independently of *all* appeals to personal or textual authority; it must be used *before* we can speak of the holiness of a Master (cf. PV I, k. 218–19), and should

raised by Hayes is resolved because there is no circle to begin with, whether vicious or benign.[701]

The Problem with the Linear Approach

The fundamental problem with this otherwise seemingly quite reasonable assessment of the proof for the Buddha's authority is that it fails to explain the purpose of Dharmakīrti's lengthy and apparently complex arguments for the Buddha's authority in *Pramāṇavārttika* 2. If the Buddhist teachings (or at any rate all the most important ones) are all already vouched for by perception and inference, what need is there to ground those teachings in the authority of the Buddha?

Two possibilities suggest themselves. First, advocates of the linear approach

---

function without any dependence upon the words of writers of treatises (*śāstrakāra*) (cf. PV IV, k. 48–59). Indeed, for us to be able to assess a teacher by examining his teachings, it is essential that there be no beliefs on questions of the authority of someone's words at the time we analyse the truth of those words via inferences. This is clearly brought out by the insistence in PV IV, k. 48–49, that *vastubalapravṛttānumāna* is the method for assessing propositions in treatises, and *hence* that there can be no beliefs or acceptances at the time of making such an inference. In short, Dharmakīrti was himself arguably aware of a potential circularity and wished to avoid it by insisting that *vastubalapravṛttānumāna* had to be belief-neutral."

701. As an example of Tillemans' thinking on this topic, consider the following passage (1993: 23): "Steinkellner, in his 1983 article, may have given us some clues as to what was being meant [in a previous citation from Vetter 1964]. In this article the Buddha was characterized as 'the final source and judge of any validity and usefulness in any kind of cognition' (1983: p. 276). Skipping the question as to whether the Buddha is a *real pramāṇa*, or is only one in the Tibetan *sgras brjod rigs kyi sgo nas* sense, it is nonetheless clear that Dharmakīrti did maintain that the Buddha was all-knowing. Does this mean that he is the *final source and judge* of any validity in any kind of cognition, including presumably the inferences establishing that he is *pramāṇabhūta*? That would lead to circularity by a very direct route: a full or even adequate evaluation of the proof of the Buddha's authority would presuppose the truth of that very same proof's conclusion. It is, however, hard to find any convincing evidence to support the view that the point of Dharmakīrti's *Pramāṇasiddhiparicched a* [i.e., PV 2] was that the Buddha is literally the final source and judge of the *validity* of all other *pramāṇas*. Even if the Buddha's being all-knowing meant that he knew the validity or invalidity of all cognitions, it seems that Dharmakīrti's position was that the truth of the Buddha's words—which is *at least* a necessary condition for establishing *pramāṇabhūta*—could and *should* be judged independently of our accepting the Buddha as being authoritative. In other words, we come back to Ngag dbang bstan dar's point that the Buddha's authority or all-knowingness should not be used as a logical reason (*hetu*) to establish that his words are authoritative. And if that is so, then there is no circle." Note that Tillemans does not offer any evidence for his claim that "Dharmakīrti did maintain that the Buddha was all-knowing."

might simply assert that the proof has nothing to do with the grounding of scriptures in the Buddha's authority. Instead, they might argue for a motive for the proof of the Buddha's authority that is similar to the motive we postulated in our first hypothesis concerning Śāntarakṣita and Kamalaśīla's specific demonstration of omniscience: that is, the demonstration is designed to allow judicious persons who desire to engage in the Buddhist path to justify their action of going for refuge to the Buddha. It seems that something along these lines informs the thinking of Ngag dbang bstan dar, at any rate, who speaks of the determination of the teacher as authoritative as a "cause and condition" for entering the teaching.[702]

The second explanation for the motive behind the proof of the Buddha's authority would preserve the intuition that the proof of the Buddha's authority is intended to ground the Buddhist scriptures, but it would limit that grounding to radically inaccessible or *atyantaparokṣa* matters. As far as I know, no contemporary scholar has explicitly argued that Dharmakīrti's motivation in establishing the authority of the Buddha was to ground scripture in this restricted manner, although Tillemans has emphatically argued for the related point that scripturally based inferences (*āgamāśritānumāna*) must be limited to *atyantaparokṣa* matters, a point which seems well supported by the *Pramāṇavārttikasvopajñavṛtti*.[703] Now, it is undeniable that Dharmakīrti accepts the use of scripturally based inference—and even urges its use—for practical purposes when there is no other way.[704] On some readings of Dharmakīrti's position, moreover, it is the credibility or authority of the scripture's author that serves to justify acceptance of a scriptural statement concerning a radically inaccessible entity.[705] Thus, it is certainly legiti-

702. In Ngag dbang bstan dar's text, for example, we find the following statement (section 19 in Tillemans' edition): *yang bstan pa skyon med yin pa rgyu mtshan du byas nas ston pa po tshad ldan gyi skyes bur nges pa dang / de nas ston pa tshad ldan gyi skyes bur nges pa des rgyu dang rkyen byas nas de'i bstan pa la 'jug dgos pa yin pas . . . / /*. Tillemans (1993: 42–43) translates as follows "On the other hand, one ascertains that the teacher is an authoritative person by taking as the reason the fact that the teaching is faultless, and then, with this ascertainment that the teacher is an authoritative person as cause and condition, one should then enter into his teaching. . . ." Since going for refuge is often seen as the first step of "entering the Buddha's teaching," I see Ngag dbang bstan dar's analysis of the motive behind the proof of the Buddha's authority in PV 2 as similar to my first hypothesis.

703. See Tillemans 1990: 32 and 1993: 16.

704. See especially Tillemans 1990, 1999a.

705. This is the position that Tillemans (1993: 15–16) dubs the "transfer of credibility" method of justifying scripturally based inference; we discuss this in the following section.

mate to consider the possibility that the *pratiloma* portion of Dharmakīrti's proof is intended to allow Buddhists to rely on the scriptures for knowledge of radically inaccessible matters.

Nonetheless, even this rather limited appeal to the Buddha's credibility as a way to ground scriptures has frequently received a rather halfhearted reception by later Buddhist epistemologists.[706] Śāntarakṣita and Kamalaśīla are no exception to this trend, and we will soon see that their skepticism about appeals to an author's credibility presents a serious stumbling block for our second hypothesis as well, even when that hypothesis is restricted to suggest that only *atyantaparokṣa* matters are grounded in the Buddha's credibility. To understand how this is so, we must take a closer look at the theory of scripturally based inference as it is found in the *Pramāṇavārttika*, the *Tattvasaṃgraha*, and the *Tattvasaṃgrahapañjikā*.

The Presentation of Scripturally Based Inference

At the outset of the section in which he considers the conditions under which a statement may serve as a scripturally based inference, Dharmakīrti offers a verse setting out an initial set of criteria that must be in place:

> A statement (*vākya*) that is a worthy subject of examination is one that is coherent (*saṃbaddha*), offers a suitable method, and cites some human aim. Other statements are not worthy subjects of examination.[707]

By themselves, however, these criteria do not suffice to render a statement eligible to be relied upon as a scripturally based inference. Further restrictions are announced in *Pramāṇavārttika* 1.215, which is the locus of a method that comes to be called the *threefold analysis*[708] for testing whether an author's statements may be considered reliable when it comes to radically inaccessible entities. The verse states:

706. Tillemans (1993: 16) emphasizes Ngag dbang bstan dar's doubts about the validity of the process by which statements concerning radically inaccessible matters that are attributed to an author whose words on empirical (i.e., *pratyakṣa* and *parokṣa*) matters can be shown to be true are to be accepted merely on that basis.

707. PV 1.214: *saṃbaddhānuguṇopāyaṃ puruṣārthābhidhāyakam / parīkṣādhikṛtaṃ vākyam ato 'nadhikṛtaṃ param //*. Translation from Dunne 2004: 361–62. Also cited at TSP *ad* TS 1–6 (B 2,18–19).

708. The term comes from the Tibetan commentarial tradition: *dpyad pa gsum*.

> Its [i.e., a scripture's] trustworthiness consists of not being contradicted by perceptual awareness and by the two kinds of inference with regard to both the observable (*dṛṣṭa*) and unobservable (*adṛṣṭa*) things (*artha*) that are the objects (*artha*) of those statements.[709]

According to this method, a scripturally based inference requires that one first determine whether the statements in question are reliable in matters that are independently verifiable through perception and inference. That is, using ordinary perception one first determines that everything the statements claim concerning perceptible (*pratyakṣa*) matters is true; and then, using ordinary inference, one further verifies that everything said about inferable (*parokṣa*) matters is also true. The third step is to verify that none of statements' claims concerning radically inaccessible (*atyantaparokṣa*) matters contradict either these other, independently verifiable propositions or each other. If the statements pass all three of these tests, then the statements are said to be "purified," and one is justified in relying on their claims concerning radically inaccessible matters. Notice that according to this method, the criterion for testing the reliability of the scripture is not the credibility of the author but rather the overall trustworthiness of the scripture itself.

Śāntarakṣita and Kamalaśīla advocate this method as well. In the last chapter of the *Tattvasaṃgraha* and the *Pañjikā* they apply this method to the speech of the Buddha. We can start by citing the relevant verse:

> [The Sugata's speech] is coherent (*saṃbaddha*), with a suitable method [for achieving its aims]; it sets forth that which is useful for humans (*puruṣārtha*); it does not in the least contradict the two means of trustworthy awareness with regard to the object that is seen as well as [that which is unseen].[710]

709. PV 1.215: *pratyakṣeṇānumānena dvividhenāpy abādhakam / dṛṣṭādṛṣṭārthayor asyāvisaṃvādas tadarthayoḥ //*. The two kinds of inference are the ordinary *vastubalapravṛttānumāna* form of inference and scripturally based inference. Regarding the terms observable (*dṛṣṭa*) and unobservable (*adṛṣṭa*), my understanding is that the observable refers to the objects of both perception and ordinary inference while the unobservable (or "nonempirical") refers to the supersensible objects of scripturally based inference.

710. TS 3342 (*atīndriyārthadarśiparīkṣā*): *saṃbaddhānuguṇopāyaṃ puruṣārthābhidhāyakam / dṛṣṭe 'py arthe pramāṇābhyām īṣad apy aprabādhitam //*. Cf. PV 1.214, cited just above in n. 707. The term *dṛṣṭa* here refers to that which is empirically observable, either through perception or inference; its counterpart is *adṛṣṭa*, the nonempirical.

The first half of this verse is clearly modeled on *Pramāṇavārttika* 1.214, cited above. The second half of the verse represents a shorthand way of referring to the threefold analysis as presented in *Pramāṇavārttika* 1.215. This becomes clear in Kamalaśīla's commentary, which starts off with a question about whether the speech of non-Buddhist teachers such as Kapila might not be acceptable as scripturally based inference, since they are also coherent and are oriented toward a human aim. The question and the relatively lengthy response are as follows:

> [Question:] Well, is not all this the case for the speech of Kapila and the others? [Answer:] Here he says, "It does not in the least contradict" and so on. In saying "with regard to the [object that is] seen" he intends that which is the object as well as that which is not the object of perception and inference. "The two means of trustworthy awareness" are perception and inference. "It does not contradict [them]" since things exist in the way that they are taught [by him]. That is, the [Buddha] maintained that the five aggregates, which are characterized as (1) blue and so on; (2) happiness, suffering, and so on; (3) the grasping of cognitive signs; (4) attachment and so on; and (5) awareness are perceptible. And it is not possible for it to be otherwise. And those things that are held to be not perceptible are indeed not perceptible—things that others maintain are perceptible, such as happiness as the conjunction (*saṃniveśa*) with form, sound, and so on, and substance, activity, universals, conjunctions, and so on. Likewise, those things that he maintained to be the objects of inference that operates through the force of a real entity (*vastubalapravṛttānumāna*) are indeed like that (*tathābhāva eva*); for example, the nobles' four truths. And those things that he asserted are not the objects of that [kind of inference] indeed are not its objects—things such as the self (*ātman*) and so on that others maintain are the objects of inference that operates through the force of real things. The words "as well as (*api*)" show that the [speech of the Sugata] is also not mistaken with regard to that which is not seen. That is, he first explained the nature of attachment and so on and the nonvirtue that arises from it. Then, in order to eliminate that [attachment and its effect] by means of what contradicts the vision of a self that is that cause of that [attachment], he taught the antidote, which is just the vision of selflessness. But such is not the case for scriptures like those of Kapila and the others, which do not contradict the

> cause of that [attachment] and which advise such things as ritual bathing and fire sacrifice.[711]

Here we see all three elements of the threefold analysis: there is the test by perception in which all that is claimed to be perceptible is shown to be perceptible and all that is claimed to be not perceptible is shown to be not perceptible. There is the test by inference in which all that is claimed to be inferable is shown to be inferable and all that is claimed to be not inferable is shown to be not inferable. And finally there is the test of the statements on radically inaccessible matters, in which such statements are shown to be not in contradiction with the findings of the two means of trustworthy awareness or among themselves.[712] As we can see, on the "purification" or threefold analysis model, the credibility of the author does not play any overt role in determining whether a statement may be used as a scripturally based inference.

The credibility of the author does, however, come into play for Dharmakīrti in his statements at *Pramāṇavārttika* 1.216–17 and *Svopajñavṛtti ad cit.* The first of these two verses recapitulates Dignāga's statement on the classification of the speech of a credible person as inference, adding that one relies on a credible person's testimony only "because there is no other way" (*agatyā*). The

711. TSP *ad* TS 3342 (*atīndriyārthadarśiparīkṣā*, B 1063,6–17): *nanu caitat sarvaṃ kapilādivākyeṣv apy astīty āha dṛṣṭe 'pītyādi / dṛṣṭe pratyakṣānumānaviṣayatvenābhiprete / pramāṇābhyāṃ pratyakṣānumānābhyām / aprabādhitaṃ yathānirdiṣṭasyārthasya tathābhāvāt / tathā hi nīlādisukhaduḥkhādinimittodgrahaṇarāgādibuddhilakṣaṇasya skandhapañcakasya pratyakṣatvenābhimatasya nānyathātvaṃ saṃbhavati / apratyakṣatvena cābhimatānām apratyakṣateva / yathā paraiḥ pratyakṣābhimatānāṃ rūpaśabdādisaṃniveśānāṃ sukhādīnāṃ dravyakarmasāmānyasaṃyogādīnāṃ ca / tathā vastubalapravṛttānumānaviṣayatvenābhipretānāṃ tathābhāva eva / yathā caturṇām āryasatyānām atadviṣayatveneṣṭānāṃ cātadviṣayatvam eva / yathā parair vastubalānumānaviṣayatvenābhimatānām ātmādīnām / apiśabdād adṛṣṭe 'pi na vikriyeti darśitam / tathā hy atra rāgādirūpaṃ tatprabhavaṃ cādharmam uddiśya tatprahāṇāya tannidānātmadarśanavirodhena nairātmyadarśanam eva pratipakṣo deśito na tu kapilādiśāstravat tannidānāviruddhaḥ snānāgnihotrādir upadiṣṭaḥ //*. Cf. PVSV *ad* PV 1.215, on which this passage is clearly based. The reading *cādharmam* in place of B and G: *vā dharmam* is based on D, vol. *'e*, 302a6–7: *de ltar 'dod chag la sogs pa'i ngo bo dang chos ma yin pa de las byung bar bstan nas*....

712. As we see here, although the process has been characterized as a "threefold analysis," it might be better thought of as an analysis consisting of five steps. That is, for both perception and inference, the scripture must in fact be "purified" in *two* ways, one positive and one negative. The final test is the test of noncontradiction between the statements made about radically inaccessible entities (i.e., the nonempirical) and entities that are amenable to perception and inference (the empirical).

second of these verses, however, appears to offer an alternative to the threefold analysis, a method we can call a *transfer of credibility*,[713] although it is also possible (but far from certain) that Dharmakīrti intends this method not as an alternative but rather as a complement to the earlier method.[714] According to this second method, one is justified in using statements as scripturally based inferences only after one has verified that the statements are correct on the most important matters (*pradhānārtha*), which in the present context means that the statements are correct on the crucial soteriological questions of what is to be taken up (*heya*), what is to be abandoned (*upādeya*), and how these are to be accomplished in order to attain liberation or *nirvāṇa*. This method appears to be considerably looser than the threefold analysis. For one thing, it does not explicitly require that we test *all* the claims in the statements but only those that concern the most important matters. In addition, it does not explicitly require that the statements on *atyantaparokṣa*

713. For the term, see Tillemans 1993: 15–16, who in his discussion of the method contained in PV 1.217 explains that certain Tibetan authors, notably Ngag dbang bstan dar and Mkhas grub rje, conceived of this method as resting on the logical evidence of the author of two statements being the same (*rtsom pa po gcig yin pa'i rtags*). The idea seems to have been that (15) "if an author is correct in his statements about a set of states of affairs X, which are more profound states than those in the set Y, then we can infer he is correct about Y," a procedure which the above authors and Tsong kha pa have compared with (16) "Āryadeva's position in *Catuḥśataka* XII k. 280, a *kārikā* where Āryadeva argues that *because* the Buddha was right on *śūnyatā* we can infer that he was right on [*atyanta*] *parokṣa* too." Apparently, however, both Mkhas grub rje and Ngag dbang bstan dar had difficulty in accepting this procedure—with its (16) "distinctively inductive aspect"—as concordant with Dharmakīrti's overall system. Mkhas grub rje presented differing accounts in his *Sde bdun rgyan yid kyi mun sel* and his *Rnam 'grel ṭīk chen*, in the latter text only allowing (16) "one watertight method for assessing scripture in Dharmakīrti: the threefold analysis." On this view, the method in PV 1.217 (16) "is just a way of showing a particular *dṛṣṭānta*, but not a *hetu*." On the other hand, Mkhas grub rje does seem to allow for the second method as a full-fledged alternative to the threefold analysis in his *Sde bdun rgyan yid kyi mun sel*. Although there are arguments for interpreting the second method as presenting a particular instance of the application of the threefold analysis rather than as an alterative method (Tillemans refers us to Candrakīrti's remarks in his *Vṛtti* on *Catuḥśataka* 12.280; see Tillemans 1993: 17n29), Dharmakīrti's own references to the "speech of a credible person" (*āptavacana*) and to the pointlessness of the speaker making a false statement without a purpose tend to support an interpretation of the verse as offering a viable alternative for judging scripture based on the credibility of the author. As Tillemans comments, however, the (16) "change or vacillation in mKhas grub rje's thought ... may even stem from a genuine obscurity in Dharmakīrti's own position."

714. Dharmakīrti introduces the verse by stating that "Or else, in another way, credible speech [or: the speech of a credible person] is said to be an inference because it is trustworthy" (*athavānyathāptavādasyāvisaṃvādād anumānatvam ucyate*).

matters be free from conflict with statements on *pratyakṣa* and *parokṣa* matters (it is impossible, however, to imagine Dharmakīrti granting scripturally based inference status to statements that *did* contain such contradictions).[715] Finally, and most problematically, Dharmakīrti in his commentary seems to imply that this method depends on the most important matters having been spoken by a credible person (*āpta*), despite the problems that we examined above that arise as a result of his immediately subsequent apparent denial (at *Pramāṇavārttika* 1.218–19 and *Svopajñavṛtti ad cit.*) on the ability to know that any particular person is indeed an *āpta*.

Unlike Dharmakīrti, Śāntarakṣita and Kamalaśīla do not seem to overtly consider the *transfer of credibility* option for determining whether a statement can serve as a scripturally based inference. Like Dharmakīrti, however, these authors do seem to offer a second alternative to the threefold analysis, which consists in a method grounded in "faith" (*śraddhā*). The passage in which this alternative method is found occurs in the general context of Śāntarakṣita and Kamalaśīla's critique of the Mīmāṃsaka commitment to the authorless and eternal status of the Veda. The passage is found in a section of the text dedicated to the refutation of the Mīmāṃsaka's notion of the power or capacity (*śakti*) of words, the supersensible and eternal connection between words and their meanings. For Buddhists, one consequence of holding such a position would be that ordinary persons (which they point out are, in any case, the only kind of persons that Mīmāṃsakas are willing to accept) would not have access to the meaning of the Veda. Nonetheless, because they would have no choice, people would be forced to try to learn the meaning from other ordinary people, which would naturally be futile.

In the *Tattvasaṃgraha* and the *Pañjikā*, the Mīmāṃsaka opponent responds to this argument by noting that the Buddhist tradition, with its humanly authored scriptures, is in the same predicament. The meaning of the scriptures must always be learned from fallible (i.e., unenlightened) persons, thus throwing the whole project of gaining certainty from scriptures into doubt. Śāntarakṣita gives the following retort:

> [Response:] This is not right, because [people] engage in that

715. PVSV *ad* PV 1.217 specifically notes that the statements are "not contradicted" (*anuparodhāt*), indicating that the criteria for contradiction that were set forth in PV 1.215 should carry over to this second method as well. Indeed, PV 4.48–52 (translated in Tillemans 2000: 78–82) bolsters this impression. Not only do these verses argue that a treatise's statements on *atyantaparokṣa* objects should not be accepted until the treatise's claims concerning *pratyakṣa* and *parokṣa* objects have been verified, they also indicate that it is invalid to accept the claims concerning *atyantaparokṣa* entities if they contradict the treatise's (verified) claims on *pratyakṣa* and *parokṣa* matters.

> [text which is authored by a person] due to faith (*śraddhā*) or else (*api vā*) [people engage in the text] due to doubt about a [supersensible] object, [but only] when the [subject] matter has been purified through perception and inference.[716]

The purification of the text mentioned in the second half of this statement corresponds to the method of the threefold analysis discussed above. Kamalaśīla explains that the purification of the text is what allows one to engage with that text even when one has doubts.[717] The first half of this statement, however, seems to provide an alternative method (indicated by the phrase *api vā*) for how one can rely on scriptures: namely, as it says, through faith. What did Śāntarakṣita mean by this? Might this be an expression of the transfer of credibility idea that has appeared so problematic to interpreters of Dharmakīrti? Since Śāntarakṣita himself says nothing more, we must look to Kamalaśīla's commentary for an idea:

> "In that" means in that [text] which has a human author and which contains desired teachings on what is to be abandoned and the means to do so, [i.e., texts whose teachings are] useful for [the accomplishment of] human aims. That is, the wise Buddhists engage [with the text] observing reason alone (*nyāyam eva*) and not due to mere rumors [of the text's excellence]. "Due to faith" (*śraddhayā*) simply means due to confidence (*abhipratyayena*), i.e., due to the certainty (*niścayena*) that is produced through deep

716. TS 2773cd–2774ab (*śrutiparīkṣā*): *na tatra śraddhayā vṛtter arthasaṃśayato 'pi vā // pratyakṣeṇānumānena viśuddhe viṣaye sati /*. Although Jha does not do so in his translation, it seems necessary to read 2773cd together with 2774.

717. At TSP *ad* 2773cd–2774ab (*śrutiparīkṣā*, B 892,13–17), Kamalaśīla raises an objection and then clarifies Śāntarakṣita's position as follows: *yady evaṃ yena kenacid āgamena kiṃ na bhavān pravartate / sandehasya sarvatra tulyatvād ity etac codyanirākaraṇāyedam āha / pratyakṣeṇetyādi / yatra pratyakṣānumānābhyām abhimatasyārthasya tathābhāvo na virudhyate tena pravartamānaḥ śobheta saty api saṃśaye / na tu yatrānyathābhāvas tatra dṛṣṭapramāṇoparodhitānarthasaṃśayasyodbhūtatvāt //*. "[Objection:] Well, if that is the case, then why do you not engage with just any text whatsoever, since all of them are equally doubtful? [Response:] In order to dispel this objection, he says, 'When the [subject] matter has been purified through perception and inference' and so on. Even when there are doubts, it would be appropriate to engage with a text in which the reality of the intended meaning is not contradicted by either perception or inference. But [it would] not [be appropriate to engage in a text] where it is otherwise, since in that case there would arise a doubt that [the meaning of the text] was wrong due to its being in conflict with means of trustworthy awareness regarding the empirical [i.e., that which is amenable to perception and inference]."

> contemplation of reasoning. For confidence with regard to a thing is reasonable only when [that thing] is established through the means of trustworthy awareness (*pramāṇasiddha*); it is not [reasonable] with regard to other [things], because there will be no cessation of doubt with regard to those [things].[718]

I think we must acknowledge that this explanation has nothing to do with the idea of a transfer of credibility or of faith in the author of the scripture. If anything, in this interpretation, the method that proceeds on the basis of "faith" is actually stricter than the method that corresponds to the threefold analysis, since this method requires certainty (*niścaya*) based on reasoning (*nyāya*), which turns out to be the real meaning of faith in Kamalaśīla's view.

Of course, the mere absence of explicit evidence for the transfer of credibility method in the *Tattvasaṃgraha* and the *Pañjikā* does not by itself rule out the possibility that the proof of the Buddha's omniscience is for the purpose of grounding the Buddhist scriptures on radically inaccessible matters. Below, we will consider some explicit statements that the authors of the *Tattvasaṃgraha* and the *Pañjikā* make that seem to indicate that such is not, however, their aim. But before we do so, we must first consider an important aspect of Śāntarakṣita and Kamalaśīla's understanding of scripturally based inference, and that is its provisional nature.

The Provisional Nature of Scripturally Based Inference

Kamalaśīla makes his most important statement about the nature of scripturally based inference in the opening section of the *Pañjikā*, where he is discussing the crucial question of how a judicious person can, under a set of very particular circumstances, act on the basis of a mere statement (as, for example, when a judicious person decides to read a text on the basis of the statement of the treatise's aim). Kamalaśīla readily grants the point that a mere statement has no connection to reality, but then he counters that this is irrelevant, since it is nonetheless established that judicious persons sometimes act

718. TSP *ad* TS 2773cd (*śrutiparīkṣā*, B 891,22–892,6): *tatreti / puruṣopadiṣṭe heyāditattve sopāye puruṣārthopayogini / tathā hi tatra nyāyam evānupālayantaḥ saugatāḥ sudhiyaḥ pravartante na pravādamātreṇa / śraddhayeti / abhisaṃpratyayena yuktinidhyānajena niścayeneti yāvat / pramāṇasiddha evārthe 'bhisaṃpratyayasya yujyamānatvāt / nānyatra / tatra saṃśayānativṛtteḥ /*. I read *puruṣopadiṣṭe* in the first line on the basis of the Tibetan, D, vol. *'e*, 210b3: *de la zhes bya ba ni skyes bu'i don la nye bar mkho ba'i dor bar bya ba la sogs pa'i de kho na nyid thabs dang bcas pa skyes bus nye bar stan pa la ste /*. B 891,23 has *puruṣe tadiṣṭe*. G 735,21 has *puruṣo yadiṣṭe* {*pauruṣeye, adṛṣṭe,-*}.

on account of statements without thereby losing their judiciousness. As he says, echoing Dharmakīrti:

> However, if it were established that no judicious person whatsoever acted on account of a statement, only then would it be true [that judicious persons only act out of certainty] for all [cases]. For some people, having heard about the great blessings and dangers of acting or not acting in relation to some results that are not directly perceptible, being unable to abide without relying on the authority of a scripture, are observed to act on account of a statement. And to that degree there is not any loss of their judiciousness, because their action is just as an expedient means (*abhyupāyena*). For apart from scripture there is no other expedient means for action with regard to an object that is a radically inaccessible entity (*atyantaparokṣārtha*). And one must necessarily act according to scripture (*āgama*) [when it comes to such radically inaccessible entities]. That is, those who accept a contradictory scripture would be injudicious; but when there is action through reliance on a noncontradictory scripture, how could the [persons] not be judicious, since that [kind of scripture] is a proper means (*samyagupāya*)?[719]

Here we see clearly that Kamalaśīla does accept scripturally based inference as a valid justifier of action. Like Dharmakīrti, Kamalaśīla seems to accept that there are at least some cases in which it is necessary—or even required—

719. TSP *ad* TS 1–6 (B 4,21–5,4): *kiṃ tu yadi vākyān na kasyacit prekṣāvataḥ pravṛttir astīty etat siddhaṃ bhavet tadā sarvam evaitat syāt / yāvatā dṛśyante hi kecid apratyakṣaphalānāṃ keṣāṃcit pravṛttinivṛttyor mahāśaṃsāpāyaśravaṇād anāśrityāgamaprāmāṇyam āsitum aśaknuvanto vacanāt pravartamānāḥ / na caitāvatā teṣāṃ prekṣāvattāhānir abhyupāyenaiva pravṛtter na hy āgamād ṛte 'tyantaparokṣārthaviṣaye pravṛttāv anyo 'bhyupāyo 'sti / avaśyaṃ ca pravartitavyaṃ tv āgamāt / vyāhatāgamaparigrahaṃ hi kurvāṇā aprekṣāpūrvakāriṇaḥ syuḥ / avyāhatāgamasamāśrayeṇa tu pravṛttau kathaṃ na prekṣāvanto bhaveyus tasyaiva samyagupāyatvāt /*. Cf. PVSV *ad* PV 1.214: *nāyaṃ puruṣo 'nāśrityāgamaprāmāṇyam āsituṃ samarthaḥ / apratyakṣaphalānāṃ keṣāṃcit pravṛttinivṛttyor mahānuśaṃsāpāyaśravaṇāt tadbhāve virodhādarśanāc ca / tat sati pravartitavye varam evaṃ pravṛtta iti /*. Translated in Dunne 2004: 361: "A person cannot proceed without relying on the instrumentality of scripture because: [1] he has heard that, in the case of some activities whose effects are not perceptible, engaging or not engaging in those activities will have some extremely praiseworthy or disastrous results; and [2] there is no observed contradiction in that being the case. He would thus act, thinking 'If this is to be done, it is best that it be done thus.'" For Gn 108: *-āpāpa* read *-āpāya* with PVT (243a) and TSP *ad* TS 1–6.

to accept a scriptural statement on a radically inaccessible entity. The presence of this statement at the outset of the *Pañjikā* indicates that Kamalaśīla accepts Dharmakīrti's basic position on scripturally based inference.

However, as Kamalaśīla mentions, although scripturally based inference may be a proper means (*samyagupāya*), it is also an "expedient means" (*abhyupāya*) since it does not yield certainty. The point is that one relies on a scripturally based inference only when there is no other way, just as one relies on the statement of the aim of a treatise as the basis of one's decision whether to read the treatise or not because one has no choice but to do so. The passage above continues as follows:

> Nor is it correct to say that [judicious people] act just through certainty with regard to that [scripture], having determined the correctness of the scripture due to its composition by an extraordinary person, because those who lack transcendental vision are not capable of ascertaining whether a person is extraordinary. And neither is it the case that judicious people should *not* act due to scripture. For similarly, in this case as well, having heard a statement of the aim and so on that is not contradictory, those who act upon those texts will be persons who act judiciously, because their action will be just an expedient means. For in the case of action here as well, there is no other expedient, because before engaging [with the treatise], the meaning of the treatise is a radically inaccessible entity (*atyantaparokṣa*).[720]

Here Kamalaśīla stresses a number of significant points. First, he again states that one does not rely on a scripture due to the credibility of the author (being composed by an "extraordinary person," or *puruṣātiśaya*, is equivalent to being composed by an *āpta*). This seems to be an explicit rejection of the transfer of credibility method of grounding scriptures. Next, he again clarifies that scripturally based inference is provisional, being an "expedient means" or "provisional means" (*upāya, abhyupāya*).[721] Finally—and quite

720. TSP *ad* TS 1–6 (B 5,4–9): *na cāgamasya puruṣātiśayapraṇītatayā yathārthatvam avadhārya tatra niścayād eva pravartanta iti yuktaṃ vaktuṃ / puruṣātiśayasyaivāparadarśanair niścetum aśakyatvāt / na cāgamān na pravartante prekṣāvanto 'pi / tadvad ihāpi / avyāhataprayojanādivākyaśravaṇāc chāstreṣu pravartamānāḥ prekṣāpūrvakāriṇo bhaviṣyanti / upāyenaiva pravṛtteḥ / na hy atrāpi pravṛttāv abhyupāyāntaram asti / śāstrārthasya prāk pravṛtter atyantaparokṣatvāt /.*

721. This is quite similar to what we find in Dharmakīrti's PVSV and the commentaries

interestingly in light of the theory earlier considered according to which the status of the omniscient being changes from radically inaccessible to inferable for the intelligent—he states that the meaning of the treatise is radically inaccessible *before* one engages with the text, with the implication being that the status of the contents of the treatise shifts from *atyantaparokṣa* to *parokṣa* after we have read and understood the arguments contained within it.

All of this seems to indicate Kamalaśīla's acceptance of the idea of relying on a scripturally based inference in those cases where the scripture has been "purified" through the threefold analysis and where there is no other way. Even though one does not attain certainty through such a scripturally based inference, one does not thereby lose one's judiciousness—in part because one has no choice and in part because one only accepts the scriptural statement provisionally. The implication seems to be that one proceeds on the basis of the scripturally based inference because it allows one to proceed along a path that is oriented toward eventually reaching a place where one *can* verify for oneself whether what has been said is true.

Some Explicit Statements on the Motive Behind the Proof

Earlier, when considering the term *śṛṅgagrāhikayā* in the *Tattvasaṃgraha* and the *Pañjikā*, we encountered a passage in which Kumārila charges that a mere proof of omniscience in general would entail the fault of *pratijñānyūna*, or "inadequacy of the proposition."[722] The problem, according to Kumārila,

---

thereon. As Śākyabuddhi (PVT 242b5) and Karṇakagomin (390) make clear, for instance, it is not that a scripturally based inference is truly real (*bhāvika*) in the manner of the trustworthy awarenesses of perception and ordinary inference. Translated in Dunne 2004: 361n3: "In other words, the Ācārya [Dignāga] did not say that knowledge from scripture is an inference by claiming that it is actually [or truly] (*bhāvika*) instrumental. Rather, it is instrumental with regard to the way in which a person should proceed." As Tillemans (1999b: 45) has argued, one accepts a scripturally based inference "because we are not, as far as we can judge, precluded from doing so and because we want to or need to do so for our spiritual goals." Like the calculated risk of the judicious person who decides to read a treatise after hearing about its purported subject and aim, Tillemans (45) states that relying on a scripturally based inference is a case of making "an informed, but fallible, choice," since "certainty is not [obtained] from that [scripture]." Cf. PVSV *ad* PV 1.318: *nāto niścayaḥ* /.

722. TS 3229 (*atīndriyārthadarśiparīkṣā*): *naraḥ ko 'py asti sarvajñas tat sarvajñatvam ity api / sādhanaṃ yat prayujyeta pratijñānyūnam eva tat* //. Translated in n. 618 above. Pathak (1892) presents slight variations in this verse according to the *Aṣṭasahasrī* of Vidyānanda: *naraḥ ko 'py asti sarvajñañ sa tu sarvajña ity api / sādhanaṃ yat prayujyeta pratijñāmātram eva tat* //. TS 3229–33 are also preserved in the Jain author Anantakīrti's *Bṛhatsarvajñasiddi* ; see Frauwallner 1962. According to Pathak (1929), the same verses

is that a proof of omniscience has, necessarily, it seems, the purpose of establishing that a particular teacher is credible so that one may be justified in relying upon that person's verbal testimony. If one seeks only to show that "there is someone who is omniscient" (*naraḥ ko 'py asti sarvajñaḥ*), then even if the proof were successful (and it is not, of course, from Kumārila's perspective), one would still not be justified in relying on the scriptures of one's own teacher, who would remain unestablished as omniscient. Kamalaśīla summarizes this criticism attributed to Kumārila as follows:

> The fault of the thesis known as the inadequacy of the proposition (*pratijñānyūna*) is when one proposes (*pratijñāyate*) one thing when one desires to prove something else. And in this case, one wishes to prove the omniscience of one's own teacher, not [to prove omniscience] in general. That is to say, judicious people do not search for an omniscient person wantonly (*vyasanitayā*), but rather [they search for such a person] out of their desire to act and to refrain from acting [with regard to Dharma and Adharma], thinking "I will act or I will refrain from acting having understood Dharma and Adharma according to the speech of that [person]." And a person is not at all helped with regard to action by this general demonstration, because there is no certainty regarding that [other person's] speech without the recognition of [that] particular [person as being omniscient]. Therefore, just that particular [person] should be established by the person who desires [guidance with regard to] action; hence, the general proposition is just an inadequate proposition.[723]

When Śāntarakṣita gets around much later to answering the charge that the proof of omniscience entails the fault of an inadequate proposition, he says that he has already shown that such is not the case.[724] He then refers us

are quoted and refuted by Pātrakesari, who states that Kumārila is attacking Samantabhadra and Akalaṅkadeva.

723. TSP *ad* TS 3229–30 (*atīndriyārthadarśiparīkṣā*, B 1016,21–1017,13): *anyasmin sādhayitum iṣṭe yad anyat pratijñāyate tat pratijñānyūnaṃ pakṣadoṣaḥ / iha ca svasya śāstuḥ sarvajñatvaṃ sādhayitum iṣṭaṃ na sāmānyena / tathā hi na vyasanitayā sarvajño 'nviṣyate prekṣāvatā / kiṃ tarhi / tadvacanād dharmādharmau jñātvā pravartiṣye nivartiṣye veti pravṛttinivṛttikāmatayā / na ca sāmānyena siddhenāpi tena pravṛttiṃ prati puruṣasya kaścid upayogo 'sti viśeṣaparijñānam antareṇa tadvacanāniścayāt / tasmāt sa eva viśeṣaḥ pravṛttikāmena sādhanīya iti sāmānyapratijñānaṃ pratijñānyūnam eva /.*

724. TS 3590–91 (*atīndriyārthadarśiparīkṣā*). See n. 728 below.

to a statement he made at the outset of that part of the general demonstration dedicated to establishing the possibility of omniscience which he claims shows that he has already demonstrated that the fault of an inadequate proposition does not apply. Let us now examine that earlier statement.

The context of the statement is the turning point in the general demonstration, where Śāntarakṣita has just finished his rebuttal of Kumārila's refutation and established that, at the very least, one cannot conclude that omniscience is impossible. He is about to continue with the remainder of the general demonstration, the portion where omniscience is shown to be a real possibility through reasoning about the nature of mental qualities and so on. He then says a curious thing: he mentions that even if the demonstration of total omniscience is futile (*niṣphala*), the wise Buddhists make an effort to establish it anyway "with a different intention."[725] The comment is difficult to interpret, in large part because Śāntarakṣita does not explain what he means by the phrase "with a different intention." But the matter is also complicated by the fact that Śāntarakṣita introduces the distinction between dharmic and total omniscience right at this point.

Kamalaśīla's commentary is also tough to unpack. He first explains that the reference to the proof of omniscience as futile hearkens back to a verse from the *pūrvapakṣa*, in which Kumārila states, "Constructing a demonstration of [a person who has] detailed knowledge of the entirety of the components and appearances [of the world] is futile, like an investigation into the teeth of a crow."[726] Concerning the phrase "with a different intention," Kamalaśīla says:

> First of all, our primary demonstration is indeed of the Blessed One's knowledge of the causes for attaining heaven and liberation; but the demonstration of his knowledge of all things without exception is a consequence of that [earlier demonstration] (*tatprāsaṅgikam*). Since there is no contravening means of

725. TS 3307–8 (*atīndriyārthadarśiparīkṣā*): *niḥśeṣārthaparijñānasādhane viphale 'pi ca / sudhiyaḥ saugatā yatnaṃ kurvanty anyena cetasā // svargāpavargasaṃprāptihetujño 'stīti gamyate / sākṣān na kevalaṃ kiṃ tu sarvajño 'pi pratīyate //*. "And even if the demonstration of a person who knows all things without exception is futile, still, wise Buddhists make an effort [to construct such a demonstration] with a different intention. Not only do they directly know that there is one who knows the causes for attaining heaven and liberation, but also they [indirectly] recognize that there is one who is omniscient [in the total sense]."

726. TS 3137 (*atīndriyārthadarśiparīkṣā*): *samastāvayavavyaktivistarajñānasādhanam / kākadantaparīkṣāvat kriyamāṇam anarthakam //*.

> trustworthy awareness for the fact that the Blessed One's knowledge engages with other [objects of cognition] also, no one can refute that he is omniscient due to directly knowing all things without exception. Therefore, it is not right for judicious persons to reject that. Rather, for those who desire to attain omniscience (*sarvajñatvādhigamārthinaḥ*), it is reasonable to act with that as their goal (*tadarthapravṛtti*).[727]

This short section of commentary contains two significant elements. First, it sets out the twofold structure of the specific demonstration, in which one initially establishes the Buddha's dharmic omniscience and then establishes total omniscience as a consequence of that. Second, it shows the motive for this demonstration, which is to allow those who desire omniscience to undertake practices that are for the purpose of attaining omniscience. This second component is what concerns us here.

Kamalaśīla's statement about the motive tells us that the demonstration of the Buddha's omniscience allows people to act with omniscience as their goal, but it does not tell us in what way it does so. It is possible, on the basis of this passage, to conceive along with Kumārila that the motive behind the demonstration of the Buddha's omniscience is in fact to ground the Buddhist scriptures, at least when it comes to radically inaccessible matters. In this case, those who want to engage with the Buddhist path and attain omniscience can rely on those scriptures as scripturally based inferences because they would know that their author was omniscient. This certainly remains a possibility, although it seems unlikely, and it is this possibility that keeps the second hypothesis for Śāntarakṣita and Kamalaśīla's motive alive. However, there is another way to read the passage, and this way has the support of Kamalaśīla's commentary on the passage in which Śāntarakṣita rejects the charge that the Buddhist's general demonstration entails the fault of the inadequacy of the proposition.

Recall that when he gets around to answering the charge, Śāntarakṣita tells us that he has already dispensed with the problem of *pratijñānyūna*, and he refers us to his earlier statement (which we have just examined) where

727. TSP *ad* TS 3308 (*atīndriyārthadarśiparīkṣā*, B 1044,15–20): *mukhyaṃ hi tāvat svargamokṣasaṃprāpakahetujñatvasādhanaṃ bhagavato 'smābhiḥ kriyate / yat punar aśeṣārthaparijñātṛtvasādhanam asya tat prāsaṅgikam / anyatrāpi bhagavato jñānapravṛtter bādhakapramāṇābhāvāt sākṣād aśeṣārthaparijñānāt sarvajño bhavan na kenacid bādhyata iti / ato na prekṣāvatāṃ tatpratikṣepo yuktaḥ / kiṃ tu ye sarvajñatvādhigamārthinas teṣāṃ tadarthapravṛttir yuktā ceti darśitaṃ bhavati //.*

he mentions the wise Buddhists' "different intention" for the demonstration.[728] The connection between the two sets of verses and accompanying commentary is thus explicit, and we should not hesitate to consider them together. Here again, Śāntarakṣita does not explain the "different intention," but Kamalaśīla makes the following statement:

> Moreover, we do not establish omniscience so that we may implement (*anuṣṭhāna*) that which we have understood to have been spoken by an omniscient person; rather, it is for the sake of those who wish to attain the state of omniscience that we establish the elimination of faults and the perfection of good qualities, for Buddhists strive for human aims only through inferences that function through the force of real entities (*vastubalapravṛttānumāna*) and not through mere words.[729]

We see here a more precise explanation of the Buddhists' "different intention" in the demonstration as a whole. Again, the emphasis is on practice, but there is also a further explanation of the mechanism by which the demonstration serves to enable practitioners to practice. That is, it seems that, as we speculated above, the specific demonstration really must be seen as a corollary of the general demonstration; for it is the general demonstration, which establishes "the elimination of faults and the perfection of good qualities," that is the compelling argument that allows one to engage with the Buddhist path in a rational manner—on the basis of *vastubalapravṛttānumāna* and perception alone. In this passage, Kamalaśīla seems to explicitly deny

728. TS 3590–91 (*atīndriyārthadarśiparīkṣā*): *nara ko 'py asti sarvajña ityādy api na sādhanam / pratijñānyūnatādoṣadṛṣṭam ity upapāditam // niḥśeṣārthaparijñānasādhane viphale 'pi hi / sudhiyaḥ saugatā yatnaṃ kurvantītyādinā purā //*. "Previously it was established, moreover, that the demonstration (*sādhana*) that 'there is someone who is omniscient' is not demolished by the fault of the inadequacy of the proposition. [Such was established] by the phrase 'for even if the demonstration of the knowledge of all things whatsoever is fruitless, the wise Buddhists make an effort' and so on."

729. TSP *ad* TS 3591: *kiṃ ca nāsmābhiḥ sarvajñoktatvam avagamya tadanuṣṭhānāya sarvajñaḥ prasādhyate / kiṃ tarhi / ye sārvajñapadaprāptīcchavas tadarthaṃ doṣakṣayo guṇotkarṣaś ca prasādhyate / yato vastubalapravṛttānumānata eva saugatāḥ puruṣārtheṣu ghaṭante na pravādamātreṇa //*. Reading *ex conj.*: *doṣakṣayo guṇotkarṣaś ca prasādhyate* instead of the reading found in G, B, and J (308b2): *doṣakṣayo guṇotkarṣāya prasādhyate /*. I base this reading on two factors. First, the Tibetan sources (D, vol. *'e*, 324a2 and P) attest *nyes pa zad pa dang yon tan 'phel ba sgrub par byed te //*. Second, the conjunct *śca* in the script of J resembles closely the combination of *āya*. For an example of the *śca* conjunct in this script see J 308b1: *tat pratipannakaś catvāra ....*

that the purpose of the overall proof is to ground scriptures, and he even seems to denigrate the reliance on scriptures that one associates with scripturally based inference. If this reading is accurate, it would seem that our second hypothesis concerning the motivation behind the specific demonstration must be incorrect, at least for Kamalaśīla (the situation is somewhat less clear for Śāntarakṣita).

At the same time, this reading leads us again to the frustrating impasse where the specific demonstration appears to have no rationale. Another factor speaking against the rejection of our second hypothesis is the fact that, as we have seen, Kamalaśīla accepts that judicious persons may, under certain circumstances, rely upon scripturally based inferences to guide their actions in relation to radically inaccessible entities. We saw the example of how a judicious person may engage with (i.e., listen to or read) a treatise on the basis of the mere proclamation of its subject matter and not thereby lose his or her judiciousness. As a final element in our consideration of the "grounding scriptures" hypothesis for the specific demonstration, then, we need to examine more closely whether and in what ways Śāntarakṣita and Kamalaśīla understand that a judicious person has need of a scripturally based inference to ground his or her faith in some radically inaccessible matter.

Faith in Radically Inaccessible Entities

We have seen above the importance that Kamalaśīla ascribes to faith (defined as certainty concerning possibility) in great beings, and how that importance lends credence to the first hypothesis. If the second hypothesis is to retain its plausibility, we must equally show that for Śāntarakṣita and Kamalaśīla there is some important way in which acceptance of radically inaccessible entities based on scripturally based inference is necessary for the judicious person to make progress on the spiritual path. The *Tattvasaṃgraha* and the *Pañjikā* make reference to a number of *atyantaparokṣa* matters, but it is only in relation to one of them—as far as I can tell—that we find any hint of the idea that faith in some radically inaccessible entity might be necessary for spiritual progress. I speak of the connection between karmic causes and their effects (*karmaphalasaṃbandha*).

Evidence suggesting this interpretation is found in the chapter of the *Tattvasaṃgraha* and the *Pañjikā* called the "Investigation of Scripture" (*śrutiparīkṣā*). The context is a discussion of the Mīmāṃsaka claim that the words of the Veda are true because they give rise to an awareness that is free from doubt, in the same way that direct perception of a real entity, such as a fire, gives rise to the certain conviction that one is, in fact, experiencing fire.[730] Śāntarakṣita's initial response to this claim is to deny that certainty arises from Vedic statements concerning supersensible (*atīndriya*) entities.[731] He then seems to soften somewhat and to grant the possibility of a kind of psychological certainty, or "unshakability" (*niṣkampya*), arising in the minds of Vedic scholars. But he states that this unshakability is the result of faith (*śraddhā*) and that it does not differ from the unshakable convictions of Buddhists concerning the misfortune that will arise in future lives due to the sacrifice of animals. The relevant verses read:

> But that unshakable opinion that arises for the Vedic scholars (*śrotriya*) whose minds are under the control of faith is the same [as that which arises] for others due to other [statements]. That is, for Buddhists and so on there arises the unshakable conviction that misfortune and suffering are produced [in a future life] due to sacrifices that involve the slaughter of animals.[732]

730. The argument here is related to another Mīmāṃsaka claim, namely that of the "intrinsic trustworthiness" (*svataḥprāmāṇya*) of all means of trustworthy awareness. The Mīmāṃsaka's point is that in order for an awareness to be false, there must arise a second, contravening awareness in relation to the first awareness that conclusively shows that awareness to be wrong (as, for example, when after seeing a mirage one arrives at the place and discovers that there is no water there). When no such contravening awareness arises, the original awareness may be accepted as true. Regarding the Vedic sentences, as for example, "one who desires heaven should perform a sacrifice" (*svargakāmo yajeta*), no contravening awareness ever arises in any place, with regard to any person, in any situation, or at any time. Thus, the awareness that arises upon hearing the statement must be true. See, e.g., ŚBh 1.1.2 (quoted in TSP *ad* TS 2386–87, *śrutiparīkṣā*, B 795,11–14): *na ca svargakāmo yajetety ato vacanāt saṃdigdham avagamyante bhavati vā svargo na vā bhavatīti / na ca viniścitam avagamyamānam idaṃ mithyā syāt / yo hi janitvā pradhvaṃsate naitad evam sa mithyāpratyayaḥ / na caiṣa deśāntare puruṣāntare 'vasthāntare kālāntare viparyeti / tasmād avitathaḥ //*. See also D'Sa 1980.

731. See TS 2388–89 (*śrutiparīkṣā*): *naivaṃ saṃśayasaṃjāter viparītānyavākyavat / prekṣāvanto hi naiteṣāṃ bhedaṃ paśyanti kaṃcana // nātīndriye hi yujyete sadasattāviniścayau / niścayo vedavākyāc ced anyādṛg na kim anyataḥ //*. "It is not the case [that certainty ensues from Vedic sentences] since there is the arisal of doubt, just as in the case of another sentence that asserts the opposite [i.e., that heaven is not the result of sacrifice]. Indeed, judicious persons do not perceive even the slightest difference between these two [cases]. For the definitive determinations of existence and nonexistence do not apply to supersensible [entities]. If there were certainty from a Vedic sentence, then why would there not be [certainty] from another [sentence] that was otherwise [i.e., that stated things to be otherwise]?"

732. TS 2390–91 (*śrutiparīkṣā*): *śrotriyāṇāṃ tu niṣkampyā buddhir eṣopajāyate /*

This statement by Śāntarakṣita can probably be considered as evidence that Śāntarakṣita accepts that the details of karmic causality cannot be proven by belief-neutral reasoning but must be accepted as a matter of faith. If so, then we have at least one radically inaccessible matter that could be a candidate for a matter in need of grounding by reference to the Buddha's omniscience, credibility, or authority.

The emphasis on faith as a kind of unshakability that occurs for Buddhists and non-Buddhists alike contrasts somewhat with the picture of faith as certainty that we earlier saw Kamalaśīla advocating. One possibility that should be considered is thus that Śāntarakṣita and Kamalaśīla do not have precisely the same view in this matter. It is possible that Śāntarakṣita allows a greater scope for a kind of faith than does his student and commentator Kamalaśīla, who is then forced into the awkward exegetical position of redefining his teacher's references to faith. In support of this idea is the fact that Kamalaśīla remains uncharacteristically taciturn in commenting on Śāntarakṣita's verses cited just above. In any case, Śāntarakṣita's verses do seem to lend credence to the idea that the judicious Buddhist must rely on scripture in order to know that the slaughter of animals necessarily leads to misfortune and suffering in a future life.

Not all the passages that touch on the future effects of karma in the *Tattvasaṃgraha* and the *Pañjikā* support this interpretation, however. Earlier, we briefly saw that Kamalaśīla holds reasoned confidence (*abhisaṃpratyaya*) in the connection between actions and their results to be one of the causes of nonerror (*aviparyāsa*), a prerequisite for both worldly and spiritual attainment. For Kamalaśīla, the implication of this statement is that one accepts the principle that ethically positive (*śubha*) actions lead to desired (*iṣṭa*) results whereas ethically negative (*aśubha*) actions lead to undesired (*aniṣṭa*) results.[733] Both authors of the *Tattvasaṃgraha* and the *Pañjikā* also hold that the connection between actions and results continues after the present life into the next life and beyond (metaphorically called the "other world" or *paraloka*), and that the existence of this continuity of lives can be definitively demonstrated.[734]

We have evidence that Śāntarakṣita and Kamalaśīla understand that the

śraddhāvivaśabuddhīnāṃ sānyeṣām anyataḥ samā // tathā hi saugatādīnāṃ dhīr akampyopajāyate / apāyaduḥkhasaṃbhūtir yāgāt prāṇivadhānvitāt //.

733. TSP *ad* TS 1 (B 14,6): *tatra karma śubhāśubham / tatphalaṃ ceṣṭāniṣṭam //.*

734. Kamalaśīla calls those who reject past and future lives *nāstika*s, whereas those who accept rebirth are called *āstika*s. Jha is quite right to note in his translation (1939, vol 2: 893) that in this context "'*nāstika*' is not the same as 'Atheist.'" The demonstration of past

basic principle of the connection between karmic causes and their results is *not* a radically inaccessible matter for ordinary persons, even if the details of the working out of karmic effects in future lives, such as, for example, the fact that killing in the present life necessarily leads to a particular kind of suffering in a future life (and not just to suffering in general), may be radically inaccessible. We see this argument at play in the "Investigation of the Connection between Actions and Results" (*karmaphalasaṃbandhaparīkṣā*), where the authors respond to an argument that states that in the Buddhist view of selflessness, there would be no incentive for people to undertake ethically positive activities, since there is no person who perdures over time to enjoy the fruits of that activity. The answer to this problem is that even ordinary persons, if they are sufficiently skillful, can determine the regular patterns or "restrictions" (*niyama*) that pertain between karmic actions and their effects, such that they will know that ethically positive activities such as giving and so on will indeed bring about further positive mental states while ethically negative activities will not do so. Kamalaśīla's analysis is as follows:

> But skillful ordinary persons, due to correctly understanding momentariness and selflessness through reasoning and scripture in this manner realize reality (*tattva*); they establish that [things have] the nature of dependent arising. Having determined the restrictions that pertain between causes and their effects, [such persons recognize that] "momentary mental tendencies (*saṃskāra*) capable of giving rise to benefit for oneself and others arise, one after the other in succession, from giving and so forth when these are preceded by compassion and so on, but [such mental formations] do not arise from harm and so on." Therefore, they engage in actions that are good and so on.[735]

The implication of this passage is that an ordinary person who has determined

---

and future lives occurs in the "Investigation of the Lokāyatas" (*lokāyataparīkṣā*), but it is too complex for us to enter into here.

735. See TSP *ad* TS 540–41 (*karmaphalasaṃbandhaparīkṣā*, B 228,12–16): *ye 'pi pṛthagjanakalyāṇā evaṃ yuktyāgamābhyāṃ yathāvat kṣaṇikānātmatayor avabodhād abhisaṃbuddhatattvās te 'py evaṃ pratītyasamutpādadharmatāṃ pratipadyante / karuṇādipūrvakebhyo dānādibhyaḥ svaparahitodayaśālinaḥ saṃskārāḥ kṣaṇikā evāparāpare paramparayā samutpadyante / na tu hiṃsādibhya ity atas te hetuphalapratiniyamam avadhārya śubhādikriyāsu pravartante /*. Reading *kṣaṇikānātmatayor avabodhād* instead of *kṣaṇikātmatayor avabodhābhi* in G and B based on D, vol. *ze*, 256a2: *... skad cig ma dang bdag med pa rab rtogs pa'i phyir ... /*.

the momentary nature of the mindstream can determine that good actions give rise to mental states that bring about the benefit of both self and others while negative actions do not. If such persons also determine through reasoning that future lives do indeed exist, they will also understand that these positive and negative effects of present actions continue into the next life, even if they do not know all the details of the effects that such actions will have in the next life.

At the same time, Kamalaśīla's use of the phrase "through reasoning and scripture" (*yuktyāgamābhyām*) is conspicuous in this passage, since it is, to my knowledge, the only place in the *Pañjikā* where it is found, despite being a standard Buddhist trope.[736] We also know that Kamalaśīla generally does not put much stock in scripture, as he states in the *Madhyamakālaṃkārapañjikā* that it is a mere "ornament" (*alaṃkāra*; Tibetan: *rgyan*) for reasoning that a philosopher must employ so that uneducated people will not think the reasoning to be the concoction of a subtle or sophistic logician and thus come to despise his work.[737] The reference to scripture in this context, then, may be a way of indicating that there are some aspects of the connection between karmic actions and their effects that should be considered radically inaccessible and whose existence one may only affirm through scripture. The question would then be whether it were really necessary for a judicious person to gain such knowledge of the details of karma in order to make spiritual progress or whether just knowing that good actions lead to beneficial results might be enough.

736. At least, I have not so far been able to locate this phrase in any other section of the TSP. It is interesting as well that this phrase also occurs at PV 2.133 and appears to refer to the methods that a person must use to attain liberation. But see, however, the comments of Devendrabuddhi (55a) and Śākyabuddhi (114a), who seem to interpret the meaning to be that one might use scriptures to prompt one's initial investigation but that the final justification for one's actions must be reasoning alone. See also Franco 1997: 33n43.

737. See MAP 21,12–21: *dad pas rjes su 'brang ba rnams kyang nges pa mi skye bas yongs su tshim par mi 'gyur ro // kyang zhes bya ba'i sgras ni sems log pa rnams lta smos kyang ci dgos zhes ston par byed do // dngos po'i stobs kyis zhugs pa smos pa ni lung las grags pa'i rjes su dpag pa bsal ba'i phyir te / de yang lung dang 'dra bas de dang bcas te de yang nges par mi byed pa'i phyir tshim par mi 'gyur ro // rigs pa ni nges pa skyed par byed pas yongs su tshim par byed pa yin no // ji ste gal te de lta na go ba rigs pa kho nas chog mod / lung gis ci zhig bya zhe na / ma yin te / lung ni rigs pa'i rgyan yin pa'i phyir ro // de lta ma yin na 'di ni rtogs ge pa sgam pos brtags pa yin no zhes mi mkhas pa kha cig gis brnyas par yang 'gyur ro //.*

Scripturally Based Inference as a Rhetorical Tool

Assuming for the moment, then, that judicious persons do *not* need to rely on scripturally based inference for anything that is soteriologically crucial to their practice, do the authors of the *Tattvasaṃgraha* and the *Pañjikā* advocate any *other* legitimate uses for scripturally based inference? Although it is not a very obvious instance, I believe that we do find an example of what these authors would understand as a completely legitimate and judicious use of a scripturally based inference. This is a use of scripturally based inference as a rhetorical device, which the judicious person relies upon in the context of a debate when the opponent has himself offered what amounts to nothing more than a scriptural proclamation in order to defend a point. The logic here is the logic of debate: if the opponent strays from the realm of belief-neutral reasoning, offering nothing more than a scriptural passage as evidence, then the proponent, too, will have the right to rely upon a scriptural statement of his choosing, without being required to offer belief-neutral evidence.

There is in the *Tattvasaṃgraha* and the *Pañjikā* at least one such example, which occurs in the "Investigation of Scripture." The context is a discussion of the *pralaya*, the universal destruction that many Indian traditions, including Buddhist traditions, accept as occurring on a cyclical basis. The background for the discussion is the Mīmāṃsaka claim that the meaning of words is eternally fixed and does not depend upon the establishment of a convention (*vyavahāra*). In order to uphold this view, it is necessary for the Mīmāṃsakas to deny the existence of the *pralaya*, at least in the sense of a truly universal destruction, since that would require that the meaning of words would also be destroyed. In addition, Kumārila argues, if everything were destroyed, there would be no one left who could then establish the conventions that others hold account for the meanings of words. For this reason, he says, the Mīmāṃsakas deny the existence of this kind of *pralaya*.[738] Instead, the term *pralaya* can only mean some limited form of destruction, as in the destruction of particular families or locales.[739]

In responding to this claim, Śāntarakṣita asserts that the Mīmāṃsaka cannot

738. See ŚV, *saṃbandhākṣepaparihāra*, 42: *pratyuccāraṇanirvṛttir bhāṣya eva nirākṛtā / sargādau ca kriyā nāsti tādṛk kālo hi neṣyate //*. Cited in a variant form at TS 2273 (*śrutiparīkṣā*): *pratyuccāraṇanirvṛttir na yuktā vyavahārataḥ / sargādau ca kriyā nāsti tādṛk kālo hi neṣyate //*.

739. TS 2274–76 (*śrutiparīkṣā*): *iṣyate hi jagat sarvaṃ na kadācid anīdṛśam / na mahāpralayo nāma jāyate pāramārthikaḥ // rātrir vā pralayo nāma līnatvāt sarvakarmaṇām / divasaḥ sṛṣṭisaṃjñaś ca sarvaceṣṭātisarjanāt // deśotsādakulotsādarūpo vā pralayo bhavet / pralaye tu pramāṇaṃ naḥ sarvocchedātmake na hi //*.

refute the possibility that the Veda will suffer destruction, whether by a limited form of destruction or by the unrefuted (*avyāhata*) universal destruction advocated by Buddhists, and therefore the Mīmāṃsaka argument fails. It is the notion of the "unrefuted universal destruction" that interests us here. Kamalaśīla explains its significance in his commentary:

> But you describe destruction in the form of the destruction of a locale and so on; but that [destruction] Buddhists describe as having the nature of destruction in the form of fire, water, and wind reaching to the limits of the billionfold world system—downward to the limit of the elemental wind sphere [and] upward successively to the limits of the first, second, and third *dhyāna*s—because it is not refuted by any means of trustworthy awareness, is therefore "unrefuted" (*avyāhata*); so that because it cannot be negated, it is doubtful [i.e., possible] even in relation to Brahmā and so on. Therefore, the destruction of the Veda is possible in the case of both these two forms of *pralaya*, and there is the uncertainty (*kampana*) of an erroneous meaning [in the sense that the original meaning of the Veda could have been lost].[740]

In this passage, Kamalaśīla mentions various aspects of the *pralaya* theory as it is presented in Buddhist sūtras and treatises, making reference to a number of common features of traditional Buddhist cosmology. These features, which include such things as the realms of meditation (*dhyāna*), are all radically inaccessible entities for ordinary beings. Kamalaśīla acknowledges this fact by stating that their destruction cannot be negated and so must remain doubtful.

Śāntarakṣita and Kamalaśīla's argument against the theory that the meaning of the Veda is eternally fixed does not depend on the argument based on the traditional Buddhist theory of universal destruction. Instead, the theory is introduced as a rhetorical device to highlight the fact that the Mīmāṃsaka's claim that *no* such destruction occurs is equally beyond the scope of the means of trustworthy awareness. Although the authors do not explicitly name this

740. TSP *ad* TS 2670–72 (*śrutiparīkṣā*, B 867,19–23): *kiṃ tu yo 'yaṃ bhavatā deśotsādādirūpapralayo varṇito yaś ca bauddhair agnyambuvāyusaṃvartanīyasvabhāvaḥ paryantatas trisāhasramahāsāhasralokadhātumaryādo 'dhastād vāyumaṇḍalāvadhir upariṣṭād yathākramaṃ prathamadvitīyatṛtīyadhyānaparyantaḥ so 'yaṃ pramāṇenābādhitatvād avyāhato 'śakyaniṣedhatvād brahmāder api śaṅkyate / ato 'smin dvividhe 'pi pralaye vedasya dhvaṃsaḥ sambhāvyate viparītārthakalpanaṃ ca /.*

as an instance of a scripturally based inference, it is certainly an instance of scripture being cited as evidence for some inaccessible reality. What is interesting, however, is that this appears to be a case where there is no particularly pressing soteriological need for the judicious person to rely upon scripture. Instead, this is an occasion where one's opponent in debate has resorted to an unverifiable claim (i.e., there is no universal destruction), which seemingly opens the door for these thinkers to draw equally on their own tradition's unverifiable claims in the course of the argument.

Summation of Findings Concerning the Second Hypothesis

The second hypothesis for the motives behind the specific demonstration states that the demonstration is intended to ground Buddhist scriptures in the credibility or omniscience of the Buddha, their author. After examining this hypothesis from various angles, we have not reached an unambiguous result. On the one hand, we have ample evidence that the authors, and perhaps especially Kamalaśīla, want to ground the Buddhist path in the belief-neutral reasoning of *vastubalapravṛttānumāna*. Scripturally based inference seems to be relegated to less-than-crucial contexts, such as the rhetorical context just examined, or the context in which one wonders about the details of karmic causality. It seems fairly certain that neither Śāntarakṣita nor Kamalaśīla hold that scripturally based inference is *necessary* for the judicious person who wants to attain omniscience and to put the Buddhist teachings into practice. If so, then we have not really discovered any convincing reasons to accept the second hypothesis. If we accept, however, that the authors wish to allow Buddhists to draw on and refer to Buddhist scriptures in a purely rhetorical fashion, then we can perhaps accept a limited version of the second hypothesis, whereby the motive for the specific demonstration includes grounding Buddhist scriptures on radically inaccessible matters only and for provisional or expedient reasons alone.

Third Hypothesis: Writing for Non-Buddhists

The third hypothesis concerning the motivation for the specific demonstration of the Buddha's omniscience in the *Tattvasaṃgraha* and the *Pañjikā* distinguishes itself most obviously from the previous two hypotheses on the question of the audience for whom the proof is intended. Here, rather than viewing the specific demonstration as directed at Buddhists or potential Buddhists, this hypothesis holds that the proof is intended for those non-Buddhists determined to judge a teaching not by its rationality but by the extraordinary qualities of the teacher. A similar hypothesis concerning

Dharmakīrti's proof of the Buddha's authority in *Pramāṇavārttika* 2 has been advanced by Franco, who argues that the entire *Pramāṇasiddhi* chapter is open to a "double reading," in which "we can read the text as a proof that the Buddha is *pramāṇabhūta* in the Buddhist or more specifically in Dignāga's sense, but also as a proof that he is an *āpta* in the Nyāya-Vaiśeṣika and Sāṅkhya-Yoga sense."[741]

I cannot analyze Franco's arguments in relation to *Pramāṇavārttika* 2, but when it comes to the arguments in the *Tattvasaṃgraha* and the *Pañjikā*, there is one tangible piece of evidence to support a similar claim. It comes at the very end of the *Pañjikā*, and although it is intended by Kamalaśīla as a response to a specific objection, its implications are wide enough to encompass the chapter as a whole. The context is an objection to the effect that when considered from the Vijñānavāda perspective that Śāntarakṣita and Kamalaśīla prefer, certain problems will arise for the doctrine of the Buddha's omniscience whether one endorses a system in which awarenesses are innately endowed with images (*sākāravāda*) or systems in which awarenesses are devoid of images (*nirākāravāda*). Śāntarakṣita, in effect, declines to answer this objection. Kamalaśīla explains why:

> Previously we, conforming to (*sthita*) the Vijñānavāda, reflected on [cognitions] without images. In the present context, when we—having accepted external objects [provisionally]—are demon-

741. Franco 1997: 29. Franco's basic argument for this claim (1997: 35–42) runs as follows. First, he rightly points out the problem that we have already raised—the apparently superfluous nature of the proof of the Buddha's authority if all of the Buddha's teachings can be established through reason (35). Next, he cites PV 1.217 and PVSV *ad cit.*, where Dharmakīrti appears to endorse a version of scripturally based inference that depends on the credibility of an author (36). According to Franco, this version of scripturally based inference "comes close to the strategy in the *Pramāṇasiddhi*-chapter" and it is in order to lend credence to this process that Dharmakīrti feels compelled to rationally establish the "most important part (*pradhānārtha*) of the Buddha's teaching, namely, the four noble truths" (37). In this, Franco sees a similarity with Vātsyāyana's system for determining the credibility (*āptatva*) of an author on the basis of that author's true statements on verifiable matters such as medicine. All this leads Franco to conclude that "Dharmakīrti writes also, or perhaps primarily, for a non-Buddhist audience" (37). While I am sympathetic with Franco's hypothesis, I cannot help wishing that his formulation of the evidence for this claim were somewhat stronger. For instance, an extended argument for the nobles' four truths, as one finds in PV 2, could be intended for a Buddhist audience, or at least for an audience open to becoming Buddhist; it does not in any *obvious* sense represent an attempt to convince non-Buddhists by reference to some "common ground shared with Brahmanical philosophers" (38).

> strating omniscience to you Mīmāṃsakas, who are addicted to external objects, it would not at all be useful to do that [analysis from the Vijñānavāda perspective again] for you externalists (*bahirarthavādin*).[742]

Kamalaśīla goes on to explain that whether cognitions are endowed with images or are devoid of them is irrelevant when the discussion is taking place on the level of analysis where external objects are provisionally accepted. Since the same question arises in relation even to ordinary cognitions, the externalists must also provide a solution to this problem. And whatever answer they provide, Śāntarakṣita and Kamalaśīla will accept as applying to the omniscient Buddha as well. Although this passage concerns one specific problem, it illustrates that Śāntarakṣita and Kamalaśīla conceive of their defense of omniscience as a response to certain non-Buddhists whose ontological presuppositions they do not share but on whose terms they argue in order to make their point. This is very much in keeping with our earlier observations concerning the rhetorical frame for the final chapter of the *Tattvasaṃgraha* and the *Pañjikā* and the way in which the last three chapters of the work as a whole are directed exclusively at Mīmāṃsakas.

Above, we have also seen that the final chapter of the *Tattvasaṃgraha* and the *Pañjikā* contains at least two supplemental demonstrations concerning the Buddha's special qualities, namely, the argument that his teachings are vouched for by the Veda and the argument for his great compassion. We noted that these supplemental arguments do not appear to play an explicit role in the specific demonstration of omniscience, even though they clearly concern the historically specific figure of the Buddha. If we allow that at least part of the intended audience for the *Tattvasaṃgraha* and the *Pañjikā* was non-Buddhist, these arguments can then be interpreted as being offered not on strictly Buddhist terms but rather in terms that should be, in theory at least, acceptable to the opponents. In this way, we can account for their apparently less "strict" character: Śāntarakṣita and Kamalaśīla know that these arguments are not cogent for rational Buddhists, but they offer them anyway in the hopes of convincing those whose rationality is not sufficiently developed to understand this fact.

742. TSP *ad* TS 3645 (*atīndriyārthadarśiparīkṣā*, B 1130,15–17): *yeyam asmābhir vijñānavādasthitair nirākāracintā prāg akāri sā sāmpratam bāhyārthābhiniviṣṭān bhavato mīmāṃsakān prati bahirartham abhyupetya sarvajñe pratipādyamāne bhavatāṃ bahirarthavādināṃ katham api nopayujyata eva kartum //.*

Résumé of the Three Hypotheses

In the preceding sections we have considered three hypotheses for the motivation of the specific demonstration of the Buddha's omniscience in the final chapter of the *Tattvasaṃgraha* and the *Pañjikā*, each of which is relevant in relation to a particular audience. The first hypothesis states that the specific demonstration is directed at judicious persons who have already been convinced by the general demonstration of the possibility of omniscience and who would now like to further engage with the practices of the Buddhist path. The specific demonstration of the Buddha's omniscience is intended to allow such persons to go for refuge in the Buddha, thus initiating their engagement with the Buddhist path.

The second hypothesis states that the specific demonstration is directed at those Buddhists who, for the purposes of their practice or for some rhetorical purposes, need or desire to ground certain Buddhist scriptural statements concerning radically inaccessible entities in the credibility of the Buddha. In considering this second hypothesis, we rejected the interpretation that the specific demonstration is for the purpose of grounding the Buddhist teachings generally; if the second hypothesis is valid at all, it is only in relation to *atyantaparokṣa* matters such as the details of the connection between karmic actions and their effects. In analyzing this hypothesis, we examined the authors' position on scripturally based inferences, to see whether they accept that the validity of a scriptural statement on a radically inaccessible entity may be accepted on the grounds of our knowledge of the Buddha's credibility. We determined that the authors hold that a scripturally based inference is not justified in this way but rather through the threefold analysis that makes no reference to the notion of credibility. The second hypothesis, then, does not seem to hold up, even if we can point to some (fairly limited) instances in which the authors do allow for the use of scripturally based inference.

Finally, the third hypothesis states that the specific demonstration is directed toward non-Buddhists and is intended to convince them of the Buddha's credibility using arguments that may not be valid in a strictly Buddhist context but that may be effective polemically. Although acceptance of this third hypothesis would seem to conflict with our rejection of the second hypothesis (that is, either these authors do or do not wish to ground Buddhist scriptures in the Buddha's credibility), the difference in audiences allows for both interpretations to stand.

The complexity of this analysis should be taken as evidence for the rhetorical subtlety that pervades this work, and may account as well for the difficulties many have encountered in trying to determine the precise contours of these authors' views.

Motives for the Demonstration of Total Omniscience

Up to this point, this chapter has been devoted to looking at the possible motives driving Śāntarakṣita and Kamalaśīla's demonstration of dharmic omniscience in the final chapter of the *Tattvasaṃgraha* and the *Pañjikā*. This final segment of the chapter seeks to address the problem of assessing the motives driving the demonstration of total omniscience, the knowledge of all things whatsoever. Of the four elements of the overall demonstration of omniscience—the rubuttal of Kumārila, the demonstration of the possibility of dharmic omniscience, the demonstration of the Buddha's dharmic omniscience in particular, and the demonstration of total omniscience—theorizing about the motives for the demonstration of total omniscience is the most difficult.

One's first inclination is to imagine that the demonstration of total omniscience is intended to ensure that what the Buddha said concerning radically inaccessible entities is true. In other words, a natural assumption is that the demonstration is intended for the purpose of grounding Buddhist scriptures in the Buddha's total omniscience. The problem with this theory, however, is that there is no evidence that this is what Śāntarakṣita and Kamalaśīla hope for their demonstration to do. Indeed, as we have seen above in our discussion of the second hypothesis concerning the motivation for the specific demonstration, there seems to be no convincing evidence for the idea that the authors think they can ground the Buddhist teachings in the Buddha's credibility or omniscience. Everything that we have seen leads us to believe that for Śāntarakṣita and Kamalaśīla, Buddhist teachings are justified through the two means of trustworthy awareness alone. Scripturally based inference, which is not a true inference but only a provisional one, can be accepted by a judicious person under certain circumstances as a justification for undertaking certain actions, but in no instance does scripturally based inference require that one demonstrate the special qualities of the scripture's author.

A second possibility concerning the motive for the demonstration of total omniscience corresponds to our third hypothesis for the specific demonstration, namely, that the demonstration is not intended for Buddhists and judicious persons at all but rather only for those who are so habituated to the idea of authorial authority that they will only be swayed by an argument that demonstrates that the Buddha in fact did know all things whatsoever. This hypothesis is not as unlikely as it at first may sound. For, as we noted above, included in the actual audience of the *Tattvasaṃgraha* and the *Pañjikā*, whether directly or indirectly, are those with whom Buddhists would compete in formal debates before (supposedly) impartial judges. Under such circumstances, one can well imagine it to be advantageous for Buddhists to present a demonstration of their founder as omniscient in the total sense, especially when their competitors (Naiyāyikas, Jains, and so on) were arguing strenuously for the omniscience of their own founders. When we consider that things such as royal patronage, land grants, or prestige were likely at stake, it appears quite understandable that the authors would develop an argument designed to show, or perhaps to *appear* to show, that the Buddha had knowledge of all *dharma*s whatsoever.

Of course, earlier I argued that the real meaning of the demonstration of total omniscience, contrary to appearances, is actually *not* to show that the Buddha knows all the myriad details of external objects of knowledge but rather only that the Buddha has nondual awareness of his own mind.[743] Once again, Kamalaśīla's disclaimer at the end of the final chapter to the effect that the demonstration was undertaken on the opponent's metaphysical assumption of the existence of external objects tips us off to the idea that the demonstration of total omniscience can be read in two different ways.[744] For non-Buddhists who are "addicted to external objects," it may be interpreted as arguing that because the Buddha directly knows the true nature (selflessness) of all things, he therefore must know all individual things themselves. For judicious Buddhists who understand that the Yogācāra perspective is more rational than any externalist ontology, the demonstration serves only to show that the Buddha has fully realized selflessness in regard to the only object of knowledge that really matters: his own mind.

Although the conclusion that the demonstration of total omniscience contains a deliberate bivalency may initially seem strange, it really is in close keeping with many of the principles of the authors' rhetoric of reason in the work. For, as we have seen, the authors are deeply committed to a form of reasoning in which one operates at distinct levels of analysis, moving only gradually from one level to the next in dependence on the degree of agreement that one reaches with one's audience. In fact, the final portion of the *Tattvasaṃgraha* and the *Pañjikā* as a whole is rife with competing visions of omniscience, all of which appear to get the authors' endorsement *within a*

743. See pp. 234–35 above.

744. TSP *ad* TS 3645 (*atīndriyārthadarśiparīkṣā*, B 1130,15–17). See n. 742 above.

certain context. At this point in the work, the objective seems to be less to settle on the one true version of omniscience than it is to delineate a range of viable interpretations of omniscience for which judicious Buddhists may be justified in arguing in different contexts.

In fact, Kamalaśīla is explicit that the various versions of omniscience are presented from the points of view of particular streams within the Buddhist tradition and are not necessarily accepted by all Buddhists. For example, when Śāntarakṣita makes mention of an understanding of omniscience in which a yogi knows all of the past and future inferentially, on the basis of his complete knowledge of all that exists in the present time,[745] Kamalaśīla remarks that such is not accepted by Sautrāntikas, who prefer the model of omniscience based on yogic perception that we have examined earlier.[746] Later, he defends distinct versions of omniscience according to two streams of the Yogācāra tradition, a system in which awarenesses are innately endowed with images (*sākāravāda*) and a system in which awarenesses are devoid of images (*nirākāravāda*).[747] A close reading of this passage does not yield any overt preference for one version over the other. Again, the openness to multiple

745. See TS 3472 (*atīndriyārthadarśiparīkṣā*), which refers the reader to the chapter the "Investigation of the Three Times" (*traikālyaparīkṣā*). The final verses of that chapter contain this theory. See TS 1852–54 (*traikālyaparīkṣā*), which Kamalaśīla also quotes in full in TSP *ad* TS 3472 (*atīndriyārthadarśiparīkṣā*, B 1090,12–17): *pāramparyeṇa sākṣād vā kāryakāraṇatāṃ gatam / yad rūpaṃ vartamānasya tad vijānanti yoginaḥ // anugacchanti paścāc ca vikalpānugatātmabhiḥ / śuddhalaukikavijñānais tattvato 'viṣayair api // tad dhetuphalayor bhūtāṃ bhāvinīṃ caiva santatim / tām āśritya pravartante 'tītānāgatadeśanāḥ //*. See also TSP *ad* TS 1852–54 (*traikālyaparīkṣā* B 632,17–21): *atītārthāpekṣayā kāryatāṃ gatam anāgatāpekṣayā kāraṇatām / vikalpānugatātmabhir iti / savikalpair ity arthaḥ / tattvato 'viṣayair iti / āviṣṭābhilāpair jñānaiḥ svalakṣaṇasyāviṣayīkaraṇāt / tat tasmāt / hetuphalayoḥ santatiṃ bhūtāṃ bhāvinīṃ cāśritātītādideśanā yogināṃ apariśuddhānāṃ pravartante /*. Note that both Śāntarakṣita and Kamalaśīla distinguish this type of yogic knowledge of the future on the basis of inference from a buddha's knowledge that is nonconceptual and spontaneous.

746. TSP *ad* TS 3473 (*atīndriyārthadarśiparīkṣā*, B 1090,19): *etac ca sautrāntikānāṃ neṣṭam ... /*.

747. See the lengthy excursus in TSP *ad* TS 3626 (*atīndriyārthadarśiparīkṣā*, B 1122,22–1126,19). This passage has been discussed by Funayama (2007), who makes the important contribution of noting that Kamalaśīla explicitly states that the images (*ākāra*) in cognition are unreal, thus throwing considerable doubt on the later classification of Śāntarakṣita and Kamalaśīla's Yogācāra thought as a species of **satyākāravāda* (Tibetan *rnam pa bden par smra ba*). As Funayama (2007: 199) rightly points out, the TSP is the earliest extant source that we have that identified two schools of Yogācāra through the categories of *sākāravāda* and *nirākāravāda*. Further research is required to unpack how Kamalaśīla understands these terms, not only in this passage but also throughout the text

interpretations remains a hallmark of these thinkers, even when we see their tendency to be toward continually honing their vision in an attempt to eventually arrive at the final, most rational vision of all. It is to that vision of omniscience that we turn to now.

---

and in comparison with his other works, especially the MAP. See also Keira 2004 for a translation and study of some relevant sections of MAP.

7. Spontaneous Omniscience and the Perfection of Reason

EARLIER, in the introduction to this book, I defended the notion that Śāntarakṣita and Kamalaśīla can be seen as practicing a form of Buddhist *philosophia*, by which I mean that they may be seen as engaged in a spiritual path that includes, and even glorifies, rational inquiry and analysis. In the intervening pages, we have examined numerous instances of rational argumentation put forth by these authors in defense of what they understand to be the goal of their path: namely, the perfection of wisdom—known otherwise as omniscience or buddhahood. Several features of this argumentation have by now become plain. For instance, we have seen that in defending the dogma of the Buddha's omniscience, the authors are first concerned to refute a conception of religious authority according to which individuals cannot have direct knowledge of the most soteriologically critical realities (that is, Dharma and Adharma) but must rely on an authorless scripture. Further, we have also seen that while the authors are deeply commited to rational analysis, their understanding of the conventional nature of all linguistic expression lends flexibility to their conception of reason such that we may speak of the authors as engaged in a rhetoric of reason. By this I mean that these Buddhists see rational argumentation as emerging from a context that is mutually defined by speaker (or author) and audience.[748] There thus is no entirely neutral rational ground on which to stand when advancing arguments, and it is only by dint of a degree of shared ignorance that we are able to engage in rational analaysis at all.[749]

The arguments advanced in the *Tattvasaṃgraha* and the *Pañjikā* in defense of omniscience are thus *all* provisional in important respects, but this does not mean that they all hold equal weight for the authors. The reason is that the authors hold—and, as we have seen, argue strenuously for the position—

748. McClintock 2008 explores this topic.

749. McClintock 2003 explores this topic.

that it is possible to eliminate ignorance, and that some arguments therefore proceed from a place of greater ignorance than others. As we have seen, this stance leads Śāntarakṣita and Kamalaśīla to adopt a method of a sliding scale of analysis, whereby they present arguments from hierarchically ranked metaphysical positions. Most of the arguments for the Buddha's omniscience in the *Tattvasaṃgraha* and the *Pañjikā* are presented at the Sautrāntika level of analysis, and this is because the arguments are addressed to Kumārila and others whose own metaphysics most closely resembles that of the Sautrāntika level of analysis from among the various Buddhist levels of analysis that our authors utilize.

For Śāntarakṣita and Kamalaśīla, the Sautrāntika level of analysis ultimately must be abandoned when one applies rational analysis to the question of whether external objects have a singular or a multiple nature.[750] They apply this analysis at the start of the chapter known as the "Investigation of External Objects," which as we saw earlier is the final chapter of the division of the *Tattvasaṃgraha* devoted to the exploration of dependent arising.[751] This chapter is also the sole investigation in the work that is argued almost exclusively from the Vijñānavāda perspective and in which the Sauntrāntika level of analysis plays only a minimal role. It is therefore not surprising to find that the model of omniscience in this chapter diverges significantly from what we find elsewhere in the work.

That is, when objects of knowledge external to the mind are accepted, as they are on the Sautrāntika level of anlaysis, the perfection of wisdom can be understood as a relatively uncomplicated matter, especially if one's definition of maximal epistemic greatness consists primarily of the idea of knowing all that is soteriologically necessary for the attainment of liberation. We have seen this definition of epistemic maximal greatness in play in the final chapter of the *Tattvasaṃgraha* and the *Pañjikā*, where we repeatedly find statements to the effect that we are justified in considering the Buddha to be omniscient because he knows what is to be abandoned and what is to be taken up, together with the means for doing so. Controversies may of course still arise concerning the capacity or the scope of his knowledge, but in the final analysis what counts is that the Buddha can be said to have knowledge of the most important things (*pradhānārtha*), or, to use Kumārila's favored terms, Dharma and Adharma. But when objects of knowledge external to the mind are refuted on the Vijñānavāda level of analysis, the description of

750. This analysis, which Śāntarakṣita has famously elaborated in his MA and MAV, has become known as the neither-one-nor-many argument.

751. See section pp. 98–102 above.

the Buddha's knowledge undergoes a radical shift. For whatever else can be said about the Buddha's knowledge, it now cannot include objects of knowledge external to the Buddha's mind. Indeed, as we will see, the authors maintain that on this level of analysis, the most rational position to hold is that the Buddha's perfect wisdom must consist in nondual reflexive awareness of his own mind. This is where the model of spontaneous omniscience comes in as a means of accounting for the Buddha's teaching with its apparent dependence on subject-object dualism and knowledge of others' minds.

Spontaneous Omniscience

The "Investigation of External Objects" chapter of the *Tattvasaṃgraha* and the *Pañjikā* is a rich source for a study, yet to be written, on Śāntarakṣita and Kamalaśīla's understanding of Yogācāra, and especially on where exactly they stand on the question of whether awareness is endowed with an image (*sākāra*) or not (*nirākāra*).[752] Here, we can only hint at some aspects of what such a study might reveal, for our focus must remain on the more specific question of the authors' understanding of a buddha's omniscient knowledge. As indicated above, the chapter begins with a résumé of the argument that external objects of knowledge cannot exist since they have neither a single nor a multiple nature.[753] This argument is elaborated again later in the chapter,

752. See n. 747 above.

753. The argument commences at TSP *ad* TS 1964 (*bahirarthaparīkṣā*, B 670,20–671,18): *tatrābhyāṃ prakārābhyāṃ vijñaptimātratābhiṣṭā / bāhyasya pṛthivyādisvabhāvasya grāhyasyābhāve grāhakasyāpy abhāvāt / saty api vā saṃtānāntare grāhyagrāhakalakṣaṇavaidhuryāt / tatra prayogaḥ / yad yaj jñānaṃ tat tat grāhyagrāhakatvadvayarahitam / jñānatvāt / pratibimbajñānavat / jñānaṃ cedaṃ svasthanetrādijñānaṃ vivādāspadībhūtam iti svabhāvahetuḥ / na cāvyāptir asya hetor mantavyā / tathā hi na tāvat pṛthivyādibāhyo 'rtho 'sya grāhyo vidyate tasyeikānekasvabhāvaśūnyatvāt / prayogaḥ / yad ekānekasvabhāvaṃ na bhavati na tat sattvena grāhyaṃ prekṣāvatā / yathā vyomotpalam / ekānekasvabhāvarahitāś ca parābhimatāḥ pṛthivyādaya iti vyāpakānupalabdhiḥ / tṛtīyarāśyantarābhāvenaikatvānekatvābhyāṃ sattvasya vyāptatvād vyāpyavyāpakabhāvānupapatir viparyaye bādhakaṃ pramāṇam iti nānaikāntikatānantarasya hetoḥ / nāpi viruddhatā sapakṣe bhāvāt / atrāsya hetor asiddhatām udbhāvayan yathoktaṃ bhūtānyeva na santīti nyāyo 'yaṃ para iṣyatām iti* /. "Now the fact [of things being] consciousness alone is asserted through these two methods: (1) because when external natures (*svabhāva*) such as earth do not exist as objects (*grāhya*), then a subject (*grāhaka*) does not exist either; or (2) because even though other mindstreams exist, they are devoid of being characterized as object and subject. Here the proof-statement is as follows: Whatever is an awareness (*jñāna*) is devoid of the duality of object and subject, because it is awareness, like the awareness of a reflection. And

and is a cornerstone of the shift to Vijñānavāda. As is also well known, the same argument is also used by these authors in their various Madhyamaka writings to demonstrate that the mind is devoid of inherent existence.[754] Although the authors stop shy of taking this step in the *Tattvasaṃgraha* and the *Pañjikā*, their Madhyamaka leanings are nonetheless on display in the form of their argumentation, especially as the distinction between external objects and real objects is not always strictly maintained.

The chapter is important for its preservation of a number of Buddhist and non-Buddhist objections to Vijñānavāda ideas, including two significant segments with direct bearing on the problem of the Buddha's omniscience. Both segments consist of responses to objections from a Buddhist opponent, Śubhagupta.[755] The first passage occurs in the context of Śubhagupta's objections to Dharmakīrti's famous *sahopalambhaniyama* reason for asserting that awareness never arises without an image. Briefly, this reason states that an awareness (*jñāna*) is always endowed with an image (*ākāra*) of its object of knowledge (*jñeya*) because of the restriction (*niyama*) that awarenesses and their images are always apprehended (*upalambha*) simultaneously, or together (*saha*).[756] Śāntarakṣita and Kamalaśīla accept that this reasoning also shows that awareness and its image are not different:

---

the awareness that is taken as the locus of the debate (*vivādāspadībhūta*) is the awareness such as a healthy ocular awareness. This is a reason by essential property (*svabhāvahetu*). And one should not think that there is no pervasion of this reason [by the *sādhya*]. That is to say, in the first place, no object, or external thing such as earth and so on, is found to belong to that [awareness], since that [alleged external object] is empty of having either a single or a multiple nature. The proof-statement is as follows: whatever does not have either a single or a multiple nature is not apprehended as real by judicious persons, as for example a sky-lotus. And the earth and so on, which are asserted by others [to have true existence], are devoid of having either a single or a multiple nature. Therefore [the non-reality of those things is established through] nonperception of the pervader. Real things are pervaded by the two [possibilities of] being either single or multiple, since there is no other third possibility. Therefore, since the relation between the pervaded and the pervader is not reasonable [when the subject is an unreal thing], there is a contravening trustworthy awareness in the contrapositive. Thus, the subsequent (*anantara*) evidence is not inconclusive. Nor is the evidence contradictory, since it exists in the homologous domain (*sapakṣa*). Here this evidence is not unestablished, and expressing this [Śāntarakṣita] said [in TS 1887] 'the elements do not exist, therefore this system (*nyāya*) should be asserted as best.'"

754. See Tillemans 1982, 1983, and 1984; Keira 2004; Blumenthal 2009.

755. On Śubhagupta, see n. 396 above.

756. For an extensive treatment of this reason in the works of Dharmakīrti and his followers, see Iwata 1991. See also PVin 1.54ab (Steinkellner ed., 2007: 40):

> Whenever there is some awareness that is an awareness of something, it is certain that that [object of awareness] is not different from that [awareness itself] and that [that awareness] is not different from that [object of awareness].[757]

In contrast, Śubhagupta holds both that external objects exist and that awareness is *not* endowed with an image of its object of knowledge. He also argues in his *Bāhyārthasiddhikārikā* ("Verses on the Proof of External Objects") that Dharmakīrti's *sahopalambhaniyama* reason is incoherent on the grounds that the term "together" (*saha*) cannot make sense if the intention of the demonstration is to show that awarenesses and their images are not, in fact, two different things.[758]

As part of his argument, Śubhagupta takes advantage of a tension present in much of Yogācāra thinking: namely, that the Yogācāra wants to deny objects of knowledge external to the mind yet still maintain the existence of *other mindstreams* different from one's own.[759] In other words, the Yogācāra generally seeks to avoid solipsism while still advocating a species of idealist metaphysics. This tension becomes particularly acute when the Buddha's omniscient knowledge is considered, since it is generally taken as a dogma of omniscience in Indian thought that one of its features is to know the minds and mental functions of others.[760] Śubhagupta offers several criticisms of the *sahopalambhaniyama* reason, including that simultaneous apprehension would entail many absurdities; for example, the Buddha's mind would

---

sahopalambhaniyamād abhedo nīlataddhiyoḥ. Cf. also PV 3.390: *nārtho 'saṃvedanaḥ kaścid anarthaṃ vāpi vedanam / dṛṣṭaṃ saṃvedyamānaṃ tat tayor nāsti vivekitā //*.

757. TS 2029 (*bahirarthaparīkṣā*): *yat saṃvedanam eva syād yasya saṃvedanaṃ dhruvam / asmād avyatiriktaṃ tat tato vā na vibhidyate //*.

758. See TSP *ad* TS 2029–30 (*bahirarthaparīkṣā*, B 692,2–3), corresponding to BASK 71: *sahaśabdaś ca loke 'smin naivānyena vinā kvacit / viruddho 'yaṃ tato hetur yady asti sahavedanam //*. "And in the world, the word *simultaneous* (*saha*) is never [applied] without what is other. Therefore if there is the awareness of [two things as being] simultaneous, then this evidence is contradictory." There are several variants in the Sanskrit. The Tibetan as recorded in the TSP at D, vol. *'e*, 120b4 is: *'jig rten 'di na lhan cig sgra / gzhan med par ni gang na'ang med / gal te lhan cig rig yod na / de'i phyir gtan tshigs 'di 'gal lo //*.

759. For Kamalaśīla's statement of this principle, see the opening commentary on the "Investigation of External Objects," TSP *ad* TS 1964 (*bahirarthaparīkṣā*, B 671,8). For Dharmakīrti's defense of the existence of other minds in the Yogācāra system, see Katsura 2007.

760. Cf. n. 360 above.

become multiple, since it would be held to be not different from its object, the many minds of sentient beings. Kamalaśīla records Śubhagupta as saying:

> [Objection:] Furthermore, just as if there were the rule of simultaneous apprehension, then the Buddha's cognition whose object (*vijñeya*) is the mental content (*citta*) of other mindstreams (*saṃtānāntara*) would become multiple [like its objects]; likewise, if there were the simultaneous apprehension of mind and mental functions, there would be no singularity either. Therefore, the reason is inconclusive.[761]

Kamalaśīla responds as follows:

> [Answer:] This is all incorrect, for in this context the intended meaning of "single apprehension" (*ekopalambha*) is not that there is the apprehension of [many] things by one [single apprehender]. Rather, there is just the mutual apprehension of awareness and the object of awareness as single and not as separate. For the apprehension of the awareness is precisely the [apprehension] of the object of awareness; and [the apprehension] of the object of awareness is precisely [the apprehension] of the awareness.[762]

In other words, the point of invoking the *sahopalambhaniyama* reason is primarily to show that all awareness is devoid of subject-object duality and also that all awareness is reflexive awareness (*svasaṃvedana*, *svasaṃvitti*). In

761. TSP *ad* TS 2029–30 (*bahirarthaparīkṣā*, B 692,18–21): *yathā kila buddhasya bhagavato yad vijñeyaṃ santānāntaracittaṃ tasya buddhajñānasya ca sahopalambhaniyame 'py asty eva ca nānātvaṃ tasya tathā cittacaittānāṃ saty api sahopalambhe naikatvam ity ato 'naikāntiko hetur iti //*. Reading *sahopalambhaniyame 'py* in accord with the Tibetan at D, vol. *'e*, 121a5: *lhan cig dmigs pa nges pa yin pa yang* instead of B 692,19: *sahopalambhaniyamo 'py*. Although J 210b2 does not record an *api*, the editor of G recognized the need for the particle and presents the following reading at G 568,6: *sahopalambhaniyame '(pya) sty eva*. This passage resembles BASK 77: *gal te thams cad mkhyen pa yi / ye shes shes bya sems kun na / de tshe gcig pu kho na yis / dmigs pa grub pa gang du brjod*. Cf. also BASK 86: *thams cad mkhyen pa'i ye shes kyi / myong par bya ba brgyud gzhan la / bsgos pa'i chos rnams gang dag [yin] / de dag gis kyang ma nges te / rtogs med ji ltar thams cad mkhyen //*.

762. TSP *ad* TS 2029–30 (*bahirarthaparīkṣā*, B 692,22–693,1): *tad etat sarvam asamyak / na hy atraikenaivopalambha ekopalambha ity ayam artho 'bhipretaḥ / kiṃ tarhi / jñānajñeyayoḥ parasparam eka evopalambho na pṛthag iti / ya eva hi jñānopalambhaḥ sa eva jñeyasya ya eva jñeyasya sa eva jñānasyeti yāvat /*.

other words, all awareness reflexively knows itself, because its nature is one of illumination.[763]

A few lines later, Kamalaśīla attempts to clarify how the Buddha can know others' minds if the Buddha's mind is truly nondual. It is here that we begin to see the doctrine of spontaneous omniscience articulated, insofar as Kamalaśīla indicates that the Buddha accomplishes the aims of sentient beings spontaneously, through the power of his previous vows and without any apprehension of them!

> Also, it is not the case that the Blessed Buddha's mind determines (*avasīyate*) the mental moments that are occurring in the mind-streams of others, since that Blessed One is free from the stains of the perceived (*grāhya*) and the perceiver (*grāhaka*) because of being free from all obscurations (*sarvāvaraṇa*). As it is said, "There is no apprehended object for that one, nor any apprehension by him; [he is] free even of the quality of having another cognition as an object." But the obtainment of success [on his part] is merely in terms of his power (*ādhipatya*). As it is said, "The aims of others are continuously and spontaneously obtained through the previously established aspirations (*pūrvapraṇidhāna*)." [Śāntarakṣita] will explain that omniscience is asserted due to the accomplishment of all aims (*sarvārthakāritvāt*).[764]

The first impression one gets here is that Kamalaśīla has left behind all rationality, advancing a theory in which the Buddha's awareness of others' minds,

763. See TS 1999–2001 and TSP *ad cit.* (*bahirarthaparīkṣā*, B 682,20–24).

764. TSP *ad* TS 2029–30 (*bahirarthaparīkṣā*, B 693,7–12): *na ca buddhasya bhagavataś cittena parasantānavartinaś cittakṣaṇā avasīyate / tasya bhagavataḥ sarvāvaraṇavigamena grāhyagrāhakakalaṅkarahitatvāt / yathoktam / grāhyaṃ na tasya grahaṇaṃ na tena jñānāntaragrāhyatayāpi śūnyam iti / akṣuṇṇavidhānaṃ tv ādhipatyamātreṇa / yathoktam / pūrvapraṇidhānāhitasatatānābhogavāhi parakāryam iti sarvārthakāritvāt sarvajña iṣyata iti vakṣyati //*. The last sentence probably refers to the explanation of the spontaneous Buddha in TS 2048–49 (*bahirarthaparīkṣā*), on which see p. 354–55 just below. Reading *cittakṣaṇā* with B instead of *cittalakṣaṇa* with G in accordance with D, vol. *'e*, 121b2: *sems kyi skad cig*. My interpretation of the compound in the second quotation is influenced by D, vol. *'e*, 121b3–4: *sngon gyi smon lam gyis bsgos pas rtag tu gzhan gyi bya ba la lhun gyis grub par 'jug go*. Kajiyama, in the notes to his translation of Ratnakīrti's *Saṃtānāntaradūṣaṇa*, claims that this passage indicates an affirmation of solipsism, a claim that if true would indicate a contradiction with statements earlier in this same chapter (Kajiyama 1965: 9n1). Kajiyama adds, however, that this passage was written from the perspective of ultimate truth, whereas the earlier ones were from a perspective of relative truth (10n2).

and of objects of knowledge in general, is just inconceivable. Amazingly, we find within a span of just a few lines the assertions that the Buddha has no apprehended object and no apprehension, that he accomplishes others' aims, and that this is the basis on which he may be considered omniscient! How can this be? Kamalaśīla promises that this will be explained, and indeed we find some answers in the second relevant segment of the chapter.

The answers come in a section that appears to accept Śubhagupta's assessment of Vijñānavāda as espousing that awarenesses are devoid of images (*nirākāra*), at least ultimately.[765] In this context, Śāntarakṣita and Kamalaśīla seem to reject the idea that the apprehender/apprehended relationship exists even figuratively for a buddha.[766] The commentary refers to those who assert that the Buddha apprehends or perceives others' minds as those who uphold a "view in which there is an objective referent" (*aupalambhikadarśana*).[767] Such talk leads naturally to the obvious question "If [the Buddha] does not know anything, how can he be omniscient?" Śāntarakṣita gives the following response:

> Like a wish-fulfilling tree, due to the purification of all conceptions, the sage accomplishes the aim of worldly beings, even without being shaken. Even though he is unseeing, everyone says the Jina is omniscient, because he knows everything simultaneously as an effect [of his previous vows].[768]

Kamalaśīla comments as follows:

> "Unseeing" means that he does not see, i.e., does not perceive, and therefore he is unseeing. [People] say that he is omniscient due to his perfection of the aims of the entire world in accord with what is auspicious, which comes about spontaneously from the force

765. This accords with passages found elsewhere in the TSP, including the long excursus at TSP *ad* TS 3626 (*atīndriyārthadarśiparīkṣā*, B 1122,22–1126,19). See Funayama 2007.

766. TS 2046 (*bahirarthaparīkṣā*) states it clearly: awareness does not apprehend anything else: *sākāraṃ tan nirākāraṃ yuktaṃ nānyasya vedakam / iti bauddhe 'pi vijñāne na tu cintā pravarttate //*. Cf. also MAP *ad* MA 92 (Ichigō 1985: 300–301).

767. TSP *ad* TS 2047 (*bahirarthaparīkṣā*, B 699,21–23).

768. TS 2048–49 (*bahirarthaparīkṣā*): *kalpapādapavat sarvasaṅkalpapavanair muniḥ / akampo 'pi karoty eva lokānām arthasampadam // tenādarśanam apy āhuḥ sarve sarvavidaṃ jinam / anābhogena niḥśeṣasarvavitkāryasaṃbhavāt //*.

of his previous vows, like a wish-fulfilling tree; it does not come about through the force of perception.[769]

I think that there can be no doubt that this represents the authors' ultimate perspective on omniscience in the *Tattvasaṃgraha* and the *Pañjikā*, and probably at their Madhyamaka level of analysis as well. Not only does it occur in their final chapter dedicated to the explication of the reality of dependent arising, it is also the answer that they give to their fellow Buddhists when pushed on the question of the actual nature of the Buddha's awareness. It is also the only scenario that resolves the tensions inherent in the problem of how the Buddha can be a speaker if he has eliminated all desire (including, presumably, the desire to speak).[770]

In fact, the spontaneous omniscience model also makes a brief appearance in the final chapter of the *Tattvasaṃgraha* and the *Pañjikā*. Here again, we encounter the idea that the Buddha's teachings are merely a matter of his innate power (*ādhipatya*), proceeding spontaneously as if from a wish-fulfilling gem in accord with the needs and desires of sentient beings, and

769. TSP *ad* TS 2048–49 (*bahirarthaparīkṣā*, B 700,11–13): *adarśanam iti / nāsya darśanam upalambho 'stīty adarśanaḥ / pūrvapraṇidhānabalād anābhogena kalpataruvad yathābhavyam aśeṣajagadarthasaṃpādanāt sarvajñam āhur nopalambhabalāt /*.

770. Śāntarakṣita and Kamalaśīla offer another solution to this quandary, according to which the Buddha is understood in fact to *have* conceptions (and therefore also potentially the desire to speak), but he is understood to have only unafflicted conceptions, which are conducive to the welfare of the world. See TS 3596–97 (*atīndriyārthadarśiparīkṣā*), which takes the form of an objection and a response: *vikalpāsaṃbhave tasya vivakṣā nanu kīdṛśī / prahīṇāvaraṇatvād dhi vikalpo nāsya vartate // naivaṃ kliṣṭo hi saṃkalpas tasya nāsty āvṛtikṣayāt / jagaddhitānukūlas tu kuśalaḥ kena vāryate //*. "[Objection:] If conceptuality is impossible for him, how could there be any kind of intention to speak? Since [as you assert] he has eliminated the obstructions, there is no conceptuality for him. [Response:] That is not so, for that one has no afflicted notions (*saṃkalpa*) because he has eliminated the obscurations. But who would deny that he has positive [conceptions] that are conducive to the benefit of the world?" The text goes on from here to explain that the conceptions that arise for the Buddha do not taint him, because, like a magician, he knows that they are unreal. See TS 3598–99 (*atīndriyārthadarśiparīkṣā*): *na ca tasya vikalpasya so 'rthavattām avasyati / taṃ hi vetti nirālambaṃ māyākārasamo hy asau // māyākāro yathā kaścin niścitāśvādigocaram / ceto nirviṣayaṃ vetti tena bhrānto na jāyate //*. "And he does not consider that conception to have an object, for like a magician, he knows that it is without an objective referent, just as a magician knows that the mind that ascertains an object such as a horse [when in fact that appearance is just an illusion] is objectless. Therefore no error arises." This solution to the problem of how the Buddha can be a speaker appears to be one step short of the final solution in which the Buddha's teachings are spontaneous and utterly devoid of conceptuality.

powered, as it were, by the vows made by the Buddha when he was still a bodhisattva (and therefore still engaged in erroneous concepts and erroneous perception). The idea is first raised as part of the challenge attributed to Sāmaṭa and Yajñaṭa near the end of the *pūrvapakṣa* section. Kamalaśīla summarizes the Mīmāṃsaka characterization of the Buddhist position as follows:

> Someone [i.e., some Buddhist] might think: He does not teach anything at all because he remains always in a nonconceptual meditative concentration (*samādhi*). But, through his power (*ādhipatya*), representations (*vijñapti*) of various teachings of the Dharma appear to the fortunate. As it is said, "On a certain night, the Tathāgata awakened, and on a certain night he attained *parinirvāṇa*. Between these [two nights] the Tathāgata did not utter or speak even a single syllable. Why is that? It is because the Tathāgata is always absorbed in meditative concentration. But those who are to be disciplined through teachings that are given voice through syllables hear words issuing from the mouth, the *uṣṇīṣa*, and the *ūrṇā* of the Tathāgata."[771]

The scriptural passage cited here is very similar to one that is cited in Candrakīrti's *Prasannapadā*, where it is attributed to the *Tathāgataguhyasūtra*. In Candrakīrti's work, the citation is followed by several verses from the same sūtra, including one that uses another metaphor to explain the Buddha's spontaneous teachings:

> Moved by the wind, mechanical chimes are caused to make a

771. TSP *ad* TS 3240–42 (*atīndriyārthadarśiparīkṣā*, B 1019,17–22): *syād etat / naivāsāv upadiśati kiñcit sarvadā nirvikalpasamādhisthitatvāt / kiṃ tu tadādhipatyena vicitradharmadeśanā pratibhāsā vijñaptayo bhavyānāṃ bhavanti / yathoktam / yasyāṃ rātrau tathāgato 'bhisambuddho yasyāṃ ca parinirvṛtaḥ / atrāntare tathāgatena ekam apy akṣaraṃ nodāhṛtaṃ na pravyāhṛtam / tat kasya hetoḥ / satatasamāhito hi tathāgataḥ / api tu ye 'kṣararutadeśanā vaineyikās te tathāgatasya mukhād uṣṇīṣād ūrṇāyāḥ śabdaṃ niḥsarantaṃ śṛṇvantītyādi /*. The quotation in this passage, with some variation, is found also in Prajñākaramati's commentary on Śāntideva's BCA 9.36, where is it followed first by a citation of TS 3240–42 and then by a citation of *Niraupamyastava* 7 (attributed to Nāgārjuna). A very similar quotation is found as well in Candrakīrti's *Prasannapadā* on Nāgārjuna's MMK 18.7 and MMK 25.24, where the source for the quotation is recorded as the *Tathāgataguhyasūtra*, which corresponds to the third text preserved in the Ratnakuṭa section of the Tibetan Bstan 'gyur, the *Āryatathāgatācintyaguhyanirdeśanā*. See next note.

> sound. There is no speaker here, and yet sounds still come forth. Likewise, due to previous purification, the Buddha's speech comes forth when moved by the aspirations of all beings, but the Buddha has no conceptuality.[772]

Candrakīrti goes on to quote the *Āryasamādhirāja*, which describes a scene in which even the grasses, trees, and mountains will resound with the Buddha's teachings, and whereby a single sound emitted by the Buddha is perceived as diverse teachings by those of various inclinations.[773] The mechanism by which such is said to occur is the power of the Buddha's previous vow, made when still a bodhisattva, to be of maximal aid to all sentient beings. Such teachings are clearly common to many Indian texts, and we know that they were shared by Jains as well.[774]

In the final chapter of the *Tattvasaṃgraha*, we find a challenge to such ideas embedded in the verses attributed to the otherwise unidentified Mīmāṃsakas, Sāmaṭa and Yajñaṭa. Here, we see reference made to teachings issuing spontaneously through the Buddha's power even from inanimate objects like walls and so on.[775] In what looks like a very reasonable response to this notion, Sāmaṭa and Yajñaṭa are represented as saying that such doctrines may be fine if one is already imbued with faith, but for those who lack such faith, some reasoning (*yukti*) should be provided.[776] They go on in the next few verses to urge that, in any case, teachings that issue spontaneously from walls and so on could not be trusted since one would not be able to verify their provenance.[777] Given that Śāntarakṣita and Kamalaśīla profess to follow a path of reason and not one of mere faith, one would expect them

772. *Prasannapadā* on Nāgārjuna's MMK 18.7 (Poussin ed., 366,9–367,2): *yathā yantrakṛtaṃ tūryaṃ vādyate pavaneritaṃ / na cātra vādakaḥ kaścin niścarantyatha ca svarāḥ // evaṃ pūrvasuśuddhatvāt sarvasattvāśayeritā / vāg niścarati buddhasya na cāsyāstiha kalpanā //.*

773. See *Prasannapadā* on Nāgārjuna's MMK 18.7 (Poussin ed., 367,12–368,3).

774. Jaini 1974: 79; Dundas 1992: 32.

775. TS 3240–41 (*atīndriyārthadarśiparīkṣā*): *tasmin dhyānasamāpanne cintāratnavad āsthite / niścaranti yathākāmaṃ kuṭyādibhyo 'pi deśanāḥ // tābhir jijñāsitānarthān sarvān jānanti mānavāḥ / hitāni ca yathābhavyaṃ kṣipram āsādayanti te //.* Reading *dhyānasamāpanne* with G in place of *jñānasamāpanne* as found in B.

776. TS 3242 (*atīndriyārthadarśiparīkṣā*): *ityādi kīrtyamānaṃ tu śraddadhāneṣu śobhate / vayam aśraddadhānās tu ye yuktīḥ prārthayāmahe //.*

777. TS 3243–45 (*atīndriyārthadarśiparīkṣā*): *kuṭyādiniḥsṛtānāṃ ca na syād āptopadiṣṭatā / viśvāsaś ca na tāsu syāt kenemāḥ kīrtitā iti // kiṃ nu buddhapraṇītāḥ syuḥ kiṃ nu brāhmaṇavañcakaiḥ / krīḍadbhir upadiṣṭāḥ syur dūrasthapratiśabdakaiḥ // kiṃ*

to react strongly to the charge that their explanations are good for the faithful alone.

Yet when Śāntarakṣita and Kamalaśīla get around to answering this objection near the end of the chapter, they seem to rely on a rather cheap trick. That is, rather than answering the substance of the charge—namely, that the doctrine of the spontaneous Buddha sounds good to those who have faith in it but lacks convincing evidence for judicious persons—they instead complain that their Mīmāṃsaka opponents have incorrectly applied the rules of formal reasoning. The gist of the complaint is that the Mīmāṃsaka opponents have not followed through on the implication of their objection. As Śāntarakṣita states:

> For here, the context is the statement, "And thus not possessing all objects [of knowledge] he is not able to teach." And in this regard, wise persons say, "If he were to have no capacity to teach, then what?" At this point, you should say, "Then there would be no scripture." But [in fact,] you then say, "Let it be thus [that the Buddha has no capacity to speak]; but have you seen the speaker [of those scriptures]?" If you urge an objection through the means of a *prasaṅga*, then the undesired consequence is this: "If speakerhood is not accepted, then there would be no scripture. But if a scripture promulgated by that one [is accepted], then you must accept his speakerhood."[778]

Although not very satisfying as a response to Sāmaṭa and Yajñaṭa, in terms of the arguments that we examined earlier on the question of religious authority, Śāntarakṣita and Kamalaśīla's answer here makes good sense. The point in this chapter and this context is not how to reconcile the Buddha's nonconceptual awareness and lack of desire with his ability to teach. Rather, the point that Śāntarakṣita and Kamalaśīla wish to drive home is that the Buddha *is* the author of the Buddhist scriptures, and that since the Buddhist scriptures can be independently confirmed to be trustworthy, there-

vā kṣudrapiśācādyair adṛṣṭair eva kīrtitāḥ / tasmān na tāsu viśvāsaḥ kartavyaḥ prājñamānibhiḥ //. Cf. ŚV, *codanā*, 138–40.

778. TS 3601–4 (*atīndriyārthadarśiparīkṣā*): *tathāvyāptaś ca sarvārthaiḥ śakto naivopadeśane / ity etat prakṛtaṃ hy atra tatra cāhur mahādhiyaḥ // tasyopadeśane śaktir na syāc cet kiṃ tadā bhavet / tato bhavadbhir vaktavyam āgamo na bhaved iti // tatrāpy āhur bhavatv evaṃ kiṃ dṛṣṭo 'sau tvayā vadan / prasaṅgasādhanenedam aniṣṭaṃ codyate yadi // na ced vaktṛtvam iṣyeta nāgamopagamo bhavet / tatpraṇetāgameṣṭau tu tasya vaktṛtvam iṣyatām //*.

fore their author must be considered trustworthy as well.[779] The Buddhist scriptures thus are the evidence for their author's omniscience, where this is understood as maximal epistemic greatness. And according to Śāntarakṣita and Kamalaśīla, the Mīmāṃsakas have not offered any refutation or undesired consequence in relation to this idea.[780]

The Perfection of Reason?

What counts for maximal epistemic greatness depends, of course, on the level of analysis from which one considers the problem. At the highest level of analysis, maximal epistemic greatness appears to be a kind of purified *unknowing* that nevertheless allows disciples to encounter a buddha who seems to be omniscient but who does not engage in the dualistic process of ordinary knowing. Although this doctrine may look dubious to Sāmaṭa and Yajñaṭa, as well as to many modern readers, there is a logic to this end result. As we have seen, although these authors are committed to the idea that reason is the final arbiter of truth for human beings, we have also seen that for these thinkers, truth—like all linguistic concepts—is a conventional designation that operates only within a dualistic context that imagines the existence of a knowing subject separate from an object of knowledge. Reason is like a tool that demolishes this dualism, but in doing so it also finally must demolish itself. The perfection of reason thus results in the perfection of wisdom—a state in which neither the knower nor the known can be ultimately distinguished. Only through the power of compassion, which took the form of a prior aspiration to omniscience, does the unknowing Buddha appear to know all to those who are ready to hear his teachings.

Reason, then, can never be removed from the embodied process of human investigation and inquiry—nor can it be entirely free of ignorance. All reasoning, and all knowing, implies relationships and contexts; there can be no decontextualized reason or rationality removed from the embodied process of human investigation and inquiry. As we have seen, this approach to reason is what allows the authors of the *Tattvasaṃgraha* and the *Pañjikā* to embrace a sliding scale of analysis, whereby different—and sometimes contradictory—premises and conclusions are upheld in diverse contexts. Ultimately, however, *all* premises and conclusions must be seen as provisional, since when knowledge and its acquisition are analyzed through reason, one increasingly

779. See TS 3611–18 (*atīndriyārthadarśiparīkṣā*).

780. See TS 3605–9 (*atīndriyārthadarśiparīkṣā*) and TSP *ad cit.* (B 1118,24–1119,16).

discovers ways in which the process of knowing cannot withstand such rational analysis. That is, when one attempts to apply a context-free ideal of reason to the process of knowing, one gradually discovers that knowing is not, in fact, rational in the manner assumed.

What then does this kind of contingent rationality look like? One answer may come by turning once again to Perelman and Olbrechts-Tyteca's notion of the universal audience. As we have seen, these authors argue in *The New Rhetoric* that philosophical discourse is generally addressed to a universal audience of rational beings. At the same time, however, *all* audiences—whether universal *or* particular—need to be understood to be constructions of the author. That is, in Perelman and Olbrechts-Tyteca's words, "Each individual, each culture, has thus its own conception of the universal audience."[781] As one interpreter of this theory astutely observed, this means that "All such [philosophical] arguments are subject to the paradox that speakers must presuppose a concept of timeless validity, a concept clearly subject to contingency."[782]

Śāntarakṣita and Kamalaśīla are not exempt from this paradox. They, too, must construct a universal audience, and I have argued that they do so in the *Tattvasaṃgraha* and the *Pañjikā* in their construction of the figure of the judicious person. Yet while they have constructed a universal audience, one might also argue that these Buddhist thinkers are more aware of its constructed nature than are many other champions of reason and rationality—both in their own times and in ours. Thus, the judicious person is urged to use reason to remove the ignorance that gives rise to all conceptions, including even such centrally important (because useful) conceptions as the "judicious person," the "means of trustworthy awareness," "reason," and so on. Thus reason remains an indispensable and constant element informing all aspects of religious life up until the final stage of omniscience or buddhahood. We might even say that for the authors of the *Tattvasaṃgraha* and the *Pañjikā*, reason *is* religion, for it is only by means of reason that one can finally transcend the mistaken addiction to the belief that ordinary, transactional forms of reasoning can ever yield fully nonerroneous and context-independent knowledge. By the same token, the conventional, contextual, and provisional nature of reason allows for a plurality of rational perspectives. Since reason eventually leads one to relinquish *all* views, there really is *no* final view—thus leaving a great deal of room for a multiplicity of views along the way.

781. Perelman and Olbrechts-Tyteca 1969: 33.

782. Gross 1999: 207.

Bibliography

Abbreviations

AA	*Abhisamayālaṃkāra* of Maitreya
AAA	*Abhisamayālaṃkārāloka* of Haribhadra
AK	*Abhidharmakośa* (*kārikā*) of Vasubandhu
AKBh	*Abhidharmakośabhāṣya* of Vasubandhu
B	Bauddha Bharati Series editions of TS/P and of the AKBh
BASK	*Bāhyārthsiddhikārikā* of Śubhagupta
BCA	*Bodhicaryāvatāra* of Śāntideva
D	Sde dge edition of the Tibetan canon
G	Gaekwad's Oriental Series edition of TS/P
Gn	Gnoli edition of PVSV
J	Jaisalmer manuscript of TS and TSP
JMS	*Jaiminimīmāṃsāsūtra* of Jaimini
MA	*Madhyamakālaṃkāra* of Śāntarakṣita
MĀ	*Madhyamakāloka* of Kamalaśīla
MAP	*Madhyamakālaṃkārapañjikā* of Kamalaśīla
MAV	*Madhyamakālaṃkāravṛtti* of Śāntarakṣita
MAv	*Madhyamakāvatāra* of Candrakīrti
MAvṬ	*Madhyamakāvatāraṭīkā* of Jayānanda
MMK	*Mūlamadhyamakakārikā* of Nāgārjuna
MN	*Majjhima Nikāya*
MSA	*Mahāyānasūtrālaṃkāra* of Maitreya/Asaṅga
NB	*Nyāyabindu* of Dharmakīrti
NBh	*Nyāyabhāṣya* of Vātsyāyana
NK	*Nyāyakaṇikā* of Vācaspatimiśra
NS	*Nyāyasūtra* of Akṣapāda Gautama
NV	*Nyāyavārttika* of Uddyotakara
P	Peking edition of the Tibetan canon

Pat	Patna manuscript of TS and TSP
PDS	*Padārthadharmasaṃgraha* of Praśastapāda
PS	*Pramāṇasamuccaya* of Dignāga
PSV	*Pramāṇasamuccayavṛtti* of Dignāga
PV	*Pramāṇavārttika* of Dharmakīrti
PVBh	*Pramāṇavārttikabhāṣya* of Prajñākaragupta
PVin	*Pramāṇaviniścaya* of Dharmakīrti
PVP	*Pramāṇavārttikapañjikā* of Devendrabuddhi
PVSV	*Pramāṇavārttikasvopajñavṛtti* of Dharmakīrti
PVṬ	*Pramāṇavārttikaṭīkā* of Śākyabuddhi
PVV	*Pramāṇavārttikavṛtti* of Manorathanandin
PVV-n	Vibhūticandra's notes to PVV; included in Sāṅkṛtyāyana's edition of PVV
RĀ	*Ratnāvalī* of Nāgārjuna
ŚBh	*Śābarabhāṣya* of Śabarasvāmin
SDV	*Satyadvayavibhaṅga* of Jñānagarbha
SDVP	*Satyadvayavibhaṅgapaṇjikā* of Śāntarakṣita
SN	*Saṃyutta Nikāya*
SS	*Sarvajñasiddhi* of Ratnakīrti
ŚV	*Ślokavārttika* of Kumārila
TS	*Tattvasaṃgraha* of Śāntarakṣita
TSP	*Tattvasaṃgrahapañjikā* of Kamalaśīla (called simply *Pañjikā* in this book)
TS/P	TS together with TSP
VN	*Vādanyāya* of Dharmakīrti
VNV	*Vādanyāyavipañcitārthā* of Śāntarakṣita
VV	*Vyomavatī* of Vyomaśiva

Primary Sources

Akalaṅkadeva. *Aṣṭaśatī.*

(1) Śrīmad Vijayanemisūrīśvara and Vijayodayasūri, eds. *Aṣṭasahasrī Vṛtti of Vidyānānda and the Aṣṭasahasrītātparyavivaraṇam of Yośovijaya.* Ahmedabad: Śrīrājanagarastha Śrījaina Granthaprakāśaka Sabhā, 1937.

Akṣapāda Gautama. *Nyāyasūtra.* [NS]

(1) In Tārānātha Nyāya-Tarkatīrtha and Amarendramohan Tarkatīrtha, eds. *Nyāyadarśanam: With Vātsyāyana's Bhāṣya, Uddyotakara's Vārttika, Vācaspati Miśra's Tātparyaṭīkā and Viśvanātha's Vṛtti.* Delhi: Munshiram Manoharlal Publishers, 1985. [Reprint of Chaukhambha Sanskrit Series 18–19, 1936–44.]

(2) Ganganatha Jha, trans. *The Nyāya-Sūtras of Gautama with the Bhāṣya of Vatsyāyana and the Vārttika of Uddyotakara.* 5 vols. Delhi: Motilal Banarsidass, 1984.

Āryadeva. *Catuḥśataka.*

(1) Karen Lang, ed. and trans. *Āryadeva's Catuḥśataka: On the Bodhisattva's Cultivation of Merit and Knowledge.* Copenhagen: Akademisk Forlag, 1986.

Asaṅga. *Bodhisattvabhūmi.*

(1) Nalinaksha Dutt, ed. *Bodhisattvabhūmi: Being the XVth Section of Asaṅgapāda's Yogācārabhūmi.* Tibetan Sanskrit Works Series 7. Patna: Kashiprasad Jayaswal Research Institute, 1966.

Bhāviveka. *Madhyamakahṛdaya.*

(1) Dīpaṃkaraśrījñāna and Tshul khrims rgyal ba, trans. *Dbu ma'i snying po'i tshig le'ur byas pa.* D, *dbu ma*, vol. *dza*, 1a1–40b7.

Bhāviveka. *Tarkajvālā.*

(1) Dīpaṃkaraśrījñāna and Tshul khrims rgyal ba, trans. *Dbu ma'i snying po 'grel pa rtog ge 'bar ba.* D, *dbu ma*, vol. *dza*, 40b7–329b4.

Buddhaghosa. *Visuddhimagga.*

(1) Henry Clarke Warren, ed. *Visuddhimagga of Buddhaghosācariya.* Harvard Oriental Series 41. Cambridge, MA: Harvard University Press, 1950.

(2) Bhikkhu Ñāṇamoli, trans., *The Path of Purification*. 2 vols. Colombo: R. Semage, 1956–57.

Candrakīrti. *Catuḥśatakaṭīkā*

(1) Kōshin Suzuki, ed. *Sanskrit Fragments and Tibetan Translation of Candrakīrti's Bodhisattvayogācāra-catuḥśatakaṭīkā*. 3 vols. Institute for Comprehensive Studies of Buddhism, Taishō University. Tokyo: The Sankibo Press, 1994.

Candrakīrti. *Madhyamakāvatāra*.

(1) Tilakalaśa and Pa tshab nyi ma grags, trans. *Dbu ma la 'jug pa*. D, *dbu ma*, vol. *'a*, 201a1–219a7. Revised by Kanakavarma and Pa tshab nyi ma grags.

Candrakīrti. *Madhyamakāvatārabhāṣya*.

(1) Louis de la Vallée Poussin, ed. *Madhyamakāvatārabhāṣya par Candrakīrti, traduction tibétaine*. St. Petersburg: Bibliotheca Buddhica 9, 1907–12. Reprint, Osnabrück: Biblio Verlag, 1970.

(2) Tilakalaśa and Pa tshab nyi ma grags, trans. *Dbu ma la 'jug pa'i bshad pa*. D, *dbu ma*, vol. *'a*, 220a1–347a7. Revised by Kanakavarma and Pa tshab nyi ma grags.

Candrakīrti. *Prasannapadā*.

(1) Louis de la Vallée Poussin, ed. *Madhyamakavṛtti: Mūlamadhyamakakārikās (Madhyamakaśāstra) de Nāgārjuna avec la Prasannapadā Commentaire de Candrakīrti*. St. Petersburg: Bibliotheca Buddhica 4, 1903–13. Reprint, Osnabrück: Biblio Verlag, 1970.

(2) P. L. Vaidya, ed. *Madhyamakaśāstra of Nāgārjuna with the Commentary "Prasannapadā" by Candrakīrti*. Buddhist Sanskrit Texts Series 10. Darbhanga: Mithila Institute, 1960.

Candrakīrti. *Triśaraṇasaptati*.

(1) Per K. Sorensen, ed. and trans. *Triśaraṇasaptati: The Septuagint on the Three Refuges*. Wiener Studien zur Tibetologie und Buddhismuskunde 16. Vienna: Arbeitskreis für Tibetische und Buddhistische Studien, University of Vienna, 1986.

Candrakīrti. *Yuktiṣaṣṭikāvṛtti*.

(1) Cristina Anna Scherrer-Schaub, ed. and trans. *Yuktiṣaṣṭikāvṛtti. Commentaire à la soixantaine sur le raisonnement ou Du vrai enseignement*

de la causalité par le Maître indien Candrakīrti. Mélanges chinois et bouddhiques 25. Brussels: Institut Belge des Hautes Études Chinoises, 1991.

Devendrabuddhi. *Pramāṇavārttikapañjikā*. [PVP]
(1) Subhutiśrī and Dge ba'i blo gros, trans. *Tshad ma rnam 'grel kyi 'grel pa*. D *tshad ma*, vol. *che*, 1a–326b.

Dharmakīrti. *Nyāyabindu*. [NB]
(1) In Dalsukhbhai Malvaniya, ed. *Nyāyabindu of Dharmakīrti with the Nyāyabinduṭīkā of Dharmottara and Durvekamiśra's Dharmottarapradīpa*. Tibetan Sanskrit Works Series, vol. 2. Patna: Kashi Prasad Jayaswal Research Institute, 1955. 2nd ed., 1971.

Dharmakīrti. *Pramāṇavārttika* and *Pramāṇavārttikasvopajñavṛtti*. [PV and PVSV]
(1) Rāhula Sāṅkṛtyāyana, ed. *Dharmakīrti's Pramāṇavārttika with a Commentary by Manorathanandin*. With the notes of Vibhūticandra. *Journal of the Bihar and Orissa Research Society* 24 (1938).
(2) Raniero Gnoli, ed. *The Pramāṇavārttikam of Dharmakīrti: The First Chapter with the Autocommentary*. Serie Orientale Roma 23. Rome: Istituto Italiano per il Medio ed Estremo Oriente, 1960.
(3) Yūsho Miyasaka, ed. *Pramāṇavārttika-kārikā (Sanskrit and Tibetan)*. Naritasan Shinshoji: *Acta Indologica* 2, 3, 4 (1971–72).
(4) Hiromasa Tosaki, ed. and trans. [PV 3] *Bukkyō Ninshikiron no Kenkyū*. 2 vols. Tokyo: Daitōshuppansha, 1979 and 1985.
(5) Ram Chandra Pandeya, ed. *The Pramāṇavārttikam of Ācārya Dharmakīrti with the Commentaries "Svopajñavṛtti" of the Author and "Pramāṇavārttikavṛtti" of Manorathanandin*. Delhi: Motilal Banarsidass, 1989.

Dharmakīrti. *Pramāṇaviniścaya*. [PVin]
(1) Tilmann Vetter, ed. and trans. *Dharmakīrti's Pramāṇaviniścaya, 1. Kapitel: Pratyakṣam* [PVin 1]. Vienna: Verlag der Österreichischen Akademie der Wissenschaften, 1966.
(2) Ernst Steinkellner, ed. *Dharmakīrti's Pramāṇaviniścayaḥ, 2. Kapitel: Svārthānumānam. Teil 1: Tibetischer Text und Sanskrittexte* [PVin 2]. Vienna: Verlag der Österreichischen Akademie der Wissenschaften, 1973.

(3) Ernst Steinkellner, trans. *Dharmakīrti's Pramāṇaviniścayaḥ, 2. Kapitel: Svārthānumānam. Teil 2: Übersetzung und Anmerkungen* [PVin 2]. Vienna: Verlag der Österreichischen Akademie der Wissenschaften, 1979.
(4) Takashi Iwata, trans. "Pramāṇaviniścaya III (I)." *Wiener Zeitschrift für die Kunde Südasiens* 39 (1995): 151–79. "Pramāṇaviniścaya III (II)." *Wiener Zeitschrift für die Kunde Südasiens* 41 (1997): 207–31.
(5) Ernst Steinkellner, ed. *Dharmakīrti's Pramāṇaviniścaya: Chapters 1 and 2.* Beijing and Vienna: China Tibet Publishing House and Austrian Academy of Sciences Press, 2007.

Dharmakīrti. *Vādanyāya.* [VN]
(1) Rāhula Sāṅkṛtyāyana, ed. *Dharmakīrti's Vādanyāya with the Commentary of Śāntarakṣita. Journal of the Bihar and Orissa Research Society* (Appendix). Patna: 21.4 (1935) and 22.1 (1936).
(2) Dwarakidas Shastri, ed. *Vādanyāyaprakaraṇa of Acharya Dharmakīrti with the Commentary Vipanchitārthā of Acharya Śāntarakṣitakṛta.* Varanasi: Bauddha Bharati Series, 1972.
(3) Michael Torsten Much, ed. and trans. *Dharmakīrtis Vādanyāyaḥ.* 2 vols. Vienna: Verlag der Österreichischen Akademie der Wissenschaften, 1991.

Dharmottara. *Nyāyabinduṭīkā.*
(1) Dalsukhbhai Malvania, ed. *Paṇḍita Durveka Miśra's Dharmottarapradīpa, Being a subcommentary on Dharmottara's Nyāyabinduṭīkā, a commentary on Dharmakīrti's Nyāyabindu.* Tibetan Sanskrit Works Series. Patna: Kashiprasad Jayaswal Research Institute, 1955. 2nd rev. ed., 1971.

Dignāga. *Ālambanaparīkṣā.*
(1) S. Yamaguchi and H. Meyer, eds. and trans. "Dignāga, Examen de l'objet de la connaissance (*Ālambanaparīkṣā*), textes tibétain et chinois et traduction des stances et du commentaire, éclaircissements et notes d'après le commentaire tibétain de Vinītadeva." *Journal Asiatique* (1929): 1–65.
(2) Fernando Tola and Carman Dragonetti, ed. and trans. "Dignāga's Ālambanaparīkṣāvṛtti." *Journal of Indian Philosophy* 10 (1982): 105–34.

Dignāga. *Nyāyamukha.*
(1) Giuseppe Tucci, trans., *The Nyāyamukha of Dignāga.* Materialen zur Kunde des Buddhismus 15. Heidelberg: O. Harrassowitz, 1930.

(2) Shōryū Katsura, ed. and (Japanese) trans. In 7 articles in *Bulletin of the Faculty of Letters of Hiroshima University*, 1977, 1978, 1979, 1981, 1982, 1984, 1987.

Dignāga. *Pramāṇasamuccaya* and *Pramāṇasamuccayavṛtti*. [PS and PSV]

(1) H. N. Randle, *Fragments from Diṅnāga*. Royal Asiatic Society Prize Publication Fund, vol. 9. London: Royal Asiatic Society, 1926.

(2) Masaaki Hattori, ed. and trans. *Dignāga on Perception, being the Pratyakṣapariccheda of Dignāga's Pramāṇasamuccaya*. Harvard Oriental Series 47. Cambridge, MA: Harvard University Press, 1968.

(3) Masaaki Hattori, ed. *The Pramāṇasamuccayavṛtti of Dignāga with Jinendrabuddhi's Commentary, Chapter Five: Anyāpoha-parīkṣā*. Tibetan text with Sanskrit fragments. Memoirs of the Faculty of Letters, Kyoto University 21 (1982).

Haribhadra. *Abhisamayālaṃkārāloka*. [AAA]

(1) Giuseppe Tucci, ed. *The Commentaries on the Prajñāpāramitās, vol. 1: The Abhisamayālaṅkāra of Haribhadra*. London: Arthur Probsthain, 1932.

(2) P. L. Vaidya, ed. *Aṣṭasāhasrikā Prajñāpāramitā with Haribhadra's Commentary Called Āloka*. Darbhanga: Mithila Institute, 1960.

(3) U. Wogihara, ed. *Abhisamayālaṃkārāloka Prajñāpāramitāvyākhyā*. 3 vols. Tokyo: Toyo Bunkyo, 1932–37. Reprint, 1973.

Haribhadra Sūri. *Sarvajñasiddhi*.

(1) Muni Hemacandra Vijaya, ed. *Śri-Haribhadrasūri-viracitā Sarvajñasiddhiḥ*. Sirpur, 1963.

Hemacandra. *Pramāṇamīmāṃsā*.

(1) Sukhalalji Sanghavi, ed. Calcutta: Singhi Jaina Series 9, 1939.

(2) Satkari Mookerjee and Nathmal Tatia, eds. and trans. *A Critique of Organ of Knowledge*. Varanasi: Tara Publications, 1970.

Jaimini. *Jaiminimīmāṃsāsūtra*. [JMS]

(1) In Yudhiṣṭhira Mīmāṃsaka, ed. *Jaiminīya Mīmāṃsābhāṣya*. 4 vols. Bahālagarh: Rāmalāl Kapūr Ḍrasṭ Pres, 1984.

Jayānanda. *Madhyamakāvatāraṭīkā*. [MAvT]

(1) Jayānanda and Kun dga' grags, trans. *Dbu ma la 'jug pa'i 'grel bshad*. D, *dbu ma*, vol. *ra*, 1a1–365a7.

Jayanta Bhaṭṭa. *Āgamaḍambara.*

(1) V. Raghavan and Anantalal Thakur, eds. *Āgamaḍambara: Otherwise Called Ṣaṇmatanāṭaka of Jayanta Bhaṭṭa.* Darbhanga: Mithila Institute, 1964.

(2) C. Dezső, ed. and trans. *Much Ado About Religion by Bhaṭṭa Jayanta.* Clay Sanskrit Library. New York: New York University Press and JJC Foundation, 2005.

Jayanta Bhaṭṭa. *Nyāyamañjarī.*

(1) Gaṅgādhara Śāstrī Tailaṅga, ed. *Nyāyamañjarī.* Varanasi: Vizianagaram Sanskrit Series 8, 1895.

Jñānagarbha. *Satyadvayavibhaṅga* and *Satyadvayavibhaṅgavṛtti.* [SDV and SDVV]

(1) Malcolm David Eckel, ed. and trans. *Jñānagarbha's Commentary on the Distinction Between the Two Truths.* Albany: State University of New York Press, 1987.

Jñānaśrīmitra. *Yoginirṇayaprakaraṇa.*

(1) Anatalal Thakur, ed. *Jñānaśrīmitranibandhāvali (Buddhist Philosophical Works of Jñānaśrīmitra).* Patna: Kashi Prasad Jayaswal Research Institute, 1987.

Kamalaśīla. *Madhyamakālaṃkārapañjikā.* [MAP]

(1) Masamichi Ichigō, ed. *Madhyamakālaṃkāra of Śāntarakṣita with his own commentary or Vṛtti and with the subcommentary or Pañjikā of Kamalaśīla.* Kyoto: Buneido, 1985.

(2) Surendrabodhi, Prajñāvarma, and Ye shes sde, trans. *Dbu ma'i rgyan gyi dka' 'grel.* D, *dbu ma,* vol. *sa,* 84a1–133b4.

Kamalaśīla. *Madhyamakāloka.* [MĀ]

(1) Śīlendrabodhi and Dpal brtsegs rakṣita, trans. *Dbu ma snang ba.* D, vol. *sa,* 133b4–244a7.

Kamalaśīla. *Sarvadharmaniḥsvabhāvasiddhi.*

(1) Śīlendrabodhi and Dpal brtsegs rakṣita, trans. *Chos thams cad rang bzhin med par grub pa.* D, vol. *sa,* 273a4–291a7.

Kamalaśīla. *Tattvasaṃgrahapañjikā.* [TSP]

(1) Embar Krishnamacharya, ed. *Tattvasaṃgraha of Śāntarakṣita with the Commentary of Kamalaśīla.* 2 vols. Gaekwad's Oriental Series 30–31. Baroda: Central Library, 1926.

(2) Dwarikadas Shastri, ed. *Tattvasaṃgraha of Ācārya Shāntarakṣita with the Commentary 'Pañjikā' of Shrī Kamalaśīla.* 2 vols. Varanasi: Bauddha Bharati Series 1, 1968.

(3) Devendrabhadra and Grags 'byor shes rab, trans. *De kho na nyid bsdus pa'i bka' 'grel.* D, *tshad ma,* vol. *ze,* 133b1–363a7 and vol. *'e,* 1a1–331a7.

(4) Ganganatha Jha, trans. *The Tattvasaṅgraha of Shāntarakṣita with the Commentary of Kamalashīla.* 2 vols. Gaekwad's Oriental Series 80. Baroda, 1937 and 1939. Reprint, Delhi: Motilal Banarsidass, 1986.

Karṇakagomin. *Pramāṇavārttikasvavṛttiṭīkā.*

(1) Rāhula Sāṅkṛtyāyana, ed. *Karṇakagomin's Commentary on the Pramāṇavārttika of Dharmakīrti.* Patna: 1935–36. Reprint, Kyoto: Rinsen, 1982.

Kumārila Bhaṭṭa. *Ślokavārttika.* [ŚV]

(1) K. Sāmbaśiva Śāstrī, ed. *Mīmāmsā Ślokavārttika with the Commentary Kāśikā of Sucaritamiśra.* Trivandrum: CBH Publications, 1990. Photo offset of 1913 ed.

(2) Dwarikadas Shastri, ed. *Ślokavārttika of Śrī Kumārila Bhaṭṭa with the Commentary Nyāyaratnākara of Śrī Pārthasārathi Miśra.* Prāchyabhārati Series 10. Varanasi: Tārā Publications, 1978.

(3) Ganga Sagar Rai, ed. *Ślokavārttika of Śrī Kumārila Bhaṭṭa with the Commentary Nyāyaratnākara of Śrī Pārthasārathi Miśra.* Varanasi: Ratna Publications, 1993.

(4) Ganganatha Jha, trans. *Ślokavārttika with the Commentaries "Kāśikā" and "Nyāyaratnākara."* Delhi: Sri Satguru Publications, 1983. Originally published 1908.

Kundakundācārya. *Pravacanasāra.*

(1) A. N. Upadhye, ed. and trans. *Pravacanasāra: Prakṛt Text with Sanskrit Commentaries of Amṛtacandra and Jayasena with Hindi Commentary of Hemarāja and English Translation.* Dharampur: Shrimad Rajchandra Ashram, 1964.

Maitreya/Asaṅga. *Abhisamayālaṃkāra.*

(1) Theodore Stcherbatsky and Eugene Obermiller, eds. *Abhisamayālaṃkāra Prajñāpāramitopadeśaśāstra.* Bibliotheca Buddhica, 23. St. Petersburg. Reprint, Delhi: Sri Satguru Publications, 1992.

(2) U. Wogihara, ed. *Abhisamayālaṃkārāloka Prajñāpāramitāvyākhyā.* 3 vols. Tokyo: Toyo Bunkyo, 1932–37. Reprint, 1973.

Maitreya/Asaṅga. *Mahāyānasūtrālaṃkāra.* [MSA]

(1) Sylvain Lévi, ed. and trans. *Mahāyāna-Sūtrālaṃkāra: Exposé de la doctrine du Grand Véhicule selon le système Yogācāra.* 2 vols. Paris: Librarie Ancienne Honoré Champion, 1907–11.

(2) S. Bagchi, ed. *Mahāyānasūtrālaṃkāra.* Buddhist Sanskrit Texts 13. Darbhanga: Mithila Institute, 1970.

Majjhima Nikāya. [MN]

(1) Bhikkhu Ñāṇamoli and Bhikkhu Bodhi, trans. *The Middle Length Discourses: A New Translation of the Majjhima Nikāya.* Boston: Wisdom Publications, 1995.

Maṇḍanamiśra. *Bhāvanāviveka.*

(1) Bhatta, V. P., ed. and trans. *Maṇḍana Miśra's Distinction of the Activity, Bhāvanāviveka: With Introduction, English Translation with Notes, and Sanskrit Text.* Delhi: Eastern Book Linkers, 1984.

Maṇḍanamiśra. *Vidhiviveka.*

(1) Mānavali Upāhva Tailanga Rāmaśāstri, ed. *Vidhiviveka: Śrīmād-ācārya-Maṇḍanamiśra-viracitaḥ Vidhivivekaḥ Nyāyakaṇikākhyayā Vyākhyayāsamalāṃkṛtaḥ.* Varanasi: 1907.

(2) Mahaprabhu Lal Goswami, ed. *Vidhiviveka of Śrī Mandana Miśra. With the Commentary Nyāyakanikā of Vācaspati Miśra.* Varanasi: Tārā Printing Works, 1986.

Manorathanandin. *Pramāṇavārttikavṛtti.* [PVV]

(1) Rāhula Sāṅkṛtyāyana, ed. *Dharmakīrti's Pramāṇavārttika with a Commentary by Manorathanandin.* With the notes of Vibhūticandra. *Journal of the Bihar and Orissa Research Society* 24 (1938).

(2) Ram Chandra Pandeya, ed. *The Pramāṇavārttikam of Ācārya Dharmakīrti with the Commentaries "Svopajñavṛtti" of the Author and "Pramāṇavārttikavṛtti" of Manorathanandin.* Delhi: Motilal Banarsidass, 1989.

Nāgārjuna. *Mūlamadhyamakakārikā*. [MMK]
(1) P. L. Vaidya, ed. *Madhyamakaśāstra of Nāgārjuna with the Commentary "Prasannapadā" by Candrakīrti*. Buddhist Sanskrit Texts Series 10. Darbhanga: Mithila Institute, 1960.
(2) J. W. de Jong, ed. *Mūlamadhyamakakārikāḥ*. Madras: Adyar Library and Research Center, 1977.

Nāgārjuna. *Ratnāvalī* (or *Rājaparikathāratnamālā*). [RĀ]
(1) Michael Hahn, ed. *Nāgārjuna's Ratnāvalī*. Bonn: Indica et Tibetica Verlag, 1982.
(2) Giuseppe Tucci, ed. "The Ratnāvalī of Nāgārjuna." *Journal of the Royal Asiatic Society*, 1934 and 1936.
(3) Ngawang Samten, ed. *Ratnāvalī of Ācārya Nāgārjuna with the Commentary by Ajitamitra*. Sarnath: Central Institute of Higher Tibetan Studies, 1990.

Prajñākaragupta. *Pramāṇavārttikabhāṣya*.
(1) Rāhula Sāṅkṛtyāyana, ed. *Pramāṇavārttikabhāṣya or Vārttikālaṃkāra of Prajñākaragupta*. Tibetan Sanskrit Works Series 1. Patna: Kashi Prasad Jayaswal Research Institute, 1953.

Praśastapāda. *Padārthadharmasaṃgraha*. [PDS]
(1) Jitendra S. Jetly, ed. *Praśastapādabhāṣyam with the Commentary Kiraṇāvalī of Udayanācārya*. Gaekwad's Oriental Series 154. Baroda: Oriental Institute, 1971.
(2) Johannes Bronkhorst and Yves Ramseier, eds. *Word Index to the Praśastapādabhāṣya*. Delhi: Motilal Banarsidass, 1994.
(3) Ganganatha Jha, trans. *Padārthadharmasaṃgraha of Praśastapāda with the Nyāyakandalī of Śrīdhara*. Varanasi: Chaukhambha Orientalia, 1982.

Ratnakīrti. *Saṃtānāntaradūṣaṇa*.
(1) In Anantalal Thakur, ed. *Ratnakīrti-Nibandhāvaliḥ (Buddhist Nyāya Works of Ratnakīrti)*. Patna: Kashi Prasad Jayaswal Research Institute, 1975.
(2) Yūichi Kajiyama, trans. *Indogaku Bukkyōgaku Kenkyū* (*Journal of the Japanese Association of Indian and Buddhist Studies*) 25 (1965): 9–24.

Ratnakīrti. *Sarvajñasiddhi.* [SS]

(2) In Anantalal Thakur, ed. *Ratnakīrti-Nibandhāvaliḥ (Buddhist Nyāya Works of Ratnakīrti).* Patna: Kashi Prasad Jayaswal Research Institute, 1975.

(3) Gudrun Bühnemann, trans. *Der Allwissende Buddha: ein Beweis und seine Probleme: Ratnakīrtis Sarvajñasiddhi, übersetzt und kommentiert.* Wiener Studien zur Tibetologie und Buddhismuskunde 12. Vienna: Arbeitskreis für Tibetische und Buddhistische Studien, 1980.

Śabarasvāmin. *Śābarabhāṣya.* [ŚBh]

(1) In Yudhiṣṭhira Mīmāṃsaka, ed. *Jaiminīya Mīmāṃsābhāṣya.* 4 vols. Bahālagarh: Ramlal Kapoor Trust Press, 1984.

(2) Erich Frauwallner, ed. Partial edition in *Materialien zur ältesten Erkenntnislehre der Karmamīmāṃsā.* Vienna: Verlag der Österreichischen Akademie der Wissenschaften, 1968.

Śākyabuddhi. *Pramāṇavārttikaṭīkā.* [PVṬ]

(1) Subhitiśrī and Dge ba'i blo gros, trans. *Tshad ma rnam 'grel kyi 'grel bshad.* D, *tshad ma*, vols. *je* 1–328a and *nye* 1–282a. P 5718.

(2) M. Inami, K. Matsuda, and T. Tani, eds. *A Study of the Pramāṇavārttikaṭīkā by Śākyabuddhi from the National Archives Collection, Kathmandu. Part I: Sanskrit Fragments Transcribed.* Studia Tibetica 23. Tokyo: Toyo Bunkyo, 1992.

Saṃyutta Nikāya.

(1) Bhikkhu Bodhi, trans. *The Connected Discourses of the Buddha: A New Translation of the Saṃyutta Nikāya.* Boston: Wisdom Publications, 2000.

Śāntarakṣita. *Madhyamakālaṃkāra.* [MA]

(1) Masamichi Ichigō, ed. *Madhyamakālaṃkāra of Śāntarakṣita with his own commentary or Vṛtti and with the subcommentary or Pañjikā of Kamalaśīla.* [Includes English translation of verses.] Kyoto: Buneido, 1985.

(2) Surendrabodhi and Ye shes sde, trans. *Dbu ma rgyan gyi tshig le'ur byas pa.* D, *dbu ma*, vol. *sa*, 53a1–56b3.

Śāntarakṣita. *Madhyamakālaṃkāravṛtti.* [MAV]

(1) Masamichi Ichigō, ed. *Madhyamakālaṃkāra of Śāntarakṣita with his own commentary or Vṛtti and with the subcommentary or Pañjikā of Kamalaśīla.* Kyoto: Buneido, 1985.

(2) Śīlendrabodhi and Ye shes sde, trans. *Dbu ma'i rgyan gyi 'grel pa*. D, *dbu ma*, vol. *sa*, 56b4–84a1.

Śāntarakṣita. *Satyadvayavibhaṅgapañjikā*.
(1) Prajñāvarma, Jñānagarbha, and Ye shes sde, trans. *Bden pa gnyis rnam par 'byed pa'i dka' 'grel*. D, *dbu ma*, vol. *sa*, 15b2–52b7.

Śāntarakṣita. *Tattvasaṃgraha*. [TS]
(1) Embar Krishnamacharya, ed. *Tattvasaṃgraha of Śāntarakṣita with the Commentary of Kamalaśīla*. 2 vols. Gaekwad's Oriental Series 30–31. Baroda: Central Library, 1926. Reprint, Baroda, 1984 and 1988.
(2) Dwarikadas Shastri, ed. *Tattvasaṃgraha of Ācārya Shāntarakṣita with the Commentary "Pañjikā" of Shrī Kamalaśīla*. 2 vols. Varanasi: Bauddha Bharati Series 1, 1968.
(3) Guṇākaraśrībhadra, Dpal lha btsan po, and Zhi ba 'od, trans. *De kho na nyid bsdus pa'i tshig le'ur byas pa*. D, vol. *ze*, 1a1–133a7. P 5764.
(4) Ganganatha Jha, trans. *The Tattvasaṅgraha of Shāntarakṣita with the Commentary of Kamalashīla*. 2 vols. Gaekwad's Oriental Series 80. Baroda, 1937 and 1939. Reprint, Delhi: Motilal Banarsidass, 1986.

Śāntarakṣita. *Vādanyāyavipañcitārthā*. [VNV]
(1) Rāhula Sāṅkṛtyāyana, ed. *Dharmakīrti's Vādanyāya with the Commentary of Śāntarakṣita*. *Journal of the Bihar and Orissa Research Society* (Appendix). Patna: 21.4 (1935) and 22.1 (1936).
(2) Dwarikadas Shastri, ed. *Vādanyāyaprakaraṇa of Acharya Dharmakīrti with the Commentary Vipanchitārthā of Acharya Śāntarakṣitakṛta*. Varanasi: Bauddha Bharati Series 8, 1972.
(3) Kumāraśrībhadra, 'Phags pa shes rab, and 'Bro seng dkar śākya 'od, trans. *Rtsod pa'i rigs pa'i 'grel pa don rnam par 'byed pa*. D, *tshad ma*, vol. *zhe*, 51a3–151a6.

Śubhagupta. *Bāhyārthasiddhikārikā*. [BASK]
(1) E. Mikogami, ed. *Śubhagupta no Bāhyārthasiddhikārikā*. Ryūkoku Daigaku Ronshū 429 (1980): 2–44.
(2) S. Matsumoto, ed. and trans. [Partial.] "Sahopalambha-niyama." *Sōtōshū Kenyūin Kenyūsei Kenkyū Kiyō* XII (1980).

Śubhagupta. *Sarvajñasiddhikārikā*.
(1) Jinamitra and Dpal brtsegs rakṣita, trans. *Thams cad mkhyen pa grub pa'i tshig le'ur byas pa*. D, vol. *zhe*: 188b3–189b2.

Uddyotakara. *Nyāyavārttika*. [NV]
(1) In Tārānātha Nyāya-Tarkatīrtha and Amarendramohan Tarkatīrtha, eds. *Nyāyadarśanam: With Vātsyāyana's Bhāṣya, Uddyotakara's Vārttika, Vācaspati Miśra's Tātparyaṭīkā & Viśvanātha's Vṛtti*. Delhi: Munshiram Manoharlal Publishers, 1985. [Reprint of Chaukhambha Sanskrit Series 18–19, 1936–44.]

Umāsvāti. *Tattvārthasūtra*.
(1) Sukhalāl Saṃghavī, ed. and (Hindi) trans. *Tattvārthasūtra: Vivecanasahita*. Varanasi: Pārśvanāth Vidyāśram Śodh Saṃsthān, 1976. Reprint, 1993.

Uṃveka. *Ślokavārttikavyākhyātātparyaṭīkā*.
(1) S. K. Ramanatha Shastri, ed. *Ślokavārttikavyākhyātātparyaṭīkā*. University of Madras Sanskrit Series 13 (1940).

Vācaspatimiśra. *Nyāyakaṇikā*. [NK]
(1) Tailaṅgarāma Śāstri Mānavallī, ed. *Vidhivivekaḥ Śrīmadācārya Maṇḍanamiśraviracitaḥ Pūjyapādaśrīmad Vācaspatimiśranirṇitayā Nyāyakaṇikākhyayā Vyākhyayā Samalāṃkṛtaḥ*. Varanasi: 1903–7.
(2) Mahaprabhu Lal Goswami, ed. *Vidhiviveka of Çrī Maṇḍana Miśra with the Commentary Nyāyakaṇikā of Vāchaspati Miśra*. Varanasi: Tara Printing Works, 1978.

Vācaspatimiśa. *Nyāyavārttikatātparyaṭīkā*.
(1) In Tārānātha Nyāya-Tarkatīrtha and Amarendramohan Tarkatīrtha, eds. *Nyāyadarśanam: With Vātsyāyana's Bhāṣya, Uddyotakara's Vārttika, Vācaspati Miśra's Tātparyaṭīkā & Viśvanātha's Vṛtti*. Delhi: Munshiram Manoharlal Publishers, 1985. [Reprint of Chaukhambha Sanskrit Series 18–19, 1936–44.]

Vasubandhu. *Abhidharmakośa* and *Abhidharmakośabhāṣya*. [AK and AKBh]
(1) Dwarikadas Shastri, ed. *Abhidharmakośa and Bhāṣya of Ācārya Vasubandhu with Sphuṭārthā Commentary of Ācārya Yaśomitra*. Varanasi: Bauddha Bharati Series 5–9, 1970.
(2) Prahlad Pradhan, ed. *Abhidharmakośabhāṣyam of Vasubandhu*. Tibetan Sanskrit Works Series 8. Patna: Kashi Prasad Jayaswal Research Institute, 1967. Revised ed., 1975.
(3) Louis de la Vallée Poussin, trans. *L'Abhidharmakośa de Vasubandhu*. 6 vols. Paris/Louvain: P. Guethner, 1923–31.

Vātsyāyana. *Nyāyabhāṣya*. [NBh]
(1) In Tārānātha Nyāya-Tarkatīrtha and Amarendramohan Tarkatīrtha, eds. *Nyāyadarśanam: With Vātsyāyana's Bhāṣya, Uddyotakara's Vārttika, Vācaspati Miśra's Tātparyaṭīkā & Viśvanātha's Vṛtti*. Delhi: Munshiram Manoharlal Publishers, 1985. [Reprint of Chaukhambha Sanskrit Series 18–19, 1936–44.]

Secondary Sources

Aklujkar, Ashok. 1972. "The Authorship of the Vākyapadīya-vṛtti." *Wiener Zeitschrift für die Kunde Südasiens* 16: 181–98.

Anālayo, Ven. 2006. "The Buddha and Omniscience." *The Indian International Journal of Buddhist Studies* 7: 1–20.

Arnold, Dan. 2005. *Buddhists, Brahmins, and Belief: Epistemology in South Asian Philosophy of Religion*. New York: Columbia University Press.

Avramides, Anita. 1997. "Intention and Convention" in B. Hale and C. Wright, eds., *A Companion to the Philosophy of Language*, 60–86. Oxford: Blackwell Publishers.

Bareau, André. 1969. "The Superhuman Personality of Buddha and Its Symbolism in the *Mahaparinirvāṇasūtra* of the Dharmaguptaka" in J. M. Kitagawa and C. H. Long, eds., *Myths and Symbols: Studies in Honor of Mircea Eliade*, 9–21. Chicago: University of Chicago Press.

Bhaskar, B. 1976. "Conception of Omniscience in Jainism and Buddhism" in *Buddhism and Jainism*. Cuttach.

Bhatt, Govardhan P. 1989. *The Basic Ways of Knowing*. 2nd rev. ed. Delhi: Motilal Banarsidass. Originally published 1962.

Bhattacaryya, B. 1926. "Foreword" in E. Krishnamacharya, ed., *Tattvasaṃgraha of Śāntarakṣita with the Commentary of Kamalaśīla*, i–cxvii. Baroda: Gaekwad Oriental Series.

Bhattacharyya, H. M. 1967. "Omniscience (*sarvajñatā*) and the Metaphysic of Knowledge (*adhigama*) in Jainism." *Kaviraj Abhinānadana Grantha*. Luknow.

Biardeau, Madeleine. 1964. *Théorie de la connaissance et philosophie de la parole dans le brahmanisme classique*. Paris, La Haye: Mouton.

———. 1968–69. "Jāti et Lakṣaṇa." *Wiener Zeitschrift für die Kunde Südasiens* 12–13: 75–83.

Blumenthal, James. 2009. "Śāntarakṣita's 'Neither-One-Nor-Many' Argument from *Madhyamakālaṃkāra* (*The Ornament of the Middle Way*)" in

J. Garfield and W. Edelglass, eds., *Buddhist Philosophy: Essential Readings*, 46–60. Oxford: Oxford University Press.

Bronkhorst, Johannes. 1981. "Yoga and Seśvara Sāṃkhya." *Journal of Indian Philosophy* 9: 309–20.

———. 1983. "God in Sāṃkhya." *Wiener Zeitschrift für die Kunde Südasiens* 27: 149–64.

———. 1996. "God's Arrival in the Vaiśeṣika System." *Journal of Indian Philosophy* 24: 289–94.

———. 2000. "The Riddle of the Jainas and Ājīvikas in Early Buddhist Literature." *Journal of Indian Philosophy* 28: 511–29.

———. 2009. *Buddhist Teaching in India.* Boston: Wisdom Publications.

Bühnemann, Gudrun. 1980. *Der Allwissende Buddha, ein Beweis und seine Probleme: Ratnakīrtis Sarvajñasiddhi, übersetzt und kommentiert.* Wiener Studien zur Tibetologie und Buddhismuskunde 12. Vienna: Arbeitskreis für Tibetische und Buddhistische Studien, University of Vienna.

Butzenberger, Klaus. 1996. "On Doubting What There Is Not: The Doctrine of Doubt and the Reference of Terms in Indian Grammar, Logic and Philosophy of Language." *Journal of Indian Philosophy* 24: 363–406.

Cabezón, José Ignacio. 1999. "Incarnation: A Buddhist View." *Faith and Philosophy* 16.4: 449–71.

Chakrabarti, Arindam. 1997. "Rationality in Indian Philosophy" in E. Deutsch and R. Bontekoe, eds., *A Companion to World Philosophies*, 259–78. Oxford: Blackwell Publishers.

Chatterjee, Asim Kumar. 1978. *A Comprehensive History of Jainism [up to 1000 A.D.]*. Calcutta: Firma KLM Private Limited.

Chatterjee, K. N. 1988. *Tattvasaṃgraha (Sthirabhāvaparīkṣā).* Calcutta: Vijaya-Veeṇā.

Chemparathy, George. 1969. "Two Little-Known Fragments from Early Vaiśeṣika Literature on the Omniscience of Īśvara." *Adyar Library Bulletin* 33: 117–34.

———. 1972. *An Indian Rational Theology: Introduction to Udayana's Nyāyakusumāñjali*. Vienna: Publications of the De Nobili Research Library 1.

———. 1983. *L'authorité du Veda selon le Nyāya-Vaiśeṣikas*. Louvain-la-Neuve: Centre d'Histoire des Religions.

Clooney, Francis X. 1990. *Thinking Ritually: Rediscovering the Pūrva Mīmāṃsā of Jaimini*. Vienna: Publications of the De Nobili Research Library 27.

Collins, Steven. 1982. *Selfless Persons: Imagery and Thought in Theravāda Buddhism.* Cambridge: Cambridge University Press.

Conze, Edward. 1947. "On Omniscience and the Goal." *Middle Way* 22.3: 62–63.

Coomaraswamy, A. K. 1936. "Rebirth and Omniscience in Pali Buddhism." *Indian Culture* 3: 19–34.

Cox, Collett. 1992. "Attainment through Abandonment: The Sarvāstivādin Path of Removing Defilements" in R. Buswell and R. Gimello, eds., *Paths to Liberation: The Mārga and Its Transformations in Buddhist Thought*, 63–105. Honolulu: University of Hawaii Press.

Crosswhite, James. 1996. *The Rhetoric of Reason: Writing and the Attractions of Argument*. Madison: University of Wisconsin Press.

Daniélou, Alain, trans. 1989. *Manimekhalai (The Dancer with the Magic Bowl) by Merchant-Prince Shattan*. New York: New Directions Publishing.

Davidson, Ronald M. 2002. *Indian Esoteric Buddhism: A Social History of the Tantric Movement*. New York: Columbia University Press.

Dayal, Har. 1932. *The Bodhisattva Doctrine in Buddhist Sanskrit Literature*. London: Keegen Paul, Trench, Trubner. Reprint, Delhi: Motilal Banarsidass, 1978.

Demiéville, Paul. 1987. *Le Concile de Lhasa: Une controverse sur le quiétisme entre bouddhistes de l'Inde et de la Chine au VIII siècle de l'ère chrétienne*. Paris: College de France, Institut des Hautes Etudes Chinoises. Originally published 1952.

Dezső, Csaba, ed. and trans. 2005. *Much Ado about Religion, by Bhaṭṭa Jayanta*. Clay Sanskrit Library. New York: New York University Press and JJC Foundation.

Dixit, K.K., trans. 1974. *Pt. Sukhlalji's Commentary on Tattvārthasūtra of Vācaka Umāsvāti*. Ahmedabad: L. D. Institute. Series No. 44.

Dośi, Becaradāsa. 1989. *Jaina Sāhitya kā Bṛhad Itihāsa*. 5 vols. Varanasi: Parśvanātha Vidyāśrama Śodha Saṃsthāna.

Dreyfus, Georges. 1991. "Dharmakīrti's Definition of *Pramāṇa* and Its Interpreters" in E. Steinkellner, ed., *Studies in the Buddhist Epistemological Tradition*, 19–38. Proceedings of the Second International Dharmakīrti Conference. Vienna: Verlag der Österreichischen Akademie der Wissenschaften.

———. 1995. "Is Dharmakīrti a Pragmatist?" *Asiatische Studien/Études Asiatiques* 49.4: 671–91.

———. 1997. *Recognizing Reality: Dharmakīrti's Philosophy and Its Tibetan Interpretations*. Albany: State University of New York Press.

D'Sa, Francis X. 1974. "Offenbarung ohne einen Gott" in G. Oberhammer, ed., *Offenbarung, Geistige Realität des Menschen: Arbeitsdokumentation eines Symposiums zum Offernbarungsbegriff in Indien*, 93–105. Vienna: The De Nobili Research Library.

———. 1980. *Śabdaprāmāṇyam in Śabara and Kumārila: Towards a Study of the Mīmāṃsā Experience of Language*. Vienna: The De Nobili Research Library.

Dube, S. N. 1980. *Cross Currents in Early Buddhism*. Delhi: Manohar.

Duerlinger, James. 2003. *Indian Buddhist Theories of Persons: Vasubandhu's "Refutation of the Theory of a Self."* London and New York: RoutledgeCurzon.

Dundas, Paul. 1992. *The Jains*. London and New York: Routledge Press.

Dunne, John D. 1996. "Thoughtless Buddha, Passionate Buddha." *Journal of the American Academy of Religion* 64.3: 525–56.

———. 2004. *Foundations of Dharmakīrti's Philosophy*. Boston: Wisdom Publications.

———. 2007. "Realizing the Unreal: Dharmakīrti's Theory of Yogic Perception." *Journal of Indian Philosophy* 34: 497–519.

Dunne, John D., and Sara L. McClintock, trans. 1997. *The Precious Garland: An Epistle to a King*. Boston: Wisdom Publications.

Dwivedi, R. C., ed. 1994. *Studies in Mīmāṃsā*. Dr. Mandan Mishra Felicitation Volume. Delhi: Motilal Banarsidass.

Eckel, Malcolm David. 1987. *Jñānagarbha's Commentary on the Distinction between the Two Truths*. Albany: State University of New York Press.

———. 1992. *To See the Buddha: A Philosopher's Quest for the Meaning of Emptiness*. San Francisco: Harper San Francisco.

———. 2008. *Bhāviveka and His Buddhist Opponents*. Cambridge MA: Harvard University Press.

Edgerton, Franklin. 1977. *Buddhist Hybrid Sanskrit Grammar and Dictionary*. 2 vols. Delhi: Motilal Banarsidass. Originally published New Haven: Yale University Press, 1953.

Eltschinger, Vincent. 1997. "Bhāvaviveka et Dharmakīrti sur *āgama* et contre la Mīmāṃsā (2)." *Asiatische Studien/Études Asiatiques* 51.4: 1095–1104.

———. 1999. "Śubhagupta's *Śrutiparīkṣā* (vv. 10cd–19) and Its Dharmakīrtian Background" in S. Katsura, ed., *Dharmakīrti's Thought and Its Impact on Indian and Tibetan Philosophy*, 47–61. Proceedings of the Third International Dharmakīrti Conference. Vienna: Verlag der Österreichischen Akademie der Wissenschaften.

———. 2000. *"Caste" et Philosophie Bouddhique: Continuité de quelques arguments bouddhiques contre le traitement réaliste de dénominations sociales*. Wiener Studien zur Tibetologie und Buddhismuskunde

47. Vienna: Arbeitskreis für Tibetische und Buddhistische Studien, University of Vienna.

———. 2001. *Dharmakīrti Sur les* Mantra *et la Perception du Supra-sensible.* Wiener Studien zur Tibetologie und Buddhismuskunde 51. Vienna: Arbeitskreis für Tibetische und Buddhistische Studien, University of Vienna.

———. 2005. "Recherches sur la Philosophie Religieuse de Dharmakīrti: I. Le Bouddha comme Śāstṛ et comme Sugata." *Asiatische Studien/Études Asiatiques* 59.2: 395–442.

———. 2007a. "On 7th and 8th Century Buddhist Accounts of Human Action, Practical Rationality and Soteriology" in B. Kellner et al., eds., *Pramāṇakīrti: Papers Dedicated to Ernst Steinkellner on the Occasion of His 70th Birthday*, part 1: 135–62. Vienna: Arbeitskreis für Tibetische und Buddhistische Studien, University of Vienna.

———. 2007b. *Penser l'autorité des Écritures: La Polémique de Dharmakīrti Contre la Notion Brahmanique Orthodoxe d'un Veda Sans Auteur, Autour de* Pramāṇavārttika I.213–68 *et* Svavṛtti. Vienna: Verlag der Österreichischen Akademie der Wissenschaften.

———. 2007c. "Studies in Dharmakīrti's Religious Philosophy: 4. The *Cintā-mayī Prajñā*" in Piotr Barcerowicz et al., eds., *Proceedings of the International Conference "Logic and Belief" (Warsaw, May 2006)*. Warsaw: Warsaw Indological Studies 3: 453–91.

———. 2008. "Pierre Hadot et les Exercises Spirituels: Quel Modèle pour la Philosophie Bouddique Tardive?" *Asiatische Studien/Études Asiatiques* 62.2: 485–544.

Endo, Toshiichi. 1997. *Buddha in Theravāda Buddhism: A Study of the Concept of Buddha in the Pāli Commentaries.* Dehiwela, Sri Lanka: Buddhist Cultural Centre.

Filliozat, Pierre-Sylvain. 1988. *Grammaire Sanskrite Pāṇinéene.* Edited by Henri Hierche. Collection Connaissance des Langues. Paris: Picard.

Franco, Eli. 1987. *Perception, Knowledge and Disbelief: A Study of Jayarāśi's Scepticism.* Stuttgart: Franz Steiner Verlag. Alt- und Neu-Indische Studien 35. 2nd ed., Delhi: Motilal Banarsidass, 1994.

———. 1991. "The Disjunction in *Pramāṇavārttika, Pramāṇasiddhi* Chapter Verse 5c" in E. Steinkellner, ed., *Studies in the Buddhist Epistemological Tradition*, 339–51. Proceedings of the Second International Dharmakīrti Conference. Vienna: Verlag der Österreichischen Akademie der Wissenschaften.

———. 1997. *Dharmakīrti on Compassion and Rebirth*. Wiener Studien zur Tibetologie und Buddhismuskunde 38. Vienna: Arbeitskreis für Tibetische und Buddhistische Studien, University of Vienna.

———. 1999. "Two Circles or Parallel Lines?" in S. Katsura, ed., *Dharmakīrti's Thought and Its Impact on Indian and Tibetan Philosophy*, 63–72. Proceedings of the Third International Dharmakīrti Conference. Vienna: Verlag der Österreichischen Akademie der Wissenschaften.

Frauwallner, Erich. 1953, 1956. *Geschichte der Indischen Philosophie*. 2 vols. Salzburg: Otto Müller Verlag.

———. 1957a. "Vasubandhu's Vādavidhiḥ." *Wiener Zeitschrift für die Kunde Süd- und Ostasiens* 1: 104–45

———. 1957b. "Zu den buddhistischen Texten in der Zeit Khri-Sroṅ-Lde-Btsan's." *Wiener Zeitschrift für die Kunde Süd- und Ostasiens* 1: 95–103.

———. 1958. "Die Erkenntnislehre des Klassischen Sāṃkhya-systems." *Wiener Zeitschrift für die Kunde Süd- und Ostasiens* 2: 84–139.

———. 1961. "Landmarks in the History of Indian Logic." *Wiener Zeitschrift für die Kunde Süd- und Ostasiens* 5: 125–48.

———. 1962. "Kumārila's Bṛhaṭṭīkā." *Wiener Zeitschrift für die Kunde Süd- und Ostasiens* 6: 78–90.

Funayama, Toru. 1992. "A Study of *kalpanāpoḍha*: A Translation of the *Tattvasaṃgraha* vv. 1212–63 by Śāntarakṣita and the *Tattvasaṃgrahapañjikā* by Kamalaśīla on the Definition of Direct Perception." Kyoto: Zinbun 27 (1992): 33–128. [Appendix II: A List of Corrections to Shastri's Edition, pp. 120–21.]

———. 1995. "Arcaṭa, Śāntarakṣita, Jinendrabuddhi, and Kamalaśīla on the Aim of a Treatise (*prayojana*)." *Wiener Zeitschrift für die Kunde Südasiens* 39: 181–201.

———. 1999. "Kamalaśīla's Interpretation of 'Non-erroneous' in the Definition of Direct Perception and Related Problems" in S. Katsura, ed., *Dharmakīrti's Thought and Its Impact on Indian and Tibetan Philosophy*, 73–99. Proceedings of the Third International Dharmakīrti Conference. Vienna: Verlag der Österreichischen Akademie der Wissenschaften.

———. 2007. "Kamalaśīla's Distinction between the Two Sub-schools of Yogācāra. A Provisional Survey" in B. Kellner et al., eds., *Pramāṇakīrti: Papers Dedicated to Ernst Steinkellner on the Occasion of His 70th Birthday*, part 1: 187–202. Vienna: Arbeitskreis für Tibetische und Buddhistische Studien, University of Vienna.

Ganeri, Jonardon. 2001. *Philosophy in Classical India: The Proper Work of Reason*. London and New York: Routledge.

Gillon, Brendan. 1991. "Dharmakīrti and the Problem of Induction" in E. Steinkellner, ed., *Studies in the Buddhist Epistemological Tradition*, 53–58. Proceedings of the Second International Dharmakīrti Conference. Vienna: Verlag der Österreichischen Akademie der Wissenschaften.

Gillon, Brendan S., and Richard P. Hayes. 1991. "Introduction to Dharmakīrti's Theory of Inference as Presented in *Pramāṇavārttika Svopajñavṛtti* 1–10." *Journal of Indian Philosophy* 19: 1–73.

Gokhale, Pradeep P. 1992. *Inference and Fallacies Discussed in Ancient Indian Logic (With Special Reference to Nyāya and Buddhism)*. Delhi: Sri Satguru Publications.

Goldman, Robert P., and Sally J. Sutherland. 1980. *Devavāṇīpraveśikā: An Introduction to the Sanskrit Language*. Berkeley: University of California, Center for South and Southeast Asia Studies.

Gómez, Luis O. 1975. "Some Aspects of the Free-Will Question in the Nikāyas." *Philosophy East and West* 25.1: 81–90.

Gonda, Jan. 1955. "Reflections on Sarva– in Vedic Texts" in *Indian Linguistics*, vol. 16 (Chatterji Jubilee Volume). Madras: Linguistic Society of India. Reprinted in J. Gonda, *Selected Studies. Vol. 2: Sanskrit Word Studies*. Leiden: E. J. Brill, 1975.

Griffiths, Paul J. 1989. "Buddha and God: A Contrastive Study in Ideas about Maximal Greatness." *The Journal of Religion* 69: 502–29.

———. 1990. "Omniscience in the *Mahāyānasūtrālaṃkāra* and Its Commentaries." *Indo-Iranian Journal* 33: 85–120.

———. 1991. *Apology for Apologetics: A Study in the Logic of Interreligious Dialogue*. Maryknoll, NY: Orbis.

———. 1994. *On Being Buddha: Maximal Greatness and the Doctrine of Buddhahood in Classical India*. Albany: State University of New York Press.

———. 1998. "Scholasticism: The Possible Recovery of an Intellectual Practice" in J. I. Cabezón, ed., *Scholasticism: Cross-Cultural and Comparative Perspectives*, 177–235. Albany: State University of New York Press.

———. 1999a. *Religious Reading: The Place of Reading in the Practice of Religion*. New York and Oxford: Oxford University Press.

———. 1999b. "What Do Buddhists Hope for from Antitheistic Argument?" *Faith and Philosophy* 16.4: 506–22.

Griffiths, Paul J., Noriaki Hakamaya, John P. Keenan, and Paul L. Swanson, eds. and trans. 1989. *The Realm of Awakening: A Translation and Study of the Tenth Chapter of Asaṅga's Mahāyānasaṃgraha*. New York and Oxford: Oxford University Press.

Gross, Alan. 1999. "A Theory of the Rhetorical Audience: Reflections on Chaim Perelman." *Quarterly Journal of Speech* 85: 203–11.

Hacking, Ian. 1982. "Language, Truth and Reason" in M. Hollis and S. Lukes, eds., *Rationality and Relativism*. Cambridge, MA: The MIT Press.

Hadot, Pierre. 1995. *Philosophy as a Way of Life: Spiritual Exercises from Socrates to Foucault*. Ed. with an introduction by A. I. Davidson. Translated by M. Chase. Oxford: Blackwell.

———. 2002. *What Is Ancient Philosophy?* Translated by M. Chase. Cambridge, MA and London: The Belknap Press of Harvard University Press.

Halbfass, Wilhelm. 1979. "Observations on Darśana." *Wiener Zeitschrift für die Kunde Südasiens* 23: 195–203.

———. 1980. "Karma, Apūrva, and 'Natural' Causes" in Wendy D. O'Flaherty, ed., *Karma and Rebirth in Classical Indian Tradition*, 268–302. Berkeley: University of California Press.

———. 1981. "Darśana, Ānvīkṣikī, Philosophie" in *Indien und Europa: Perspektiven ihrer Geistigen Begegnung*, 296–327. Basel and Stuttgart: Schwabe.

———. 1988. *India and Europe: An Essay in Understanding*. Albany: State University of New York Press.

———. 1992. *On Being and What There Is: Classical Vaiśeṣika and the History of Indian Ontology*. Albany: State University of New York Press.

Harrison, Paul. 1982. "Sanskrit Fragments of a Lokottaravāda Tradition" in L. A. Hercus, ed., *Indological and Buddhist Studies: Volume in Honour of Professor J. W. de Jong on His Sixtieth Birthday*, 211–34. Canberra: Faculty of Asian Studies.

———. 1995. "Some Reflections on the Personality of the Buddha." Otani University: *The Otani Gakuho (The Journal of Buddhist Studies and Humanities)* 74.4: 1–29.

Hattori, Masaaki. 1960. "Bāhyārthasiddhikārikā of Śubhagupta." *Indogaku Bukkyōgaku Kenkyū* (*Journal of the Japanese Association of Indian and Buddhist Studies*) 8.1: 400–395.

———. 1968. *Dignāga on Perception: Being the Pratyakṣapariccheda of Dignāga's Pramāṇasamuccaya*. Harvard Oriental Series 47. Cambridge, MA: Harvard University Press.

———. 1980. "Apoha and Pratibhā" in M. Nagatomi et al., eds., *Sanskrit and Indian Studies in Honor of Daniel H. H. Ingalls*, 61–74. Dordrecht and Boston: D. Reidel Publishing.

Hayes, Richard P. 1984. "The Question of Doctrinalism in the Buddhist Epistemologists." *Journal of the American Academy of Religion* 52: 645–70.

———. 1988. *Dignāga on the Interpretation of Signs*. Studies of Classical India 9. Dordrecht: Kluwer Academic Press.

———. 1997. "Whose Experience Validates What for Dharmakīrti?" in P. Bilimoria and J. N. Mohanty, eds., *Relativism, Suffering and Beyond: Essays in Memory of Bimal K. Matilal*, 105–18. Delhi: Oxford University Press.

Hertzberger, Radhika. 1986. *Bhartṛhari and the Buddhists: An Essay in the Development of Fifth and Sixth Century Indian Thought*. Studies of Classical India 8. Dordrecht: D. Reidel (Kluwer).

Hoffman, Frank J. 1987. "The Pragmatic Efficacy of *Saddhā*." *Journal of Indian Philosophy* 15: 399–412.

Houben, Jan E. M. 1995. *The Saṃbandha-Samuddeśa (Chapter on Relation) and Bhartṛhari's Philosophy of Language*. Groningen: Egbert Forsten.

Ichigō, Masamichi. 1985. *Madhyamakālaṃkāra of Śāntarakṣita with his own commentary or Vṛtti and with the subcommentary or Pañjikā of Kamalaśīla.* Critically edited with a translation of the kārikās and an introduction. Kyoto: Sangyo University, 1985.

Iida, Shotaro. 1980. *Reason and Emptiness: A Study in Logic and Mysticism.* Tokyo: Hokuseido Press.

———. 1985. "Bhāvaviveka's Argument for the Omniscience of the Buddha" in R. N. Dandekar and P. D. Navathe, eds., *Proceedings of the Fifth World Sanskrit Conference: Varanasi, India: October 21–26, 1981*. New Delhi: Rashtriya Sanskrit Sansthan: 524–35.

Inami, M., and T. Tillemans. 1986. "Another Look at the Framework of the *Pramāṇasiddhi* Chapter of *Pramāṇavarttika*." *Wiener Zeitschrift für die Kunde Südasiens* 30: 123–42.

Iwata, Takashi. 1984. "One Interpretation of the *Saṃvedana*-Inference of Dharmakīrti." *Indogaku Bukkyōgaku Kenkyū* (*Journal of the Japanese Association of Indian and Buddhist Studies*) 33.1: 397–394.

———. 1991. *Sahopalambhaniyama: Struktur und Entwicklung des Schlusses von der Tatsache dass Erkenntnis und Gegenstand ausschliesslich zusammen wahrgenommen werden, auf deren Nichtverschiedenheit.* 2 vols. Stuttgart: Franz Steiner Verlag.

Jackson, Roger. 1988. "The Buddha as *pramaṇabhūta*: Epithets and Arguments in the Buddhist 'Logical' Tradition." *Journal of Indian Philosophy* 16.4: 335–65.

———. 1991. "Dharmakīrti's Attitude Toward Omniscience" in M. A. Dhaky, ed. *Aspects of Jainology: Vol. 3. Pt. Dalsukh Bhai Malvania Felicitation Volume I*. Varanasi: P. V. Research Institute.

———. 1993. *Is Enlightenment Possible? Dharmakīrti and rGyal tshab rje on Knowledge, Rebirth, No-Self and Liberation.* Ithaca, NY: Snow Lion Publications.

———. 1999. "Atheology and Buddhalogy in Dharmakīrti's *Pramāṇavārttika*." *Faith and Philosophy* 16.4: 472–505.

Jaini, Padmanabh S. 1974. "On the Sarvajñatva (Omniscience) of Mahāvīra and the Buddha" in L.S. Cousins et al., eds., *Buddhist Studies in Honor of I. B. Horner*, 71–90. Dordrecht: Reidel.

———. 1979. *The Jaina Path of Purification.* Berkeley: University of California Press.

———. 1992. "On the Ignorance of the Arhat" in R. Buswell and R. Gimello, eds., *Paths to Liberation: The Mārga and Its Transformation in Buddhist Thought*, 135–45. Honolulu: University of Hawaii Press.

Jalakīkar, Mahāmahopādhyāya Bhīmācārya. 1978. *Nyāyakośa or Dictionary of Technical Terms of Indian Philosophy.* Revised and re-edited by Mahāmahopādhyāya Vāsudev Shāstri Abhyankar. Poona: The Bhandarkar Oriental Research Institute.

Jayatilleke, K. N. 1963. *Early Buddhist Theory of Knowledge.* London: Allen & Unwin.

Jenkins, Stephen. 1999. "The Circle of Compassion: An Interpretive Study of *Karuṇā* in Indian Buddhist Literature." Unpublished Ph.D. dissertation: Harvard University.

Jha, Ganganatha, trans. 1937 and 1939. *The Tattvasaṅgraha of Shāntarakṣita with the Commentary of Kamalashīla.* 2 vols. Baroda: Gaekwad's Oriental Series 80. Reprint, Delhi: Motilal Banarsidass, 1986.

———. 1942. *Pūrva-Mīmāṃsā in Its Sources.* Library of Indian Philosophy and Religion, 1. Ed. by S. Radakrishnan. Benares: Benares Hindu University.

———. 1978. *The Prabhākara School of Pūrva Mīmāṃsaka.* Delhi: Motilal Banarsidass.

———. 1983. *Ślokavārttika with the Commentaries "Kāśikā" and "Nyāyaratnākara."* Delhi: Sri Satguru Publications. First ed., 1908.

Jha, Ujjwala Panse. 1998. "Kumārila Bhaṭṭa on Yogic Perception." *Journal of the Indian Council of Philosophical Research* 15.3: 69–78.

Kajiyama, Yūichi. 1957. "Introduction to the Logic of the Svātantrika-Mādhyamika Philosophy." *Nava-Nalanda Mahavihara Research Publication* 1: 291–331.

———. 1963. "Trikapañcakacintā: Development of the Buddhist Theory on the Determination of Causality." *Miscellanea Indologica Kiotiensia* 4.5: 1–15.

———. 1965. "Controversy Between the Sākāra- and Nirākāra-vādins of the Yogācāra School—Some Materials." *Indogaku Bukkyōgaku Kenkyū* (*Journal of the Japanese Association of Indian and Buddhist Studies*) 14.1: 429–18.

———. 1966. *An Introduction to Buddhist Philosophy: An Annotated Translation of the Tarkabhāṣā of Mokṣākaragupta*. Kyoto: Memoirs of the Faculty of Kyoto University, no. 10.

———. 1973. "Three Kinds of Affirmation and Two Kinds of Negation in Buddhist Philosophy." *Wiener Zeitschrift für die Kunde Südasiens* 17: 161–75.

———. 1978. "Later Mādhyamikas on Epistemology and Meditation" in M. Kiyota, ed., *Mahāyāna Buddhist Meditation: Theory and Practice*, 114–43. Honolulu: University of Hawaii Press.

Kang, Sung Yong. 2003. *Die Debatte im alten Indien: Untersuchungen zum Sabhāṣāvidhi und verwandten Themen in der Carakasaṃhitā Vimānasthāna 8.15–28*. Reinbek: Verlag für Orientalistischen Fachpublikationen.

Kapstein, Matthew. 2000. *The Tibetan Assimilation of Buddhism: Conversion, Contestation and Memory*. Oxford and New York: Oxford University Press.

———. 2001. *Reason's Traces: Identity and Interpretation in Indian and Tibetan Buddhist Thought*. Boston: Wisdom Publications.

Kariyawasam, Tilak. 2001. "Some Aspects in the Development of Early Buddhist Conception of Omniscience in Theravāda and in Early Mahāyāna Buddhism" in Prof. Lily de Silva Felicitation Committee, eds., *Buddhist Studies in Honour of Professor Lily de Silva*, 135–51. Kandy, Sri Lanka: Department of Pali and Buddhist Studies, University of Peradeniya.

Katsura, Shōryū. 1984. "Dharmakīrti's Theory of Truth." *Journal of Indian Philosophy* 12: 215–35.

———. 1991. "Dignāga and Dharmakīrti on *apoha*" in E. Steinkellner, ed., *Studies in the Buddhist Epistemological Tradition*, 129–44. Vienna: Verlag der Österreichischen Akademie der Wissenschaften.

———. 1992. "Dignāga and Dharmakīrti on *adarśanamātra* and *anupalabdhi*." *Asiatische Studien/Études Asiatiques* 46: 222–31.

———. 2007. "Dharmakīrti's Proof of the Existence of Other Minds" in B. Kellner et al., eds., *Pramāṇakīrti: Papers Dedicated to Ernst Steinkellner on the Occasion of His 70th Birthday*, part 1: 407–21. Vienna: Arbeitskreis für Tibetische und Buddhistische Studien, University of Vienna.

Katz, Nathan. 1982. *Buddhist Images of Human Perfection: The Arahant of the Sutta Piṭaka Compared with the Bodhisattva and the Mahāsiddha*. Delhi: Motilal Banarsidass.

Kawasaki, Shinjō. 1963. "Criticism of the Buddhist Idea of Sarvajña as Found in the *Tattvasaṃgraha*" [in Japanese]. *Indogaku Bukkyōgaku Kenkyū* (*Journal of the Japanese Association of Indian and Buddhist Studies*) 11.2: 548–49.

———. 1974. "Quotations in the Mīmāṃsā Chapter of Bhavya's *Madhyamaka-hṛdaya-kārikā*." *Journal of the Japanese Association of Indian and Buddhist Studies* 22.2: 1120–27.

———. 1977, 1987, 1988. "Study of the Mīmāṃsā Chapter of Bhavya's *Madhyamaka-hṛdaya-kārikā*—Text and Translation—(1) pūrva-pakṣa." *Studies in Philosophy* 2 (1977): 1–16; Institute of Philosophy, University of Tsukuba; "Sanskrit and Tibetan Texts—(2) uttara-pakṣa." *Studies in Philosophy* 12 (1987): 1–23; "Sanskrit and Tibetan Texts—(3) uttara-pakṣa with the Sarvajña Chapter." *Studies in Philosophy* 13 (1988): 1–42.

———. 1992a. "Discrepancies in the Sanskrit and Tibetan Texts of Bhavya's *Madhyamaka-hṛdaya-Tarkajvālā* (the IXth and Xth Chapters)" in S. Ihara and Z. Yamaguchi, eds., *Tibetan Studies: Proceedings of the 5th Seminar of the International Association for Tibetan Studies*, 131–43. Vol. 1. Narita: Naritasan Shinshoji.

———. 1992b. *Issaichi Shisô no Kenkyû (A Study of the Buddhist Concept of an Omniscient Being)* [in Japanese]. Tokyo: Shunjūsha.

———. 1995. "The Buddhist Concept of an Omniscient Being: History of the Sarvajña Study and Its Significance." *Studies in Philosophy: Ronshū Proceedings* 22. Institute of Philosophy, University of Tsukuba.

Keira, Ryusei. 2004. *Mādhyamika and Epistemology: A Study of Kamalaśīla's Method for Proving the Voidness of All Dharmas*. Wiener Studien zur Tibetologie und Buddhismuskunde 59. Vienna: Arbeitskreis für Tibetische und Buddhistische Studien, University of Vienna.

Keira, Ryūsei, and Noboru Ueda. 1998. *Sanskrit Word Index to the* Abhisamayālaṃkārāloka Prajñāpāramitāvyākhyā. Tokyo: The Sankibo Press.

Kellner, Birgit. 1996. "There Are No Pots in the *Ślokavārttika*—Kumārila's Definition of the *abhāvapramāṇa* and Patterns of Negative Cognition in Indian Philosophy." *Journal of the Oriental Institute (Baroda)* 46.3–4: 143–67.

———. 1997. *Nichts Bleibt Nichts*. Die buddhistische Kritik an Kumārilas *abhāvapramāṇa*. Übersetzung und Interpretation von Śāntarakṣitas *Tattvasaṃgraha* vv. 1647–90 mit Kamalaśīlas *Pañjikā*. Wiener Studien zur Tibetologie und Buddhismuskunde 39. Vienna: Arbeitskreis für Tibetische und Buddhistische Studien, University of Vienna.

Kenny, Anthony. 1979. *The God of the Philosophers.* Oxford: Clarendon Press.

Keyt, Christine Mullikin. 1980. "Dharmakīrti's Concept of the 'Svalakṣaṇa.'" Unpublished Ph.D. dissertation, University of Washington.

Kher, Chitrarekha. 1972. "Some Aspects of the Concept of Omniscience (*sarvajñatā*) in Buddhism." *Annals of the Bhandarkar Oriental Research Institute* 53: 175–82.

Kimura, T. 1978. "Sarvajñasiddhiparīkṣā" [in Japanese]. *Indogaku Bukkyōgaku Kenkyū* (*Journal of the Japanese Association of Indian and Buddhist Studies*) 27.1: 447–43.

Kirkham, R. L. 1992. *Theories of Truth: A Critical Introduction.* Cambridge, MA: MIT Press.

Krasser, Helmut. 1991. *Dharmottaras kurze Untersuchung der Gültigkeit einer Erkenntnis: Laghuprāmāṇyaparīkṣā.* Teil 1: Tibetischer Text und Sanskritmaterialien. Teil 2: Übersetzung. Beiträge zur Kultur- und Geistesgeschichte Asiens 7. Vienna: Verlag der Österreichischen Akademie der Wissenschaften.

———. 1992. "On the Relationship between Dharmottara, Śāntarakṣita, and Kamalaśīla" in S. Ihara and Z. Yamaguchi, eds., *Tibetan Studies: Proceedings of the 5th Seminar of the International Association of Tibetan Studies*, 151–58. Narita: Naritasan Shinshoji.

———. 1995. "Dharmottara's Theory of Knowledge in his *Laghuprāmāṇyaparīkṣā.*" *Journal of Indian Philosophy* 23: 247–71.

———. 2001. "On Dharmakīrti's Understanding of *pramāṇabhūta* and his Definition of *pramāṇa.*" *Wiener Zeitschrift für die Kunde Süd-Asiens* 45: 173–99.

———. 2005. "Are Buddhist Pramāṇavādins non-Buddhistic? Dignāga and Dharmakīrti on the Impact of Logic and Epistemology on Emancipation." *Horin* 11: 129–46.

Krasser, Helmut, and Ernst Steinkellner. 1989. *Dharmottaras Exkurs zur Definition gültiger Erkenntnis im Pramāṇaviniścaya.* Tibetischer Text, Sanskritmaterialien und Übersetzung. Beiträge zur Kultur- und Geistesgeschichte Asiens 2. Vienna: Verlag der Österreichischen Akademie der Wissenschaften.

Kunst, Arnold. 1939. *Probleme der Buddhistischen Logik in der Darstellung des Tattvasaṃgraha.* Krakow: Nakladem Polskiej Akademii Umiejetnosci.

———. 1946–47. "Kamalaśīla's Commentary on Śāntarakṣita's Anumāṇaparīkṣā of Tattvasaṃgraha. Tibetan Text with Introduction and Notes." *Mélanges chinois et bouddhiques* 8: 106–216.

———. 1977. "Some Aspects of the *Ekayāna*" in L. Lancaster, ed., *Prajñāpāramitā and Related Systems: Studies in Honor of Edward Conze*, 313–26. Berkeley: University of California Press.

Lalou, Marcelle. 1953. "Les textes bouddhiques au temps du roi Khri-sroṅ-lde-bçan." *Journal Asiatique* 241: 313–53.

Lamotte, Étienne. 1974. "Passions and Impregnations of the Passions in Buddhism" in L. Cousins et al., eds., *Buddhist Studies in Honor of I. B. Horner*, 91–104. Dordrecht: D. Reidel.

Lasic, Horst. 1999. "Dharmakīrti and His Successors on the Determination of Causality" in S. Katsura, ed., *Dharmakīrti's Thought and Its Impact on Indian and Tibetan Philosophy*, 233–42. Proceedings of the Third International Dharmakīrti Conference. Vienna: Verlag der Österreichischen Akademie der Wissenschaften.

Lopez, Donald S. 1988a. "Do *Śrāvaka*s Understand Emptiness?" *Journal of Indian Philosophy* 16: 65–105.

———. 1988b. "Sanctification on the Bodhisattva Path" in R. Kieckhefer and G. Bond, eds., *Sainthood: Its Manifestations in World Religions*. Berkeley: University of California Press.

———. 1992. "Paths Terminable and Interminable" in R. E. Buswell and R. M. Gimello, eds., *Paths to Liberation: The Mārga and Its Transformations in Buddhist Thought*, 147–92. Honolulu: University of Hawaii Press.

———. 1995. "Authority and Orality in the Mahāyāna." *Numen* 42.1: 21–47.

Makransky, John J. 1997. *Buddhahood Embodied: Sources of Controversy in India and Tibet*. Albany: State University of New York Press.

Matilal, Bimal K. 1970. "Reference and Existence in Nyāya and Buddhist Logic." *Journal of Indian Philosophy* 1: 83–110.

———. 1971. *Epistemology, Logic, and Grammar in Indian Philosophical Analysis*. The Hague and Paris: Mouton.

———. 1977. *Nyāya-Vaiśeṣika*. A History of Indian Literature. Vol. 7. Wiesbaden: Otto Harrassowitz.

———. 1982. *Logical and Ethical Issues of Religious Belief*. Calcutta: University of Calcutta Press.

———. 1986a. "Buddhist Logic and Epistemology" in B. K. Matilal and Robert Evans, eds., *Buddhist Logic and Epistemology*. Dordrecht: D. Reidel: 1–30.

———. 1986b. *Perception: An Essay on Classical Indian Theories of Knowledge*. Oxford: Oxford University Press.

———. 1986c. "Sva-samvedana: Self-Awareness" in Julius J. Lipner and Dermott Killingly, eds., *A Net Cast Wide: Investigations into Indian Thought in Memory of David Friedman*. Newcastle upon Tyne: Grevatt and Grevatt: 74–79.

———. 1998. *The Character of Logic in India*. Ed. by J. Ganeri and H. Tiwari. Albany: State University of New York Press.

———. 2001. *Philosophy, Culture and Religion: Collected Essays*. Delhi: Oxford University Press.

Matsumoto, Shiro. 1980. "Sahopalambha-niyama" in *Sōtōshū Kenyūin Kenyūsei Kenkyū Kiyō* 12. Contains Tibetan text of vv. 65–82 of Śubhagupta's BASK with Sanskrit fragments and English translation.

May, Jacques, trans. 1959. *Candrakīrti Prasannapadā Madhyamakavṛtti.* Douze chapitres traduits du sanscrit et du tibétain, accompagnés d'une introduction, de notes et d'une édition critique de la version tibétain. Paris: Adrien-Maisonneuve.

McClintock, Sara L. 2000. "Knowing All through Knowing One: Mystical Communion or Logical Trick in the *Tattvasaṃgraha* and *Tattvasaṃgrahapañjikā*." *Journal of the International Association of Buddhist Studies* 23: 225–44.

———. 2002. *Omniscience and the Rhetoric of Reason in the Tattvasaṃgraha and the Tattvasaṃgrahapañjikā*. Unpublished Ph.D. dissertation, Harvard University.

———. 2003. "The Role of the 'Given' in the Classification of Śāntarakṣita and Kamalaśīla as Svātantrika-Mādhyamikas" in Georges B. J. Dreyfus and Sara L. McClintock, eds., *The Svātantrika-Prāsaṅgika Distinction: What Difference Does a Difference Make?*, 125–71. Boston: Wisdom Publications.

———. 2008. "Rhetoric and the Reception Theory of Rationality in the Work of Two Buddhist Philosophers." *Argumentation* 22: 27–41.

McDermott, Charlene. 1978. "Yogic Direct Awareness as a Means of Valid Cognition in Dharmakīrti and Rgyal-tshab" in M. Kiyota, ed., *Mahāyāna Buddhist Meditation: Theory and Practice*, 144–66. Honolulu: University of Hawaii Press.

Mikogami, Eshō. 1979. "Some Remarks on the Concept of *arthakriyā*." *Journal of Indian Philosophy* 7: 79–94.

———. 1989. "Śubhagupta's Criticism of the Vāsanā Theory: Disputes between Realists and the Vijñānavādins." *Ryūkoku Daigaku Ronshū* 434–35: 31–46.

Mimaki, Katsumi. 1976. *La Réfutation bouddhique de la permanence des choses (sthirasiddhidūṣaṇa) et la preuve de la momentanétié des choses (kṣaṇabhaṅgasiddhi)*. Paris: Publications de l'institut de civilisation indienne, fascicule 41.

———. 1987–88. "*Bahirārthsiddhikārikā* kk. 59–60 de Śubhagupta." *Indologica Taurinensia* 14 (Professor Colette Caillat Felicitation Volume): 275–83.

Mimaki, Katsumi, et al. 1989. *Y Kajiyama: Studies in Buddhist Philosophy*. Selected papers. Kyoto: Rinsen.

Mohanty, Jitendranath. 1984. "*Prāmāṇya* and Workability: Response to Potter." *Journal of Indian Philosophy* 12: 329–38.

———. 1992. *Reason and Tradition in Indian Thought: An Essay on the Nature of Indian Philosophical Thinking*. Oxford: Clarendon Press.

Monier-Williams, Monier. 1899. *A Sanskrit-English Dictionary*. Oxford: Clarendon Press. Reprint, Tokyo: Meicho Fukyukai Co., 1986.

Mookerjee, Satkari. 1935. *The Buddhist Philosophy of Universal Flux: An Exploration of the Philosophy of Critical Realism as Expounded by the School of Dignāga*. Calcutta: University of Calcutta. 2nd ed., New Delhi: Motilal Banarsidass, 1975.

———. 1960. "The Omniscient as the Founder of a Religion." *Nālandā: The Nava-Nālandā Mahāvīra Research Publication* II: 1–44.

Moriyama, Seitetsu. 1984a. "Kamalaśīla and Haribhadra's Refutation of the Satyākāra and Alīkākāra-vādins of the Yogācāra School." *Indogaku Bukkyōgaku Kenkyū* (*Journal of the Japanese Association of Indian and Buddhist Studies*) 33.1: 393–89.

———. 1984b. "The Yogācāra-Madhyamika Refutation of the Position of the Satyākāra and Alīkākāra-vādins of the Yogācāra School: A Translation of Portions of Haribhadra's *Abhisamayālaṃkārāloka Prajñāpāramitāvyākhyā*." Kyoto: *Bukkyō Daigaku Daigakuin Kenkyū Kiyō (Proceedings of the Graduate School of Bukkyō University)*, part I (March 1984): 1–58; part II (October 1984): 1–35; part III (December 1984): 1–28.

———. 1991. "The Later Mādhyamika and Dharmakīrti" in E. Steinkellner, ed., *Studies in the Buddhist Epistemological Tradition*, 199–210. Proceedings of the Second International Dharmakīrti Conference. Vienna: Verlag der Österreichischen Akademie der Wissenschaften.

Much, Michael Torsten. 1986. "Dharmakīrti's Definition of 'Points of Defeat' (*Nigrahasthāna*)" in B. K. Matilal and R. D. Evans, eds., *Buddhist Logic and Epistemology: Studies in the Buddhist Analysis of Inference and Language*, 133–42. Dordrecht: D. Reidel.

———. 1991. *Dharmakīrtis Vādanyāyaḥ*. Teil I: Sanskrit-Text. Teil II: Übersetzung und Anmerkungen. Vienna: Verlag der Österreichischen Akademie der Wissenschaften.

Nagatomi, Masatoshi. 1957. "A Study of Dharmakīrti's *Pramāṇavārttika*: An English Translation and Annotation of the *Pramāṇavārttika*, Book I." Unpublished Ph.D. dissertation, Harvard University.

———. 1959. "The Framework of the *Pramāṇavarttika*, Book One." *Journal of the American Oriental Society* 79: 262–66.

———. 1967–68. "Arthakriyā." *Dr. V. Raghavan Felicitation Volume, Adyar Library Bulletin* 31–32: 52–72.

———. 1979. "*Mānasa-pratyakṣa*: A Conundrum in the Buddhist *Pramāṇa* System" in M. Nagatomi et al, eds., *Sanskrit and Indian Studies: Essays in Honor of Daniel H. H. Ingalls*, 243–60. Dordrecht: D. Reidel.

Nance, Richard. 2007. "On What Do We Rely When We Rely on Reasoning?" *Journal of Indian Philosophy* 35: 149–67.

Nash, Ronald H. 1983. *The Concept of God: An Exploration of Contemporary Difficulties with the Attributes of God.* Grand Rapids, MI: Zondervan Publishing House.

Naughton, Alexander T. 1989. "The Buddhist Path to Omniscience." Unpublished Ph.D. dissertation, University of Wisconsin–Madison.

Nozick, Robert. 1981. *Philosophical Explanations*. Cambridge, MA: Belknap Press.

Nussbaum, Martha C. 1994. *The Therapy of Desire: Theory and Practice in Hellenistic Ethics*. Princeton, NJ: Princeton University Press.

Oberhammer, Gerhard. 1963. "Ein Beitrag zu den Vāda-Traditionen Indiens." *Wiener Zeitschrift für die Kunde Süd- und Ostasiens* 7: 63–103.

———. 1974. "Die Überlieferungsautorität im Hinduismus" in G. Oberhammer, ed., *Offenbarung, Geistige Realität des Menschen: Arbeitsdokumentation eines Symposiums zum Offernbarungsbegriff in Indien*, 41–92. Vienna: The De Nobili Research Library.

———. 1984. *Wahrheit und Transzendenz: Ein Beitrag zur Spiritualität des Nyāya*. Vienna: Verlag der Österreichischen Akademie der Wissenschaften.

Obermiller, Eugene. 1933a. *Analysis of the Abhisamayālaṃkāra*. London: Luzac.

———. 1933b. "The Doctrine of the Prajñāpāramitā as Exposed in the *Abhisamayālaṃkāra* of Maitreya." *Acta Orientala* 11: 1–133, 334–54.

Oetke, Claus. 1999. "The Disjunction in the Pramāṇasiddhi" in S. Katsura, ed., *Dharmakīrti's Thought and Its Impact on Indian and Tibetan Philosophy*,

243–51. Proceedings of the Third International Dharmakīrti Conference. Vienna: Verlag der Österreichischen Akademie der Wissenschaften.

Ono, Motoi. 2000. *Prajñākaraguptas Erklärung der Definitions gültiger Erkenntnis.* (*Pramāṇavārttikālaṃkāra* zu *Pramāṇavārttika* II 1–7). Teil I: Sanskrit-Text und Materialien. Beiträge zur Kultur- und Geistesgeschichte Asiens 34. Vienna: Verlag der Österreichischen Akademie der Wissenschaften.

Pathak, K. B. 1892. "The Position of Kumārila in Digambara Jaina Literature" in *The Transactions of the Ninth International Orientalists Congress*, 186–214. London.

———. 1929. "Śāntarakṣita's Reference to Kumārila's Attacks on Samantabhadra and Akalaṅkadeva." *Annals of the Bhandarkar Oriental Research Institute* 11: 155–64.

———. 1930–31. "Śāntarakṣita, Kamalaśīla, and Prabhācandra." *Annals of the Bhandarkar Oriental Research Institute* 12: 81–83.

———. 1931. "Kumārila's Verses Attacking the Jain and Buddhist Notions of an Omniscient Being." *Annals of the Bhandarkar Oriental Research Institute* 12: 123–31.

Patil, Parimal. 2008. *Against a Hindu God: Buddhist Philosophy of Religion in India.* New York: Columbia University Press.

Pemwieser, Monika. 1991. "Materialien zur Theorie der Yogischen Erkenntnis im Buddhismus." Unpublished M.A. thesis, University of Vienna.

Perelman, Chaïm. 1982. *The Realm of Rhetoric.* Trans. by W. Kluback. Notre Dame, IN: University of Notre Dame Press.

———. 1989. "The New Rhetoric" in R. D. Dearin, ed., *The New Rhetoric of Chaim Perelman: Statement and Response.* Lanham, MD: University Press of America: 37–42. Originally published in 1971.

Perelman, Chaïm, and Lucie Olbrechts-Tyteca. 1969. *The New Rhetoric: A Treatise on Argumentation.* Trans. by J. Wilkinson and P. Weaver. Notre Dame, IN: University of Notre Dame Press.

Perrett, Roy W. 1989. "Omniscience in Indian Philosophy and Religion" in Roy W. Perrett, ed., *Indian Philosophy of Religion*, 125–42. Dordrecht: Kluwer.

———. 1999. "Is Whatever Exists Knowable and Nameable?" *Philosophy East and West* 49/4: 401–14.

Plantinga, Alvin. 1993. *Warrant: The Current Debate.* New York and Oxford: Oxford University Press.

Potter, Karl. 1963. *Presuppositions of India's Philosophies.* Englewood Cliffs, NJ: Prentice Hall.

———. 1968–69. "*Astitva, Jñeyatva, Abhidheyatva.*" *Wiener Zeitschrift für die Kunde Süd- und Ostasiens* 12–13: 275–89.

———. 1984. "Does Indian Philosophy Concern Justified True Belief?" *Journal of Indian Philosophy* 12: 307–27.

Poussin, Louis de la Vallée. 1929. "Some Notes on the Tattvasaṃgraha." *Indian Historical Quarterly* 5: 354–55.

Prévèreau, Raynald. 1994. "Dharmakīrti's Account of Yogic Intuition as a Source of Knowledge." Unpublished M.A. Thesis, McGill University.

Raghavan, V., and Anantalal Thakur, eds. 1964. *Āgamaḍambara: Otherwise Called Ṣaṇmatanāṭaka of Jayanta Bhaṭṭa*. Darbhanga: Mithila Institute.

Raja, K. Kunjunni. 1963. *Indian Theories of Meaning*. Adyar Library Series 91. Madras: The Adyar Library and Research Centre.

Ram-Prasad, Chakravarthi. 2000. *Knowledge and the Highest Good: Liberation and Philosophical Inquiry in Classical Indian Thought*. Basingstoke: Macmillan Press.

———. 2007. *Indian Philosophy and the Consequences of Knowledge: Themes in Ethics, Metaphysics and Soteriology*. Hampshire (England) and Burlington, VT: Ashgate Publishing.

Randle, H. N. 1930. *Indian Logic in the Early Schools: A Study of the Nyāyadarśana in its Relation to the Early Logic of Other Schools*. Oxford: Oxford University Press.

Rani, Vijaya. 1982. *The Buddhist Philosophy as Presented in the Mīmāṃsā-Śloka-Vārttika*. Delhi and Ahmedabad: Parimal Publications.

Ricoeur, Paul. 1976. *Interpretation Theory: Discourse and the Surplus of Meaning*. Fort Worth: The Texas Christian University Press.

Rotman, Andy. 2009. *Thus Have I Heard: Visualizing Faith in Early Indian Buddhism*. Oxford: Oxford University Press.

Ruegg, David Seyfort. 1969. *La Théorie du Tathāgatagarbha et du Gotra*. Publications de l'Ecole Française d'Extrême-Orient. Vol. 70. Paris: A. Maisonneuve.

———. 1970. "On Ratnakīrti." *Journal of Indian Philosophy* 1: 300–309.

———. 1971. "On the Knowability and Expressibility of the Absolute Reality in Buddhism." *Indogaku Bukkyōgaku Kenkyū* (*Journal of the Japanese Association of Indian and Buddhist Studies*) 20: 1–7.

———. 1981a. "Autour du *lTa ba'i khyad par* de Ye śes sde (version de Touen-Houang, Pelliot Tibétain 814)." *Journal Asiatique:* 207–29.

———. 1981b. *The Literature of the Madhyamaka School of Philosophy in India*. Wiesbaden: Otto Harrassowitz.

———. 1982. "Towards a Chronology of the Madhyamaka School" in L. A. Hercus et al., ed., *Indological and Buddhist Studies: Volume in Honour of Professor J.W. de Jong on His Sixtieth Birthday*, 505–30. Canberra: Faculty of Asian Studies.

———. 1994a. "La notion du voyant et du 'connaisseur suprême' et la question de l'authorité epistemique." *Wiener Zeitschrift für die Kunde Südasiens* 38: 403–19.

———. 1994b. "*Pramāṇabhūta*, **Pramāṇa(bhūta-)puruṣa*, *Pratyakṣadharman* and *Sākṣātkṛtsdharman* as epithets of the *Ṛṣi*, *Ācārya* and *Tathāgata* in Grammatical, Epistemological and Madhyamaka Texts." *Bulletin of the School of Oriental and African Studies* 57.2: 303–20.

———. 1995a. "Some Reflections on the Place of Philosophy in the Study of Buddhism." *Journal of the International Association of Buddhist Studies* 18: 145–81.

———. 1995b. "Validity and Authority or Cognitive Rightness and Pragmatic Efficacy? On the Concepts of *pramāṇa*, *pramāṇabhūta* and *pramāṇa(bhūta) puruṣa*." *Asiatische Studien/Études Asiatiques* 49: 817–28.

Sakai, Masamichi. 2010. "Dharmottaras Erklärung von Dharmakīrtis *kṣaṇikatvānumāna* (*Pramāṇaviniścayaṭīkā* zu *Pramāṇaviniścaya* 2 vv. 53–55 mit Prosa." Unpublished Ph.D. dissertation. University of Vienna.

Sāṅkṛtyāyana, Rāhula. 1938. "Search for Sanskrit Mss. in Tibet." *Journal of the Bihar and Orissa Research Society* 24: 137–61.

Scharfstein, Ben-Ami. 1997. "The Three Philosophical Traditions." In E. Franco and K. Preisendanz, eds., *Beyond Orientalism: The World of Wilhelm Halbfass and Its Impact on Indian and Cross-Cultural Studies*. Amsterdam and Atlanta: Rodopi.

Scherrer-Schaub, Cristina Anne. 1981. "Le term *yukti*: primière etude." *Asiatische Studien/Études Asiatiques* 35: 185–99.

———, ed. and trans. 1991. *Yuktiṣaṣṭikāvṛtti: Commentaire à la soixantaine sur le raisonnement ou Du vrai enseignement de la causalité par le Maître indien Candrakīrti. Mélanges chinois et bouddhiques* 25. Bruxelles: Institut Belge des Hautes Études Chinoises.

Schmithausen, Lambert. 1965. *Maṇḍanamiśra's Vibhramavivekaḥ. Mit einer Studie zur Entwicklung der Indischen Irrtumslehre*. Sitzungsberichte Philosophisch-Historische Klasse 247/1. Vienna: Verlag der Österreichischen Akademie der Wissenschaften.

———. 1969. *Der Nirvāṇa-Abschnitt in der Viniścayasaṃgrahaṇī der Yogācārabhūmiḥ*. Vienna: Verlag der Österreichischen Akademie der Wissenschaften.

———. 1973. "Spirituelle Praxis und Philosophische Theorie im Buddhismus." *Zeitschrift für Missionswissenschaft und Religionswissenschaft* 3: 161–86.

———. 1976. "On the Problem of the Relation of Spiritual Practice and Philosophical Theory in Buddhism" in *German Scholars on India: Contributions to Indian Studies*, vol. 2: 235–50. New Delhi: Cultural Department of the Embassy of the Federal Republic of Germany.

Shah, Nagin J. 1967. *Akalaṅka's Criticism of Dharmakīrti's Philosophy*. Ahmedabad: L. D. Institute of Jainology, No. 11.

Shastri, Dharmendra Nath. 1964. *Critique of Indian Realism: A Study of the Conflict Between the Nyāya-Vaiśeṣika and the Buddhist Dignāga School.* Agra: Agra University.

Shastri, N. A. 1967. "Bahyartha Siddhi Karika." *Bulletin of Tibetology* (Gangtok) 4.2: 1–96.

Siderits, Mark. 1985. "Word Meaning, Sentence Meaning, and *Apoha*." *Journal of Indian Philosophy* 13: 133–51.

———. 1986. "Was Śāntarakṣita a 'Positivist'?" in B. K. Matilal and R. D. Evans, eds., *Buddhist Logic and Epistemology*, 193–206. Dordrecht: D. Reidel.

———. 1987. "Beyond Compatibilism: A Buddhist Approach to Freedom and Determination." *American Philosophical Quarterly* 24.2: 149–59.

———. 1999. "Apohavāda, Nominalism and Resemblance Theories" in S. Katsura, ed., *Dharmakīrti's Thought and Its Impact on Indian and Tibetan Philosophy*, 341–48. Proceedings of the Third International Dharmakīrti Conference. Vienna: Verlag der Österreichischen Akademie der Wissenschaften.

———. 2008. "Paleo-Combatibilism and Buddhist Reductionism." *Sophia* 47: 29–42.

Silk, Jonathan. 2002. "Possible Indian Sources for the Term *Tshad ma'i skyes bu* as *Pramāṇapuruṣa*." *Journal of Indian Philosophy* 30: 111–60.

Sin, Fujinaga. 2000. "Determining Which Jaina Philosopher Was the Object of Dharmakīrti's Criticisms." *Philosophy East and West* 50.3: 378–84.

Singh, Ramjee. 1974. *The Jaina Concept of Omniscience*. Ahmedabad: L. D. Institute of Indology.

———. 1979. *The Concept of Omniscience in Ancient Hindu Thought*. New Delhi: Oriental Publishers & Distributors.

Solomon, Esther A. 1962. "The Problem of Omniscience (*sarvajñatva*)." *Adyar Library Bulletin* 26.1–2: 36–77.

———. 1976. *Indian Dialectics: Methods of Philosophical Discussion*. Vol. 1. Ahmedabad: Gujarat Vidya Sabha.

———. 1978. *Indian Dialectics : Methods of Philosophical Discussion*. Vol. 2. Ahmedabad: Gujarat Vidya Sabha.

Soni, Jayandra. 1996. "The Notion of *Āpta* in Jaina Philosophy." The 1995 Roop Lal Jain Lecture. Centre for South Asian Studies, University of Toronto.

———. 2000. "Basic Jaina Epistemology." *Philosophy East and West* 50.3: 367–77.

Steinkellner, Ernst. 1963. "Zur Zitierweise Kamalaśīla's." *Wiener Zeitschrift für die Kunde Süd- und Ostasiens* 7: 116–50.

———. 1971. "Wirklichkeit und Begriff bei Dharmakīrti." *Wiener Zeitschrift für die Kunde Südasiens* 15: 179–211.

———. 1977. "Jñānaśrīmitra's *Sarvajñasiddhiḥ*" in L. Lancaster, ed., *Prajñāpāramitā and Related Systems: Studies in Honor of Edward Conze*, 383–93. Berkeley: University of California Press.

———. 1978. "Yogische Erkenntnis als Problem im Buddhismus" in G. Oberhammer, ed., *Transzendenzerfahrung: Vollzugshorizont des Heils: Das Problem in indischer und christlicher Tradition*, 121–34. Vienna: De Nobili Research Library.

———. 1981. "Philological Remarks on Śākyamati's *Pramāṇavārttikaṭīkā*" in K. Bruhn and A. Wezler, eds., *Studien zum Jainismus und Buddhismus: Gedenkschrift für Ludwig Alsdorf.* Alt- und Neu-Indische Studien 23. Wiesbaden: Franz Steiner Verlag.

———. 1982. "The Spiritual Place of the Epistemological Tradition in Buddhism." Todaiji Temple, Nara. *Nanto Bukkyō* 49: 1–18.

———. 1983. "*Tshad ma'i skyes bu*: Meaning and Historical Significance of the Term" in vol. 2 of E. Steinkellner and H. Tauscher, eds., *Proceedings of the Csoma de Körös Symposium*, 275–84. Wiener Studien zur Tibetologie und Buddhismuskunde 11. Vienna: Arbeitskreis für Tibetische und Buddhistische Studien, University of Vienna.

———. 1990. "Is Dharmakīrti a Mādhyamika?" in David S. Ruegg and Lambert Schmithausen, eds., *Panels of the VIIth World Sanskrit Conference*, vol. 2: *Earliest Buddhism and Madhyamaka*, 72–83. Leiden: E. J. Brill.

———. 1994. "Buddhist Logic: The Search for Certainty" in Y. Takeuchi et al., eds., *Buddhist Spirituality: Indian, Southeast Asian, Tibetan and Early Chinese*. London: SCM Press.

———. 1999. "Yogic Cognition, Tantric Goal and Other Methodological Applications of Dharmakīrti's *kāryānumāna* Theorem" in S. Katsura, ed., *Dharmakīrti's Thought and Its Impact on Indian and Tibetan Philosophy*, 349–62. Proceedings of the Third International Dharmakīrti Conference. Vienna: Verlag der Österreichischen Akademie der Wissenschaften.

Steinkellner, Ernst, and Helmut Krasser. 1989. *Dharmottaras Exkurs zur Definition gültiger Erkenntnis im Pramāṇaviniścaya*. Vienna: Verlag der Österreichischen Akademie der Wissenschaften.

Steinkellner, Ernst, and Michael T. Much. 1995. *Texte der erkenntnistheoretischen Schule des Buddhismus*. Systematische Übersicht über die buddhistische Sanskrit-Literatur 2. Göttingen: Vandenhoeck & Ruprecht.

Subrahmania, K. A. Iyer. 1969. *Bhartṛhari: A Study of the Vākyapadīya in the Light of the Ancient Commentaries*. Deccan College Building Centenary and Silver Jubilee Series. Poona: Deccan College.

Sukhlalaji, Sanghvi Panditji. 1957. "Sarvajñatā aur uska Artha" in *Darśana aur Cintana: Pandita Sukhalalajike Hindi lekhoma sangraha*. Ahmedabad: Sukhalalaji Sanmāna Samiti.

———. 1961. *Advanced Studies in Indian Logic and Metaphysics*. Calcutta: R. K. Maitra. Indian Studies Past and Present.

Taber, John A. 1986–92. "Further Observations on Kumārila's *Bṛhaṭṭīkā*." *The Journal of Oriental Research Madras* 56–62: 179–89.

———. 2005. *A Hindu Critique of Buddhist Epistemology: Kumārila on Percetion, The "Determination of Perception" Chapter of Kumārila Bhaṭṭa's* Ślokavārttika. *Translation and Commentary*. London and New York: RoutledgeCurzon.

Tātia, Nāthmal. 1951. *Studies in Jaina Philosophy*. Varanasi: Jaina Cultural Research Society.

Thakur, Anantalal. 1972. "Śāntarakṣita and Kamalaśīla." *Journal of the Ganganatha Jha Kendriya Sanskrit Vidyapeetha (Ganaganatha Jha Research Institute, Allahabad)* 28.1–2: 663–74.

Tillemans, Tom J. F. 1982. "The 'Neither One Nor Many' Argument for *Śūnyatā* and Its Tibetan Interpretations: Background Information and Source Materials." *Etudes de Lettres* (University of Lausanne) 3: 103–28.

———. 1983. "The 'Neither One Nor Many' Argument for *Śūnyatā* and Its Tibetan Interpretations" in E. Steinkellner and H. Tauscher, eds., *Contributions on Tibetan and Buddhist Religion and Philosophy*, 305–20. Wiener Studien zur Tibetologie und Buddhismuskunde 11. Vienna: Arbeitskreis für Tibetische und Buddhistische Studien, University of Vienna.

———. 1984. "Two Tibetan Texts on the 'Neither One Nor Many' Argument for *Śūnyatā*." *Journal of Indian Philosophy* 12: 357–88.

———. 1986. "Dharmakīrti, Āryadeva and Dharmapāla on Scriptural Authority." *Tetsugaku: The Journal of the Hiroshima Philosophical Society* 38: 31–47. Reprinted in Tillemans 1999b.

———. 1990. *Materials for the Study of Āryadeva, Dharmapāla and Candrakīrti*. The *Catuḥśataka* of Āryadeva, chapters XII and XIII, with the commentaries of Dharmapāla and Candrakīrti: Introduction, translation, Sanskrit, Tibetan, and Chinese texts, notes. 2 vols. Wiener Studien zur Tibetologie und Buddhismuskunde 24.1 and 24.2. Vienna: Arbeitskreis für Tibetische und Buddhistische Studien, University of Vienna.

———. 1993. *Persons of Authority. The* sTon pa tshad ma'i skyes bur sgrub pa'i gtam *of A lag sha Ngag dbang bstan dar: A Tibetan Work on the Central Religious Questions in Buddhist Epistemology*. Tibetan and Indo-Tibetan Studies 5. Stuttgart: F. Steiner Verlag.

———. 1995. "Remarks on Philology." *Journal of the International Association of Buddhist Studies* 18: 269–77.

———. 1999a. "How Much of a Proof Is Scripturally Based Inference (*āgamāśritānumāna*)?" in S. Katsura, ed., *Dharmakīrti's Thought and Its Impact on Indian and Tibetan Philosophy*, 395–404. Proceedings of the Third International Dharmakīrti Conference. Vienna: Verlag der Österreichischen Akademie der Wissenschaften. Reprinted in Tillemans 1999b.

———. 1999b. *Scripture, Logic, Language: Essays on Dharmakīrti and His Tibetan Successors*. Boston: Wisdom Publications.

———. 2000. *Dharmakīrti's Pramāṇavārttika: An Annotated Translation of the Fourth Chapter (parārthānumāna)*. Vol. 1 (k. 1–148). Vienna: Verlag der Österreichischen Akademie der Wissenschaften.

Tindale, Christopher W. 1999. *Acts of Arguing: A Rhetorical Model of Argument*. Albany: State University of New York Press.

Toulmin, Stephen E. 1958. *The Uses of Argument*. Cambridge: Cambridge University Press.

———. 2001. *Return to Reason*. Cambridge, MA: Harvard University Press.

Tripāṭhī, Rām Śaṅkar. 1990. *Sautrāntikadarśanam*. Sarnath: Central Institute for Higher Tibetan Studies.

Tucci, Giuseppe. 1929. *Pre-Diṅnāga Buddhist Texts on Logic from Chinese Sources*. Baroda: Gaekwad's Oriental Series 49. Reprint, Chinese Materials Center, 1983.

———. 1958. *Minor Buddhist Texts II: First Bhāvanākrama of Kamalaśīla*. Sanskrit and Tibetan Texts with English Summary. Rome: Istituto Italiano per il Medio ed Estremo Oriente.

van Bijlert, Vittorio A. 1989. *Epistemology and Spiritual Authority: The Development of Epistemology and Logic in the Old Nyāya and the Buddhist School of Epistemology with an Annotated Translation of Dharmakīrti's Pramaṇavārttika II (Pramāṇasiddhi) vv. 1–7*. Wiener Studien zur Tibetologie und Buddhismuskunde 20. Vienna: Arbeitskreis für Tibetische und Buddhistische Studien, University of Vienna.

van der Kuijp, Leonard. 1983. *Contributions to the Development of Tibetan Epistemology from the Eleventh to the Thirteenth Century*. Wiesbaden: Franz Steiner Verlag.

———. 1999. "Remarks on the 'Person of Authority' in the dGa' ldan pa / dGe lugs pa School of Tibetan Buddhism." *Journal of the American Oriental Society* 119.4: 646–72.

Verpoorten, Jean-Marie. 1987. *Mīmāṃsā Literature*. A History of Indian Literature. Vol. 6, Fasc. 5. Wiesbaden: Otto Harrassowitz.

———. 1994. "The 24th Chapter of the *Tattvasaṃgraha*: Refutation of the Mīmāṃsā Doctrine of *Vedāpauruṣeyatva*" in R. C. Dwivedi, ed. *Studies in Mīmāṃsā*, 117–29. Dr. Mandan Mishra Felicitation Volume. Delhi: Motilal Banarsidass.

Vetter, Tilmann. 1964. *Erkenntnisprobleme bei Dharmakīrti*. Vienna: Verlag der Österreichischen Akademie der Wissenschaften.

———. 1990. *Der Buddha und seine Lehre in Dharmakīrtis Pramāṇavārttika*. Der Abschnitt über den Buddha und die vier edlen Wahrheiten im Pramāṇasiddhi Kapitel. Eingeleitet, ediert und übersetzt. Wiener Studien zur Tibetologie und Buddhismuskunde 12. Vienna: Arbeitskreis für Tibetische und Buddhistische Studien, University of Vienna. 2nd rev. edition. Originally published in 1984.

Watanabe, Shigeaki. 1987. "Śubhagupta's *Sarvajñasiddhikārikā*" in *Proceedings of the Naritasan Institute of Buddhist Studies* 10: 55–74. [Includes Tibetan text and Japanese translation.]

———. 1988. "Tattvasaṅgraha XXVI, kk 3247–3261 et kk 3622–3646." *Journal of Naritasan Institute for Buddhist Studies* 11: 501–33.

Watanabe, Shoko. 1985. "Glossary of the Tattvasaṃgrahapañjikā." *Acta Indologica* V.

Wayman, Alex. 1958. "The Rules of Debate According to Asaṅga." *Journal of the American Oriental Society* 78: 29–40.

Wezler, Albrecht. 1982. "Manu's Omniscience: On the Interpretation of Manusmṛti II,7" in Günther-Dietz Sontheimer and Paramesvara Kota Aithal, eds., *Indology and Law: Studies in Honor of Professor J. Duncan M. Derret*, 79–105. Beiträge zur Südasienforschung 77. Wiesbaden.

Williams, Paul. 1989. *Mahāyāna Buddhism: The Doctrinal Foundations*. London and New York: Routledge.

———. 1998a. *Altruism and Reality: Studies in the Philosophy of the Bodhicaryāvatāra*. Surrey, England: Curzon Press.

———. 1998b. *The Reflexive Nature of Awareness: A Tibetan Madhyamaka Defence*. Surrey, England: Curzon Press.

Wood, Thomas E. 1991. *Mind Only: A Philosophical and Doctrinal Analysis of the Vijñānavāda*. Honolulu: University of Hawaii Press.

Xing, Guang. 2005. *The Concept of the Buddha: Its Evolution from Early Buddhism to the* Trikāya *Theory*. London and New York: RoutledgeCurzon.

Yaita, Hideomi. 1987. "Dharmakīrti on the Authority of Buddhist Scriptures (*āgama*)—an annotated translation of the *Pramāṇavārttika-svasvṛtti* ad v. 213–217" in *Nanto Bukkyō* 58: 1–17. Nara: Todaiji Temple.

———. 1988. "Dharmakīrti on the Person Free from Faults, Annotated Translation of the *Pramāṇavārttikasvavṛttiḥ* at v. 218–223." *Proceedings of the Naritasan Institute of Buddhist Studies* 11: 433–45.

Yao, Zhihua. 2005. *The Buddhist Theory of Self-Cognition*. London and New York: Routledge.

Index of Translated Passages

All references to TS and TSP are to the Buddha Bharati edition (B) and verse numbers.

Other Texts

General Index

natural relation (*svabhāvapratibandha*), 83, 178–79, 193, 247, 254n590, 262
negative concomitance (*vyatirekavyāpti*), 83n217, 193–94, 204n489, 254n590, 262
neither-one-nor-many argument, 91n245, 348n750
New Rhetoric, 4, 5, 10, 49, 65, 360
Ngag dbang bstan dar, 314–17, 321n713
niḥśreyasa. *See* highest good
nirākāravāda. *See* image, doctrine that cognition is devoid of
nirmāṇikakāya. *See* emanation body
nirupadhiśeṣanirvāṇa. *See* nirvana without remainder
nirvāṇa, 116n302, 192, 212n513, 250, 321, 356
  false, 122n316, 123n317
  non-abiding (*apratiṣṭhitanirvāṇa*), 89
  without remainder (*nirupadhiśeṣanirvāṇa*), 121n314
nirvikalpa. *See* nonconceptual
niścaya. *See* certainty
noble one (*arhat, arhant*), 29, 29n74, 89, 116n302, 121n313, 125n321, 126n327–28, 136–38
nobles' four truths, 190n462, 319, 340n741
  as the Buddha's core teaching, 29–30, 130, 248, 250, 270
  knowledge of, 33, 36
  as a model of sickness that must be cured, 15n29
nonconceptual (*nirvikalpa, kalpanāpoḍha*), 81, 198–200, 227, 289n658, 356
nonerroneous (*abhrānta*), 32, 81, 107, 199, 207, 360
nonperception (*anupalabdhi*), 71n175, 159, 172–73, 176–79, 185, 191n464, 211, 254, 256, 350n753
Nussbaum, Martha, 15n29
nyāya. *See* reasoning, formal
Nyāyakaṇikā, 54n124, 229n542, 296n699
Nyāyasūtra, 27n70, 68, 68n160, 69, 75n189, 128n332, 266n618, 308n686
Nyāyaviniścaya, 68n162

O

Oberhammer, Gerhard, 27n70, 308n686
obscuration (*āvaraṇa*), 108–9, 123–32, 241, 353
  afflictive (*kleśāvaraṇa*), 195, 250
  epistemic (*jñeyāvaraṇa*), 251
  removal of, 121, 141, 191–92, 250, 285, 355n770
omniscience (*sarvañja*)
  capacity, 31–32, 36, 137n344, 307n684
  contours of in India, 23–35
  connotations of, 132–44
  general demonstration of, 43–44, 159–160, 165–235, 248, 257, 265–66, 268, 272, 285–86, 299, 303–4, 329, 331
  gradual model of, 33
  instantaneous, 33
  logical, 25, 26n66
  rational defense of, 3, 12, 23, 110, 246, 305, 347
  specific demonstration of, 44, 104, 160–61, 181, 220, 237–85, 303–10, 330–32, 339, 341–43
  spontaneous, 36, 38–39, 347–60
  See also dharmic omniscience; total omniscience
one-vehicle (*ekayāna*), 122n316

P

Pāli texts, 23–25, 28–32, 36, 42, 125n325
parārthānumāna. *See* inference, for another
parokṣa. *See* remote entity
particular (*svalakṣaṇa*), 77–78, 83, 87, 101–2, 140, 225–29
Patañjali, 23
Pathak, K. B., 155n383, 327n722
Paṭisambhidāmagga, 31, 125n325
pedagogy, 56, 130
Pemwieser, Monika, 54n124, 158n388, 201n482, 214n518
perception (*pratyakṣa*), 60, 71, 77, 155, 198

R

scholastic, 91–95
See also *pramāṇa* theory
reductio ad adsurdum (*prasaṅga*), 61n142, 74n183, 150, 358
reflexive awareness (*svasaṃvedana, svasaṃvitti*), 33, 143, 162, 172n416
as awareness of self, 234, 352–53
contrasted with knowing all particulars, 141, 349
nothing other than awareness itself, 216–18
vividness of, 81, 289n657
religious authority (*pramāṇabhutatā*), 4, 12–13, 38–42, 97, 102–5, 246
of the Buddha, 138, 347
circular approach to the demonstration of, 311–15
Dharmakīrti on, 135
linear approach to the demonstration of, 311, 313–15
Mīmāṃsaka theories of, 103–4, 151, 358
progressive (*anuloma*) phase of proof for, 157–59, 187, 189, 246, 249n576, 314
regressive (*pratiloma*) phase of proof for, 157–59, 237, 246–47, 249n576, 305, 314, 317
See also trustworthiness
remote entity (*parokṣa*), 83–84, 117, 134, 178, 188, 239, 250, 257–58, 297, 318
rhetoric of reason, 1–13, 45, 344–46, 359–60
Ricoeur, Paul, 50n118
root of virtue, 170, 187, 187n455
Rotman, Andy, 301n677
Ruegg, David Seyfort, 118n306

S

Sa skya, 150n373, 158n386
Śabarasvāmin, 57, 152, 239, 263
Sabba Sutta, 25
śābda. *See* verbal testimony
sahopalambhaniyama reason, 350–52
Sakai, Masamichi, 137n343
sākāravāda. *See* image, doctrine that cognition is endowed with
śakti. *See* capacity
Śākyabuddhi, 84n222, 94, 94n256, 157, 191n464, 327n721, 336n736
sāmānyalakṣana. *See* universal
Sāmaṭa, 152, 155–56, 161, 225, 356–59
sāmbhogikakāya. *See* enjoyment body
Sāṃkhya, 23, 25n63, 75, 98
saṃsāra
cause of, 108, 192
fear of, 116–18
liberation from, 20n44, 27–30, 37, 39, 107, 121–22, 212, 224, 235, 285
saṃśaya. *See* doubt
samyaksaṃbodhi. *See* perfect and complete awakening
Saṃyuta Nikāya, 25n62
Sandaka Sutta, 40n108
Sāṅkhya-Yoga, 340
Śāntideva, 18, 92n248, 123n317, 356n771
śaraṇagamana. *See* going for refuge
sarvajñatva, 132–34, 140, 155
Sarvāstivāda, 32–35, 101
Satyadvayavibhaṅga, 3n4
Sautrāntika, 37, 86–89, 97, 102, 142, 151, 156, 162–63, 345, 348
scripturally based inference (*āgamāśrayānumāna*), 316–27, 330, 337–39, 342–43
credibility of, 258–59, 264, 304
Dharmakīrti on, 253, 312, 340n741
and radical inaccessibility, 41, 84, 304, 332
Siderits, Mark, 27n69
Sin, Fujinaga, 136n341
Singh, Ramjee, 31n85, 135n341, 308n686
single moment of cognition, 28, 31, 33, 142, 233
sliding scale of analysis, 12, 36, 85–86, 91, 111, 132, 141, 152, 348, 359
Ślokavārttika, 152, 163, 171
Solomon, Esther, 69n166
soteriology, 20–22, 108, 199, 321
soteriological aims, 118
soteriological necessity, 246, 248, 337, 339, 347–48
soteriological relevance, 36, 55, 128–34, 139, 141, 167, 188–89, 219, 221, 242

About the Author

SARA L. MCCLINTOCK is an assistant professor of religion at Emory University, where she teaches undergraduate and graduate courses in Indian and Tibetan Buddhism. She obtained her bachelor's degree in fine arts from Bryn Mawr College, her master's in world religions from Harvard Divinity School, and her doctorate in religion from Harvard University. She has spent time as a researcher at the Central Institute for Higher Tibetan Studies in Sarnath and the University of Lausanne, and has taught at Carleton College and the University of Wisconsin–Madison. Her interests include both narrative and philosophical traditions in South Asian Buddhism, with particular focus on issues of metaphysics, hermeneutics, and rhetoric. Her work includes articles on these themes, as well as a translation, with John Dunne, of Nāgārjuna's *Ratnāvalī*. She has also co-edited a volume of articles on Indian and Tibetan Madhyamaka with Georges Dreyfus, *The Svātantrika-Prāsaṅgika Distinction: What Difference Does a Difference Make?* Her current research centers on the intersection of philosophical and literary conceptions of time and timelessness in Indian and Tibetan Buddhism.

About Wisdom

Wisdom Publications is dedicated to making available authentic Buddhist works for the benefit of all. We publish translations of the sutras and tantras, commentaries and teachings of past and contemporary Buddhist masters, and original works by the world's leading Buddhist scholars. We publish our titles with the appreciation of Buddhism as a living philosophy and with the special commitment to preserve and transmit important works from all the major Buddhist traditions.

Wisdom Publications
199 Elm Street
Somerville, Massachusetts 02144 USA
Telephone: 617-776-7416
Fax: 617-776-7841
Email: info@wisdompubs.org
www.wisdompubs.org

Wisdom is a nonprofit, charitable 501(c)(3) organization affiliated with the Foundation for the Preservation of the Mahayana Tradition (FPMT).

Studies in Indian and Tibetan Buddhism
Series Titles Previously Published

Among Tibetan Texts
History and Literature of the Himalayan Plateau
E. Gene Smith

Approaching the Great Perfection
Simultaneous and Gradual Methods of Dzogchen Practice in the Longchen Nyingtig
Sam van Schaik

Buddhism Between Tibet and China
Matthew T. Kapstein

The Buddhist Philosophy of the Middle
Essays on Indian and Tibetan Madhyamaka
David Seyfort Ruegg

Buddhist Teaching in India
Johannes Bronkhorst

A Direct Path to the Buddha Within
Gö Lotsāwa's Mahāmudrā Interpretation of the Ratnagotravibhāga
Klaus-Dieter Mathes

Foundations of Dharmakīrti's Philosophy
John D. Dunne

Freedom from Extremes
Gorampa's "Distinguishing the Views" and the Polemics of Emptiness
José Ignacio Cabezón and Geshe Lobsang Dargyay

Luminous Lives
The Story of the Early Masters of the Lam 'bras in Tibet
Cyrus Stearns

Mipham's Beacon of Certainty
Illuminating the View of Dzogchen, the Great Perfection
John Whitney Pettit

Reason's Traces
Identity and Interpretation in Indian and Tibetan Buddhist Thought
Matthew T. Kapstein

Resurrecting Candrakīrti
Disputes in the Tibetan Creation of Prāsaṅgika
Kevin A. Vose

Scripture, Logic, Language
Essays on Dharmakīrti and His Tibetan Successors
Tom J. F. Tillemans

The Svātantrika-Prāsaṅgika Distinction
What Difference Does a Difference Make?
Edited by Georges Dreyfus and Sara McClintock

Vajrayoginī
Her Visualizations, Rituals, and Forms
Elizabeth English